# BEGINNINGS & BEYOND

## FOUNDATIONS IN EARLY CHILDHOOD EDUCATION

### SECOND EDITION

## Ann Miles Gordon

*Executive Director*
*National Association of Episcopal Schools*
*New York, New York*

## Kathryn Williams Browne

*The Bing School*
*Stanford University*
*Stanford, California*

**Guest Editors**
*EDITH M. DOWLEY*
*K. EILEEN ALLEN*
*JOSEPH H. STEVENS, JR.*
*THELMA HARMS*
*DAVID ELKIND*
*BETTYE M. CALDWELL*

**Contributor**
*GAY SPITZ*
*Salinas, California*

 Delmar Publishers Inc.®

# NOTICE TO THE READER

For Dan and David, who redefined the step-parent role

—AMG

To Campbell Williams Browne, whose smile invites and encircles us all with its love of life

—KWB

Cover photographs by Mark Roberts

*Delmar Staff*
Executive Editor: Susan Newkirk
Associate Editor: Jay Whitney
Editing Manager: Gerry East

Project Editor: Mary Ormsbee
Design Coordinator: Susan Mathews
Production Coordinators: Linda Helfrich
                        Judith Block

For information, address Delmar Publishers Inc.,
2 Computer Drive West, Box 15-015
Albany, New York 12212-5015

Printed in the United States of America
Published simultaneously in Canada
by Nelson Canada,
A Division of International Thomson Limited

10 9 8 7 6 5 4 3 2

**Library of Congress Cataloging in Publication Data**
Gordon, Ann Miles.
    Beginnings and beyond.

    Bibliography: p.
    Includes index.
    1. Early childhood education. 2. Early childhood education—Curricula. 3. Child development. I. Browne, Kathryn Williams. II. Title.
    LB1140.2.G578   1989        372'.21              88-29921
    ISBN 0-8273-3410-9
    ISBN 0-8273-3411-7 (instructor's guide)

# CONTENTS

# PREFACE

Revising a book is a lot like redecorating the infant's room as the child grows into a toddler and preschooler. It is still the child's room, but certain elements reflect changes in time, attitudes, knowledge, and culture. So it is with this second edition of *Beginnings and Beyond*.

## FEATURES OF THE TEXT

Each and every chapter has been modified to meet what our experience and that of students, instructors and reviewers suggested. There is new data on program effectiveness, controversies, and professionalism. Some material has less emphasis in response to the ever changing field of early childhood education.

There is a *greater emphasis* on:

- pluralism and diversity
- infant, toddler, and school-age children
- "how-to"s—more applied examples to tie theory to practice
- family support and parent growth
- crisis in child care today
- cross referencing material from one chapter to another
- becoming a teacher

There is an *expanded view* on:

- evaluation and testing
- developmentally appropriate practices and materials
- guidance techniques
- developmental theory and its application
- playgrounds and physical play
- objectives and goals in curriculum planning
- stress
- children and TV

There is *new material* on:

- accreditation
- children and AIDS
- family ecology, family support, and family values
- educational reform
- advocacy
- reality of the child care profession
- ethics
- current issues and future trends
- appendices

A brand new feature, expanding on the success of the Guest Editorials at each section opening, is the *Focus* discussion—a shorter, more concentrated statement from prominent educators: Bernard Spodek, Bretta Weiss, Janice Hale-Benson, John Flavel, Diane Eyer, Alice Honig, Elizabeth Jones, Robert Calfee, Ellen Galinsky, and Heather Clarke. Combined with the viewpoints expressed in the Guest Editorials, they give the student an enlarged vision of the field, its problems, issues, attitudes, and history.

New photographs and charts, plus a new layout in this edition will appeal to instructors and students by making the information more accessible.

We constantly sought for balance between calling the issue or topic to the student's attention and providing an in-depth discussion. The introductory nature of the text made this creative tension necessary. We know, however, that good instructors who use *Beginnings and Beyond* will bring their own depth and emphasis to the material we present. As we say further along in the text, curriculum exists only when children meet materials and bring to life mere paper plans. So, too, will *Beginnings and Beyond*. The basics are here, the beginning is set forth. Take it and make it your own with your own issues, zest, questions, and concerns. Breathe life into these pages by using this book the way it fits your needs: Start at the back, in the middle, with the last chapter; omit, add, and create what you know is the best course for your students, and enable them to move from beginnings to beyond.

# PHILOSOPHY

As in the earlier edition, *Beginnings and Beyond* is based on the premise that as teachers of young children we are in the business of helping them "get started." We are aware of how important beginnings are. So, too, we are committed to helping new teachers in their beginnings—to make sense of what they are doing without losing the excitement of teaching, yet with an increasing understanding of the underlying relationship between children's behaviors and good teaching techniques. In understanding typical, predictable child growth and behavior, new teachers acquire a foundation for building good programs, for determining good teaching styles, for establishing good physical environments in which optimal growth is fostered, and for promoting good support systems between home and school.

The collegial association of this book is unique. From its original concept through the current revision it has been a professional collaboration of exceptional order. It is a relationship that was forged as teachers, has culminated in this text, and has used the philosophy of teaching espoused in *Beginnings and Beyond.* Teaching is a collaborative effort between student and teacher, teacher and teacher, parent and teacher. We team wrote it as we team taught it—only from a distance of 3,000 miles. Model working relationships are based on mutual respect; we share that with our readers in the hope that they will integrate that respect as part of their own philosophy of teaching.

# ABOUT THE AUTHORS

*Ann Miles Gordon* has been in the field of early childhood for more than 25 years as a teacher of young children, a teacher of parents, and a teacher of college students. She has taught in laboratory schools, church-related centers, and private and public preschool and kindergarten programs. While at Stanford, Ann was a head teacher at the Bing School for seven years and a lecturer in the Psychology Department. For ten years she also served as an adjunct faculty member in four different colleges, teaching the full gamut of early childhood courses. Today, Ann is the executive director of the National Association of Episcopal Schools, where her commitment and interest in education stretches the full age range from infancy through high school. More than 500 early childhood programs are a part of her network. Ann is the mother of two grown children, Andy and Libby Miles.

*Kathryn Williams Browne,* most recently a lecturer in the Psychology Department of Stanford University, has been a head teacher at the Bing School of Stanford for more than a decade. Her teaching experiences include nursery school, parent cooperatives, full-day child care, pre-kindergarten and bilingual programs, as well as kindergarten and first grade. Kate's background in child development and research led her to choose early childhood education, for to truly understand child development, one needs to be with children. The professional adventure of *Beginnings and Beyond* has now taken a new meaning, as her work with groups of children is supplemented by living with her own two children. The balance and pull of career and family give this edition a special flavor—part of the growth and challenge of the field of early childhood education.

# ACKNOWLEDGMENTS

Professional formation comes to a teacher in different ways. For us, the many years spent at The Bing School of Stanford University were pivotal in shaping our professional growth and development. "Bing," as we affectionately know it, was the setting where we practiced and honed the experiences and philosophy set forth in this text. We will always be grateful to our colleagues from Bing who enthusiastically supported and encouraged the first and now the second edition of *Beginnings and Beyond.*

Some of the photo credits belong to the current Bing family—children, parents, and faculty who happily agreed to photo sessions and permissions. Thanks also to Gay Ellsworth of Stride Rite Children's Centers in Cambridge, MA; Evelyn French of Trinity Preschool, New York City; Family Service Association of San Mateo County in Burlingame, CA; Stephanie Barry Agnew of Palo Alto, CA; Linda DeFilippo of Plaza Day Care Center in Niskayuna, NY; and to the University of Chicago Library. We gratefully acknowledge the extensive contribution their photographs have made. Any photos not otherwise credited were taken by the authors.

We are especially thankful for the important contribution of our guest contributors. Through their Guest Editorials and *Focus* discussions, they generously shared insights and perspectives that broaden the scope of *Beginnings and Beyond,* and add a lively dimension for the student reader.

Reviewers make a significant contribution when they offer candid and constructive suggestions that clarify and focus the writing. Ours were especially helpful and we extend our thanks to:

Delores Taylor
Bellevue Community College

Diane Eyer
Cañada College

Margaret Budz
Triton College

Joan Lawson
Hudson Valley Community College

Ned Sauls
Wayne Community College

Dona Mese
Cambrian College

Gale Spear
Austin Community College

We thank Jay Thorp of the School of Education at Stanford University for arrangements of work space, general assistance, and support. We also thank former Bing School teachers Susan Wickizer, Joan Ehrenreich Tananbaum, and Becky Cooper for materials on which they collaborated over the years, and to Libby Miles for editorial clarity throughout. As always, we appreciate the wisdom and advice that Gay Spitz, Karen McLaughlin, and Eileen Allen share on a regular basis. We also want to recognize the indelible stamp that Adele Morse O'Connell placed on the first edition.

To our families we give a hearty thanks for putting up with late meals and lost weekends as we tried to meet our ever-present deadlines. Marty, Julia, and Campbell Browne and David Gordon, thank you!

Finally, we would like to publicly acknowledge the deep personal and professional relationship which has grown out of *Beginnings and Beyond.* Each of us received from the other a depth of support, humor, and affection that enhanced the written words, the philosophy, and the finished product. This collaboration has deepened over the life of *Beginnings and Beyond* to one of mutual respect and admiration—a bonus to a friendship begun long ago.

# SECTION 1

# EARLY CHILDHOOD EDUCATION IN THE SHIPYARDS

*Edith M. Dowley*

If you are thinking about working with young children as a career, perhaps you are wondering how early childhood education compares in prestige and importance with elementary or secondary education. Does it have a background of tradition? Is it truly a profession with the potential for growth and change? Can a student preparing to work with young children today look forward to a challenging, intellectually stimulating, and rewarding future in an early childhood profession?

My career with young children began during the Great Depression, a time of arrested economic growth and widespread unemployment. My undergraduate major and minors were in fields where job opportunities were, at the time, apparently hopeless. However, with the help of wise counselors and some very good luck, I spent two years in graduate study with outstanding professors of child development and worked as an assistant with nursery school teachers chosen as models of artistic technique and effective nurturers of young children. I found working with children so challenging and rewarding, I made it my life's work! Forty years later, when I "retired," I could truthfully say I was never disappointed.

All but two of those years were spent in university settings where research and theory questioned, modified, and sometimes changed our attitudes, interpretations, and reactions to child growth and behavior. They were years of growing and learning, of planning, struggling, and some accomplishments. No two years—actually no two days—were ever the same.

But this editorial is about a different, unforgettable experience I had with young children, far removed from a university setting, in a period of national crisis. It occurred during World War II, in an innovative project that not only was a remarkable solution to a problem for those times, but that also has special relevance and appropriateness, I believe, for the 1980s.

In early 1943, the Kaiser Shipbuilding Corporation was faced with the necessity of

# What Is the Field of Early Childhood Education?

employing more women to meet the stepped-up schedule for producing warships in their two shipyards in Portland, Oregon. Of the 12,000 women already employed, one third of them were mothers who had no place to leave their preschool children while they worked. Absenteeism among women was running 50 percent higher than among men and was contributing to slow-downs in production that seriously affected the war effort. The reasons most women gave for being late or for missing work were that the baby-sitter did not show up or a child was ill and could not be left at home until seen by a doctor. Henry Kaiser, reportedly in typical fashion, responded to the dilemma by saying that if mothers were worried about leaving their children, he would provide them with nurseries. He resolved to build the finest child care centers in the country.

Within a few weeks, architects were drawing plans for two child service centers to be placed at the entrances to the shipyards—one at Swan Island and the other at Oregon Yard. Paid for by the United States Maritime Commission and absorbed as part of the cost of building ships, these centers turned out to be not only very fine centers, but also the largest child care centers in the world.

Dr. Lois Meek Stolz, a well-known leader in the fields of child development and early childhood education, was chosen by Edgar Kaiser to direct the two child service centers. She planned the entire children's program and made provisions for staffing the centers. She brought James L. Hymes, Jr., former editor of *Progressive Education,* to the program as Manager of the Child Service Centers, and she recruited Dr. Miriam Lowenberg, a well-known nutritionist, to be responsible for the children's nutritional needs.

## THE STAFF

Each center had a supervisor who was responsible for the total operation over all three shifts—day, swing, and graveyard. There were group supervisors, head teachers, assistant teachers, dieticians, and nurses under her direction. In addition, each center had a social worker who served as a liaison between the teachers in the centers and the parents in the shipyard. All of the staff members were recruited from nursery school training centers throughout the United States. All of the teachers had college degrees, and the supervisors and most of the head teachers had master's degrees and years of experience with children. They were young, energetic women "chosen for their comfortable qualities as well as for their scientific knowledge" (Jean Muir, from an article she wrote for the *Oregon Journal,* Sunday, December 12, 1943).

## THE SETTING

The teaching staff began arriving in late October as the finishing touches were being made on the buildings. They found, to their delight, that the centers, although temporary, were beautifully and functionally designed. Each center was built around a large, octagonally shaped courtyard with four wading pools where children could play away from the hazards of traffic. The courtyard itself was grass-covered, with a hard-surfaced area designed for wheel toys that extended around the perimeter. Because of the long rainy season in Portland, covered porches, equipped with jungle gyms, climbing boxes, slides, and large, hollow blocks, connected the interior rooms to the grassy areas. Children could thus enjoy vigorous outdoor play every day of the year, regardless of the weather.

A cog-wheel plan of architecture provided for 15 rectangular playrooms (26' by 49') extending out from a central circular corridor. Between and opposite every two playrooms were smaller rooms for teachers' meetings, special play, or story times. Each of the 15 playrooms had windows on two sides to provide light and interesting views of the outside world. Window seats, low enough for children to sit on, were built so that the children could curl up on them and watch the ships, cars, trucks, and cranes in the busy shipyard below where their parents were working. This proved to be a special delight as darkness came and the yards were lighted, showing the outlines of the ships and their reflections in the water.

The interior colors were soft pastel shades of blue, yellow, and apricot, depending on the exposure of the individual room. Adult-height counterspace covered the expansive shelving where children could readily reach the many unit blocks, toys, games, books, and puzzles that were neatly and meaningfully stored there. Children's lockers, arranged like a dressing room unit, provided hooks for coats and jackets, a shelf for caps, mittens, and art work to take home, and a place for safekeeping of special possessions. Each room had its own toilet room with toilets and wash basins scaled to child size. Wash cloths and towels provided by the center were hung on hooks within the children's reach and marked with individual symbols matching the ones on their lockers.

There was a large room in each center, separated from the playrooms, where children could be cared for when they were ill. Comfortable cribs, like those used in children's hospitals, were placed in glass-sided cubicles that allowed children quiet places to sleep, eat, or sit up and play while recovering from colds, coughs, earaches, or upset tummies. A registered nurse was on duty at all times in the infirmary, and teachers planned and provided the play materials and projects for both the bed patients and those who were up and about.

Each center had a fully equipped, large, modern kitchen that was adequate for serving meals and snacks, over a 24-hour day, to some 400 children and their teachers. Large, heated rolling carts were available to deliver the china, silverware, and food to each room, where children were served at small, low tables. Usually, five children and a teacher dined together each day as a "family."

The architects thoughtfully included one additional feature: several large, square bath tubs raised two steps above the floor. These tubs allowed teachers, when necessary or desirable, to bathe a child without bending over. These tubs also provided safe places for children to "swim" and splash and engage in relaxing water play.

## OPENING DAYS

The teaching staff, of which I was a part, arrived in Portland about two weeks before the centers opened. Until we found more permanent places to live, we were housed in a dormitory for female workers at the Swan Island shipyard. Each evening, we met with Dr. Hymes and the supervisors, building a common but shared philosophy about child care and our roles as educators. During the days, we prepared the playrooms in anticipation of the day when the children would arrive.

Oregon Center, where I was a group supervisor, opened its doors on November 8, 1943, to children, age 18 months to six years, of parents working on the day and swing shifts. On that day, a total of 67 children came to the center. We were, of course, very disappointed in this turnout. We realized, however, that the majority of people in the area had never even heard of a nursery school and were not able to imagine a children's center that would stay open twelve months a year, six days a week, and twenty-four hours a day! So we planned "open house" on Sundays and invited the public to tour the centers. We went down into the shipyards to talk to the workers about the child services available. Feature articles with many photographs appeared in the local newspapers. Gradually, more children were enrolled. By Christmas of that year, there were over 100 children being cared for in the center. In January, the graveyard shift was started, as was a Saturday and after-school program for older children. By August 27th, when Oregon Shipyard went on a seven-day work week, the Center was operating seven days a week, with an average daily attendance of 370 children.

Everything possible was done to keep workers on the job of building ships. Parents paid only nominal fees for child service: 75 cents a day for one child in a family and 50 cents for each additional child, paid by the week. If a child came seven days a week, parents were only charged for six days.

## THE CHILDREN

The children we worked with in the Center were much the same as the children most of us had worked with before. Each was a unique individual, with distinctive characteristics and special needs. They had strong ties to their parents and families and depended on them for love, approval, and support. Mothers or fathers brought the children to their rooms at the Center each day before their shifts began, and picked them up after the shift ended. Day-shift children often spent nine or more hours in the Center as that was the longest shift. Day-shift parents were always in a hurry, it seemed, and were less able to spend time helping their children make the transition from home to school. Separating from their mothers and fathers was painful for some children at first. It was probably hardest of all for the

18-month-olds and two-year-olds to adjust to being left with strangers in a strange place for such long hours. Some of these little ones, most of whom had not yet begun to talk, cried for long periods and were difficult to comfort. Some refused to let anyone remove their coats, snowsuits, or hats all day, clinging to them as perhaps the last link with home and mother. They would stay on their feet, apart from the others even during snacks or meal times, unwilling to sit or to accept food from a strange table. Eventually, hunger would overcome this reluctance, and when teachers wisely left finger foods within their sight and reach, they devoured them quickly and covertly. Sleep, too, overcame them, even though they steadfastly resisted lying on a nursery school cot when invited to nap. Still in their heavy outdoor clothing, they would drop to the floor, asleep. Then, a teacher would carefully place the child on a cot close to an open window. The child would waken hours later, refreshed and on the way to trusting a smiling, loving teacher and the safety of the nursery school environment.

After working out in the cold and rain for long hours at a stretch, day-shift parents were very tired and in a hurry at the end of the day when they came to pick up their children. Some were cross and impatient as they hurried their preschoolers to avoid missing the bus or car-pool ride. There was no time to talk over their child's day with the teacher. So, teachers communicated with parents about their children by writing brief comments next to a child's name on a chart hung outside the playroom door. These comments had to be worded with great tact, we discovered. Even such comments as "John didn't finish his lunch" or "Betsy didn't take a nap today" could result in angry scolding or slapping of the child. We tried to emphasize the positive behaviors in our messages in order to make each child appear more lovable and interesting to parents.

For the children on the swing shift, life was quite different. They usually arrived early after a leisurely day at home or out shopping with their parents. Mothers and fathers on their way to work often stayed for a while at the center, reading stories or looking at toys or interesting things tne children described to them the night before. There was a more relaxed atmosphere in the playrooms during the swing shift than during the day shift. This was evident in the conversations between children, and especially in their dramatic play. In contrast to the day-shift children, who rarely used the doll corner to "keep house," swing-shift children meticulously swept the floor, made the doll beds, set the table, bathed and dressed the dolls, and sat down quietly for pretend tea parties. In contrast, day-shift children, especially the four-year-olds, turned the sink and stove upside down in the doll corner and "launched them" in noisy excitement. They were more aggressive in their play and more destructive of play materials. They probably had fewer occasions to observe their mothers making beds, preparing meals, or enjoying homemaking tasks.

Swing-shift children were served supper as a group, after which they had time to play, listen to stories, enjoy music and play games, paint pictures and, in summertime, play outside until dark. They then undressed and went to bed. The children were then awakened and dressed before their tired parents arrived.

## ADDITIONAL SERVICES

The Center also tried to provide time-saving services to parents that might relieve some of the stresses under which they worked. Home Service Foods began in January of 1944. Precooked meals, planned by Dr. Lowenberg, were prepared in the centers' kitchens. Priced at fifty cents each, one order was ample for a working man or woman, and a single portion would serve two preschool children. These ready-packaged meals were ordered two or more days in advance and contained the main course and dessert, the foods that usually required the most preparation time. Directions were included for heating and serving, and suggestions for additional foods to round out the meal were offered.

In time, other services were added, such as mending children's clothes, buying their shoelaces, and haircutting. In February, a program of immunizations was begun. Children whose parents had not been able to arrange for the necessary shots required for nursery school attendance were able to receive their shots at the Center. Teachers, in the absence of parents, brought children in turn to the Center's physician, holding them on their laps to reassure and comfort them while they got their shots.

## PARENT-TEACHER INTERACTIONS

Parent-teacher conferences were usually difficult to arrange. We found ways to talk briefly with a mother by walking with her to a waiting bus or car. Teachers invited parents into the playrooms to see the art work of their children or to view special block buildings preserved for their admiration.

Parent meetings took place occasionally when dinner was served to the mothers and fathers in one room while their children had dinner in another. Group supervisors went down into the shipyard to talk to a parent when it seemed necessary. On these occasions, I found myself surrounded by fathers and mothers who eagerly asked "What was my child doing when you left?" As parents realized how much teachers knew and cared about their children, they made time for interviews and shared their problems and pleasures with them.

## PROGRAM RESULTS

One of the most gratifying aspects of the Kaiser experience was the steady growth and change we observed in the children. The outdoor play, regular sleep and rest, and especially the excellent nutrition wrought dramatic improvements in the health and appearance of many of the children. Before the centers opened, some of the children had no regular meal times but ate whatever "handouts" (usually bread) were made available to them by neighbors or caretakers. When they first came to the centers, bread was the only food some children would eat. After the children seemed comfortable with the nursery school routines, Dr. Lowenberg omitted bread from the meals entirely. The hungry children began to taste and enjoy a wide variety of unfamiliar flavors and textures. Later on, when bread was again included in the form of small sandwiches, they were accepted as just another food.

Patience and planning reduced aggression and destructive behavior and, as children were convinced that their teachers really liked them and cared what happened to them, they confided in them their fears and worries and sought comfort and assurance from them. An emerging sense of trust freed the children to develop confidence in their bodies. Their motor skills increased, their self-esteem was enhanced, and they grew more friendly, more tolerant of one another, and more giving.

We also saw measurable growth in language development. Opportunities to develop the ability to listen to a teacher's direction, to enjoy longer and more complex stories, and to verbalize shared experiences with pets or on walks was part of the program planning.

Many good things happened in the Child Service Centers in the Kaiser Shipyards—for children, for parents, for the industry, for all of us. We all had a part in winning the war as "champion shipbuilders," as we were told, and for that we were proud. The head of the Maritime Commission told the teachers that, without their help, it would have been impossible to keep the shipyards in production seven days a week. Parents told us that when they were tired and tempted to sleep late on Sunday morning, their children would awaken them, saying "Get up, get up. If you don't go to work, we don't get to go to school." When the centers were closed in 1945 at the end of the war, records showed that "3,811 children were taken care of—a total of 250,000 child care days—which freed almost 2 million working hours for the women" (Stanford University Campus Report, Interview with Lois Stolz, March 30, 1983).

But I think the most remarkable, the best thing that happened was that, in a time of war, when mothers of preschool children worked eight and nine hours a day, six or seven days a week, the lives of almost 4,000 children were made happy, healthy, and in some ways, better than they ever were before. This could only happen as a combination of skillful professional planning, strong professional leadership, and some of the best teachers the nursery school profession has ever prepared. I believe that all children deserve to benefit from that combination, especially in their early years.

You who are beginning the study of early childhood education have many career paths open to you. Ours is a profession that is constantly growing, branching out in many directions and ready to meet emerging challenges in flexible, innovative ways. At present, employment prospects may look discouraging and preschool teachers' salaries substandard, but these conditions must change. In a society where 50 percent of women work for a living, we can no longer function without a nationwide, high-quality program for the care and education of children under six years of age.

When this happens, we must wonder whether there will be enough professionally prepared specialists in the field to provide leadership. Will there be enough teachers who are knowledgeable about the nature and development of infants and young children and sensitive to their individual needs? Will there be enough enlightened and caring personnel to license and monitor (with in-service education) facilities and programs for an entire nation's children? You—and those who follow in your footsteps—hold the answers to these questions.

*EDITH M. DOWLEY was involved in early childhood education for fifty years. She was a student at the Merrill-Palmer Institute in 1933 and 1934, and a faculty member from 1945 through 1948. Dr. Dowley received her master's degree in Child Development in 1935, and taught for nine years at the University Elementary School at the University of Michigan. She was a group supervisor in the Kaiser Child Service Centers, and later became the first director of Stanford University's Bing Nursey School, a position she retained until 1975. She served as a national consultant to Project Head Start from 1965 to 1968, and from 1971 to 1972 she was a member of the California Task Force on Early Childhood Education.*

*Dr. Dowley was a visiting instructor at the University of Victoria (British Columbia, Canada) and the University of Hawaii and conducted summer workshops in Santa Barbara and Berkeley, California. The late Dr. Dowley was most recently Professor Emerita of Psychology and Education at Stanford University.*

# CHAPTER 1

## History of Early Childhood Education

## QUESTIONS for THOUGHT

- Why is it important to know about the history of early childhood education?
- What other fields have influenced the development of the early childhood philosophy? What has been their impact?
- Why are the roots of psychology and early childhood education so intertwined?
- What have been the basic themes in early education throughout history?
- How do current events—political, social, and economic—affect the direction of education?

# INTRODUCTION TO THE FIELD

Early childhood education has a rich and exciting history. The story of its development is the chronicle of people who took bold steps toward improving children's lives. Critical events have had a hand in shaping the history of early childhood education. For example, a national crisis such as a world war can bring together a community to provide for its children, as described in the guest editorial by Edith Dowley. A new model is forged through necessity and innovation, thus changing what we know about children and their care and education. Across the globe and through the centuries, the education of children has evolved.

## Why History?

Most early childhood students and many educators know little about the origins of their chosen profession. The names of Rousseau, Froebel, Montessori, and Dewey may not have much significance at this time (although many teachers are familiar with some of their techniques), but knowing something about the roots of this profession is important.

First of all, there is a sense of support that comes from knowing that history. It gives one pause to reflect that what is referred to as "education" in the 1980s stems from ancient times. Socrates, Plato, and Aristotle are a part of the philosophical foundation on which this field is built. Even in ancient Greece and Rome, schools were established where literature, the arts, and science were taught.

Knowing that early childhood *philosophy* has deep roots is inspiring and helps professionals express their ideas today. The past as well as the present and future must be considered when developing sound educational programs for young children. The *tenets* expressed by past educators help develop better methods of teaching. Looking at history gives an overview of how various ages looked at children and their learning, based on the religious, political, and economic pressures of the time. Reviewing the professional record demonstrates how the needs of society affect education. Perhaps some of

the mistakes of the past can be avoided if history is remembered.

Drawing upon knowledge of the past creates an awareness of changes in education. Into the fabric of early childhood education are woven many threads of influence that are responsible for current philosophies. By understanding and telling the story of the past, we are better equipped to interpret our own history, to have a sense of mission and purpose. As Bernard Spodek wrote, "This common sense of mission— commitment to the education, development, and well-being of young children—holds the field of early childhood education together" (Spodek, 1985).

In this chapter, the people, the ideas, and the circumstances that have influenced early childhood are introduced by examining historical forces in both Europe and America that have affected educational trends. Educational changes of a more recent nature follow. The impact of other disciplines, such as medicine and psychology, and the recurrent themes of early childhood education are also explored.

## Defining the Terms

The term *early childhood education* refers to group settings deliberately intended to effect developmental changes in children from birth to the age of entering first grade. More recent definitions include the elementary years as well. For our purposes, we shall define early childhood as from infancy through third grade. In terms of a child's life, that is roughly from birth to eight years of age. In school terms, it includes group settings for infants through the primary years of elementary school, grades one through three.

Early childhood educators thus build bridges between a child's two worlds, school (or group experience) and home. It is during these years that the foundation for future learning is set; these are the building block years, during which a child learns to walk, talk, print, and count. In later years, that same child builds on these skills to be able to climb mountains, speak a foreign language, learn cursive writing, and understand multiplication.

# WESTERN INFLUENCES

## In Ancient Times

The definition of childhood has varied greatly throughout history. For example, before the Renaissance children were considered adults by age seven. A society's definition of childhood influences how it educates its children.

Through medieval times (approximately the fifth through the thirteenth centuries), childhood hardly lasted beyond infancy. This period was largely an era of ignorance. Few members of the ruling class could read or write their names, and the monastery schools were for priests and religious instruction only. The education of children was fairly simple before the fifteenth century; there was no educational system, and the way of life was uncomplicated as well. Children learned mostly through their parents or by apprenticeship outside the family. The child was expected and encouraged to move into adulthood as fast as possible. Survival was the primary goal in life. Since the common religious belief was that people were naturally evil, children had to be directed, punished, and corrected constantly.

What little learning occurred during the Dark Ages came through the policies of Charlemagne of France, who proclaimed that the nobility should know their letters, and from a few monastery schools that maintained libraries. A new social class in the form of craft guilds began to grow as apprenticeships expanded. Although education was sparse, the seeds of learning were planted, including the introduction of the concepts of equality and brotherhood, a continuing concern of educators today.

## The Renaissance and the Reformation

With the Renaissance in the fourteenth century and the Reformation in the sixteenth century, society gradually became more enlightened. Several political, social, economic, and religious movements combined. The German school system had its beginnings estab-lished at this time and would continue to influence education in all parts of Europe. People changed the way they looked at children and their education. Towns grew and expanded, and there was an opportunity to move to new lands. Living conditions improved and infant mortality waned. Children were living longer. The acquisition of knowledge and skills at an earlier age became important. If educated, children could be expected to help their family improve its situation. Parents found they needed help in teaching their children.

## Into Modern Times

### Comenius

John Amos Comenius offered to help in teaching children. One of the best educators of the sixteenth century, he wrote the first picture book for children. Called *Orbis Pictus (The World of Pictures)*, it was a guide for teachers that included training of the senses and the study of nature. Comenius fostered the belief that education should follow the natural order of things. In other words, children's development follows a timetable of its own and their education should reflect that fact. He felt teachers must observe and work with this natural order, the timetable, to ensure successful learning. This idea was later reflected in Montessori's sensitive periods and Piaget's stages of development. Today it is recognized as the issue of *school readiness.*

Comenius also stressed a basic concept that is now taken for granted: learning by doing. He encouraged parents to let their children play with other children of the same age. He also reflected the growing social reform that would educate the poor as well as the rich.

### Locke

An important scholar and teacher in England during the 1600s, John Locke is considered to be the founder of modern educational philosophy. He based his theory of education on the scientific method and the study of the mind and learning. The purpose of education, he claimed, is to make man a reasoning creature (Cubberly, 1920). For beginners, a knowledge of the Bible and business was enough. Locke suggested

| | | |
|---|---|---|
| *Cornix* cornicatur, | à à | A a |
| The *Crow* crieth. | | |
| *Agnus* balat, | b è è è | B b |
| The *Lamb* blaiteth. | | |
| *Cicàda* stridet, | cì cì | C c |
| The *Grasshopper* chirpeth. | | |
| *Upupa* dicit, | du du | D d |
| The *Whooppoo* saith. | | |
| *Infans* ejulat, | è è è | E e |
| The *Infant* crieth. | | |
| *Ventus* flat, | fi fi | F f |
| The *Wind* bloweth. | | |
| *Anser* gingrit, | ga ga | G g |
| The *Goose* gagleth. | | |
| *Os* halat, | hà'h hà'h | H h |
| The *Mouth* breatheth out. | | |
| *Mus* mintrit, | ì ì ì | I i |
| The *Mouse* chirpeth. | | |
| *Anas* tetrinnit, | kha, kha | K k |
| The *Duck* quaketh. | | |
| *Lupus* ululat, | lu ulu | L |
| The *Wolf* howleth. | | |
| | [mum | |
| *Ursus* murmurat, | mum- | M m |
| The *Bear* grumbleth. | | |

**FIGURE 1.1**  *Orbis Pictus,* by John Comenius, is considered the first picture book written for children.

that such instruction should be pleasant, with playful activities as well as drills. Locke's influence on education was not felt strongly at the time. Later, however, his best ideas were popularized by Rousseau, such as the notion that the teacher must work through the senses to help children reach understanding. Today, teachers still emphasize a sensory approach to learning, helping children gain experience by touch, smell, and taste as well as by hearing and sight. Giving children

reasons for what happens is based on Locke's belief in helping children to learn to reason.

## Rousseau

After Comenius, new thoughts were everywhere in Europe. Locke offered some educational challenges, and Darwin brought a change to science. The time was ripe for new ideas about childhood. Jean Jacques Rousseau, a writer and philosopher of the middle

1700s, brought forth the idea that children were not inherently evil, but naturally good. He reasoned that education should reflect this goodness and allow spontaneous interests and activities of the children. Soon, children were actively involved in their own education. Each child was considered unique and valuable. While he was not an educator, Rousseau offered insights that were valuable. He suggested that school atmosphere should be less restrained and more flexible to meet the needs of the children. He insisted on using concrete teaching materials, leaving the abstract and symbolism for later years. Rousseau maintained that sense perception was the key to education. His _naturalism_ has affected thinking of educators ever since. Pestalozzi, Froebel, and Montessori were greatly influenced by him. In Europe, his ideas had a ripple effect that sent waves across the Atlantic Ocean.

Rousseau's ideas are still followed today in early childhood classes. Free play is based on Rousseau's belief in children's inherent goodness and ability to choose what they need to learn. Using concrete rather than abstract materials for young children is still one of the cornerstones of developmentally appropriate curriculum in the early years.

### Pestalozzi

Swiss educator Johann Heinrick Pestalozzi helped develop some classic principles of education. Like Rousseau, he used nature study as part of the curriculum and believed that good education meant the development of the senses. Pestalozzi stressed the idea of the _integrated curriculum_ which would develop the whole child. He wanted education to be of the hand, the head, and the heart of the child. Teachers were to guide self-activity through intuition, exercise, and the senses. Along with intellectual content, he proposed that practical skills be taught in the schools. He differed from Rousseau in that he proposed teaching children in groups rather than using a tutor with an individual child. Pestalozzi's work detailed some procedures for mothers to use at home with their children. He could well be named the first home trainer.

### Froebel

The work of Friedrich Wilhelm Froebel was perhaps the major influence on childhood education of the 1800s. He is known to us as the father of the kindergarten, not only for giving it a name, but for devoting his life to the development of a system of education for young children. The German word _kindergarten_ means "children's garden," and that is what Froebel felt best expressd what he wanted for children under six years of age. Since his own childhood had been unhappy, he resolved that early education should be pleasant. He advocated the radical thought that children should be able to play, to have toys, and to be with trained teachers. He started the first training school. Over one hundred years ago, Froebel's kindergartens included blocks, pets, and fingerplays. Froebel observed children and came to understand how they learned and what they liked to do. He developed the first educational toys, which he termed "gifts." Some of his theories about children and their education later influenced Montessori and were reflected in the educational materials she developed.

Every day, teachers in centers and homes across the country practice the Froebelian belief that a child's first educational experiences should be a garden: full of pleasant discoveries and delightful adventure, where the adults' role is to plant ideas and materials for children to use as they grow at their own pace.

> When the children are just making friends with the teacher and with each other, it is very interesting and profitable for them to formulate their mite of knowledge into a sentence, each one holding his ball high in the air with the right hand, and saying:
> My ball is red like a cherry.
> My ball is yellow like a lemon.
> My ball is blue like the sky.
> My ball is orange like a marigold.
> My ball is green like the grass.
> My ball is violet like a plum.

**FIGURE 1.2** Fingerplays, which are common activities in today's early childhood programs, were also a part of Froebel's kindergarten programs. (Excerpted from Wiggins and Smith, _Froebel's Gifts,_ Boston and New York: Houghton Mifflin Co., 1895, p. 22)

**FIGURE 1.3** Maria Montessori designed materials, classrooms, and a learning method for young children. (Courtesy of American Montessori Society, New York, N.Y.)

## Montessori

At the turn of the century, Maria Montessori became the first female physician in Italy. She worked in the slums of Rome with poor children and with mentally retarded children. Sensing that what they lacked was proper motivation and environment, she opened a preschool, Casa di Bambini, in 1907. Montessori designed materials, classrooms, and a teaching procedure that proved her point to the astonishment of people all over Europe and America.

Before her, no one with "medical and psychiatric training had yet spelled out so clearly" the needs of the growing child (Robison, 1983). Her medical background added credibility to her findings and helped her ideas gain recognition in this country. Through her enlightenment, child-sized furniture and materials are now used in classrooms. By focusing on the *sequential steps of learning,* Montessori developed a set of learning materials still used widely today. One of her most valuable contributions was a theory of how children learn. She believed that any task could be reduced to a series of small steps. By using this process, children could learn to sweep a floor, dress themselves, or multiply numbers.

Montessori materials are graded in difficulty and emphasize her interest in self-help skills. To foster this, she developed frames with buttons and laces so children could learn to be responsible for themselves when dressing. The layout of the room and the distribution and presentation of materials furthered this concept. Montessori placed great emphasis on the environment—the "prepared environment," as she called it. A sense of order, a place for everything, and a clear rationale are hallmarks of the Montessori influence.

Her procedures as well as her materials contain *self-correcting* features. Nesting cylinders, for example, fit together only one way and are to be used that way. Montessori supported earlier educational ideas of sensory development; she felt that cognitive abilities stem from sensory discrimination. Thus, most of her equipment was *tactile* and enhanced the senses as well as the mind. (See Chapter 2 for more information on Montessori programs.)

# AMERICAN INFLUENCES

## Colonial Days

The American educational system began in the Colonies. When thinking of Colonial America, people often envision the one-room schoolhouse. Indeed, this was the mainstay of education in the New England Colonies. Although home teaching of the Bible was not uncommon, children were sent to school primarily for religious reasons. Everyone needed to be able to read the Bible, the Puritan fathers reasoned. All children were sent to study, though historically boys were educated before girls. Not only the Bible was used in school, however; new materials like the New England Primer and the Horn Book were also used.

In the South, it was a different story. Plantation owners imported tutors from England or opened small private schools to teach just their sons to read and write. While the reasons were different, the results were similar: a very high percentage of adult readers. From these came the leaders of the American Revolution and the new nation.

The Revolutionary War brought the establishment of both the Union and religious freedom. By affirming fundamental principles of democratic liberty, the Founding Fathers paved the way for a system of free, common, public school systems, the first the world had seen (Cubberly, 1920). However, after the Revolutionary War, there were no significant advances in education until the late 1800s. Leaders like Thomas Jefferson felt that knowledge ought to be available to all, but that opinion was not widely shared. Most of the post-Revolutionary period focused on growing crops and pioneering the frontier, not teaching and educating children. Even by the 1820s, education for the common man was not readily available. Industrialization in both the North and South did little to encourage reading and writing skills. Manual labor and machine-operating skills were more important. While public schools were accepted in principle, in reality no tax basis was established to support them.

| My Pedagogic Creed—John Dewey | What It Means Today |
|---|---|
| 1. ". . . I believe that only true education comes through the stimulation of the child's powers by the demands of the social situations in which he finds himself." | This tells us that children learn to manage themselves in groups, to make and share friendships, to solve problems, and to cooperate. |
| 2. ". . . The child's own instinct and powers furnish the material and give the starting point for all education." | We need to create a place that is child-centered, a place that values the skills and interests of each child and each group. |
| 3. ". . . I believe that education, therefore, is a process of living and not a preparation for future living." | Prepare the child for what is to come by enriching and interpreting the present to him. Find educational implications in everyday experiences. |
| 4. ". . I believe that . . . the school life should grow gradually out of the home life . . . it is the business of the school to deepen and extend . . . the child's sense of the values bound up in his home life." | This sets the rationale for a relationship between teachers and parents. Values established and created in the home should be enhanced by teaching in the schools. |
| 5. ". . . I believe, finally, that the teacher is engaged, not simply in the training of individuals, but in the formation of a proper social life. I believe that every teacher should realize the dignity of his calling." | This says that the work teachers do is important and valuable. They teach more than academic content; they teach how to live. |

**FIGURE 1.4** John Dewey's Pedagogic Creed. John Dewey expressed his ideas about education in an important document titled, *My Pedagogic Creed* (Washington, D.C.: The Progressive Education Association, 1897).

## John Dewey

By the end of the 1800s, however, a nationwide reform movement had begun. In education, the *Progressive Movement,* as it was called, got its direction primarily through one individual, John Dewey (1858-1952).

Dewey was the first real American influence on American education. Raised in Vermont, he became a professor of philosophy at both the University of Chicago and Columbia University. In the years that followed, Dewey would be responsible for one of the greatest impacts on American education of all time.

Dewey believed that children were valuable and that childhood was an important part of their lives. Like Froebel, he felt that education should be integrated with life and should provide a training ground for cooperative living. As did Pestalozzi and Rousseau, Dewey felt that schools should focus on the nature of the child. Until this time, children were considered of little consequence. Childhood was rushed. Children as young as seven were a regular part of the work force—on the farms, in the mines, and in the factories. Dewey's beliefs about children and learning are summarized in Figure 1.4.

A new kind of school emerged from these ideals. Even the buildings began to take on a different look. Movable furniture replaced rows of benches. Children's projects, some still under construction, were found everywhere. The curriculum of the school began to focus on all of the basics, not just a few of the academics. If a group of six-year-olds decided to make a woodworking table, they would first have to learn to read in order to understand the directions. After calculating the cost, they would purchase the materials. In building the table, geometry, physics, and math were learned along the way. This was a group effort that encouraged children to work together in teams and so school became a society in miniature. Children's social skills were developed along with reading, science, and math. The teacher's role in the process was one of ongoing support, involvement, and encouragement.

The contribution of John Dewey to American education cannot be underestimated. As described in Figure 1.4, Dewey's ideas are part of today's classrooms in several ways. His child-oriented schools are a model of day care centers and family day care homes, as learning and living are inseparable. As the following sections on kindergarten and nursery schools illustrate, John Dewey had a vision that is still alive today.

## Kindergarten

The word *kindergarten*—which is German for "children's garden"—is a delightful term. It brings to mind the image of young seedlings on the verge of blossoming. The similarity between caring for young plants and young children is not accidental. Froebel, the man who coined the word kindergarten, meant for that association to be made. As a flower opens from a bud, so too does a child go through a natural unfolding process. This idea—and ideal—are part of the kindergarten story.

The first kindergarten was a German school started by Froebel in 1837. Over a dozen years later, in 1856, Margaretha Schurz, a student of Froebel, opened the first kindergarten in the United States. It was for German-speaking children and held in her home in Wisconsin. Schurz inspired Elizabeth Peabody of Boston, who opened the first English-speaking kindergarten there in 1860. Peabody, in turn, after studying kindergartens in Germany, influenced William Harris, superintendent of schools in St. Louis, Missouri. In 1873, Harris allowed Susan Blow to open the first kindergarten in the United States that was associated with the public schools.

Froebel's concepts became well-established and are a cornerstone of early childhood philosophy. Froebelian kindergartens emphasized the importance of play and the value of childhood. His curriculum consisted of "gifts"—objects for children to use and manipulate to discover concepts and learning. Some of Froebel's gifts were a ball of yarn, a cube, a cylinder, and a sphere. Activities, songs, and fingerplays were developed that used these gifts as learning tools. Until close to the turn of the century, Froebel's philosophy remained the mainstay of kindergarten education.

By early 1900, however, the voices of dissent were being heard. Froebel's ideas had come under the scrutiny of Hall, Dewey, and others. A classic clash of

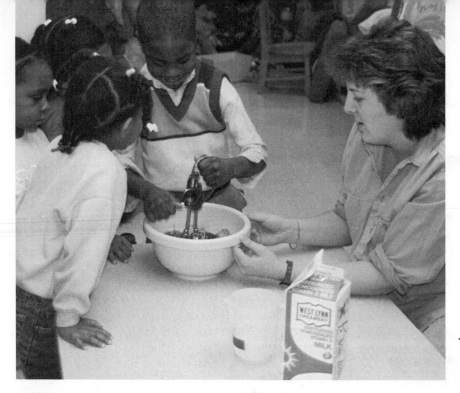

**FIGURE 1.5** Schools patterned after John Dewey's philosophy involved children in activities of practical, real-life nature, such as cooking the meal of the day. (Courtesy of Stride Rite Children's Centers, Cambridge, Mass.)

ideals developed between followers of Froebel (conservatives) and those of Dewey's new educational viewpoint (progressives). Support for the latter came from those who saw kindergartens as a social service. Many of the kindergartens started in the late 1800s were established by churches and other agencies that worked with the poor. It was an era of rising social conscience, and the reasons for helping the less fortunate were not unlike the rationale that led to the creation of Head Start and Follow-Through sixty years later.

Critics of Froebel took exception to his seemingly rigid approach. The emphasis in a Froebelian kindergarten was on teacher-directed learning. Dewey's followers preferred a more child-centered approach, with teachers serving as facilitators of children's learning. It is the same tension that exists today between the "back to basics" movement and the supporters of open education. The progressives found fault with the "gifts" of Froebel's curriculum. Those who followed Dewey believed that "real objects and real situations within the child's own social setting" should be used (Read and Patterson, 1980). Froebel was viewed as too

structured and too symbolic; Dewey was perceived as child-oriented and child-involved. Even the processes they employed were different. Froebel believed in the unfolding of the child's mind and learning, whereas Dewey stressed the child's "potential developed through social interaction" (Broman, 1978).

The debate raged for another 25 years. The progressives succeeded in influencing the content of kindergarten programs, retaining some of Froebel's basic concepts. "The reform of kindergarten education continued through the 1920s and 1930s leading to the creation of the modern American kindergarten..." (Spodek, 1972).

Patty Smith Hill of Teacher's College, Columbia University, was an outstanding innovator of the time and one of the Progressive Movement's most able leaders. It was she who founded the National Association for Nursery Education (NANE). Now the largest association of early childhood educators, it is known today as the National Association for the Education of Young Children (NAEYC). She believed strongly in basing curricula and programs on the nature and needs of the children, and she was one of the major education experimenters of her day. She was

> . . . guided by principles of democracy and respect for individuals. She argued for freedom and initiative for children, as well as a curriculum relevant to children's lives. It was she who originated large-muscle equipment and materials suitable for climbing and construction, a departure from the prescribed small-muscle activities of the Froebelians. Patty Hill also urged unification of kindergarten and first grade work, but her objective was not to start 5 year olds on first grade work, we today might readily assume. Rather, emphasis was on giving six year olds the opportunity for independent, creative activities before embarking on the three R's.
>
> (Cohen and Randolph, 1977)

These ideas became the backbone of kindergarten practice. Regardless of controversy within, kindergartens were still on the fringes of the educational establishments as a whole. However, when the 1960s highlighted the problems of the poor and their failure in schools and society, kindergarten and the early years were brought back into the spotlight. Today, the kindergarten is found in some form in nearly every country of the world. While the content of the program and the length of the day vary widely in the United States, kindergarten is available in every one of the United States. For a discussion of the development of teachers in kindergarten, see Dr. Spodek's *Focus* discussion.

# Nursery Schools

## *Establishment in America*

Early childhood educators took Dewey's philosophy to heart. Their schools reflected the principles of a *child-centered* approach, active learning, and social cooperation. By the 1920s and 1930s, early childhood education had reached a professional status in the United States. Nursery schools and day nurseries went beyond custodial health care. They fostered the child's total development. The children were enrolled from middle- and upper-class homes as well as from working

families. However, until the 1960s, nursery schools served few poor families.

Parent education was acknowledged as a vital function of the school and led to the establishment of *parent cooperative schools*. The first of these parent participation schools was developed in 1915 at the University of Chicago. A group of faculty wives started the Chicago Cooperative Nursery School.

Research centers and child development laboratories were started in many colleges and universities. Among them were:

| | |
|---|---|
| 1919 | Bank Street School *between WW I + WW II* |
| 1921 | Columbia Teacher's College Laboratory Nursery School |
| 1922 | Ruggles Street Nursery School and Training Center |
| 1922 | Merrill-Palmer Institute Nursery School |
| 1923 | Bowling Green Nursery |
| 1923 | Cambridge Nursery |
| 1926 | Vassar College Nursery School |
| 1926 | Smith College Nursery School |
| 1927 | Mills College Nursery School |

These *laboratory schools* were active in expanding the knowledge of how important a child's early years are.

## *Lucy Sprague Mitchell*

Early childhood education in the United States grew out of John Dewey's progressive movement largely because of Lucy Sprague Mitchell and her contemporaries. Raised in an environment of educational and social reform, Mitchell developed the idea of schools as community centers as well as places for children to learn to think. As Greenberg (1987) explained, she gathered together, in a democratic, cooperative venture, many talented people to brainstorm, mastermind, and sponsor:

- A remarkable Bureau of Educational Experiments

- A school to implement and experiment with these principles

- A laboratory to record and analyze how and why they function as she knew they did (and as we know they do!)

# EARLY CHILDHOOD PRACTITIONERS

*Bernard Spodek*

One way to understand early childhood education practice today is to look at how practice and practitioners evolved. A century ago, practitioners of early childhood education were not called teachers, but rather *kindergarteners.* They worked in the newly established kindergartens brought over from Germany by women trained in the educational practices of Friedrich Froebel. The change to *teacher* was paralleled by a slow but steady increase in the required level of preparation.

Kindergartners were originally trained in a modified form of apprenticeship. Directors of kindergartens would also train novices, who would work with children under supervision while studying Froebel's philosophy and practices. Often the novices would be put through the same kindergarten activities as were the children. Although kindergarten programs were originally freestanding institutions, they were slowly integrated into public education, becoming part of the elementary school. The kindergarten with its rich, child-centered program influenced the primary grades so that art, music, science, and social studies were included along with the basic academic skills.

As kindergartens became part of the public schools, normal schools, which prepared elementary teachers, began to prepare kindergarten teachers as well. The early normal schools were parallel institutions to the high school, which at that time was primarily preparing students for college. Later, normal schools evolved into one- and two-year post-secondary programs, then adding liberal arts education and becoming four-year colleges and universities. In the process, the preparation of kindergarten teachers became closely related to the preparation of elementary teachers.

- A teachers' college to promote them
- A workshop for writers of children's literature (a new genre—a number of currently famous authors of juvenile books attended) and
- A bulletin to disseminate it all, as well as disseminating what a plethora of progressive educators were up to elsewhere, *beginning in 1916!*

By establishing Bank Street College of Education (and its laboratory school), Lucy Sprague Mitchell emphasized the link between theory and practice, namely, that the education of young children and the study of how children learn are intrinsically tied together.

## *Abagail Eliot*

The nursery school movement was pioneered by Abagail Eliot. A graduate of Radcliffe College and Harvard University, she was the director of the Ruggles Street Nursery School and Training Center, which opened in Boston in 1922. Eliot has made some observations about those early years:

*On the "new school":* "The big difference—the new idea—was program. I had visited many day nurseries in Boston as a social worker. I can remember them even now: dull green walls, no light colors, nothing pretty—spotlessly clean places, with rows of white-faced, listless little children sitting, doing nothing. There was a drabness, an emptiness, a nothingness. In the new nursery school, the children were active . . . alive . . . choosing . . . gay, busy, happy. That was the difference . . . "

*On parents:* "Parents chose to send their children to nursery schools. They wanted nursery school

The development of the nursery school in the 1920s provided a new avenue for early childhood teachers. The nursery school teacher became responsible for the education and nurturance of young children, usually ages three and four. The child study movement and later the field of child development evolved along with the nursery school. Teachers of young children were expected to know more about child development research and theory.

Though nursery schools were primarily half-day programs, they influenced day nurseries, originally designed as custodial agencies, to include education programs. The day care teacher was expected to know more about children than was the nursery school teacher, since day care teachers were responsible for the health and welfare of children, as well as their education. Assistant teachers and teacher aides with less training augmented the work of teachers in kindergartens, nursery schools, and child care centers, allowing for lower child:adult ratios in the classroom.

With the possible exception of day care staffs, in which economic pressures have limited development, early childhood teachers are becoming better educated than in the past. Teachers are also being prepared to teach in a broader array of programs, in a variety of institutions, and for a range of ages (such as birth through four or three through eight).

The field continues to be concerned with the need for increased competence and increased professionalism in early childhood teachers. Not only must we have more teachers of young children, we need better prepared teachers. There must also be increased recognition of competence in early childhood teachers. Certification and credentialing of early childhood practitioners, perhaps at varying professional levels, will increase recognition and professionalism. Recognition will also come with higher teacher salaries and higher status for those who work with young children, both within and outside the field of education.

*Bernard Spodek, Ed.D., is a professor of early childhood education at the University of Illinois.*

---

for the child's own good . . . I remember telling one of the early graduating classes at the Nursery Training School: 'If the nursery school movement does not result ultimately in better homes, it will be a failure.'"

*On learning:* "There was a conviction back then, too, that children learn so much from each other . . . I think the early schools were committed to the belief that the physical and mental life of children are inseparable. You cannot educate the mind without the body, and vice versa."

(Hymes, 1978)

# Midcentury Developments

## *The Depression*

It was during the Depression, World War II, and the postwar years that the American public focused more sharply than ever before on the needs of young children. These were times when the general public became aware of the importance of early childhood. Government-funded nursery schools later became the Works Progress Administration (WPA) nursery schools, which hired unemployed teachers. Government support from 1941 (Lanham Act War Nurseries) continued until 1946 when the Lanham Act schools were turned over to the states or closed.

## *Kaiser Child Care Centers*

During World War II, funds were provided to deal with the common situation of mothers working in war-related industries. Further support came from industry during World War II. An excellent model for child care operated from 1943 to 1945 in Portland, Oregon. It was the Kaiser Child Care Centers. Kaiser became the world's largest such center and functioned "round the clock" all year long. A number of services were made available on site. An infirmary was located nearby for both mothers and children. Hot meals were made available for mothers to take home when they picked up their children. Lois Meek Stolz was the director of the centers, and James L. Hymes, Jr., the manager. Edith Dowley, who was one of the teachers, describes in detail the environment and experiences of this remarkable project in the guest editorial that introduces this section. Stolz and Hymes describe the centers this way:

> . . . The centers were to have three distinctive qualities. One, they were to be located not out in the community but right at the entrance to the two shipyards, convenient to mothers on their way to and from work. They were to be industry-based, not neighborhood-centered. Two, the centers were to be operated by the shipyards, not by the public schools and not by community agencies. They were to be industrial child care centers, with the cost borne by the Kaiser company and by parents using the service. Three, they were to be large centers, big enough to meet the need. In the original plan each center was to serve a thousand preschool children on three shifts.
>
> (Hymes, 1978)

These centers served 3,811 different children. As Hymes points out, they provided 249,268 child care days. They had freed 1,931,827 woman work-hours. Once the war ended, though, the workers left. Child care was no longer needed, and the centers closed. The model they provide for child care remains exemplary, especially in light of the need for high-quality, full-day child care today.

## Head Start

After the war, few innovations took place until a small piece of metal made its worldwide debut. Sputnik, the Soviet satellite, was successfully launched in 1957 and caused an upheaval in educational circles. Two questions were uppermost in the minds of most Americans: Why weren't we first in space? What is wrong with our schools? The emphasis in education quickly settled on engineering, science, and math in

the hope of catching up with Russian technology.

The civil rights struggle in the early 1960s soon followed. In pointing out the plight of the poor, education was highlighted as a major stumbling block toward equality of all people. It was time to act, and Project Head Start was conceived as education's place to fight the "war on poverty." The same goals of Froebel and Montessori formed the basis of Head Start: helping disadvantaged preschool children.

Beginning in 1965, Project Head Start organized summer programs for children four and five years old. All children whose socioeconomic status predicted school failure were eligible. After the first summer, the experiment was expanded to the academic year as well. This was an exciting time—a national recognition of the needs of young children and a hope for a better quality of life. Three major points included in the Head Start program are noteworthy:

- *Compensatory education*—programs that compensate for inadequate early life experiences.
- *Parental involvement*—inclusion of parents in planning, teaching, and decision making.
- *Community control*—local support and participation.

These three objectives combined to reinforce the goals of the program in real and concrete ways. Head Start was an attempt to make amends, to compensate poor children by preparing them for school and educational experiences. Parents, by being required to participate at all levels, were educated along with their children. The purpose of the community-based governing boards was to allow the program to reflect local values and concerns. Concurrently, underprivileged, poor people were being encouraged to take part in solving some of their own problems.

The spirit of Head Start was infectious. As a result of community interest in Head Start, there was a burst of enthusiasm for many programs for the young child. Because of Head Start's publicity, there has been an expanding enrollment in nursery school, kindergarten, and day care programs. Thanks to Head Start, there is national attention to the need for providing good care and educational experiences for young children. Head Start programs are still alive and well today. We will discuss them further in Chapter 2.

# INTERDISCIPLINARY INFLUENCES

Several professions enrich the heritage of early childhood. This diversity was apparent from the beginning; the first nursery schools drew from five different professions: social work, home economics, nursing, psychology, and medicine. Three of the most consistent and influential of those disciplines were medicine, education, and child psychology.

## Medicine

The medical field has contributed to the study of child growth through the work of several physicians. These doctors became interested in child development and extended their knowledge to the areas of child rearing and education.

### Sigmund Freud

Few can deny that Dr. Freud made important contributions to modern thinking. The father of personality theory, he drastically changed how we look at childhood. Freud reinforced two specific ideas: (1) a person is influenced by his early life in fundamental and dramatic ways, and (2) early experiences shape the way people live and behave as adults. Thus, psychoanalytic theory is mostly about personality development and emotional problems. Although the impact of psychoanalysis on child psychology is not as great as it was 25 years ago, it still contributes significantly to the study of early childhood. Though he was not involved directly in education, Dr. Freud influenced its development.

### Arnold Gesell

As a qualified physician, Dr. Gesell was concerned with growth from a medical point of view. Gesell began studying child development when he was a student of G. Stanley Hall, an early advocate of child study. The data collected by Gesell and his colleagues have become the recognized norms of how children grow and develop.

Gesell's greatest contribution was in the area of child growth. He saw maturation as an innate and powerful force in development. "The total plan of growth," he said, "is beyond your control. It is too complex and mysterious to be altogether entrusted to human hands. So nature takes over most of the task, and simply invites your assistance" (Gesell, Ames, and Ilg, 1977). This belief became known in psychological circles as the *maturation theory*.

Through the Gesell Institute, guides were published using this theory. With such experts as Dr. Frances Ilg and Dr. Louise Bates Ames, Gesell authored articles that realistically portrayed the child's growth from birth to adolescence.

### Benjamin Spock

Spock's book, *Baby and Child Care*, was a mainstay for parents in the 1940s and 1950s. In a detailed "how-to" format Dr. Spock preached a common-sense approach that helped shape the childhood of many of today's adults. He suggested that mothers use the playpen less and allow children freedom to explore the world first-hand. To that end, he asked parents to "child proof" their homes—a radical thought at the time. The word "permissiveness," as it relates to child rearing, became associated with Dr. Spock's methods.

Dr. Spock has become an outspoken advocate for causes that extend his ideas. He is an active critic of those forces, be they economic, social, or political, that destroy people's healthy development. In his own words:

> I'll summarize my thoughts this way: Child care and home care, if well done, can be more creative, make a greater contribution to the world, bring more pleasure to family members, than 9 out of 10 outside jobs. It is only our mixed-up, materialistic values that make so many of us think the other way around.
>
> (Spock, 1976)

### T. Berry Brazelton

Dr. Brazelton is a well-known pediatrician who supports and understands the development of infants and toddlers. His pediatric guide to parents deals with both physical and emotional growth. His writings speak to the parents' side of child raising, such as setting limits, or listening to what children say and observing what they do. Brazelton (1974) discusses the two-year-old and sharing this way:

> Understanding such concepts as fair and unfair, of giving and receiving and the process of sharing, all demands a kind of self-awareness. If a child is not sure of his own limits and of his own strengths, he cannot afford to allow his toys, equivalent to parts of himself, to be passed out to someone else, trusting that they will come back. At the same time, the ability to do so is evidence of an awareness of behavior in others comparable to his own and denotes the beginning of an awareness of non-self.

## Education

Early childhood is one part of the larger professional field known as education. This includes elementary, secondary, and college or postsecondary schools. Along with John Dewey and Abagail Eliot, several other influences from this field bear attention.

### The Macmillan Sisters

In the first three decades of this century, these two sisters pioneered in early education. Nursery schools in Britain and America probably were developed because of the drive and dedication of the Macmillan sisters.

Both women had broad international backgrounds. They grew up in North America and Scotland. Margaret studied music and language in Europe. She was well read in philosophy, politics, and medicine. Rachel studied to become a health inspector in England.

Health studies of 1908-1910 showed that 80 percent of children were born in good health, but that by the time they entered school, only 20 percent could be classifed that way. Noticing the deplorable conditions for children under five, the Macmillan sisters began a crusade for the slum children in England. Their concern extended beyond education to medical and dental care for young children. In 1910 they set up a clinic in Deptford, a London slum area, which became an open-air nursery a year later. The Macmillans called it a "nurture school." Later, a training college nearby was named for Rachel. With no private financial resources, these two women faced tremendous hardships in keeping their school open. It is to their credit that Deptford still exists today.

The Macmillan theory of fresh air, sleep, and bathing proved successful. "When over seven hundred children between one and five died of measles, there was not one fatal case at Deptford School" (Deasey, 1978). From the school's inception, a primary function was to research the effects of poverty on children.

Of the two sisters, Margaret had the greatest influence at the school at Deptford. Abagail Eliot writes of her:

> Miss Macmillan invented the name [nursery school]. She paid great attention to health: a daily inspection, the outdoor program, play, good food—what she called "nurture." But she saw that an educational problem was also involved and she set to work to establish her own method of education for young children. This was why she called it a "school."

(Hymes, 1978)

### The Child Study Movement

A survey of education influences is incomplete without mentioning the child study movement in the 1920s and 1930s. It was through the child study movement that education and psychology began to have a common focus on children. Besides the Gesell Institute, many research centers and child development laboratories were established at colleges and universities around the country. Their inception reflects the interest of several disciplines in the growth of the young child. Schools of psychology looked for children to observe and study; schools of education wanted demonstration schools for their teachers-in-training and for student-teacher placement. Schools of home economics wanted their students to have first-hand experiences with children. These on-campus schools provided a place to gather information about child development and child psychology.

One important member of this movement was Susan Isaacs. Her work with young children in England's Malting House School was an experiment in the application of John Dewey's principles. Dr. Isaacs created a school with materials that stimulated curiosity about the real world and emphasized children's innate drive toward learning to solve problems of their own choosing. She developed the first advanced course in child development for teachers. Today Susan Isaacs is remembered for her innovative work with children and for being the "Mother of Early Childhood Graduate Study."

This period of educational experiment and child study led to an impressive collection of normative data by which we still measure ranges of ordinary development. Broman (1978) sums up the influence of the movement this way:

> From the beginning of the child study movement in the 1920s . . . early childhood was not a major emphasis in education until after the War on Poverty and the establishment of Head Start in 1965. The child study movement, however, was the impetus that began the search for the most appropriate means of educating young children.

### The British Infant School

Developed by Robert Owen in the early nineteenth century, the British infant schools enrolled children at 18 months and had a strong commitment to social reform (Spodek, 1985). In England, the term *infant school* refers to the kindergarten and primary grades. Then in 1967, the Plowden Report proposed a series of reforms for the schools. These changes paralleled those of American early childhood education. As a result, many American teachers in both the preschool and primary grades adapted the British infant school approach to their own classrooms.

Three aspects of this *open school* style that received the most attention were:

**1.** *Vertical, or family, groupings.* Children from five to eight years of age are placed in the same classroom. Several teachers may combine their classes and work together in teaching teams. Children may be taught by the same teachers for two or three years.

**2.** *Integrated day.* The classroom is organized into various centers, for math, science, and the arts. The teacher moves from one child or center to another as needed. Play is often the central activity, with an emphasis on follow-through with children's ideas and interests as they arise.

**3.** *Underlying concept.* There is a fundamental belief that the process of thinking takes precedence over the accumulation of facts. Learning how to think rather than stockpiling data is encouraged. How to identify and solve problems is valued more than having a finished product. Teachers focus on the child's current learning rather than on the future.

Just as Owen's ideas took hold in America in the nineteenth century, so, too, did the twentieth-century version of the infant school fire the imaginations of teachers in the United States. Their tenets of open education are developmentally appropriate for both preschool and primary schools (Bredekamp, 1988).

## Psychology

The roots of early childhood education are wonderfully diverse, but one tap root is especially deep: the connection with the field of psychology. In this century particularly, the study of people and their behavior is linked with the study of children and their growth. Initially, child development was mostly confined to the study of trends and descriptions of changes.

Since World War II, the scope and definition of child development have changed radically. Developmental psychologists now study the process associated with those changes. Specifically, child development focuses on language acquisition, the effect of early experiences on intellectual development, and the process of attachment to others. Such is the world of early childhood—it is no wonder that we are so closely tied to the world of psychology.

There is no one theory or name that encompasses all of developmental psychology. Indeed, there are many. The major theories, their creators, and their influence on early education will be discussed in depth in Chapter 4.

| | |
|---|---|
| 1592–1670 | Johann Amos Comenius (E) *Orbis Pictus,* 1657 *learning by doing* |
| 1712–1788 | Jean Jacques Rousseau (E) *naturalism* |
| 1746–1826 | Johann Heinrich Pestalozzi (E) *How Gertrude Teaches Her Children,* 1801 *integrated curriculum* |
| 1782–1852 | Friedrich Wilhelm Froebel (E) *Songs for Mothers* and *Nursery Songs Kindergarten* *1837* |
| 1804–1894 | Elizabeth Peabody (E) National movement for kindergarten |
| 1843–1916 | Susan Blow (E) First U.S. public kindergarten *1856* |
| 1856–1939 | Sigmund Freud (P) |
| 1858–1952 | John Dewey (E) *My Pedagogic Creed,* 1897 |
| 1860–1931 | Margaret Macmillan (E) Founder of Deptford School |
| 1868–1946 | Patty Smith Hill (E) Founder of Columbia Laboratory School and NANE (now NAEYC) |
| 1870–1952 | Maria Montessori (M) |
| 1874–1949 | Edward L. Thorndike (P) |
| 1878–1958 | John B. Watson (P) |
| 1878–1967 | Lucy Sprague (E) Founder of Bank Street College of Education and its laboratory school |
| 1880–1961 | Arnold Gesell (M) *The Preschool Child,* 1923 |
| 1885– | Susan Isaacs (E) Founder of early childhood education and advanced study |
| 1896–1980 | Jean Jacques Piaget (P) *The Language and Thought of the Child,* 1926 |
| 1902– | Erik H. Erikson (P) *Childhood and Society,* 1950 |
| 1903– | Benjamin Spock (M) *Baby and Child Care,* 1946 |
| 1904– | B.F. Skinner (P) *The Behavior of Organisms,* 1938 |
| 1908–1984 | Sylvia Ashton Warner (E) New Zealand kindergarten teacher, developed "organic reading" and "key vocabulary" concepts |
| 1913– | Abagail Eliot (E) Founder of Ruggles Street School |
| 1915– | Jerome Bruner (P) |
| 1918– | T. Berry Brazelton (M) *Infants and Mothers,* 1969 |
| 1925– | Albert Bandura (P) |
| 1929– | Jerome Kagan (P) |
| 1929– | Burton White (M) |

(E): Educator
(P): Psychologist
(M): Medical person

*[handwritten margin notes: "Notable — how did — what third" ; "Susan B. Anthony?" ; "Civil War 1861 — time line"]*

**FIGURE 1.6** The timeline of influential people in early childhood education stretches across the centuries and includes the works and ideas of the influential educators throughout history.

*[handwritten margin note: Decrease reform? change in edua]*

# THEMES IN EARLY CHILDHOOD EDUCATION

When we review the colorful and rich history of early childhood education, three major themes emerge. These same themes reappear and are reflected in the ensuing thought and theory of each age.

## Ethic of Social Reform

The first theme is that of the ethic of social reform. Early childhood education programs often have had the expectation that schooling for the young will lead to social change and improvement. Montessori, the Macmillans, and Head Start all tried to improve children's health and physical well-being by attending first to the physical and social welfare aspects of children's lives. Educators today still assert that tired,

undernourished children are not ready to learn or to be educated. Social reform can go a step further, such as with Head Start, improving the whole family situation and involving the community in its efforts.

## Importance of Childhood

The second theme is the importance and uniqueness of childhood. Before 1700 or so, Western society showed little concern for children. Infanticide was persistent, if not actually accepted. Once families and society began to value children, life changed dramatically for the young. The saying "As the twig is bent, so grows the tree" could apply to all children and their early childhood learning experiences as well as to an individual child. When people accepted the importance of childhood, they began to take responsibility for a quality life for children. Society began to

| Year | School and Founder | Location |
|---|---|---|
| 1837 | First kindergarten (Froebel) | Germany |
| 1856 | First American kindergarten (Schurz) | Wisconsin |
| 1873 | First American public school kindergarten (Blow) | Missouri |
| 1907 | Casa di Bambini (Montessori) | Italy |
| 1911 | Deptford School (Macmillan Sisters) | England |
| 1919 | Bank Street College (Mitchell/Johnson) | New York |
| 1921 | Columbia Teacher's College Laboratory School (P.S. Hill) | New York |
| 1921 | Iowa Research Station | Iowa |
| 1921 | Summerhill (Neill) | England |
| 1922 | Merrill-Palmer Institute (White) | Michigan |
|  | Ruggles Street Nursery School (Eliot) | Massachusetts |
| 1926 | Smith College Nursery School | Massachusetts |
|  | Vassar College Nursery School | New York |
|  | Yale Guidance Nursery (Gesell) | Connecticut |
| 1927 | Mills College Nursery School | California |
| 1943 | Kaiser Child Care Centers (Stolz) | Oregon |
| 1946 | Bing Nursery School, Stanford (Dowley) | California |
| 1962 | Perry Preschool Project (Weikart) | Michigan |
| 1965 | Head Start | United States |
| 1830s and 1967 | British Infant Schools (Owen, Plowden Report) | England |

**FIGURE 1.7**   Since the early 1900s, early childhood education has provided children with excellent schools both here and abroad.

provide for the health and physical welfare of children and came to understand the necessity to care for their minds.

Modern early childhood teachers believe the early years form the foundation for later development, physically, intellectually, socially, and emotionally. Children need special attention during these years. Childhood is fundamentally different from adulthood; it needs to be understood and respected as such. Public recognition of that need has created a wealth of programs for the young not dreamed of at any other time in history.

## Transmitting Values

The third recurrent theme in our educational heritage is that of transmitting values. What children should ultimately *do* and *be* is at the core of all child-rearing practices, whether in the home or the school. Values—be they social, cultural, moral, or religious—have been the essence of education for centuries. For example, the Puritan fathers valued hard work and Biblical theology. Therefore, schools of their time taught children to read in order to learn the Bible. Rousseau, Froebel, Montessori, and Dewey valued the child. Their work reflected a belief in the worth and dignity of childhood. They transmitted these values into the educational thought and practices we have inherited. Finally, the initiators of Head Start realized the child's self-worth would be enhanced by valuing cultural heritage. Therefore, an awareness and appreciation of ethnic heritage became an integral part of the Head Start curriculum.

Teaching children to live in a democratic society has always been valued in the United States. In the curriculum from kindergarten through college, this belief is reflected as we educate our children for citizenship. It is how we define these values and how we teach them that are the critical issues in education.

These three themes have been at the center of early education for centuries. Occasionally, one theme dominates, as it did in the 1960s when the desire for social reform led to the creation of Head Start. At other times they seem indistinguishable from one another. Together, they have shaped the direction of early

childhood education as we know it today. As we learn more about children, society, and ourselves, the 1990s will be a time to reconsider and redefine our aims and directions. It is a formidable challenge—and a worthy one.

## INTEGRATING HISTORY WITH THEORY

The history of early childhood education is like a tapestry—woven of many influences. A broad field such as medicine is a thread in this cloth, as is the passion of a Patty Smith Hill or a Lucy Sprague Mitchell. The history forms the theory on which we base our teaching, and every child, every class, every experience forms another thread in the weaving.

Events of history have had a hand in shaping early childhood education. Forces such as war (which produced the Kaiser Shipyards project) and the state of the economy (which brought the War on Poverty and Head Start) bring about change and development in how children are cared for in this country.

Several fields of study and a number of professions have added to our knowledge of children and, therefore, have affected educational theory. From the professions of education, medicine, and psychology, early childhood education has developed a theory of what is best for children. The medical model offered a view of childhood that is both maturational and environmental. Psychology confirmed this blending of nature and nurture and offered observational study as a basis for educational practice. As a result, early childhood theory includes both an attention to physical growth and developmental stages and a respect for personal experience in learning. The field of education brought to early childhood theory the components of a holistic approach to child and family, variable grouping of children and activities, and a sensitivity to the social and reform possibilities of educating our young. These influences will be described at length in Chapter 4.

The individuals who created our history have had a profound effect on early childhood theory. Their strong and passionate beliefs have captured our imaginations and fueled our commitment to enhancing

**FIGURE 1.8** Childhood is a special time of life.

the well-being of children. What John Dewey, Lucy Sprague Mitchell, and Susan Isaacs all had in common was a drive to extend themselves on behalf of young children. Thus, early childhood theory has a *personal* component, an emotional investment that gives each early childhood teacher and caregiver a sense of belonging to a larger cause. The work that has gone before goes on through us and extends beyond us—to children of all ages and any era.

From this blending of professional discoveries and personal commitment comes a challenge. Early childhood history calls on teachers to learn from the past and to know the theories on which the profession is based. These theories must be continually tested in the classroom and refined as they apply to children every day. In this way, the profession stays relevant and legitimate. Finally, early childhood education history affirms the value of being connected with others and

remaining steadfastly committed to the common cause of young children. As the NAEYC Code of Ethics states:

I will know about, abide by, and advocate for laws and regulations that enhance the quality of life for young children.

I will support the rights of children to live and learn in environments that are responsive to their developmental needs.

I will improve my competencies in providing for children's needs.

I will appreciate each child's uniqueness, thus enhancing the child's self-respect. (NAEYC, 1988)

# SUMMARY

This chapter traces the roots of early childhood education from ancient times. Knowing this history gives teachers a sense of support and inspiration. An historical overview offers insights that illuminate present program and societal needs and prevent future mistakes. It helps us appreciate the legacy left by others.

Early childhood education involves children from infancy through the primary years. The term itself offers its own professional challenges:

EARLY: How do YOUNG children grow and learn best?

CHILDHOOD: How do CHILDREN think, feel, learn?

EDUCATION: How can children LEARN and be TAUGHT?

These questions have been addressed by educators in Europe and America throughout history. Their answers have influenced educational philosophy and practice and, in turn, have been affected by the social and political forces of the day. The most notable modern developments in this country have been the advent of nursery schools and kindergartens, the Kaiser Child Care Center in World War II as a day care model, and Head Start.

Early childhood education itself is an interdisciplinary field. Important contributions have come from medicine, education, and psychology.

Certain themes emerge in early childhood education with a study of its history. The ethic of social reform, the importance of childhood, and the transmission of values have been at the core of this field throughout history.

The contributions of many pioneers leave us dreams for the young children of our society. This can give meaning to our lives as teachers as we continue to create a climate for the child who will make history tomorrow.

## REVIEW QUESTIONS

1. Identify and describe five key people who influenced the field of early childhood education. With whom would you like to have studied or worked? Why?

2. Match the name with the appropriate phrase. Put them in the order that best matches your own theory of early childhood education. State your reasons.

| | |
|---|---|
| Rousseau | "prepared environment" |
| Montessori | "nurture" school |
| Froebel | children are naturally good |
| Dewey | father of kindergarten |
| Spock | common-sense approach |
| Macmillan Sisters | first picture book for children |
| Comenius | Progressive Movement |

3. Define early childhood education in your own words. Include age ranges and what you believe to be its purpose. Contrast this to the text definition and defend your position.

4. Name three institutions or living persons who are influencing the history of early childhood today. Describe your reactions to each, and how they have influenced your educational philosophy. *Head Start; NAEYC; Barry Brazelton*

5. Maria Montessori made several contributions to education. What are some of her theories and how did she adapt them for classroom use? How are Montessori materials or teaching methods used in your classroom? *Sequential steps of learning prepared environment self correcting activities*

# L E A R N I N G   A C T I V I T I E S

*Choose 1*

1. Find out when and by whom the school or center in which you are student teaching was started. What were some of the social, economic, and political issues of those times? How might they have affected the philosophy of the school?

✓ 2. Write your own pedagogic creed. List five of what you consider to be the most important beliefs you hold about educating young children. How do you see those beliefs expressed in school today?

3. Make a list of the values you think are important to teach children. In an adjoining column, add the ways in which you would help children learn those values. In other words, list the materials and curriculum you would use. *respect for others self respect (esteem)*

# B I B L I O G R A P H Y

Braun, S.J., and Edwards, E.P. *History and Theory of Early Childhood Education.* Belmont, Calif.: Wadsworth Publishing Co., 1972.

Brazelton, T. Berry, M.D. *Toddlers and Parents.* Delacorte Press, 1974.

Bredekamp, Sue (Ed.). *Developmentally Appropriate Practice.* Washington, D.C.: NAEYC, 1986.

Bredekamp, Sue (Ed.). "NAEYC Position Statement on Developmentally Appropriate Practice in the Primary Grades, Serving 5- Through 8-Year-Olds." Washington, D.C.: *Young Children,* Vol. 3, No. 2, January 1988.

Cleverley, J.F.; and Phillips, D.C. *Visions of Childhood,* 2nd edition. New York: Teachers College Press, 1986.

Cohen, Dorothy H., and Randolph, Marguerita. *Kindergarten and Early Schooling.* Englewood Cliffs, N.J.: Prentice-Hall, 1977.

Cubberley, E.P. *A Brief History of Education.* Boston: Houghton Mifflin, 1920.

Dewey, John. *Democracy and Education: An Introduction to the Philosophy of Education.* New York: Macmillan, 1916.

Froebel, F.W. *The Songs and Music of Friedrich Froebel's Mother Play.* Arranged and prepared by Susan Blow. New York; Appleton & Co., 1895.

Gesell, A.L.; Ames, L.A.; and Ilg, F.L. *The Child From Five to Ten.* New York: Harper and Row, 1977.

Greenberg, Polly. "Lucy Sprague Mitchell: A Major Missing Link Between Early Childhood Education in the 1980s and Progressive Education in the 1890s-1930s." Washington, D.C.: *Young Children,* Vol. 42, No. 5, July 1987.

Hill, P.S. "The Function of the Kindergarten." Washington, D.C.: *Young Children,* Vol. 42, No. 5, July 1987.

Hymes, James L., Jr. *Early Childhood Education: Living History Interviews.* Carmel, Calif.: Hacienda Press, 1978.

Lazerson, M. "The Historical Antecedents of Early Childhood Education." In Gordon, I.J. (ed.), *Early Childhood Education (Part II).* National Society for the Study of Education, University of Chicago, 1972.

Macmillan, M. *The Nursery School.* New York: E.P. Dutton and Co., 1919.

National Association for the Education of Young Children. *Montessori in Perspective.* Washington, D.C.: 1966.

NAEYC. "Commitment to Children." 1988 Membership Card.

Pence, A.R. "Infant Schools in North America: 1825-1840." In Kilmer, S. (Ed.), *Advances in Early Education and Day Care,* Vol. 4, 1986.

Spock, Benjamin. "Taking Care of a Child and a Home: An Honorable Profession for Men and Women." *Redbook Magazine,* April 1976, pp. 22, 25, 115.

Spodek, Bernard. *Teaching in the Early Years.* Englewood Cliffs, N.J.: Prentice-Hall, 1972.

Spodek, B. "Early Childhood Education's Past as Prologue: Roots of Contemporary Concerns." Washington, D.C.: *Young Children,* Vol. 40, No. 5, July 1985.

Spodek, B.; Saracho, O.N.; and Peters, D.L. *Professionalism and the Early Childhood Practitioner.* New York: Teachers College Press, 1988.

# CHAPTER 2

## Types of Programs

*(handwritten: → working / infant toddler / pre-school / 3-4 / & 5)*

## QUESTIONS for THOUGHT

- What are some of the different types of early childhood programs?
- *(32)* What basic principles are common to most programs for young children?
- What is the range of early childhood education, and which programs correspond to the various age levels?
- *(52)* Why is there an increase in the number of infant/toddler programs?
- *(56)* What types of kindergarten programs are there?
- *(55)* Around which programs are there controversies—and why?
- How does the role of the teacher differ in each of the early childhood settings?
- *(60)* What criteria affect programs in early childhood?
- How do Head Start and Follow-Through differ from other early childhood programs? *(social reform)*
- *(53)* *(55)* How do infant/toddler programs differ from preschool programs, and how do they differ from one another? *(lower teacher ratio)* *(envir.)* *(greater commn. parents)*

# DIVERSITY OF PROGRAMS

From the types available to the numbers of children who attend these schools, the name of the game in early childhood programs is diversity. Early childhood programs abound; every community has some type of schooling for the young child. The range can encompass a morning nursery school for toddlers, an infant-parent stimulation program, or a full child care service for three-to-six-year-olds. Some programs run for only a half-day; others are open from 6:00 A.M. until 7:00 P.M. Still other centers accept children on a drop-in basis. Churches, school districts, community-action groups, parents, governments, private social agencies, and businesses may run schools.

Schools exist to serve a number of needs, which often overlap. Some of these are:

1. caring for children while parents work

2. enrichment programs for children

3. educational programs for parent and child

4. an activity arena for children

5. academic instruction

Programs generally reflect the needs of society as a whole. Millions of mothers of children under six are in the labor force as never before. Early childhood schools provide a wide range of services for children from infancy through eight years of age to meet some of that need.

In the human life cycle, early childhood is a period of maximum dependency. The various programs available reflect this in a number of ways. The teacher-child ratio varies in relation to the child's age; infants, at the higher end of the dependency scale, require more teachers per child in a classroom than do five-year-olds. The program itself reflects the age group it serves. The size of the group, the length of the program, and the equipment used relate to the enrolled children's capabilities and needs. Even the daily schedule mirrors the dependent relationship between the child and the teacher. Bathrooming, snack and meal routines, as well as clothing needs, call for longer periods of time in a toddler group than in a class of four-year-olds.

Diversity is apparent, too, in the philosophy expressed by the specific program. Some schools, such as Montessori programs, follow a very clear, precise outline based on a philosophical approach developed by Maria Montessori at the turn of the century. Other schools are more eclectic; they draw from a number of theories, choosing those methods and ideas that best suit their needs.

## Some Basic Tenets

Preschools vary greatly in their educational goals and practices, their methods of instruction, and even in the kind of social "mood" or atmosphere they create. Yet, varied as they are, most early childhood programs share some common principles.

The NAEYC has established a list of criteria for high-quality early childhood programs, based on a consensus of thousands of early childhood professionals. These tenets are fundamental to any early childhood program desiring to provide quality teaching and nurturing of young children:

1. Interactions between children and staff provide opportunities for children to develop an understanding of self and others and are characterized by warmth, personal respect, individuality, positive support, and responsiveness.

2. The curriculum encourages children to be actively involved in the learning process, to experience a variety of developmentally appropriate activities and materials, and to pursue their own interests in the context of life in the community and the world.

3. Parents are well informed about the program and welcomed as observers and contributors.

4. The program is staffed by adults who understand child development and who recognize and provide for children's needs.

5. The program is efficiently and effectively administered with attention to the needs and desires of children, parents, and staff.

6. The program is sufficiently staffed to meet the needs of and promote the physical, social, emotional, and cognitive development of children.

7. The indoor and outdoor physical environment fosters optimal growth and development through opportunities for exploration and learning.

8. The health and safety of children and adults are protected and enhanced.

9. The nutritional needs of children and adults are met in a manner that promotes physical, social, emotional, and cognitive development.

10. Systematic assessment of the effectiveness of the program in meeting its goals for children, parents, and staff is conducted to ensure that good quality care and education are provided and maintained.

(NAEYC, 1984)

These are the 10 essential components on which a program is judged for accreditation through NAEYC's Academy of Early Childhood Programs.

# THE CORE OF EARLY CHILDHOOD EDUCATION

What do programs for the young child look like? How are the similarities and differences expressed in school settings? What marks a program as unique? The answers to these questions can be found by looking at some of the most common programs in early childhood education.

## The Traditional Nursery School

At the core of early education is what is labeled *traditional nursery school:* a place for 2½-to-five-year-olds designed for educational experiences. This includes nursery schools, the variations of day care centers and their sister programs, laboratory schools, and parent cooperatives.

The philosophy of these schools is best described by Katherine Read in her now classic book, *The Nursery School: A Human Relationships Laboratory.* First published over 35 years ago, this book serves as an encyclopedia of the traditional nursery school, its methods, and its philosophy.

The idea of a school as a place of human activity mirrors the thoughts of Dewey, Piaget, Erikson, and others. Read develops this philosophy fully, with an educational model that emphasizes the human needs, growth patterns, and relationships in a young child's life. Developmentally, a traditional nursery school focuses on social competence and emotional well-being. The curriculum encourages self-expression through language, creativity, intellectual skill, and physical activity. The basic underlying belief is the importance of interpersonal connections children make with themselves, each other, and adults.

In theory, the objectives of traditional nursery schools are prescribed. The schools have some general characteristics in common, like the daily schedule (see Figure 2.1). The schedule reflects the values for the school. For example, large blocks of time are devoted to free play, emphasizing the importance of play. In this way, children learn to make their own choices, select their own playmates, and work on their interests and issues at their own rate. A dominant belief is that children learn best in an atmosphere free from excessive restraint and direction.

A typical daily schedule also indicates an awareness of the developing child's characteristics and needs.

| | |
|---|---|
| 9:00 | Children arrive at school |
| 9:00–9:45 | Free play (indoors) |
| 9:45 | Cleanup |
| 10:00 | Singing time (large group) |
| 10:15–10:30 | Toileting/snack time (small groups) |
| 10:30–11:30 | Free play (outdoors) |
| 11:30 | Cleanup |
| 11:45 | Story time |
| 12:00 | Children leave for home |

**FIGURE 2.1**  A sample schedule for traditional half-day nursery schools, the core of early education programs.

Programs attend to the physical and health needs (toileting, snacks, fresh air). There is a balance of activities (indoors and out, free choice, and teacher-directed times). Closer inspection of the environment reveals a wide variety of activities (large- and small-muscle games, intellectual choices, creative arts, social play opportunities).

Then, too, there is the clear acknowledgment of change and the time it takes children to make and adjust to changes. Children must have plenty of time for arrival and departure from school, greetings, cleanup, and transition times between activities. The amount of time given to any one part of the day's activities directly reflects the values the school endorses.

There are also aspects of the traditional model that are not immediately evident by looking at a daily schedule. The role of the teacher and methods of teaching are important. Nursery schools assume that young children need individual attention and should have personal, warm relationships with important adults. Therefore, the groups of children are generally small, often fewer than 20 in a class. The teacher-child ratio is low, as few as six to ten children for each teacher. Teachers learn about children's development and needs by observation and direct interaction, rather than from formalized testing. They work with children individually and in small groups (perhaps three or four) and often teach through conversation and materials. Always, the teacher encourages the children to express

**FIGURE 2.2** An essential component in every program: individual attention and warm relationships. (Courtesy of Michael DiBari, University of Miami.)

themselves, their feelings, and their thinking. And, as Read puts it:

> . . . A large part of the teacher's role is helping children learn to learn. Some teaching may be done through games that encourage the use of the senses, the imagination, and problem-solving capacities. Throughout her teaching, the teacher respects the individual interests, styles, and rates of learning of the children.
>
> (Read and Patterson, 1980)

Such rapport between teacher and pupil fosters self-confidence, security, and belonging. Proponents of the traditional nursery school believe that these feelings promote positive self-image, healthy relationships, and an encouraging learning environment.

There are several programs within the traditional preschool framework. Three important variations on the theme are: child care centers, laboratory schools, and parent cooperative nursery schools.

## Child Care Centers

Some of the first nursery schools in England operated from 8:00 A.M. until 4:00 or 5:00 P.M. It was only later in America that the nursery school evolved into a part- or half-day program. Child care, then, is not a modern phenomenon. Child care center patterns differ from those of half-day nursery schools. By definition, a *child care center* is a place for children who need care for a greater portion of the day. The school schedule is extended to fit the hours of working parents. The program roughly models what ordinarily happens in the routines of a child's day at home. Therefore the adults who work in a child care center have somewhat different responsibilities and training. Child care centers are for infants and toddlers, as well as for the 2½-to-five-year-old range. In this section, the focus is on those centers for the nursery school age range.

Child care has a number of unique qualities.

**Scheduling.** Compare the nursery school schedule to the child care schedule (see Figure 2.3). The morning

starts slowly. Children arrive early since their parent(s) must go to work. The center will usually supply breakfast; midmorning and midafternoon snacks supplement a noon lunch. A nap period for one to two hours for all the children gives a needed rest and balances their active, social day with quiet, solitary time. The program also includes extended experiences outside the school—field trips, library story hour, or swimming lessons—since children spend the major portion of their waking hours on-site. As the day draws to a close, children gather together quietly, with less energy and activity.

| | |
|---|---|
| 7:00–8:30 | Arrival/breakfast; limited indoor play |
| 8:30 | Large group meeting |
| 8:45–9:45 | Free play (inside) |
| 9:45 | Cleanup/toileting |
| 10:00 | Snack time (small groups) |
| 10:15–11:30 | Free play (outside) |
| 11:30 | Cleanup/handwashing |
| 12:00 | Lunch |
| 12:30 | Toothbrushing/toileting |
| 1:00–2:00 | Nap time |
| 2:00–3:00 | Free play (outside) |
| 3:00 | Group time |
| 3:15 | Snack time (small groups) |
| 3:30–5:00 | Inside and outside free play/ library hour |
| 5:00 | Cleanup |
| 5:15–5:30 | Departure |

**FIGURE 2.3** A typical full-day care schedule. Most child care programs combine education and caring for basic needs.

**Licensing.** There are no national standards or policies regarding licensing of child care facilities. Many local and state governments, however, do require licensing of child care centers and family day care homes. Nor is there one central licensing agency. Depending upon the state, a license may be issued by the Department of Health, Department of Education, or Department of Social Welfare. Certification of child care workers is again left to local options.

Early childhood professional groups are calling for increased standardization of licensing procedures to ensure that children are receiving the best possible care in safe and healthy environments. The primary concern is to establish effective licensing policies that are reinforced and will ensure that all programs will provide adequate care to meet the basic developmental needs of children. Standardized licensing regulations will protect children at all economic levels. All children will be treated equally whether they attend a family day care home in Houston, a Head Start classroom in Jacksonville, a child care center in Harlem, or a public school extended day program in Sacramento. The same minimum standards will apply to adult:child ratios, suitable safety precautions, health and nutrition needs, and the amount of training and preparation required of caregivers.

The need for standards arises out of recent changes in early childhood. The number of children in out-of-home care settings has increased. Many are infants and toddlers, a younger population than previously served. Children are spending longer hours in child care, and there are more programs sponsored by a variety of agencies such as churches, public schools, and private for-profit firms. With this diverse mix, a common set of standards for licensing is imperative to ensure the best possible care for all children who need these services. (See Chapters 3, 9, 10, and 15 for further discussion of licensing, regulations, and standards for early childhood programs. Of particular note is the *Focus* discussion on page 297 by Sue Bredekamp regarding NAEYC's accreditation program.)

While professionalization of centers is worthwhile, implementation is controversial and costly. The question arises as to which agency should rightfully evaluate licensing and enforce the policies and procedures established by law. Many see it as a natural extension of the state Department of Education. Others argue equally for the Department of Social Welfare or Board of Health.

Until government and professionals can agree on implementation, enforcement, and funding, licensing of child care facilities and personnel will remain an unsolved issue.

**Staffing.** What does child care mean for teachers? First, they must be aware of and trained to deal with the parenting side of teaching. The children may need more nurturing, clearer consistency in limits, and established routines. At the same time, they need individual flexibility and understanding and regular private time with caring adults.

Parents' needs also may be greater and require more of the teachers' time. Teachers should communicate with and support parents effectively. Parents want to trust their children's teachers and be relaxed with them. Teachers in a child care center find it valuable to take the time to be good listeners and clear communicators to parents about their child; this builds the trust and support that is so vital when working with young children. Child care parents may require extra effort; they have full-time jobs as well as child-rearing responsibilities draining their energies. It takes a strong team effort on the part of the teacher and the parent to make sure the lines of communication stay open.

The teaching staff undoubtedly has staggered schedules, perhaps a morning and an afternoon shift. Administration of this type of program is therefore more complex. An effort must be made to ensure that all teachers get together on a regular basis to share the mutual information and details about the children in their care. Both shifts must be aware of what happens when they are not on-site in order to run the program consistently.

### Need for Child Care

Child care in the United States used to be primarily *custodial*, providing basic health and physical care. But times have changed. Full day care is an American way of life, providing enriched programs for total development. Thousands of families rely on child care centers. Fifty percent of all mothers of preschool children and more than half of all married mothers with children younger than two years old are in the labor force (Children's Defense Fund, 1988). According to the U.S. Census Bureau statistics, 1987 was a landmark year as women with children younger than one year old in the workforce passed the fifty percent mark. When more than half the new mothers in the U.S. are in the labor force, it reflects a way of life, not a trend (*New York Times* editorial, 1988). The rising divorce rate, single-parent families, the women's movement, and the economy have all contributed to a greater need than ever for child care.

Good, affordable, accessible child care that will meet the increasing needs of American families is one of today's most critical issues. The distinction between day care (stressing the protective, custodial services) and early education (emphasizing schooling) has appropriately blurred. Today, child care professionals recognize the concept of child care inherent in all programs for young children and the concept of education as an integral part of caring for young children.

This desire to link child care services with educating the young child is best expressed by the trend toward labeling many early childhood programs "child care" rather than the traditional "day care." This new term implies that child care is a permanent part of American life, including both teaching and nurturing functions. It removes some of the stigma previously attached to day care as primarily a babysitting, custodial function. The one exception to this terminology seems to be family day care. Although many family day care providers are trained and provide quality programs, the label "day care" persists. It appears that the words "family day care" are appropriate in this case because they serve to distinguish a type of child care program from regular, ongoing family child-rearing. See also Chapter 15, Care and Education.

## *Child Care Controversy*

Child care issues are continually debated. Some see child care outside the traditional home setting as undermining the role of mother, family, and therefore society. Many question the effects on children who spend so much of their early years in group care.

The issue is complex and related to economic trends as well as social forces. Families need and want child care. Child care exists as a response to the trend toward working mothers. It is a solution to economic and social pressures, not a cause.

The impact of child care on children, families, and the community is not yet fully understood. Some experts continue to urge mothers to stay at home with their young children (White, 1981). Yet over a dozen

studies investigating child care found "no consistent adverse effect of out-of-home child day care" (O'Connell, 1983). Most research shows that child care has either positive effects or no effects on intelligence and little impact on children's attachment to parents. There is some question that child care may increase the rate of aggressiveness in later life, yet the same children were seen by teachers as more curious and more intelligent (Bee, 1985). Ongoing research can help answer the critical questions regarding the effect of child care on a child's development, on parent-child relationships, and on the quality of child care.

The focus of the child care debate centers on a few core problems:

- The quality of child care varies. In the United States, there are more than 60,000 licensed child care centers and more than 161,000 licensed child care homes. Yet most children receive care from unlicensed homes (Kutner, 1988).

- Licensing itself may carry little assurance of quality programs. Standards and enforcement vary widely. Some states have none. Twelve states exempt religiously affiliated child care centers from complying with regulations.

- The low wage scales of child care workers affect the quality, stability, and experience of staff who are caring for children. Two out of every three child care workers earn wages below the poverty level (Children's Defense Fund, 1987).

- Research on a number of critical issues in infant child care, such as age of entry and social development, is now under way. More research is needed to investigate an array of influences in the infant's life, such as prenatal care, the quality of the infant program, and characteristics of the family (Phillips, 1987).

- Obtaining affordable child care for those who need it is a major concern. The typical costs for child care in the United States in 1988 was $3,000 per year. That is one-third the annual poverty-level income for a family of three. A single parent working full-time at a minimum wage would have to spend 90 percent of that income to provide child care for two children (Children's Defense Fund, 1987).

38

- There is a shortage of child care programs, especially for infants.
- Safety and health are additional concerns.

The reader will also want to see Chapter 15 for another discussion of child care in America as well as EllenGalinsky's *Focus* discussion on the child care crisis on page 442.

Work in child care is long, intense, and coupled with undesirable wages. This creates high staff turnover and low morale. Full-time child care is expensive. Sometimes it is too costly for poorly paid or underemployed parents to pay for quality child care. Occasionally, a center will cut corners to keep tuition reasonable, but the results of these shortcuts are usually detrimental to children.

Regardless of disagreements about the effects, child care outside the home is a fact of life for millions of children. It is the only choice for many parents, and the most sensible one for others. Therefore, the issue is not whether there should be child care, but how to provide the highest quality care. Two variations in child care may provide some of the solutions.

## *Family Day Care*

This type of service cares for children in ways reminiscent of an extended family grouping. The child care provider takes in small numbers of children in the family residence. The group size can range from two to twelve, but recent research shows that most homes keep a low adult:child ratio, enrolling fewer than six children (Stevens, 1982).

The home setting, sometimes right within the child's own neighborhood, offers a more intimate, convenient, and possibly less expensive service for working parents. The children in a *family day care* home can range from infants to school-age children who are cared for after regular school hours.

**Advantages.** Family day care has many advantages. It is especially good for children who do well in small groups or whose parents prefer them in a family-style setting. Women who want to remain at home with one or more children of their own have found family day

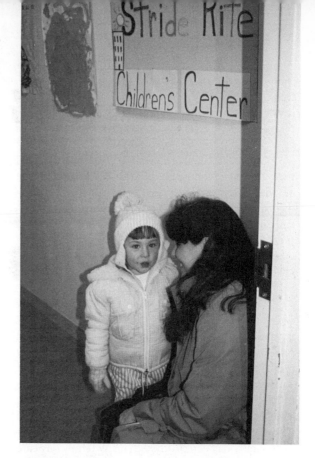

**FIGURE 2.4** More and more corporations and businesses help parents by offering on-the-job child care facilities. (Courtesy of Stride Rite Children's Centers, Cambridge, Mass.)

care meets this need while giving them a chance to increase the family's income. And those who have begun careers in this area feel a sense of budding professionalism.

**Disadvantages.** Family day care has its disadvantages, too. Many homes are unregulated; that is, they are not under any sponsorship or agency that enforces quality care. Many offer little more than baby-sitting or custodial care. In a review of recent research about family day care, agency- or group-regulated homes had the best care (Stevens, 1982). In such homes, the child care providers interacted more frequently with the children than did those in unregulated homes. The quality of these interactions and the types of activities offered were more stimulating and beneficial to the

**FIGURE 2.5**  Family day care can be within the child's own neighborhood. (Courtesy of Family Service Agency of San Mateo County, Calif.)

children's growth and development. The environment as a whole, in the regulated child care homes, was more satisfactory: the food was more nutritious and the providers taught and helped the children more. Significantly, the child care providers in these regulated homes also had more training in early childhood education.

The overwhelming majority of family day care is provided by women in unregulated homes, according to Stevens' review. Blacks, Hispanics, and Caucasians share equally as child care providers. Sponsorship of a regulating agency, be it by government or a family service association, proved to be positive in terms of both quality of child care and training of providers.

This type of care could be a star in the galaxy of child care options. Small and personalized, it offers parents an appealing choice of home-based care. It is obvious, though, that further regulation of standards, availability of training for providers, and an awareness of the advantages of family day care need to be addressed. For those who need child care, this should be a viable alternative; for those who want to work at home, this type of career should be given serious consideration.

## Employer-Sponsored Child Care

*Employer-sponsored* child care refers to child care facilities on or near the job site and supported by the business or industry. Hospitals, factories, colleges, and military bases often provide this service.

The role of industry and business in group child care has an outstanding, if brief, history. The most notable example in this country is the Kaiser Shipyard Centers during World War II. When child care was equated with a national cause—winning the war—government and industry joined forces to provide quality child care in industrial settings. Recently this model has been examined as one way businesses can

**FIGURE 2.6**  Routines, such as naps, provide a balance to an active and busy day at the child care center. (Courtesy of Trinity Preschool, New York, N.Y.)

support working parents' efforts to find quality child care.

The number of women working outside the home and the increase in single-parent families encourage us to look at the workplace as a logical solution for child care needs. Advocates claim many benefits for both industry and people. They suggest that:

- Absenteeism drops when stable and convenient child care is available on or near the parent's work site.

- Employees are likely to stay on the job longer and employers will need to do less recruiting by offering child care services at reasonable cost and close to work.

- There can be tax advantages to businesses that provide child care services.

- There is a greater sense of loyalty because employees feel more positive about working for companies that provide this benefit.

- There is a greater opportunity for parents to spend more time with their children, going to and from work, during breaks, and at lunch time.

- Children understand their parents' role outside the home when these two worlds are brought into relationship with one another.

Studies now show that child care can be cost effective in business terms, and more businesses are realizing that involvement in employee child care issues can have a positive effect on profits. Three national studies have found that employers viewed improved recruitment, retention of workers, lower absenteeism, and higher employee morale as translating into reduced costs (Galinsky, 1986).

A growing number of employers are offering some kind of child care assistance programs. Three thousand business firms throughout the United States provide a range of services:

- child care information and referral
- after-school care
- flexible work schedules and leave-of-absence policies
- counseling services
- seminars and discussion groups with child development experts
- nursing services for sick children
- on-site child care centers
- training and licensing of family day care providers
- discounts provided with local child care centers
- direct financial assistance through vouchers
- child care as an optional benefit in the compensation package

In a half-dozen areas around the country, child care centers are being built as an integral part of new office park developments (Child Care Information Exchange, 1986).

The critical issue is not concerned so much with on-site facilities for care of employees' children. (For instance, employers who do not have their own programs could provide vouchers for child care in other settings. They could also offer, as a benefit to attract working parents, reimbursement for some portion of their employees' child care.) Helping parents with placement in other centers or offering flexible time schedules is as much a part of the issue as child care itself.

However, an even larger issue addresses women in the work force and parents' relationships to their families. A small but growing number of businesses deal with this issue of balancing work and parenthood in a unique way: around the country in corporate boardrooms, parenting seminars are available to employees during business hours. Led by qualified child development specialists, parents discuss some of the difficulties they face as working people who are also mothers and fathers. Early childhood professionals must explore new avenues with business and industry to assist the working parent, especially the working mother, so that "the workplace of the future . . . is fully supportive of employees in their dual roles as workers and family members" (Galinsky, 1986).

## Laboratory Schools

The college and university laboratory schools were among the first preschools established in the United States. They usually focus on teacher training, research, and innovative education. These schools serve as standards for model programs in early childhood education. They add to our knowledge of children, child development, and teaching methods. An important part of education in the United States, they are often supported or subsidized by the college.

As part of the child study movement, laboratory schools gathered information previously unknown about children and child development. Early ones include Bank Street School in 1919, begun by Harriet Johnson, and the laboratory nursery school at Columbia Teacher's College, started in 1921 by Patty Smith Hill. In the late 1920s, Vassar, Smith, and Mills colleges all opened laboratory schools. Shortly after World War II, Edith Dowley started the Bing Nursery School at Stanford University. Much more recently, community-college campuses have followed the lead of these pioneers. Campus child care centers have begun to combine child care services with the laboratory function of teacher training in one setting. The types and roles of the schools vary, depending on the educational philosophy and needs of the college and its students.

Regardless of their specific purposes, laboratory schools enlarge our understanding of children. They are often excellent places for beginning teachers to learn ways of teaching children. They encourage the joining of psychology, medicine, and other related fields to early education, and they serve as professional models for the public at large for what is good in child care and education.

The isolation of college campuses sometimes restricts the number and type of children who enroll. The program itself is tailored to meet the needs of student teachers who, under the guidance of skilled people, do much of the teaching. College calendars may be unable to accommodate the needs of children for full-time and year-round care. In addition, teachers trained in a laboratory school atmosphere will have to adjust to the realities of subsequent school settings.

## Parent Cooperatives

*Parent cooperatives* are those schools organized and run by parents. This type of early childhood setting offers a unique opportunity for parents to be involved in the education of their child. The very first parent cooperative, the Chicago Cooperative Nursery School, was started in 1915 by faculty wives at the University of Chicago.

Parent cooperative schools may offer half-day or full-day child care programs and are usually nonprofit organizations. They are similar to other nursery schools, with two notable exceptions. First, parents organize and maintain the school: they hire the teachers, buy supplies and equipment, recruit members, raise funds, influence school philosophy, and manage the budget. Traditionally, parents or their substitutes were required to participate in the classroom on a regular basis. In light of current family work patterns and the unavailability of many parents, this requirement has been modified in most programs. More professional teachers are hired, or other parents who are available are paid to substitute for parents who cannot work at the center.

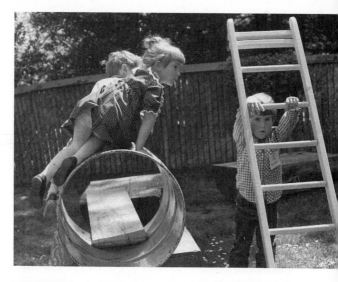

**FIGURE 2.7** An ideal outside environment in a laboratory school, The Bing School of Stanford University.

Cooperative schools work well for many reasons. Popular with young families, they have low operating costs, the appeal of being with parents in similar circumstances, and the mutual support that is generated among members of a co-op. Friendships grow among parents who share child rearing as participants in their own and in their child's education. But what a co-op does not cost in dollars, it may cost in time. By their very nature, cooperatives can exclude working parents unless another adult is able to substitute for them in classroom participation. Maintenance is very much the parents' responsibility; they must regularly schedule work parties to refurbish the facility.

Depending upon the size of the school, parents hire one or more professional teachers. These teachers must be able to work well with adults, have curriculum-building skills, and model good guidance and discipline techniques. Since many parent cooperatives require a weekly or monthly parent meeting, the teaching staff must also be competent in parent education. Child development and child-rearing topics are part of almost any cooperative nursery school discussion and require a practiced teacher to lead. The role of the teacher in this setting, then, is two-fold: to provide for a sound educational experience for young children and to guide and direct parents in their own learning.

# Church-Related Schools

*Church-related schools* are those owned or operated by an individual congregation or other recognized church organization. Many different denominations sponsor a variety of educational and child care programs.

Throughout this nation's history, churches have demonstrated their concern for the welfare of children and their families. It was the churches that established many of the early schools, advocating the education of children. At the turn of the century, church day nurseries and settlement houses cared for children of immigrants and poor working mothers. Later, hospitals and orphanages were founded, and churches spoke out for children's rights and the creation of child labor laws. In each era, depending on social and economic conditions, the churches have responded to the needs of children.

## *Role in Child Care*

It is no surprise, then, to find that churches are deeply involved in child care today: they are probably the single largest group of child care providers in the country. They also play an indirect part as landlords to programs not under church sponsorship (Lindner et al., 1983).

Church-housed programs are broad-based. Toddler groups, full- and part-time nursery classes, all-day care, and after-school care are typical. Some churches sponsor programs for children with special needs and children of migrant farm workers. They serve the community-at-large and rarely restrict participation to their own congregations or denominations.

Religious or spiritual development is not the explicit aim of the majority of programs for preschoolers. Churches are committed to caring for children of working parents, providing a warm and loving environment to help children develop positive self-esteem (Lindner et al., 1983). The teaching of religious values to children in this age group is not

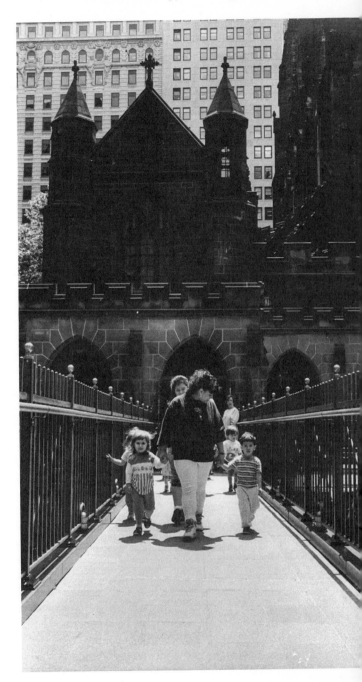

**FIGURE 2.8** Churches are the largest single providers of child care in the country today, even on Wall Street. (Courtesy of Trinity Preschool, New York, N.Y.)

common practice in most child care settings. The policy will vary, however, with each individual setting.

### Academic Church Schools

For those parents who seek alternative education in a religious context, church schools fill the need. Many denominations serve children from early childhood through senior high. The relationship with the individual church organizations and the academic philosophy will vary from setting to setting.

### Controversy Over State Regulation

Most religious groups support the need for regulations and abide by licensing procedures even if their state exempts them. However, a bitter battle is being waged in the courts by a few fundamentalist Christian churches that object to state regulation and licensing of child care centers. In some of the twelve states that currently exempt church-affiliated centers from licensing requirements, building and fire codes must be met. In other states, centers can negotiate for which regulations they will meet.

Those churches seeking exemption claim a threat to their rights under the First Amendment, which guarantees the freedom of religion. They claim that the intentional ministry of their child care centers protects them from interference by the state. Their opponents argue that exempting church-sponsored schools from regulation is unfair and is in violation of *their* First Amendment rights.

Early childhood professionals, joined by many church leaders, are deeply concerned that exemption from even the most minimal standards not only undermines the national effort to create uniform standards for child care but threatens the safety and welfare of children. In a landmark decision (Gold, 1988), a U.S. District Court in Richmond, Virginia, upheld the exemption of religiously affiliated child care centers from meeting state licensing requirements. This decision will surely affect pending suits in other states. The controversy will continue so long as the court actions are being decided and bears close observation by all in the early childhood field.

The National Council of Churches, representing 15 major Protestant denominations, states the case clearly in its *Policy Statement on Child Care:*

> . . . It is important that no child care program be exempt from securing a child care license . . . Child care licensing is an official acknowledgement of the public responsibility to maintain health, safety, and developmentally appropriate conditions for children during the time they spend in child care. Licensing is a form of consumer protection for children and their parents.
>
> (National Council of Churches, 1987)

## For-Profit Child Care

A fast-growing business in the world of child care, the for-profit center, offers a variety of programs to meet parents' needs. Infant and toddler programs, preschools, kindergartens, before and after school care, as well as summer sessions accommodate working parents. A number of national chains have emerged on the child care scenes, highlighting the growth of the child care industry in general. The growth of national chains has been dramatic: From 237 in 1974 to a total of 2,285 in 1987. Two out of three child care centers in the United States now operate on a for-profit basis (Neugebauer, 1988).

## Other Schools

To serve the scope of human needs today, some early childhood programs focus on caring for children in a very specific context. Many high schools now have on-campus child care programs. Some serve as laboratory facilities to introduce adolescents to child care principles and practices before they become parents.

Others are part of a growing trend to provide support services to teenage parents. Young mothers are encouraged to complete their high school education by returning to campus with their young children. Parents are required to participate in parent education classes along with regular academic subjects where they discuss child-rearing policies and parent concerns. They also spend time in the children's classroom, applying their skills under the supervision of professional child care workers.

The aim of this program is to help meet the long-term needs of adolescent parents by providing educational skills necessary to secure a job. At the same time, valuable support and training for parenthood helps teenagers deal with the reality of the young children in their lives.

Hospitals also provide group settings for children who are confined for a period of time. Schools for the handicapped address the needs of specific disabilities, offering a combination of educational, medical, and therapeutic services. Children who attend these schools may or may not be mainstreamed part-time into other school settings.

### Homeless Children

The plight of homeless children raises questions about program needs for this new and tragic phenomenon. Families with children now represent more than one-third of the homeless population (Children's Defense Fund, 1988). These children attend schools closest to the shelter in which they stay for a brief time, then change schools when their parents move to another shelter. Many times these are children who already experience problems and failures in school. State and federal legislation is now being enacted to ensure full and equal educational opportunities for homeless children.

# SCHOOLS WITH A MESSAGE

## Head Start

### Beginnings

Head Start began as part of this country's social action against poverty in the mid-1960s (see Chapter 1). The implication of this program was clear: if underprivileged, disadvantaged, poverty-stricken children could be exposed to a program that enhanced their schooling, their intellectual functions might increase, and these gains would help break the poverty cycle. To that end, the Office of Economic Opportunity created

Head Start, a federally funded school program for low-income children and their families. Head Start served youngsters from ages two to five in both half-day and full-day classes. The schools were administered by any one of several agencies: the local government, school districts, or Model Cities projects.

One of Head Start's most valuable contributions was its *comprehensive* program. Beyond intellectual development was a concern for health, nutrition, and physical growth. The child was seen as a whole, requiring medical, dental, and nutritional assessment as well as intellectual growth. Some Head Start programs were specifically tailored to handicapped and bilingual children.

Head Start was for children *and* their families. Parents were required to be involved at all levels: in the classroom as teacher aids and on governing boards. Parents helped to define and direct each Head Start center; parent involvement was a major underlying philosophy.

Community interest and support is an ongoing Head Start objective. Head Start attempts to involve neighborhood resources and functions under local rule. Programs reflect not only the child but the culture as well. The curriculum encourages activities that enhance self-esteem, especially as it relates to the child's ethnic heritage and cultural background.

### Guiding Objectives and Principles

- Improve the child's physical health and physical abilities.

- Help the emotional and social development of the child by encouraging self-confidence, spontaneity, curiosity, and self-discipline.

- Improve the child's mental processes and skills with particular attention to conceptual and verbal skills.

- Establish patterns and expectations of success for the child that will create a climate of confidence for his future learning efforts.

- Increase the child's capacity to relate positively to family members and others, while at the same time strengthening the family's ability to relate positively to the child and his problems.

- Develop in the child and his family a responsible attitude toward society and foster constructive opportunities for society to work together with the poor in solving their problems.

- Increase the sense of dignity and self-worth within the child and his family.

(Evans, 1975)

These objectives could apply to any good nursery or kindergarten class. They take on an added dimension, though, when viewed as part of the total effort of Project Head Start, which was designed to be comprehensive enough to ensure appropriate programs for children and flexible enough to meet individual needs within the family and community.

### Head Start Today

Head Start has had a rocky twenty-year history, struggling against budget cuts and controversy over its effectiveness. Today, Head Start still fulfills its initial purpose: 90 percent of Head Start children are from families who live on less than poverty-level incomes. Yet, owing to lack of funding, Head Start is currently able to reach only 18 percent of the children who need its services (CDF, 1988).

Four conditions in U.S. life today underscore the need for the comprehensive philosophy of Head Start. According to Washington and Oyemade (1985), they are:

- The high number of households headed by females, who are more likely to experience poverty than those headed by men or two parents. This is sometimes called "the feminization of poverty."

- The number of teenaged parents who generally drop out of school, have inadequate skills and job training, and are likely to be welfare recipients.

- The number of working mothers, especially those who have children under six.

- The increasing pressure on low-income families to become economically self-sufficient and get out of the poverty cycle.

These trends are not isolated from one another; indeed, they are interrelated and compound one another. Head Start, with its emphasis on family support and community involvement, seems to have a mandate for future generations. Although it has been successful in helping to "move children and their families toward self-sufficiency . . . Head Start . . . can be even more instrumental in reducing the enormous harm to the next generation that poverty can cause" (Washington and Oyemade, 1985).

### Evaluating Head Start's Effectiveness

Has Head Start fulfilled its promise? As soon as the program began, so did the research to evaluate its effectiveness. Evaluating any program is complicated,

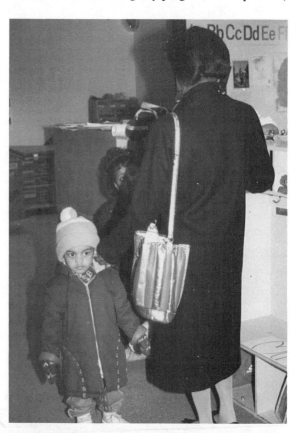

**FIGURE 2.9** The need for quality child care has increased as thousands of mothers enter the work force. (Courtesy of Stride Rite Children's Centers, Cambridge, Mass.)

and Head Start is no exception. Research findings take on great importance when large numbers of children and governmental dollars are at stake. Three research studies demonstrate the types of controversies and the variety of findings.

The first major evaluation was conducted by the Westinghouse Learning Corporation on the first 104 Head Start centers. The study concluded that the gains made by Head Start children over non-Head Start children did not persist after the first few years of school. The Westinghouse study has been criticized for flawed research criteria, and its findings have been disproved by subsequent research. However, the damage to the reputation and image of Head Start took its toll.

Two studies have helped considerably to erase the negative effects of the Westinghouse report: The Consortium for Longitudinal Studies and the Perry Preschool Project.

## The Consortium for Longitudinal Studies

This consortium was formed in the mid-1970s as positive results from other early intervention programs were published. Child development researchers across the country pooled data from a number of smaller studies in the hope that clear trends regarding early intervention could be identified. Brown (1985) notes two significant findings: 1) That Head Start children were less likely to be placed in special education classes and 2) that early intervention programs were associated with a significant increase in IQ and school achievement. Brown further notes that after this report was published, government funding for Head Start was increased for the first time in a decade.

## The Perry Preschool Project

This study presents convincing evidence of the effectiveness of early intervention programs for disadvantaged children. It is the first longitudinal study, begun in the mid-1960s, to measure the effects of preschool education and to track the children from preschool years through age 19.

One hundred twenty-three black children from poor families, with IQs ranging from 60 to 90, were randomly assigned to two groups. The first group were placed in high-quality early childhood programs at age three; the other group did not attend preschool. The results showed great differences between the children who had the advantage of a high-quality program and those who did not. Disadvantaged children who attended preschool significantly outperformed those who did not.

The children attending the preschool program were more successful in high school, were nearly twice as likely to attend college or job training, and were more likely to hold jobs and be self-sufficient. They also were less likely to be involved in juvenile crimes or welfare dependency. Fifty percent fewer teen pregnancies occurred in this group than in the group with no preschool experience.

The Perry Preschool Project is also noteworthy because it is the first study of its kind to suggest the economic impact of early intervention. Because most of the children in the high-quality early childhood program required less remedial education, had better earning prospects, and were less costly to the welfare and justice systems, early intervention in education was shown to be cost-effective. The estimated value gained over the lifetime of the students in the preschool program "may be more than seven times the cost of one year's operation of the program." (Berrueta-Clement, et al., 1984). That assessment of economic benefits captured the attention of state and federal legislators during an election year and provided the impetus for extensive legislative action. (See the section on David Weikart in Chapter 4.)

Finally these studies provide sufficient data to support the need for expanded early intervention programs for young children. It will surely be written in the history books that Head Start, as one of the most ambitious efforts made ever on behalf of young children in the United States, was instrumental in creating an awareness of this need.

## Follow-Through

Once Head Start got underway, its children began to graduate and continue on into elementary school. Project Follow-Through is a set of federally funded programs for children from kindergarten through third grade. People asked: What is happening to the "head start" these children had in school? Can the whole idea of compensatory education work at all? Or is there something about elementary school that fails to build upon the gains made in preschool?

Project Follow-Through attempts to answer the last question by providing some model programs for impoverished grade-school children. Follow-Through, started in 1968, is a smaller project than Head Start— and more experimental. The programs operate across the country, in both urban and rural settings. The children in any one group come from a variety of ethnic backgrounds, or from a single population. Sponsors include universities, research centers, and communities.

Educational models of Follow-Through differ widely in philosophy and teaching techniques. The Bank Street Model uses a classic child development approach, while the Direct Instruction Model is academically oriented. The Tuscon Early Education Model emphasizes language development, the Florida Project concentrates on parents and infants in the home, and the Behavior Analysis Model uses behavior-modification principles. Each separate model is striking in its diversity, yet contributes to an interesting experiment in planned variations.

How have these programs helped children? Attempts to evaluate Follow-Through are as complicated as those for Head Start. Generally, it seems that programs tend to be successful in meeting their particular goals. For example, the Cognitively Oriented Curriculum Model (based on Piaget's theory) has been successful in meeting its stated goal of increasing children's use of verbal language. The Florida Project demonstrates how early education begins in the home. It appears that the more specific the program format, the greater the chance for success.

Compensatory education is a difficult process. There are no easy solutions to the problems of poverty, the realities of ghetto life. Continued support of experimental research and educational programs is one way to try to find ways to help our children—all our children—succeed.

# Open Schools

Open education—sometimes called open schools or informal education—is a term used to describe child-centered learning environments often associated with the British infant schools. It is based on the belief that children learn and grow at different rates, that they are eager and curious about learning, and that they learn best when they are able to pursue their own interests. Open school philosophy uses play as the principal means for learning. Not only do children learn from each other as they play in a mixed-age group, they grow through a rich and varied learning environment.

The emphasis in an open classroom is on the integration of the total curriculum, rather than on the separate subject matter. Academic skills—reading, writing, number concepts—comprise a natural part of all learning. Music can include math and counting; science discussions develop language arts; and dramatic play can spur writing. The stress is on the learning process—what happens when child and materials meet. Their play encourages children to explore, manipulate, and construct; classroom space encourages this. Activity areas, or centers of interest, are set up throughout the room. Children self-select where and with whom they want to spend their time, be it with clay, at woodworking, or at one of the table games.

Teachers facilitate, or guide, setting up the environment to promote independence and self-sufficiency so that they are free to interact with children. Team teaching is ideal for the open classroom; several teachers can provide the amount of supervision, organization, and planning necessary for success. "Good informal instruction is hard work" (Elkind, 1982).

If this description sounds vaguely familiar, it should since it applies to many typical nursery schools and kindergartens. The philosophy has a familiar ring to it. Didn't John Dewey speak of self-initiated learning, social cooperation, active education, and respect for the individual? And before him, Comenius, Rousseau, Pestalozzi, and Froebel all promoted similar concepts. In some ways, open education is the Progressive Movement revisited.

The British aided the revival of open education in the United States today since many schools pattern themselves after the British infant school model. American educators, excited by the British response to open learning, helped to revive local commitment to those principles. Numerous American educators trekked to England to see how open schools worked there, and so they reappeared in the United States education scene in the 1970s. Several Follow-Through models—the Bank Street Model and the EDC Open Education Model—use the open school approach to learning. The open school has come to mean an approach, a philosophy, that is practiced in many types of early childhood settings—nursery schools, day care centers, and elementary schools.

The open school is not without criticism, much of which centers around the lack of formal instruction. The deemphasis in direct instruction of reading and writing is questioned. Supporters of open schools counter that the child-centered approach in fact leads to a high motivation to read and write.

While loosely structured classrooms may prove challenging and stimulating to some children, others may find the lack of structure difficult. More traditional programs offer clear goals that are measured by evaluation and testing. The open school's approach includes the children in the planning and evaluation of some of the learning that takes place. If the experiences in an open classroom are not integrated into the total curriculum and the learnings not related in some meaningful way, they remain merely good—but isolated—experiences for the child. "Done well," says Elkind, "open education can be a model of truly humanistic education; done poorly, it can be a disaster" (Elkind, 1982).

Open education allows for a child to respond individually and personally to the experience. The freedom of choice, the development of problem-solving skills, the respect for initiative, are based on the strong belief that allowing children this kind of involvement reflects back to them their worth and dignity. For that reason alone, open classrooms continue to exemplify the best in humanistic education.

# Montessori

Maria Montessori began working with slum children in the early 1900s in Rome, Italy. Her school, the Casa di Bambini, was open to children from the ages of 2½ to seven years. Montessori's approach to learning has had a continuing influence in education since those early years. Of her work, three features stand out: (1) adapting school work to the individual rather than molding the child to fit the curriculum; (2) insisting on freedom for children in selection of materials and choice of activities; and (3) training of the senses and practical life issues.

## The Program

The most striking feature of the Montessori classroom is its materials. Many are made of wood and designed to stress the philosophy of learning through the senses. Color, texture, and quality of craftsmanship of the materials appeal to the hand as well as the eye; they demand to be touched. "Smooth" and "oval" take on new meaning as a child runs a finger around Montessori-designed puzzle shapes.

Montessori materials have other unique characteristics besides their tactile appeal. They are self-correcting—that is, they fit together or work in only one way so that children will know immediately whether or not they are successful. Montessori curriculum presents the materials in a sequence, from simplest to most difficult. Many of the learning tasks have a series of steps and must be learned in a prescribed order. Whether sponging a table clean or using the number rods, the child is taught the precise order in which to use the materials. Montessori developed curriculum materials and tasks that related to real life. "Practical life" activities range from cleaning tasks (hands, tables) to clothing tasks (lacing, buttoning, or tying garment closures).

In a Montessori classroom, children work by themselves at their own pace. They are free to choose the materials with which they want to "work"—the word used to describe their activity. Children must accomplish one task before starting another, one including the replacing of the materials on the shelf for someone else to use.

The prepared environment in a Montessori program has child-sized furniture and equipment—one of Froebel's ideas that Montessori used. Materials are set out on low shelves, in an orderly fashion, to encourage children's independent use. Only one set of any materials—their shape, form, and the way they are presented for children to use—are the vehicles for learning.

The teacher in the Montessori setting has a prescribed role, one of observing the children. Teachers become familiar with skills and developmental levels, then match the child to the appropriate material or task. There is little teacher intervention beyond giving clear directions for how to use the materials. Group instruction is not common; learning is an individual experience.

### The Controversy

Some controversy surrounds the Montessori method, its schools, its training. Limitations of the Montessori philosophy most frequently cited follow. They highlight the difference between the Montessori system and the mainstream of American education.

- *Lack of social interaction among children and between teachers and children.* Notably, the absence of dramatic play equipment that would foster peer interchange.

- *Lack of self-expression.* Children are discouraged from exploring and experimenting with materials in their own way. Creative arts are not part of the pure Montessori method. No vehicle is provided for self-expression through fantasy, imagination, or creative play.

- *Lack of stimulation for language development.* Since children are encouraged to work alone and teachers interact with them in fairly structured ways, many opportunities for verbal exchange are lost. Again, creative arts and dramatic play provide options, if they are available.

- *Lack of gross-motor equipment or emphasis.* Only fine-motor skills are emphasized in most of the Montessori materials. Outdoor play is not an integrated part of the Montessori curriculum.

In a review of the research (Chattin-McNichols, 1981), it was found that the Montessori programs have positive results in divergent thinking and school readiness. Montessori was regarded as inferior to other programs in the areas of vocabulary recognition, verbal-social participation, and Piagetian conceptual development. Montessori performs as well as any other program in general intelligence achievement in academic areas, attention, concentration, and distractability strategies. Both sides of the issue call for continued research concerning the effects of a Montessori school experience.

Today, this country is interpreting Montessori education differently. Many Montessori schools are adding curriculum areas of art, dramatic play, and large-motor development. There is also greater teacher flexibility to promote social interaction.

Maria Montessori has found her way into nearly every early education program in existence today. Many schools regularly use materials she designed: the alphabet sandpaper letters, the graduated cylinders, and the number rods are common in preschools and elementary math labs. Whether labeled so or not, much of the material and equipment as well as many of the teaching techniques in use today originated with this dynamic woman nearly one hundred years ago.

She is firmly established in early childhood history of the past and of the future. The Montessori method should be weighed in light of contemporary knowledge and be tailored to meet the needs of vigorous, eager, often needy children of the 1980s and 1990s.

## MONTESSORI MEETS THE NEEDS OF AMERICAN PARENTS IN THE 1980s AND 1990s

*Bretta Weiss*

The biggest issue for the majority of American families now and in the immediate future is child care—the kind of care that is safe and affordable, and which can function long hours each day.

Two other current hot issues involving children are: What should today's teachers be teaching and what should children be learning?

It is time for American parents and educators to look again at the educational philosophy and strategies of Dr. Maria Montessori.

Dr. Montessori's philosophy was developed largely from her scientific observations of children whose parents were both working full time. The curriculum and strategies that emerged closely parallel what leaders in early education today identify as developmentally appropriate practices.

It was Montessori who conceptualized a "prepared environment" for children, in which each individual's physical, social, emotional, and cognitive needs would be nurtured.

She recognized and accommodated that force which drives children to move freely, to use all their senses in exploring their world, and to interact with other children and adults as well as with materials in the environment. Each Montessori environment has an age span of three years—family grouping—to encourage language development as well as social interaction. The learning materials that Montessori invented are concrete, real, and relevant to the lives of young children. They are sequential and self-correcting and provide appropriate challenges.

The Montessori environment also provides the answer to the second question confronting American parents and teachers, which really is: Should teachers be teaching what is sometimes labeled "moral education?" In a Montessori classroom the answer is inevitably "Yes."

In a society where confusion appears to rule the realm of values, the young child in a Montessori "children's house" is encouraged to learn self-care, care for the environment, and care for all persons and living things within the environment. From this learning comes respect and responsibility for self, for others, and for the world in which he or she will play an active part.

The Montessori teacher models honorable traits of character and looks at each child as unique and worthy of respect, no matter what the child's peculiar outlook or level of ability might be. Montessori saw the goal of education as the formation of the child.

Finally, as to the question of what a child should learn, the Montessori approach emphasizes the cogency of learning how to learn. Learning today's facts may or may not be relevant to tomorrow's needs. But learning *how to learn* provides the master tool necessary for life.

Montessori's vision of the child and of education takes direct aim at our most serious problems of what kind of education is best for and most encourages the preparation of tomorrow's citizens.

In her last book she wrote:

One of the most urgent endeavors to be undertaken on behalf of the reconstruction of society is the reconstruction of education [to awaken] those marvellous powers which today remain hidden . . . Then there will appear the child who is destined to form a humanity capable of understanding and controlling our present civilization. (*The Formation of Man,* p. 98).

*Bretta Weiss is the National Director of the American Montessori Society.*

# EXTENDING THE AGE RANGE

## Infant/Toddler Programs

There has been a dramatic rise in recent years in the demand for and availability of group care for infants and toddlers. The early 1970s produced a great deal of research concerning the infant/toddler, enhancing public awareness of the potential of children this age. Greater resources and information became available, creating an awareness of the implications for programs that focus specifically on the infant or toddler. Research by Brazelton, White, Honig, Caldwell, Keister, and others has informed us where and how and why we can offer enrichment and learning opportunities to the youngest of children. And we know that this can take place in group care settings under professional guidance.

The trend toward group care for infants and toddlers is affected by the rising number of women in the work force who combine child rearing and careers and by the increasing single-parent families where the parent must work.

Gonzales-Mena and Eyer (1980) define the infant/toddler age group: Infancy is from babyhood until the child learns to walk. Then he or she is called a toddler until almost three years old.

Infant/toddler centers fall into several categories. They may be full day care centers or they may be part-time. They may be more educational, with parent involvement programs, than centers for group care. Most are a combination of physical care coupled with intellectual stimulation and parent development.

Parent relationships are an important part of any program for young children, but especially so when babies and toddlers are involved. The general intention of these centers is to provide care that is supplemental to family life and that supports the child's family structure. In order to do that, the caregiver at an infant/toddler center involves the parents in the everyday decisions about the care of their child, provides them with information about the child's day, and strengthens the child's sense of belonging to that particular family.

## Philosophy of Infant/Toddler Care

Current research has enlarged the understanding of the growth process of babies. Piaget defined this time as the sensorimotor stage, and Erikson states that trust and autonomy are the critical lessons to be learned at this age (see Chapter 4). Through these insights, we have come to view the infant more and more as an involved person, one who experiences a wide range of intellectual and emotional abilities. The prevalent philosophy of quality infant/toddler programs recognizes the "personhood" of the baby (Honig, 1981). This means that the infant/toddler is treated with the same consideration as any child. Although they may appear to be helpless beings, babies are in fact persons with feelings, rights, and an individual nature. Gonzales-Mena and Eyer (1980) hold that the infant/toddler deserves "respect as a full human being regardless of age or helplessness."

This philosophy implies that taking care of infants or toddlers is not just a case of thrusting bottles in their mouths when they are hungry or putting them in a playpen to amuse themselves. The caregiver in a quality infant/toddler center understands that feeding, diapering, and playing are, in fact, the curriculum of this age group. Caregiving routines are at the heart of the infant/toddler program. The challenge for the caregiver is to find ways to use these daily routines to interact, develop trust and security, and provide educational opportunities. The term *"educaring,"* coined by Magda Gerber, describes the combination of factors that "stress the importance of respectful, responsive, and reciprocal adult-infant interaction" (Gonzales-Mena and Eyer, 1980). In many cases, the caregiver's (or educarer's) role extends to helping parents use these same common occurrences to promote the optimum development of their child.

## What Is Good Infant/Toddler Care?

Just what is meant by "quality" infant/toddler care? What are the factors that combine to provide the best environments for these youngsters?

The first and overriding purpose of infant and toddler education is "good basic caregiving" (Cataldo, 1983). Once that purpose is understood and met, then

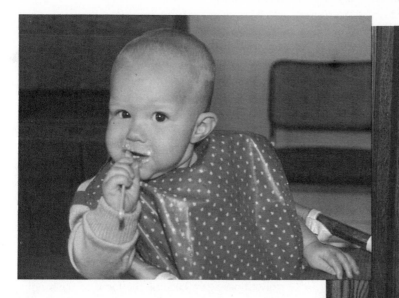

**FIGURE 2.10** The infant and toddler achieving independence: "I can do it myself!" (Photo at right courtesy of Trinity Preschool, New York, N.Y.)

two important goals are: (1) To fully develop the sequence of specific skills and abilities thought to express and enhance competence and to foster understanding of self and others, and (2) to develop a personal and social self and be valued and supported in the growth of personality and effective social relationships (Cataldo, 1983).

To accomplish these goals requires individual attention and affection, as well as spontaneous and informal interaction between caregivers and babies. Through the security of daily routines and frequent contact, self-esteem is fostered.

Infant and toddler education differs from preschool education in several important ways. These differences stem from the very nature of infants and toddlers and their needs. According to Cataldo (1983) infant and toddler education is "more intense . . . more physical . . . more personal" than working with preschoolers. Infant/toddler education owes its overall philosophy to the traditional tenets of early childhood education; these basic principles are extended to meet the specific requirements of this more vulnerable age group.

In infant and toddler programs as compared with preschool programs, there is a need for:

- more one-to-one physical care
- immediate response from adults
- more follow-up to experiences and activities
- use of ordinary routines as learning opportunities
- skills that go beyond teaching: mothering, being a playmate
- intentional rather than discovery learning
- keener attunement to interpreting need and distress signals in young children

Good programs for infants and toddlers, then, are distinctly arranged for them and are not simply modified versions of what works well in a program for three-year-olds. The high level of adult dependency, the rapid growth changes from birth to age three, and the interrelationship among developmental areas (see Chapter 3) call for certain elements in a program for babies and toddlers:

- A low number of children per caregiver, the optimum for infants being one caregiver to four infants and for toddlers, one to six (Lally, et al., 1986).
- Infants should not relate to more than two different adults during the day (Lally, et al., 1986).
- Programs should be designed to allow for caregivers to spend between 10 and 15 percent of their time on a one-to-one basis with each of the children in their care (Slaughter, 1981).
- The quality and training of caregivers is a key factor. They should be responsive adults who are sensitive to the awakening social, emotional, and intellectual needs of the infant and toddler.
- The stability and continuity of the staff is important. There should be a minimum amount of staff turnover, with plenty of time allotted for introduction of new personnel to the children.

The distinction between programs for infants and those for toddlers is also important to note. Just as a scaled-down version of preschool is not a toddler program, neither is a scaled-down version of a good day for toddlers an appropriate model for infants. The mobility of the toddler, for instance, requires different amounts of space and time in the schedule than are required for infants. Babies sleep more their first year of life; their rhythm of eating, sleeping, and playing must be met. Babies thrive when someone responds to their smiles and developing skills. Common routines such as diapering create the curriculum as caregivers talk with the babies about what they are doing and what is happening to them. Caregivers get babies to focus on themselves in a gentle, extensively personal involvement. Good programs for babies recognize their capacities and the extent of their awareness of themselves and others in their environment.

Routines again become the focus of the toddler day but in a somewhat different way. Mealtimes and toileting provide daily opportunities for toddlers to explore and to express their emerging sense of self. Handwashing—even eating—becomes a time to fill, to taste, to dump, to pick up. Again, the curriculum emerges from a developmental need toddlers have of "Me! Mine!" To foster that independence, that wanting to "do it myself," routines that allow for experimentation, mistakes, and messes make a good toddler curriculum.

## Issues

There are many important issues surrounding quality infant/toddler care. First, good care costs money. The factors that combine to make a quality program—low teacher:child ratio, small groups, individual attention—raise the costs to make infant/toddler care one of the most expensive child care programs. Second, critics of child care—any child care—raise even greater fears about the negative effects on family life and the harmful aspects of group care for the very young. Ignoring the statistics, they do not seem to realize that the question is hardly one of whether or not child care should exist. The need for child care for young children is well documented.

According to the Children's Defense Fund (1988), the availability of child care lags behind the need: By

1995 more than three-quarters of all school-age children and two-thirds of all preschool children will have mothers in the labor force. That means 15 million children under the age of six will need some kind of child care service.

Honig (1985), calling infant/toddler caregiving "the scarcest commodity in the world of child care," lists a number of challenges to these programs:

- the quality of the caregiver
- the stability of the staff
- the expensive staff:infant or staff:toddler ratio of at least 1 to 4
- the need for a rich language experience integrated into daily routines
- the need to build a prosocial curriculum that promotes children to care for and about one another
- the necessity for caregivers to devote individual attention for both learning and caregiving, balancing between the group and the individual child
- the need to support and renew staff so they in turn will be supportive to parents and serve as appropriate resources
- the need to promote a sense of choice and control to young children throughout the curriculum and routines of caregiving
- the critical need for ongoing training for caregivers

Honig's own research supports these statements, as do other sources. The most critical question regarding infant attachment has been answered by research also. Bee (1985) cites research by Rutter in 1982 that indicated infants raised in child care situations developed as strong attachments to their parents as did infants raised in their own homes by their parents.

The task for the early childhood professional seems clear. Learn what the issues are, defend policies that reflect high standards, and be prepared to further influence group care for infants and toddlers that is of the highest quality.

# Kindergarten

Today's kindergartens reflect a broad picture. Kindergartens are found in elementary schools, churches, private schools, and as part of preschool child care centers. The school day may be 2½ hours long, a half-day, or (of increasing frequency) a full-day session. Age of enrollment varies from 4½ to six years old. Children may be required to attend school every day or just part of the week. Teachers may be trained in elementary school methods, in nursery school, or in a specialty, such as Montessori methods.

Kindergartens are universally available throughout the United States and have a significant impact in early education. In 1965 only 47 percent of five-year-olds were enrolled in kindergarten; 20 years later that figure reached 90 percent (Spodek, 1986). All states now have publicly supported kindergarten, but attendance is mandatory in only 22 of them. Two states subsidize prekindergarten programs, and the largest U.S. school system, New York City, initiated full-day kindergartens in 1983.

Three current debates bring kindergarten issues into focus. One is concerned with the length of the kindergarten day, a second with lowering the kindergarten age to four. The third is about the increasing formal skills training found in many kindergarten classes. Each topic deserves careful consideration.

There are three types of schedules for kindergarten programs: 67 percent are half-day; 22 percent are full-day, every day; and 7 percent are full-day on alternating days (Jalongo, 1986). The advantages and disadvantages of each are explored in Figure 2.11 on pages 56-57.

In the United States, the compulsory age for kindergarten ranges from five to eight. Lowering the age for beginning school to four years raises questions about the nature of prekindergarten programs and their relationship to kindergarten. Would they be compressed into one year? How would readiness be determined? What would happen to four-year-olds who were not ready for kindergarten? What would the curriculum of the kindergarten look like?

At the present, kindergarten programs range from relatively traditional classes to highly structured, academically oriented classes. The first approach, in

| POSSIBLE ADVANTAGES FOR: | Full-Day Daily | Full-Day/Alternating Days | Half-Day |
|---|---|---|---|
| THE CHILD | more chances for participation and individualization | more gradual induction into school | the most gradual orientation to school of the three options |
| | increased opportunity to participate in total school experience (special events, remedial programs, enrichment activities) | fuller participation in school activities than with half-day | |
| | more contact with teacher and peers | | child who has difficulty being separated from parents may adapt more readily |
| | incidence of grade retention and special education placement may be reduced disadvantaged child may benefit greatly (from learning environment, health screening, school lunch program, etc.) | disadvantaged child may derive some benefit over half-day | |
| | children with siblings at the same school can travel to and from school together | | |
| THE PARENTS | professional child care throughout most of the day decreases child care expenses for working parents | child care throughout several days on a regular schedule might decrease child care expenses | parents who plan to spend more time at home with their child can do so |
| | transportation generally provided | | |
| | better communication with teachers may be possible | | |
| THE SCHOOL | expanded curriculum possible | no additional teaching staff necessary | fewer teachers required |
| | utilization of empty classrooms in low enrollment schools | | |
| | greater efficiency in scheduling | classroom space and supplies the same as half-day | less space, equipment, and supplies than full-day |
| | elimination of an additional bus run | reduction in transportation costs over half-day | |
| | government subsidy increased in some states | | |
| | enrollment increase when children in private full-day kindergartens transfer to public school | | |

| POSSIBLE DISADVANTAGES FOR: | *Full-Day Daily* | *Fulll-Day/Alternating Days* | *Half-Day* |
|---|---|---|---|
| THE CHILD | less mature children may be frustrated by the learning environment | less instructional time than full-day option | limited instructional time |
|  | adjustment to school may be more difficult | schedule may be difficult to remember and follow | assignment to morning or afternoon group may be problematic for child |
|  | formal academics may be introduced before the child has attained readiness | children may not feel the room is "theirs" | teacher, room and resources are usually shared with others |
| THE PARENTS | parents who prefer to spend more time at home with their child may feel pressured to comply with the full-day program | working parents may find child care for non-school days only more difficult to arrange | transportation not provided in some districts |
|  |  |  | large numbers of children assigned to one teacher may deter parent-teacher interaction |
| THE SCHOOL | additional specially trained staff required | less efficiency in schedule | less efficienty in schedule |
|  | more space, equipment and supplies necessary | teachers may find that continuity of program is difficult to maintain | increased transportation costs (if provided) |
|  |  | teachers often have two complete classes of children each week | too much of total instructional time available spent getting started and preparing to leave |
|  |  |  | teachers often have two complete classes of children each day |

**FIGURE 2.11**  Comparing three kindergarten schedules. Reprinted from Jalongo, M. (1986). "What is happening to kindergarten?" *Childhood Education* 62 (3) 158–159. Reprinted by permission of M. Jalongo and the Association for Childhood Education International, 11141 Georgia Avenue, Suite 200, Wheaton, Md. Copyright © 1986 by the Association.

which curriculum is based on play, tends to focus on social adjustment to school as a whole and on developmental patterns. Creativity is valued, large blocks of free-play time are provided, and process is emphasized over content.

The academically oriented programs have emerged over the past 20 years. In what is usually called an instructional or cognitive model, achievement in mathematics, language, and reading is stressed. Direct teacher instruction in skill-specific tasks is common, as are workbooks. Product is emphasized

over process. Many of these programs seem inconsistent with the developmental and learning styles of five- and six-year-olds and are viewed as preparation for advancement to first grade rather than as the more traditional bridge between preschool or home and formal education.

For further discussion on the negative effects of early academics, see Chapter 3 for developmental ranges and Word Pictures for appropriate expectations. See Chapter 10 for standardized testing and for Sue Bredekamp's *Focus* article. See Section 5 for

David Elkind's *Guest Editorial* on "Miseducation." See Chapter 11 for developmentally appropriate curriculum and Elizabeth Jones's *Focus* discussion, and Chapter 13 for Robert Calfee's *Focus* discussion on reading. In Chapter 15 this issue is discussed in various sections: See Stress; Education Reform; Curriculum; and Back to Basics, as well as other related topics.

So the issues and controversies are set. Today's child faces a world of unbelievable complexity. All kinds of values are changing, from the roles of men and women, to the growing scarcity of resources, to the real threat of extinction. No one innovation, either in materials or approaches, has shown itself to be the answer to society's—or kindergarten's—problems. Recent research and evaluation have begun to pose questions that need answers. As those answers emerge, keep in mind that

> . . . We need to explore all dimensions of the kindergarten curriculum if we are to determine whether it is adequate for children in today's society. We need to evaluate curriculum from a developmental point of view, asking whether what we are teaching young children is developmentally appropriate. We need to evaluate it from a cultural context dimension, asking whether what we are teaching is worthwhile . . . [w]e need to evaluate it from a knowledge dimension, asking whether the way we are teaching children is consistent with the forms of knowledge taught, and thus can be tested by the child.
>
> A look at all three of these dimensions of the kindergarten curriculum can provide us with the basis for determining an appropriate one for today's kindergarten.
>
> (Spodek, 1986)

Spodek (1986) further suggests that if we are to use our knowledge of kindergarten programs "wisely and justly," the following guidelines should direct our actions:

- Kindergartens should be available to all children.
- Kindergarten programs should support children's developmental needs.

- Kindergartens should support children's individual growth patterns.
- Kindergarten should be taught by qualified individuals.
- Kindergartens should provide bridges within children's lives.

Standardized testing and screening, an important prekindergarten issue, are discussed in Chapter 10, Evaluating for Effectiveness.

## After-School Programs

*After-school programs* are designed for children after they finish their regular academic day. This type of care is usually available for children in kindergarten through third grade. Some family day care homes provide this service, as do individual programs designed specifically for the five-through-eight-year-old.

Generally, by the time children reach the age of eight or nine, they stay at home or engage in extracurricular activities at school or in the community. Younger children need adult supervision and access to appropriate materials and activities when they finish their school day. There is a critical need for safe, recreational programs for children of this age. It has been estimated that between two and six million children are left alone to take care of themselves before and after school. In the 1984-85 Census Bureau report, one million school-age children claimed that they took care of themselves after school (*Education Week*, 1987). Only four percent of all schools operate an after-school program to serve the needs of these children.

What happens to these children after school? For the kindergartener, school may be over at noon. From 1:30 to 3:00 P.M., first-, second- and third-graders are released from their school day. Too often these children are sent home with a house key around their necks or in their pockets. They are instructed to look after themselves and possibly a younger sibling until the parent (or parents) comes home from work. These *"latch key" children,* as they are known, are a young and vulnerable population. The early childhood community has embraced their obvious need for good after-school programs.

The essentials of after-school care reflect the needs of the parents, teachers, and children involved. Flexible hours, reasonable tuition rates, and clear lines of communication are of primary importance to parents. To ensure continual care, scheduling must take into consideration the elementary school calendar. Holidays, conference times, and minimum-day schedules of schools must be considered. Opportunities to extend the after-school program can originate from the use of community resources such as library story hours, swimming facilities, and parks.

In planning, the teaching staff must be aware of how their program differs from the rest of the child's normal school day. Knowing that this is probably the third environment, set of rules, and adult supervision that the child has faced that day is uppermost in the minds of the teachers. Carlson et al. (1980) identify four components necessary for success. Children need:

- *A time for sharing*. Small conversational groups where children can relate the day's happenings with an interested adult and their after-school friends.

- *To control the experience*. Children actively participate in group planning of short- and long-term projects and activities. Children move freely, choosing between indoor and outdoor activities, with many choices in a supervised, guided, free-play environment.

- *Vigorous activity*. Outdoor play, indoor climbers, slides, and other large-motor equipment are popular. Self-directed chasing games are important.

- *Challenging curriculum*. Craft materials requiring increasingly complex fine motor and planning skills are successful with this age group. Table activities, such as origami, checkers, Chinese checkers, marbles, card games, charades, and puppetry add to the necessary stimulation.

Children need the safety, the creative opportunity, and the emotionally supportive relationships that after-school care can provide. As the trend of working mothers continues, more of these programs will appear as a natural extension of responsible child care.

**FIGURE 2.12**   After school: A time for sharing snacks and friendship. (Courtesy of Maria C. Hiller, Midland College, Tex.)

| Criteria Affecting Programs | For Example |
| --- | --- |
| 1. The age of the children served | Is it a toddler group? Infant care? A specific age group? A multiage group? |
| 2. The philosophy expressed | Is there one overriding philosophy, such as Montessori or behavior analysis? Is it an eclectic school, combining several approaches? |
| 3. The goals of the program | Are the objectives academic preparation? Custodial care? Enrichment for preschoolers? Socialization? Parent education? |
| 4. The purpose for which it was established | For profit? As a laboratory for research? As a place for parents to meet? As a social service vehicle? |
| 5. The sponsoring agency and its requirements | To whom is the program responsible? The federal government? A family service agency? School district? Church board? Employer? Private individual? How does that agency influence and affect the program? |
| 6. The quality and training of the teaching staff | Do all teachers have degrees or credentials in early childhood? What kind of experience is required? Is there an opportunity for in-service training and continuing education? |
| 7. The physical environment | What is the amount and shape of space available indoors and out? |
| 8. The general population served | What is the ethnic makeup of the surrounding community? What languages are spoken? What are the economic status and family patterns in the neighborhood? Will it serve the handicapped and disabled? |
| 9. The financial stability | Is money available for equipment and supplies? Is the budget sufficient to pay child care workers reasonable salaries? Is the financial base sound? Will funding end? |

FIGURE 2.13   Chart of criteria affecting programs.

# CRITERIA AFFECTING PROGRAMS

There are many factors that determine exactly what type of program will best serve the young child.

Some of these variables emerged through the descriptions of the many kinds of settings available for children today. Programs in early childhood are defined by the elements listed in Figure 2.13. Any one program is a combination of these factors. At one time or another, each factor was given specific and serious consideration regarding its impact on the program desired.

# SUMMARY

Educational facilities for young children reach a broad population. They serve children from infancy through elementary-school age. There is an array of programs available, which varies for philosophical reasons as well as because of ages of children enrolled. Early childhood teachers have a wide range of programs from which to choose—as do parents.

The traditional nursery school and its sister programs of child care, laboratory schools, and parent cooperatives form the core of early childhood programs. The intervention models of the 1960s and 1970s— Head Start and Follow-Through—are variations on the theme. They are specific attempts to provide early education and intervention to children caught in

poverty's cycle. Other schools, such as Montessori or behavior analysis programs, are based on clearly stated principles with outlined procedures for teachers and children.

In reflecting the needs of society, it is no wonder that extended day programs have been created. Not only are children being cared for in group situations before and after school hours, they are being placed in the group settings at an earlier age. The 1970s gave rise to numerous infant/toddler programs. After-school care is becoming common in many communities.

As varied as they are, there is also a certain similarity among all programs for young children. Consideration must be given to a number of factors when reviewing the needs of young children and their families. Some of these elements are the ages of the children the program will serve, the qualifications and experience of the teaching staff, the funding base and financial support available, and the goals of the program to meet the needs of all children and their families. With so many choices, those who desire child care will find options that suit their specific needs.

# REVIEW QUESTIONS

1. Match the program with the appropriate description:

Montessori                    Educaring
Follow-Through                Staggered staff schedules
Infant/Toddler                Community involvement
Day Care                      Prepared environment
Head Start                    Elementary school

2. Name and describe the three sister programs within traditional preschool boundaries. *Cooperative child care Cooperatives/lab schools*

3. Why are some early childhood programs called "intervention" schools? *Head Start outcome*

4. Are there differences among preschool and kindergarten programs? Between infant and toddler programs? What are they? Should there be a difference? Why?

5. What are some of the criteria that affect all children's programs?

6. What has been the unique contribution of the Perry Preschool Project and how do you see this affecting legislation, program development in early childhood, and the early childhood profession?

7. What is the controversy regarding for-profit child care centers? Are you for or against the idea of child care centers making a profit? Why?

8. What is the kindergarten age requirement in your state? How does your local school district interpret this requirement?

## LEARNING ACTIVITIES

1. Choose one program and describe how you would operate that type of class. Include the daily schedule, number and skill level of teachers, types of parent contacts, and the activities for children.

2. Consider how each of these problems might be handled in each of these different programs:

   Problems:  One child hits another
              Parent doesn't pay tuition on time
              A child who withdraws from social contact
              A child who wanders

   Programs:  Montessori
              Day care
              Parent cooperative

3. What role would children's social skills play in these settings:
   Traditional nursery school
   Montessori
   Kindergarten
   Infant/Toddler

4. What are the licensing regulations for child care in your area? Describe the steps necessary in your town to open a
   - nursery school.
   - child care center.
   - family day care home.

5. Which government agencies are involved in the licensing procedure?

## BIBLIOGRAPHY

Bee, Helen. *The Developing Child.* Cambridge, Mass.: Harper & Row, 1985.

Berrueta-Clement, J.R.; Schweinhart, L.J.; Barnett, W.S.; Epstein, A.S.; and Weikart, D.P. *Changed Lives: The Effects of the Perry Preschool Program on Youths Through 19.* Ypsilanti, Mich.: High/Scope Press, 1984.

Bredekamp, Sue (ed.). "NAEYC Position Statement on Developmentally Appropriate Practice in the Primary Grades, Serving 5- Through 8-Year-Olds." *Young Children,* January 1988, pp. 64-84.

Brown, Bernard. "Head Start—How Research Changed Public Policy." *Young Children,* July 1985, pp. 9-13.

Carlson, Nancy A., et al. "After-Kindergarten Day Care: A Challenge to the Community." *Young Children,* November 1980, pp. 13-20.

Cataldo, Christine Z. *Infant and Toddler Programs.* Reading, Mass.: Addison-Wesley Publishing, 1983.

Chattin-McNichols, John P. "The Effects of Montessori School Experience." *Young Children,* July 1981, pp. 49-66.

*Child Care Information Exchange,* November 1986, pp. 7-8.

Children's Defense Fund. *A Call for Action to Make Our Nation Safe for Children: A Briefing Book on the Status of American Children in 1988.* Washington, D.C., 1988.

Children's Defense Fund. *Child Care: The Time Is Now.* Washington, D.C., 1987.

Cole, Luella. "Basic Ideas of the Montessori Method." In Coopersmith and Feldman (eds.), *The Formative Years.* San Francisco: Albion Publishing Co., 1974.

*Education Week,* May 13, 1987. "Census Bureau Finds Working Mothers Increasingly Dependent on Child Care." p. 8.

Elkind, David. "Humanizing the Curriculum." In *Early Childhood Education,* Annual Edition. Guilford, Conn.: The Dushkin Publishing Group, 1982.

Elkind, David. "Montessori Education: Abiding Contributions and Contemporary Challenge." *Young Children,* January 1983, pp. 3-10.

Evans, Ellis. *Contemporary Influences in Early Childhood Education.* New York: Holt, Rinehart and Winston, 1975.

Galinsky, Ellen. *Investing in Quality Child Care: A Report for AT&T,* 1986.

Glazer, Judith S. "Kindergarten and Early Education/Issues and Problems." *Childhood Education,* September/October 1985, pp. 13-18.

Gold, Deborah, L. "Church Day Care Wins Exemption from State Law." *Education Week,* May 25, 1988, p. 1.

Gonzales-Mena, Janet, and Eyer, Dianne W. *Infancy and Caregiving.* Palo Alto, Calif.: Mayfield Publishing Co., 1980.

Honig, Alice. "What Are the Needs of Infants?" *Young Children,* November 1981, pp. 3-10.

Honig, Alice S. "High Quality Infant/Toddler Care: Issues and Dilemmas." *Young Children,* November 1985, pp. 40-46.

Jalongo, Mary Renck. "What Is Happening to Kindergarten?" *Childhood Education,* January/February 1986, pp. 154-160.

Kutner, Lawrence. "Searching for the Best in Day Care." *The New York Times,* February 4, 1988, p. C1.

Lally, J. Ronald; Provence, Sally; Szanton, Eleanor; and Weissbourd, Bernice. "Developmentally Appropriate Care for Children from Birth to Age 3." In Bredekamp, Sue (ed.), *Developmentally Appropriate Practice.* Washington, D.C.: National Association for the Education of Young Children, 1986.

Lindner, Eileen; Mattis, Mary C.; and Rogers, June. *When Churches Mind the Children.* Ypsilanti, Mich.: High/Scope Press, 1983.

Modigliani, Kathy; Reiff, Marianne; and Jones, Sylvia. *Opening Your Door to Children: How to Start a Family Day Care Program.* Washington, D.C.: National Association for the Education of Young Children, 1987.

National Association for the Education of Young Children. *Accreditation Criteria and Procedures of the National Academy of Early Childhood Programs.* Washington, D.C.: 1984.

Neugebauer, Roger. "How's Business? Status Report #4 on For-Profit Child Care." *Child Care Information Exchange,* January 1988, pp. 29-34.

*New York Times* Editorial "Mothers With Babies—and Jobs." June 19, 1988, p. 26.

O'Connell, Joanne Curry. "Research in Review: Children of Working Mothers: What the Research Tells Us." *Young Children,* January 1983, pp. 62-70.

Phillips, Deborah A. "Sparing the Rod and Escaping the Regulators: Religious Exemptions from Child Care Regulations." *Child Care Information Exchange,* September 1987, pp. 9-12.

Ramey, Craig T. "Consequences of Infant Day Care." In Weissbourd and Musick (eds.), *Infants: Their Social Environment.* Washington, D.C.: National Association for the Education of Young Children, 1981.

Ramsey, Marjorie, and Bayless, Kathleen. *Kindergarten: Programs and Practices.* St. Louis: C.V. Mosby Co., 1980.

Read, Katherine, and Patterson, June. *The Nursery School and Kindergarten.* New York: Holt, Rinehart and Winston, 1980.

Slaughter, Diana T. "Social Policy Issues Affecting Infants." In Weissbourd and Musick (eds.), *Infants: Their Social Environment.* Washington, D.C.: National Association for the Education of Young Children, 1981.

Spodek, Bernard (ed.). *Today's Kindergarten: Exploring the Knowledge Base, Expanding the Curriculum.* New York: Teacher's College Press, 1986.

Stevens, Joseph H., Jr. "The National Day Care Home Study: Family Day Care in the United States." *Young Children,* May 1982, pp. 59-66.

Wallis, Claudia. "The Child Care Dilemma." *Time,* June 22, 1987, pp. 54-60.

White, Burton L. "Viewpoint: Should You Stay Home with Your Baby?" *Young Children,* November 1981, pp. 11-17.

# SECTION 2

# WHO IS THE CHILD?

*K. Eileen Allen*

Who is the child? In search of the answer I propose a counter question: "Who are we?" Unless we, the teachers of young children, know ourselves we cannot know the child. Yet children are always in process, always evolving, always changing. And so should we be. If we are to be truly effective teachers we must recognize that scientific, social, and political forces are continuously at work, directly and indirectly, influencing us in our efforts to answer "Who is the child?"

Child development was a fairly new discipline in the early 1940s. Already we had entered an age of smugness, even conceit, about the state of our knowledge. Almost exclusively, the biological-maturationist theory of development governed the thinking, teaching, and practices in the field of early childhood. And little wonder—the evidence was most convincing, given the state of the art. Few questioned the prevailing thesis, that the underpinnings of all development lay in sequential, biological changes based on hereditary "givens" mapped out almost from the moment of conception. Thus, when asked, "Who is the child?" we responded confidently that the child was a product of its genetic inheritance with everything the child would be determined long before birth.

This deterministic philosophy was actually the forerunner of the normative movement. A generation of researchers, led by Arnold Gesell, assessed groups of infants and children during the first months and years of life, charting the sequences of development at each of many age levels. Out of this seminal research came two pervasive guidelines: one, the theory that maturation occurred "independent of experience"; two, the "ages and stages" stereotyping. Catch phrases such as the *terrible twos*, the *trusting threes*, and even the *fearless fours* became the banners of our trade. We never questioned the elitism nor the homogeneity of the groups of children on whom the normative data were based. Nor did we question the often unwarranted conclusions derived from those data.

In spite of the problems associated with oversubscribing to an "ages and stages" philosophy, we did acquire invaluable knowledge about physical characteristics and developmental sequences that will serve us well for as long as we study children. Further, even though the biological-maturationist point of view lost much of its impact for a time, it has reemerged in recent years in a number of research projects as a possible explanation for

# Who Is
# the Young Child?

various aspects of temperament and even intelligence in the developing child.

In the 1960s an about face was heard in answer to "Who is the child?" In seeming chorus, social, political, and scientific sources answered that the child was a product of its environment. The popular refrain was that everything the child would become depended largely on early experiences, especially those experiences that occurred during the child's first five years. What was responsible for this major shift in theoretical position?

Learning theorists (starting long ago with John Locke and his tabula rasa, or "blank slate" concept of development) had been slowly building a strong case for the power of the environment in determining a child's developmental outcome. An increasingly robust body of research was demonstrating that the consequences of a child's behavior became the crucial factor in determining the skills a child would acquire: children tended to learn those responses that produced success or positive results and to avoid experiences that ended in failure or negative results.

Again, there followed a period of naivete and of over-subscribing—this time to the theoretically baseless assumption that the child was little more than a puppet, a passive recipient of what the environment provided or failed to provide. To the credit of all, this fallacy was short-lived. Learning theory broadened its research base to focus on social learning and on observational learning. As an example: the mother-neonate studies gave evidence that the human infant was anything but passive. We discovered that the neonate was an active observer, imitator, and responder who could and did evoke additional responses from significant persons in the environment thereby prompting further responding from the infant. Of course, such interactions were not always benign. A placid, cuddly baby who expressed needs clearly and at regular times was likely to have different early learning experiences from those of a colicky infant who was tense, fussy, and unpredictable in crying, eating, and sleeping patterns.

Almost concurrent with these analyses of development came a changing view of intelligence. No longer was intelligence viewed as fixed and innate, unfolding in ways comparable to a child's developing physical capacities. Instead, the theory, as put forth by Piaget, was that the development of intelligence—or cognition—was analogous to a layering or building block process. In this process, interaction with the environment provided critical nourishment for the child's intellectual development. J. Mc V. Hunt, theorizing further from Piaget's writings, described cognitive development as the direct result of the child's exploration of the environment. By actively playing with or manipulating a variety of objects and events that were familiar in many respects, but which also contained elements just a bit beyond the child's immediate knowledge base, cognitive development thrived. And so an interactionist theory of development, a melding of maturational and environmental forces, began to take form.

Other forces, both social and political, were at work, too. The Civil Rights Movement and its exposure of the inequities in our educational system, together with the repudiation of a wholly deterministic viewpoint of development, led to compensatory early education programs for minority and poverty children. Not long after, we came to recognize that the needs and rights of handicapped children must also be respected. These children, and those in our poverty sector, were as much a part of the answer to "Who is the child?" as were the vast majority of children who were fortunate enough to be spared physical or environmental trauma and deprivation.

The inclusion of poor children, minority children, and handicapped children in our response to "Who is the child?" expanded our understanding of developmental processes. True, even at the height of our "ages and stages" period, we touted the need to recognize individual differences among children, and to value each child's uniqueness. But did we really believe it, especially if the child was unkempt or poor, slow or from a different culture? I think not. Today, having broadened our developmental perspective, there is wide recognition that every child is a special child with a unique personality, learning style, and interest. Every child is deserving of genuine respect for the uniqueness of his or her family history and cultural background.

With this growing esteem for the differences among children, families, and cultures, we also began to develop a different attitude toward parents. Instead of viewing ourselves as the experts—and parents as humble targets or objects of our expertise—we came to see parents as partners, *senior partners,* in promoting a child's development. We faced up to the reality that it is they, not us, who will continue to provide support and carry the primary responsibility for the child's socialization and developmental progress. We came to recognize, too, that the more delayed or the more impaired the child, the greater the need for us to listen to parents, seek their help, and work in close partnership with them.

What else have we learned from broadening our definition of the child to include *all* children, regardless of physical, cognitive, or social-economic differences? Most notable is a reaffirmation that the child is, indeed, more than a sum of its parts. True, we have always espoused the "whole child" or holistic approach to development, but the concept tended to be didactic rather than applied. Only through the combination of service, research, and clinical training activities in interdisciplinary settings devoted to retarded, handicapped, and high-risk infants and children did rigorous evidence of the essential interrelatedness of all areas of development come to light. In such settings, we came to see how futile it was to view any problem from a single perspective. We learned that more often than not, a language delay, for example, stemmed from physical, neurological, nutritional, psychological, and social factors interacting in complex combinations with other events in the child's environment.

Where does this leave us in formulating an answer to "Who is the child?" The here and now of child development in this last decade of the twentieth century most assuredly can boast a broad and sophisticated knowledge base. But history has taught us to be cautious. It seems that the more we know about the developing child, the more there is to learn. Perhaps the best answer to the question is that we are still searching.

*K. EILEEN ALLEN is Professor Emeritus from the Department of Human Development at the University of Kansas, where she has taught for the past fourteen years. Earlier, Professor Allen had been involved in her home state of Washington in the field of early childhood at many levels—as a lay teacher in a parent cooperative when her own children were young; as head teacher in the Developmental Psychology Laboratory Preschool at the University of Washington in Seattle; and as Coordinator of Early Childhood Education, Research, and Teacher Training, also at the University of Washington.*

*Professor Allen has been in the field for more than thirty years, and has been involved with many breakthroughs in child development and early education. She helped design and implement one of the earliest training programs for Head Start teachers in the Northwest; she and her colleagues published much of the precedent-setting behavioral research done in the naturalistic environment of the preschool; she was part of one of the first service, training, and research programs to center on an interdisciplinary approach to early intervention with young handicapped children; and she directed one of the earliest First Chance Network Model Preschools demonstrating the principles of mainstreaming young handicapped children. More recently she was selected as a Congressional Science Fellow by the Society for Research in Child Development and by the American Association for the Advancement of Science. Now Professor Allen focuses much of her public speaking and publishing on public policy following her year on Capitol Hill.*

*After retiring from the University of Kansas, Professor Allen returned to live in her home in Seattle. She continues to write and has just had her sixth text book published. She is also engaged in consulting and teaching at both the community college and university levels.*

# CHAPTER 3

## Defining the Young Child

Jill

Tyrannosaurus
Rex

## QUESTIONS for THOUGHT

- What is the age range for early childhood?
- What are some of the basic characteristics of each age?
- How does the development of one area of growth affect other areas?
- What are the implications for teaching children of varying levels of development?
- What are some cautions to take when interpreting age-level characteristic charts? How are they useful?
- Who is the whole child?
- Who are special-needs children?
- What are some of the common types of handicaps found in preschoolers?
- What is mainstreaming?
- Who is the "hurried child"?

**FIGURE 3.1** Children: Alike, yet different. (Courtesy of Cricket Rowe, Eckerd College, Fla.)

## Defining the Child

Children—who are they? When entering a class room, questions arise in teachers' minds about the youngsters they see:

- What do children say?
- What can children do?
- What do children think?
- How do children feel?

Glancing around the room brings an awareness of the group as a whole. Individuals blur among a number of children, all the same size and same age. At this point, they are hardly more than a list of names with ages attached. Quickly, however, a teacher becomes conscious of a single child here and there. In this assortment of small people, different sizes, shapes, and colors emerge.

## Through the Teacher's Eyes

### *Physical Impressions*

Teachers usually begin to define children by their physical characteristics. Initially, their differences are most obvious by the way they look.

Eric is a tall blonde. He is much larger than his just-three age would indicate. He has long slender fingers and arms to match. His movements are fluid; he lopes across the room toward the easel.

Lamar's short stocky build and constant swagger lend the impression that he is a pretty tough character. His coffee-and-cream complexion, soft, curly hair, and smile offset that image.

Natalie at four is a study in perpetual motion. Green eyes flashing, arms and legs waving, she ignores the bulk of her diaper as she propels herself down the slide. There is little indication that the mild case of spina bifida she has inhibits her motor activities. It certainly hasn't affected her daring.

Nothing will heighten an awareness of the individuality of each child more than working in the classroom. Teachers quickly learn what makes each child special. By watching and observing children, teachers accumulate a great deal of detailed information. Adults learn what children really look like as children move their bodies, change expressions and assume a posture. A teacher can sense whether Sonja is happy, hurt, or hurried by the way she moves and how she looks. Rodrigo's face mirrors his distress or his delight. The observant teacher learns to read children for evidence of their social, emotional, physical, and intellectual growth. Children quite naturally express these characteristics with their whole body; each child's response is unique.

## Children's Behaviors

Children's behaviors are so individual; they show their own personal responses to life. They relate to people in ways that express their original nature. Dina has an ability to get her peers to wait on her; Sean trails the teachers for constant companionship. Their responses to the classroom environment are also singular. Ginny becomes overstimulated and loses control; Clark stands and watches other children for long periods of time before he joins in. Teachers become aware of individual differences in the skill level of children. They notice that of the five children at the art table, for instance, only one of them is holding scissors correctly and cutting paper.

## How Children Are Alike

The similarities of the many children in a class are striking. The more they are different, the more they are the same. There seems to be a natural discrepancy here. Teachers can see the differences—wide differences—yet there are common characteristics within the age group itself. Six toddlers working on an art project exhibit six different personal styles, yet typically, they all become distracted and leave their projects half finished. Observation of children—how they look and how they act—helps the teacher see each child as an individual. When many children in a classroom are observed, behaviors common to that age become clear. There is enough standard behavior appropriate to

certain age levels that allows for some generalizations about children's behavior.

Descriptions of these common characteristics date back to a classic collection of research by Gesell and Ilg. Beginning on page 78 are a series of "word pictures" depicting these *age level characteristics* from infancy through age five. In looking at individual children or a group, these descriptions are helpful in understanding the nature of the child and normal growth.

## How Children Differ

Watching and working with children exposes how very different each child is. What makes children differ so, especially when they have so many features in common? Megan gives the tire swing a big push. Ariel shrieks with delight, but Hans bursts into tears and screams to get off. What accounts for the wide range of behaviors evident when you observe any group of children?

**Genetic Makeup.** This certainly accounts for some of the differences. Each child is a unique combination of *genes* that "contributes to the emergence and nature of every human trait from the color of the eyes...to the individual's ultimate intelligence and creativity" (Gardner, 1982).

**Environment.** The effects of the world on inherited genes also play a role. The number and kinds of experiences children have affect how they develop. The attitudes with which children are raised, their culture, their socioeconomic status, the kinds of caregiving they experience, and their community combine in countless ways to affect growth. Good, nutritious food, adequate play space, interested and stimulating adults, the quality of life in the neighborhood, and family stability and relationships affect individual development. Whether a child lives in the South Bronx or Beverly Hills, environmental factors interact with genes to create a single, individual person.

The small child who stands at the classroom door is the sum total of the physical, intellectual, social, and emotional factors of home and heredity. What nature provides, the world shapes and bends. Using intelligence as an example, Gardner (1982) states the interdependency of environment and genetics this way: "The limit of intelligence is fixed by genetics, but the actual intelligence achieved reflects the diverse environments."

There are three other factors concerning the developmental scheme of things that account for individual differences.

**Children Grow and Develop at Different Rates.** Each child has an inner mechanism for monitoring growth. It is a timetable that varies from child to child. It means that each child is ready to learn at a given time, which may or may not coincide with the rest of the group. This readiness factor must be respected.

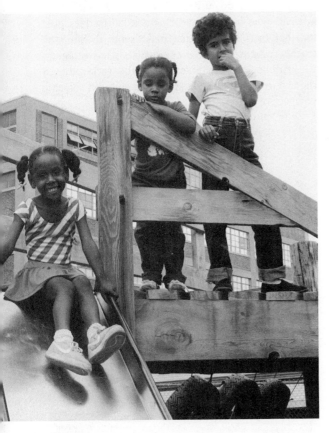

**FIGURE 3.2** Even within one classroom, children come in different sizes and shapes. (Courtesy of Stride Rite Children's Centers, Cambridge, Mass.)

**Development Is Predictable and Follows a Sequence.** Period of rapid growth and activity are followed by periods of calmness and consolidation. *Behavioral swings* at the half-year mark are common in many children. The pleasant, well-balanced three-year-old may become shy and begin to stutter at three-and-one-half. The age at which this occurs is not as important as the sequence in which it happens. The important thing to remember is that children will exhibit markedly different behaviors in the period of one short year. Teachers prepare for these times and appreciate them as a normal course of events for the growing child.

**There Is a Set of Developmental Tasks.** These challenge children at every stage in their growth. Teachers will recognize where children are in the mastery of these tasks, knowing that normal development will account for the inherent differences in children.

### *Implications for Teaching*

The differences in children's development must be accounted for when planning a program for a group. How do teachers take all these factors into consideration? How do they meet the needs of the individual child while addressing the concerns and interests of the total group?

**Program Planning.** Teachers generally begin by planning individual and group activities according to the age level of the class they teach, knowing that certain behavior patterns exist. Planning begins around the known similarities, the developmental tasks and age-appropriate behavior common to that group of children. Goals are set for the children based on these general characteristics. As the school year progresses, teachers observe individuals and the group and change the developmental goals as needed. Individual differences in children are incorporated into the planning; activities selected allow for a variety of responses from children at different stages of development. A pasting activity encourages creativity in the most adept three-year-old and still allows the less-skilled two-year-old to explore the feel of the paste on fingers and hands.

Programs are planned to meet the needs and challenges of the whole group.

Grouping of children by rigid age levels seems contrary to our understanding of individual rates of growth, readiness factors, and wide ranges of abilities. It is a convenient, though arbitrary, system of teaching children. The implication for teachers is clear: plan for the age level with the understanding and appreciation of the variations in development even within a one-year span. Know the child; know what to expect and what development has taken place. Look at the stages of growth for the age level just below and just above the one in which you teach.

**Teachers' Response.** The key word for teachers is *acceptance.* Teachers must not only accept the differences in children, they must plan for them. In doing so, they show respect for the individuality of each child in the class. Accepting the way children reveal themselves fosters the uniqueness that makes each one a special person.

See Chapter 5, The Teacher's Role, for specific suggestions on how teachers plan to accommodate the individuality of children, particularly the sections Self-awareness; Attitudes and Biases; Ten Essentials to Successful Teaching; and A Student Teacher's Guidelines for Beginning. The curriculum chapters, 11 through 15, demonstrate other examples of planning for a wide range of skills. It might be useful, too, to read Chapter 9, Creating Environments, particularly the self-help environment and the anti-bias curriculum.

## Through Children's Eyes

Another way to define children is to look at them from their own point of view. What does it mean to look at the world through children's eyes? What is a child's perspective on the world?

Adults carry into the classroom a great many perceptions about children. Having the advantage of many more years of experience, they tend to forget how much they know! The child they see is sometimes blurred through a great many filters. These filters are attitudes, concepts, experiences, and prejudices. What looks mundane to an adult, such as a trip on the subway, fills children with the joy and wonder of discovery.

To view a classroom through the eyes of a child, one must set aside the filtered lenses of the grown-up world. The young child in the classroom is of the here and now and likes what is familiar and known. The preschooler takes pleasure in common, everyday experiences, learns by doing, and uses all five senses. Though aware of a great many things, the young child is not interested in depth of learning. This may be due to a short attention span or because there is just so *much* to learn about.

The teacher learns to look through children's eyes—what interests them, what they avoid, who their friends are, how they respond in a variety of situations, and how they learn. When Kitty must play it safe with a friend who is less timid than she or Jacques puts together facts in ways that make sense to him, the teacher recognizes these as expressions of individuality.

Adults find that by looking at the world through the eyes of a child, they gain a different and valuable perspective as teacher.

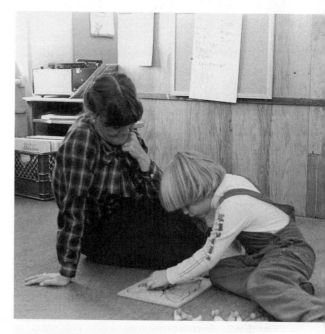

**FIGURE 3.3** Adults see children through many filters. What is it like to look through children's eyes?

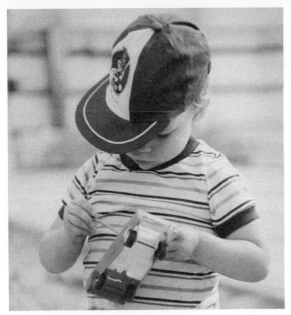

Courtesy of Ray Otto, Silver Lake College, Wis.

Courtesy of Carol A. Mullins.

Courtesy of Galen Noles.

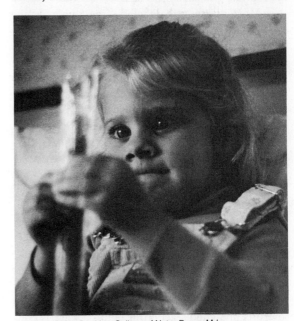

Courtesy of Lisa Deakins, College of Notre Dame, Md.

**FIGURE 3.4**   Children explore and develop in their own way, according to their own inner clock.

# DEVELOPMENTAL RANGES

Each developmental phase has characteristic traits. In the following pages some of the classic normative data collected by Gesell is combined with theories of Piaget, Elkind, and Erikson to demonstrate what children have in common at various ages. Despite the wide range of individual differences at all ages, there are some characteristics children share that are worth keeping in mind. These common behaviors help teachers prescribe programs and plan activities and curricula. They lend perspective. Word pictures of a child, taken from age-level charts, help teachers know what to expect and when to expect it. By using the charts as a reference, teachers lessen the risk of expecting too much or too little of children at any given age. If, for instance, four-year-olds typically "tell tall tales," teachers' responses to their stories reflect that awareness. The fun of making up a story and the use of imagination are acknowledged, but there is not a concern that the child is lying. Age-level characteristics give a frame of reference with which to handle daily situations and a basis for planning appropriate guidance measures.

Most classes are labeled "the two's," "the three's," and so on. Schools enroll children according to a chronological order based on whether a birthday falls before or after an *arbitrary* deadline. Yet most child development texts no longer use the narrow one-year age span when setting out behavior characteristics. Larger, more inclusive groupings of Infant, Toddler, Preschooler, and so on are common. The reason for this change is "that individual differences are so great and growth patterns so diverse that any delineation of common characteristics for a particular age level is bound to be deceptive and misleading" (Elkind, 1978). That point of view has merit; age-level charts can be misunderstood unless used with discretion.

One consideration is what use teachers will make of the charts. It is important to know what range of behaviors occur and to be able to recognize them as normal patterns of growth. That helps to define and interpret the child's action in light of what is considered typical. Guidance and discipline are based on an awareness of the expected behaviors common to a given age range. Many so called "problem behaviors" are normal behaviors of the age in which they occur. This does not imply a passive approach; teachers and parents do not ignore undesirable behavior because the child is "going through a stage." Instead adults seek to guide and direct children in ways that enhance

their overall growth. Four-year-olds test limits and are resistant to controls. The wise teacher accepts the testing of power and individuality, yet still maintains necessary limits to behavior.

Use the charts with care. A profile of the whole child is helpful, but avoid the tendency to overclassify. Look and listen to the children in the classroom in order to interpret theory. Balance your impressions with classroom experience of real children. Interpretation of the charts must not focus on what the child *cannot* do. Instead, use them to get a perspective on the wide range of developmental norms a child exhibits over several of the chronological age groupings. Always look at the word picture for the group just below and just above the age level of the children you are assessing. Those children will undoubtedly exhibit some of the developmental behaviors appropriate to all three groups you check.

The word picture on the infant to one-year-old is deliberately vague on the ages when some developmental characteristics might appear. The rapid rate of growth combined with individual growth patterns make it difficult to predict with any surety when Garth will indeed sit up by himself unaided, but he is likely to accomplish that task within one or two months on either side of the average age cited.

The expression "hurried child," so aptly used by David Elkind in his book of the same name in the early 1980s, has come to mean a disregard for activities and curriculum geared to a child's appropriate developmental level. Instead, children are forced to sit and pay attention far longer than their bodies or minds can tolerate; attempts are made to teach reading and writing before children are developmentally prepared; and curriculum for fours, fives, and sixes include content best suited for later years. The following charts can be invaluable in helping early childhood professionals plan appropriate curriculum and activities for young children. Word pictures can be used to tailor curriculum planning to an individual child or a particular class or group on the basis of known developmental standards. See also Crises in Children's Lives, Chapter 15.

# The Value of Word Pictures

There are several things to keep in mind for the age-level charts to be a valuable teaching tool. It is very important to realize that these norms of development refer to average or typical behavior. They cannot be applied to an individual child too literally. If you were to look at a class of six-year-olds using the profiles, for instance, you would find that probably half of the children would fit the majority of the description. Some of them would not yet have reached this level of development and some would have already gone through this stage. Shawna might well fit the general description of the six-year-old at a physical level. Her language and intellectual levels may be closer to a seven-year-old, while her social skills may be typical of many four-year-olds. There may very well be characteristics that Shawna will *never* exhibit. It won't work to use the chart as a measuring stick, comparing one child to another, since children develop at their own rates and in their own ways.

Remember that children probably go through most of the stages described, and in the same sequence. But they will do so in ways that reflect their own rate of growth and their own background. Use these characteristics not to pit children against each other to see who is developing faster, but to compare the child to himself. Looking at Dwayne, it helps to know where he is in relation to most two-year-olds, but more important, where he is now, six months from now, a year from now, and what he was like a year ago. A clear picture of his rate of growth emerges. His recent change of behavior, for instance, might be attributed to the 2½-year-old stage of *disequilibrium,* even though Dwayne is chronologically two years, nine months. See also Child Development and Cultural Diversity in Chapter 4.

# Word Pictures

Four basic developmental areas are included in the word pictures:

- *Physical/Motor Development.* Includes gross motor, fine motor, and perceptual motor.
- *Language Development.* Includes children's utterances, pronunciation, vocabulary, sentence length, and the ability to express ideas, needs, and feelings. It includes receptive language (do they understand what they hear?) and verbal levels (what do they say?)
- *Intellectual Development.* This generally means the ability to perceive and think. Includes curiosity, memory, attention span, general knowledge, problem solving, analytical thinking, beginning reading, computing skills, and other cognitive processes.
- *Social-Emotional Development.* Includes a child's relationship with himself and others, self-concept, self-esteem, and the ability to express feelings.

The following word pictures are designed to help classroom teachers. Characteristics listed are:

- behaviors most common to the age group
- those that have implications for children in group settings
- those that suggest guidance and disciplinary measures
- those that have implications for planning developmentally appropriate curriculum

**FIGURE  3.5**  Word Picture for the Infant.

## SOCIAL-EMOTIONAL

0-1 month:  cries to express emotions; bonding begins
4-10 weeks:  social smiles
2 months:  begins social games
3 months:  distinguishes familiar faces;
      turns head toward human voice;
      smiles in response to a smile;
      kicks, smiles, waves in response;
      cries when left alone;
      recognizes parent
4 months:  genuine laugh;
      smiles when spoken to;
      loves attention
5 months to 1 year:  stranger anxiety
6 months:  distinguishes between voices;
      smiles, babbles at strangers;
      develops attachment;
      begins to play imitation games;
      plays peek-a-boo;
      sensitive to parental moods
8 months:  laughs out loud
9 months:  screams to get own way

Play is activity only for present moment.
Fears unfamiliar: people, places, things.
Beginning sense of separate self.

## LANGUAGE

0-1 month:  turns head in response to voices;
      cries to express needs
6-8 weeks:  coos
Gestures to communicate:
   pushes objects away, squirms,
   reaches out to people, pouts,
   smacks lips, shrieks, points
2 months:  voluntary vocal sounds
3 months:  babbles
6-12 months:  imitation sound games
Responds to variety of sounds.
Makes vowel sounds.
Acquires receptive language.
Cries to communicate
12 months:  first words

## PHYSICAL/MOTOR

By 1 year:  grows 10 to 12 inches, triples birth weight,
      lengthens by 40%, doubles brain size, grows
      full head of hair
Bounces in crib
Uses whole-body motions
 4 months:  sees, grasps objects
 5 months:  examines fingers;
      sits when propped
 6 months:  rolls over;
      discovers feet;
      teething begins
 7 months:  crawls
 8 months:  sits up unaided;
      pulls to standing position;
      pincer grasp established
 9 months:  creeps
10 months:  feeds self with spoon
11 months:  stands alone; cruises
12 months:  first steps
Late infancy:  can move hands in rotation to
      turn knobs
Newborn motor activity is mostly reflexes.

## INTELLECTUAL-COGNITIVE

0-1 month:  responds to mother's voice;
      senses function, especially pain, touch
10 weeks:  memory is evident
4 months:  smiles of recognition
7-10 months:  solves simple problems (knocks over
      box to get toy)
8 months:  begins to believe in permanence of objects;
      follows a simple instruction
8-12 months:  intentionality in acts
11 months:  begins trial-error experimentation
12 months:  plays drop/retrieve games, pat-a-cake
Explores with hands and fingers
Smiles, vocalizes at image in mirror

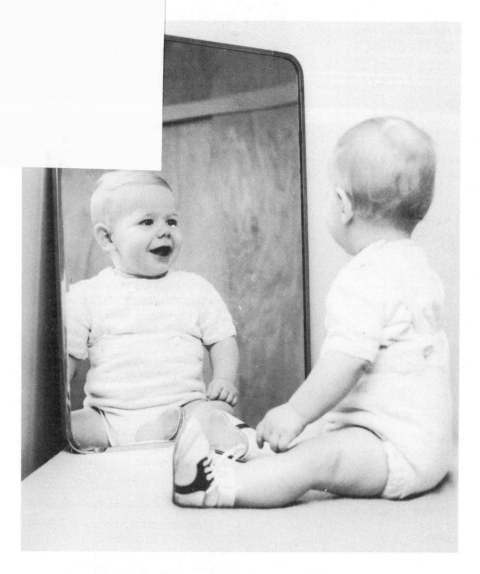

**FIGURE 3.5**    Around eight months, the infant laughs aloud.

**FIGURE 3.6** The toddler in action—a whole body explorer. (Photo courtesy of Thaddeus Cunejo, NMSU.)

**FIGURE 3.6** Word Picture for Toddlers.

## SOCIAL-EMOTIONAL

Almost totally egocentric
Likes to be noticed; loves an audience
Lacks inhibitions
Insists on own way
Likes doing things by self
Assertive, independent
Adapts easily
Plays by self in playpen
Refers to self by name
Laughs loudly at peek-a-boo
Cries when left alone
Curious
Relates to adults better than children
Active, eager
Talks mostly to self
Usually friendly
Strong sense of ownership

## LANGUAGE

Some two-word phrases
Enjoys vocalizing to self
Babbles in own jargon
Uses "eh-eh" or "uh-uh" with gestures
Names closest relatives
Repeats adults' words
Points to communicate needs, wants
Shakes head "no" to respond
Responds to directions to fetch, point
Obeys verbal requests
Answers "What's that?"
Understands simple phrases
Uses 5 to 50 words

## PHYSICAL/MOTOR

Awkward coordination; chubby body
Tottering stance
Creeps when in a hurry
Walks with increasing confidence
Walks with feet wide apart, arms out, head forward
Finds it difficult to turn corners
Goes up and down stairs holding on
Backs into chair to sit down
Can squat for long periods of time
Motor-minded: constant motion
Loves to pull/push objects
Runs with stiff, flat gait
Uses whole-arm movements
Carry and dump becomes a favorite activity
Scribbles
Turns pages two or three at a time
Zips/unzips large zipper
Likes holding objects in both hands

## INTELLECTUAL-COGNITIVE

Points to objects in a book
Matches similar objects
Fits round block in round hole
Loves opposites: up/down, yes/no
Imitates simple tasks
Interest shifts quickly
Short attention span
Follows one direction
Gives up easily, but easily engaged
Conclusions are important: close doors, shut books
Thinks with feet; action-oriented
Builds tower of three to four small blocks

**FIGURE 3.10**   Word Picture for Six- and Seven-Year-Olds.

## SOCIAL-EMOTIONAL

**Six-year-old**
Likes to work, yet often does so in spurts
Does not show persistence
Tends to be a know-it-all
Free with opinions and advice
Brings home evidence of good schoolwork
Observes family rules
Gender-role stereotypes are rigid
Friends easily gained, easily lost
Finding a place with peers
Tests and measures self against peers
Makes social connections through play
Friends are of same sex
Believes in rules except for self
Active, outgoing
Own activities, pleasure take precedence
Charming
Proud of accomplishments

**Seven-year-old**
More serious
Sensitive to others' reactions
Eager for home responsibilities
Tractable and polite at home
Complaining, pensive
Shame is common emotion
Leaves rather than face criticism, ridicule, disapproval
Complains of unfair treatment, not being liked
Shows politeness and consideration for adults
Enjoys solitary activities
First peer pressure: needs to be "in"
Wants to be one of the gang
Relates physical competence to self-concept
Impatient

## LANGUAGE

**Six- and seven-year-olds**
Enjoy putting language skill to paper
Talk *with* adults rather than *to* them
Chatter incessantly
Dominate conversations
Speech irregularities still common
Learning to print/write
Acquisition of new words tapers off
Bilingual capacities nearly complete if English is second language
Ability to learn new language still present

## PHYSICAL/MOTOR DEVELOPMENT

**Six- and seven-year-olds**
Growth has slowed
Basic skills developed; need refinement
Need active play to let off steam
Like to test limits of own bodies
Enjoy acrobatics
Value physical competence
Work at self-imposed tasks
Need daily legitimate channels for high energy
Learn to ride two-wheelers
Enjoy challenges in balancing—skating, skiing
Motor development is tool for socializing
Bones growing and solidifying
Boisterous, enjoy stunts
Like to roughhouse but may get hurt
Susceptible to fatigue
Visual acuity reaches normal
Hungry at short intervals
Insatiable taste for sweets, especially after school

(continued on next page)

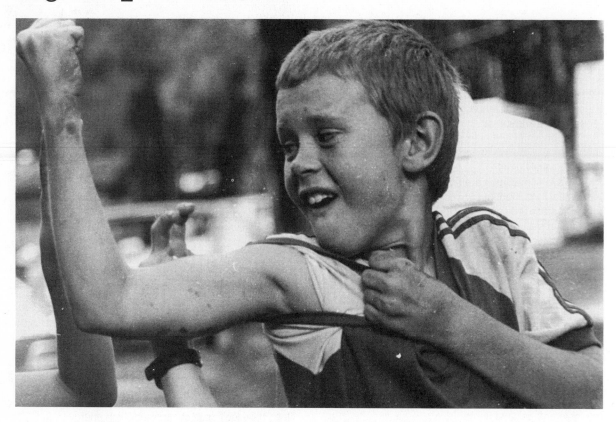

INTELLECTUAL-COGNITIVE

**Six- and seven-year-olds**
Work in spurts, not persistent
Letter and word reversal common
Learn to read
Can consider others' point of view
Use logic, systematic thinking
Can plan ahead
Enjoy collecting: sorting, classifying
Beginning math skills
Can sequence events and retell stories
Concepts of winning/losing are difficult
Like games with simple rules
May cheat or change rules
Appetite for "real" knowledge
Want "real" things: watches and cameras that work
Sift and sort information
Can conceptualize situations

**FIGURE 3.11 Cont.** To the six- and seven-year-old, physical skills relate to self-esteem. (Photo courtesy of John Weiss, Northern Arizona University, Flagstaff.)

# THE WHOLE CHILD

The concept of "the whole child" is based on the accepted principle that all areas of human growth and development are interrelated. It is only for the purpose of studying one area or another in depth that such categories are created. The four developmental areas labeled in the preceding Word Pictures help focus on certain aspects of a child's normal development. In reality, all areas of growth are "intertwined and mutually supportive" (Allen and Marotz, 1989).

## Each Child Is Unique

There are several reasons to consolidate different developmental areas into one person. The first is the uniqueness of the children. Each one is a sum total of a multitude of parts and, as such, is different from anyone else. Individual natures and learning styles affect the way teachers will teach two children of the same age in the same class.

## Growth Is Interrelated

The second reason is that one area of development affects the other. A child with a hearing loss is likely to have language delay as well; thus, the physical development affects the language part of growth. The child who has trouble making friends (social) is likely to exhibit his unhappiness (emotional) in the school yard (physical) and in the math period (intellectual). The interdependence of the areas of development have some positive aspects as well. The child who has a good breakfast and starts the school day with parent interest is ready to tackle new puzzles and new relationships. The kindergartener who masters using scissors is ready to try printing: the fine-motor skills enhance the cognitive task of learning the alphabet.

One way for new teachers to look at this concept of development is to plot the relationships visually. Think of each area of development as a circle. There are four of them: physical-motor, language, intellectual, and social-emotional. Try to connect them so that they intersect one another, as shown in Figure 3.12.

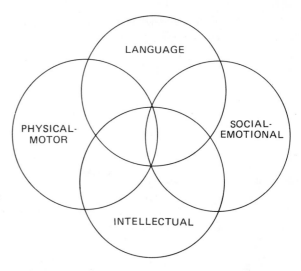

**FIGURE 3.12**  How areas of growth are interrelated: Each area of growth is affected by and influences every other area of development.

Think how each area might affect or interact with the others. Can physical development affect how children feel about themselves? Of course; children who appreciate their body and its power feel confident in what they can do. How do intellectual skills interact with language development? When children have mastered their primary language, they can then clarify some of their thought processes. The emphasis on the circularity of the child's growth and development is a primary concept.

Normal physical development, for instance, depends on meeting not only the child's physical (adequate nutrition) needs but psychological (nurturing caregivers/parents) and social (adequate play/exploration) needs as well. Social development is aided by the ability to communicate verbally; a well-developed attention span helps the child develop fine motor skills; relating to others is more successful if intellectual problem-solving skills are already mature.

Three-year-olds frequently pose the question, "Why?" as part of their intellectual curiosity. A teacher matches that understanding with the age-level characteristic of "listening in order to learn" and knows that the child understands some explanations. Thus, intellectual and language development areas influence one another.

Two-year-old Gabe, who has difficulty relaxing, responds better at naptime if allowed to cling to a familiar object or toy. Motor and emotional growth interact with each other in this case.

## Valuing Wholeness

The whole-child approach is seen from a medical point of view as well. *Holistic* medicine is basically an attempt to view health care from a "wellness" rather than illness perspective. From this comes the idea of preventive medicine, which attempts to maintain the body in a healthy state, rather than wait for treatment until infection or disease has invaded.

What does this have to do with educating children? It is an attitude that begins with a belief in the "wellness" of children, their innate goodness and trustworthiness. A two-year-old who says, "No!" exhibits signs of "wellness" and is to be accepted as behaving normally. Young children wiggle and squirm during naptime. The deadly quiet of 25 kindergarteners in a room may indicate anxiety and concern rather than accomplishment. In other words, rather than viewing behavior as "wrong," it is important to notice and value whether what a child is doing is a sign of "wellness."

The concept of the whole child strongly suggests the uniqueness of the person. Although they are often discussed separately, the areas of development (social, emotional, physical, and intellectual) cannot be isolated from one another. They each make a valuable contribution to the total child.

## CHILDREN WITH SPECIAL NEEDS

Two types of children come under the category of children with special needs. The handicapped child and the gifted child extend the definition of "Who is the child?". They are discussed separately in this section. Chapter 15 also contains a discussion on Special Education.

**FIGURE 3.13** Handicapped child in classroom setting with other children. (From Machado and Meyer, *Early Childhood Practicum Guide,* Delmar Publishers, 1984, p. 150. Used with permission.)

## The Handicapped Child

More and more of the children in early childhood classrooms have a handicap or disabling condition. Five-year-old Pete, blind from birth, has been in nursery school for three years. Chrissy, a multi-handicapped four-year-old, has her daily program in a special school supplemented by attending the child care center three afternoons each week. Travis is a child with *Down's syndrome,* and this is his first experience in a school not restricted to *atypical* children.

These children have some obvious characteristics that qualify them for special-needs status. Other children with less apparent handicaps also fall into this category. The term *special needs* includes a great many handicapping conditions that may or may not be noticeable.

Allen (1980) suggests three conditions under which a child is considered handicapped. To be so designated, a child's normal growth and development is (1) delayed; (2) distorted, atypical, or abnormal; or (3) severely or negatively affected. This definition includes the physical, mental, emotional, and social areas of development.

Approximately 15 to 20 percent of all children in the United States will exhibit some form of atypical development and need special services (Bee, 1985). These are children who did not develop according to normal standards. They exhibit a wide range of atypical disorders ranging from short-term behavior problems to long-term physical, mental, and emotional disabilities.

Figure 3.14 lists some typical handicaps and disabilities found in early childhood classes. For further information concerning a specific one, the student will want to consult a special education textbook.

In the course of normal development, any one area of a child's growth is affected by the development of the whole child. This is true for the handicapped child also; the disability may have led to problems in other areas of growth. A child with a profound hearing loss is often delayed in speech production or language abilities and suffers social isolation due to the inability to hear and speak with peers. A Down's syndrome child may have the intellectual capacity to put simple puzzles together but may not yet have the language to engage verbally in songs and fingerplays.

Some disabilities are in and of themselves multi-handicapping, affecting several growth areas. A typical Down's syndrome child, for instance, may have congenital heart defects, mental retardation, eye abnormalities, poor physical coordination, and speech dis-

| *Social-Emotional* | *Physical/Motor* |
|---|---|
| Self-destructive behavior | Visual impairment |
| Severe withdrawal | Blindness |
| Dangerously aggressive to self and others | Perceptual motor |
| Noncommunicative | Orthopedic handicaps: |
| Moodiness |    Cerebral palsy |
| Tantrums |    Spina bifida |
| Hyperactive |    Loss of limbs |
| Severely anxious |    Muscular dystrophy |
| Depressed | Hearing impairments |
| Phobic | Deafness |
| Psychotic | |
| Autistic | |
| | |
| *Speech and Language* | *Intellectual* |
| Hard of hearing | Mental retardation |
| Deafness | Brain injury |
| Stuttering | Brain dysfunction |
| Articulation problems | Dyslexia |
| Cleft palate | Learning disabilities |
| Chronic voice disorders | |
| Learning disabilities | |

*Health Impairments* (of a chronic nature or requiring prolonged convalescence)

| | |
|---|---|
| Severe asthma | Diabetes |
| Epilepsy | Tuberculosis |
| Hemophilia | Cystic fibrosis |
| Congenital heart defects | Down's syndrome |
| Severe anemia | Sickle-cell anemia |
| Malnutrition | Tay Sachs disease |

**FIGURE 3.14**   *A variety of handicapping conditions.* (Adapted from Kiernan et al., n.d.)

orders. Children who have cerebral palsy, a central nervous system disorder, often have other disabling conditions such as mental retardation, epilepsy, and hearing, visual, and speech problems (Kiernan et al., n.d.).

Children with *learning disorders* are found in almost every classroom; they usually make up approximately 1 percent of the school population. Two types of learning disorders about which early childhood practitioners should know are 1) *dyslexia*, the most common disorder, in which a child has problems reading; and 2) *dysgraphia*, in which a child has problems writing (Bee, 1985).

According to Bee (1985), a child with a learning disorder develops normally in other respects and has no obvious brain damage, but the task of reading seems to highlight several areas of difficulty: problems of visual perception, inability to integrate visual and auditory information, impaired memory, problems with language, and difficulty distinguishing the separate sounds in words. This wide range of symptoms, the number of potential causes, and the varying degrees to which children exhibit the symptoms makes learning disorders difficult to diagnose.

Parents are usually the first to notice that their child is not developing according to the norms. They may ask the child's teacher to watch for signs of deafness, lack of necessary motor skills, or language imperfections. Since early diagnosis and intervention are important, teachers should take these requests seriously and should begin to assess the child's overall skills. With the parents, they can then plan appropriate follow-through. This may include a consultation with a physician for further developmental screening and testing. If both parents and teachers feel there is a potential problem, the task is to help identify it and secure the services needed.

The teacher's role is to observe the child and provide current information, to support the parents through their concern, to find appropriate resources for them (such as social service agencies, public health offices, private and public schools), to assist with future placement for child care, and to be available for consultation with others who are working in the best interests of the child. The early childhood professional is not an expert in diagnosing learning disabilities but can be effective in helping parents secure proper referrals and treatment.

Attention to the problems of the handicapped in our society has reached national proportion only recently. Since the mid-1960s there has been significant public recognition of and the advent of public funding for the educational programs for the handicapped. Prior to that, public—and private—attitudes seemed to be ones of shame and segregation. Past generations hid the handicapped in their homes or secluded them in institutions. Slowly, reform took place. Keeping the handicapped out of sight gave way to providing separate opportunities for them. Schools, classes, and recreational programs were started exclusively for handicapped persons. Public consciousness is now sufficient to understand that many disabled people can lead useful and productive lives, and that all people with handicaps are not retarded. The current practice of integrating the handicapped into ongoing programs in schools—the mainstream of American life—is not only more humane, but practical as well.

Over the years a small number of schools had routinely accepted children with special needs. The idea gained national attention in 1972 when Head Start required that a minimum of 10 percent of its enrollment be reserved for handicapped children. Head Start led the way toward large-scale mainstreaming. In 1975, Public Law 94-142, the Education for All Handicapped Children Act, passed. This so-called "Bill of Rights for the Handicapped" guarantees free public education to those from three to 21 years of age who are handicapped. An individualized program for each person is mandatory, to be worked out in concert with the child's parents. Early childhood educators are fulfilling the requirements of that legislation. Public school systems faced with providing preschool programs for handicapped and disabled children are turning to private preschools to fill the need when their own services are unavailable or inadequate.

On the tenth anniversary of P.L. 94-142, the

United States Department of Education published these findings:

- The number of students enrolled in special education classes had risen.
- The greatest increase was among those classified as "learning disabled."
- That increase was matched by a decrease in the number of students categorized as mentally retarded.
- Most special education students are in mainstreaming situations.

The success of P.L. 94-142 means that thousands of handicapped children who would have been denied any educational opportunities a decade ago are now in school. Further, they are being integrated in schools with their nonhandicapped peers.

A more recent bill, P.L. 99-457, the Education of the Handicapped Amendments Act of 1986, should have an even more profound impact for early childhood educators. Sections of this law provide funding for handicapped children who were not included in the previous law: infants, toddlers, and three-to-five-year-olds. Before P.L. 99-457 was passed, only six states offered any services to handicapped infants at birth. Almost every state has indicated it will participate under the new bill. The states must have the programs established by 1990 or lose their funding for all handicapped programs.

The preschool programs are essentially an extension of P.L. 94-142 services, which provide for the least restrictive environments for educating handicapped children. The infant/toddler amendment is new, however. Another critical aspect of this law is that it allows for the inclusion of "developmentally delayed" youngsters and leaves local agencies the opportunity to include the "at risk" child in that definition. The vague definitions give local agencies the opportunity to define handicapping conditions in terms of local needs.

The importance of this legislation cannot be underestimated by those in and entering the field of early childhood. All states receiving funds under this law must provide programs for preschoolers by 1990. Clearly, the integration and transition of handicapped children in early childhood programs will require knowledgeable teachers. Early chidhood educators of the 1990s would be wise to avail themselves of special education courses now in order to meet this challenge. Many states now require such course work before certification; others will surely follow in order to fulfill the mandates of P.L. 99-457.

## Mainstreaming

The term *mainstreaming* refers to the process of integrating handicapped children into classrooms with the nonhandicapped. Children disabled by physical, intellectual, or emotional problems enroll in classes with other youngsters their age who are not handicapped.

Placement in the classroom is not all there is to mainstreaming. Planning and care must be given to ensure that

- Teachers foster interactions between handicapped and nonhandicapped children that promote healthy social relationships.
- Teachers recognize that every handicapped child has strengths as well as deficits and build upon those strengths.
- Teachers receive training and guidance in the critical task of working with handicapped and *developmentally disabled* children in their classes.
- Teachers work with parents to plan and implement the child's program.
- Handicapped children are actively involved and accepted in the total program.
- Handicapped children are helped to take advantage of, to the fullest extent of their capabilities, all the activities the school has to offer.
- Children's individual handicaps are addressed and taken into consideration in program planning and that procedures and curriculum are adapted to fit the children with special needs.

Mainstreaming is an important concept for all children. For the nonhandicapped it is an opportunity to learn to accept differences in people. In the early education center much of the curriculum is directed toward fostering the child's self-esteem and self-worth. Teaching is dedicated to helping youngsters see themselves and others as important and valuable. Mainstreaming the handicapped presents an opportunity to extend that principle to the full range of human characteristics.

For the handicapped child in a mainstreamed classroom, the large numbers of children who serve as age-appropriate behavior models is important. Many handicapped children have not had an opportunity to hear the language of their normal peer group. They may not know how to play with another child or how to communicate in socially acceptable ways. In the mainstreamed classroom, with sensitive and knowledgeable teachers, handicapped children are helped to realize their potential as growing and learning children.

Teachers are a key factor in the successful integration of the handicapped. Their attitude is critical; they must be committed to teaching all children, regardless of their intelligence or skill levels, with equal caring and concern.

Handicap legislation makes strong demands on parents to be intimately involved with their child's program. Parent involvement greatly improves the child's chances for success (Allen and Marotz, 1989). Teachers and parents work together on a planned, consistent set of expectations. The child's confidence is reinforced at home and at school for the same achievements. Parents of handicapped children find support from other parents since they share common child-rearing concerns. Teachers learn a great deal about handicaps from the parents of the children who are mainstreamed. This helps them become more effective teachers and aware of the special needs of the handicapped child.

Fortunately, the preschool teacher rarely needs to face the task of mainstreaming alone. Almost every early childhood center has access to a team of professionals who can provide the child, the family, and the teaching staff with effective therapeutic activities. Their combined knowledge helps teachers understand the specific handicap and plan an appropriate curriculum for each child. Together, teachers, clinicians, and parents work out a well-rounded program. This is called an *interdisciplinary approach* to teaching.

## The Gifted Child

The child who is *gifted* demonstrates an intellectual and creative potential superior to that of most children in the same age range. Bee (1985) defines gifted children as "those whose *rate* of intellectual development is greatly in excess of the norm." Gifted children are found in all social, economic, and cultural groups.

Traditionally, gifted children have been identified as those scoring 130 to 150 on standard IQ tests. At the preschool level, formal testing procedures to identify gifted and talented children are not common. Therefore, early childhood educators should be aware of some traits gifted children display so they can recognize potentially gifted children in their care.

In intellectual and academic areas, gifted children have long attention spans, learn rapidly, have good memories and advanced vocabularies. They ask a lot of questions and are able to express their ideas easily. Independent and imaginative, gifted children may be bored by normal activities.

Socially, the gifted child is sought after by peers yet may be uneasy about relationships with other children. Planning and organizing skills are evident in their artwork and other creative endeavors. The gifted child is content to be alone, spending time in purposeful activity. Their use of humor is more advanced than children the same age; originality is typically characteristic of the gifted.

One of the most fascinating studies of gifted children—in fact, the study that is the cornerstone of the gifted child movement—is the Terman Study of the Gifted, which began at Stanford University in 1921. Lewis M. Terman, who developed the Stanford-Binet intelligence test, picked 1,500 California public school children who had scores ranging between 135 and 200 on the test. This longitudinal study is now in its seventh decade; many of the participants are in their seventies and eighties. It is the longest psychological study ever conducted. This body of work has provided the most complete informaton to date on gifted children, spanning the grade school years through retirement. Its initial purpose was to dispel the perception, common at that time, that bright children grow into maladjusted and eccentric misfits.

Instead, the study found that the exceptionally bright child is, in later life, more successful, better educated, better satisfied, healthier, more socially adept and popular with peers, better adjusted, and a more productive member of society than the average American. It must be noted that the families from which these exceptional children came were middle class, advantaged, and with an enriched environment.

A recent study by the Sid W. Richardson Foundation highlights a common concern about gifted programs and the exclusion of children from backgrounds other than those cited in the Terman study. The Richardson study calls for opening programs for the gifted to a larger group of "able learners" (Olson, 1985), dropping labels such as "gifted" and "talented," promoting students on the basis of their mastering a subject or skill, and looking for eligible students among populations "excluded from opportunity by ethnic or economic circumstances" (Olson, 1985). Other reports similarly call for making nontraditional students a priority in programs for gifted children.

The current definition of "gifted" limits programs to those children who are intellectually exceptional. There is a call among other gifted-education experts to enlarge the definition to include, for example, children who are gifted in music, art, and physical skills as well as children who are handicapped.

Gifted children, once identified, need to be challenged. In some cases the children may be advanced to an older group, moving on to kindergarten or first grade. A more common approach in early childhood has been in the area of curriculum enrichment. In this way the child remains with age-level peers in order to develop social skills. Some schools segregate gifted children by placing them in special classes exclusively for those identified as being gifted.

The teacher's role with the gifted preschool child is that of providing challenge and stimulation. Curriculum areas are developed in more complex ways. The gifted child is ready to learn in greater depth; the teachers provide added materials and activities that will help the child probe the extent of their interests. The nongifted children in the same classroom benefit from this enrichment; each responds according to his or her abilities. Teachers of children who have special gifts and talents can meet their unique needs in a regular school setting at the same time they provide a rich curriculum for the nongifted student.

## The Role of the Early Childhood Educator

Early childhood teachers are well prepared to work with children at their own pace—a key factor in teaching the gifted and an underlying principle of early childhood education. However, the logistics of having gifted children in a class can present challenges in curriculum planning.

Parents of the gifted child will need support and encouragement as well as guidance in dealing with their child's exceptionality. Together, teachers and parents can explore what will best suit each individual child so that this giftedness may be nurtured and challenged at home and at school.

Integrating children with special needs into classroom settings can pose problems if teachers are not aware of how to deal with children who represent both ends of the broad spectrum of normal development. Individual attention is a necessity; so is a climate that supports self-help, interdependence, and responsibility. Successful integration of the classroom requires more planning and preparation on the part of the teaching staff to see that the needs of all the children are being met. Teachers are called on to facilitate and support peer interaction between the mainstreamed children and those without handicaps on a more frequent and consistent basis. The average early childhood teacher can learn from special education courses, from the parents of special-needs children, and from medical specialists how to adapt teaching strategies for an integrated program. Knowing how to work with parents of special needs children, especially in the area of communication, is a critical factor for teachers. It is also important to keep in mind that most early childhood professionals are not trained diagnosticians but can assist parents in identifying potential problems as they observe children in the classroom setting.

## SPECIAL NEEDS OF BLACK CHILDREN

The following *Focus* discussion by Dr. Janice

Hale-Benson outlines some of the critical issues that she believes affect the achievement of Black students. After reading this essay, the reader may want to reflect on The Anti-Bias Curriculum in Chapter 9, and in Chapter 15 the sections on At Risk: Children in Need; The Family and Its Values; Diversity; Peace Education: Living with Diversity; and Teaching Values.

---

# FOCUS

## EARLY CHILDHOOD AND BLACK AMERICAN CHILDREN

*Janice Hale-Benson*

Early childhood education can play an important role in closing the achievement gap between African-American and white children. One explanation for the difficulty Black children experience in school is that they are required to master at least two cultures in order to achieve upward mobility in school and the workplace.

It is possible that African-American male children may have to master three divergent cultures. I make the point elsewhere (Hale-Benson, 1986) that African-American males have a culture that is distinct from both white male culture *and* Black female culture. Their culture is not recognized and may even be assaulted at school because it is not understood.

Most elementary school classes are taught by women, which creates a feminine orientation in the classroom. Increasingly we will find, as we enter the twenty-first century, that most inner city classrooms will contain a majority of minority children being taught by white female teachers. White female teachers tend to be more comfortable with and knowledgeable about the behavioral characteristics of white female children and, to a lesser degree, white male children.

Cornbleth and Korth (1980) suggest that there is a cultural configuration in classrooms that places Black male children at a disadvantage. In order to achieve, Black males in particular must acquire behavioral characteristics that are incongruent with the culture they bring to school.

It is important to acknowledge this dual socialization that is required of Black children because early childhood education can play an important role in fostering biculturalism in African-American children, thereby reducing the conflict within the child which depletes his energy and clouds his perceptions.

The "intervention" strategies of the 1960s are passe. Recent research by Black scholars (Rashid, 1981; Hale-Benson, 1986) has rejected the notion that African-American children are culturally or cognitively deprived. They are seen as members of a culture endowed with specific modes of cognition.

Early childhood educational and caregiving settings must search for cultural continuity—not intervention. Rashid suggests that:

The preschool experience must therefore provide a dynamic blend of African-American culture and that culture which is reflected in the Euro-American educational setting . . . The African-American child who only sees the Euro-American cultural tradition manifested in the preschool environment can only conclude that the absence of visual representation of his culture connotes his essential worthlessness (p. 60).

*Visions for Children* is an early childhood education program I have designed to demonstrate the recommendations outlined in my book, *Black Children: Their Roots, Culture and Learning Styles* (1986). This research/demonstration program, funded by the Cleveland Foundation, operates in Cleveland, Ohio, and is delivered in a day care format.

This demonstration program is designed to articulate a pedagogy that begins in early childhood and includes an interrelated learning environment drawn from African-American culture, teaching strategies that complement African-American learning styles, and materials relevant to the African-American experience.

Important questions addressed by this model in seeking cultural continuity are:

1. What is a unified approach to creating an inter-related learning environment for Black children that achieves this cultural continuity?

2. How can an educational program be designed that moves Black children away from a poverty/remedial track toward an academically oriented preschool experience?

3. How can Black children be connected to the future and acquire experiences with computers that are embedded in their learning styles?

4. How can the Black community achieve a holistic education for Black children in which they are educated about Afro-American culture and heritage in all of its diversity throughout the curriculum at the same time that they learn about other cultures?

5. How can standardized testing be demystified for Black parents so that they can facilitate their children's performance on such measures?

6. How can the lower academic performance of Black male children be improved? How can the overriding feminine orientation of early childhood classrooms be reduced and more tolerance of male culture and specifically Black male culture be introduced?

7. How can more information be provided to Black parents about how to provide a road map to achievement for their children? The high motivation that Black parents provide for their children to achieve has been well documented by scholars. What seems to be missing is being able to identify the mechanisms for achievement and skill in resolving stumbling blocks along the way.

8. How can parents and teachers assist Black children in coping with the world in which they live as well as changing the world around us?

9. How can existing patterns in teaching children to handle aggression be improved so that aggression works for them instead of against them? How can parents and teachers teach social skills so that children learn nonviolent techniques of interpersonal conflict resolution? How can social skills be taught in such a way that children are able to negotiate mainstream institutions as well as Afro-American culture?

For cultural and educational reasons, the schools need to accommodate instruction to the learning styles of Black children. Early child care settings need to build bridges between the culture Black children bring to school and the equal educational outcomes they must achieve in order to survive and become upwardly mobile in American society.

*Janice Hale-Benson is a professor of Early Childhood Education at Cleveland State University.*

# SUMMARY

The child in early childhood programs ranges from the dependent infant to the outgoing eight-year-old. In those few short years teachers witness tremendous physical, intellectual, social, and emotional gains.

The child learns to crawl, walk, run, climb, throw a ball, write with a pencil, use scissors, hold a spoon, and manipulate toys. Both large and small muscles are called into play throughout each stage of development.

Language development is equally impressive. The nonverbal infant becomes fluent, sometimes in more than one language. Intellectual gains coincide as children become able to express thoughts, solve problems, and exhibit growth in their reasoning powers.

Socially, the child learns to relate to family members, schoolmates, teachers, and other adults. Every range of human emotion is developed during these early years as children learn appropriate ways to express and release their feelings.

Teachers notice that children share many common characteristics at the same time they display wide individual differences. Profile charts—word pictures—describing normal development help teachers understand when a particular behavior is likely to occur. With advance notice, then, teachers can plan activities and curricula that appeal to children at every age level; disciplinary and guidance measures can match the child's specific level of development.

Yet it is obvious that growth and development do not proceed normally for all children. Two groups of children have special needs within the early childhood classroom. The handicapped who are mainstreamed require particular attention to their individual disabilities, and teachers need special skills to help them integrate handicapped and nonhandicapped children. Gifted children also require attention; their exceptional abilities must be challenged and stimulated within the regular early childhood program.

## REVIEW QUESTIONS

1. Match the word picture to the age group in which it belongs:

   | | |
   |---|---|
   | Plays peek-a-boo | fours |
   | "Me" is prominent pronoun | fives |
   | Draws recognizable man | threes |
   | Avid "me-too"er | threes |
   | Grasps cup with two hands | twos |
   | Beginning to share | infants |
   | Silly, loves nonsense | twos |
   | Time concept is now | fours |
   | A great talker | twos |
   | Smiles at self in mirror | infants |

2. Name one way children are alike and one way they differ from one another. Describe the curriculum planning implications for the teacher of these differing children.

3. One area of development affects another. List two ways that social or emotional problems can affect other areas of growth.

4. What are some of the reasons for using the concept of the whole child in early education?

5. What are some of the advantages of mainstreaming children with special needs? What are some of the difficulties that must be overcome for successful integration of special-needs children?

6. What are some of the contributing factors to raising a gifted child?

7. Do you agree or disagree with Janice Hale-Benson's theory regarding Black children? How important is it to know and understand the culture of children we teach?

## L E A R N I N G   A C T I V I T I E S

1. Select two children who are approximately the same age. Compare their physical and social development. How are they alike? How are they different? What do you think accounts for these differences?

2. Observe a handicapped child who has been mainstreamed. How does the teacher promote social interaction? Define the type of handicap.

3. Look at the word picture for a three-year-old. Compare it with a three-year-old you know. What behavior do you see that falls within the range of the chart? What is different?

4. Observe a class of handicapped children who are being mainstreamed. What would you do to foster interactions between the handicapped and non-handicapped children? What verbalizations are used about a child's handicapping condition and do the nonhandicapped children seem to understand how their friends are similar to them as well as different? Do you think mainstreaming is a good idea? Why or why not?

5. Using the Word Pictures, how would you design an appropriate art activity for children who are 18 months old? What kind of playground experience would you provide for a three-year-old? How would you schedule a day for a six-year-old you were babysitting? Justify your answers by citing specific developmental references.

## B I B L I O G R A P H Y

Allen, K. Eileen, and Marotz, Lynn. *Developmental Profiles: Birth to Six.* Albany, N.Y.: Delmar Publishers, 1989.

Allen, K. Eileen. *Mainstreaming in Early Childhood Education.* Albany, N.Y.: Delmar Publishers, 1980.

Allen, K. Eileen; Holm, V.A.; and Schiefelbusch, R.L. *Early Intervention—A Team Approach.* Baltimore: University Park Press, 1978.

Ames, Louise B., and Ilg, Frances L. *Your One-Year-Old.* New York: Dell, 1983.

———. *Your Two-Year-Old.* New York: Dell, 1976.

———. *Your Three-Year-Old.* New York: Dell, 1976.

———. *Your Four-Year-Old.* New York: Dell, 1976.

———. *Your Five-Year-Old.* New York: Dell, 1979.

———. *Your Six-Year-Old.* New York: Dell, 1979.

Bee, Helen. *The Developing Child.* Cambridge, Mass.: Harper & Row, 1985.

Cornbleth, Catherine, and Korth, Williard. "Teacher perceptions and teacher-student interaction in integrated classrooms." *Journal of Experimental Education,* Summer 1980, Vol. 48, pp. 259-263.

CRC Education and Human Development, Inc. *Mainstreaming Preschoolers.* Belmont, Mass.: U.S. Government Printing Office, series.

Elkind, David. "Humanizing the Curriculum." In *Early Childhood Education,* Annual Edition. Guilford, Conn.: The Dushkin Publishing Group, 1982.

Elkind, David. *The Hurried Child: Growing Up Too Fast, Too Soon.* Reading, Mass.: Addison-Wesley, 1982.

Flax, Ellen. "Economic Concerns Aiding Programs for Gifted." *Education Week,* May 13, 1987, p. 1.

Gardner, Howard. *Developmental Psychology.* Boston: Little, Brown and Co., 1982.

Hale-Benson, Janice. *Black Children: Their Roots, Culture and Learning Styles.* Baltimore, Md.: The Johns Hopkins University Press, 1986.

Kiernan, Shari, et al. *Mainstreaming Preschoolers: Children with Orthopedic Handicaps.* Washington, D.C.: U.S. Department of Health, Education, and Welfare, n.d.

Olson, Lynn. "Programs for Gifted Students Fragmented, Inadequate, Study Says." *Education Week,* January 16, 1985, p. 5.

Rashid, H.M. "Early childhood education as a cultural transition for African-American children." *Educational Research Quarterly,* 6:55-63, 1981.

Viadero, Debra. "Study Documents Jump in Special Education Enrollments." *Education Week,* March 2, 1988, p. 17.

———. "Most States Adopt Program for Handicapped Preschoolers." *Education Week,* April 1, 1987, p. 1.

# CHAPTER 4

## Developmental and Learning Theories

## QUESTIONS for THOUGHT

- What psychological theories are basic to early childhood education today?
- Who are the main speakers for each school of thought?
- What are the psychosocial stages of early childhood?
- What are the tenets of behaviorist theory?
- How does a cognitive theory explain children's thinking processes?
- What is the hierarchy of human needs?
- How does maturation theory describe growth?
- How can development and learning theories be applied to the classroom and work with young children?

# INTRODUCTION

Early childhood education draws from several fields of study. The connection with the field of psychology is particularly strong. Much of what we know about children today comes from child development and child psychology research. As educators, we apply those findings in the classroom. Our knowledge base comes directly from psychological studies.

- How do children develop?
- What do they learn, and in what order?
- What do people need in order to be ready to learn?
- What affects learning?
- Do all people develop in the same ways?
- What are the similarities and differences in growth and development?

Psychologists and educators have been asking themselves these questions for years. In the twentieth century a great deal has been discovered about these issues. The basic quest for knowledge about learning and development has given early educators much to consider in developing their own ideas about children.

Initially, the study of child development was mostly confined to the study of trends and descriptions of age changes. As this century has progressed, the scope and definition of child development have changed radically. Developmental psychologists now study how psychological processes begin, change, and develop. Specifically, child development focuses on language acquisition, various early effects on later intellectual development, and the process of attachment to others. Early childhood teachers should know how children develop and how they learn. Therefore, it is important to have a background in both developmental psychology and learning theories.

There is no one set of principles that encompasses all developmental and learning theories. We have chosen three theories that are commonly accepted as major components of the child development field. A fourth comes from a medical model and outlines developmental norms of growth and behavior. Another does not always appear in child psychology texts but highlights some of the processes of working with children. The five theories we will outline are commonly known as (1) psychodynamic theory, (2) behaviorist theory, (3) cognitive theory, (4) maturation theory, and (5) humanistic theory.

Since the field of child development is broad, encompassing a wide variety of opinion and fact, not all the experts agree, or even think alike. Indeed, there are differences among them about how children grow, think, and learn, and what motivates them. Each theory describes children and their processes in a different way. The teacher thus has a diversity of thought on which to establish a professional philosophy.

# PSYCHODYNAMIC THEORY

Psychodynamic theory is about personality development and emotional problems. Dr. Sigmund Freud first put forth this theory, and his ideas were expanded upon by Anna Freud (his daughter), Carl Jung, Karen Horney, and others. Although Freud's interest was abnormal adult behavior and its causes, his conclusions have a major effect on our conception of childhood and its place in the life span.

To Freud, the personality was the most important aspect of development, more central to human growth than language, perception, or cognition. He thought that the personality developed in a fixed pattern of stages that emerged as the body matured naturally. But even though the sequence of the stages might be firm, how children were treated while going through those stages determined whether they developed healthy or abnormal personalities. In particular, the mother-child relationship was important in each stage. Thus, the interaction between the child's wishes and needs and how these were treated (by the mother or other adults) was a focal point for proper development.

All psychoanalytic explanations of human development emphasize the critical importance of relationships with people and the sequence, or stages, of personality development. The psychoanalyst Erik Erikson expanded and refined Freud's theory of development. It is Erikson whose ideas have most affected early childhood education.

# Erik Erikson

Erik Homberg Erikson is perhaps the most influential psychoanalyst alive today, certainly a key figure in the study of children and development. His interest in children and education has been a lifelong one, including a teaching background in progressive and Montessori schools in Europe. After clinical training in psychoanalysis, he remained interested in the connections between psychotherapy and education. Erikson became the first child analyst in the Boston area. He continues to work in various universities in this country, without any formal degree of his own.

# Erikson's Theory of Human Development

Erikson's theory of human development, like those of Freud and Piaget, states that life is a series of stages through which each person passes, with each stage growing from the previous ones. He proposes eight stages of psychosocial development, each representing a critical period for the development of an important quality or virtue. Positive growth allows the individual to integrate his or her physical and biological development with the challenges that the social institutions and culture present. Each stage is characterized by a pair of basic emotional states. Balance is the key word in Erikson's framework: the forming of a balance between a child's wishes and the demands of the environment, of a mentally healthy dose of each emotion, is the base for personality strength.

In other words, every growing organism passes through certain developmental stages. A stage is a period during which certain changes take place. What one achieves in each stage is based on the developments of the previous stages, and each stage presents the organisms with certain kinds of problems to be solved. When children succeed, they go on to attack new problems and grow through solving them.

Everyone has certain biological, social, and psychological needs that must be satisfied in order to grow in a healthy manner. Medicine has learned much about physical needs—diet, rest, exercise. There are also basic intellectual, social, and emotional needs that

| Stage | Description | Challenge _relationships to others_ |
|---|---|---|
| Stage One | The newborn | Trust vs. mistrust |
| Stage Two | Toddlers | Autonomy vs. shame and doubt |
| Stage Three | Childhood | Initiative vs. guilt |
| Stage Four | School | Competence (or Industry) vs. inferiority |
| Stage Five | Adolescence | Search for identity vs. role confusion |
| Stage Six | Young adulthood | Intimacy (love and friendship) vs. isolation (loneliness) |
| Stage Seven | Grown-ups | Caring for the next generation (generativity) vs. stagnation |
| Stage Eight | Old age | Integrity vs. despair |

**FIGURE 4.1** Erikson's theory of psychosocial development centers on basic crises that people face from birth to old age. This stage theory of development proposes that these conflicts are part of the life process, and that successful handling of these issues can give a person the "ego strength" to face life positively. (Adapted from Hubley and Hubley, 1976.)

must be met for an organism to be healthy. Psychology, such as Eriksonian theory, can speak to these needs. Whether these needs are met or unfulfilled will affect development.

## Stage 1: Trust vs. Mistrust (Birth to One Year)

Erikson's first stage is roughly the first year of life and parallels Freud's oral-sensory stage. Attitudes important to development are the capacity to trust—or mistrust—inner and outer experiences. By providing consistent care, parents help an infant develop a basic sense of trust in self and an ability to trust other people. They give affection and emotional security as well as provide for physical needs. Inconsistent or inadequate care prevents the infant from trusting the world. In extreme cases, as shown

by Spitz's classic studies on infant deprivation (Spitz, 1946), lack of care can actually lead to infant death. A less extreme case might form isolation or distrust of others, such as in schizophrenia. Given a solid base in early trust, though, the infant develops the virtue, or strength, of hope.

When working with infants and toddlers, teachers must take special care to provide a predictable environment and consistent caregiving. Babies are totally dependent on adults to meet their needs; they are particularly vulnerable to difficulties because they have few skills for coping with discomfort and stress. It is critical, therefore, that they be cared for by warm, positive adults who are sensitive and respond affectionately to an infant's needs as soon as they arise. In this way the very young develop the trust in the world that will support their growth into the next stage.

**FIGURE 4.2** An Eriksonian crisis in a young child's life. The child who has successfully mastered the first of Erikson's psychosocial conflicts will then be able to cope with future challenges. In this instance, the child who takes initiative (grabbing a toy) also can feel guilt (returning it).

## Stage 2: Autonomy vs. Doubt (Two to Three Years)

The second stage, corresponding to the second and third years of life, parallels the muscular-anal period in Freudian theory. The child learns to manage and control impulses, and to use both motor and mental skills. To help a child develop a healthy balance between autonomy and shame, parents should consider how to handle their toddlers' toilet training and growing curiosity to explore. Restrictive or compulsive parents may give the child a feeling of shame and doubt, causing a sense of insecurity. Successful growth in this stage gives a child the strength of will.

When teaching children of this age, adults help children feel ready to explore their world through a full range of activities that employ their senses. Play is encouraged, with plenty of "yes" in the environment. Budding curiosity means high energy, so the daily schedule should include plenty of time for active movement and flexibility to deal with fluctuating energy and mood. Toileting is a learned behavior just as eating, dressing, painting, and singing are; a relaxed attitude about this area helps the child gain mastery without shame. Allowing for plenty of "two steps forward, one back" acknowledges the child's natural doubts and the balancing that happens in this stage.

## Stage 3: Initiative vs. Guilt (Three to Five or Six Years)

The third stage of Eriksonian theory corresponds to the preschool and kindergarten years and parallels Freud's genital stage of development. Out of a sense of autonomy grows a sense of initiative. The child is ready to plan and carry out thoughts and ideas. The parent can encourage the child's natural curiosity to plan and execute activities that are constructive and cooperative. An overly restrictive parent may raise a child with an excessive sense of guilt and inhibition. On the other hand, parents or teachers giving no restraints signal to the child no clear idea of what is socially acceptable and what is not. The key strength that grows out of this stage is purpose.

Teaching children of this age is both exhilarating and exasperating. The child who takes initiative is ready to meet the world head-on and wants to do it "all by myself," which may include both putting on a jacket and hitting someone who has said something unkind. The environment that can respond to a child's interests, both in theme and at the moment, will be interesting and successful. At the same time, teachers must be prepared with a small set of logical limits (or "rules") and the means to follow through kindly and firmly when those limits are tested. Socializing at this age is the very point of the emotional states of initiative and guilt; children must have enough freedom to develop their own ways to deal with one another and still develop a sense of fairness and conscience.

## Stage 4: Industry vs. Inferiority *competence* (Six to 12 Years)

Erikson's fourth stage, beginning with the primary school years and ending with puberty, parallels Freud's latency period. The major theme in this stage is mastery of life, primarily by adapting to laws of society and things. For most children, this means finding a place in one's own school, be it in a classroom, on a soccer field, or at a club meeting. Children are ready to apply themselves to skills and tasks and to receive systematic instruction in the culture. They also need to handle the "tools of the tribe" (Erikson, 1963), and to experience both achievement and disappointment. In the United States, these tools include pencils, reading and arithmetic books, and computers, as well as balls and bats. The danger for the child lies in feeling inadequate and inferior to such tasks. A parent or teacher who overemphasizes children's mistakes could make them despair of ever learning, for instance, the multiplication tables or cursive handwriting. At the same time, adults must encourage children to work toward mastery. Parents must not let their children restrict their own horizons by doing only what they already know. Particularly in social situations, it is essential for children to learn to do things *with* others, as difficult and unfair as this may sometimes be.

# Applying Erikson's Theory to Work with Children

How can teachers apply Erikson's theory of psychosocial development to young children? First, Erikson has a clear message about the importance of play. Second, the theory helps shape guidelines for the role of adults in children's lives.

Early childhood teachers have long held that play is a critical part of children's total development. Most schools for children under six have periods of time allotted for play called "choice time" or "free play." Erikson supports these ideas explicitly by stating that the sense of autonomy and of initiative are developed mainly through social and fantasy play. He suggests that child's play is "the infantile form of the human ability to deal with experiences by creating model situations and to master reality by experiment and planning . . . . To 'play it out' in play is the most natural self-healing measure childhood affords" (Erikson, 1964).

The adult, from a psychoanalytic point of view, is primarily an emotional base and a social mediator for the child. That is, the adult is the interpreter of feelings, actions, reasons, and solutions. The adult helps children understand situations and motives so that they can solve their own problems. The adult looks at each child's emotional makeup and monitors the progress through developmental crises. Since the infant must learn to trust the world, the parent needs to be responsive and satisfy the basic needs of food, warmth, and love. In a toddler's world, the teacher and parent must allow the child, in Erikson's words:

> . . . to experience over and over again that he is a person who is permitted to make choices. He has to have the right to choose, for example, whether to sit or whether to stand, whether to approach a visitor or to lean against his mother's knee . . . whether to use the toilet or to wet his pants. At the same time he must learn some of the boundaries of self-determination. He inevitably finds that there are some walls he cannot climb, that there are objects out of reach, that, above all, there are innumerable commands enforced by powerful adults.
>
> (Erikson, 1969)

In preschool and kindergarten, a teacher allows children to take initiative and does not interfere with the results of those actions. At the same time, teachers and parents provide clear limits so that the children can learn what behaviors are unacceptable to society.

The issues of early childhood, from Erikson's theory, are really our own issues. Since the remnant of these crises stay with us all our lives, teachers must be aware of their own processes to fully appreciate the struggles of children.

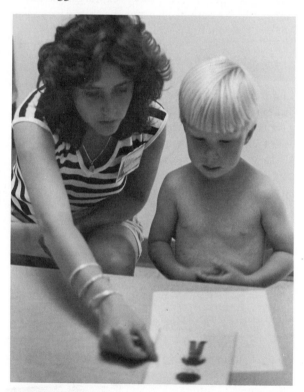

**FIGURE 4.3** Research to examine theory and psychological processes will further our knowledge of child development.

# BEHAVIORIST THEORY

Behaviorism is the most pragmatic and functional of the modern psychological ideologies. Behaviorist theories describe both development and learning. Developed during the 1920s and continually modified today, behaviorism is "the most distinctively

American contribution to psychology" (Suransky, 1982). There are countless developmental psychologists and researchers who have defined and expanded upon this idea, several of whom are mentioned later in this chapter. To summarize the behaviorist theory, we have chosen four theorists: John Watson, Edward Thorndike, B.F. Skinner, and Albert Bandura.

## The Behaviorists

What is known today as "behaviorism" begins with the notion that a child is born with a "clean slate," a *tabula rasa* in John Locke's words, on which events are written throughout life. The conditions of those events cause all important human behavior.

John B. Watson was an American theorist who studied the experiments of Russian scientist Ivan Pavlov. He then translated those ideas of conditioning into human terms. In the first quarter of this century, Watson made sweeping claims about the powers of this classical conditioning. He declared that he could shape a person's entire life by controlling exactly the events of an infant's first year. One of his ideas was to strictly discourage emotional ties between parents and children, though he later modified this. Nonetheless, he gave scientific validity to the idea that teachers should set conditions for learning and reward proper responses.

Edward L. Thorndike also studied the conditions of learning. After working with animals and their problem-solving abilities, he decided that people took an active part in their learning. He set forth the famous "stimulus-response" technique. A stimulus will recall a response in a person; this forms learned habits. Therefore, it is wise to pay close attention to the consequences of behavior and to the various kinds of reinforcement.

B.F. Skinner took the idea of "tabula rasa" one step further. He created the doctrine of the "empty organism." That is, a person is like a vessel to be filled by carefully designed experiences. All behavior is under the control of one or more aspects of the environment. Furthermore, Skinner maintains that there is no behavior that cannot be modified.

Behaviorists often insist that only what can actually be observed will be accepted as fact. Only behavior can be treated, they say, not feelings or internal states. This contrasts to the psychodynamic approach, which insists that behavior is just an indirect clue to the "real" self, that of inner feelings and thoughts.

Skinner's ideas have probably stirred up more controversy, and caused more emotional response, than those of any other psychologist of our time. Some people might argue that Skinnerian concepts tend to depersonalize the learning process and treat people as puppets. Others say that behaviorist psychology has made us develop new ways to help people learn and cope effectively with the world.

Albert Bandura has developed another type of learning theory, called social learning. As behaviorists began to accept that what people said about their feelings and internal state was valid data, they looked at how children became socialized. Socialization is the process of learning to conform to social rules. Social-learning theorists watch how children learn these rules and use them in groups. They study the patterns of reinforcement and reward in socially appropriate and unacceptable behavior.

According to Bandura:

> Children acquire most of their social concepts —the rules by which they live—from models whom they observe in the course of daily life, particularly parents, caregivers, teachers, and peers. Social learning theory [suggests] the models most likely to be imitated are individuals who are nurturant—warm, rewarding, and affectionate. Attachment also affects the process: the most significant or influential models are people to whom the child is emotionally tied.
>
> (Fong & Resnick, 1986)

From this arose a new concept known as modeling. This is what used to be known as learning and teaching by example. For instance, children who see their parents smoking will likely smoke themselves. Any behavior can be learned by watching it, from language (listening to others talk) to fighting (watching violence on television).

# Theory of Behaviorism and Learning

What is behavior, or learning, theory all about? Many texts have been written on this set of principles; every child development text of the day cites behavior and social-learning concepts. Most early education texts will make mention of the system of positive reinforcement; that is, how to praise children so that they are likely to repeat the desired behavior.

Learning takes place when an organism interacts with the environment. Through experience, behavior is modified, or changed. In the behaviorist's eyes, three types of learning occur: (1) classical conditioning; (2) operant conditioning; and (3) observational learning or modeling. The first two are based on the idea that learning is mostly the development of habit. What people learn is a series of associations, forming a connection between a stimulus and response that did not exist before. The third is based on a social approach. Figure 4.4 summarizes these three types of behaviorist learning processes.

## Classical Conditioning

Classical conditioning can be explained by reviewing Pavlov's original experiments. A dog normally salivates at the sight of food, but not when he hears a bell. By pairing the sound of a bell with the sight of food, the dog "learns" to salivate when he hears the bell, whether or not food is nearby. Thus, the dog has been conditioned to salivate (give the response) for both the food (unconditioned stimulus) and the bell (conditioned stimulus).

## Operant Conditioning

Operant conditioning is slightly different from classical conditioning in that it focuses on the response rather than the stimulus. It also involves reinforcers, or those things that are likely to increase behaviors that produce pleasant results. Most people are likely to increase what gives them pleasure (be it food or attention), and decrease what gives them displeasure (such as punishment, pain, or the withdrawal of food or attention). The behaviorist tries to influence the organism by controlling these kinds of reinforcement.

For example, you would like Claire to begin to use a spoon instead of her hands to eat. Before conditioning, you talk to her whenever she eats. During the conditioning period, you can give attention (a positive reinforcer), each time she picks up a spoon during feeding times, and ignore her when she uses her hands. Afterward, she is more likely to use a spoon, and less often her hands. This is an example of a positive reinforcer, something that increases the likelihood of the desired response.

The reinforcers can be both positive and negative. Circle time is Jimmy's favorite activity at school. Yet he has difficulty controlling his behavior and consistently disrupts the group. Before condi-

|  | Classical Conditioning | Operant Conditioning | Social Learning |
|---|---|---|---|
| Kind of behavior | Reflexive | Voluntary | Voluntary |
| Type of learning | Learning through association | Learning through reinforcement | Learning through observation and imitation |
| Role of learner | Passive | Active or passive | Active |

**FIGURE 4.4** Behaviorist learning processes. Classical conditioning, operant conditioning, and social learning are three ways to develop learned behavior. Each describes how certain kinds of behavior will be learned and what role the learner will take in the process.

tioning, he is told that if he talks to his neighbors and shouts responses at the teacher, he will be asked to leave the circle. During the conditioning period, Jimmy is praised whenever he pays attention, sings songs, and does not bother those around him (positive reinforcement). When he begins to shout, he is told to leave and return when he can sing without shouting (negative reinforcement). A negative reinforcer is used to "stop a child from acting in a particular way . . . by arranging for him to terminate a mildly adversive situation immediately [his having to leave the group] by improving his behavior" (Krumboltz and Krumboltz, 1972). Jimmy, by controlling his own behavior, could end his isolation from the group.

Reinforcement, both positive and negative, is a powerful tool. It is important for adults to realize that it can be misused. It is wise to be careful, particularly in the case of negative reinforcement. An adult may not be gentle with a negative reinforcer when angry with a child's inappropriate behavior. Educators and parents should be aware of the possibilities and check their own responses.

**FIGURE 4.5** A shared smile is a simple and powerful reinforcement.

## Modeling

The third kind of conditioning is called "observational learning" or "modeling." Social behavior is particularly noteworthy to early childhood professionals, as most work with children in groups and thus witness social behavior constantly. Any behavior that involves more than one person can be considered social. One of the most negative social behaviors is aggression. It is this type that Albert Bandura researched, finding that much of it is learned by watching others.

Aggression is a complex issue, involving various definitions and behaviors. To illustrate social-learning theory, Bandura and others interpret aggression to mean behavior intended to inflict harm or discomfort to another person or object. Bandura showed a short film of aggressive behavior to young children. The original mid-1960s studies are summarized below:

Each child in Bandura's experiment viewed one of three films. In all three films, a man hit, kicked, and verbally abused an inflated Bobo doll in ways that young children are unlikely to do spontaneously. The films differed in what happened to the model after the aggressive sequence. In one film the model was lavishly rewarded with praise and foods that appealed to preschoolers, such as candy and caramel popcorn. In another film the model was punished in a dramatic way, including severe scolding and a spanking. The third film simply ended after the model's aggressive behavior, with no consequences following the aggression. After viewing one film, each child in the experiment was allowed to play in a room with a Bobo doll, all the toys used in the aggressive film, and a variety of other toys.

(McClinton and Meier, 1978)

The results are most impressive, especially to those working with young children. The level of aggression was directly related to what the children saw as the consequences in the film. When offered prizes, they imitated almost exactly what their model had done. Also, children appeared more likely to attack another child after viewing the attacks on the Bobo doll in film. Further studies have shown that children's level of aggression is higher right after viewing the film, but less so when shown it again six months later (McClinton and Meier, 1978). Regardless of the controversy that may surround any study of children's aggression, or the effects of watching filmed violence on youngsters, the social-learning theory deserves serious consideration. The effect of television watching on children is extremely important and will be discussed in Chapter 15.

## Applying Behaviorist Theory to Work with Children

Behaviorist theories make a strong case for how the environment influences our behavior. A teacher, a parent, any adult who works closely with children, can use this knowledge to arrange the environment in such a way that positive learning is enhanced. Thus, early childhood educators pay close attention to how to arrange furniture, materials, the daily schedule. The way teachers interact with children is critical to changing their behavior.

Adults are powerful reinforcers and models for children. A learning situation is comprised of many cues; it is up to adults to know what those cues are and how to control them. Teachers who use behavior modification techniques know both what children are to do and how they will be reinforced for their behavior. The issues of using this kind of control, and the ethics involved, are of deep concern to everyone. The extremes of behaviorist theory suggest programmed instruction and interaction that many early educators reject. Each teacher and program must consider the impact of this theory and how to apply it to classroom and client.

The implications of behaviorist theory for teachers are farreaching. What children learn is shaped by the circumstances surrounding the learning. Experiences that are enjoyable are reinforcing. From the peek-a-boo game with an infant to a seven-year-old's first ride on a skateboard, an experience is more likely to be repeated and learned if it is pleasant.

Social learning is particularly powerful in the lives of young children. Adults must be mindful of their own behavior, and that it is a source of learning. Watching children as young as two years old play "family" or "school" will convince the most skeptical critic that any behavior is learnable and can become part of children's behavioral repertoire.

## COGNITIVE THEORY

Adult: What does it mean to be alive?
Child: It means you can move about, play—that you can do all kinds of things.
Adult: Is a mountain alive?
Child: Yes, because it has grown by itself.
Adult: Is a cloud alive?
Child: Yes, because it sends water.
Adult: Is wind alive?
Child: Yes, because it pushes things.
(Peters and Willis, 1978)

How can we tell what children are thinking? How do children learn to think, and what do they think about? Once we begin to ask these questions, we enter the realm of knowledge about how people "know" and "think," and how they learn to do it.

## Jean Piaget

Jean Jacques Piaget (1896-1980) was one of the most exciting research theorists in child development. A major force in child psychology, he studied both thought processes and how they change with age. Jean Piaget's ideas serve as our guide to the cognitive theory because of the thoroughness of his work. He had great influence on child psychology, theories of learning, intellectual development, even philosophy. He became the foremost expert on the development of knowledge from birth to adulthood.

How did Piaget find out about such matters? A short review of his life and ideas reveals a staggering volume of work and a wide scope of interests. Born at the turn of the century, Piaget built on his childhood curiosity in science and philosophy by working with Dr. Simon at the Binet Laboratory (Simon and Binet devised the first intelligence test). While recording children's abilities to answer questions correctly, he became fascinated with children's incorrect responses. He noticed that children tended to give similar kinds of wrong answers, and that they made different kinds of mistakes at different ages.

Thus, Jean Piaget launched into a lifelong study of intelligence. He believed that children think in fundamentally different ways from adults. He also developed a new method for studying thought processes. Rather than using a standardized test, he adapted the psychiatric method of question and response. Called the "methode clinique," it lets people's answers guide the questions. Therefore, it focuses on the child's own natural ways of thinking. This method is discussed in detail in Chapter 6.

Piaget then began studying children's thought processes. With his wife, one of his former students, he observed his children. He also began to look closely at how actively children engage in their own development. He studied the development of logic and looked at children's understanding of scientific and mathematical principles. In his final works, he returned to his original interest, that of the study of knowledge itself. Prolific his entire life, Jean Piaget has given us a complex theory of intelligence and child development that will influence us for some time. He has recorded, in a systematic way, how children learn, when they learn, and what they learn.

## Theory of Cognitive Development

What are the concepts of cognitive theory? Detailing all Piaget's ideas is impossible. What follows are several tenets that explain the nature of intelligence and its functions.

Piaget's theory relies on both maturational and environmental factors. It is called maturational because it sets out a sequence of cognitive (thinking) stages that are governed by heredity. For example, heredity affects our learning by (1) how the body is structured biologically, and (2) automatic, or instinctive, behavior, such as an infant's sucking at birth. It is an environmental theory because what experiences children have will directly influence how they develop.

Thinking and learning is a process of interaction between a person and the environment. Piaget also sets out that all species inherit a basic tendency to organize their lives and adapt to the world around them. In doing so, an organism "figures out" what the world is all about, and then works toward surviving in that world. Regardless of their age, all people use two basic processes of adaptation, accommodation, and assimilation. Figure 4.6 demonstrates how these processes work.

---

*Assimilation:* Taking new information and organizing it in such a way that it fits with what the person already knows.

*Example:* Annie sees an airplane while walking outdoors with her father. She knows that birds fly. So, never having seen this flying thing before, she calls it a "bird." This is what we call *assimilation.* That is, she is taking in this new information and making it fit into what she already knows. Children assimilate what they are taught into their own world as they play, such as playing at "taking turns" with their dolls or making a triangle with wood and nails after being shown a picture of one by an adult.

*Accommodation:* Taking new information and changing what is already thought to fit the new information.

*Example:* Aaron is at the grocery store with his mother and newborn baby. He calls the lady in line "pregnant" although she is simply overweight. After being corrected, he asks the next person he sees, "Are you pregnant or just fat?" This is what we call *accommodation.* That is, having learned that all large people with large bellies aren't pregnant, he changes his knowledge base to include this new information. Children accommodate to the adult world as they are taught to use a spoon, the toilet, a computer.

---

**FIGURE 4.6** In Piagetian theory, the processes of assimilation and accommodation are basic to how all people organize their thoughts and therefore to all cognitive development.

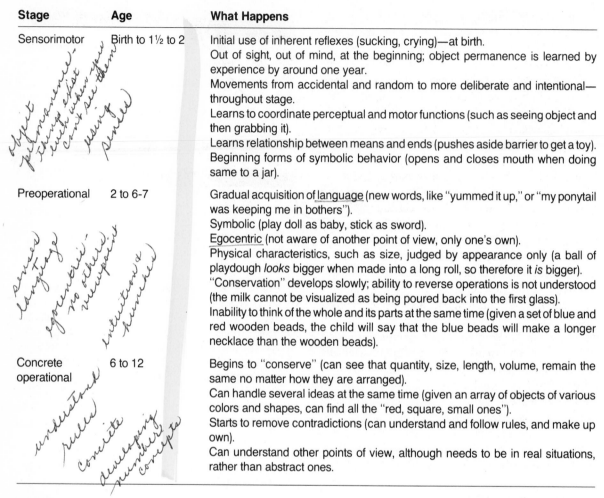

| Stage | Age | What Happens |
|---|---|---|
| Sensorimotor | Birth to 1½ to 2 | Initial use of inherent reflexes (sucking, crying)—at birth. Out of sight, out of mind, at the beginning; object permanence is learned by experience by around one year. Movements from accidental and random to more deliberate and intentional—throughout stage. Learns to coordinate perceptual and motor functions (such as seeing object and then grabbing it). Learns relationship between means and ends (pushes aside barrier to get a toy). Beginning forms of symbolic behavior (opens and closes mouth when doing same to a jar). |
| Preoperational | 2 to 6-7 | Gradual acquisition of language (new words, like "yummed it up," or "my ponytail was keeping me in bothers"). Symbolic (play doll as baby, stick as sword). Egocentric (not aware of another point of view, only one's own). Physical characteristics, such as size, judged by appearance only (a ball of playdough *looks* bigger when made into a long roll, so therefore it *is* bigger). "Conservation" develops slowly; ability to reverse operations is not understood (the milk cannot be visualized as being poured back into the first glass). Inability to think of the whole and its parts at the same time (given a set of blue and red wooden beads, the child will say that the blue beads will make a longer necklace than the wooden beads). |
| Concrete operational | 6 to 12 | Begins to "conserve" (can see that quantity, size, length, volume, remain the same no matter how they are arranged). Can handle several ideas at the same time (given an array of objects of various colors and shapes, can find all the "red, square, small ones"). Starts to remove contradictions (can understand and follow rules, and make up own). Can understand other points of view, although needs to be in real situations, rather than abstract ones. |

**FIGURE 4.7** In their early childhood, children will pass through the sensorimotor and preoperational stages and enter the stage of concrete operations.

Piaget theorizes that thinking develops along certain lines. This coincides with his idea that people tend to organize themselves, and the stages of thinking are the psychological structures that go along with trying to adapt to the environment. Such a series of stages goes beyond individual differences in thinking styles. It focuses on internal structures rather than on external conditions as behavioral theory does. Piaget identifies four major stages of cognitive development:

| | |
|---|---|
| Sensorimotor stage | zero to two years |
| Preoperational stage | 1½ to six or seven years |
| Concrete operational | six to 12 years |
| Formal operational stage | 12 years to adulthood |

Each person of normal intelligence will go through these stages in this order, although the rate will change depending on the individual and his or her experiences. Figure 4.7 details the stages of early childhood.

Children progress from one stage to the next, changing their thinking depending on their level of maturation and experience with the environment. The *Focus* discussion by Dr. John Flavell describes how children think about thinking. Certain physical skills, such as fine-motor coordination, will determine how much a child is capable of doing. Environmental factors, such as the kinds of experiences adults and the world provide, influence the rate of growth. Throughout the process, both accommodation and assimilation are at work in a child's mind. Children take in new knowledge and decide how it fits with what they already know.

## Applying Cognitive Theory to Work with Children

What can teachers learn from this complicated theory? Piaget's writings do not apply directly to classroom methods or subject matter per se, and therefore careful interpretation is required. In fact, he never claimed to be an educator. However, Piaget's theories provide a framework, or philosophy, about children's thinking. Piagetian theory has some implications for both environment and interactions.

### Materials

Children need many objects to explore, so that they can later incorporate these into their symbolic thinking. Such materials need to be balanced among open-ended ones (such as sand and water activities, basic art and construction materials), guided ones (cooking with recipes, conducting experiments, classification and seriate materials), and self-correcting ones (puzzles, matching games, such as some of the Montessori materials). It is important to remember that young children need to be involved with concrete objects and to explore and use them in their own ways, which include both sensorimotor and beginning symbolic play.

### Scheduling

Children need lots of time to explore their own reality, especially through the use of play. A Piagetian

**FIGURE 4.8**   Young children need materials and time to explore the world on their own.

classroom would have large periods of time for children to "act out" their own ideas. Also, there should be time scheduled for imitation of adult-given ideas (songs, fingerplays, and stories).

### Teachers

Children need teachers who understand and agree with a developmental point of view. The teacher who knows the stages and levels of thinking of the children will be one who can guide that class into new and challenging opportunities to learn and grow.

To encourage thinking and learning, teachers should refrain from telling children exactly how to solve a problem. Rather, the teacher should ask questions that encourage children to observe and pay attention to their own ideas. Teachers:

- Use or create situations that are personally meaningful to children.

- Provide opportunities for them to make decisions.
- Provide opportunities for them to exchange viewpoints with their peers (Williams & Kamii, 1986).

### *Awareness*

Perhaps more important is the awareness on the part of all adults that all children have the capability to reason and be thinkers if they are given appropriate materials for their stage of development. Teachers must remember that young children:

1. Think differently than adults.

2. Need many materials to explore and describe.

3. Think in a concrete manner and often cannot think out things in their heads.

4. Come to conclusions and decisions based on what they see, rather than on what is sensible and logical.

5. Need challenging questions, and the time to make their own decisions and find their own answers.

The thoughts and ideas of Jean Piaget are impressive, both in quantity and quality. The collective works of this man are extremely complex, often difficult to understand. Yet they have given us a valuable blueprint. Clearly, Jean Piaget has provided unique and important insights into the development of intelligence and children.

It is Piaget's genius for empathy with children, together with true intellectual genius, that has made him the outstanding child psychologist in the world today and one destined to stand beside Freud with respect to his contributions to psychology, education, and related disciplines. Just as Freud's discoveries of unconscious motivation, infantile sexuality, and the stages of psychosexual growth changed our ways of thinking about human personality, so Piaget's discoveries of children's implicit philosophies, the construction of reality by the infant, and the stages of mental development have altered our ways of thinking about human intelligence.

(Elkind, 1977)

# MATURATION THEORY
## Arnold Gesell

As noted in Chapter 1, Arnold Gesell was a physician intrigued with the notion that children's internal clock seemed to govern their growth and behavior. In the 1950s, he established norms for both physical-motor growth and the behaviors that accompany that development. The Gesell Institute, which fosters the work of Dr. Louise Bates Ames and others, continues to provide guidelines for how children mature from birth to puberty.

## Theory of Maturation

*Maturation,* by definition, is the process of physical and mental growth that is determined by heredity. The maturation sequence takes place in relatively stable and orderly ways. Maturation theory holds that much growth is genetically determined from conception. This theory differs from behaviorism, which asserts that growth is determined by environmental conditions and experiences, and cognitive theory, which states that growth and behavior are a reflection of both maturation and learning.

Maturation and growth are interrelated and occur together. Maturation describes the *quality* of growth; that is, while a child grows in inches and pounds, the nature (or quality) of that growth changes. Maturation is qualitative, describing the way a baby moves into walking, rather than simply the age at which the baby took the first step. Growth is *what* happens; maturation is *how* it happens.

Studies have established that the maturation sequence is the same for all children, regardless of culture, country of origin, or learning environment. But there are two vital points to remember:

- Although maturation determines the sequence of development, the precise age is *approximate*. The sequence of developmental stages may be universal, but the rate at which a child moves through the stages varies tremendously.
- Growth is *uneven*. Children grow in spurts. Motor

development may be slow in some stages, fast in another. For instance, a baby may gain an ounce a day for two months, then only half a pound in an entire month. Usually there is a growth spurt at puberty, with some children at 13 nearly their adult height, others not yet five feet tall. This unpredictability brings, again, much individual variation.

## Applying Maturation Theory to Work with Children

Maturation theory is most useful in describing children's growth and typical behavior. In Chapter 3, these normative data are used to develop Word Pictures that describe common characteristics of children at different ages. Such charts will help adults understand behavior better and will keep them from expecting too much or too little. Teachers can use developmental norms to understand typical growth by remembering that there is great individual variation and uneven growth. Further, maturation theory has inspired excellent developmental norms that help parents, teachers, and physicians alike determine whether a child's growth is within the normal range.

# HUMANISTIC THEORY

## The Humanists

As the field of psychology began to develop, various schools of thought arose. By the middle of this century, two "camps" dominated the American psychological circles. The first, known as psychodynamic, included the Freudians and is best known to us through the works of Erik Erikson. The second, called behaviorism, began with Watson and Thorndike, and was later expanded by Skinner and Bandura.

In 1954, Abraham Maslow published a book that articulated another set of ideas. He called it

. . . the Third Force (or Humanistic Psychology), which is developing a new image of man, . . . the work of *many* men. Not only this, but it is also paralleled by independent advances and discoveries in other fields as well. Thus, there is rapidly developing a new image of society and all of its institutions. So, also, there is a new philosophy of science, of education, of religion, of psychotherapy, of politics, of economics, etc, etc, etc. Taken together these developments can be called single aspects of a comprehensive philosophy of *everything*.

(Goble, 1970)

This theory has a place in early childhood education because it attempts to explain how people are motivated. Specifically, humanistic theory is centered on people's needs, goals, and successes. This was a change from the study of mental illness, as in psychotherapy, or the study of animal behavior, in the case of much behaviorist research. Instead, Dr. Maslow studied exceptionally mature and successful people. Others, such as Carl Rogers, Fritz Perls, Alan Watts, and Erich Fromm added to what was known about healthy personalities. The humanists developed a comprehensive theory of human behavior based on mental health.

## Maslow's Theory of Human Needs

Maslow's theory of self-actualization is a set of ideas about what people need in order to become and stay healthy. He asserts that every human being is motivated by a number of basic needs, regardless of age, sex, race, culture, or geographic location. According to Maslow (1962), a basic need is something:

- Whose absence breeds illness.
- Whose presence prevents illness.
- Whose restoration cures illness.
- Preferred by the deprived person over other satisfactions, under certain conditions (such as very complex, free-choice instances).
- Found to be inactive, at a low ebb, or functionally absent in the healthy person.

These needs, not to be denied, form a theory of human motivation. It is a hierarchy, or pyramid, because there is a certain way these needs are inter-related, and because the most critical needs form the foundation from which the other needs can be met.

## Applying Humanistic Theory to Work with Children

The basic needs are sometimes called "deficiency needs" because they are critical for a person's survival, and a deficiency can cause a person to die. Until those are met, no other significant growth can take place. How well a teacher knows that a hungry child will ignore a lesson, or simply be unable to concentrate. A tired child often pushes aside other learning materials and experiences until rested. The child who is deprived of basic physiological needs may be able to think of those needs only; in Maslow's words, "such a man can fairly be said to live by bread alone" (Maslow, 1954). The humanists would strongly advocate a school breakfast or lunch program, and support regular rest and nap-times in programs with long hours.

Once the physiological needs are satisfied, the need for safety and security will emerge. Maslow points at insecure and neurotic people as examples of what happens when these needs are left unfulfilled. These people act as if a disaster is about to occur, as if a spanking is on the way. Given an unpredictable home or school, a child cannot find any sense of consistency, and so is preoccupied with worrying and anxiety. Maslow would advise teachers to give freedom within limits, rather than either total neglect or permissiveness.

The growth needs begin to emerge when the basic needs have been met. Higher needs are dependent on those primary ones. They are what we strive for in order to become more satisfied and healthy people. Figure 4.9 describes both basic and growth needs in detail.

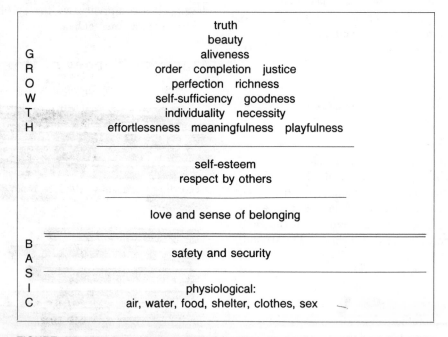

```
                        truth
                        beauty
  G                    aliveness
  R           order   completion   justice
  O             perfection   richness
  W            self-sufficiency   goodness
  T              individuality   necessity
  H     effortlessness   meaningfulness   playfulness
        _____

                     self-esteem
                   respect by others
        _____

                 love and sense of belonging
        ═══════════════════════════════════════════

  B
  A                  safety and security
  S     _____
  I
  C                   physiological:
        air, water, food, shelter, clothes, sex
```

**FIGURE 4.9** Abraham Maslow studied healthy personalities and found that what people need for growth is universal. One tenet of humanistic psychology is the hierarchy of basic and growth needs. (Adapted from Maslow, 1954)

## Love and Belonging

The need for love and belonging is often expressed directly and clearly by the young children in our care. A lack of love and sense of belonging stifles growth. In order to learn to give love later in life, one has to learn about love by receiving it as a child. This means learning early about the responsibilities of giving as well as receiving love.

## The Esteem Needs

The need for esteem can be divided into two categories: self-respect and esteem from others. "Self-esteem includes such needs as a desire for confidence, competence, mastery, adequacy, achievement, independence, and freedom. Respect for others includes such concepts as prestige, recognition, acceptance, attention, status, reputation, and appreciation." (Goble, 1970)

## Self-Actualization

Self-actualization is what gives a person satisfaction in life. From the desire to know and understand the world and people around us comes a renewal of self-knowledge. For the early childhood educator, these needs are expressed in the enthusiasm, curiosity, and natural "drive" to learn and try. In meeting these needs, a person finds meaning for life, an eagerness to live, and a willingness to do so.

Children must have their physical and basic emotional needs met before these requirements of higher cognitive learning can be fulfilled. Moreover, the child who seems stuck in a particular "needs area" will likely stay there until that basic need is satisfied. A hungry, insecure, or hurt child is a poor learner. Teachers must continually advocate better physical and social conditions for all children.

Maslow's theory has important implications for child care. Children's basic needs are teachers' first concern: Teachers must ensure that children are properly clothed, fed, and rested as well as safe and secure. Only then are they ready to address curriculum and skill development.

# OTHER PSYCHOLOGISTS

To complete our discussion of psychology and early education, the contributions of several others are worth mentioning. All have added to our knowledge about children's thinking and learning (Bruner, Flavell, Kagan, and Weikart), their personality and social development (Ainsworth, Kohlberg, Maccoby), and infancy (White). Unfortunately, the list is necessarily far shorter than the numbers of excellent researchers who have contributed to the growing body of knowledge of early childhood development. We include these eight to emphasize the vital links between psychology, developmental research, and early childhood education.

## Mary Ainsworth

Mary Ainsworth has done extensive research in children's attachment to others, particularly the mother-child bond. She has described in detail the many facets of mothers' behavior towards their infants, showing how patterns of attachment are expressed in children's personalities. Her work reinforces the notion that children secure in their relationships with their parents are more outgoing and freer to venture into the world than those children whose parental attention and attachment is less intense. Ainsworth's observations of babies with their mothers and strangers has resulted in techniques and classifications that others use to study child rearing.

## Jerome Bruner

Jerome Bruner is another rich resource of knowledge about learning and thinking. His work is in the area of cognitive development. Like Piaget, Bruner theorizes a progression of development through a fixed sequence of stages. A noteworthy and yet unresolved exception to Piaget's theory is in the relationship of language and thought. Piaget suggests that language is an abstract of thought, and thus children's language helps their thinking. Bruner claims that language and thought are essentially separate until the primary years. While language itself can be very complex at an earlier age (at three or four), cognitive thought does not become equally complex until later (at six or seven). Bruner has taken a special interest in education. As a professor at Harvard, he directed a group of intellectual scholars that produced a book on the study of the process of education. It is this involvement in the educational field and the practical issues that provide a critical and all-too-rare link between psychology and education.

## John Flavell

John Flavell is a cognitive-developmental theorist whose research has contributed significantly to what we know about the child's mind and thought structures. What is of particular interest to early childhood teachers is the extensive work he has done in perceptual development of preschoolers (see the *Focus* discussion in this chapter). Flavell has detailed the changes in developmental levels of perception, use of language, and strategies for remembering (encoding and retrieval strategies). He, as much as any other, has brought Piaget to the attention of American educators and psychologists.

## FOCUS

## THE EARLY DEVELOPMENT OF CHILDREN'S KNOWLEDGE ABOUT THE MIND

### *John H. Flavell*

The development of children's knowledge about the mind is currently a very exciting research area within the field of developmental psychology. Researchers are investigating such interesting topics as children's basic understanding of belief, their ability to infer the perspectives of other people, and their knowledge of the physical-mental and appearance-reality distinctions. How does development proceed in this area? According to my theory, it proceeds from an earlier developmental level in which children understand *cognitive connections* to a later level in which they understand *mental representations*.

The theory claims that by two or three years of age children have learned that they and other people can be *cognitively* (perceptually, intellectually, emotionally) *connected* to things in the external world in a variety of ways. That is, they understand at least roughly what it is for themselves and others to see or not see something (visual connection), to hear it, taste it, smell it,

dream of it, pretend with it, want it, like it, fear it, be angry with it, and so on. They are also not as egocentric at this age as Piaget thought. For example, if a card containing a picture of a dog on one side and a cat on the other is held up between them and the experimenter, they can infer that the experimenter sees the dog when they view the cat side and vice-versa. That is, they do not egocentrically assume that the other person always sees whatever they see—that others' "connections" are always identical to their own.

At ages four and five children move to a new developmental level in which they understand that it is possible to *mentally represent* the very same thing in two or more very different ways—a possibility that escapes the younger child. Here are two illustrations of this developmental difference as shown in recent research. A story character sees that a cookie box contains cookies, and then conspicuously leaves the scene. While he is gone, someone takes the cookies out of the box and puts a pencil in there instead. What will the story character think is in the box when she returns, the child subjects are asked. "Cookies" says the five-year-old, grinning at the trick. "A pencil" says the three-year-old, sober-faced and uncomprehending. The experimenter puts a white object behind a blue filter and asks the children what color the object presently appears to be, and what color it really and truly is. "Blue," "white," correctly answers the five-year-old. "Blue," "blue," says the three-year-old. The older child recognizes that although the contents of the box and the object behind the filter are only one thing out there in the world, they can be mentally represented in people's heads in more than one way: as "cookies" as well as "pencil" in the first example, and as "white" as well as "blue" in the second.

What are the implications for early childhood educators and parents? Expect some understanding of the mental world by three-year-olds but not too much. Because they do not yet understand mental representations very well, they will have trouble recognizing that another person may view or interpret things differently than they do. For the same reason they may have trouble distinguishing how things seem or appear from how they really are. For them, if something *seems* dangerous (the menacing-looking shadow in their unlit bedroom) it *is* dangerous, and if it *seems* nondangerous (the friendly-acting stranger) it *is* nondangerous. We often think of young children as naive, credulous, gullible, trusting, and the like. Their inadequate understanding that things may not be as they appear might be partly responsible for this impression.

*Dr. John H. Flavell is a professor of Psychology at Stanford University, where his research concerns children's cognitive development.*

## Jerome Kagan

Jerome Kagan has researched a number of issues related to child development for more than 20 years. His writings range from works on children's play, achievement, and readiness to coauthorship of one of the most widely used child development texts. He has made contributions to the cognitive-developmental theory, particularly in the development of patterns of attention and temperament in very young children. Kagan maintains that cognitive activity begins in the first year, earlier in life than Piagetian theory states. His work emphasizes the distinctions between natural intellectual abilities, which all children have to some extent, and acquired cultural knowledge. This clarification is particularly helpful when mainstreaming and when working with retarded children.

## Lawrence Kohlberg

Lawrence Kohlberg is best known as a theorist in social development, but he has also addressed educational practice. His work on gender constancy clarifies the role of cognition in learning one's sex role. Building on Piagetian dimensions of moral development, Kohlberg's theory of moral development involves both social growth and intellectual reasoning. People move from stage to stage as a result of their own reasoning power and as they see for themselves contradictions in their own beliefs. For instance, children in stage 1 obey rules only to avoid punishment. They move to the next stage as they understand that conforming to rules will bring them rewards, such as having favors returned. Only later, in adolescence, does a person generally conform primarily to please others or follow rules for their own sake. Kohlberg has also helped translate Piaget's theories into curriculum. Moreover, his comparison of Piagetian principles to other theories and programs (such as the Montessori and Bank Street models) has made Piaget's theories more understandable.

## Eleanor Maccoby

Eleanor Maccoby is a developmental psychologist whose work has revealed the realities—and myths—surrounding sex differences and their effect on behavior from infants to adults. Her writing has provided a forum for open-minded discussion of how people grow and the complex interaction between heredity and environment that makes child development so fascinating.

## David Weikart

David Weikart has directed research and development in cognitive theory and its application to education since the late 1960s. He initiated the Ypsilanti Perry Preschool Project, a longitudinal study of how preschool affects disadvantaged children (see Chapter 2), and he has been instrumental in developing a cognitively oriented approach to teaching and curriculum, using Piagetian theory. Weikart's works detail the relationships of curriculum, teaching, and learning in preschool education. Under his leadership, the High/Scope Foundation has grown to become a major source of applied educational research and practical work with teachers.

## Burton White

Burton White is best known for his work with infants. White studied infant eyesight to determine both field of vision and focus points. His work in infant stimulation tells what kinds of environmental stimuli will encourage a baby to look at and reach out to what is offered. His research has helped establish descriptive data about children from birth to three years old, as well as how to work with them.

## USING DEVELOPMENTAL AND LEARNING THEORIES

As beginning teachers it is important to think about what *you* believe about children, development, and learning. As you do, try to avoid the pitfall of taking sides. Instead, integrate theory into your daily work with children by comparing the major developmental and learning theories.

## Similarities Among the Theories

All five theories we have discussed attempt to explain how children grow, more in the socio-emotional and cognitive areas than in the physical and motor areas. Maturation theory is the only one of the five that includes physical growth and motor development. In other words, these theories do not try to explain the workings of the body as much as the mind and heart. In general, the theories do not dictate curriculum for the classroom, though behaviorism does recommend teaching/learning techniques. Each theory posits that learning follows an orderly, if not always smooth, path from birth to adulthood. They all see later learning as growing from previous experiences. They all agree that learning must be real, rewarding and, except in extreme cases, connected to an important person or people in early life. Figure 4.10 summarizes the five major theories and principal theorists.

## Differences Among the Theories

More obvious are the differences among the various theories. All four have a particular focus, but not the same one. In developmental terms, Erikson covers the psychosocial area. The behaviorists and Piagetians tend to concentrate on cognitive growth. Maturational theory rests on physical-motor development, although theorists have derived behavior in other areas as well. Gesell's maturation theory concentrates on the larger behaviors that heredity dictates. Maslow builds a framework including physiological, affective, and intellectual needs. Three of the five are developmental theories; that is, they describe changes in children as the result of combination of growth (controlled mostly by maturation and heredity) and interaction with the environment. Maslow's theory of self-actualization is less developmental than descriptive of overall human needs, though it is clear that in early childhood the basic needs predominate over higher ones that occur later in life.

*testable* (handwritten)

| Theory | Major Theorists | Important Facts |
|---|---|---|
| Psychosocial | Erik Erikson | Maturational emphasis<br>Stage theory of social and emotional development<br>Crises at each level<br>Teacher: Emotional base, social mediator |
| Behaviorist | John Watson<br>Edward Thorndike<br>B. F. Skinner<br>Albert Bandura | Environmental emphasis<br>Stimulus-response *association*<br>Conditioning (classical and operant) *reinforcement*<br>Reinforcement (positive and negative)<br>Modeling - *social learning*<br>Teacher: Arranger of environment and reinforcer of behavior |
| Cognitive | Jean Piaget | Maturational and environmental emphasis *new info*<br>Assimilation and accommodation - *replace old*<br>Stage theory of cognitive development *ideas*<br>Teacher: Provider of materials and time and supporter of children's unique ways of thinking |
| Maturation | Arnold Gesell | Emphasis on heredity<br>Normative data *word pictures*<br>Teacher: Guider of behavior based on what is typical and normal |
| Humanist | Abraham Maslow<br>Erich Fromm<br>Fritz Perls<br>Carl Rogers | Environmental emphasis *how people are motivated*<br>Mental health model *freedom w/e*<br>Hierarchy of human needs *limits*<br>Teacher: Provider of basic and growth needs |
| Others | Jerome Bruner *Piaget*<br>Jerome Kagan *Piaget*<br>Eleanor Maccoby<br>David Weikart<br>Burton White | Learning and thinking<br>Child development research/text<br>Sex differences research<br>Cognitive-oriented curriculum *Perry Preschool*<br>Infant research |

(handwritten left margin annotation: *adult active*)
(handwritten annotation: *new ideas fill in old*)

*Flavell - perceptual development* (handwritten)

**FIGURE 4.10**  Each of the major theories of development or learning describes children and their growth in a different way.

Behaviorist theory emphasizes changes that occur in the environment. Cognitive and psychosocial ideas are stage theories, explaining growth as a series of steps through which all children pass, regardless of environment. Behaviorists spell out how the children learn no matter what age or stage they may have achieved, while the two stage theorists claim that what and how a child learns is tied to a stage of development. Humanists tend to look at learning as paralleling the child's internal affective state, rather than a stage of growth or external environmental conditions.

Most early childhood educators are eclectic in their theoretical biases. That is, they have developed their own philosophies of education based on a little of each theory, as summarized in Figure 4.9. Each teacher has an obligation to develop a clear set of ideas of how children grow and learn. We are fortunate to have choices. Most educators agree on some basic tenets based, in part, on theories of development and learning.

1. Children's basic physiological needs and their needs for physical and psychological safety must

be met satisfactorily before they can experience and respond to "growth motives." [Maslow]

2. Children develop unevenly and not in a linear fashion as they grow toward psychosocial maturity and psychological well-being. A wide variety of factors in children's lives, as well as the manner in which they interpret their own experiences, will have a bearing on the pattern and rate of progress toward greater social and emotional maturity. [Erikson, the behaviorists, maturationists]

3. Developmental crises that occur in the normal process of growing up may offer maximum opportunities for psychological growth, but these crises are also full of possibilities for regression or even negative adaptation. [Erikson]

4. Children strive for mastery over their own private inner worlds as well as for mastery of the world outside of them. [Erikson, Piaget]

5. The child's interactions with significant persons in his life play a major part in his development. [Erikson, the behaviorists, Piaget, and Maslow]

# Developmental Research Conclusions

## Results

To keep in mind the real child underneath all these theories, teachers apply developmental research to their own classroom settings. Figure 4.11 consolidates what developmental research has found and how it can be put into practical use with young children.

| Developmental Research Tells Us: | Teachers Can: |
|---|---|
| 1. Growth occurs in a sequence. | Think about the steps children will take when planning projects. Know the sequence of growth in their children's age group. |
| 2. Children in any age group will behave similarly in certain ways. | Plan for activities in relation to age range of children. Know the characteristics of their children's age group. |
| 3. Children grow through certain stages. | Know the stages of growth in their class. Identify to family any behavior inconsistent with general stages of development. |
| 4. Growth occurs in four interrelated areas. | Understand that a person's work in one area can help in another. Plan for language growth, while children use their bodies. |
| 5. Intellectual growth: Children learn through their senses. Children learn by doing; adults learn in abstract ways, while children need concrete learning. Cognitive growth occurs in four areas: perception (visual, auditory, etc.) | Have activities in looking, smelling, tasting, hearing, and touching. Realize that talking is abstract; have children touch, manipulate, act out what they are to do. Provide materials and activities in matching, finding same/different, putting a picture with a sound, taste, or with a symbol. |
| language | Provide opportunities to find and label things, talk with grown-ups, friends, tell what it "looks like," "smells like," etc. |
| memory | Know that by three, a child can often remember 2–3 directions. |

**FIGURE 4.11** Developmental research tests theories of growth and learning to find out about children and childhood.

| Developmental Research Tells Us: | Teachers Can: |
|---|---|
| reasoning | Know that memory is helped by seeing, holding objects and people. |
| | Recognize that it is just beginning, so children judge on what they *see,* rather than what they reason they should see. |
| | Be sure adult explanations aid in understanding reasons. |
| | Practice finding "answers" to open-ended questions such as "How can you tell when you are tired?" |
| 6. Social growth: | Expect that children will know their ideas only. |
| The world *is* only from the child's viewpoint. | Be aware that the rights of others are minimal to them. |
| Seeing is believing. | Remember that if they cannot see the situation, they may not be able to talk about it. |
| Group play is developing. | Provide free-play sessions, with places to play socially. |
| | Understand that group play in structured situations is hard, because of "self" orientation. |
| Independence increases as competence grows. | Know that children test to see how far they can go. |
| | Realize that children will vary from independent to dependent (both among the group, and within one child). |
| People are born not knowing when it is safe to go on. | Understand that children will need to learn by trial and error. |
| Adult attention is very important. | Know the children individually. |
| | Be with the child, not just with the group. |
| Young children are not born with internal mechanism that says "slow down." | Move into a situation before children lose control. |
| 7. Emotional growth: | Watch for what each person's self-image is becoming. |
| Self-image is developing. | Give praise to enhance good feelings about oneself. |
| | Know that giving children responsibilities helps self-image. |
| | Talk to children at eye level. Children learn by example. |
| | Model appropriate behavior by doing yourself what you want the children to do. |
| 8. Physical growth: | Not expect perfection, in either small- or large-muscle activity. |
| Muscle development is not complete. | |
| Muscles cannot stay still for long. | Plan short times for children to sit. |
| Large muscles are better developed than small ones. | Give lots of chances to move about, be gentle with expectations for hand work. |
| Hand preference is being established. | Watch to see how children decide their handedness. |
| | Let children trade hands in their play. |
| A skill must be done several times before it is internalized. | Have available materials to be used often. |
| | Plan projects to use the same skill over and over. |
| Bowel and bladder control is not completely internalized. | Be understanding of "accidents." |
| | If possible, have toilet facilities available always, and keep them attractive. |

**FIGURE 4.11   Cont.**

## Decision Making in Teaching

Knowledge of child development can help teachers in the many decisions they must make daily concerning their classrooms, the curriculum, and, most important, the children. Consistent and effective teachers have a solid foundation in learning and developmental theory. Instead of basing a decision on whim or the heat of the moment, the thoughtful teacher can use theory along with sharp observation skills to set realistic goals for each child.

Consider, for instance, how useful child development information is in the following circumstances:

15-month-old Kenya and Peter are crying and fussy this morning. The teacher pauses, then realizes that neither has been outdoors yet or eaten a snack. Scheduling regular times for active movement keeps children comfortable; knowing children's physical developmental needs (maturation theory; Maslow) will help these children.

Mario and Therese, both in wheelchairs, joined the first grade class last month, but their parents report that neither wants to come to school. The teacher, recognizing their need to feel part of the class and their classmates' need to get acquainted with newcomers, pairs children in a project to design and build wheel toys for pets. By knowing the children's need for competence (Erikson) and level of cognitive thinking (Piaget), she encourages these six-year-olds toward greater mutual understanding and social skills.

Preschoolers Jared and Panya have been arguing about who has brought the "best" toy to child care. Knowing of their egocentrism (Piaget), the teacher realizes that both are right, but that they may be unable to see this themselves. By praising each child's toy in their presence, the teacher uses herself as a model (behavioral social learning theory) and demonstrates how the two children—and their toys—can play together.

Finally, the teacher well versed in child development theory can offer this information to parents. Parents can share the intimate, in-depth view of their children while teachers offer their perspective regarding learning and growth. Together, parents and teachers can make decisions about the child on the basis of concrete, truthful information.

## Conditions for Learning

Teachers also look for the best conditions for learning. Caring for children means providing for total growth, in the best possible environment. Developmental theory helps define conditions which enhance learning and from which positive learning environments are created. Research on all theories extends the knowledge of children and learning.

Coupled with practical application, both theory and research have helped all to recognize that:

1. *Learning must be real.* We teach about the children's bodies, their families, their neighborhoods, and their school. We start with who children are and expand this to include the world, in their terms. We give them the words, the ideas, the ways to question and figure things out for themselves.

2. *Learning must be rewarding.* Practice makes better, but only if it is all right to practice, to stumble and try again. We include the time to do all this, by providing an atmosphere of acceptance and of immediate feedback as to what was accomplished (even what boundary was just overstepped). Also, practice can make a good experience even better, as it reminds children in their terms of what they can do.

3. *Learning must build on children's lives.* We help connect the family to the child and the teacher. We know important family events and help the family support happenings at school. For children learning goes on wherever they may be, awake and asleep. Parents can learn to value learning and help it happen for their child.

**4.** *Learning needs a good stage.* Healthy bodies make for alert minds, so good education means caring for children's health. This includes physical health, and emotional and mental health, too. Psychological safety and well-being are theoretical terms for the insight, availability, and awareness teachers bring to their classrooms. On the lookout for each child's successes, we prevent distractions in the way furniture is arranged, how noisy it is, how many strangers are around. Mental health is both emotional and intellectual. We try to have a variety of materials and experiences, and a flexible schedule, when someone is pursuing an idea, building a project, finishing a disagreement. As long as we care for children, we will have our hands full. With the theoretical underpinnings presented here, we have the tools with which to make our own way into the world of children and of early childhood education.

# CHILD DEVELOPMENT AND CULTURAL DIVERSITY

In many ways, each child is like every other. Certain universals hold for all children, and knowing them, teachers can apply child development and learning theories. There are limits on such application, however, because some differences among children exist as a result of cultural commonalities and each child's uniqueness. Caldwell (1983) outlines these three areas so that teachers can make child development useful without overgeneralizing:

First, all children have the same needs and rights, go through the same developmental stages, and have the same developmental goals. Cross-cultural research on Piagetian theory has demonstrated that the stages of development are invariant and hold true world-wide, although the ages vary between cultures and among individuals.

Second, children are like each other in some ways; for example, there are similarities within cultural groups. Certain cultural and social expectations will bring about commonalities in how soon youngsters use writing tools or in ways of self-expression. This means that, while all two-year-olds

are in the process of developing language, the actual rate of vocabulary increase will differ according to how important language expression is to the cultural and familial groups. What certain children have in common may be broad—from patterns of socializing to cognitive style—but is culture-bound. Teachers without appropriate knowledge of their students' cultures run a risk of misapplying developmental theories and norms.

Third, each child is like no other in many respects. What is unique comes from genetic make-up, temperament, energy level, sensory sensitivity, interests, and motivation, to name several. Child development and learning theories have limits. They can foster a global outlook about children in general, but these theories must be viewed in light of both cultural diversity and a respect for individuality. With the theoretical underpinnings presented here, teachers have the tools with which to make their own way into the world of children and of early childhood education.

# SUMMARY

The twentieth century has been called "the century of the child." Developmental and learning theories of this century form the cornerstone of our knowledge about children. What we know about how children grow, learn, and adapt to the world around them is critical in our quest for greater understanding of the people we serve. Our field is greater for the contributions of several schools of study. Psychoanalyst Erik Erikson's theory of psychosocial development gives us insight into children's feelings and how their emotional and social lives affect their learning. The behaviorists, a distinctively American group of psychologists, demonstrate how much we can learn of human affairs by applying the methods of science. Jean Piaget, a "giant in the nursery school" (Elkind, 1977), opens our eyes to a stage theory of growth and shows us how active children are in their own learning. Arnold Gesell offers U.S. developmental norms. Abraham Maslow, a humanistic psychologist, establishes a hierarchy of needs, reminding us that the basic physical and psychological needs must be met before higher learning can take place.

In learning about these theories, we are more able to formulate our own philosophy of education. By tracing our roots to these learning theories, we show our willingness to make a commitment to children. What we know about growth and development helps us fight for our most important resource—our children.

## R E V I E W   Q U E S T I O N S

1. Match the theorist with the appropriate description:

   B.F. Skinner          Sex differences
   Abraham Maslow        Attachment *mother child*
   Jean Piaget           Social learning
   Albert Bandura        Psychosocial development
   Mary Ainsworth        Behaviorism
   Eleanor Maccoby       Developmental norms
   Erik Erikson          Cognitive theory
   Arnold Gesell         Self-actualization *humanism*

2. Describe Piaget's four stages of cognitive development and their implications for early childhood education.

3. Name at least three psychologists who have contributed to the knowledge of development. Describe your reaction to each.

4. Given five theories of learning and development, which one would most likely advocate large blocks of free play? An early academic program? Open-ended questioning by teachers? Regular early mealtime?

## L E A R N I N G   A C T I V I T I E S

1. You are a teacher in a large urban child care center. Your children arrive by 7:00, and usually stay until after 5:00 each day. What would you do first thing in the morning? Use Maslow's hierarchy of needs to justify your answer.

2. What do you think of cartoons? From a social learning perspective, what kind of television would you have your daughter watch?

3. You are a teacher in a middle-class suburban preschool. What do you know about your group's needs and developmental stage? What does their cultural background tell you about what to teach? How will you find out about what each child is ready to learn?

# B I B L I O G R A P H Y

Bee, Helen. *The Developing Child.* New York: Harper & Row, 1985.

Caldwell, Bettye. "Child Development and Global Diversity." Future 8 OMEP World Assembly, Geneva, Switzerland, August 1983.

DeVries, Rheta, and Kohlberg, Lawrence. *Programs of Early Education.* White Plains, N.Y.: Longman's, 1987.

Elkind, David. "Giant in the Nursery School—Jean Piaget." In Hetherington, E.M., and Parke, R.D. (eds.), *Contemporary Readings in Psychology.* New York: McGraw-Hill, 1977.

Erikson, E.H. "A Healthy Personality for Every Child." In Mussen, Paul H.; Conger, John J.; and Kagan, Jerome (eds.), *Child Development and Personality,* 3rd ed. New York: Harper and Row, 1969.

Erikson, E.H. *Childhood and Society,* 2nd ed. New York: W.W. Norton and Co., 1963.

Erikson, E.H. "Toys and Reasons." In Haworth, M.R. (ed.), *Child Psychotherapy: Practice and Theory.* New York: Basic Books, 1964.

Fong, Bernadine, and Resnick, Miriam. *The Child: Development Through Adolescence.* Palo Alto, Calif.: Mayfield, 1986.

Gardner, Howard. *Developmental Psychology.* Boston: Little, Brown and Co., 1982.

Ginsberg, Herbert, and Opper, Sylvia. *Piaget's Theory of Intellectual Development.* Englewood Cliffs, N.J.: Prentice-Hall, 1969.

Goble, Frank G. *The Third Force: The Psychology of Abraham Maslow.* New York: Grossman Publishers, 1970.

Hubley, John, and Hubley, Faith. *Everyone Rides the Carousel.* Santa Monica, Calif.: Pyramid Films, 1976.

Krumboltz, John, and Krumboltz, Helen. *Changing Children's Behavior.* Englewood Cliffs, N.J.: Prentice-Hall, 1972.

McClinton, Barbara S., and Meier, Blanche G. *Beginnings: Psychology of Early Childhood.* St. Louis: C.V. Mosby Co., 1978.

Maslow, Abraham H. *Motivation and Personality.* New York: Harper and Row, 1954.

Moyer, Joan. "Child Development as a Base for Decision Making." *Childhood Education,* May-June 1986.

Murphy, Lois B., and Leeper, Ethel M. "Conditions for Learning." Washington, D.C.: U.S. Department of Health, Education, and Welfare, 1973.

Peters, Donald L., and Willis, Sherry L. *Early Childhood,* Life-Span Human Development Series. Monterey, Calif.: Brooks/Cole Publishing Co., 1978.

Spitz, R.A., and Wolf, K.M. "Anaclitic Depression: An Inquiry into the Genesis of Psychiatric Conditions in Early Childhood, II." In Freud, A., et al. (eds.), *The Psychoanalytic Study of the Child,* Vol. II. New York: International Universities Press, 1946.

Williams, C.K., and Kamii, Constance. "How Do Children Learn by Handling Objects?" *Young Children,* 42, No. 1, November 1986.

# SECTION 3

GUEST EDITORIAL

# EFFECTIVE TEACHING: A COMMITMENT TO OPTIMAL CHILD DEVELOPMENT

## Joseph H. Stevens, Jr.

Effective teaching with young children requires commitment, knowledge, and skill: commitment to assisting children's optimal development; knowledge of the factors which promote that development; and skill in behaving and arranging the environment in ways consistent with that knowledge. To do this well requires some self-awareness: insight about one's own competencies, as well as an ability and willingness to formulate a professional point of view—an open, working philosophy. Construct that point of view. Inform it through study of research and theory. Hone it by reflecting on your experiences with children and your teaching practices. Have coworkers scrutinize it. Work to enlarge it. Expect it to change.

Consider the following incident and what you would do were you the teacher in this classroom.

Timmy and Kwansa, two black five-year-old boys, have been building with Lego blocks for about ten minutes. Jeff, one of two white children in the class, walks over, points to Kwansa's building, and says, "That's my house!" Kwansa looks up, stares dead at Jeff, and shouts, "No, it's not!" He pauses, then, "You're not building with me!" Timmy and Kwansa turn back to their work. Jeff continues to look as they work; he sits down about two feet away, looks over at the box of Legos, then glances back at Kwansa, and says, "I hate you!" No reply from Timmy or Kwansa as they talk, smile at each other, and add more buildings. Five minutes later they have three blocks of houses, stores, and garages. Jeff has moved off to the side with some Rig-A-Jigs and has started building an airplane.

Not so cute, but certainly revealing. If you had overhead this incident, what would you have done? Why? What hypotheses about the social development and social skills of Timmy, Kwansa, and Jeff does this incident generate? If this behavior is typical of Jeff,

126

# Who Are the Teachers of the Young Child?

what might be appropriate learning objectives for him? How would you arrange the materials, equipment, daily schedule, learning activities, and grouping of the children to achieve these? How would you intervene—directly or indirectly? What social behaviors would you model, suggest, or praise? With which ones do you begin? How do you assist parents in working toward similar objectives at home? Are there alternative strategies? What do research and theory say about the relative effectiveness of the alternatives? What do you do tomorrow with Timmy, Kwansa, and Jeff? How will you know if it works? This is the business of teaching.

Many competencies are required of the effective early childhood teacher. Some are: keen observational skills; knowledge of child development; adherence to a strong ethical code; commitment to educational experiences that support cultural diversity and literacy; deftness in constructing, implementing, and evaluating activities targeted to foster specific developmental growth; participation in activities to foster one's own professional development; and skill in integrating the classroom program with the child's life at home.

Skill in assessing children's behavior and their perspective of the world, as well as those environmental factors that influence their behavior, is a cornerstone of good teaching. Children teach adults about child development and about education when those adults are sensitive and systematic observers. I like to remember Maria Montessori's description of how she developed the Method—through watching how children played with materials.

The burgeoning knowledge base in child development continually challenges us to judiciously apply what we learn. For example, consider what we know now about the effects of divorce, how children learn to read, how nutrition affects learning and development, and the teacher's role in promoting oral language. Extensive research on the development of infant attachment has provided guidance about key caregiving behaviors infant workers need to manifest. This research has also convinced us that infant day care need not be detrimental to a child's emotional development. Research on the long-term consequences of high-quality preschool education for low-income children has affirmed for state and national legislators the importance of early education. Effective application requires regular reading of professional journals like *Young Children, Child Care Quarterly, Journal of Applied Developmental Psychology,* and *Topics in Special Education,* among others.

Increasingly, children in early childhood programs represent a variety of ethnic and cultural backgrounds. A major task for teachers is to increase children's literacy about their and others' cultures without promoting stereotypes. A starting point is attitudinal—recognition that each ethnic group has a distinct culture (customs, language, dress, values, often a world view) and sense of peoplehood that distinguish it from its cultural counterparts. Promoting cultural literacy among children means helping them gain first-hand knowledge about these cultural aspects of various groups. We can help expose children to these broad cultural themes, and at the same time, we can help children see the diversity *within* cultures and the diffusion of cultural practices.

A central task of the teacher is curriculum development. All teachers must assess children's development, plan instruction, implement those plans, and evaluate whether the objectives were achieved; this process is curriculum development. It is through this systematic process that we are most likely to provide programs that promote children's development—programs that are effective. It is on this process that teachers must focus that commitment, that knowledge, and that skill. This is clearly no mean endeavor, one that anyone can do. It *is* one in which skilled professionals can make a difference.

*PROFESSOR STEVENS was a teacher in a research and demonstration program for preschool children and was administrator of a prekindergarten program. For the past several years, he has been actively involved in early childhood teacher education. His research has examined the effectiveness of home-based early childhood programs, the influence of teenage and adult parents' social support systems on their childrearing skill, and factors related to the socialization of parenting from early adolescence through adulthood. He has served as Professor of Education and (by courtesy) Professor of Psychology and Human Development at George Peabody College for Teachers, Vanderbilt University. Dr. Stevens is currently a professor in the Department of Early Childhood Education at Georgia State University in Atlanta.*

# CHAPTER 5

## The Teacher's Role

tOKATE

HiKATE.

## QUESTIONS for THOUGHT

- What makes the teacher's role complex?
- What qualifications does a good teacher possess?
- What is team teaching in early childhood?
- What are the essentials for successful teaching?
- How does my own personal development relate to my growth as a teacher?
- What is a professional code of ethics?
- How do I make the most of my student teaching experience?
- What are some of the common problems associated with student teaching, and how can I avoid them?
- What does it mean to be a member of the teaching profession?

# WHO ARE THE TEACHERS OF THE YOUNG CHILD?

Group time for the 3½-year-olds is about to begin. The teacher, Paul, is well prepared and ready. He has chosen dinosaurs as his topic after hearing two children arguing about how to pronounce tyrannosaurus the day before. That morning, Paul gathered pictures of dinosaurs, small plastic models of prehistoric animals, a record with songs and stories about dinosaurs and several picture books. He put pictures of dinosaurs on the wall, borrowed a copy of "Danny and the Dinosaur" from another classroom, and learned a fingerplay about dinosaurs from his coteacher Margarita.

But where are the children? Group time was scheduled to begin five minutes ago. Two or three at a time, children begin to join Paul on the rug. They are coming in from outdoors; some are going to the bathroom before they sit down. Kendra, another teacher, is with them. "Has anyone here ever seen a dinosaur?", Paul asks. Before the words are out, Phillip wanders in from outside, his face covered with sand, and crying softly. Margarita takes him to the bathroom where Kendra will help him clean up.

Paul begins again but the children are restless. Angelo puts his arm around Fatima and she pushes him away. Erika and Andrew, sitting close by, are watching them with avid interest. No one responds to Paul's question. Some of the children are looking at him, some seem lost in their own thoughts, and others are still pulling at the velcro of their shoes. Several are making faces and noises at their neighbors. For Max, the lull is too tempting, and he launches into a monologue about his sister's new toy. Paul simultaneously nods encouragement to the children who are watching him, frowns at Angelo, tells Max to listen, and brings out a picture of a dinosaur. Margarita has rejoined the group in time to hear them shout, "I saw one of those!", "I have one at home like that!", "They scare me—", "I don't like them."

Capitalizing on the children's interest, Paul and Margarita pass around the small plastic dinosaurs. Willie refuses to share them with anyone, Marcus growls and shoves one near Jennifer's face. She screams; Kendra, who has brought the last child from the bathroom, moves near to comfort Jennifer and guide Marcus. All 25 children are now in place and Paul continues leading a discussion about dinosaurs. The book sits unused, the fingerplay forgotten, as the teachers invite the children to join them in a dinosaur dance. Thus, five to eight minutes have passed in the lives of three early childhood teachers.

Teachers of young children come into early childhood for many reasons. Paul spent several years with emotionally disturbed children and wants to gain some experience with normal youngsters. Margarita began as a Head Start teacher, and Kendra was active in a parent cooperative school. The teachers in the next classroom have different stories. Elva, mother of two elementary-school children, wanted part-time work to earn extra income. During high school, Karen worked part time at a child care center and thought she might like to make a full-time career of child care. Roger helped raise his younger brothers and sisters, while Ann and Al always wanted to be teachers.

All of these people had different motivations, but all were drawn into the early childhood classroom. What prompted that decision may have had something to do with the nature of teaching at this early age.

## Comparison to Teaching in Other Educational Settings

### Differences

The nature of teaching in the early years is unlike that of other age groups. Early childhood teachers are more involved in small-group activity than many elementary- and secondary-school teachers. The bulk of teaching and learning in the preschool takes place through teacher-child interactions rather than through lectures and demonstrations. Play is the learning medium in a classroom for preschoolers, but reserved for recess time in other grades. Children in early childhood settings generally have a choice of activities, while schools for older children are structured so that all the students do the same thing at once. Outdoor play periods in the preschool actively involve the teachers since young children require more supervision than older ones. Even the classrooms are set up differently. There is an abundance of materials and child-sized equipment to invite children's interest and inter-action; no rows of desks line up neatly in the early childhood room.

Working closely with other adults is an unusual aspect to teaching in the early years. A staff, a team of teachers, is common to many preschools, whereas a fourth- or fifth-grade teacher generally teaches alone most of the day. Being sensitive to the role of the secretary, bus driver, cook, and janitor is important in an early childhood setting where everyone on the staff works together to create the best possible program for children.

Teachers in early childhood education have close and frequent contact with parents of the children they teach. Regularly scheduled parent conferences, parent assistants/volunteers in the classes, and daily contact with parents when they deliver and pick up their children combine to give the early childhood teacher an opportunity to develop closer home-school relations. (Parent-teacher rela-tions will be discussed more fully in Chapter 8.)

In place of textbooks and worksheets, however, the early childhood professional provides an ever-changing array of materials for children to explore. Collecting and observing real polliwogs brings mean-ing to the term "science"; a basket filled with small plastic bears encourages counting, ordering, and other mathematical concepts; easel painting and pasting activities are preliminary to reading and writing term papers. The curriculum for the early years is experiential and concrete.

Early childhood teachers, like their colleagues in the upper grades, spend a fair amount of time outside the classroom in lesson preparation and planning. Another common factor among all teachers is the assessment of children's progress; the dif-ferences are in the methods used. Grades and report

**FIGURE 5.1** Learning takes place through teacher-child interactions—on the floor, at a table, in the play yard.

cards are common tools of elementary, middle, and secondary schools. Teachers of young children use methods that are more appropriate to the age level of the very young: (1) anecdotal reports, (2) observation notes, (3) forms that measure various developmental areas of growth, (4) consultations with others who teach the child, and (5) oral reports to parents in a conference setting.

### Similarities

At first glance, the differences in teaching pre-school and older children outweigh any similarities. There is one common element, however, that links the two. Early childhood teachers teach what other teachers teach. The curriculum in the early years is as rich in math, science, social studies, history, language, art, and geography as it is in any other grade. Academic content is presented in the pre-school in ways appropriate to the age and develop-mental level of the students.

# THE TEACHER'S ROLE

## Definitions

Over the years the teacher's role in the early childhood classroom has been defined in many ways. The number and variety of tasks teachers perform are innumerable and hard to label. According to Sizer (1985):

> . . . Teaching is, of course, a form of theater . . . Like acting, teaching demands much of personality . . . teaching is being on show . . . A good teacher is self-confident . . . good teachers are patient, and patience flows out of confidence . . . Teaching is a complex craft, one class never being quite the same as another . . . Like writing, teaching is science, art, and craft.

Beyer (1968) calls the teacher a "viewer of children, a catcher of their signals, and a perceptive responder." Spodek (1972) lists teacher tasks:

> . . . (the teacher) functions as lecturer, story teller, group discussion leader, traffic director, mediator of conflicts, psychological diagnostician, custodian, assigner of academic work, and file clerk.

An early pioneer in the field, Jessie Stanton, takes a more humorous view:

> . . . She should have a fair education. By this I mean she should have a doctor's degree in psychology and medicine. Sociology as a background is advisable. She should be an experienced carpenter, mason, mechanic, plumber, and a thoroughly trained musician and poet. At least five years practical experience in each of these branches is essential . . . Now at 83, she's ready!

> (Beyer, 1968)

It would be difficult to improve on any and all of these job descriptions. They are accurate and awesome, yet this diversity is exactly what makes teaching in the early years so appealing. The multiple roles a teacher plays add challenge to the job. Nor are these descriptions exhaustive; the list could include adult educator, parent resource, faculty member, chief purchasing agent, nurse, program planner, staff supervisor, business manager, treasurer, personnel director, employee, and employer. (The role

**FIGURE 5.2** Teachers model learning, listening, and loving.

of the teacher in relationship to parents and programs as a whole will be further discussed in Chapters 8 and 10, respectively.)

Perhaps the job would seem more manageable and less overwhelming to the new teacher if some of the responsibilities were categorized. What teachers do with children is not all there is to teaching. Much of the work takes place outside the classroom. It is helpful to look at the teacher's role in another way. What are the things a teacher does with children? What are the things a teacher does after the children go home? How does the teacher interact with other adults in the early childhood setting?

## In the Classroom

### Interacting with Children

It is no secret that most teachers find their greatest satisfaction and challenges in the first role—

who and what they are with children. The teacher-child interactions, the spur-of-the-moment crisis, the intense activity, the on-the-spot decisions, the loving and nurturing, go far in making one "feel" like a real teacher. Helping Rhonda get a good grip on the hammer, soothing Josh and Benno after they bump heads, and talking with Alexa about her drawing are at the heart of teaching young children. These encounters are enjoyable and provide moments for interactive teaching opportunities. These times help establish good relationships with the children. It is during these spontaneous, anything-can-happen-and-probably-will times that teachers display their craftsmanship. The real art of teaching comes on the floor of the classroom. All teaching skills are called upon in short order. Responses are automatic and sometimes unplanned. Teachers intuitively call upon their knowledge base, their experience, and their proven techniques. Almost unconsciously, they reach back in their minds for all those things they know about children. Throughout the school day they apply that combination of knowledge and know-how.

> The creative genius of a teacher is in the ability to find ways to interact with each child according to that child's needs, to stretch an attention span, motivate a child to persist at a task, or provide opportunity to experiment with materials, actively and autonomously.
>
> (Honig, 1979)

## Managing the Classroom

A teacher spends a lot of time being a classroom manager. Being a successful manager is a little like being a successful juggler. Both require the ability to think about and react to more than three things at once. With a simple gesture, a significant look, or merely moving nearby, the teacher maintains the ongoing activity.

Anticipating a clash between Nathan and Julie, the teacher Miriam intervenes, redirects them, and moves away. At the same time she has kept a watchful eye on Bobby at the bathroom sink. Passing close to Francie, she touches the child's shoulder in brief acknowledgment, smiling down as Francie struggles with the doll's dress. Miguel and Lea run up to her, grab her by the skirt and hand, and pull her toward the science display. They need to ask her something about the snake...NOW! Jake, the handyman, has come into the classroom wanting to know exactly which of the climbers needs repair. Sarah, the parent volunteer, waves to her; it's time to check on the corn bread baking in the kitchen. Quickly, the teacher files a mental note of the names of the children who accompany Sarah to the kitchen. As she reaches for a copy of *Ranger Rick* (the one with the great snake pictures in it), she observes Angie and her father entering the room. They both look upset. Telling Miguel and Lea she will return, the teacher walks over to greet the latecomers. As she moves past Doug, the student teacher, she comments on how well his language game is going and suggests he continue for another five minutes. Glancing at the clock, she realizes it is almost cleanup time. Her assistant, Chuck, watches her. She looks his way, and a nonverbal signal passes between them. Without a word, they both understand that snacks will be a little late today. Angie's father begins to explain their delay as the teacher bends down to invite the child to come and look at the new snake cage with her.

In this setting, the teacher has a major role in supervising a number of people. Aides and volunteers, student teachers, and visitors add to the richness of a program. But it is the teacher who coordinates and supervises their various functions. From the description, it is clear that the teacher's role as a supervisor and manager includes being:

- caretaker for a safe environment
- observer of and listener to children
- on-the-spot teacher trainer for students, aides, and volunteers
- on-site supervisor for student teachers
- a liaison and communicator with parents

## Setting the Tone

Teachers, obviously, are at the center of activity. Directly or indirectly they control much of the action. Since teachers are responsible for what occurs in the classroom, they must have a finger on its pulse at all times. As part of the juggling act, the teacher takes that pulse while moving around the class or yard. But something else happens. Throughout the day, from the moment of arrival, the teacher puts into effect another vital element. The teacher *sets the tone,* creating an atmosphere in which teachers and children will work and play. The skill with which it is done can make the critical difference between a classroom that is alive and supportive and one that is chaotic or apathetic. Because personality has such impact in the early childhood setting, the teacher creates more than an environmental mood, does more than provide the setting and the learning activities.

The teacher establishes what will be the *emotional framework.* This is done with body movements, by the tone of voice, facial expressions or lack of them, and nonverbal as well as verbal gestures. The way the children respond reflects this tone.

This interaction between the atmosphere the teacher creates and the child's behavior sets the tone. Young children are very sensitive to adult moods and attitudes. The teacher who is upset or angry invites the children to react with their own tense brand of activity. A teacher who exudes calm and confidence, strength and support, will inspire a more relaxed, comfortable atmosphere in which children can learn and grow. If the teacher is punitive and harsh, the tone of the classroom will reflect that. On the other hand, if teachers act on their beliefs that children deserve respect and are intelligent, capable human beings, they will create an entirely different climate. And the children will respond in kind.

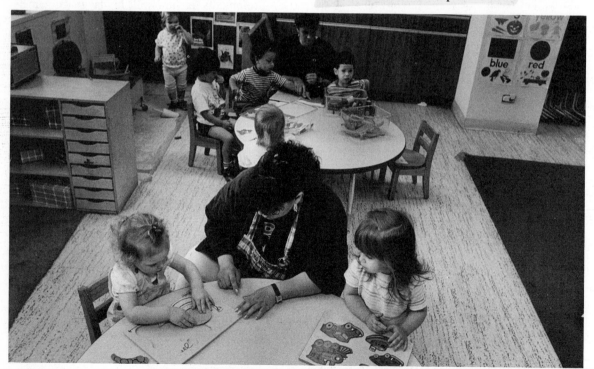

**FIGURE 5.3**   The teacher determines the quality of the child's school experience. She provides a supportive atmosphere in which children can learn. (Courtesy of Trinity Preschool, New York, N.Y.)

Normal behavior for the young child includes tantrums, crying, resistance, curiosity, impatience, emotional swings, noise, and self-centeredness. This is the time to achieve a sense of their own separate self. They need a place to work through the developmental stages that their needs and nature indicate. The atmosphere that a teacher creates is a key element in that process.

The way teachers handle fights, react to tears, the words they use, and the voices raised communicate a direct message to the child. The understanding, the soothing, the warmth, the acceptance, create a climate where children feel safe, secure, and guided. This requires teachers who respect childhood, the individuality of children, their growing patterns, their emerging feelings, and their special capacity to learn. The end result is that preschoolers will thrive in an atmosphere influenced by teachers who understand this time of tension and growth in their lives.

### Planning and Evaluating Curriculum

As teachers move through the school day interacting with children, managing the classroom, sensing the tone, they consciously or unconsciously evaluate what is happening:

- The relay race outdoors produced more tears than cheers; most of the children were interested in participating when the game started but drifted away. Why?
- The Cuisenaire rods were never touched today. How can we make this a more inviting activity?
- The toddlers are beginning to participate fully in the "Eensy Weensy Spider" fingerplay. What might they like to learn next?

The teacher notes where and how children played, the quality of their interactions, and possible "next steps" in curriculum. These notes are then discussed with other staff members at the end of the day or in weekly planning sessions.

Effective ways to develop curriculum planning are discussed in Chapter 11. It is important to note here, in discussing the role of the teacher, that the process has its roots in what the teacher sees happening in the classroom as children play and learn. Early childhood teachers use their observation skills, collect data as they work with children, and build curriculum around their knowledge of actual classroom practice and behavior.

## Outside the Classroom

But what of those after-hours tasks that are a part of any total teaching effort? There are quite a few of these responsibilities that may be taken for granted. This part of the job may not be as gratifying as working directly with children, yet teachers must understand why it is important.

A good classroom is often dependent on how teachers spend their time away from the children. Many of the tasks that give added strength and depth to a teacher's curriculum are those which, out of necessity, must be accomplished after hours. The two most obvious jobs that fall into this category are paperwork and meetings.

**FIGURE 5.4** Teachers' responsibilities extend beyond the classroom.

## Paperwork

Preschool teachers keep records on a variety of subjects; the type and kind will vary from school to school. The philosophy of the school, the number of children, the background of the teaching staff, and the purpose for the records will determine the amount the teachers will write. In schools that rely on government funding, record keeping is not optional. The children's progress, the teacher's performance, the program itself, must be evaluated on a regular basis. The data collected will be used to justify the continuation of the program; thus, the paperwork becomes critical to survival. Laboratory schools, teacher training centers, and other programs consider periodic developmental reports on the children as a natural part of teaching; they guide the teacher in more objective ways than casual observations.

While report writing and record keeping may be considered time-consuming, they are essential to any good early childhood program. The ultimate reason for collecting data is to give a more complete and up-to-date picture of each child. Once teachers understand the importance and value of ongoing records, they set about the task readily.

Children's progress reports demonstrate a school's commitment to good child development practices. Teachers see them as a means for parent education and information. Curriculum plans and learning activities sprout from such reports and records. It wasn't until such data was collected for entry into first grade that the kindergarten teachers realized most of the children were not sufficiently skilled with the scissors. They were able to plan curriculum experiences around this need and provide an opportunity for the classes to learn a necessary task.

Teachers also find that the social-emotional growth recorded periodically provides information from which insight and interpretation can develop. It may be just a brief note taken on the run, a thoughtful anecdote written at length after class, or a checklist of the child's favorite activities. All of these serve to give teachers a greater understanding of the role they play. If maintaining reports after school hours supports that role, they accept the job willingly.

## Meetings

Meetings are probably the most time-consuming of all out-of-class jobs. The teacher may need to communicate with the other people who are involved in the lives of the children, directly or indirectly. Parents, other teachers, baby-sitters, doctors, and social workers are some of the people with whom a teacher may want to confer. Teachers attend many different kinds of meetings. Figure 5.5 lists the most common.

## Other Responsibilities

Some of a teacher's after-hours activities are intended to fortify and vitalize the classroom. Therefore, teachers:

- Organize and collect materials for use in class. They might collect space shuttle books from the library, find out if the bagel factory will allow field trips, or cut 18 pumpkin shapes while watching television. Teachers are also responsible for maintaining an orderly classroom. They might add pictures to the bulletin board, obtain new books and records, or replenish curriculum materials.

- Purchase materials and equipment that cannot be ordered. They know that the kitchen needs new mixing bowls, the supply room is low on red construction paper, and someone has to pick up fabric for pillow covers.

- Make phone calls. This is a quick and efficient way of keeping in touch. Teachers may call parents to check on children who are sick or absent. For children with special needs, teachers may need to contact doctors, therapists, and other specialists.

- Attend professional conferences and workshops and visit and observe other school settings. This type of ongoing professional education helps teachers keep abreast of the field.

- Attend in-service training events or study for an advanced degree in an area related to early childhood education.

| *Staff Meetings* | *Professional Meetings* |
|---|---|
| Held usually once a week for individual teaching teams. Purpose is to plan curriculum, set goals, and discuss children's progress. Faculty meetings for all school personnel may be held less frequently. | Attendance at workshops, seminars, in-service training. Local, state, and national conferences are sponsored by the National Association for the Education of Young Children, Association for Childhood Education International, and Child Care Coordinating Council. |
| *Parent–Teacher Conferences* ✓ | *Student–Teacher Conferences* |
| May be offered on a scheduled basis or they may be called by either parents or teachers as needed. Each school defines its own policy as to the number and frequency of parent contacts. | In schools used as training sites, teachers arrange time with individual students assigned to their class. |
| *Parent Education Meetings* | *Home Visits* |
| Many schools offer evening programs for parents. Teacher attendance may or may not be required. | May or may not be optional. Some schools schedule them before opening day. Otherwise teachers must arrange them on their own time. |

**FIGURE 5.5**  Teachers attend many different types of meetings, which help them create better programs, learn more about children, and learn how to become better teachers.

These duties are a part of the job of teaching young children but many will be shared with other teachers on the team or at the school. Though time-consuming, these responsibilities add to the creativity and care that teachers express for their classes.

# THE TEACHER AS A PERSON

## Personal Qualities

A teacher's personality has influence and impact. When a teacher exhibits a sense of trust, security, and support, the children echo those feelings and behaviors. Children learn to trust by being trusted; they learn respect by being respected. Children learn to understand others by being understood themselves. They learn responsibility by being treated as responsible human beings. The personal qualities of their teachers should include traits that foster those learnings.

Good teachers should have dedication, compassion, insight, flexibility, patience, energy, and self-confidence. Teachers should also be happy people who can laugh and use their sense of humor wisely. Liking children is part of wanting to work with them; teachers then feel that the job they are doing is important. Teachers need to be fair-minded, showing concern for all, regardless of color or creed. Physical and mental well-being are important, as is a demonstrated sense of responsibility and reliability. Teachers who can be both warm and loving, yet firm when expressing disapproval, have good teaching qualities.

Today, the well-rounded teacher, while maintaining a professional commitment, has other interests as well. Good teachers have an involvement with the world outside the walls of the child care center. They want to help children understand some of the real-life issues and concerns. They know that their interest in the world at large transmits itself to children.

Quality teachers personalize teaching, integrating their individuality into their work in appropriate ways. By exposing the human qualities they possess, teachers strengthen the bond between themselves and the children.

This basic description is a framework, a checklist of personal attributes, a place to begin to look at the human side of teaching. Men and women who are able to nurture and comfort children treat them as real persons and value them as children. Expressing this takes practice so that teachers do not intrude on children's well-being. Teachers do not have to sentimentalize childhood or tolerate misbehavior because it is "cute." Children deserve teachers who understand their nature and respect the limits of behavior.

> . . . The best teachers are the ones who are struggling to become more than they are, on any given day, and who demonstrate to their students that this quest to learn and to grow, to accept failure and go on to new challenges, is what life is all about.
>
> (LeShan, 1985)

**FIGURE 5.6** A positive self-concept and a willingness to be open to new experiences are hallmarks of a good teacher of young children. (Courtesy of Stephanie Barry Agnew.)

## Self-Awareness

To be the best teacher possible, understanding and accepting oneself is vital. *Self-awareness* will make a difference in the way teachers relate to children. Each teacher must ask, "Who and what and why am I? And how does knowing this bring some meaning into my life? How does it affect my life as a teacher?"

Teachers may also begin to realize something about themselves. They know how and why children learn as they do, but what do they know about themselves as learners? How do teachers communicate an authentic appreciation of learning unless they have a sense of it in their own lives? Teachers might well ask themselves: "Do I see myself as a learner? Where does my learning take place? How? What happens to me when something is hard or when I make a mistake? Do I learn from other teachers? Do I learn from children?" Teachers' recognition of themselves as learning, growing persons gives an added degree of sincerity to teaching.

Asking—and then answering—these questions helps teachers gain insights into their own behavior as adults alone and as adults who work with children. In perceiving themselves as learners, for instance, they might see a similarity between their own learning style and that of some of the children in the class. Pausing to look at their own behavior when faced with a difficult task or in handling a mistake helps teachers remember what children experience each day. Opening themselves up to the possibility of learning from students stretches teachers' capacity to grow into relationships with children based on mutual respect and trust. Opening themselves to learning from other teachers creates a foundation for mutual support, collegiality, professional mind-stretching, and deepening of friendships. The first step is self-awareness; the second step is self-acceptance. Adults who work with young children weave these insights into what they are learning about children. They also adopt these insights into their relationships with parents and other staff members. When teachers take the time to look at their own style of behavior and how it affects others, they place themselves on a par with children as learning, growing people.

Self-knowledge—examining values and personal qualities—takes courage and a willingness to risk oneself. Children, other teachers, and parents will respond. Accepting oneself is where to begin in accepting children.

## Attitudes and Biases

Facing *prejudices* about children may be one of the most difficult things for a beginning teacher. Personal histories are filled with biases. Most people are not familiar with ethnic cultures other than their own and therefore may be uncomfortable with persons who are different. They have been raised to know what is "good" behavior (at least what their family thinks is such) and what is "naughty." Teachers have strong opinions, born of their own experiences, as to how parents should treat their children. Children who are messy, who have odors, whose clothes are too big or too small, bother some teachers. Some of these biases can be resolved. Home visits and parent demonstrations of ethnic, religious, and cultural observances, can awaken an appreciation for the diversity of humankind. Sometimes teachers may be forced into further soul searching and reflection before they can untangle their anxiety and attitudes. Our feelings show in our contacts with children, and we do not want those feelings to damage their self-acceptance or self-appreciation. The question is not one of liking or disliking any child, it is one of teacher understanding and acceptance. By achieving that sense of acceptance, teachers are better able to accept all the children with whom they work, regardless of their "likeability."

## Teacher Burnout

Job *burnout* often results when a person is faced with a demanding work load, uncertain or inadequate rewards, and other pressures that damage work effectiveness. At its most extreme, teacher burnout can drive a good professional out of the field altogether. In other cases, skilled teachers become lackadaisical workers. Rather than searching for excellence and innovative methods or curriculum, they become disgruntled and disillusioned. The teacher approaching burnout has little to give except criticism and low morale. Teacher burnout is an occupational hazard of substantial proportions.

Our job is one of human service, of caring for people dependent upon us. It is inherent in the job that child care workers and teachers are vulnerable to the stress of this daily demand. Teachers do not have the luxury of putting an irate parent or upset child "on hold." And too few have the time or money for regular vacations and sabbaticals to recharge professional and personal batteries.

Furthermore, when a teacher begins to deteriorate from job stress and overwork, that individual is not the only one affected. Children, fellow workers, families are all touched when a skilled and dedicated teacher feels powerless and discouraged.

> If burnout in the early childhood setting affected only individuals in isolation, it might be far less devastating. But it can multiply like a cancer, affecting the morale of others on the staff and ultimately their collective capacity to give to and nurture young children. The statistics are painfully obvious: staff turnover averages 15 to 30 percent in child care centers, well above other professions. Equally significant, many potential workers are taking a serious second look at child care jobs and passing them up for more lucrative and less stressful positions.
>
> (Jorde, 1982)

It is up to all of us as early childhood professionals to work together to give each other support— both moral and financial. Our profession is at once difficult and rewarding. We have the capacity to develop early warning signals of stress and to plan strategies at our work sites to deal effectively with such times. If administrators and teachers regularly communicate, problems that add to burnout will be brought to attention. If the school offers opportunities for job advancement as well as varied kinds of professional involvement, teachers are likely to find their jobs stimulating rather than overly stressful.

# BECOMING A TEACHER

The heart of teaching is, of course, what happens when you begin to work in a classroom every day. The teaching role is not restricted to working with children, though. Numerous adults must be met, tolerated, worked with, and included in the total teaching picture. Some of these people may be:

- other professional teachers, aides, and student teachers

- volunteers

- program directors and administrators

- school support personnel: clerical and janitorial staffs, food service workers, bus drivers

- parents

- consultants and specialists

The majority of these interactions will be with other teachers, and these relationships are among the most important a teacher can have.

The beginning teacher may join a team of teachers or may teach in a small class alone. This will depend on many factors, including the age level of the children, licensing or accrediting requirements, the size of the classroom, and the school's philosophy and practices. With infant programs, for instance, there is a higher ratio of adults per child (NAEYC suggests as optimal a ratio of 1 to 4), so it is more likely there will be several teachers in one classroom. Together they will shape, direct, and participate in that program as a team of teachers. The team approach is common in many nursery schools and child care centers where larger groups of children attend. Kindergarten, first, and second grade teachers generally teach alone in self-contained classrooms, sometimes with an aide. In extended day, after-school programs, high school and college students may make up the rest of the team.

Most teams of teachers are comprised of people with varying skills, experience, and training. A typical group will have a lead or head teacher—someone who is trained in child development or early childhood education. Assistants with less experience and training add support. Student teachers, interns, and volunteers may round out the group. A resource teacher—someone who specializes in art, music, or physical development, for instance—may also be available on a part-time basis.

Many state regulations mandate a minimum number of adults in the early childhood setting, and this minimum varies with the ages of the children. The prescribed ratio of adult to children changes as the children mature and become able to function in more independent ways.

There are many reasons why teaching in teams is such an integral part of so many early childhood programs. The advantages are numerous:

**Adult Role Models.** A team of teachers provides a wide range of adult models for children. Teachers who are male, female, young, middle-aged, older, or of varying ethnic backgrounds bring to the teaching experience equally diverse attitudes, approaches to children, interests, skills, and knowledge to share. In the team-teaching setting, teachers have an opportunity to model good social relationships for children in the way they treat each other. Children learn how to accept differences in people as they watch adults interact with others on the team.

**Support for Children.** Team teaching is supportive for children. The absence of one teacher is not as disruptive when the children can count on other familiar faces. Children learn to trust the teaching environment, since someone they know is always there. In this way, they are introduced to change in a less abrupt manner.

**Support for Teachers.** Team members can share problems with each other and be understood. Learning to work together on a team promotes admiration and respect for one another. This can be a great teaching tool: adults working cohesively, communicating with one another, and being friends.

**Workload Reduction.** Teams lighten the workload. There are more people available to do the paperwork

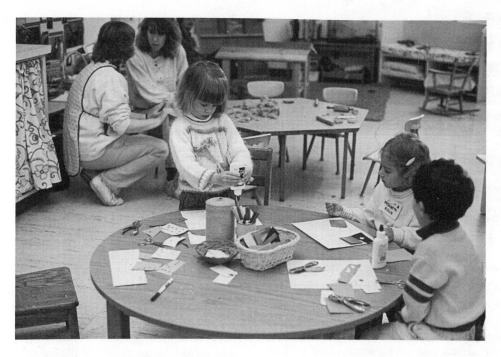

**FIGURE 5.7** Members of a teaching team need frequent communication with one another. (Courtesy of Stephanie Barry Agnew.)

and record keeping, to maintain the room and yard, and to help clean up and set up. There is a sharing of the teaching tasks, whether it is curriculum planning, parent conferencing, or teaching and caring for the children.

**Program Enrichment.** Team teaching adds richness to the program. A team of teachers can share talents and resources. All team members can teach to their strengths, and can work on weaknesses with the support of the team. Clara may be superb with small groups of children but ineffective at music. Jon loves music, plays a guitar, and dances with the children. These two teachers can learn from each other.

Most of the disadvantages of team teaching stem from communication problems among team members. The following ten guidelines to successful teaching are particularly useful for team situations. Teachers new to the team teaching process will want to discuss them with other team members.

Good teachers are "complicated human beings

with strengths and weaknesses, talents and limitations, good days and bad days" (LeShan, 1985). They work at becoming good teachers by developing skills in interpersonal relationships, primarily with other adults: teachers, administrators, and parents. Communication problems and conflicts arise in every teaching situation. The following guidelines will help teachers promote good working relationships. These guidelines focus on working with others in the school setting; parent-teacher relationships are discussed in Chapter 8.

## Ten Essentials of Successful Teaching

Ten essential attributes of successful teaching are:

**1.** open and frequent communication

**2.** self-awareness

3. a satisfying role

4. mutual respect and acceptance

5. team spirit and empathy

6. flexibility

7. a willingness to share the spotlight

8. clearly defined roles

9. professionalism

10. evaluation

Each of these attributes is discussed in the following paragraphs.

## Open and Frequent Communication

The ability and opportunity to communicate thoughts, concerns, and feelings to others are perhaps the most important factors in promoting good inter-personal relationships. Communication takes many forms: verbal and nonverbal, written and spoken, even body language.

Teachers must continually seek out opportunities for formal and informal communication with others on the staff. Seeking such opportunities may mean taking advantage of the faculty lounge during lunch hour or arriving five minutes early to catch someone before children arrive. For those who work on teaching teams, set-up and clean-up times can be used to discuss issues, modify strategies, and resolve misunderstandings. The three basic reasons for developing successful communication links with others on the teaching staff are to share information, to contribute new ideas, and to solve problems.

In a teaching situation, important information centers on activities in the classroom and the children themselves. Information about children and their families is shared, just as child development strategies are. For example: "Sheila's grandmother died yesterday, so she and her family may need some extra support and attention for a while."

New ideas keep teachers challenged. Teachers enjoy sharing a recent article from *Young Children,* a new discipline strategy, or a successful art activity.

New ideas keep teaching alive and fresh. For example: "Tom developed a new format for our parent-teacher conferences that works very well. You might want to try it."

Every organization and every classroom will encounter problems at some time. Differences in opinion, approach, personality, and style among adults and children are inevitable. Good teachers recognize and accept such problems and conflicts as a part of their challenge to teach, and they work with others to solve them. For example: Meg, the teacher's aide who has been with the preschool for a year, constantly belittles the student teacher's efforts to conduct group time and refuses to do her share when they are assigned to the same activity. The head teacher confronts Meg privately about her attitudes and performance, stating her concern about Meg's behavior. She listens carefully to Meg's explanation and grievances. As they continue to talk, the head teacher acknowledges Meg's own hurt feelings and suggests they might look at some ways to support and encourage the efforts of the beginning teacher. Meg appreciates being included and offers to work with the student teacher on her group-time leadership, an area in which Meg is highly skilled.

## Self-Awareness

Beginning teachers may feel inadequate at first in their relationships with others on the staff. This feeling has a lot to do with their self-perceptions. Once teachers know and accept themselves, they can apply their new self-awareness to their relationships with fellow workers.

To promote growth through self-knowledge, teachers might ask themselves: What are my strengths and weaknesses, and how do they complement or conflict with others in my place of work? As part of a staff, do I prefer to follow or to lead, to plan programs or to carry out plans developed by a coworker? In what teaching situations do I feel uncomfortable, and why? What have I done lately to learn more about myself?

Again, asking and then answering these questions helps teachers develop a greater capacity for

**FIGURE 5.8**   As a teacher, how do I make a difference in this child's life? What special talents do I have that contribute to this group of children? What am I learning about myself as a teacher? What does it take to "become" a teacher? (Courtesy of Stride Rite Children's Centers, Cambridge, Mass.)

self-understanding, or self-awareness. Our personalities are made up of a vision of who we are and who we can be. Both these visions powerfully affect our classroom behavior. The vision of what one can be is especially pertinent to the teaching relationship.

Some aspects of self-awareness help teachers relate to one another in different ways. Once Wanda assesses herself as a follower, she might begin to observe those who lead and the qualities that make them successful leaders. She might also ask them how they go about planning their program or developing relationships. Ultimately, she might risk

taking on some leadership herself after watching others and consulting with them about ways to take the initial steps. If a teacher acknowledges that working with parents or with difficult children makes for uncomfortable feelings, then that teacher can approach another person and ask for help in learning to handle such situations. Self-awareness helps us learn; teachers use information about themselves to help themselves become better teachers, better parents, better communicators, better citizens.

### A Satisfying Role

Among a group of people working together in a school setting, each person must have a satisfying role to play. That means each person must be appreciated for the special something he or she brings to the group. Beginning teachers must consider: Is there a place in my school (or on my team) that is uniquely mine? How can my special talents and experiences contribute to the success of this program? One way teachers find their own unique role is to identify the roles of other teachers: "I see you are the one who always makes sure we maintain the classroom pets in good health." Or, "Geraldo seems to be the champion of the difficult child. He has such insights into working with hard-to-handle children." Modeling this technique for other teachers is a good way to learn about the whole team as well as one teacher's unique contribution. At staff meetings, teachers could be asked to name their own particular strength. Alternatively, each staff member may be asked to identify the strength of one other person on the team. Just as teachers tell children they have qualities and capabilities that set them apart, teachers need to tell one another.

### Mutual Respect and Acceptance

All members of a school or center staff have an obligation to learn about the people with whom they work—to know their diverse personalities, experiences, strengths and weaknesses, stages of professional development, educational philosophies, and social and cultural values. Appreciating and accepting the individuality of other team members is as important to the success of the program as is working directly with children. This knowledge is also the basis for resolving differences. The climate of trust and the nonthreatening atmosphere gained through mutual respect allow each staff member to contribute openly and innovatively to the program.

In the interest of developing a respect for and acceptance of the uniqueness of each staff member, teachers should ask themselves: What do I have in common with my coworkers, and what unique qualities do they bring to this school at this time? What do I expect from my coworkers: emotional support? intellectual stimulation? candid feedback?

### Team Spirit and Empathy

A sense of being a team happens in a school setting not by accident, but by conscious effort. Every member of the staff must be committed not only to working together day by day but also to the long-term goals of the early childhood program. This commitment means being empathetic to the moods, feelings, and needs of coworkers, whether by sharing the workload, being tactful in disagreements, or being positive in suggesting change.

To develop empathetic and supportive relationships with fellow staff members, teachers should ask themselves: How can I relate to and be supportive of my coworkers? Have I ever been in their shoes? What did I feel like when I lost control of the children in my activity center? What strategy worked for me when I had to deal with Kim's destructive behavior? What can I do to promote and sustain high morale among my coworkers?

### Flexibility

Just as it is important to change with and adapt to the varying needs of children, so is it crucial to respond to the needs of other staff members with a give-and-take approach. Flexibility involves a willingness to offer and accept negotiation and compromise in order to preserve the effectiveness of the whole staff's effort. Beginning teachers should ask themselves: Do I demonstrate a willingness to change with the changing needs of my coworkers, or do I adhere rigidly to preset plans or attitudes? Am I open to new ideas proposed by others? Am I sufficiently prepared to handle changes within the classroom setting? How can I get better at this?

All teachers should periodically assess themselves with a quick flexibility test. People tend to get rigid and set in their teaching habits. For example: the last time you were asked to alter your daily schedule or to postpone a field trip, did you: Say "no" immediately? Give it serious consideration overnight? Use it as a way to make trade-offs ("I'll do it if you take kitchen duty for me next week")? Say "yes" immediately? Discuss it with the rest of the staff first and gain consensus? A quick assessment like this indicates how flexible or inflexible you are.

The next step is to look at what you do when you have a new idea to propose. How do you present it? Negotiate it? Was it accepted or denied? What strategies work well?

Finally, you might want to look at how you prepare children for changes. How did you make children comfortable with the new staff member? With the new room arrangement? With a change in the daily routines? What strategies work well with children, and how are they adaptable to working with adults? Teachers who expect children to be flexible and open to change must model that quality for them.

### A Willingness to Share the Spotlight

Unless held in check, tension among staff members can arise from a sense of competition, which may appear in subtle ways. We must be willing to admit that other teachers are just as dedicated to children and deserving of their affections as we are. Especially crucial when working on a teaching team is a willingness not only to share the credit for progress, but also to share the responsibility for resolving problems when they arise. We should ask ourselves: How do I feel when another teacher is praised by a parent or preferred by a child? Am I quick to acknowledge my coworkers' achievements?

### Clearly Defined Roles

An understanding of the role a teacher is expected to play in each particular setting is essential for the smooth functioning of that early childhood program and for the teacher's own sense of well-being. A checklist or job description may be helpful in reinforcing the appropriateness of the actions taken or the responsibilities assumed by a given teacher. In team teaching situations, besides understanding one's own role, one needs to know what others' jobs entail. Clearly defined teacher roles also serve as a guard against legal and ethical problems. Teachers should ask themselves: Do I know the extent of the responsibilities for this particular teaching assignment? If working on a team, do I fulfill my responsibilities as a team member, or do I allow others to take over some of my least-liked responsibilities?

## Professionalism

Professional attitudes and behavior are a critical part of the teaching effort. Personal grievances must be kept out of the classroom and the teachers' lounge. Teachers should be encouraged to relate to one another as peers, colleagues, and professionals, whatever the level of their development. There is no place in the early childhood setting for petty gossip, ill will, or exclusive cliques.

Many schools have established appropriate channels through which individual problems can be resolved. These channels are described in a series of personnel policies and generally require that individuals try to work out their differences on a one-to-one basis. If that is not possible, the head teacher or center director, possibly with a member of the personnel committee of the center's board, acts as a mediator. If a member of the staff does not feel satisfied with the results, the personnel policies usually spell out some kind of grievance procedure to follow next. This ensures each member of the staff a hearing at the highest level and a resolution to the situation. Obviously, the most productive route is for the two people involved to discuss problems when they first occur.

Taking personal differences to someone who can help solve them usually means going directly to the person in question, not complaining about that individual in the kitchen or parking lot. Everyone on the staff can model professional behavior for the others. Teachers should ask themselves: Do I behave in a professional manner? Can I keep confidences? Do I confront those with whom I have differences in an attempt to work them out?

### Evaluation

No teacher can become truly successful unless provisions are made for ongoing evaluation. Being judged by one's peers is part of the privilege in claiming membership in the teaching profession. Evaluations should provide a teacher with a clear picture that confirms strengths and pinpoints potential areas for growth. Assessment of another's performance should be communicated in an affirming, not a criticizing, manner. (Evaluation of programs and people is discussed more thoroughly in Chapter 10.) Teachers should ask themselves: When in the position of assessing others, do I evaluate them fairly and share my observations with them in a supportive way? Do I accept evaluation as an essential part of teaching? Am I responsive to the thoughts and opinions of others?

## THE TEACHER AS A PROFESSIONAL

## Attitudes and Background

There is a body of knowledge, an educational foundation, that is assumed of anyone entering the early childhood profession. There are also some basic teaching skills that are necessary. These include methods and techniques appropriate for teaching the very young child. Yet there is more if one is to be called a true *professional*.

Being a member of the teaching profession goes beyond an accumulation of methods, coursework, and teaching experiences. Being a professional teacher suggests an attitude about teaching. It is not simply an eight-hour-a-day job, or an occupation chosen lightly. Teachers are called to the profession when they believe they can indeed make a difference in the lives of the children. While that may at first

**FIGURE 5.9** Professional attitudes and behavior are crucial. Teachers and administrators can relate to one another as colleagues and coworkers.

sound *altruistic,* it reflects a dedication to teaching that exceeds the desire for a job or a steady paycheck.

There are professional expectations, starting with having a common background with others in the field. This includes studying child development and human behavior, family relations, parent education and development, and curriculum planning. Some practical teaching experience under the guidance of a master teacher is assumed, as is a familiarity with observation and recording techniques. This foundation of knowledge and experience provides the framework for professional development. Teachers gradually acquire further skills on the job. They learn to juggle three or four interactions with children at once and develop the skill of stopping an argument by a mere look or a quick gesture. Thus, the process of becoming a professional teacher is an orderly progression along a continuum of development.

This progression of teaching skills has been described by Lilian Katz (1977) as consisting of four distinct stages of teacher development. See Appendix A for a description and definition of each stage.

# Professional Development

## Developing a Professional Code of Ethics

As teachers mature, they turn their attention to issues and concerns outside themselves. Many of these issues, whether they are called so or not, are related to ethical conflicts and moral principles. Teachers are, after all, human beings, and that entails genuine conflict about behavior. Doing what is right becomes difficult at times; knowing what is right may be elusive. Even identifying what is right—an ethical conflict—may not be obvious.

Every day, situations arise with parents, other teachers, and administrators that require teachers to make some hard choices. Some cases are clearly ethical dilemmas: suspected child abuse by a parent or teacher, talking about children and their families outside of school, or the firing of a staff member without due cause. Others, some of which are common occurrences, may not seem as obvious. Some everyday examples are:

**When Parents:**

- Ask you to advance their child into the next higher reading group against your advice

- Urge you to slap their child to control disruptive behavior

- Attempt to gossip with you about another staff member

**When Another Teacher:**

- Suggests a private staff meeting outside of school with a select group of teachers

- Refuses to take a turn cleaning out the animal cages

- Regularly is absent from staff meetings

- Disagrees with the school's educational philosophy and continues to teach in ways that differ from the approved methods in that setting

- Goes to the school administrator with a complaint about a staff team member

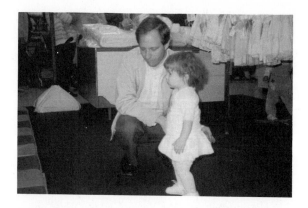

**FIGURE 5.10** Ethical questions arise daily. This father is encouraging his daughter to hit back at any child that hits her. What do you say to him? How do you handle this situation?

**When the Administrator:**

• Insists on adding one more child to an already overenrolled class

• Makes personnel decisions based on friendship, not performance

• Backs a parent who complains about a teacher without hearing the teacher's side of the story.

These are ethical problems that occur daily in any teacher's life. They are not problems of an abstract or impersonal nature. Just what are ethics? Essentially, they are the moral guidelines by which we govern our own behavior and that of society. "Ethics is nothing more than systematic critical reflection about our obligations," says philosopher Kenneth Kipnis (1987).

We can strictly define ethics as "the system or code of morals of a particular philosopher, religion, group, or profession." This definition suggests that a personal code of ethics can be supported by a professional code of ethics. A code of ethics is a set of statements that helps us deal with the temptations inherent in our occupations. It helps us act in terms of what is right rather than what is expedient (Katz and Ward, 1978).

Why might the early childhood profession need such a code? A primary reason is that the choices

teachers make should be based not simply on personal values and preferences but "on values, judgments, and ethical commitments shared by the professional society or association of which they are a member" (Katz and Ward, 1978).

A code of ethics provides collective wisdom and advice from a broad base in the profession. It states the principles by which each individual can measure and govern professional behavior. It says that a group or association has recognized the moral dimensions of its work. It provides teachers with a known, defined core of professional values—those basic commitments that any early childhood educator should consider inviolate. This protects teachers and administrators from having to make hard ethical decisions on the spur of the moment, possibly on the basis of personal bias. An established professional code supports the teacher's choice by saying, "It isn't that *I* won't act this way: *No early childhood educator* should act this way" (Kipnis, 1987).

How does a group go about creating an ethical code for itself? The National Association for the Education of Young Children is actively engaged in this process with its membership of over 50,000 early childhood professionals. A Commission on Professional Ethics has been established. Surveys in the journal *Young Children* have identified some of the ethical issues of most concern to those in the field of early childhood education: (1) discussing a child or family in a nonprofessional setting, (2) implementing policies that are not good for children because the program requires them, (3) letting children do an activity that may not be worthwhile or appropriate, (4) knowing that a program is in violation of state regulations, and (5) dealing with conflicting requests from divorced or separated parents (Feeny and Sisko, 1986).

A beginning list of basic core values has emerged from this work. These are "the purposes that each professional should have in common with others" (Kipnis, 1987), and they form the basis of agreement for the profession. Examples of such core values include:

• Recognition of each individual as a unique human being

- Appreciation of the special vulnerability of children and their need for safe and healthy environments

- The critical need to establish and maintain communication with families

- Recognition by childhood professionals that the term "family" can be represented in many forms

- Respect for confidentiality and the right of the child and family to privacy

- Use of developmentally appropriate instructional techniques for children

- Support for the right of all children, regardless of income or other circumstances, to have access to quality early childhood programs

(Feeney, 1987; Feeney, 1988; Kipnis, 1987)

Out of this work, the NAEYC hopes to develop guidelines for ethical behavior in early childhood education, an important contribution to the ongoing life of teachers, children, and parents everywhere.

Teachers may find it helpful to discuss their ethical concerns with colleagues. Some schools provide in-service programs for the staff where these issues are raised. Other schools have a code of ethics for their employees to follow.

### *Continuing Education*

Creative and stimulating classes are the product of teachers who continue to learn more about how to teach. After the initial stage of teaching, many teachers begin to seek new challenges and new ways to improve the quality of their teaching. Usually, this leads to some form of *continuing education,* such as participation in workshops, courses, or seminars. If time to pursue continuing education is not built into a teacher's schedule, there may be other options:

- In-service training programs may be brought into the school setting. Resource people can be invited to lead the staff in discussions about children's behavior, parent relationships, assessment charts, or science curriculum.

- Various members of the teaching staff can develop a program of their own, offering their expertise to fellow faculty at an in-service meeting.

- A computer specialist, art resource teacher, or movement expert can be invited to visit the classrooms, instructing children and providing staff with some useful ideas and plans.

- A family therapist can be invited to speak at a staff meeting about strategies for supporting families in crisis.

- A library for teachers, stocked with professional books, journals (such as *Young Children*), and newspapers (such as *Education Week*) can provide a teacher with the means to keep up with current trends and practices and to improve teaching skills in the classroom.

- Parents who are professionals in a variety of fields can be utilized whenever possible to enrich the knowledge and skills of the staff.

## Setting Professional Goals

As teachers raise their sights beyond "How will I survive?" to "Where am I going?", they begin to set goals for themselves and their teaching career. They develop both long- and short-term objectives for themselves, establishing a framework for professional growth.

The goals that are set will vary with individual teachers. For Jim, this could mean developing a brand new curriculum for his class of two-year-olds. Susan might choose to work toward having greater parent support in her classroom. Thea and Frank might decide to develop a workshop on sensorimotor skills. Stephanie wonders about using her skills with children and computers to go into business for herself. Cassie would like to create a calendar of parent meetings and events for the school year. Whether in the area of children's programs, administration, staff relations, or their own professional development, teachers can learn, grow, and change. (See Chapter 10 for evaluation and goal-setting techniques.)

## Professional Affiliations

Teachers who are beginning to perceive themselves as professionals may choose to join one of the professional organizations related to the early childhood field. One of the largest, the National Association for the Education of Young Children (NAEYC), has local and state affiliate groups through which one can become a member. NAEYC offers a range of services to its members, including conferences and publications such as the journal, *Young Children*. The Association for Childhood Education International (ACEI) has a similar function, whereas the Society for Research in Child Development (SRCD) focuses on child psychology, research, and development.

## THE STUDENT TEACHER

Beginning teachers of young children cannot expect to successfully blend all of the many facets of a teacher—personal, team, and professional identity —at once. Certainly, teaching young children carries with it the obligation to understand and accept the many roles and responsibilities associated with the title of "teacher." However, beginning teachers must also be committed to the time and energy needed to *become* that total teacher.

Student teaching can be a great deal of fun as well as a unique learning experience. Textbook theories come alive as children naturally demonstrate child development concepts. Student teachers expect to learn about individual child growth and development; many are surprised to discover that they also learn how children function in groups and with adults. For students in a teacher training program, *practice teaching* may be the first hands-on opportunity to work directly with children.

Planning and executing activities that fit the needs and abilities of the child are another part of the student teacher's role. They provide an opportunity to test curriculum ideas, to see what happens when child meets materials. Working with an experienced teacher who models highly polished skills is an

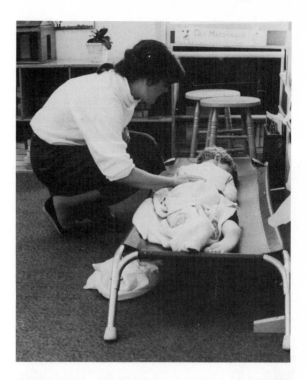

**FIGURE 5.11** The student teacher has many responsibilities.

important part of the experience. The student becomes part of a faculty for a short period of time. Identification with a number of professionals can help the student find a teaching identity, and working as part of a team is supportive to the beginning teacher.

Yet we know that student teaching is not always fun. It is a time for intensive self-searching and self-revelations. Many students' own school experiences loom before them and intimidate their confidence. Planning lessons takes long hours. Students may still have doubts about being a teacher at all. It is uncomfortable to feel judged and criticized by others. This is a time of anxiety for most beginning teachers. But remember, even the poised, confident, and always-does-the-right-thing master teacher was once a beginning teacher.

# Orientation to the Role of Student Teacher

Beginnings for student teachers are just as important as they are for young children. A child's first days of school are planned very carefully: Attempts are made to ease the separation process for parents and child, new children are shown where to put their belongings, daily schedules are explained, the locations of the bathroom and drinking fountain are pointed out, and the basic rules of the child care center are outlined.

Likewise, there are some strategies for easing the transition from student to student teacher. The key to making the most of an initial teaching experience is to anticipate some of the common pitfalls and develop a plan for dealing with them if they arise.

## *Before School Starts*

The following guidelines will help to make the first days of your student teaching assignment a satisfying and positive experience:

- Contact the teacher before the first day of school. Try to meet together before school begins. Find out how to get there, where to park, and where to put your materials. Find out where the class meets and at what time. Be sure to ask at what time to arrive and when to leave. Are there any meetings to attend? If so, when and where are they held? What is the age group, the size, and the makeup of the children in the class? Are there special children and what are their needs? Get a copy of the daily schedule.

- On the first day you visit, introduce yourself to the administrative and auxiliary staff of the school. Be sure to learn their names, for they can help you in many ways.

- Find out what is expected during the first few days. Will you observe or actively participate? Will you be assigned to follow another teacher for a day or so? Ask these questions to learn the general format of the school day and to get a feeling for the student participant's role. Then relax and concentrate on the children.

**FIGURE 5.12** The student teacher comes to class prepared to participate fully. He learns to be with children in meaningful ways without becoming the focus of their attention.

- Visit the room to which you will be assigned to become acquainted with its layout. Tour the yard as well. Continue to look around the rest of the school if there is time. The janitor's room, the kitchen, nurse's office, and storeroom are all important places to identify.

- Share with the teacher any special skills or talents you may have, such as playing the harp or knowing how to use sign language. The teacher can help utilize these skills in new ways with young children. Sharing something of importance with young children is one way to establish closer relationships and adds confidence that will carry over into other areas of teaching. Let the teacher know about any other experiences with children: babysitting, camp counseling, or eight younger brothers and sisters. Be sure to let the teacher know of any course requirements you must meet by this experience.

- At some point in this initial meeting, the teacher will probably ask about goals and expectations for the student teaching experience. What would you like to get out of the time you spend in this classroom? It may be just a desire to work with children or a more definite goal to work with children for a specific reason. There may be short-term goals: to be at ease in a classroom setting. Some may be long term and specific: do a cooking activity in three weeks or lead a group time by the end of the semester. By establishing some common goals, the teacher will be able to guide a course so that those goals will be realized.

- Evaluation is an important part of the goal-setting process. Suggestions, constructive criticism, and feedback can be looked at more objectively when goals are clear. Students need to know how their work is affecting the classroom, the children, and the other teachers. Set a time together for receiving feedback; this may be each day after class or only once a week. At this time, your needs, questions, and reactions can be addressed by the teacher. You will also learn whether you have met the expectations of the teacher, the school, and the program.

# Guidelines for Beginning

After the first few sessions, things will begin to go more smoothly. The routine will become second nature. Most of the children's names will be familiar, and the student teacher will assume a place in this group of children and adults. Background information from the teacher and class participation help ease the adjustment. Once this level of comfort is reached, some of the more challenging aspects of working with young children can be addressed. The following suggestions will help ease the first week's anxieties.

## *Student Behavior*

**Dress Appropriately.** Be sure to dress for the job and the season. A teacher who is worried about getting paint or clay on clothes will not be relaxed with the children. Dress warmly for the outdoors in cold weather. Wear sturdy, waterproof shoes when it is wet. Summer clothing should be equally practical. Smocks or aprons are quite common when supervising some of the messier activities.

**Be Prompt.** Arrive at school on schedule. Five or ten minutes late can make the difference between a well-organized day and one that never quite makes it. Don't spend the day trying to catch up. It is the student's responsibility to inform the teacher if he or she will be absent. As a member of a teaching team, a student's presence is very important. The team needs to know in advance if the student will be absent in order to make adjustments. Get the master teacher's home phone number as well as the school office number.

**Know Where Things Are.** Find out where equipment and materials are stored—the glue, construction paper, art supplies. Look at what scrounge materials are available, where the key to the rabbit cage is kept, and where the laundry room is located.

**Use Professional Ethics.** Children and parents are not to be discussed outside of the school setting. Their privacy is to be protected at all times. The way Carlos described the guinea pig or Andrea's original songs make amusing stories, but be sure to change the children's names to protect their privacy.

## *Interacting with Children*

**Move in Slowly.** When interacting with children, move in slowly. Make a practice of sitting back and watching to see what children are doing before getting involved.

**Maintain Your Role as Teacher.** Do not play games with the children or entertain them. When that happens, it becomes an adult-centered activity instead of a child-centered one. Help the children keep their attention focused on the game they are playing, the other children, or on the materials they are using. It is easy to fall into the trap of becoming the center of their interest. One of the lessons student teachers learn is how to be with children in interesting and meaningful ways, yet not be the focus of their attention.

**Give Children Time.** Allow plenty of time for children to do for themselves. Let them help as much

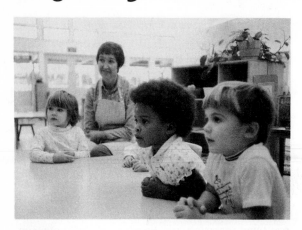

**FIGURE 5.13** How do you help children wait for snacks? Can you think of something interesting for them to watch? A good teacher models interest and attention; children quickly imitate.

as possible, whether it is putting away the music instruments or pulling on their snow pants. Give them time to do as much as they can possibly do without help. Children will vary; some will need five minutes to struggle into their boots, and others will have coats on and zippered in less than one.

**Help Children Wait.** It is almost impossible for children to wait, but there are some ways to help them when it becomes necessary. Make sure that the next activity is ready to go. Have some fingerplays or songs ready if children get restless while waiting. If possible, have an area of the schoolroom available for quiet reading for those who finish first.

**Be Alert to the Whole Group.** Know where the children and other teachers are and what they are doing, even when they are not in the immediate area. Develop this skill by consciously thinking about where all the children are and what is happening in the rest of the room or yard. This takes practice but it is never too soon to start. Try to anticipate situations and to help children and teachers before being asked.

**Never Leave Children Unsupervised.** Notify the teacher in charge if you must leave the area, and work

out an arrangement that will provide full coverage of all the activities.

**Maintain the Environment.** Keep the room and yard in order as the day moves along. Involve children in the clean-up process. Model a sense of social concern with a few simple acts. Wipe finger paint off the front of the sink before another child comes along. Pick up the sand toys, and put them on the shelf in an attractive arrangement for the next class. These thoughtful deeds show children another aspect of living in a group and caring about one another. Remember, however, the first priority is to be with children.

**Use Your Voice and Tone Effectively.** Go over to a child, bend down, and speak quietly, but distinctly. Children are more likely to listen to an adult who is close and low than to one that shouts from across a room. Learn to use verbalizations to get children to cooperate. Listen to other teachers in the room. See what works for them.

**Never Shove or Use Force.** Avoid picking up children to get them where they are supposed to go. Such acts show great disrespect for children and their sense of growing up in a world populated by people so much larger. Do not undermine their budding feelings of strength and competency.

## Relating to Other Adults

**Never Interfere When Another Teacher Is Solving a Problem.** Unless specifically invited to join in, allow other teachers the courtesy of dealing with the situation alone. It can be confusing to children to have too many adults involved and runs the risk of giving the children mixed messages.

**Ask Questions.** It is not always possible for others to know of difficulties; be sure to ask for help when needed. It may not be clear how a teacher handled an argument between Chloe and her mother or why the room was rearranged. Be sure to ask since the school staff is there to help the student learn. In most teacher training centers, the staff is used to being

**FIGURE 5.14** Through experience, teachers learn to handle large groups of children. Learning to develop interesting group times is a skill that is practiced over many years.

challenged. Many teachers enjoy a chance to respond to, "Tell me why you did it that way," especially when asked in a positive, nonthreatening way.

**Maintain Communication.** Keep other team members informed of significant events or problems that occur. The teacher in charge will want to know the details of Aaron's fall from the climber or Sarita's sand-throwing episode. Some problems will require the assistance of another teacher. Parent questions and concerns should be redirected to the staff.

**Consult Your Master Teacher.** In planning a lesson or activity, consult the teacher so plans can be integrated into the established curriculum. Work together on selecting age-appropriate activities and the best time and place for them. Ask for help to evaluate the lesson; get some feedback from a staff member who saw the activity. Many times students are overcritical of their initial efforts. An experienced

teacher can help draw out the positive aspects as well as look at what didn't work so well.

Keep these guidelines in mind to avoid some of the common pitfalls of student teaching. But remember, they are only guidelines. Students must add their own experiences, insights, and interpretations. With the support of the teaching staff, confidence will grow, together with an understanding of what it means to be a total teacher.

## THE WHOLE TEACHER

"Teachers deliberately build their programs on their best knowledge of why they are teaching, whom they are teaching, what they are teaching and how they are teaching" (Hymes, 1974). This integration of knowledge and training, experience and life, is referred to by several names. Some say "real" teachers. Others refer to the "total" teacher. A common phrase is the "whole" teacher. Any one of these terms is an apt reflection of the relationship between how teachers view children and how they see themselves. There is a meshing of the emotional, physical, intellectual, and social aspects of each human being, adult or child.

What happens when this blending occurs? During the first few years in the classroom, teachers consolidate their various official functions—merging their teacher training and experience with their personal style and nature. To discover and define the role of a teacher means to develop a personal teaching style. This is the sum of one's response to teaching, and it is unique to each teacher. When it happens, a beginning teacher becomes aware of "feeling" like a teacher. The strengths and convictions one has as a person blend with those one has as a teacher; they become inseparable. What teachers do and what teachers are become woven together. And in adding the personal teacher to the professional teacher, the sum becomes greater than two, allowing the whole teacher the freedom to grow in insight and understanding.

---

**F O C U S**

# CAREER OPTIONS IN EARLY CHILDHOOD EDUCATION

*Dianne Widmeyer Eyer*

This is an exciting time to be considering a career in early childhood education! National awareness of the issues of children and families is exploding. Twenty million mothers are working; the need for child care has increased 60 percent in the last five years. Few fields of work provide such an obvious career ladder. This is a profession that fosters personal growth. But this is also a field that contains a bewildering mix of satisfactions and frustrations, diversities and challenges.

To assist you in considering your interest area and the education necessary for career development, the following overview of career options is divided into four areas: direct service to children and families, indirect service, community involvement, and open options. Salaries can change dramatically according to where and for whom you work, and your own education and experience.

and skills in planning and program organization. They may require course work in related fields of study.

- Teacher in an early childhood education program
- Director of a child care facility
- Family day care provider: caring for children in your home
- Nanny or *au pair:* caring for children in child's home
- Foster parent: short-term care of children from families in stress
- Social worker or adoption agent
- Pediatric nurse or school nurse
- Family therapist or parent educator
- Pediatrician

## Direct Service to Children and Families

The following career choices incorporate an understanding of children's developmental needs

## Indirect Service to Children and Families

These career options emphasize an awareness of technological advances, staying current with the changing marketplace, and appreciating various family needs and lifestyles.

- Curriculum specialist: addressing specific classroom needs
- Instructional technologist: incorporating computer advances into the classroom
- Child development researcher
- Early childhood education specialist: a teacher of teachers
- Program consultant: assisting a variety of child care programs and individual needs
- Consumer advocate: emphasizing either product design or toy safety

## Community Involvement

Early childhood education, combined with other areas of study, can develop into specialized career options that focus on specific community issues. In addition to advanced education, public relations skills and a clear sense of personal commitment are required.

- Licensing worker: state or local level
- Legislative advocate for children
- Specialist in child care law
- Environmental consultant in early childhood education
- Interior designer for children's spaces
- Governmental planning agent for children's issues
- Consultant in bilingual education
- Infant specialist
- Nutrition specialist for children

Suggested second majors for the career options listed in this area include political science, law, social work, interior design, architecture, urban planning, bilingual education, special education, infant development, nutrition, and recreation.

## Open Options

For those individuals who are particularly creative and independent, several career areas are just beginning to acknowledge the needs of children and families. These open options offer tremendous opportunity for growth and innovation.

- Communications consultant: emphasis on radio or television
- Script writer or editor: for radio, television, or film
- Freelance writer: journalism and early childhood education combination
- Author of children's books
- Children's photographer
- Microcomputer specialist or program consultant

Selecting a career is a complex and highly personal process. Having numerous choices often makes that process all the more difficult. To clarify this experience for yourself, you need some time to really think about what you enjoy doing and what your skills and abilities are. Consider what degree of involvement you want with children and how much education you are planning to pursue. Talk with experienced persons already in the field and visit area programs. Be sure that you visit your local colleges and universities for their program guides. Stay alert to the issues and needs within your community. Persistance, innovation, and timing can combine to create a career in early childhood education in which you can truly feel that you make a difference in children's lives.

*Dianne Eyer is the Program Coordinator for Early Childhood Education for the San Mateo County Community College District.*

# SUMMARY

Teachers of young children share with other teachers a variety of subject matter. The curriculum in the early childhood school is rich in math, science, language, social studies, geography, and the like. The format for these learning experiences is a "hands-on" approach. Teachers set out materials, equipment, and activities that invite children's interest and interaction.

In some areas the early childhood teacher differs from others in the field of education. Team teaching, teacher-child interactions, small-group emphasis, and adult relationships are more common in the early years than in other types of schools.

The teaching role is not restricted to working just with children. Teachers must learn to interact with numerous adults—primarily parents, other teachers, and administrators. Teaching roles will vary, depending on whether or not you teach alone or on a team. Team teaching is common in many early childhood programs and has many advantages. By keeping in mind ten essentials for successful teaching, all early childhood teachers can assure themselves of optimal working conditions in their setting.

Early childhood teachers have multiple roles. They supervise and manage the classroom, interact with children and a number of adults, and they set the emotional tone. Much of what they do occurs away from children. There are meetings to attend, reports to write, parent conferences to hold, and materials to purchase. These after-hours duties add to the depth of classroom experiences the teacher provides for the children.

Ethical situations arise frequently, calling on the teacher or administrator to make difficult choices about children and their lives. A professional code of ethics sets out standards of behavior based on core values and commitments all early childhood professionals share. It can support decisions individuals have to make in the best interests of children.

The student teacher gains valuable experience working directly with children under the supervision of a mature teacher. Some of the initial anxieties are overcome by following general guidelines for student teaching. Further help comes from looking at some common problems and ways to avoid them.

As they grow and gain confidence, teachers pass through several stages of professional development and search for ways to be more effectively challenged. As they integrate teaching style and personality, they become whole teachers.

## R E V I E W   Q U E S T I O N S

1. What do you think are the five most important qualifications a teacher of young children should have? Why? Which do you possess? Which are most difficult for you?

2. Make a line down the center of a paper. On one side write a list of what you like about teaching. On the other side, list those aspects of teaching that you don't like. How can you address those that you don't like and make them more positive?

3. Give several reasons why team teaching is important in the early years.

4. List some of the common problems associated with student teaching. How can you avoid them?

5. Describe a teacher you would want to teach your own child.

6. Finish the following statement: "Teaching is _____."

## L E A R N I N G   A C T I V I T I E S

1. Draw a picture of the first classroom you remember. Place furniture in it and note where your friends sat, where you sat, where the teacher sat. Down one side of the paper write one-word descriptions of what you felt when you were in that classroom.

2. Write an advertisement for yourself as a teacher. *résumé*

3. Have you ever had a teacher who was "different"? Describe the person. What did you like most about that teacher? What did you like least? Would you hire that teacher? Why?

4. Write your own code of ethics.

5. Read the ethical situations posed on pages 146-147. Think about how you would solve them. Discuss your answers with a member of your class, a teacher, and a parent.

6. Observe a teacher working in a team situation and one who works alone in a classroom. What seem to be the advantages of each? Disadvantages? Which would you prefer for your first year of teaching? Why? Your third year? Your seventh year?

7. Do you disagree with any core values listed on pages 141–142? What are they? How would you change them? Discuss your response with another teacher, another student, your class instructor.

## B I B L I O G R A P H Y

Beyer, Evelyn. *Teaching Young Children.* New York: Western Publishing, 1968.

Feeney, Stephanie. "Ethics Case Studies: The Working Mother." *Young Children,* November 1987, pp. 16-17.

_____. "Ethics Case Studies: The Divorced Parents." *Young Children,* March 1988, pp. 48-49.

Feeney, Stephanie, and Kipnis, Kenneth. "Professional Ethics in Early Childhood Education." *Young Children,* March 1985, pp. 54-58.

Feeney, Stephanie, and Sisko, Lynda. "Professional Ethics in Early Childhood Education: Survey Results." *Young Children,* November 1986, pp. 15-20.

Gordon-Nourok, Esther. *You're a Student Teacher!* Sierra Madre, Calif.: Southern California Association for the Education of Young Children, 1979.

Honig, Alice. *Parent Involvement in Early Childhood Education.* Washington, D.C.: National Association for the Education of Young Children, 1979.

Hymes, James L., Jr. *Teaching the Child Under Six.* Columbus, Oh.: Charles E. Merrill, 1981.

Katz, Lilian G. *Talks With Teachers.* Washington, D.C.: National Association for the Education of Young Children, 1977.

Katz, Lilian G. "Ethics Case Studies: The Working Mother." *Young Children,* November 1987, p. 18.

Katz, Lilian G., and Ward, Evangeline H. *Ethical Behavior in Early Childhood Education.* Washington, D.C.: National Association for the Education of Young Children, 1978.

Kipnis, Kenneth. "How to Discuss Professional Ethics." *Young Children,* May 1987, pp. 26-30.

LeShan, Eda. *When Your Child Drives You Crazy.* New York: St. Martin's Press, 1985.

Sizer, Theodore R. *Horace's Compromise.* Boston: Houghton Mifflin, 1985.

Spodek, Bernard. *Teaching in the Early Years.* Englewood Cliffs, N.J.: Prentice-Hall, 1972.

Spodek, Bernard, ed. *Teaching Practices/Reexamining Assumptions.* Washington, D.C.: National Association for the Education of Young Children, 1977.

# CHAPTER 6

## Observation:
## Learning to
## Read the Child

## QUESTIONS for THOUGHT

- Why is observing children an important teaching tool?
- How do observations help us understand people and their behavior?
- What is the difference between fact and inference?
- How can observations be used to compare individual behavior and general developmental growth?
- What are some of the ways to record observations?
- What are the guidelines to follow when observing and recording behavior?

# INTRODUCTION

Children are fascinating. They are charming, needful, busy, creative, unpredictable, and emotional. At school, at home, in the grocery store, and in the park, children demonstrate a variety of behaviors. There is the happy child pumping hard on the swing. The angry, defiant child grabs a book or toy and runs away. The studious child works seriously on a puzzle.

These pictures of children flash through the mind, caught for an instant as if by a camera. These minipictures of children working, playing, and living together can be very useful to teachers. Good observing skills can help teachers capture those moments in a child's life. Memory leaves just the impression. The written word is an opportunity to check impressions and opinions against the facts.

# What Is Observation?

Teachers learn to make mental notes of the important details in each interaction:

That's the first time I've seen Karen playing with Bryce. They are laughing together as they build with blocks.

For five minutes now, Teddy has been standing on the fringes of the sand area where the toddler group is playing. He has ignored the children's smiles and refused the teacher's invitiation to join in the play.

Antonio stops climbing each time he reaches the top of the climbing frame. He looks quickly around and if he catches a teacher's eye, he scrambles down and runs away.

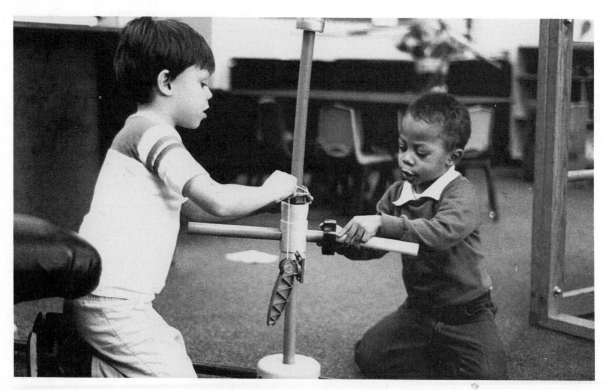

**FIGURE 6.1** These two children are seen playing together for the first time. What can teachers learn by observing their play about their use of materials? The way they make friends? How they solve problems? (Courtesy of Denise Strus.)

Through their behavior, these three children reveal much about their personalities. The teacher's responsibility is to notice all the clues and put them together in meaningful ways. The teacher sees the obvious clues as well as the more subtle ones. The way observations are put together with other pertinent information becomes critical. The first child, Karen, has been looking for a special friend. Now that she has learned some ways to approach other children that don't frighten and overwhelm them, children want to play with her. Teddy's parents divorced two weeks ago. It appears he is just beginning to feel some of that pain and has become withdrawn at school. At home, Antonio is expected to do things right the first time. At school, he generally attempts only what he knows he can do without making a mistake.

These simple observations, made in the midst of a busy morning at school, give vital information about each child's abilities, needs, and concerns. It is a more developed picture. Children are complex human beings who respond in many ways. Teachers can observe these responses and use their skills to help each child grow and learn.

Observation is more than ordinary looking. It takes energy and concentration to become an accurate observer. Teachers must train themselves to record what they see on a regular basis. They need to discipline themselves to distinguish between detail and trivia as well as learn to spot biases that might invalidate the observation. Once acquired, objective observation techniques help give a scientific and professional character to the role of early childhood education.

## Seeing Children Through Observation

Play is the work of childhood. It is the way children express themselves and how they show what they are really like. By observing play, teachers can see children as they are and as they see themselves. Much of what children do gives clues to their inner beings.

The stage is set; the action begins as soon as the first child enters the room. Here, teachers can see children in action and watch for important behavior. All that is needed is to be alert to the clues and make note of them:

> Allison, normally a cocky, competent three-year-old, wavers in her confidence as she enters school. She knows her best friend, Andy, will be absent today.
>
> Charlie, full of bravado on the first grade playground, refuses to perform a simple coloring task. He tells the teacher, "I can't do it. I don't know how."

Developing sound observational skills enables teachers to better meet the social, emotional, and intellectual needs of each child.

What are children telling us about themselves? Which actions are most important to note? The teacher makes a point to observe children at critical moments. An alert teacher will notice the way a child enters school each morning. Tina always clings to her blanket after her Dad leaves her at school. Lasauna bounces in each day ready to play the

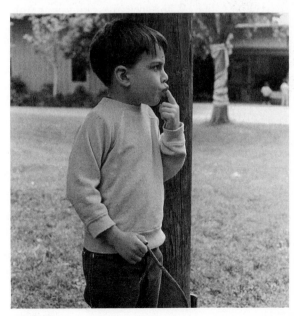

**FIGURE 6.2** Observing children closely reveals their feelings and needs.

moment she walks in the door. David says good-bye to his grandmother, then circles the room, hugging each adult before settling into an activity. These children show the observant teacher something about their needs. A good observer will continue to watch, taking note of these early morning scenes. One can interpret these behaviors later, seeing how they apply to each child and how behavior changes over time.

Another important behavior to watch is how children use their bodies. The basic routines of eating, napping, toileting, and dressing show how they take care of themselves. Whether Chris learns how to put his jacket on by himself indicates his skills in other areas requiring initiative and self-sufficiency. It also shows whether or not children are developing an awareness of themselves as separate, independent beings.

Seeing children in relation to other people is a third area to notice. Teachers see whom children choose as playmates and whom they avoid. They can tell what children will look for in friends. The observant teacher will also make note of the adults in each child's life. Who does the child seek for comfort? For questions? Who takes care of the child outside of school? Who picks the child up from school each day?

Finally, in selecting play materials and equipment, children show what they like to do, how well they use the environment, and what they avoid. Teachers observe whether or not a child picks materials that are challenging. Bethany starts each morning in the art area, then plays with puzzles before taking care of the animals. Conor prefers the blocks and dramatic play areas and lately has been spending more time in the cooking corner. Observing children at play and at work can tell us how they learn and what methods they use to gain information.

# Why Observe?

## *To Become More Objective*

Observing children helps teachers become more objective about the children in their care. When making observation notes, teachers look first at what the child is doing. This is different from looking at how a child ought to be doing something. The teacher becomes like a camera, recording what is seen without immediately judging it. This *objectivity* can balance the intense, personal side of teaching.

Teachers are influenced in their work by their own early childhood experiences. They have notions about how children learn, play, grow, or behave because of the way they were raised and trained. Moreover, when teachers are in the thick of activity, they see only a narrow picture. To pull back, take some notes, and make an observation gives the teacher a chance to see the larger scene.

Teams of teachers help each other gain perspective on the class, an individual, a time of the day. Observations can be a means of validating one teacher's point of view. By checking out an opinion or idea through systematic observation, teachers get a sense of direction in their planning.

Additionally, all teachers develop ideas and impressions about children when they spend time with them. Some children seem shy, some helpful, some affectionate, aggressive, cooperative, stubborn, and so on. These opinions influence the way teachers behave and interact with children. The child thought to be aggressive, for instance, is more likely to be blamed for starting the quarrel when one occurs nearby. It is no accident that the children teachers consider more polite are the ones who are often given special considerations. The problem stems from teacher biases, and these can be misleading. Assumptions made about a child often stereotype the child (or the group) rather than illuminate it. This gives both teachers and children a narrow view of themselves and others.

Cohen and Stern (1978) suggest that to become a careful observer is to become in part a scientist. A good observer makes a clear distinction between fact and *inference,* between real behavior and an impression or conclusion drawn from it. Being aware of the difference between what actually happens and one's opinion and conclusions about those events is critical to good teaching. Refer to Figure 6.6 for an illustration of these differences. By separating what happens from what you *think* about it or how you *feel* about it, you are able to distinguish between fact and inference. That does not mean teachers have to become aloof; their eyes can reflect both warmth and a measure of objectivity at the same time. The picture of the child from a teacher's view is often based on one or two events, not necessarily repeated or typical of the child. Thus, it is not a true picture of the child at all.

No one can be free from bias, nor is that the point. The impressions and influences made can provide valuable insights into children. The important first step in observation, though, is to separate what children *do* from what teachers think or feel about it. This can only be done with an awareness of one's own biases. Knowing personal influences and prejudices, coupled with observation and recording skills, prepares teachers to focus on actual behaviors.

### To Link Theory with Practice

Observations are a link between theory and practice. All teachers gain from making this connection. New teachers can see the pages of a textbook come alive as they watch a group of children. They can match what they see with what they read. By putting together psychology and medical research with in-class experiences, teachers gain a deeper understanding of the nature of children.

### To Help Parents

Parents benefit from observations. A collection of notes about an individual child can be used in parent conferences. The teacher shares fresh, meaningful examples that demonstrate the child's growth and abilities. The child's teachers also gain a perspective when the notes are accumulated and discussed with parents. Problems become more clear and plans can be made to work together. Results can be further tested through continuing observation.

### To Use as an Assessment Tool

Notes, time samplings, and running records serve as an informal way to assess children's skills and capabilities. Observation can be used as a tool for

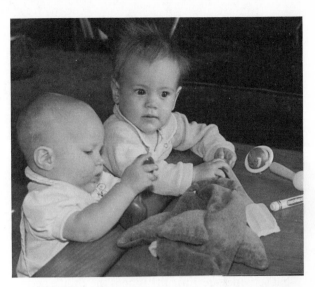

**FIGURE 6.3** Observations bring theory to life. What can these babies do with objects? Is the environment safe? Challenging? How does observing answer these questions?

teachers to check the accuracy of their own impressions. Comparing notes with other teachers, with parents, or with anyone familiar with the classroom or the child in question refines a teacher's own objective observation skills. The results lead directly into curriculum planning for the class. Teachers observe the room arrangement and use of space. Does the traffic flow easily or are children stuck in play areas and can't get out? Many classroom problems can be solved if teachers will take time to make observations. They can observe what happens in the block corner at cleanup time. Who always cleans up? Who avoids it? Or they look at play patterns and find out who children play with or who plays alone. Observations can clarify which children are having problems and give teachers a sense of when and where the trouble starts.

More frequently teachers are called upon to set specific goals for the children in their classes and for the overall class performance. They justify what they do and why and document children's progress. In this way teachers are accountable to their clients: the children, the parents, and the public. Learning to assess children's skills and behavior and to document it is becoming increasingly important to the early childhood educator. Formal assessment techniques such as screening are described in Chapter 10.

# UNDERSTANDING WHAT WE OBSERVE

The goal of observing children is to understand them better. Teachers, students, and parents collect a great deal of information by watching children. Observational data helps adults know children in several significant ways.

## Children as Individuals

How do children spend their time at school? What activities are difficult? Who is the child's best friend? By watching individual children, teachers help them learn at their own pace, at their own rate of development, in their own time. By watching carefully, they find out each child's learning style. When teachers know how each child functions, they can choose activities and materials to match interests and skills. This is called *individualized curriculum:* tailoring what is taught to what a child is ready and willing to learn.

Observing helps a teacher spot a child's strengths and areas of difficulty. Once these are known, teachers plan intervention measures, helping to make the school experience successful for the child. The following example shows how individualizing the curriculum can bring about changes in behavior that help children succeed.

The teachers were concerned about Jody, age 4½, who had minimal small-motor skills. She used scissors in a "hedge-clippers" fashion and had an awkward grip when using a pencil. Jody also found it difficult to fit puzzle pieces together. She avoided all areas that required the use of those skills: art, table toys, woodworking, and cooking. A check with her parents revealed two important facts: Jody had trouble handling table utensils and couldn't button her sweater. They said there was no provision at home for her to pursue any fine motor activities. Knowing

of Jody's interest in airplanes, the teachers used that to draw Jody into areas of the curriculum she didn't ordinarily pursue. Small airplanes were added to the block corner and airplane stencils were placed near the art table. A large mural of an airport was hung on the fence and children were invited to paint on it. One day children cut airplane pictures out of magazines and used them on a collage. Simple airplane puzzles were placed on the puzzle table. Felt shapes and small plastic airplanes in the water table helped draw Jody toward activities requiring fine motor skills. Jody's parents supplied her with a special art box at home, full of crayons, scissors, pens, water colors, and stencils. As her small-motor skills increased and refined, Jody became a more confident and happier child. By the end of three months she was a regular participant in all areas of the school and seemed to be enjoying her newfound interest in art materials.

## Children in General

When recording behavior, teachers see growth patterns emerge. These trends reflect the nature of human development. Both Jean Piaget and Erik Erikson used this technique to learn how children think and develop socially and emotionally. Gesell studied large numbers of children to get developmental *norms* of physical growth. Parten and Dawes watched hundreds of preschoolers and arrived at the definitive description of children's play patterns and quarreling behavior. For today's early childhood educator, observing children can provide the answer to these questions:

- What might you expect when a two-year-old pours juice?

- How will the second grade class respond to a field trip?

- What will children do when their parents leave them at school the first day?

- What is the difference between the attention span at storytime of a two-year-old and a five-year-old?

- What kind of social play is typical for the four-year-old?

- How does an infant move from crawling to walking upright?

Observation gives a feeling for group behavior as well as a developmental yardstick to compare individuals within the group. Teachers determine age-appropriate expectations from this. It is important, for example, to know that most children cannot tie their own shoes at four, but can be expected to pull them on by themseves. A general understanding aids in planning thoughtful and challenging curriculum. Teachers in a class of three-year-olds, for instance, know that many children are ready for eight- to 10-piece puzzles, but that the 20-piece jigsaw will most likely be dumped on the table and quickly abandoned.

Finally, knowledge of children in general gives teachers a solid foundation upon which to base decisions about individuals. From observing many children comes an awareness of each child's progression along the developmental scale. Experienced teachers of toddlers will not put out watercolor sets, while the second-grade teacher will do so routinely. Teachers learn that it is typical of four- and five-year-olds to exclude others from their play because they will have seen it happen countless times. The 3½-year-old who is sure she is "too little" to use the toilet won't convince the knowledgeable teacher who knows that this is developmentally appropriate behavior! Decisions about single children come from watching and knowing many children. This understanding is a valuable asset when talking to parents.

## Developmental Relationships

Observing brings about an understanding of the various developmental areas and how they are related. Development is at once *specific* and *integrated*.

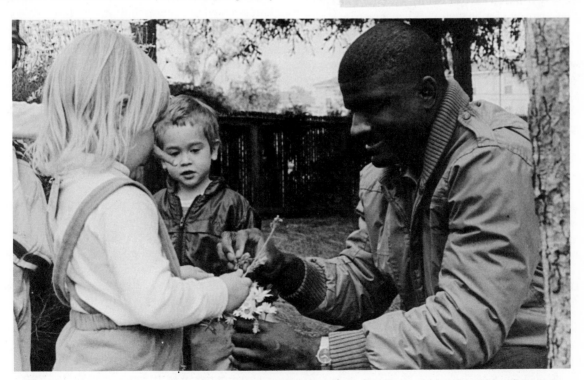

**FIGURE 6.4**  Understanding the child is the goal of observation. By noticing a child's spontaneous act of giving flowers, the teacher sees what kinds and colors are chosen, the verbal and nonverbal language in the message, and the impact on others.

Children's behavior is a mix of several distinct developmental areas and, at the same time, an integrated whole whose parts influence each other. Reference to the *whole child* implies a consideration of how development works in unison.

When observing children, one must focus on these different developmental areas. What are the language abilities of three-year-olds? What social skills do preschool children acquire? Which self-help skills can children learn before six? How does fine-motor development interact with intellectual growth? Does large-motor skill effect successful cognitive learning? How does self-concept relate to all of the other areas?

Observing these separately brings a specific definition to the term "growth." Teachers see how the pieces fit together. When teachers have an understanding of children's thought processes, they can see why children have difficulty with the concept of dual-identity, for instance. When given a set of blocks in various sizes, colors, and shapes, a four-year-old will have no difficulty finding the red ones or square ones, but may be puzzled when asked to find those that are both red and square. No wonder that same child has difficulty understanding that someone can be their best friend and like someone else at the same time.

Practiced observation will show that a child's skills are multiple and varied and have only limited connection to age. Derek has the physical coordination of a 4½-year-old, language skills of a six-year-old, and the social skills of a two-year-old—all bound up in a body that just turned three. A brief picture such as this "whole child" can be helpful to both parents and teachers.

# Influences on Behavior

Careful observation in the classroom and on the playground benefits an understanding of child growth and behavior. This includes an understanding of the influences and dynamics of that behavior.

Boaz has a hard time when he enters child care each morning, yet he is competent and says he likes school. Close observation reveals that his favorite areas are climbing outdoor games and the sandbox. Boaz feels least successful in the construction and creative arts areas, the primary choices indoors, where his school day begins.

Mari, on the other hand, starts the day happily but cries frequently throughout the day. Is there a pattern to her outbursts? Watch what happens to Mari when free play is over and group time begins. She falls apart readily when it is time to move outdoors to play, time to have snacks, time to nap, and so on.

Environmental influences have an impact on both these children. The classroom arrangement and daily schedule influence children's behavior, because children are directly affected by the restraints imposed by their activities and their time. Boaz feels unsure of himself in those activities that are offered as he starts his day. Seeing only these choices as he enters the room causes him discomfort, which he shows by crying and clinging to his dad. By adding something he enjoys, such as a sand table indoors, the teacher changes the physical environment to be more appealing and positive. Boaz's difficulties in saying goodbye disappear as he finds he can be successful and comfortable at the beginning of his day.

The cause of Mari's problem is more difficult to detect. The physical environment seems to interest and appeal to her. Upon closer observation, her crying and disruptive behavior appear to happen just at the point of change, regardless of the activities before or afterwards. It is the *time* aspect of the environment that causes difficulty for her. The teacher makes a special effort to signal upcoming transitions and to involve her in bringing them about. Telling Mari "Five more minutes until naptime" or "After you wash your hands, go to the snack table" gives her the clues she needs to anticipate the process of change. Asking her to announce cleanup time to the class lets her be in control of that transition.

Adult behavior affects and influences children. Annika has days of intense activity and involvement with materials; on other days she appears sluggish and disinterested. After a week of observation, teachers find a direct correlation with the presence of a student teacher. On the days the student is in the classroom, Annika calls out to him to see her artwork and watch her various accomplishments. It is on the days that the student is absent that Annika's activity level falls. Once a pattern is noticed, the teacher acts upon these observations. In this case, the teacher and the student teacher work together to encourage Annika's daily involvement in school. The student teacher offers Annika ideas for activities she could demonstrate to him the following day. When he is absent, the teacher tries some of his activities that Annika especially enjoys.

Children also influence one another in powerful ways. Anyone who has worked with toddlers knows how attractive a toy becomes to a child once another has it. The six-year-old who suddenly dislikes school may be feeling left out of a friendship group. Teachers need to carefully observe the social dynamics of the class as they seek to understand individual children.

## Understanding of Self

Observing children can be a key to understanding ourselves. People who develop observational skills notice human behavior more accurately. They become skilled at seeing small but important facets of human personality. They learn to differentiate between what is fact and what is *inference*. This increases an awareness of self as teacher and how one's biases affect the perceptions of children.

The values and benefits of observation are long-lasting. Only by practicing observations—what it takes to look, to see, to become more sensitive—will teachers be able to record children's behavior fully and vividly, capturing the unique qualities and personality of each child. According to Dr. Edith Dowley, observation of children can be made at three levels. First, report exactly what the child *does*. Second, express how the child seems to feel about what happened. Last, include your own impressions and interpretations. Each level describes a separate level of child development and builds on successful

mastery of the previous level to ensure accurate reporting. The challenge of observation is high, but the benefits are well worth the effort.

# RECORDING OBSERVATIONS

Once teachers and students understand why observing is important, they must then learn how to record what they see. While children are constantly under the teacher's eyes, so much happens so fast that critical events are lost in the daily routine of classrooms. Systematic observations aid in recording events and help teachers make sense of them.

## Common Elements of Observations

The key ingredients in all types of observations used in recording children's behavior are (1) defining and describing the behaviors and (2) repeating the observation in terms of several factors such as time, number of children, or activities. All observational systems have certain elements in common:

**Focus**
- What do you want to know?
- Whom/what do you want to observe?
  Child? Teacher? Environment? Group?
- What aspects of behavior do you want to know about? Motor skills? Social development? Problem-solving?
- What is your purpose?
  Study the environment?
  Observe the daily schedule?
  Evaluate a child's skills?
  Deal with negative behavior?
  Analyze transitions?
  Do research?
  Conference with parents?
  Train teachers?

**System**
- What will you do?

- How will you define the terms?
- How will you record the information you need?
- How detailed will your record be?
- Will you need units of measure? What kind?
- For how long will you record?

**Tools**

- What will you need for your observations?
- How will you record what you want to know?
  Video or tape recorder? Camera? Pencil?
  Chart?

**Environment**

- Where will you watch?
  Classroom? Yard? Home?
- What restraints are inherent in the setting?

Using these building blocks of observational systems, teachers seek a method that yields a collection of observable data that helps them focus more clearly on a child or situation. Four major methods of observing and two additional information-gathering techniques will be discussed. They are:

1. Narratives (diary descriptions, running records, specimen descriptions, anecdotal notes)

2. Time sampling

3. Event sampling

4. Modified child study techniques (Checklists, rating scales, shadow study)

5. Experimental procedures

6. The clinical method

# Types of Observations

## *Narratives*

At once the most valuable and most difficult of records, narratives are attempts to record nearly everything that happens. In the case of a young child, this means all that the child does, says,

gestures, seems to feel, and appears to think about. For instance, reread the narrative in Dr. Joseph Stevens' Guest Editoral at the beginning of this section. Notice how observation maintains a running record of the excitement and tension of the interaction while remaining an accurate, objective account of the events and behavior. Narratives are an attempt to actually recreate the scene by recording it in thorough and vivid language. Observers put into words what they see, hear, and know about an event or a person. The result is a full and dynamic report.

Narratives are the oldest and often most informative kind of report. Historically, as Arnold Gesell reported, they were used to set basic developmental norms. They are a standard technique in anthropology and the biological sciences. Irwin and Bushnell (1980) provide a detailed historical background

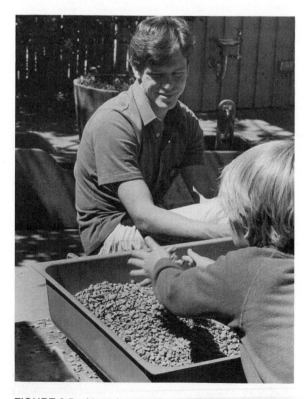

**FIGURE 6.5** Narratives can be recorded anywhere, any time. The teacher watches how children use materials and can record the quality of a child's daily play.

that traces the narrative back to Pestalozzi (1700s) and Darwin (1800s). Jean Piaget watched and recorded in minute detail his own children's growth. His observations resulted in a full report on children's thought processes and development of intelligence. *"Baby biographies,"* narratives written by parents, were some of the first methods used in child study and reached their peak of popularity in the early 1900s.

*Diary descriptions* are one form of narrative. Just as the term implies, they are, in diary form, consecutive records of everything children do and say and how they do it. The process is a natural one. In the classroom this means describing every action observed within a given time period. It might be a five-minute period during free play to watch and record what one child does. The child who is a loner, the child who wanders, and the child who is aggressive are prime candidates for a diary description. Another way to use this type of *running record* is to watch an area of the yard or room, then record who is there and how they are using the materials.

A more common form of the narrative is a modified version of a running record, or a *specimen description* as it is often called in research terms. The procedure is to take on-the-spot notes of a specific child each day. This task lends itself easily to most early childhood settings. The teachers carry with them a small notebook and pencil, tucked in a pocket. They jot down whatever seems important or noteworthy during the day. They may focus on one specimen at a time:

- A part of the environment—how is the science area being used?

- A particular time of day—what happens right after naps?

- A specific child—how often is Lucy hitting out at other children?

This system may be even less structured with all the teachers taking "on-the-hoof" notes as daily incidents occur. These notes then become a rich source of information for report writing and parent conferences.

Another form of narrative is a *log* or *journal.* A page is set aside for each child in the class. At some point, teachers write in details about each child. Since this is time-consuming and needs to be done without interruption, it helps to write immediately after school is over. Sometimes teaching teams organize themselves to enable one member of the staff to observe and record in the journal during class time. The important point is that each child's general behavior is recorded either while it is happening or soon afterward.

The challenging part of this recording technique, the narrative, is to have enough detail so the reader will be able to picture whole situations later. Using language as a descriptive tool requires a large vocabulary and skillful recorder. Whatever notes the teachers use, however brief, need to be both clear and accurate.

At the same time teachers are recording in a graphic way, they need to be aware of the personal biases that can influence observations. When we look at children, what we see is in part a result of our personal experiences, the theories we hold, and the assumptions we make. Teaching is an intensely personal activity, and what the children look like, do, and say may arouse strong feelings and reactions. Figure 6.6 compares two observations to illustrate this point. By becoming aware of our biases and assumptions, we can become more accurate and objective in our work as teachers.

Narratives are an observational technique with roots in psychology, anthropology, and biology. They can follow several formats and are an attempt to record all that happens as it happens. There are many advantages to this type of observation. Narratives are rich in information, provide detailed behavioral accounts, and are relatively easy to record. With a minimum of equipment and training, teachers can learn to take notes on what children do and say. To write down everything is impossible, so some selection is necessary. These judgment calls can warp the narrative. Also, observations of this kind require large amounts of time—just what teachers who are involved with a group of children lack. The main disadvantages of narratives, then, are the time

*drawback*
*time -*
*long*
*before*

they can take, the language and the vocabulary that must be used, and the biases the recorder may have. Even though the narrative remains one of the most widely used and effective methods of observing young children today, many teachers prefer more structured procedures because of these problems. These more definite, more precise techniques still involve some personal interpretation, but the area of individual judgment is diminished. The observational techniques discussed in the following sections also tend to be less time-consuming than the narrative.

## Time Sampling

This method collects information other than that which a narrative provides. It is less descriptive,

more specific, and requires different observational skills. A time sample is an observation of what happens within a given period of time. Developed as an observational strategy in laboratory schools in the 1920s, time sampling was used to collect data on large numbers of children and to get a sense of normative behaviors for particular age groups or sexes.

Time sampling "appears to be indigenous to research in child development" (Wright, 1967). It has been used to record autonomy, dependency, task persistence, aggression, and social involvement. Time sampling has also been used to study dependent, independent, and solitary play patterns and to record nervous habits of school children, such as nail biting and hair twisting (Prescott, 1973, and Irwin

| Poor Observation | Analysis and Comments |
|---|---|
| A. Julio walked over to the coat rack and dropped his sweater on the floor. He is <u>shy</u> (1) of teachers, so he didn't ask anyone to help him pick it up. He walked over to Cynthia <u>because she's his best friend</u> (2). He wasn't <u>nice</u> (3) to the other children when he started being <u>pushy and bossy</u> (4). He <u>wanted their attention</u> (5), so he <u>nagged</u> (6) them into leaving the table and going to the blocks like <u>four-year-old boys do</u> (7). | (1) Inference of a general characteristic.<br>(2) Inference of child's emotion.<br>(3) Observer's opinion.<br>(4) Inference with no physical evidence stated.<br>(5) Opinion of child's motivation.<br>(6) Observer's inference.<br>(7) Overgeneralization; stereotyping. |

| Good Observation | Analysis and Comments |
|---|---|
| B. Emilio pulled out a puzzle from the rack with his right hand, then carried it with both hands to the table nearby. Using both hands, he methodically took each piece out of the frame and set it to his left. Sara, who had been seated across from Emilio with some table toys in front of her, reached out and pushed all the puzzle pieces onto the floor. Emilio's face reddened as his eyes stared directly at Sara with his mouth in a taut line. His hands turned to fists, his brow furrowed, and he yelled at Sara in a forced tone, "Stop it! I hate you!" | Emilio was clearly *angry* as demonstrated in his facial expressions, hand gestures, and body movements. What is more, the way a child speaks is as revealing as what a child says when one wants to determine what a child is feeling. Muscular tension is another clue to the child's emotions. But the physical attitude of the child is not enough; one must also consider the context. Just seeing a child sitting in a chair with a red face, one doesn't know if he is embarrassed, angry, feverish, or overstimulated. We need to know the events that led to this conclusion. Then we can correctly assess the entire situation. By attempting to rid ourselves of some of these biases, we begin to see the child more clearly. |

**FIGURE 6.6** Two observations. Example A contains numerous biases, which are underlined in the left column and explained in the right column. Example B has good descriptions and is relatively free of biases.

| Child | PLAY WITH OTHERS<br>P = Parallel<br>A = Associative<br>C = Cooperative | | | | | | | | | | | | | | | | | | Total |
|-------|---|---|---|---|---|---|---|---|---|---|---|---|---|---|---|---|---|---|-------|
| | **Time Unit** | | | | | | | | | | | | | | | | | | |
| | 9:00 | | | 9:05 | | | 9:10 | | | 9:20 | | | 9:25 | | | 9:30 | | | |
| | P | A | C | P | A | C | P | A | C | P | A | C | P | A | C | P | A | C | |
| Jamal | | | | | | | | | | | | | | | | | | | |
| Marty | | | | | | | | | | | | | | | | | | | |
| Dahlia | | | | | | | | | | | | | | | | | | | |
| Keith | | | | | | | | | | | | | | | | | | | |
| Rosa | | | | | | | | | | | | | | | | | | | |
| Cameron | | | | | | | | | | | | | | | | | | | |
| Hannah | | | | | | | | | | | | | | | | | | | |

**FIGURE 6.7** Time sampling of play with others involves defining the behavior and making a coding sheet to tally observations.

and Bushnell, 1980). The definitive study using time sampling is Mildred Parten's observation in the 1930s of children's play. The codes developed in this study have become classic play patterns: parallel, associative, and cooperative play. These codes are used throughout this text (see Chapters 3, 11, and 14), as well as in the professional field to describe the interactions of children.

In a time sample, behavior is recorded at regular time intervals. To use this method, one needs to sample what occurs fairly frequently. It makes sense to choose those behaviors that might occur, say, at least once every 10 minutes. Figure 6.7 demonstrates a time-sampling procedure.

Time sampling has its own advantages and disadvantages. The process itself helps teachers define exactly what it is they want to observe. Certainly it helps focus on specific behaviors and how often they occur. Time sampling is ideal for collecting informa-

**FIGURE 6.8** Event sampling can be helpful in determining how frequently a specific event takes place. For instance, sampling the number and types of accidents for a given child or time frame helps teachers see what is happening in class. (Courtesy of Susan Thibodeau, College of Notre Dame of Md.)

tion about the group as a whole. Finally, by defining behaviors clearly and developing a category and coding system, the problem of observer bias is reduced.

Yet by diminishing this bias one also eliminates some of the richness and quality of information. It is difficult to get the whole picture when one divides it into artificial time units and with only a few categories. The key is to decide what it is teachers want to know, then choose the observational method that best suits those needs. When narratives or time samplings won't suffice, perhaps an event sampling will.

## Event Sampling

This is one of the most fascinating and intriguing techniques. With this method, the observer defines an event, devises a system for describing and coding it, then waits for it to happen. As soon as it does, the recorder moves into action. Thus, the behavior is recorded as it occurs naturally.

The events that are chosen can be quite interesting and diverse. Consider Helen C. Dawes' classic analysis of preschool children's quarrels. Whenever a quarrel began, the observer recorded how long the quarrel lasted and what took place (Irwin and Bushnell, 1980).

Observer _____  Date _____  Time _____

| Learning Center | Anna | Charlie | Leticia | Neroko | Mat | Josie | Totals |
|---|---|---|---|---|---|---|---|
| **Indoors** | | | | | | | |
| Science Area | | | | | \| | | 1 |
| Dramatic Play | \| | \| | \| | | | \| | 4 |
| Art | \| | | \| | \| | | | 3 |
| Blocks | | \| | | | | | 1 |
| Manipulatives | | | \| | \| | \| | | 3 |
| Easels | | | | \| | | | 1 |
| Music | | | \| | | \| | | 2 |
| **Outdoors** | | | | | | | |
| Water/Sand/Mud | | \| | \| | | | \| | 3 |
| Blocks | | | \| | \| | | | 2 |
| Wheel Toys | | \| | | | \| | | 2 |
| Climbers | \| | | \| | | | \| | 3 |
| Woodworking | | | | \| | | | 1 |
| Ball Games | \| | | | | | | 1 |
| Animal Care | \| | \| | | | | \| | 3 |
| **Totals** | 5 | 5 | 6 | 5 | 5 | 4 | |

**FIGURE 6.9** An activity checklist. With data collected for a week, teachers have a broad picture of how children spend their time at school and what activities interest them.

Other researchers have studied dominance and emotions. Teachers can use event sampling to look at these and other behaviors such as bossiness, avoidance of teacher requests, or withdrawal.

Like time sampling, event sampling looks at a particular behavior or occurrence. But the unit is the event rather than a prescribed time interval. Here again the behavior must be clearly defined and the recording sheet easy to use. Unlike with time sampling, the event to be recorded may occur a number of times during the observation.

For these reasons, event sampling is a favorite of classroom teachers. They can go about the business of teaching children until the event occurs. Then they can record the event quickly and efficiently. By prescribing the context within which the event occurs, some of the quality often lost in time sampling is regained. The only disadvantage is that the richness of detail of the narrative descriptions is missing.

## Modified Child Study Techniques

Since observation is the key method of studying young children in their natural settings, it makes

---

Motor Skills Observation (ages 2–4)     Child _____

Date _____ Observer _____ Age _____

Eating:                                                   Yes   No
1. Holds glass with one hand
2. Pours from pitcher
3. Spills little from spoon
4. Selects food with pincer grasp

Dressing:
1. Unbuttons
2. Puts shoes on
3. Uses both hands together (such as holding jacket
   with one hand while zipping with the other)

Fine Motor:
1. Uses pincer grasp with pencil, brushes
2. Draws straight line
3. Copies circles
4. Cuts at least 2″ in line
5. Makes designs and crude letters
6. Builds tower of 6–9 blocks
7. Turns pages singly

Gross Motor:
1. Descends/ascends steps with alternate feet
2. Stands on one foot, unsupported
3. Hops on two feet
4. Catches ball, arms straight, elbows in
   front of body
5. Operates tricycle

---

**FIGURE 6.10**   A yes/no checklist gives specific information about an individual child's skills.

good sense to develop many kinds of observational skills. Each can be tailored to fit the individual child, the particular group, the kind of staff, and the specific problem. Teachers who live in complex, creative classrooms have questions arise that need fast answers. Modified child study techniques can define the scope of the problem fairly quickly. Some of the techniques are: checklist systems, rating scales, shadow studies, and modified processes that reach both the group and the individuals in it.

*Checklists* contain a great deal of information that can be recorded rapidly. A carefully planned checklist can tell a lot about one child or the entire class. The data is collected in a short space of time, usually about a week. Figure 6.9 is an example of an activity checklist. With data collected for a week, teachers have a broad picture of how these children spend their time and what activities interest them.

If, however, teachers want to assess children's motor skills, a yes/no list is preferable. Figure 6.10 illustrates the use of such a chart.

Checklists can vary in length and complexity depending on their functions. To develop one, teachers first determine the purpose of the observation. Next they define what the children will do to demonstrate the behavior being observed. Finally comes designing the actual checklist, one that is easy to use and simple to set aside when other duties must take precedence.

Although they are easy to record, checklists lack the richness of the more descriptive narrative. For instance, by looking at the checklist in Figure 6.9 teachers will know which activities children have chosen, but they will not gain a sense of how they played in each area, the time spent there, or whether and with whom they interacted. The advantage of checklists is that they can tally broad areas of information, and teachers can create one with relative ease.

*Rating scales* are like checklists, planned in advance to record something specific. They extend checklists by adding some quality to what is observed. The advantage is that more information is gathered. A potential problem is added, since the observers' opinions are now required and could hamper objectivity.

Rating scales differ from checklists in several ways. Instead of simply recording where children are playing, the rating scales require the teacher to decide how they are playing. What is the extent of their involvement and the frequency or degree of their play? A rating scale may use word phrases ("always," "sometimes," "never") or a numerical key (1 through 5).

Developing a rating scale is simple, though a good scale can be difficult to make. The full range of behavior teachers will observe cannot always be easily reduced to discrete measurements. However, after deciding what to observe, teachers then determine what the children will do to demonstrate the action. To measure attention at group times, a scale might include the categories in Figure 6.11. Each teacher's rating scale could include a series of checkmarks that record each group time for a period of two weeks. The staff pools information by comparing notes. The result is a detailed description of (1) each child's behavior as each teacher sees it; (2) the group's overall attention level; and (3) an interesting cross-teacher comparison.

---

NEVER ATTENDS (wiggles, distracts others, wanders away).

SELDOM ATTENDS (eyes wander, never follows fingerplays or songs, occasionally watches leader).

SOMETIMES ATTENDS (can be seen imitating hand gestures, appears to be watching leader about half the time, watches others imitating leader).

USUALLY ATTENDS (often follows leader, rarely leaves group, rarely needs redirection, occasionally volunteers, usually follows leader's gestures and imitations).

ALWAYS ATTENDS (regularly volunteers, enthusiastically enters into each activity, eagerly imitates leader, almost always tries new songs).

---

**FIGURE 6.11** A rating scale measuring attention at group times requires data in terms of frequency, adding depth to the observation.

The *shadow study* is a third type of modified technique. It is similar to the diary description and focuses on one child at a time. An in-depth approach, the shadow study gives a detailed picture.

Each teacher attempts to observe and record regularly the behavior of one particular child. Then after a week or so the notes are compared. Although the notes may be random, it is preferable to give them some form and organization. Divide a sheet of paper in half lengthwise, with one column for the environment and the other column for details about the child's behavior or response. This will make it easy to glance at 15-minute intervals to collect the data. Figure 6.12 illustrates this process.

The data in a shadow study is descriptive. In this, it shares the advantages of narratives. One of its disadvantages is that teachers may let other matters go while focusing on one child. Also, the shadow study can be quite time-consuming. Still, one interesting side effect often noted is how the behavior of the child being studied improves while being observed. The disruptive behavior seems to diminish or appear less intense. It would appear that in the act of focusing on the child, teacher attention has somehow helped to alter the behavior. Somehow the child feels the impact of all this positive, caring attention and responds to it.

Modified child study techniques are particularly useful because they are tailored to fit the specific needs and interests of the teachers. Teachers know what it is they want to observe and can develop a method of recording that matches their needs and

Child's Name _____ *Jeff* _____

| Time | Setting (where) | Behavior/Response (what and how) |
|------|-----------------|----------------------------------|
| 9:00 | Arrives—cubby, removes wraps, etc. | "I can put on my own nametag" (enthusiastically). Uses thumb to push sharp end of pin; grins widely. Goes to teacher, "Did you see what I did?" |
| 9:15 | Blocks | Precise, elaborate work with small cubes on top of block structure which he built with James. "Those are the dead ones," pointing to the purple cubes outside the structure. Cries and hits Kate when her elbow accidentally knocks tower off. |
| 9:30 | Wandering around room | Semidistant, slow pace. Stops at table where children are preparing snack. Does not make eye contact with teacher when invited to sit; Ali grabs J.'s shirt and tugs at it. "The teacher is talking to you!" J. blinks, then sits and asks to help make snack. Stays 10 minutes. |

**FIGURE 6.12** A shadow study will profile an individual child in the class. This method is especially useful for studying children who seem to be having trouble in school.

the time available during school. Devising a new technique is neither easy nor quick. It takes hard work and dedicated teachers committed to improving their observational skills to record accurately what they see.

## Additional Information-Gathering Techniques

Two additional strategies are used to obtain information about a child. Because they involve some adult intervention, they do not consist strictly of observing and recording naturally occurring behavior. Still, they are very helpful techniques for teachers to understand and use.

### Experimental Procedures

Experimental procedures are those in which adult researchers closely control a situation and its variables. Researchers create a situation in which they can (1) observe a particular behavior, (2) make a hypothesis, or guess, about that behavior, and (3) test the hypothesis by conducting the experiment.

For instance, an experimenter might wish to observe fine-motor behavior in seven-year-olds to test the hypothesis that these children can significantly improve their fine-motor skills in sewing if given specific instructions. Two groups of children are tested. One group is given an embroidery hoop, thread, and needle and asked to make 10 stitches. The other receives a demonstration of how to stitch and is then given the identical task. The embroidery hoops created by both groups are then compared. Some previously agreed-upon criteria are used to quantify the fine-motor skill demonstrated by the two groups' work. The major criteria for a scientific experiment may be applied to this procedure as follows:

1. The experimenters can control all relevant aspects of the behavior. (In this case, the materials can be controlled, although previous experience with embroidering cannot.)

2. Usually, only one variable at a time should be measured. (Only fine-motor skill as it relates to embroidery is observed, not other skills such as language or information processing, or even fine-motor proficiency in printing or drawing.)

3. Children are assigned to the two groups in a random manner. (In other words, the groups are not divided by sex, age, or any other predetermined characteristics.)

Few teachers working directly with children will use the stringent criteria needed to undertake a true scientific experiment. However, it is useful to understand this process because much basic research conducted to investigate how children think, perceive, and behave utilizes these techniques. One example is the studies described in Dr. Flavell's *Focus* of Chapter 4.

### Clinical Method

The clinical method is another information-gathering technique that involves the adult directly with the child. This method is used in psychotherapy and in counseling settings, as the therapist asks probing questions. The master of *le methode clinique* with children was Piaget, who would observe and question a child about a situation as described in Chapter 4. Two examples of this method are:

> Three-month-old Jenna is lying in a crib looking at a mobile. Her hands are waving in the air. The adult wonders whether Jenna will reach out and grasp the mobile if it is moved close to her hands. Or will she bat at the toy? Move her hands away? The adult then tries it to see what will happen.

> A group of preschoolers are gathered around a water table. The teacher notices two cups, one deep and narrow, the other broad and shallow, and asks, "I wonder which one holds more, or if they are the same?" The children say what they think and why. Then, one of the children takes the two cups and pours the liquid from one into the other.

In both examples, the adult does more than simply observe and record what happens. With the

| Method | Observational Interval | Recording Techniques | Advantages | Disadvantages |
|---|---|---|---|---|
| 1. Narratives<br>Diary description | Day to day | Using notebook and pencil; can itemize activity or other ongoing behavior; can see growth patterns | Rich in detail; maintains sequence of events; describes behavior as it occurs | Open to observer bias; time-consuming |
| Specimen descriptions/ running record | Continuous sequences | Same | Less structured | Sometimes need follow-up |
| Journal | Regular, preferred daily/ weekly | Log, usually with space for each child; often a summary of child's behavior | | |
| "On-the-Hoof" Anecdotes | Sporadic | Ongoing during class time; using notepad and paper in hand | Quick and easy to take; short-capture pertinent events/details | Lack detail; need to be filled in at later time; can detract from teaching responsibilities |
| 2. Time Sampling | Short and uniform time intervals | On-the-spot as time passes; prearranged recording sheets | Easy to record; easy to analyze; relatively bias free | Limited behaviors; loss of detail; loss of sequence and ecology of event |
| 3. Event Sampling | For the duration of the event | Same as for time sampling | Easy to record; easy to analyze; can maintain flow of class activity easily | Limited behaviors; loss of detail; must wait for behavior to occur |
| 4. Modifications Checklists | Regular or intermittent | Using prepared recording sheets; can be both during or after class | Easy to develop and use | Lack of detail; tells little of the cause of behaviors |
| Rating scales | Continuous behavior | Same as for checklists | Easy to develop and use; can use for wide range of behaviors | Ambiguity of terms; high observer bias |
| Shadow study | Continuous behavior | Narrative-type recording; uses prepared recording sheets | Rich in detail; focuses in depth on individual | Bias problem; can take away too much of a teacher's time and attention |
| 5. Experimental procedures | Short and uniform | May be checklists, prearranged recording sheets, audio or video tape | Simple, clear, pure study, relatively bias free | Difficult, hard to isolate in the classroom |
| 6. Clinical method | Any time | Usually notebook or tape recorder | Relevant data, can be spontaneous, easy | Adult has changed naturally occurring behavior |

**FIGURE 6.13**  A summary chart of the major observational techniques that the early childhood professional can use to record children's behavior. (Adapted from Irwin and Bushnell, 1980.)

infant, the adult questions what Jenna's responses might be and then watches for the answer. The preschool teacher intervenes in the children's natural play to explore a question systematically with them, then listens for and observes the answers. The clinical method is not strictly an observation method, but it is an informative technique that, when used carefully, can reveal much about children's abilities and knowledge.

All these observation techniques help adults watch closely to see what is going on. Figure 6.13 summarizes these systems. It is safe to say that whenever a teacher encounters a problem—be it a child's behavior, a period of the day, a set of materials, or a puzzling series of events—the first step toward a solution is systematic observation.

## HOW TO OBSERVE AND RECORD

Learning how to observe is a serious activity and requires a great deal of concentration. Some preparations can be made beforehand so that full attention is focused on the observation. Thinking through some of the possible problems helps the teacher get the most out of the experience.

## Observing While Teaching

To make observing workable at school, it is important to keep in mind that there is no one right way to observe and record. Some teachers find certain times of the day easier than others. Many prefer to watch during free play, while others find it easier to watch individual children during directed teaching times. While some teachers keep a pencil and paper handy to write their observations throughout the day, others choose to record what they see after school is over for the day. The professional team that is committed to observation will find ways to support its implementation.

Finding an opportunity for regular observations is difficult. Centers are rarely staffed so well that one teacher can be free from classroom respon-

**FIGURE 6.14** Various observational methods translate the child's play behavior to the child's personality.

sibilities for long periods of time. Some schools ask for parent volunteers to take over an activity while a teacher observes. In one center the snack was set up ahead of time to free up one teacher to observe during group time. The environment can be arranged with activities that require little supervision when a teacher is interested in making some observations.

Some question the reliability of the data collected when children know they are being observed. Initially, children may feel self-conscious, asking pointed questions of the observer and changing their behavior as if they were on stage. However, when effective observation strategies are used (see the section in this chapter entitled How to Observe Effectively) and regular observations are done by familiar adults, children will soon ignore the observer and resume normal activity.

Teachers practice observations and recording techniques outside the classroom. Staff meetings take on an added dimension when teachers role play, devise word games, and draw up observation forms together. At home, observation strategies are used to compare notes on a segment of a television program.

The teacher who makes notes during class time has other considerations. The need to be inconspicuous while note taking is important when trying to teach and record simultaneously. Wear clothing with at least one good pocket. This ensures the paper and pencil are available when needed and the children's privacy is protected. Take care not to leave notes out on tables, shelves, or in cupboards for others to see. They should be kept confidential until added to the children's records.

Respect the privacy of the children and their families at all times. Any information gathered as part of an observation is treated with strict confidentiality. Teachers and students are careful not to use children's names in casual conversation. They do not talk about children in front of other children or themselves. It is the role of the adults to see that children's privacy is maintained. Carrying tales out of school is tempting, but unprofessional.

## The Beginning Student Observes

In some schools, observers are a normal part of the school routine. In colleges where there are laboratory facilities on campus, student observers are familiar figures. They have only to follow established guidelines for making an observation.

Many times students are responsible for finding their own places to observe children. If so, the student calls ahead and schedules a time to observe that is convenient. Be specific about observation needs, the assignment, the ages of children desired, the amount of time needed, and the purpose of the observation.

Whenever an observation is planned, it is wise to look at some practical matters before settling into the classroom. When arriving at the school, students should:

- Make themselves known to the principal, director, or teacher.

- Find out where to store personal belongings and wraps.

- Take into class only what is necessary.

The success of the observation depends on how inconspicuous the observer can be. Children are more natural if the observer blends into the scenery. By sitting back, one can observe the whole scene and record what is seen and heard, undisturbed and uninfluenced. This distancing sets up a climate for recording that aids the student in concentrating on the children.

## How to Observe Effectively

There are two main reasons for an observer to be *unobtrusive*. First, it allows for a more accurate recording of the children's activities. Second, it does not interfere with the smooth functioning of the classroom, the children, or the teachers. The following suggestions help effective observing:

- Enter and leave the area quietly. Ask the teacher where to sit. Keep in the background as much as possible. The good observer is so skilled at this that both children and teachers forget the presence of a stranger.

- Sit down in a low chair in an out-of-the-way place. Sit where the activity of the children is unobstructed. By keeping low, observers call less attention to themselves. Take care to sit outside traffic patterns so children will be able to carry on with play without interference or interruption.

- Sit at the edge of an activity rather than right in the middle of it. Against a wall or around the perimeter of the room are good vantage points for sitting. Outside, if no chair is available, blend against a wall, a fence, or a tree.

- Sometimes it may be necessary to follow children as they move from place to place. When that happens, be as inconspicuous as possible and be prepared for times when, for good reasons, the teacher might object.

- Children may occasionally ask, "What is your name? What are you doing? Why did you come here?" If asked a direct question, answer in a truthful, friendly manner, but be as brief as possible. A good response is, "I'm working." Avoid initiating conversations with children. Be as natural as possible if a child talks to you, but appear to be busy writing and observing.

- It is difficult to be in a busy classroom with children without being amused by them. Avoid a degree of response that will attract the children's attention. Laughing at them, smiling, talking, meeting their eyes, distracts them from play. It also makes the observer the center of their attention rather than their work or playmates.

- Avoid talking to other adults while observing. Sitting apart from others draws less attention to the tasks and lessens the temptation to chat. Request a brief conference before leaving to check accuracy.

- There is one time when it might be necessary to get involved with the children. If a child is in obvious danger and no one else is around, the observer should step in. Call for a teacher only if there is time. A child running out the gate toward the street or in the way of a swing needs immediate help. Two children fighting over a truck might need a teacher but are not in immediate danger.

## SUMMARY

Systematic observation and recording of children's behavior is a fundamental tool in understanding children. What children do and say and how they think and feel are revealed as they play and work. By learning to observe children's behavior, teachers

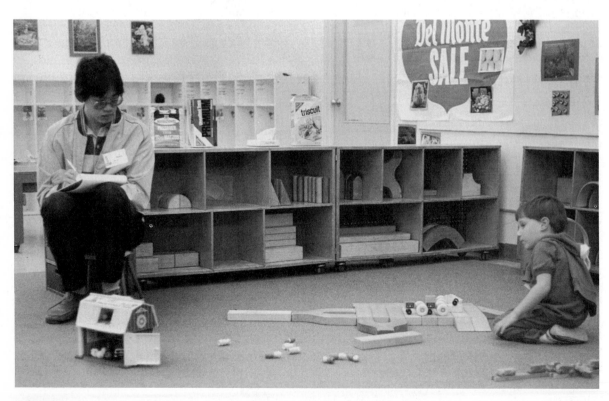

**FIGURE 6.15**  Learning to observe and record effectively takes time and practice. Remaining unobtrusive and recording quietly allows children to continue their natural behavior without distraction.

become more aware of the children's skills, needs, and concerns.

The ability to observe is a skill in itself; teachers examine their own lives and attitudes in order to achieve a measure of objectivity. Recording the observations is another skill, one that requires facility with the written word and an understanding of the purpose for observing. For an observation to be successful, teachers first decide what it is they want to find out about the child(ren).

Key ingredients to successful observations include clear definitions of the behaviors to be observed and techniques for observing and recording them. These provide the tools for gaining a deeper understanding of individual children and the group. They also enhance knowledge about the interrelationships of developmental areas. Too, one gains insight into the dynamics of child behavior and what influences are brought to bear on it. Finally, observing children can give insight and greater understanding of self.

The general types of observational techniques explored in this chapter include narratives, time sampling, event sampling, and modified child study techniques, such as checklists, rating scales, and shadow studies. Additional information-gathering techniques include experimental procedures and the clinical method.

As teachers observe and record the behavior of young children, they are aware of professional guidelines that protect children. The guidelines help ensure accurate observation and help the observer respect the privacy of the individual or group.

## REVIEW QUESTIONS

1. List four observational methods. Describe the advantages and disadvantages of each. Which would you prefer? Why? Which one(s) might best suit a beginning teacher? A parent? An experienced teacher? The director of the school?

2. Observe a child for 10 minutes. Using language as your paintbrush, make a written picture of that child's physical appearance and movements. Include a comparison of the child's size, body build, facial features, and energy level to those of other children in the class. Record as many of the body movements as you can, noting seemingly useless movements, failures, partial successes, as well as final achievements.

3. Perceptions of a person's character are in the eyes of the beholder. These perceptions affect how teachers behave with children. What color are your glasses tinted? Divide a piece of paper in half, lengthwise. On one side, list some words to describe your feelings about childhood, school, teachers, children, authority, making friends, losing friends, hitting, playing. On the other side, describe how these feelings may have influenced your teaching and helped create your own biases.

4. Teachers have noticed that several children consistently interrupt at storytime with seemingly irrelevant questions and constantly grab onto children seated nearby. What's happening—and why? What observational tools would you use to find out? What clues from individual behavior would you look for? How would you look at the group as a whole? What other information would you need?

5. What do you consider to be the three most important guidelines to follow when observing young children? Why?

## LEARNING ACTIVITIES

1. Observe a children's quarrel. What was happening for *you* when you watched? What does this tell you about your own influences in childhood? How did the teaching staff intervene? How would you? Why?

2. Try a time sample of children's play in your classroom. Observe 10 children for one minute each during free-play times, and record the type(s) of social behavior they show. Using Parten's categories, your chart would look like the one on p. 171. Compare your results with the impressions of the other teachers with whom you work. Did you come to any conclusions on how children develop socially?

| Child/Age | Unoccupied | Solitary | Onlooker | Parallel | Associative | Cooperative |
|---|---|---|---|---|---|---|
| 1. | | | | | | |
| 2. | | | | | | |
| 3. | | | | | | |
| 4. | | | | | | |
| 5. | | | | | | |
| 6. | | | | | | |
| 7. | | | | | | |
| 8. | | | | | | |
| 9. | | | | | | |
| 10. | | | | | | |
| Totals | | | | | | |

3. Observe one child in your class and jot down a brief description of her language skills. Are they typical of her age level? How could you tell? Compare your notes with the perceptions of your supervising teacher.

4. Choose two children, one you think is doing well and one who is having trouble. Observe the adult-child interactions of each. What are the differences from the *children's* point of view in the quantity and quality of those relationships? What generalizations about the importance of such relationships in the early years can you make?

5. If you can, try a shadow study on a child in your class. Choose a child you don't know much about, you have trouble working with, or who is exhibiting inappropriate behaviors. How did this study help you to see the class and school from that child's point of view?

6. Observe a group of children for 10 minutes engaged in block play. Record your observations in running record form. Now, go back over that running record and make a list of things you want to know about the children's thinking and behavior. How could you construct this list, using the clinical method, to obtain the information you need? Would you intervene nonverbally? What questions could you ask the children directly?

## B I B L I O G R A P H Y

Boehm, A. *The Classroom Observer.* New York: Teachers College Press, 1977.

Cohen, D.H., and Stern, V. *Observing and Recording the Behavior of Young Children.* New York: Teachers College Press, 1978.

Dowley, Edith M. *Cues for Observing Children's Behavior.* Unpublished paper.

Irwin, D.M., and Bushnell, M.M. *Observational Strategies for Child Study.* New York: Holt, Rinehart and Winston, 1980.

Mattick, I., and Perkins, F.J. *Guidelines for Observation and Assessment.* Washington, D.C.: Day Care and Child Development Council of America, 1972.

Stallings, J. *Learning to Look.* Belmont, Calif.: Wadsworth, 1977.

Wright, H.F. *Recording and Analyzing Child Behavior.* New York: Harper and Row, 1967.

# CHAPTER 7

## Understanding and Guiding Behavior

Happy

This one is sad

## QUESTIONS for THOUGHT

- Why do children behave the way they do?
- What are some ways in which the classroom environment affects children's behavior?
- What do teachers need to know about themselves so they can guide children with control and concern?
- What is the difference between discipline and punishment?
- Are behavior goals the same for all children? Why?
- What are some common problem behaviors found in young children?
- What are some effective ways to deal with behavior problems?
- Why is spanking harmful to children?

# UNDERSTANDING BEHAVIOR

Allie, who is four, leans across the table and scribbles on Beth's paper. Beth looks startled, calls Allie a dummy, and crumples the paper in her fist. Jason, who just turned five and is sitting next to Allie, uses his crayon to make similar marks on Allie's drawing. He laughs as Allie hits out at him. Beth calls for the teacher.

Nicole, a three-year-old, cries and clings to her mother at the entrance to school several days in a row. Her mother tells her to stop acting like a baby and thrusts her toward the teacher. She then rushes out to work.

Matt, who is 18 months old, bursts into tears when the teacher stops him as he strikes out at Pablo, who is 13 months old. The boys both reached for the same toy and Pablo got it first.

*(See page 203 and Figure 7.12 for discussing solutions to these situations).*

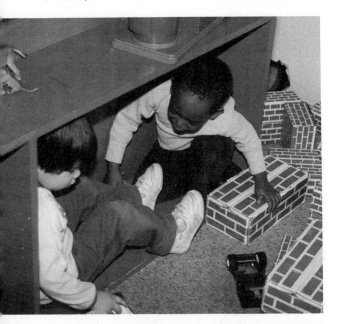

**FIGURE 7.1** Are these two boys misbehaving? Would you stop this play? Why? (Courtesy of Stride Rite Children's Centers, Cambridge, Mass.)

These are typical scenes in any early childhood center. No matter how plentiful the materials, how many or well-trained the adults, or how preplanned the program, conflicts are sure to occur. In this chapter, students will look at ways to recognize and handle such situations; how to understand and guide children's behavior in ways that will help them deal more effectively with their feelings. Helping children learn how to cope with their anger, their fears, their frustrations, and their desires is one of the most challenging jobs for a teacher.

To teach children to respect themselves and each other is a complex and difficult task. It takes experience, skill, and love and is a critical part of caring for children. Look at the examples again. What do they say about children in general? What do they say about Allie, Nicole, and Matt? How should teachers respond to these children, and how does that response influence future behavior?

## Theories

To guide children's behavior, a teacher must first understand it. This requires a solid background in child development, skills in observing, and understanding about *why* children behave and misbehave.

There are several ways of explaining what people do and why. One idea is that people's behavior is mainly a result of heredity (nature). Another is that experience and environment shape behavior (nurture). A third theory suggests that children go through "stages" at certain times of their lives regardless of their genes or home background.

Both sides have valid arguments in the nature/nurture debate. It is useful to remember that both heredity and experience affect behavior. Age and stage theory is also familiar. People speak of the "terrible two's" or say that all four-year-old girls are silly. There may be some truth to those generalities, but that does not excuse the inappropriate behavior of the various developmental stages. Teachers and parents cannot ignore misbehavior just because children are the "right" age or because of their home situations. That attitude implies adults are powerless to help children form new behavior patterns. Not true!

# ON SPANKING

...Three long-term effects of spanking are particularly significant:

1. The adult models the use of physical force as a method of problem solving or getting people to do what you want them to do. If this is a model you do not want a child to imitate, then you are sending mixed messages to the child. Children will do what you do, not what you say.

2. You lessen the overall effect of your influence by matching your presence with something painful and unpleasant; therefore undermining your own positive value for the child. This will lessen the influence praise and affection will have.

3. The emotional message of spanking is rejection of the child.

(Bee, 1985)

. . . [spanking] does not teach any constructive lessons about human relationships, and after all, that's what discipline is all about: the ways we try to teach our children to live in a civilized fashion with themselves and others. . . . You are resorting to the lowest possible level of human interaction.

(LeShan, 1985)

**FIGURE 7.2** Spanking children is a controversial issue. Two early childhood experts, one a developmental psychologist, the other a family counselor, state their views. Do you agree or disagree with them? Why?

Adults can do something about children's behavior if they understand what is happening to the child. Where does appropriate behavior come from? Why do children misbehave?

# Factors That Affect Behavior

Knowing what affects children's behavior and feelings helps adults understand and manage the misbehaving child. Teachers can anticipate problems instead of waiting for them to occur; preventive guidance measures are part of guiding children's behavior.

At least four factors affect behavior: developmental factors, environmental factors, individual or personal styles, and social and emotional needs. These factors combine aspects of both nature and nurture theories, as well as the theories of ages and stages of development.

## *Developmental Factors*

Children's growth is constant if not always smooth. Adults who work with children should be aware of developmental theory in order to know what type of behavior to expect of children at various ages.

*Case Study #1*
All the children are outdoors playing, just before lunch. Chris, who turned three years old last week, is at the sand table, when 5½-year-old Benjamin arrives. "Stop! We're the bosses here!" Benjie states with a frown. Chris returns the angry glare, hunches his shoulders, and sits down. "You can't have any sand. Get out of here. And you just messed up our road, you dummy!" shouts Benjie. Chris stands up quickly and throws sand at Benjie. They start hitting each other. (See Figure 7.3.)

The facts are that these children have been in a group setting for more than three hours and it is nearly lunch time. One child is over five years of age; the other barely three. The teacher knows that preschoolers cannot be expected to be in control of themselves over extended periods of time. Conflicts and disagreements are to be expected in any group of children. Hungry children are often ineffective problem solvers; the same situation might not be as *volatile* after lunch. It is also clear to the teacher that three-year-olds do not have the language or social

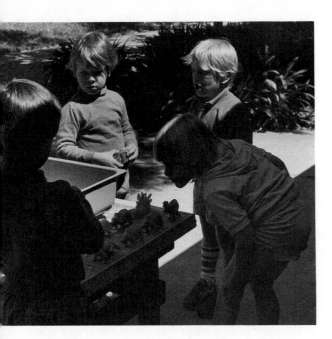

**FIGURE 7.3** "We're the bosses here!"

development skills to talk problems out with other children. Five-year-olds tend to dominate a younger peer to exercise their well-developed cognitive, social, and language skills.

Taking all of these developmental factors into consideration, the teacher *intervenes* to stop the fighting and takes both boys over to the hose to clean the sand out of their faces. In the process, the teacher encourages the children to help each other by holding the hose when the other one washes. The conversation at this time revolves around how hungry everyone must be as lunch time approaches. Benjie is encouraged to find a place for Chris; Chris is given words to use to tell Benjie where he wants to play in the sand. Benjie is asked to assume a role in helping Chris find a place; his leadership skills are put to positive use.

Developmental theory helps teachers anticipate what children will do and how they might behave. To see behavior as predictable and developmentally appropriate is to understand it more completely. This understanding guides teachers in solving behavioral problems.

Developmental guidelines also help teachers maintain reasonable expectations. When adults are aware of which behaviors are simply beyond the capabilities of children, they can help avert situations that will lead to conflicts. Asking a group of toddlers, for example, to sit quietly together for a 20-minute story is to invite misbehavior—wriggling, talking aloud, pushing, interrupting, walking away. Yet all of these are completely normal behaviors for a two-year-old in that situation. The adult's insistence on a prolonged story time is asking these children to perform beyond their current physical, social, and cognitive abilities.

## Environmental Factors

Environment for the young child is primarily home, school, or child care settings. The term environment has three distinct parts: the physical, the *temporal* (timing and scheduling), and the interpersonal. Each has an impact on children's behavior.

The physical environment is a powerful tool in controlling children's behavior. Teachers can achieve a number of behavior goals through the physical facilities of the early childhood program. Child-size furniture that fits the preschool body encourages sitting and working behavior. Room arrangements that have no long, open spaces children could use as runways encourage children to walk from place to place. Low, open shelves create an expectation that children are to help themselves in taking out and putting away the materials and equipment.

Chapter 9, Creating Environments, contains a detailed discussion of many factors that should be considered when designing spaces for young children. Many of these environmental considerations directly influence children's behavior. See also the Classroom Checklist (Fig. 7.9) on page 197.

**Materials.** In addition to arrangement of room or yard, materials affect how children behave, whether in a family day care home or an after-school sports program. The materials provided can challenge children, overwhelm them, or bore them. If materials and equipment are suitable, children will feel more at ease with themselves and be more willing to accept adults' limits and controls. The materials and equipment allow appropriate outlets for children's natural tendencies; they capture interest and attention, and this helps prevent many opportunities for misbehavior. When children are occupied with stimulating, age-appropriate materials, the amount of conflict and disruption lessens. Adding materials and equipment can help prevent fights over a favorite toy, create new interests and challenges in alternative activities, and extend children's play ideas and themes. Changing the environment when needed can help avert behavior problems. Removing attractive but breakable items reduces tears and conflicts. Some materials may prove to be too stimulating and may need to be removed for a while. Some activities may need to be limited to specific locations to control the level of activity and behavior.

**Time.** The temporal structure (Mattick and Perkins, 1974) describes the sequence of a program. When there are blocks of time to choose activities, children can proceed at their own pace without feeling pushed or hurried. They feel free to work, move, and play and are able to accept the teacher's control when it is necessary. The physical needs of eating, sleeping, and toileting are met by careful scheduling so that children are able to play without concern for the necessities of life. Schedules that do not allow enough time for cleanup, for instance, produce a frantic climate. It is when children are rushed and hurried by adults that arguments, accidents, and tears ensue. Uncooperative behavior is sometimes related to time pressures.

A consistent daily plan helps promote a feeling that the world is predictable and understandable. Children need time to work out their own problems. Hurrying and wondering what happens next create tension that results in behavior problems.

**Relationships.** These need special consideration because they determine how learning takes place. The interpersonal environment refers to all the "people" factors. An atmosphere of trust and support helps to create a sound learning environment. In early childhood centers the significant relation-

ships are those between teacher and child, children and other children, teacher and parents, and teacher and other teachers. Each type of relationship affects and influences children's behavior. When children sense a feeling of mutual support and acceptance, their play reflects that tone. Tension among adults is quickly transmitted to children, and their behavior patterns adjust to the negative influence.

Other influences affect behavior. Weather seems to affect children. Wild, windy, gray, rainy days seem to stimulate children into high and excitable behavior. Bright, sunny days also seem to influence a child's mood and temperament. Problems that upset adults can make an impression on a child. A family crisis, a new baby, or a recent divorce have impact. Sharing a room, visits from relatives, illness, television and movie shows, brothers and sisters, nutrition and health, cause children to behave in many different ways. The longer teachers work with children, the more adept they become at seeing how these various factors shape the behavior of the individual children in their class.

*Case Study #2*
It is late in the afternoon at the child care center, and it has been raining all week. Several children are playing with hollow blocks on the covered patio. Shouts and screams fill the air. Three-year-old Jonathan holds firmly to a steering wheel mounted on a large block. "It's mine! It's mine!" he yells. Sam, a four-year-old and Justo, who is 2½, pull the block toward their building. Scowling, Justo reaches toward Jonathan, grabs his arm, and raises it to his face. The teacher arrives just in time to prevent Justo from biting Jonathan.

The facts are that children find waiting and sharing difficult. When they are able to play with attractive equipment for only short periods of time, they become frustrated, resulting in more arguments over play materials. Two- and three-year-olds are just developing social skills and learning to share; they do not have the abilities of a four-year-old to negotiate for equipment. Two steering wheel blocks may not be enough for the number of children in this particular group; perhaps more should be added so that children do not have to wait as long for a turn. The rain has kept the children confined to small spaces indoors and on the patio; that adds to the tension everyone feels. Jonathan has been at school only a week, and Justo helped to celebrate his sister's first birthday yesterday. Both of these children carry with them remnants of emotional adjustments they are making.

The teacher holds Justo's arm to prevent him from biting Jonathan. "I will not let you bite children, Justo. Biting hurts. I won't let you hurt children, and I won't let you be hurt," says the teacher. Jonathan is invited to tell his side of the story and the teacher helps the children negotiate a time limit for using the steering wheels and for playing on the patio.

Environmental factors can add to the stress of behavior expectations. In this example, the amount of time, the weather, and levels of social development combined to create a situation that frustrated the children and resulted in their inappropriate behavior.

**FIGURE 7.4**  "It's mine! It's mine! I got it first!"

## Individual Styles

People seem to come equipped with a style all their own. Pregnant women can describe a child's personality while the baby is still in the womb. Mothers know of the special way infants behave that sets them apart. Parents often comment on the differences among their own children. Raised by the same parents in the same house and neighborhood, each child is a singular and original being.

Each child in a classroom is also unique, an individual like no other. All have a personal style that needs to be acknowledged and valued. Children who are not accepted for themselves may learn to hate themselves or not to trust their own instincts. A broken or timid spirit creates a timid or rebellious person.

Teachers of young children soon learn the temperamental characteristics of each child in the class. Hondi works and plays with great intensity; Norman is easily distracted. Tawana fears any change while Enrique thrives on challenges. The consistent patterns of temperament that emerge help define each child's individual style.

Research by Thomas and Chess (Bee, 1985) has identified three types of temperament in babies: the easy child, the difficult child, and the slow-to-warm-up child. The traits used to classify these children were:

- The child's activity level—the amount of movement or inactivity
- The regularity and rhythm of bodily routines such as sleep, digestion, and elimination
- The ability to adapt to change
- Initial reaction to something new
- Physical sensitivity to the total environment—light, heat, noise
- Intensity of reaction and strength of response
- Ease of distraction
- Overall negative or positive mood
- Persistence and length of attention span

These differences were observed in very young infants and seem to remain consistent as the child grows.

The implications for teachers in these findings are several. First and foremost, the research supports the concept of individual differences that are present from birth and the importance of acknowledging those differences. If parents and teachers come to know the nature of a child's temperament, they can accept that as part of the wholeness of that particular child. Discipline and guidance measures can be tailored to meet the unique needs of a slow-to-warm-up child, for instance, or a difficult child. Those strategies will need to be different from techniques used to discipline the easy child. Recognition of traits enables teachers and parents to deal with quirks of personality. How would you deal with children who exhibit extremes of the nine traits listed above? It is also useful to compare your own temperament with that of the children you teach.

Children's temperament also affects the way people deal with them. An easy child is easy to respond to; a slow-to-warm-up child may be harder to reach. Difficult children may tend to be blamed for things they did not do. Identifying traits can be useful so long as adults are careful not to label children unfairly or prematurely.

*Case Study #3*
It is midmorning at the preschool, nearing the end of free-play time indoors. Zachary has been moving about the room for 10 or 15 minutes. He has stepped on Sergio's hand as he shuffled past and he "accident'ly" knocked over Megan's five-story garage in the block corner. Now he comes to the art table where children are using water colors. To Steven and Lydia he says, "Those are ugly pictures." The teacher reminds him that hurtful words bother other people. He shouts back, "I don't care. You can't make the words go back in my mouth. And I'm not helping at cleanup time either."

The facts are that Zachary's personal style is that of a five-year-old full of himself and his power as one of the leaders in the class. He is a verbal and

**FIGURE 7.5** "You can't make the words go back in my mouth." (Courtesy of Stride Rite Children's Centers, Cambridge, Mass.)

strong child who likes to have the last word. He is also enthusiastic and plunges into activities spontaneously, sometimes without looking ahead or surveying the wreckage he leaves behind. Zachary's teacher is aware that he can be personable and cooperative if he is given options and a chance to make decisions. As they talk together about this incident, the teacher offers Zachary a valid choice: leading the bucket brigade to empty the water table or moving chairs to clear space for a movie (one of Zachary's favorite group activities). Both find satisfaction in working together in ways that acknowledge and respect Zachary's personal style.

## Emotional and Social Needs

Some behavior problems stem from the child's attempt to express social and emotional needs. These include the need to feel loved and cared for, the need to be included, the desire to be considered important and valued, the desire to have friends, and the need to feel safe from harm. Young children are still working out ways to express these needs and feelings.

Typically, since they are only just learning language and communication skills, it is often through non-verbal or indirect actions that children let us know what is bothering them. Therefore, it is also important to provide children with models of language for resolving these conflicts. It is important to let children know that we recognize they can be angry, jealous, or hurt. The supportive adult will help children find satisfying ways to cope with their social and emotional feelings.

Psychiatrist Rudolf Dreikurs has defined four categories of misbehavior that seem to stem from the child's social or emotional needs. Since children have something to gain from each type of misbehavior, Dreikurs labels the behaviors goals; namely, attention, power, revenge, and the display of inadequacy.

**Attention.** Nearly all children want attention. They prefer to get it in positive ways, but if that doesn't work, they will try to gain attention, any attention, even if it is negative. There are several appropriate responses possible. First, try to pay attention to children when they are not actively seeking attention, that is, when it is not being demanded. This will emphasize the giving nature of attention rather than the getting. Next, attend to the child's positive behavior. This shows children that their useful acts get them attention, not their negative ones. Finally, ignore their bids for attention when they misbehave or try to respond in ways children do not expect. An example of the latter would be to keep the dawdling Cleo inside until she puts on her coat, even though the rest of the class is already outside.

**Power.** Everyone likes to feel important and powerful. Power-seeking children, though, seem to think that they are important only if they are "the boss." Adults must avoid a power struggle; getting angry or using power tactics only defeats the child and shows that power over others is, in fact, valuable. Rather, choose carefully what to say and do, following through with limits or decisions calmly and deliberately. Enlist children's help; give them some valid power. By empowering these children with chances

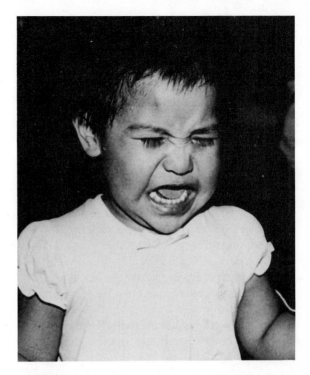

**FIGURE 7.6** Children often express their needs in non-verbal ways. It is important to understand what children are communicating when they cry. (Courtesy of Thaddeus Cunejo, NMSU.)

for positive leadership, their behavior can turn into something productive.

**Revenge.** Usually children who seek revenge feel unlovable and unimportant. Often they think others are treating them unfairly or have decided that this treatment is what they deserve. They are hurt and they try to hurt back; only by hurting others can they be important. Adults must try not to retaliate; this will only reinforce the children's belief that they are, indeed, being hurt and are unlovable.

**A Display of Inadequacy.** All children who misbehave are discouraged. The children who display *inadequacy* probably feel the most helpless. They have given up any idea of succeeding, rarely try anything new, and will not persist in any activity for long. They may also say, "I don't know" in order to keep people from expecting anything of them. Adults may get impatient or easily discouraged, or give up hope. Instead, teachers and parents should try to eliminate any criticism and praise any attempt the child makes. Do not wait for the child to succeed; praise the effort of trying.

These goals can apply to the child's interactions with adults or with other children. More than one goal may be involved, and the particular reason for misbehavior may not be obvious. When Allie scribbles on Beth's paper (in the example at the beginning of the chapter) did she just want attention or was she flexing her power? Perhaps she was, in Dreikurs' term, seeking revenge. To help Allie learn to manage her behavior, her teachers will have to weigh those possible motives against what they know of Allie's social and emotional history as well as her individual style.

In Chapter 14, Planning for the Heart and Soul, the young child's social and emotional growth is further explored.

# GUIDING BEHAVIOR
## Discipline

Discipline is one of the most common and persistent concerns of teachers and parents. Listen in the teacher's lounge or at the park and sooner or later the discussion turns to children's behavior.

Why won't Emily make her bed?

What should I do when Carl refuses to take the garbage out?

Crispin is such a whiner!

I wonder why Dominic never comes to school on time.

I wish Peggy wouldn't disrupt group time with her silliness.

How can teachers be more effective in helping children change the way they behave? "How can I get better results? What should I do now? I've tried everything," is the lament. When the subject is discipline, feelings and frustrations run high.

---

ABOUT CHOICES

–Give children choices whenever possible. This allows some control over themselves so they do not feel continually dominated by adults and helps them practice self-reliance, self-direction, and self-discipline. "Looks like there is plenty of room at the easels or at the lotto games, Seth. Where would you like to play?"

–Only give choices when you mean for the children to have a choice. Be prepared to accept their answer when a choice is offered. Make sure you present choices to children only when they really have one. "Some of the children are going inside for music now. Would you like to join them?" Do not ask, "Would you like to go home now? Clean up?" when it is not an option.

–Suggest two choices when there is the possibility of resistance. Let children know you expect them to comply with your request, but allow some decision on their part. Do not box them into a corner. "It's time to go home now. Would you like to get your artwork before or after you put on your jacket?"

–Make the choice real and valid. Acknowledge children's growing ability to deal with responsibility and help them practice making reasonable choices. "There are several kinds of nails, Stacey. Try them out to see which ones work best for you."

| Discipline | Punishment |
|---|---|
| Emphasizes what the child should *do* | Emphasizes what the child should *not* do |
| Is an ongoing process | Is a one-time occurrence |
| Sets an example to follow | Insists on obedience |
| Leads to self-control | Undermines independence |
| Helps children change | Is an adult release |
| Is positive | Is negative |
| Accepts child's need to assert self | *Makes* children behave |
| Fosters child's ability to think | Thinks *for* the child |
| Bolsters self-esteem | Defeats self-esteem |
| Shapes behavior | Condemns misbehavior |

**FIGURE 7.7** A positive approach to discipline encourages children's interaction and involvement; punishment is usually something that is done *to* a child.

## What Is Discipline?

Some of those strong feelings stem from the association of *discipline* with the word *punishment*. Discipline is generally thought of in negative terms. To many people, the words *discipline* and *punishment* are synonymous.

Figure 7.7 shows how these terms mean very different things. Discuss these differences in class and plan intervention strategies for teachers to use with Allie, Nicole, and Matt in the situations described on page 185. Match the proposed solutions with the developmentally appropriate expectations found in the Word Pictures in Chapter 3.

What does discipline mean and why does it cause uncertainty in teachers and parents? Why is there so much confusion about it?

The word discipline stems from disciple: a pupil, a follower, a learner. This suggests an important concept, that of following an example versus following rules. Children try to be like the adults they see; adults serve as models for children. How children see adults behave tends to become part of their own behavior. Adults help children learn appropriate behavior by setting good examples.

Discipline and guidance are used interchangeably. Discipline is guiding and directing children toward acceptable behavior. This includes everything parents and teachers do, everything they say, in an attempt to influence the child. Discipline is something you do with children; it is an interaction, not something adults do *to* children. In caring and understanding ways, the effective teacher helps children gain control over their own behavior. To accomplish this, teachers maintain that delicate balance between children's attempts to be independent and their need for outer controls.

It is not so much the word discipline that is significant as it is the form it takes. Children are robbed of their self-respect when they are treated harshly and made to feel they have no ability to control themselves. Shame, disgrace, and embarrassment have no part in good disciplinary procedures.

One of the goals of discipline is to help children achieve self-discipline. This happens only if adults lead in ways that support children's developing ability to control themselves. Teachers who are sensitive to this will decrease the amount of control they exercise. By gradually handing over to children the opportunity to govern their own actions, adults communicate trust. For young children, with their urge to prove themselves, their drive toward initiative, this is an important step to take. With added responsibility and trust comes an added dimension of self-respect and self-confidence. Such children feel capable and worthwhile.

Along with self-respect, the child must taste the freedom that comes with a lessening of adult controls.

Children do not learn to handle freedom by being told what to do all the time. Only when they have an opportunity to test themselves, make some decisions on their own, will they know their capabilities. Young children must learn this in safe places, with adults who allow them as much freedom as they can responsibly handle.

The essence of good discipline is summed up by Allen and Hart (1984) as follows:

> . . . Teachers want children to try out new behaviors; they want children to test the limits in a setting where it is safe to do so; and they want children to learn how to manage failure as well as success. Discipline is designed both to help children learn how to manage mistakes and to let the children know that the rules really do hold, thus making it safe for them to make mistakes.

## The Language of Discipline

Discipline has a language all its own. As beginning teachers gain experience in handling problem behaviors, they learn to use that language. The result, in most cases, is a startling *interdependence:* the more practiced teachers become in the language of discipline, the more comfortable they become in developing their own approach to disciplinary problems. And the more comfortable they are in that approach, the more effectively they use language to solve behavior problems.

The language and communication techniques in discipline are both spoken and unspoken. Teachers discover how potent the voice can be; what words will work best and when. They become aware of facial expressions and what a touch or a look will convey to children. How they use their body reflects a distinct attitude and approach to discipline. New

---

BEING POSITIVE

–Tell children what it is you want them to do. Make directions and suggestions in positive statements, not in negative forms. "Walk around the edge of the grass, Hilla, so you won't get hit by the swing," instead of, "Don't get hit!"

–Reinforce what children do right, what you like, and what you want to see repeated. This helps build the relationship on positive grounds. "Good job, Sammy. You worked hard on that puzzle."

–Give indirect suggestions or reminders, emphasizing what you want children to do. Help them refocus on the task without nagging or confrontation. "I know you are excited about the field trip, Mickey. Looks like you are almost finished putting on your jacket so we can go," instead of "Hurry and button that jacket so we can go."

–Use positive redirection whenever possible. Suggest another acceptable way for the child to do the same thing or achieve the same results. This shows children how to meet their needs by addressing the problem in direct ways. Redirection differs from diverting the child's attention to something else. It does not avoid the issue, but confronts it with an alternative method. "You two really seem to want to wrestle. Let's get the mats out so you can wrestle with each other and not interfere with music," instead of "Stop that wrestling and find something else to do."

–Give reasons for your request. Let children know in simple, straightforward statements the reasons behind your request. Children are more likely to cooperate when they can understand the reason why. "Tom, if you move those chairs, then you and Dee will have more room to dance," instead of "Move the chairs, Tom."

teachers should know how to use these tools in ways that will work best for them and the children.

**Voice.** Some adults feel that when they are speaking to children they must assume a different voice from the one they normally use. This "teacher voice" often occurs when disciplinary issues are at stake. The teacher's voice becomes tight, high-pitched, the tone increasingly strained. Teaching requires no more than a normal speaking voice. Talk to children in the same way you talk to other people. Learn to control the volume and use good speech patterns for children to imitate. In order to be heard, get close enough to speak in a normal tone; get down to the child's level. Often, lowering volume and pitch is effective.

**Words.** Children have torrents of words rained upon them in the course of a school day. Teachers fall into the trap of overusing words. Where behavior is concerned and anger or frustration aroused, some adults seem to gain release from a string of verbage. This works against good disciplinary practices. Children tend to turn off people who are excessively verbal with them. Their eyes glaze over, they become fidgety or even frightened, and the incident looses significance.

The fewer the words, the better. Simple, clear statements, spoken once, will have more impact. The child will be able to focus on the real issues involved. A brief description of what happened, a word or two about what behavior is acceptable and what isn't, and a suggestion for possible solutions are all that is necessary.

Choose words carefully. They should convey to the child exactly what is expected. "Richy, move the block closer to the truck. Then Sarah won't bump into it again," tells Richy in a positive, concrete way what he can do to protect his block building. If he had been told, "Richy, watch where you are building," he would not know what action to take to solve the problem.

**Body Expressions.** When working with small children, it is important to be aware of body height

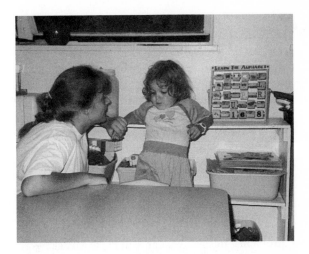

**FIGURE 7.8** Body height and position are important. Get down to the child's eye level for greater impact and involvement.

and position. Show children that respect for their size by speaking with them face to face. Sit, squat, or kneel—but get down to their level. It is difficult to communicate warmth, caring, and concern from two or three feet above a child's head.

Good discipline is founded on a loving, caring relationship between child and adult. In order to help children gain control over their impulses and monitor their own behavior, teachers must establish a sense of trust and well-being with children. The way teachers use their bodies invites or rejects close relationship and familiarity. A child will find teachers more approachable if they are seated low, with arms available, rather than standing, with arms folded.

By making full use of the senses, the impact of words can be softened. A firm grip on the hand of a child who is hitting out, a gentle touch on the shoulder, tells children the adult is there to protect them from themselves and others. Eye contact is essential. Teachers learn to communicate the seriousness of a situation through eye and facial expressions. They also show reassurance, concern, sadness, and affection this way.

Physical presence should convey to the child a message that the teacher is there, available, and interested.

**Attitude.** This is part of the unspoken language of discipline. Attitudes are derived from experience. Most adults who take care of children reflect how their own parents treated them and how they were disciplined. Some people react against the way they were raised; others tend to follow the model their parents established. Teachers find it useful to look at the way they were disciplined as youngsters and acknowledge their feelings about it. As they begin to inhibit the behavior of the children in their classes, teachers should be aware of their own attitudes. The following questions may help that process:

- Do you accept the fact that all children will have problems, misbehave, and will make mistakes?
- Do you believe children are capable of solving their own problems, and do you involve them in the process?
- Do you accept the child's right to independence and actively encourage self-reliance?
- Do you think children misbehave deliberately, to bother the teacher?
- Do you help children accept the responsibility for their own actions without blaming them?
- Are you optimistic that problems can be solved and that you and the child can work it out together?

# Good Disciplinary Practices

Children's behavior is influenced by more than just their own impulses, needs, or reactions. The three case studies show that factors beyond the scope of childhood can cause misbehavior. There are several areas over which adults have control that may cause problems for children. Three of the most common are the classroom environment, setting limits on children's behavior, and the teacher's role in guidance.

Since the classroom promotes or detracts from positive interactions and appropriate behavior, it is the first place to look for ways to improve guidance and disciplinary techniques. The goals for behavior management should be reflected in the classroom

setting. Too often, good intentions are defeated by the physical environment. The physical setting should tell children clearly and directly how to act in that space. That makes it easier for them to know what is expected and how they should behave.

Through the intentional use of the environment, the teacher indirectly influences behavior in the classroom. The schedule allows for enough time to play and clean up; there are adequate and interesting materials to use; there is a sense of order and adults are skilled in discipline techniques that work. Use the classroom checklist in Figure 7.9 to evaluate how the environment relates to your disciplinary values and is clearly related to the behavior of children.

## Consider the Limits

When teachers discipline children for unacceptable behavior, they are setting the *limits* on that behavior. Limits are the absolute control the adult puts on the child's behavior. They are the constraints set up to help children know what will or will not be tolerated. Teachers generally have two reasons for setting limits: (1) to prevent children from injuring themselves or others; and (2) to prevent the destruction of property, materials, or equipment.

Limits are a necessary part of any group or society. Every group has its bottom-line rules—rules that must be kept to ensure order and living in accord. The early childhood classroom is no exception; teachers make it clear to children what rules determine the conduct within that group. Teachers plan curriculum, arrange rooms, and follow good disciplinary practices so that a great number of rules are not necessary. Frequent exclamations of "Don't do this . . . " or "Don't do that . . . " need not be a part of the early childhood classroom when one understands the nature of setting limits.

Limits are like fences; they are protective structures that help children feel secure. Limits define the boundaries of behavior just like fences outline property lines. Fences and limits are erected and maintained to help people know how far they can go.

Fences—or limits—set up a framework in which everyone knows the rules. There is no guess work, no vague or hidden boundaries, no invisible

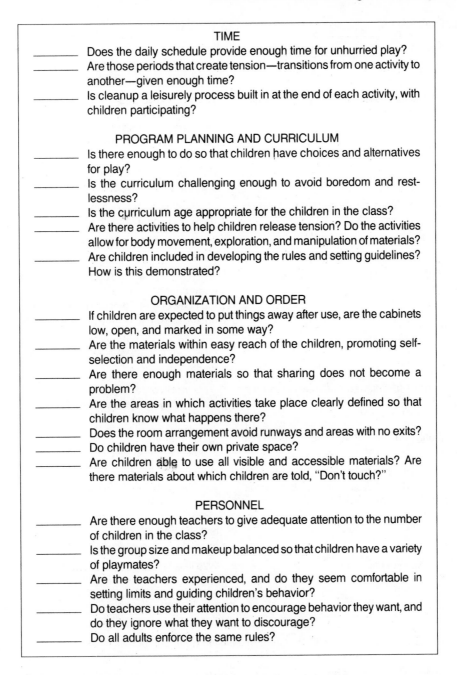

TIME

_____ Does the daily schedule provide enough time for unhurried play?

_____ Are those periods that create tension—transitions from one activity to another—given enough time?

_____ Is cleanup a leisurely process built in at the end of each activity, with children participating?

PROGRAM PLANNING AND CURRICULUM

_____ Is there enough to do so that children have choices and alternatives for play?

_____ Is the curriculum challenging enough to avoid boredom and restlessness?

_____ Is the curriculum age appropriate for the children in the class?

_____ Are there activities to help children release tension? Do the activities allow for body movement, exploration, and manipulation of materials?

_____ Are children included in developing the rules and setting guidelines? How is this demonstrated?

ORGANIZATION AND ORDER

_____ If children are expected to put things away after use, are the cabinets low, open, and marked in some way?

_____ Are the materials within easy reach of the children, promoting self-selection and independence?

_____ Are there enough materials so that sharing does not become a problem?

_____ Are the areas in which activities take place clearly defined so that children know what happens there?

_____ Does the room arrangement avoid runways and areas with no exits?

_____ Do children have their own private space?

_____ Are children able to use all visible and accessible materials? Are there materials about which children are told, "Don't touch?"

PERSONNEL

_____ Are there enough teachers to give adequate attention to the number of children in the class?

_____ Is the group size and makeup balanced so that children have a variety of playmates?

_____ Are the teachers experienced, and do they seem comfortable in setting limits and guiding children's behavior?

_____ Do teachers use their attention to encourage behavior they want, and do they ignore what they want to discourage?

_____ Do all adults enforce the same rules?

**FIGURE 7.9** Classroom checklist. By anticipating children's needs and growth patterns, teachers set up classrooms that foster constructive and purposeful behavior.

| When Setting Limits | For Example |
|---|---|
| 1. Make sure that the limit is appropriate to the situation. | "Andrew, please get down from the table. You may finish your snack by sitting in your chair or standing next to me. You may not stand on the table." |
| 2. Fit the limits to the individual child's age, history, and emotional framework. | "Sheila, you've interrupted the story too many times today. Please find a place at the puzzle table until we are finished. Remember, I told you earlier that you wouldn't be able to hear the end of the story if you yelled again." |
| | "Jamal, I know it's your first day back since you broke your arm, but it is time to listen to the story now. You and Sascha can talk together in a few minutes." |
| 3. See that the limits are consistently applied by all adults. | "I know you want to ride the red bike now but both teachers have said you already had a long turn today." |
| 4. Reinforce the same rules consistently. | "Judy, remember everyone *walks* inside. You can run outside." |
| 5. Follow through; support your words with actions. | "I can't let you tear the books. Since this is the second page this morning, you'll need to make another choice instead of the book corner." If child does not leave, begin to pick up books. Lead child firmly to another activity. |
| 6. Use simple statements; be clear and state limits positively. | "Please use a gentle voice indoors. When your voice is too loud, people can't hear one another. You may use your big loud voice outside." |
| 7. Respect the child's feelings and acknowledge them when you can. | "I know you want your mom to stay. She has to go to her job now. I'll stay with you while you feel sad and I'll take care of you until she comes back." |
| 8. Act with authority; be sure of your purpose and be confident. | "I can't let you hurt other people. Put the block down," instead of "I wish you wouldn't do that." |
| 9. Be ready to accept the consequences; have a plan for the next step, if needed. Maintain the limit. Don't avoid the situation or give in if the child threatens to fall apart or create a scene. | "I'm sorry, Sarah, but you missed your ride to school. When you play with your food it keeps you from getting dressed on time. Remember, Mrs. Allen said she wouldn't wait one more time. Screaming and kicking won't get her to turn the car around. Let's go feed the cat and think about what you might do at home today." |
| 10. Have children help in defining limits. | "We'll be taking a bus to the museum next week. What are some of the rules we should follow so that we can enjoy the trip? Wally, do you have an idea?" |

**FIGURE 7.10**  Guidelines for setting limits. Children feel safe when appropriate limits are set on their behavior.

lines to cross over. When children know where fences are, what limits, what rules apply, they do not have to continually try to find out *if* fences are there and *where* they are. "Inside those fences . . . chil-dren . . . have the complete freedom to move, to experience, to shift and change, to grow and shrink, to rest and have fun; to live, if you will" (Long, 1977).

PLAN AHEAD

–Allow plenty of time for children to respond. Give them an opportunity to decide their course of action.

–Review limits and rules periodically. Modify them as children's growth and maturation indicate. Change them as circumstances change; be flexible.

–Encourage children to talk things over. Be open to their point of view even if you cannot accept it. Let them know you are willing to listen to all sides of the conflict.

–Become aware of the climate in the room or yard. Anticipate the need for a change of pace or a different activity BEFORE children become bored or troublesome.

–Remember, it takes time and numerous opportunities for changes in behavior to occur. By using consistent guidance techniques, you will help children practice new behavior repeatedly.

A natural part of growing up is to stretch those limits and push those fences aside. This happens as children grow and mature; fences move in an ever-widening pattern. The womb first holds and protects the growing fetus; the infant is protected in the confines of the crib. The toddler has safe space defined in a playpen. The preschool child plays first in small, protected yards before moving on to the large, open playground in elementary school. Physical limits expand as the child is able to handle more freedom, more space, more responsibility. It is the same with behavioral limits.

Children may not like fences; they may resist attempts to limit their behavior. The beginning teacher must learn to set and maintain limits with confidence and authority. Children respond to how limits are set as much as to the limits themselves. Be sure children help determine limits. Keep in mind that a good disciplinary process involves children as active participants; this fosters self-discipline. Children also seem less resistant to following rules when they are a part of the limit-setting procedure. Figure 7.10 illustrates positive ways to set limits when working with young children.

For the child, limits are self-protective. Young children have not yet learned the skills to control themselves in all situations. Their behavior easily

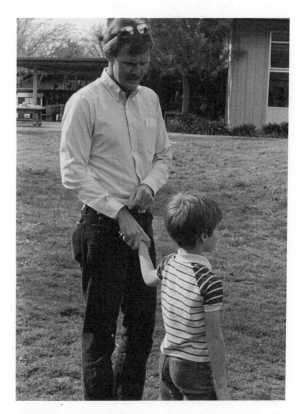

**FIGURE 7.11** Children can help to set their own limits. Good discipline practices involve children as active participants.

goes out-of-bounds. Children are just beginning to exert that inner pressure (self-control) that will help them monitor their own actions. Until then, they need adults to help them learn when and how to apply self-restraint. Limits keep them from going too far. Children can frighten themselves and others with anger, frustration, fear. They need adults who care to stop them from doing physical or emotional harm to themselves. Well-considered limits give the child freedom to try out, test, and explore avenues of self-expression in ways that will promote growth and protect budding autonomy. Children feel more secure with adults who will stop them from going too far and who help them learn to gain control.

## Consider the Teacher's Role

A teacher has direct and indirect influence on children's behavior. Some of the ways teachers deal directly with discipline is by what they say and what they do. Indirectly, a teacher's influence is felt just as strongly. Room arrangements and time schedules, attitudes and behavior can work for or against good disciplinary practices.

Teachers who are well grounded in the developmental process know that problem behaviors are normal and occur in every early childhood setting.

They realize that growing children must have a safe, secure place in which to test themselves against the world.

The teacher as a behavior model is an important element in discipline. Children pattern their responses after adult behaviors. They are aware of how teachers respond to anger, frustration, and aggression; how they solve problems and conflicts. Adults must be sure to model the desired behavior around the children they teach. To be successful models, teachers should be aware of their emotions and feelings; they do not want to compound a problem by their own reaction.

Being consistent is one of the key elements in good disciplinary practices. If adults want to develop mutual trust, the rules must be clear, fair, and enforced consistently and regularly. At the same time, children need to know what will happen if rules are not followed. This, too, should be consistent.

An emerging issue, as our population becomes more and more diverse, has to do with cultural values and discipline. Teachers may be confronted by parents with disciplinary practices that are contrary to the school's philosophy. Pressure may be exerted on teachers to apply some of those same tactics at school that parents use at home. How do teachers

---

ALWAYS AVOID
- –Methods that will shame, frighten, or humiliate children.
- –Physical abuse.
- –Comparisons among the children. This fosters competitiveness and affects self-esteem.
- –Carry-overs from the incident. Once it is over, leave it behind; do not keep reminding children about it.
- –Consequences that are too long, too punitive, or postponed. Children benefit most from immediate, short consequences.
- –Lots of rules. Set only enough to ensure a safe environment for all children.
- –Making promises you cannot keep.
- –Being overly helpful. Let children do as much as they can by themselves, including solving their own conflicts.
- –Threatening children with the loss of your affection.

maintain the school's as well as their own standards *without* communicating to the family that their values are wrong? In what position do teachers put children by telling them, "At school we do it this way"? Do children feel that something about their home and family is diminished in the teacher's eyes? Ethical issues such as these are discussed in Chapter 5, and Janice Hale-Benson's *Focus* discussion in Chapter 3 adds a unique perspective to the issue of cultural values. The anti-bias curriculum, as described in Chapter 9, suggests some strategies as well. Also see Child Development and Cultural Diversity in Chapter 4.

Children have a right to express negative feelings and air their grievances, but what about teachers? Is it ever appropriate for a teacher to show anger? If so, what are the considerations? Children are very sensitive to adult emotions. It is better to acknowledge the feeling, label it, and then discuss it together. Once it is identified, it becomes more manageable for both. Adults who express negative feelings to children must proceed carefully, stating their position clearly, honestly, and objectively, and in a low, calm voice.

> It bothers me when you call Roberto a dummy.
>
> You don't need to yell at me. I can hear you from right here. Tell me again in a quieter voice.
>
> I'm serious about this...no biting.
>
> Sometimes I get mad when children try to hurt each other.
>
> It makes me sad to see all that food going to waste. Please put just enough on your plate so that you will eat it all.

Remember that children are frightened by strong feelings; do not overwhelm them by your own behavior.

Sometimes teachers have unrealistic expectations for children, either too high or too low. They presume children have abilities and skills they do not yet possess. This may cause children to respond in inappropriate ways. It can be helpful to rehearse with children how they are expected to act. Practice sessions are especially useful when introducing a new topic or plan. One teacher rehearsed the children for their first bus ride. They practiced singing, looking out the windows, having snacks, talking with friends. A large outline of a bus was drawn with chalk on the patio floor. The children pretended to board the bus, walk down the narrow aisle, find a seat, and remember to take big steps getting up and down the steps. When the field trip day arrived, children knew several appropriate ways of behaving while on the long bus trip.

Many times children are asked to do jobs that are too complicated for them. The young child who is just learning to put on jackets and pants or to make a bed is a good example. Children may not be able to accomplish the entire job at first; it is helpful to them if the task is broken down into smaller steps. Straighten the sheet and blanket for Gordon, then let him pull the spread up over the pillow. Little by little have Gordon assume more of the bed-making job as he becomes capable.

Preventing opportunities for children to misbehave is another part of the teacher's role. Good discipline practices call for teachers to be alert to potential problems and situations *before* they result in children's inappropriate behavior. Even then, unpredictable situations occur: A child becomes tired in the middle of snack time, one of the teachers is called out of the room with a sick child, rain forces an activity to move indoors, or a scheduled event gets postponed. At these trying and typical times, a teacher's full range of abilities is called into play. Ways to help children maintain good behavior patterns in these situations include:

- *Recognizing and labeling the problem or situation.* Acknowledge the difficulties it presents to the children. Example: "You seem tired, Gus, and I know you had to wait a long time for your snack. When you have finished your juice and cracker, put your head down on the table and rest for a minute."

- *Asking children for their help.* Get them involved in working out the solutions. Example: "Mr. Gallo had to leave for a while. How can we continue with this cooking project when I need to watch the block area too? Who has an idea? What do you think would work, Henry?"

- *Assigning a job or a task to the children who are most likely to react to the crisis.* Example: "Lorraine and Paul, will you carry the special drums inside, please, while I help the toddlers put the wagons away?"

- *Always being prepared with a story to tell, songs to sing, guessing games to play or exercises to do.* Help children pass the time in an appropriate way modeled by the teacher. Give a new focus. Example: "Oh, dear. The fire truck hasn't arrived at school yet; we'll have to wait another five minutes. While we are waiting to go and see it, show me how firefighters climb ladders and slide down poles."

- *Saying what you would like to have happen.* Admit what you wish you could do to correct the situation. Example: "Oh, little Riko, I wish I could bring your mommy back right now but I can't. She has to go to work, but I will hold you until your crying stops."

Do these disciplinary practices apply even to infants and toddlers? Most certainly, but there are some special considerations that teachers should remember. Infants cry—sometimes a great deal. It is their only means of communication. When they cry they should not be ignored or chastised, but comforted. It is helpful to talk to the baby, no matter how young, and begin to identify the steps you will take to ease the distress. "Oh, Fernando, you are crying and I don't know what's wrong. Let's take a look at your diapers; maybe a change will make you more comfortable. Perhaps you are teething; I know that can hurt. Maybe you are hungry; is it time for your bottle yet?" Those soothing words as a teacher changes diapers, rubs the baby's back, cuddles and rocks, ease this time of stress. Toddlers, too, need adults to use words to express problem situations, and the examples above readily apply to working with this active and lively age group. One word of caution, however. Removing infants and toddlers from the group as a means of discipline or confining them to a playpen or crib is not appropriate. Very young children do not understand that kind of isolation.

Discipline, to be effective, should be helpful, not punitive.

Teachers can learn a great deal about the cause and effect of their discipline and guidance techniques if they are active observers in their own classrooms. When teachers observe, they can time intervention; they do not want to interfere too soon. Observations can be used to show children their actions and the consequences they have for others.

# Guidance Techniques

The following approaches, while not specifically outlined, are woven throughout the discussion of discipline and behavior management. They have many similar components. Each requires some advance thought on the part of the adult, and allows for consequences that are predictable and immediate. These methods follow good disciplinary practices by encouraging less talk and more action. Adults and children will not need to spend time arguing the situation when the outline of response is so clear.

## Parent Effectiveness Training (P.E.T.)

This outlines two techniques that have proved most helpful in child guidance. These are (1) active listening, and (2) the use of "I" messages (Gordon, 1970).

Parents and teachers can learn the art of *active listening* in order to respond to a child's feelings as well as words. The technique encourages sensitive, atuned hearing—checking on the accuracy of what is being said. To do this, teachers or parents listen carefully, trying to understand what the child is saying beyond the words being used. Then they reflect back in their own words what it is they think the child has said. The child has an opportunity to correct any misinterpretations. Further dialogue helps to clarify what it was the child meant. An example is:

Rita: I hate school!
Teacher: Sounds like you are really disappointed you didn't get a turn cooking today.
Rita: I *really* wanted to help make pancakes.

| If This Is The Behavior | Try This | For Example |
|---|---|---|
| Whining | Ignoring | Do and say nothing while whining persists. Pay attention to child when whining stops. |
| Playing cooperatively | Positive reinforcement | "You two are sure working hard on this garden! What a good team you make." |
| Refusing to cooperate | Provide a choice | "Reva, do you want to pick up the Legos off the floor or help Charlie empty the water table?" |
| Restlessness, inattentiveness | Change the activity | "This story seems long today; we'll finish it later. Let's play some music and dance now." |
| Daydreaming | Indirect suggestion | "As soon as you get your coat, Winona, we'll all be ready to go outside." |
| Arguing over the ownership of a toy | Active listening | "You really wanted to be the first one to play with the blue truck today, didn't you, Lief?" |
| Dawdling, late for snacks | Natural consequences | "Sorry, Nate, the snacks have been put away. Maybe tomorrow you'll remember to come inside when the other children leave the yard." |
| Pushing, crowding, running inside | Change room arrangement | Create larger, more open spaces so children have greater freedom of movement and do not feel crowded together. |
| Unable to take turns, to wait | Review daily schedule, equipment | Buy duplicates of popular equipment. Allow enough time for free play so children won't feel anxious about getting a turn. |
| Boisterous play | Positive redirection | "You and Sergio seem to want to wrestle. Let's go set the mats out in the other room. If you wrestle here you disturb the children who are playing quietly." |

**FIGURE 7.12** Varieties of guidance techniques. The astute teacher selects from the options available and individualizes the responses.

*"I" messages* are an adult's way of reflecting back to children how their actions have affected others. According to Gordon, a "parent simply tells a child how some unacceptable behavior is making the parent feel" (1970).

> Parent: When you scream indoors, it really hurts my ears.

> Parent: I feel sad when you tell me you don't like me.

"I" messages are honest, nonjudgmental statements that place no blame on the child, but which state an observation of the behavior and its results. They avoid accusing statements, such as "You made me . . . " and call for a framework that allows adults to state their feelings to the child.

## Natural and Logical Consequences

These enhance children's ability to take responsibility for themselves. As implied, this approach lets children experience the natural consequences of their actions. This approach, designed by Rudolf Dreikurs, emphasizes the opportunity children have to learn from the way their environment functions:

> If Libby does not eat her dinner, she can expect to be hungry later.
>
> If Kara puts her hand on a hot stove, she is likely to get burned.
>
> If Tony grabs the book away from Ben, Ben may hit him.

This method allows adults to define the situation for children without making judgments, and lets children know what to expect. The consequences are a natural result of the child's own actions. *Logical* consequences, on the other hand, are a function of what adults impose. A logical consequence of disrupting group time is removal from the group. For the adult, this means a commitment to follow through; consequences, once stated, must be enforced. It is important to give children an opportunity to choose a course of action for themselves once they have some understanding of what is likely to happen.

## Behavior Modification

This is an organized approach based on the premise that behavior is learned through *positive and negative reinforcement* or rewards. The belief is that children will tend to repeat behavior for which they get the desired results (positive reinforcement) and are likely to avoid doing things which have undesirable consequences (negative reinforcement). Positive reinforcement is used to teach new and different behaviors to a child, and help the child maintain the change. Negative reinforcement may simply involve ignoring or withdrawing attention when the child acts inappropriately. Initially, the reinforcement (or reward) must be swift and consistently applied, as often as the behavior occurs. If the desired behavior, for instance, is for Janie to always hang her coat on the hook, praise and appre-

**FIGURE 7.13** A sensitive teacher will move in and help redirect a child's behavior or activity before it becomes a problem.

ciate the effort each time Janie hangs up her wraps. Once this is a well-established routine, the reinforcement (praise) becomes less intense.

*Reinforcers,* or rewards, must be individualized to meet the needs of the child and the situation. Social reinforcers, such as smiling, interest and attention, hugging, touching, and talking, are powerful tools with young children. Food, tokens, and money are also used as reinforcers in home and school settings. The goal is that inner satisfaction will become its own reward, no matter the type of reinforcer one might use initially.

To succeed, the adult will focus on only one behavior change at a time. If parents want to use behavior modification methods to help their children arrive at the dinner table on time, then Dad does not nag about homework or Mom about a messy room. The behavior that is targeted for change becomes the primary concern until it is successfully altered.

Parents and teachers often take for granted the positive, desirable behavior in children and may forget to acknowledge these behaviors frequently. Behavior modification helps to correct that oversight. Whenever adults focus on a negative aspect of a child's behavior and make an attempt to change it, they also look at the positive qualities the child possesses and reinforces them. This keeps a balanced perspective while working on a problem.

Behavior modification enables adults to invite children to be part of the process, giving them an active part in monitoring their own behavior. Children are capable of keeping a chart of how many times they finished their plate, made the bed, or fed the dog. This chart serves as a natural reinforcer.

Each of these methods is a valuable tool for teachers. These approaches influence children to modify their behavior because they place the responsibility where it belongs: with the child. The adult informs children of the results of their actions and trusts their willingness and abilities to cooperate in a solution. The child's self-respect is left intact because no one has placed blame. By integrating these methods into a disciplinary approach, teachers enlarge the child's capacity to become increasingly self-directed and self-reliant.

### Additional Techniques

A variety of additional guidance techniques and variations can be used in resolving discipline problems. Wise teachers do not attempt to prevent children from stretching limits and controls. Instead, they help children understand and accept their feelings and learn that they can live within limits. Acting with confidence, the teacher involves children in the disciplinary process, discussing with them alternatives and options for how they act. Children learn they are held accountable for their actions and can help determine how they want to handle themselves and change their own behavior. The following are common and useful strategies found in many early childhood settings.

**Redirecting the Activity.** Sometimes the adult will want to change the activity in which the child is engaged to one that is more acceptable. For example, if Paco and Elena are throwing books off the reading loft, the teacher will want to redirect them and may

suggest throwing soft foam balls into a makeshift basket. This technique calls for the adult to make an accurate assessment of what the children really want to do. In this case, it appears they enjoy throwing from a height. Now the teacher can consider alternatives that permit the desired activity while changing the expression or form it takes: "It looks like you two are enjoying dropping things from up there. Let's figure out a way you can do that so that books won't be damaged."

The substitute activity must be a valid one, acceptable to the adults and fulfilling to the children. In most cases children are not being deliberately malicious or destructive. More than likely they are expressing curiosity, imagination, and the need to explore. Positive redirection satisfies these needs in a way that enhances children's self-concept and self-control.

**Ignoring Behavior.** When misbehavior is of a less serious nature—for instance, when a child whines constantly—it may be best to ignore it. This kind of behavior, while mildly annoying, is not harmful. To use the technique successfully, the adult chooses not to respond to the child in any way and may even become occupied elsewhere while the behavior persists. This method is based on the learning theory that negative reinforcement (the adult ignoring the child) will eventually cause the child to stop the undesirable behavior. At first there might be an increase in the misbehavior as the child tests to see whether or not the adult will truly ignore the action. Once the child sees there is nothing to gain, the behavior disappears.

**Distraction.** When the adult helps focus the child's attention elsewhere, some problems may be avoided. Very young children, especially infants and toddlers, can easily be distracted from undesirable actions. Consider the example at the beginning of the chapter in which Matt and Pablo reached for the same puzzle. A fast-thinking teacher could present Matt with another attractive one. This method calls for well-timed intervention.

**Time Out.** Removing a child from the play area is particularly appropriate when, owing to anger, hurt, or frustration, the child is out of control. Taking children away from the scene of intensity and emotion to allow them time to cool off and settle down is sometimes the only way to help them. The teacher is firm and consistent as the child is quietly removed from play. It is important that this discipline technique be used with a positive attitude and approach, not as punishment for misbehavior.

The time-out period is very much like that used in athletic events: a brief respite and a chance to stop all activity and regroup. The teacher's role is to help the child talk about the incident—the feelings involved as well as the need for self-control—and to give the child an opportunity to gain self-control before resuming play. Children can monitor themselves and choose when they are ready to return to classroom activity. Noah, who persists in knocking down other children's block structures, might be told, "You may come back to the block area when you think you are ready to play without knocking over other children's work." Noah can then assume some responsibility for how he will behave and when he is ready to return to play.

Use this technique lightly; it can be misused too easily by adults who leave the child with a sense of rejection. As with other good disciplinary techniques, it should be appropriate to the misbehavior and should help the child toward self-discipline.

**Active Problem Solving.** The principle here is to actively engage children in confronting their differences and working together to solve their problems. The adult has a sensitive role to play: that of guiding children toward solutions but not solving problems for them. Posing open-ended questions helps the adult stay focused:

"What could you do _____"
"How might she feel when _____"
"What might happen if _____"
"How can you _____"

The point is to encourage children to come up with alternative solutions. This requires an accepting attitude on the part of the teacher; all of the children's

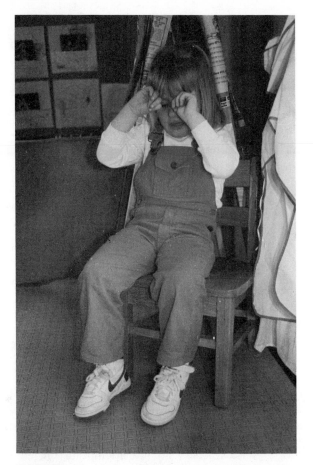

**FIGURE 7.14** Young children should not be isolated for misbehavior in ways that damage their self-esteem. (Courtesy of Stride Rite Children's Centers, Cambridge, Mass.)

suggestions must be acknowledged seriously, even if they seem unreasonable. Young children are likely to start the discussion by suggesting extreme solutions. In the case of Allie, for instance (see the first example on page 185), they might initially suggest a radical alternative: "Don't let Allie come to this school anymore." These suggestions will become tempered as other children respond; fair and reasonable solutions will eventually emerge: "Anyone who scribbles on somebody else's paper can't play at the art table any more today."

Rather than assessing blame, teachers help children think through a number of alternatives, including the consequences of what they suggest: "If we take all the crayons away, what will happen when you want to finish writing your story this afternoon?" By assisting them in anticipating the results of what they suggest, teachers can help children understand how their behavior influences and affects others. This is an early lesson in a lifelong quest to become responsible for one's own behavior.

When children help create a solution, they come away with a sense of commitment to it. This process also gives children a sense of power and control, a sense of independence, and a feeling of self-worth.

Figure 7.12 illustrates how these disciplinary techniques may be used to best advantage. See also Chapter 14, Social Development, for five steps to social problem solving.

## Teacher's Role

Guidance, discipline, and behavior management are terms that refer to the adult's role in working with children and their behavior problems. A teacher observes what the child says and does and identifies how that needs to change.

Behavior is the unspoken language through which the child acts out feelings and thoughts that adults might express in speech. Until children learn to express themselves vocally, they employ a variety of behaviors to communicate such feelings as distress, anger, anxiety, fear, hurt, and jealousy. The key to dealing with common behavior problems is the awareness that it is the adult's behavior and attitudes that must change if the child is to achieve self-control. This is probably one of the most difficult concepts for new teachers to grasp. The phrases "behavior management" or "changing children's behavior" are misleading. What really has to change is the adult's own behavior—how the teacher or parent reacts to children who misbehave. Read the various guidance techniques again and note how many of the strategies require the adult to change a response or attitude before the child can be expected to alter behavior. Teachers and parents help solve discipline problems by examining their own methods of dealing with misbehavior and choosing those that enhance children's ability to govern themselves.

Figure 7.12 lists some of the most common ways children indicate they are troubled. How many of them are likely to happen on an average day in your classroom?

## SUMMARY

The early childhood educator provides opportunities for children to express their feelings in appropriate ways and to solve their social problems constructively. Children are incapable of controlling their own impulses all the time, so caring adults are needed to guide them toward self-control. Teachers base their methods and disciplinary principles on an understanding of why children misbehave and what factors influence behavior.

Most guidance techniques begin by accepting the feelings the child expresses and verbalizing them. Then the adult sets limits on what form the behavior may take, guiding the action as needed and following through to conclusion.

The most effective methods of discipline are clear, consistent, and fair rules that are enforced in consistent, humane ways. Children should be aware of the consequences if the rules are broken.

Good disciplinary practices emphasize the positive aspects of a child's behavior, not just the problem behaviors. Guidance measures have greater meaning to children if they are encouraged to take responsibility for their own actions and are part of the problem-solving process.

## REVIEW QUESTIONS

1. What are some of the goals of children's misbehavior? What techniques can adults use to deal with children who exhibit these goals?

2. What developmental factors affect children's behavior? What environmental factors? How does a child's individual style affect behavior? What do developmental and learning theories (Chapter 4) add to the discussion?

3. How would you solve Case Study #3 if Zachary refused to make a choice between emptying the water table and moving chairs?

4. What is your own definition of discipline?

5. Why do teachers have to set limits on children's behavior? How does it help the child?

6. Describe ways children differ in temperament.

## LEARNING ACTIVITIES

1. Your three-year-old daughter always interrupts when you talk on the telephone. She cries for you to play with her, hits her brothers, and crawls into cupboards. What is she doing and why? What is your reaction? How will you solve the problem?

2. List activities that channel aggressive feelings into acceptable ways to play. After each, note the emotion or feeling the specific activity might release. *Example:* Clay—anger, frustration

3. Finish this sentence: "When I was four-years-old, the *worst* thing I ever did was. . ." How did the adults around you react? What would you do if you were the adult in charge? Discuss and compare responses with a classmate.

4. Children's literature helps us focus on disciplinary and behavior problems. Select a book from the following list. Define the problem behavior and the person creating the problem. Do you agree with the author's way of handling the situation? Suggest alternatives. When and with whom might you use this story?

Suggested books: *Noisy Nora*/Rosemary Wells
*The Man Who Wouldn't Wash His Dishes*/Phyllis Krasilovsky
*Pierre*/Maurice Sendak
*Nobody Asked Me If I Wanted A Baby Sister*/Martha Alexander

> *Benjamin and Tulip*/Rosemary Wells
> *Bread and Jam for Frances*/Russell and Lillian Hoban
> *Ira Sleeps Over*/Bernard Waber
> *Where the Wild Things Are*/Maurice Sendak
> *The Bundle Book*/Ruth Krauss
> *And to Think That I Saw It on Mulberry Street*/Dr. Seuss
> *Alexander and the Terrible, Horrible, No Good, Very Bad Day*/Judith Viorst

5. Observe a group of young children during a free play period. See whether you can identify an example of a child who might be described as an easy child, a difficult child, and a slow-to-warm-up child. What disciplinary techniques do the teachers use with each child? Are they the same? If they are different, describe the differences. How successful are the disciplinary techniques that are being used? What might you do differently?

6. How do you feel about spanking children? Were you spanked when you were a child? If so, what precipitated the spankings? Could you think of any other forms of behavior control that might have worked instead of spanking? Compare your thoughts and insights with those of another member of this class.

## B I B L I O G R A P H Y

Allen, K. Eileen, and Hart, Betty. *The Early Years.* Englewood Cliffs, N.J.: Prentice-Hall, 1984.

Bee, Helen. *The Developing Child.* New York: Harper & Row, 1985.

Dreikurs, R., and Stolz, V. *Children: The Challenge.* New York: Hawthorne Books, 1964.

Gordon, Dr. Thomas. *Parent Effectiveness Training.* New York: Peter H. Wyden, 1970.

LeShan, Eda. *When Your Child Drives You Crazy.* New York: St. Martin's Press, 1985.

Long, Barbara Ellis. *Freedom Versus Limits.* Unpublished paper, 1977.

Marion, Marian. *Guidance of Young Children.* St. Louis: C.V. Mosby, 1981.

Mattick, Ilse, and Perkins, Frances J. *Guidelines for Observation and Assessment: An Approach to Evaluating the Learning Environment of a Day Care Center.* Washington, D.C.: Day Care and Child Development Council, 1974.

Schaefer, Charles, and Millman, Howard. *How to Help Children with Common Problems.* New York: Van Nostrand Reinhold, 1981.

# CHAPTER 8

## Parents and Teachers: Partners in Education

## QUESTIONS for THOUGHT

- Why is it important to have good working relationships with parents?
- What are teachers expected to share with parents?
- What will parents share with teachers?
- How do parents get interested and involved in the classroom?
- What are the ingredients for a good parent program?
- What are the ingredients for a successful parent–teacher conference?
- What is the teacher's role in providing a supportive atmosphere for parents?
- What are some major concerns of parents?
- How do parents affect children's growth?

# HISTORICAL PERSPECTIVE

Working with parents can be one of the teacher's most satisfying responsibilities, or it can be one of the most frustrating. It is usually both. The potential is clearly present for a dynamic partnership between the most important adults in a child's life. The common goal is obvious: the welfare of the child. Each has knowledge, skills, and a sense of caring to bring to that relationship. Each has a need for the other. Partnerships usually begin with such a need. So, parents and teachers become coworkers, colleagues in a joint effort to help the child develop fully.

There is a historical *precedent* for the partnership between parents and teachers. Pestalozzi and Froebel, early eighteenth-century educators, detailed many of their procedures for home use. The involvement of the mother in the education of the child was considered important even then. When kindergartens were organized in this country, classes for parents and mothers' clubs were also started. The National Congress of Mothers evolved from that movement. Today it is the National Congress of Parents and Teachers (Spodek, 1972). This well-known organization is an integral part of most school systems and continues to promote a union between home and school, teachers and parents.

There was a period of time during the 1930s when parental involvement in education was actively discouraged. Teachers were seen as experts who wanted to be left alone to do their job. In many cases, teachers felt they did little but remedy parental mistakes. Parents in or near the classroom were barely tolerated. That trend ended in the 1940s when the need for parent support and encouragement was recognized. Closer relationships between teachers and parents were established. This view of a need for closer ties between teacher and parents, although nearly 50 years old, stands today as a commonly accepted principle.

Teacher training curricula began to reflect the change. Teachers were exposed to courses that would help them appreciate and utilize parents as coworkers in the child's development. By the 1960s, Head Start programs required parental involvement and set about developing parent education and parent training programs. Their commitment to children included a commitment to the parents of those children.

The most recent influences are still felt today. Early childhood teachers all over the country, regardless of the setting, believe in the necessity of the parent–teacher relationship. There is general agreement that at no other age is such a relationship more important than in the years before school. Teachers have come to appreciate the role parents can play and no longer fear their interference. Parents have accepted the responsibility, too. The way, then, is paved for this partnership to be successful. By changing some of their assumptions about one another, parents and teachers now stand together to support and promote children's development.

*Note:* Throughout this chapter, the terms "parents" and "parenthood" are used deliberately to include fathers as well as mothers in the process of rearing and educating children.

# PARTNERSHIP IN EDUCATION

Parents have a unique contribution to make in the child's schooling. They have different knowledge about the child from what the teacher has. They know the child's history: physical, medical, social, and intellectual. They know the child as a member of a family, and the role that child plays in the total family group. Through parents, teachers learn about the home life of the children in their classes: who they live with, in what kind of family situation, and what their life style is like. Parents bring with them a sense of continuity about the child: they provide the context with which the teacher can view the whole child. As the teacher will soon learn, the parents already know what makes their child happy or sad, or how they react to changes in routines. Thus, parents have a wealth of intimate knowledge about their child that the teacher is only just beginning to discover.

**FIGURE 8.1** The child benefits when teachers and parents share knowledge, insight, and interest.

Teachers bring to the partnership another perspective. As child development professionals, they see the child in relation to what they know are normal milestones and appropriate behaviors. They notice how each child plays with other children in the group, what seems to challenge Elizabeth and when Patrick is likely to fall apart. Unlike parents, teachers see individual children from a perspective that is balanced by the numerous other children they have taught. They observe how the child behaves with a variety of adults, sensing children's ability to trust other adults through interactions with them at school. When parents need help for themselves or for their child, teachers become resources. They may work with the parents to find psychologists, hearing and speech specialists, or other educational programs, if warranted.

By pooling their knowledge of a child, both parents and teachers gain a more complete picture of the whole child. By becoming aware of the role each plays in the life of the child, teachers and parents grow in their understanding of one another. They can respect each other's unique contribution. As they recognize their need to share valuable information, they can support one another.

## The Value of Working Together

The very first contact between parents and teachers is likely to take place within the early childhood education setting. If parents feel welcome and important, the stage is set for ongoing involve-

**Ways to Encourage Parent Involvement**

| Provide: | Develop: | Have: |
|---|---|---|
| A gathering place for parents at the school: a room where they can meet one another as they bring and take away their children. | A parent awards program to recognize and honor the parents who best exemplify good parental involvement. | Staff available at beginning and end of day to greet parents, call them by name, and comment about child's day. |
| A bulletin board near front door of school where parents can share ideas and information. Make it bilingual or multilingual when appropriate. | Resource and referral lists for housing, health, legal, and social issues that affect parents' daily lives. Help them get the help they need so they will have time to be involved in school. | Parent meetings at night or on weekends in local neighborhoods or housing projects where parents live. Provide child care. |
| In-service training for staff on effective ways to communicate and support positive home-school relationships | Surveys of and for parents to note issues of major concern. Follow up with meaningful workshops on those subjects. | School newsletters with short articles to help parents cope with critical issues: latchkey children, nutrition, absentee fathers, child abuse. Provide more than just classroom activities information. |

**FIGURE 8.2**    As more mothers of young children enter the work force and are unavailable during the school day, there is a greater challenge to create meaningful parent involvement. Fathers as well as mothers need the opportunity to participate in their children's educations.

ment in their child's education. By working closely with parents, teachers establish a pattern that can be repeated as the child grows. Parents should be involved in the school life of their child at all grade levels. Their introduction to this world of schools and teachers, then, is important.

## For the Parents

One of the greatest values of a strong parent program is the opportunity for parents to meet each other. They find that they share similar problems and frustrations, and that they can support one another in finding solutions. Friendships blossom based on mutual interests and concerns about their children.

Through close home–school relationships, parents can find ways to become more effective as parents and as teachers of their children. They can observe modeling techniques that teachers find successful in dealing with children and can learn what behaviors are appropriate at certain ages. By observing how their children relate to other adults and children, parents can come to know them better as social beings. They may become more aware of

school and community resources that are available to them and, in the person of the teacher, they now have access to a consultant who knows and understands their child and can help them when they need it.

Parents are the child's teachers too. They teach by word, by example, and by all they say and do. Through closer home–school relationships, parents can be helped to see that their everyday experiences with their children provide teachable moments, opportunities for educating their children. Teachers can support parents in their roles as teachers of their children by keeping them informed about each stage of the child's development, by showing them how to encourage language and thinking skills, by educating them to children's social needs at any given age, by providing lists of books and toys that encourage children's thinking and creative abilities as they provide the joy of reading. Teachers should make sure parents have copies of children's favorite songs, recipes that are popular at school, and information on how to teach safety habits at home. Parents need not teach a curriculum; they do need to use common household routines and experiences to encourage children's total growth. The teaching staff has a

---

**The Ten Most Important Things Parents Can Teach Their Children**

1. To love themselves
2. To read behavior
3. To communicate with words
4. To understand the difference between thoughts and actions
5. To wonder and ask why
6. To understand that complicated questions do not have simple answers
7. To risk failure as a necessary part of growing up
8. To trust grownups
9. To have a mind of their own
10. To know when to lean on adults

---

**FIGURE 8.3** A list of important basics that children can learn at home. (Adapted from Ida LeShan, *When Your Child Drives You Crazy,* New York: St. Martin's Press, 1985.)

strong role to play in helping parents learn how to do this. In Figure 8.3, Eda LeShan, a noted author and family counselor, lists some of the most important things parents can teach their children.

The majority of parents today want to learn the best way to raise their children and want to improve their child-rearing skills. Honig (1979) has highlighted six basic needs of parents:

1. Parents need knowledge about how children develop.

2. Parents need to learn how to observe young children.

3. Parents need knowledge of alternative methods of discipline and of problem avoidance.

4. Parents need to learn how to take advantage of situations and activities at home to create learning opportunities for their children.

5. Parents need language tools to simplify explanations that will make sense to a preschool child.

6. Parents need to feel they are important and how much they make a difference in their child's life.

The challenge for the early childhood professional is to create ways to meet these basic needs for parents of the 1990s.

## *For the Teachers and School*

Active parent involvement benefits the teacher and school, too. Parents are an untapped resource in most schools. The skills and talents in a group of parents multiply the people resources available to children. Some parents will want to work directly in the classroom with children; others may volunteer to help in the office, the schoolyard, or the kitchen. Parents who have jobs can sometimes arrange to take some time off to accompany a class on a field trip. There are parents who are willing to work at home, either sewing, typing, mending, building, or painting. Parents will vary in their willingness to become involved. Some may be unable to participate because of work schedules, small children to care for at home, or lack of transportation.

## *For the Children*

The children whose parents choose to take an active part in the school reap the rewards of such involvement. Research shows examples of children's gains in academic skills, positive self-concept, and verbal intelligence when extensive parental participation is required (Honig, 1979). The family is the primary source from which the child develops and grows. Schools alone may not be able to provide all that is necessary. The family of the child is needed to reinforce the learning, the attitudes, and the motivation if children are to remain interested learners. In her *Focus* discussion on page 228, Alice Honig reviews parent involvement from the view of the parent, the teacher, and the child.

## Prerequisites for a Good Parent Program

The quality of parent involvement and interest will depend on many factors. Some of the funda-

**FIGURE 8.4**   When a dad visits the block corner, new ways to build emerge.

mental components of a good parent program are:

**Support from School Personnel.** School administrators must lend their full support to the concept of parental involvement, spending both time and energy to make it work. The endorsement of the school director or principal is critical, as are teacher interest and enthusiasm. Some teachers will gladly work with parents on any project; others will support their involvement by praising and promoting parental efforts. Teachers should have a choice in the ways in which they would like to get involved. They may volunteer to serve on parent committees, open their classes to parent aides, or coordinate the parent training.

**Foundation of Needs, Concerns, and Interests of Parents.** Offering a lecture series on "Child-Rearing Practices Around the World" will not meet the needs of parents when they are asking for help in coping with children fighting on the school bus. In order to sustain parent interest, the program must also use the skills and knowledge available within that group of parents. That means someone must take the time to survey what individual parents have to offer and are willing to share. Periodic evaluation of the total program is important. Regular assessment helps to develop programs that work well for parents and the school.

**Variety.** Parents have many needs in common, but they do not all have the same needs at the same time. A good program for parental involvement reflects those needs in the number, type, and kinds of opportunities it provides. It allows the individual parent to select where, when, and how to participate. A variety of times for participations—during school, evenings, weekends—allows parents many options.

**Parents as Change Agents.** Good parent programming means that the school has something of value to offer the parents and that parents have something to contribute to the school. This implies a willingness to learn from each other, a give-and-take relationship. School administrators and teachers show parents that they have influence and can bring about change. In one school this resulted in the development of day care and extended day facilities, inclusion of a toddler program, regularly scheduled parent support groups, and the beginning of a scholarship fund. Changes do not occur all at once and are the result of sympathetic school administrators and parents who are willing to work together in constructive ways. Parents should feel that what they have to say is important; school personnel who encourage and respond to parent feedback demonstrate a commitment to parent involvement.

**Respect for Parents.** A good parent program is based on mutual respect. Do not approach parents as though they are in need of being converted to new ways to be a parent. Allow them freedom to accept what is useful and let them reject what they cannot, in good conscience, adopt for themselves. Parents will grow in self-confidence and security only if school personnel will respect their native intelligence and instincts about their own children.

# Basic Guidelines for Working with Parents

Supporting and encouraging parents in their role is part of a teacher's responsibility. Good teachers are sensitive to parent concerns and understand their needs. To insure good parent–teacher relationships, review the following guidelines:

**Prepare** parents for what they can expect from their child's school experience. School policies and a yearly calendar should be clearly stated and thoroughly reviewed with parents as the child enters school. Then parents will know what their responsibilities are, where the school can be of assistance to them, and what expectations the school has of the parents.

**Protect** the parent–child relationship. Enhance the pride children naturally feel about their mothers and fathers. Tell Maggie her eyes are just like her Dad's or mention to Kevin that his Mom will be pleased to hear he slid down the big slide. Reinforce that unique place families have in children's lives. This is particularly critical for children who spend long hours in child care centers away from their parents. Parents need teachers to support them in raising their children and they like to hear when they have done well. They take pride in doing their best and appreciate teachers who acknowledge this.

**Contact** parents frequently and on a regular basis. Keep the lines of communication open and flowing between school and home. Be sure to know the parents by name. Take advantage of the daily contact as they bring their child to and from school. It may be brief and breezy, but it is a good way to stay in touch. Be sure to find ways to touch base with those parents who do not come to school every day, by telephone, note, or home visit.

**Respect** parents for the difficult job they have, the role they play, and the persons they are. Respect their religious, cultural, social, and ethnic backgrounds and heritage. Respect their privacy. Do not allow one parent to seek information about another. Respect the right of the parent to disagree. Above all, respect the unparalleled part they play in the growth and development of their child.

**Listen** to parents. Hear them out. They, too, have accumulated experiences to share, and their views are valid. Learn to listen to them with a degree of understanding; try to hear it from their point of view. Listen to parents without judging them or jumping to conclusions; this is the basis for open communication.

# TODAY'S PARENT

There is little preparation for the job of being a parent and most mothers and fathers feel inadequate in their role. Parents are pretty much alone as they strike out in unfamiliar territory. Due to our increasingly mobile society, most couples do not live around the corner from grandparents or other family members. There is no extended family to teach new mothers and fathers some of the traditional, time-honored child-rearing skills. There is no one with whom parents can share their worries, frustrations, and concerns. So the *pediatrician's* phone number is etched in their minds, and they proceed to become the best parents they can.

More recently, an important change has taken place within young families. Raising children as a shared experience is becoming a commonly accepted way of life. Young men, influenced by changing values and attitudes toward traditional sex roles, are taking an active part in raising their families. Fathers seem aware of the critical role they play in the child's life and are making appropriate changes to see that they have the time to be with their children. Child rearing is no longer just the mother's responsibility, according to a new generation of fathers.

## Stages of Parent Development

The role of parent is not a static one; parents grow and change as their children do. The cycle of stages parents experience is only recently being recognized and studied. Identifiable stages of parental growth are described in a manner similar to the stages of growth that occur as all humans develop and as teachers develop (Galinsky, 1981).

### SIX STAGES OF PARENTHOOD

| Stage | Parent Task | Age of Child(ren) |
|---|---|---|
| 1. Image-making stage | Parents draw on their memories and fantasies of what kind of parent they want to be, prepare for changes in themselves and with other important adults. | Occurs during gestation |
| 2. Nurturing stage | Parents confront the demands of attachment, compare their images with their actual experiences. | From birth until child says "No," around 18 to 24 months |
| 3. Authority stage | Parents define the rules of the family system and their roles in it; they decide what kind of authority to be. | From 18 months to five years of age |
| 4. Interpretive stage | Parents decide how to interpret the world to their child, are concerned with how they interpret themselves to their children, how they are developing the children's self-concepts; and what kind of values, knowledge, and skills to promote. | From late preschool years until the beginning of adolescence |
| 5. Interdependent stage | Parents renegotiate the rules with their teenagers; issues of stage 3 (authority) reappear; parents form a new relationship with their almost-grown children. | The teenage years |
| 6. Departure stage | Parents evaluate their sense of success or failure—whether they have achieved the parent-child relationship they want—and redefine these new relationships. | When children leave home |

**FIGURE 8.5**   The role of a parent changes in various ways as parent and child grow older together. (Adapted from Ellen Galinsky, *Between Generations,* Reading, Mass: Addison-Wesley, 1987.)

According to Galinsky, there are six stages of parenthood. Because parents may have children of different ages, they may be going through several stages at once. Growth can occur at any time and during any stage. The tasks and issues at each stage vary (see Figure 8.5).

The advent of the first baby brings with it life-altering changes and implications. For many parents the myths about having children do not match the reality of what they experience once the baby arrives. LeMasters (1981) suggests some myths that are not borne out in day-to-day living:

• Having children is *fun*.

• Parenthood is an American priority.

• Child-rearing today is easier.

• Children can improve a marriage.

• All married couples should have children.

• All children need two parents.

As they gain confidence in themselves, as more children are added to the family, and as each family member matures in age, parents continually change. The issues they face with only one child are altered considerably when a second or third baby is born. As each of the children grow, develop, and progress through stages, parents are required to adapt. As parents modify their own myths about child-rearing to the realities they experience, they grow as parents. Changing their own behavior is a sign of growth. In other words, parents do not have a consistent or permanent pattern of child-rearing over the years (Bee, 1985).

## Patterns of Child-Rearing

One notable study of how parents behave with preschool children was published by Diana Baumrind in 1972 and reported by Bee (1985). Of the three types of parental styles identified (authoritative, authoritarian, and permissive), authoritative parents were associated with the highest levels of self-esteem, self-reliance, independence, and curiosity in children. *Authoritative* parents provided a warm, loving atmosphere with clear limits and high expecta-

tions. In a follow-up study done when the children were eight or nine, Baumrind's findings persisted.

In contrast, *authoritarian* child rearing patterns reflect high control and maturity demands combined with relatively low communication and nurturance. Authoritarian parents are dictatorial; they expect and demand obedience yet lack warmth and affection. *Permissive* patterns are essentially the reverse of authoritarian child rearing styles. There is a high level of warmth and affection but little control. Clear standards and rules are not set, nor are they reinforced consistently.

This research points out clearly how children are affected by the way their parents treat them. The role of the teacher becomes clear also—to help parents learn appropriate and effective ways to raise their children.

Incidentally, it has been noted that in lists defining characteristics of unusually effective schools, the qualities cited sound similar to those of the authoritative child-rearing style. The effective parent and the effective school each establish "clear goals and rules, good control, good communication, and high nurturance" (Bee, 1985).

## The Changing American Family

As changes in parent development styles have been recorded about individual family systems, the American family as a whole is experiencing significant alterations. Statistics gathered 20 years apart show these dramatic changes:

|  | 1965 | 1985 |
|---|---|---|
| Women who work (percentage of those older than 15) | 37 | 55 |
| Number of children | 2.9 | 1.8 |
| Median age at first marriage |  |  |
| Men | 23 | 26 |
| Women | 21 | 23 |
| Divorce rate (per 1000 couples) | 2.5 | 5.0 |
| Single-parent families (percentage with children younger than 18) | 10 | 22 |
| Premarital births (percentage of all births | 8 | 22 |

(Adapted from "The Changed American Family," *Child Care Information Exchange,* March 1987, p. 7)

For the early childhood educator the implications are clear. The critical issues facing children and their families today are adequate and affordable child care, raising children alone, raising only children, and becoming first-time parents at an older age. The challenge for the teacher is to be prepared to understand families in their various forms, and to be part of a family support system.

## Needs of Single Parents

In their eagerness to do right by their child, parents grab for help whenever and however it is offered. They devour how-to books. Television talk shows where child-rearing methods are discussed and parenting issues are raised are popular. Magazines that feature articles by noted childhood specialists are in all corner grocery stores. Parents seem willing to listen to anyone, to try anything. That is surely some measure of how lonely and frightened they feel at times.

These feelings may be particularly acute for single parents—men and women who are raising children without a partner. Between 1970 and 1986 the percentage of children younger than 18 living in single-parent households increased from 11.8 percent to 23.5 percent (Select Committee on Children, Youth and Family, 1987). It will continue to increase in the 1990s.

Faced with the economic necessity to work, single parents must cope not only with raising children alone, but with child care arrangements and costs. Particularly hard-hit are women who head single-parent households. They are more likely than men to live below the poverty level, to never have married, not to have finished high school, and to be members of a minority population.

Single parents need the early childhood professional to be part of a support system for them and their children. To best serve the interests of children, educators must be sensitive to the unique aspects of raising children alone. This means reexamining school policies and attitudes that ignore the needs of single parents. Overburdened child care professionals need to be flexible in exploring new avenues of

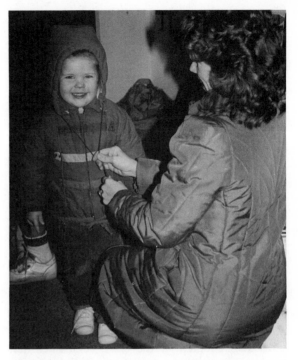

**FIGURE 8.6**  By 1995, nearly 15 million children younger than six will have mothers in the work force. (Courtesy of Stride Rite Children's Centers, Cambridge, Mass.)

home–school collaboration. They need to ask:

- What kind of involvement in a child's classroom is *possible* for a working single parent?

- How can teachers help parents feel connected even if they are unable to be at the center?

- What is appropriate support for single parents?

- How do teachers maintain the role of the professional, offering support, without getting involved with inappropriate friendships?

- How judgmental are teachers about single parents? Single women?

- How do teachers help parents and children deal with the absent parent?

- What are some of the best strategies for helping children cope with the transitions when visiting one parent or the other?

These and other similar questions must become an agenda of staff meetings, in-service for teachers, and parent-group meetings.

## The Teacher's Role

The child care specialist is often one of the first people, outside the home, to whom parents turn for help. Parents come to the center looking for teachers who know about children and who will work with them. They arrive at school confused and discouraged; being a mommy or daddy is not at all like they thought it was going to be. Helping parents with their child-rearing problems is part of a teacher's role. The way in which teachers define that role and their response to parental concerns should be carefully thought through. The following are guidelines to consider in establishing a supportive atmosphere for parents:

*Do not confuse the role of teacher and parent.* While committed to meeting the needs of the individual children in the class, remember that teachers are not and cannot be *surrogate* mothers. Allow parents to do their part of the job to the best of their ability, and teachers their part without infringing on that relationship.

*Support all parents, even those with differing opinions.* Find ways to acknowledge them and what they are trying to do even though you may be at odds with some of their child-rearing philosophies. There is a greater chance to discuss differences and affect change if there are areas where teachers and parents find agreement. Children are sensitive to adult feelings, whether they are spoken or not. A teacher should not overtly disagree with a child's parents. Differences of opinions should be discussed out of the child's hearing, but teachers should also do nothing that would undermine that parent in the eyes of his or her child.

*Respect the values of families.* Social, cultural, and religious differences and a variety of life styles, child-rearing methods, and educational philosophies are reflected in every class. It is important that parents feel accepted. Capitalize on their differences by adding a multicultural aspect to the program.

*Be friendly with parents, but do not be their friends.* The temptation to move into a social relationship with some families in your class is one that every teacher faces. When a teacher develops close relationships with one family or another, this can complicate the teacher role. It makes a teacher feel good to know that friendship is desired, but it can be confusing to parents and children. The teacher maintains a more realistic, objective picture of the child if there is some detachment. The child and the family will probably benefit most if a close relationship is postponed until the child moves on to another class.

*Ask parents instead of telling them.* A teacher-tell approach should be used sparingly. Teachers are most helpful when they begin with the parents' concerns. Suggestions will be received more favorably if teachers avoid telling parents what to do. A teacher's role is one of helping parents clarify their own goals for their children and identifying the trouble spots. Teachers then encourage and support parents as they work together to solve the problem. Parents will feel overwhelmed and inadequate if they think they must change their whole child-rearing style. The sensitive teacher will observe parents and move toward reasonable solutions.

*A little support goes a long way.* Everyone likes to be reinforced for doing a good job. Parents respond positively to a comment, a phone call, or any brief acknowledgment of their efforts. As Alex's parents enter or leave school, the teacher could mention how Alex has relaxed since they began to insist on a reasonable bedtime. A quick note, sent home with Juanita, that commends her parents for getting her to school on time would be appreciated.

*Help parents support each other.* Any group of parents represents a multitude of resources. Each parent has accumulated experiences that might prove helpful to someone else. Parents have common concerns and a lot to share with one another. The teacher can provide an arena in which sharing happens. Introduce two families to each other by suggesting that their children play together outside of school. Parent meetings, work parties, and potluck dinners are methods for getting parents involved with each other. The teacher's role can be one of providing the setting, encouraging introductions, and then letting it happen.

*Enhance parents' perception of their child.* Parents want teachers who know their child, enjoy their child, and are an advocate for their child. That means acknowledging the child's strengths and those personality traits that are particularly pleasing. Help parents to recognize the joys of parenthood, rather than focusing on the burdens.

*Focus on the parent–child relationship.* Help parents learn the "how to's" of their relationship with their child rather than the "how-to's" of developing academic skills. Concentrate on the nature of the parent–child interaction—how they get along with each other and how they interact as a family. A major concern of parents may be how to get Rhoda to stop biting her nails; how to set limits that Joel will keep; how to stop Richard and Monica from fighting at the dinner table; how to get Timmy to stop wetting his bed; how to get Allie to take care of the puppy or how to get Frannie to clean up her room. These issues are the heart and soul of parent–child relationships. Teachers have a role to play in enhancing the quality of those relationships by helping parents focus on the real "how to's."

*Accept parents for what they are.* Their feelings get aroused by teachers, schools, children's behavior, being judged, being criticized, feeling inadequate, and being told what to do. Meantime, teachers have to face their feelings about parents. The important thing to keep in mind is that parents just want to be accepted for who and what they are. As teachers accept the individuality of each child, they must accept each parent as a unique combination of traits, personalities, strengths, problems, and concerns. Parents and teachers seem frightened of one another. This is especially true of inexperienced teachers and first-time parents. Each has anxieties about what the other does—or does not do. They must work at putting the other at ease and come to some understanding and respect. Teachers who have a clear understanding of that role can help parents relax and set aside some of their fears.

# Parents with Special Needs

Parents are parents the world over and have mutual problems and pleasures as they go about bringing up their young. Their shared experiences create an automatic bond whenever parents meet. There are some parents, however, who face additional challenges in child rearing, and who may need added teacher support. These are:

- parents of children with handicaps
- single parents
- parents who both work outside the home
- divorced parents
- teenage parents
- parents who are raising children in foreign cultures
- parents who do not speak English
- older first-time parents

Any one or combination of these situations can create complex challenges for parents. A teacher should become aware of the forces at work within these families and be sensitive to their needs. Teachers should treat these parents as they do any other, it is not necessary to single them out and, indeed, such an effort may be resented. For the most part, teachers can help these parents by focusing on the many interests and concerns they share with all other parents. In some cases, additional support for these parents is needed.

- Help parents locate community resources to assist them.
- Put them in touch with other parents who have similar parenting circumstances.
- Assist them in exploring school settings for the future.
- See that they are included in all school functions.
- Learn about their special needs.
- Seek their help and advice.
- Help them establish contact with other parents who may be willing to assist in translating, transporting, baby-sitting, and sharing friendship.

# TEACHER–PARENT INTERACTIONS

## The Separation Process

When parents leave a child at school, it is a time of stress for all concerned. Each time this process occurs, the child, parents, and teachers are entering into a new and unpredictable relationship.

### The Child's Perspective

Each year, as school begins, a child enters a classroom and says good-bye to a parent. Each year this is, in some ways, a new experience for that child, no matter how long he or she might have been enrolled in school. Children returning to the same classroom will find some changes with which they must cope. There may be new teachers and new children together with some familiar faces. The room arrangement might be different enough to cause some anxiety. For most, school is a new and alien place. Each child will react differently to the situation, and it is difficult to predict how a child will respond. Some children will have had previous group experience to draw on; others will never have been a part of a group of children before.

Here are some scenes of children entering school for the first time:

> Paul, clinging to his Dad's trouser legs, hides his face from view. All efforts to talk with him are met with further withdrawal behind his father.

> Sherry bounces in, runs from her mother over to the blocks area and begins to play there. Her mother is left standing alone, just inside the classroom.

> Stacey and Virginia enter hand-in-hand. They are looking for Alejandro with whom they became acquainted in their gymnastic class. He sees them first, dashes over to where they are greeting the teacher, and beams at them. They grin at him and grab his hand.

The wide range of behavior these children exhibit is normal, predictable, and age-appropriate.

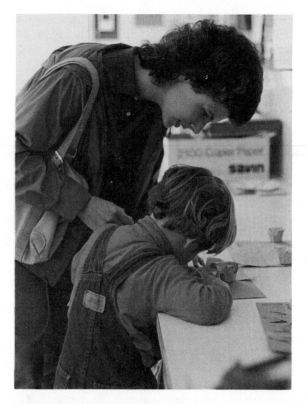

**FIGURE 8.7** Children reap the benefits of parental interest.

Each child has a natural way of dealing with the anxieties of coming to school. Their behavior will be as varied as they are themselves.

### The Teacher's Perspective

The separation process is one instance in which the teacher's role is to help the parents as much as the child. Parents and teachers must be especially clear with one another during this time. It is helpful to have written school policies and procedures so the teacher can go over the process step by step, on an individual basis, as each child enrolls, or at a general parent meeting held prior to the opening of school.

In some schools, teachers arrange to make a home visit to each child enrolled in the class before school begins. This helps the teacher know more about students before they enter school and gives children a chance to become acquainted with a teacher on their home ground.

### The Parent's Perspective

Most parents want their children to make a smooth transition from home to school. Adjustment is a gradual process; parents need encouragement and guidance as their child moves toward independence. When parents are reassured their child is acting normally, and their own anxieties are common, they relax and begin to help the child feel more comfortable.

Parents encourage their child's participation in the program by asking questions and talking together about school activities. They communicate their interest in ways to help their child meet the challenge with a minimum of stress and a maximum of enjoyment.

### The Partnership

In giving support and encouragement to both the parent and the child, the teacher helps them achieve independence from one another. Together, parents and teachers make a plan, going over the guidelines and ground rules. The teacher takes the lead, encouraging the child to move out from the parent. The teacher is there to make the decisions regarding the time of actual separation. The parent and teacher prepare children and tell them when it is time. The teacher supports the parents' exit and stands by the child, ready to give comfort, if needed. This is a time when a teacher needs to act with conviction. Parents appreciate firmness and confidence at a time when their own feelings may be *ambiguous.* Children are reassured by teachers whose attitudes express a belief in what they are doing.

Some parent–child relationships are difficult to assess, and it is not always easy or obvious for the teacher to know what to do. For most children, the separation process is a struggle between their natural desire to explore the world and their equally natural resistance to leaving what is "safe." It is during these years that children are learning to move about under their own power and to trust themselves. Coming to school can provide each child with the opportunity to grow, starting with the separation from parents. Through careful planning, close communication, and sensitivity to one another, parents and teachers will assure the child mastery of this task.

## Parent Education

Almost any contact between the teacher and the parent can be perceived as parent education. Teachers interpret children's behavior to their parents, suggest alternative ways for dealing with problems, show them toys and games that are appropriate, mention books and articles of interest to parents, and reinforce parents' interest and skills. All of these activities are

**FIGURE 8.8**  Parents like to know they make a difference.

considered parent education. Some of it is planned, some of it is spontaneous.

Parent education happens frequently, whether in a formal discussion about nightmares, or an informal chat about safe car seats. It happens as parents observe. They see how teachers respond to Kurt's name calling or the way teachers discuss plans for Kimmy's birthday celebration. They feel it when the teacher disagrees with them about cupcake and ice-cream treats at school.

Stevens and King (1976) view parent education as a type of parent involvement. They state the purpose of parent education as "the development of effective parenting skills, attitudes, and behaviors that optimize the development of young children. Parent education is most strictly those activities that are designed to enable adults to become better parents."

## Communicating with Parents

There are many ways for parents and teachers to increase their communication with one another. In doing so, teachers demonstrate that they value the

**FIGURE 8.9** There are many avenues for parent-teacher communication. These parent pockets, located just outside the classroom door, hold newsletters, notices, and even children's art. (Courtesy of Stephanie Barry Agnew.)

role parents play in their children's lives. Parents are made aware of what their children are doing in school. Five of the most common ways teachers can involve and inform parents are:

1. *Newsletters from the classroom.* They give a general idea of what the children are doing and any special events taking place in class, personal information about new babies, vacations, or other important events in the lives of the children.

2. *Bulletin boards.* Posted where parents can see them, these boards contain notices about parent meetings, guest speakers, community resources, child care, baby-sitting, clothing and furniture exchanges, and library story hours. Information regarding health programs, automobile and toy safety, and immunization clinics are also publicized.

3. *A place for parents.* An area or room at the school set aside for parent use can be an important step in letting parents know they are wanted and needed. Some schools provide space for a parent lounge, complete with a library of resource books on child rearing. If there is no available space, set up a coffee bar in the office or hall. The smallest amount of space—even a countertop with magazines—is a start.

4. *Informal contacts are the easiest and most useful lines of communication with parents.* All it takes is a phone call, a brief note, or a brief talk on a daily basis. For parents who have difficulty attending meetings or who do not accompany their child to and from school, teachers can send home a note along with a sample of artwork, or a story the child has dictated, or a photograph of the child with friends.

5. *Home visits.* Depending on its purpose, a home visit can be used to enhance communications. The visit might be set up to focus only on the relationship between the teacher and the child. Or, the visit might have a purely social function— a way for teachers to meet the whole family and

for them to get acquainted with the teachers. In any event, the teacher can use this as a bridge to build a pleasant, casual beginning with this family.

## *Parent-Teacher Conferences*

Parent conferences are the backbone of any good parent–teacher relationship. They provide a way of coming together to focus on the needs of the individual child. Conferencing can be a mutually supportive link established between the adults who are most concerned about an individual child, with the purpose of helping the child reach the fullest potential possible.

Conferences between parents and teachers are held for many reasons. The initial conference, when the child first enrolls in school, may focus on the family. Important information to share includes a brief overview of the child's development, daily habits, and interests, as well as the parents' view of the child and what the parents expect of the school. The teacher will want to assure parents that they are free to call at any time if they have questions about the school or their child. Farther into the school year, both parents and teachers will want an up-to-date assessment of the child's progress, noting especially the strengths of the child and areas where improvement is needed. Several formats to help focus the discussion are cited in Chapter 10, Figures 10.6 and 10.10.

A conference may be called at any time by either a parent or a teacher if there are concerns to discuss. A written outline listing the goals of the conference will help guide the discussion and direct it to problem areas. Every occasion when parents and teachers get together to talk about a child is a step toward building trusting relationships between home and school.

Too often, teachers are left to figure out for themselves how to have a conference that is satisfying and productive to both parties. Experience is the best teacher is an old saying that certainly has merit. The more new teachers work with parents and hold regular conferences, the more effective they become.

1. *Schedule conferences on a regular basis.* Parents and teachers should share some of the positive aspects of child growth and development and not meet only in crisis. This promotes better feelings about one another, not to mention the child, if meetings are at times other than when a problem occurs.

2. *Be prepared.* Discuss with the staff ahead of time any points they want to include. Gather together any materials, notes, and samples of the child's work that might illustrate a point.

3. *Select a quiet place, free from interruption.* If necessary, sign up for use of a conference room. Make sure that someone is available to intercept phone calls and other appointments.

4. *Have a clear purpose.* Use a written format as a guide to keep focused on the intent of the conference. This gives a brief reminder of points to be covered and serves to keep parents on the track.

5. *Put parents at ease right away.* Offer them a cup of coffee or share an amusing anecdote that just took place in the classroom. Acknowledge the important part they played in the school fair. These light, positive comments will help relax both teacher and parent.

6. *Use up-to-date information and data.* Cite examples, from teacher's observations, that occurred that morning or a few days ago. Include examples of situations that occurred when they were present. "Timmy is very empathetic for a three-year-old, isn't he? That was so clear from the way you two were talking as you came through the door today."

7. *Give them a place to shine.* Tell them what they do well—their success with car-pool crowds or in mediating fights in the yard. If they have a special talent they have shared with the class, comment on its impact on the children.

8. *Ask—don't tell.* Get them talking by asking open-ended questions. "How is that new bedtime arrangement working?" "Tell me more about Katie's eating habits." Teachers will relate these to their own knowledge and experiences with the child and then share what has worked in school, but acknowledge the difference between school and home, teacher and parent. Learn how to listen. Concentrate on what the parents are saying. Don't listen with half an ear while planning an appropriate response or comment.

9. *Avoid blaming parents.* Keep the conversation based on mutual concerns and how to help each other. Look at some alternatives together and make a plan of action. Discuss ways to check in with each other or provide for follow-through at school or home. This way the parent will have a feeling of working together rather than of being blamed.

10. *Know where and how to secure community resources and referrals.* Many parents do not know where to get a child's speech tested, or what an I.Q. test is, or where to secure family therapy. They may be unaware of play groups, gymnastic schools, library story hours, or children's museums. Be sure the school can provide this information for parents who need it.

**FIGURE 8.10** One of the most important responsibilities of the teacher is the parent conference. A good parent-teacher conference is focused and strengthens the relationship between home and school.

11. *Take time to write a brief report after the conference.* Make special note of who attended and who requested the conference, what important issues were raised by either the parents or the teacher, what solutions and strategies were discussed, and what time was agreed upon for checking in with each other regarding progress.
12. *Find a good role model.* Ask experienced teachers to share their ingredients for success. When possible, attend a parent conference with one of them. Observe what works for them and learn from their experience. Ask them to critique your own performance after a conference.

**FIGURE 8.10 Cont.**

The chart in Figure 8.10 might help the beginning teacher hold fulfilling parent conferences.

## Parental Involvement

Parental *involvement* in education includes a wide range of activities. A school that is sensitive to parents will offer a number of ways for them to become involved. The term *involvement* has many meanings, ranging from observation to policy making (Stevens and King, 1976). Parents may choose to play a minor role, if they prefer. If they choose to take a more active part, the options are limited only by school policies and attitudes. A high degree of involvement might mean that parents are serving as salaried teacher aides or as members of governing boards who help define school policy and philosophy. Acting as classroom volunteer, fund raiser, or curriculum resource person are other ways parents get involved.

### *Maintaining Privacy and Confidentiality*

The more involved parents are in the workings of the school, the more important it is to establish guidelines for protecting the privacy of all the families enrolled. When selecting parents for jobs, school administrators must be very clear about their expectations for ensuring such privacy. Parents who work in the office must be responsible enough not to carry tales out of school about any of the children, the teachers, the administration, or the other parents. They should not be expected to handle files that contain sensitive information regarding any of the children, their families, or the staff. Parents in the classroom, either as volunteers or paid aides, must come to understand the necessity for complete confidentiality. What goes on in the classroom must stay in the classroom. Whatever information teachers share with parents about a child is to be used in that classroom only. Teachers will have a responsibility here to uphold these professional standards where parents are concerned.

Classroom participation is the most direct way parents can contribute to the school program. There is always room for another pair of hands in the early childhood setting. Even parents who feel they have

**FIGURE 8.11** A good information program about a variety of issues related to children can inform parents of the need for greater child advocacy. Each April, the Week of the Young Child, sponsored by local NAEYC chapters, serves that purpose. (Courtesy of Stephanie Barry Agnew.)

"nothing to contribute" soon realize how much they are needed. They often come in expecting to do very little. They leave exhausted, smiling, and saying how much they became involved—and how fast the time passed! The sensitive teacher will let parents know that when they tie a shoelace, go on a field trip, or organize a beanbag toss, they are providing valuable help. A calendar posted on the parent bulletin board is an obvious way of saying parents are welcome.

Not all parental participation takes place at school. For parents who work and who are unable to volunteer, or for those with baby-sitting or transportation problems, other alternatives are available. Parents can work at home and still feel needed. Some of the ways these parents can add to their child's school experience are to sew new paint smocks or repair dress-up clothes, cut out materials for art projects, type newsletters, conduct parent surveys, collect collage and woodworking materials, or organize a class songbook or cookbook.

## F O C U S

# PARENT INVOLVEMENT

*Alice S. Honig*

The professionalization of parenting is a recent phenomenon. Workplaces have become cut off from family living spaces, and jobs have become esoteric. Children no longer spend days with parents learning the modes, rhythms, and technical skills of typical chores and occupations. Children are educated in specialized places called schools by professionals trained to inculcate such expertise as decoding print, reading for understanding, computation, and computer skills. Yet, society is currently bewildered and concerned by high school dropout rates and the realization that some children are ill prepared for school learning. Some children seem to lack a passionate commitment to the hard work of literacy and learning.

Slowly, we are beginning to realize the powerful importance of the oldest profession—parenting. New bridges are being built, albeit with suspicion and reluctance by some, so that parents can become intimate, involved partners with teachers in the crucial job of motivating children for solving difficult problems. Researchers, such as L. Alan Sroufe and his colleagues at Minnesota, reveal that there is a hidden key to a child's cooperation with teaching adults and to the roots of competence and persistence at difficult tasks. That key resides not only in a teacher's skillful interactions but *earlier*, in the patterns of support for emotional intimacy and attachment that parents are uniquely qualified to provide in the first years of life. Patterns of secure or insecure attachment to a parent in babyhood are connected strongly with the ways in which older toddlers approach difficult tasks that involve tool-using strategies. Toddlers who were insecurely attached as babies lack zest and enthusiasm for tackling difficult problems, cry, have temper tantrums, and act far more negatively to adult suggestions when faced with difficult learning tasks.

Thus, the urgent realization comes to us that we must respect the ancient profession, as well as the personal job, of parenting. Let's be sure that schools do not just teach history or math or car driving. Courses in child development need to be made integral components of school curricula. A high-quality infant/toddler/preschool child care setting belongs in the school as an expert practicum situation. There, students can learn techniques of tender cuddling; of reading to an energetic, bouncy toddler; or diapering a baby while carrying on responsive turn-taking cooing conversations and talk. Shop and social studies teachers can coordinate with this emphasis by focusing assignments on toys, history, and environments to optimize young children's learnings. English teachers can assign research on excellent books to read to preschoolers. A homework assignment could be to try out ways to capture toddlers' attention with various books and then to write a paper critiquing the books for babies.

Communication with parents who are sometimes bilingual or from other culture groups requires that principals sponsor workshops in awareness and sensitivity training. Parents and teachers can use transactional analysis techniques as suggested in Gordon's Parent Effectiveness Training books or Shure and Spivack's Inter-

personal Cognitive Problem Solving materials to learn communication skills. *Active listening* is a tool that every parent and teacher needs to enhance empathy—atunement to the fears, frustrations, worries, creative passions, and unique selves of young people.

Skillful sensitivity in responding to the emotional and intellectual needs of babies does not come as a free giveaway at time of birth. Parents need a Bill of Rights. They have the right to knowledge and help in learning more intimately, more perceptively, how to cherish children and how to teach them. Then, together, parents and teachers can enhance the zest for loving and learning that should be every child's birthright.

*Dr. Alice S. Honig is a professor of Child Development at Syracuse University.*

# SUMMARY

The partnership in education between parent and teacher has a long and varied history. In current practice, parents and teachers have a growing awareness of the part each has to play in the child's life. Each has a separate but important function, and each has valuable information about the child that needs to be shared.

Parents have an intimate, subjective history of the child from birth. The teacher's perspective comes from an overall knowledge of child development principles, guidance techniques, observational skills, and objectivity. By pooling their information, each has a more complete picture of the whole child. Together they share some common goals for that child. As parents and teachers become more sensitive to each other, they grow in their understanding

of their unique roles.

In order to have successful parent involvement, there must be mutual respect and strong support from the school administration. Programs that invite parent involvement must assess the needs of parents and offer a variety of ways to meet those needs. Parents want to know they are listened to and that they have the potential to effect change.

One of the first and most intensive ways parents and teacher work together is through the separation process that takes place when the child enters school. There are other basic skills teachers must have to work successfully with parents. Frequent communication and many levels of parent education are but two. Parent conferencing is a critical part of any parent effort, and the new teacher can be helped by guidelines that will ensure a good beginning.

# REVIEW QUESTIONS

1. What do you consider to be the most important reasons for teachers and parents to have good relationships? Why should parents be involved in their child's schooling? How would you balance this involvement with your career and/or family responsibilities?

2. Describe three ways you would encourage parents to participate in your classroom. Cite the advantages for the (a) children, (b) parents, and (c) teacher. Are there any disadvantages?

3. What are some of your own "Myths About Parenthood"? Make two lists, one headed "Myths Teachers Have About Parents" and another headed "Myths Parents Have About Teachers." Compare the two and then discuss them with both a parent and a teacher.

4. What are some of the key elements in a successful parent–child separation? What is the role of the teacher?

5. Are you planning to have children? Do you plan to work outside the home after they are born? What will you do about child care?

6. What differences do you see in the way you want to raise your children versus your parents' child-rearing style?

7. How do you and your friends feel about (1) women who opt for careers rather than traditional homemaking? (2) child care needs expressed by these women? (3) single women who raise children alone? What do you think influences your attitudes about these issues?

# LEARNING ACTIVITIES

1. Complete this sentence: "For me, the most difficult part of being a parent (is) would be _____." Discuss your response with another parent, a grandparent, a single person, and a teacher.

2. Interview three parents you know well. What do you see as their major concerns as they raise their children in today's world? What has surprised them the most about parenthood? Be sure to include fathers in your interview.

3. Write a newsletter for your classroom. Involve the children and let it be theirs to write.

4. On page 216, look at the five "Basic Guidelines for Working with Parents." Give an example of how you would apply each of the five principles in your classroom. Look at another classroom setting and see if you can find any way in which these are being undermined.

5. The twelfth step in "Successful Parent–Teacher Conferences" suggests that you find a good role model. Look around at the teachers you know and select one. Go through the steps suggested in number 12 and write up your response.

6. Interview a parent or parents of (1) a six-month-old baby, (2) two or more children, and (3) children with a wide age range. Using the Six Stages of Parenthood, identify where each of the parents are. Discuss.

7. Interview several single parents, both men and women. What do you see as the most critical issue they face? How do you see their children's schools supporting them? Where is there a need for improvement? What are the implications in your life regarding single parenthood?

## BIBLIOGRAPHY

Bee, Helen. *The Developing Child.* Cambridge, Mass.: Harper & Row, 1985.

Galinsky, Ellen. *Between Generations.* Reading, Mass.: Addison-Wesley, 1987.

Honig, Alice S. *Parent Involvement in Early Childhood Education.* Washington, D.C.: National Association for the Education of Young Children, 1979.

LeMasters, E.E. *Parents in Modern America.* Homewood, Ill.: The Dorsey Press, 1974.

Select Committee on Children, Youth and Families. Washington, D.C.: U.S. Government Printing Office, 1987. (Document No. 81-138).

Spodek, Bernard. *Teaching in the Early Years.* Englewood Cliffs, N.J.: Prentice-Hall, 1972.

Stevens, Joseph H., Jr., and King, Edith W. *Administering Early Childhood Education Programs.* Boston: Little, Brown and Co., 1976.

# SECTION 4

# CREATING ENVIRONMENTS FOR GROWTH AND LEARNING
## *Thelma Harms*

The environment that adults create for children is a powerful tool for teaching. Through the way we structure children's surroundings, we communicate our values, provide guidance about how children are to behave in the environment, and influence the quality of their learning. Teachers of young children need to become aware of the constant influence the environment has on the children in their care. Preschool children are much more responsive to the here and now than older children and adults because they have not yet learned to screen out distractions and make sense of confusing messages. By creating an environment that young children understand easily and manage as independently as possible, the teacher can maximize the positive influence of this dependence on the here and now.

The important aspects of environment include arrangement of space, furnishings and equipment, activities to enhance development, the daily schedule, and supervision provided by staff. This broad definition of environment makes it possible for adults to take into consideration all the factors that together create the children's surroundings. For children, interpersonal interactions are interwoven with the physical features of the setting and contribute significantly to the impact made by the total environment. Similarly, the learning activities available to the children are an important part of what they react to in the setting. The term *environment*, then, includes a lot more than the physical features and equipment.

All settings for early childhood care and education have the same basic environmental components and the same basic goal—that of meeting the needs of children, despite the fact that programs vary in length of day, size of group, number of staff and ages of children served. Consider each of the components listed below. I think you will agree that no program could meet the social, emotional, and intellectual needs of young children without doing a good job of providing environmental support for each of these areas:

1. Personal care routines

# What Is
# the Setting?

**GUEST EDITORIAL**

2. Appropriate furnishings and display space
3. Language and reasoning experiences
4. Fine and gross motor activities
5. Creative activities
6. Social development experiences
7. Personal and professional needs of the adults in the program

The first six environmental components deal with the children's needs and the seventh with those of the teaching staff. It is painfully obvious that few people consider it important to include environmental provisions for the adults in early childhood settings. Yet, wherever there are children, there are, of necessity, key adults who are responsible for those children. Unless a facility provides proper space and time for the personal and professional needs of the staff, as well as providing opportunities for staff development and parent–staff interaction, teachers will not be able to reach their professional potential, and the program will suffer. Within each early childhood setting, it is important that the administration and teaching staff arrange the environment to meet their own needs, as well as those of the children entrusted to them.

As teachers of young children, we need to ask ourselves what sorts of goals we should have for early childhood settings. A primary goal is to avoid behavior problems by setting up a soft, responsive, clearly organized and supportive environment that keeps children relaxed, happy, and responding positively. An equally important goal is to set up a predictable environment that children can easily learn to manage independently. The more independent children become, the more teachers are free to provide language and cognitive stimulation through interaction instead of devoting time to the mechanics of running the room. The third goal for early childhood settings—namely, creating a stimulating environment with lots of active learning opportunities for children—can best be carried out if the first two goals are already met.

I believe there is no better tool than observation to help teachers improve their programs. Observation keeps a teacher in touch with what is really happening for children in the program. The challenge in using observation, however, is to remain as objective as possible, which is particularly hard for teachers to do in their own programs. An environment observation guide can help focus a teacher's attention on all the important aspects of the room, including some aspects that might be new areas of awareness for the teacher. Using such a guide periodically can not only increase one's objectivity, but can also help the teacher identify where improvements are taking place and which areas need work.

Teachers who want to be effective in creating quality care and teaching environments need to continue to learn and grow by:

- Trying out new spatial arrangements.
- Trying out new ideas for activities.
- Developing positive interaction skills with children.
- Communicating with parents about their children.
- Visiting other programs.
- Using their skills of observation to objectively evaluate their own programs.

The environment influences children and staff, whether or not we consciously harness this influence. Teachers need to assume responsibility for creating an attractive, functional, and stimulating environment for children and for themselves.

*THELMA HARMS was formerly head teacher at the Harold E. Jones Child Study Center, University of California at Berkeley, in which capacity she served for 15 years. She has consulted extensively with a variety of early childhood programs, both in the United States and abroad, including day care, parent cooperatives, Head Start, public school, preschool, and kindergarten programs.*

*Dr. Harms is an active member of NAEYC and the author of a number of publications including three environmental rating scales:* The Early Childhood Environment Rating Scale *(with R.M. Clifford);* The Family Day Care Rating Scale *(with R.M. Clifford); and* The Infant-Toddler Environment Rating Scale *(with D. Cryer and R.M. Clifford). Her many curriculum materials include the four-volume* Active Learning Series for Infants, for Ones, for Twos, *and* for Threes *(Cryer, Harms, and Bourland);* The Family Day Care Education Series; *and* Cook and Learn *(with Bev Veitch). Her films,* My Art Is Me *and* Growing Up in a Scary World, *are used in teacher training, as are her many filmstrips. Much of her work has been focused on increasing parental involvement in education, and on clarifying the many underlying factors that have an impact on the quality of early childhood education, whatever the setting. She is presently Director of Curriculum Development, Frank Porter Graham Child Development Center, and Clinical Associate Professor, School of Education, both at the University of North Carolina at Chapel Hill.*

# CHAPTER 9
## Creating Environments

## QUESTIONS for THOUGHT

- What does the term *environment* mean?
- What criteria are used in planning the optimum environment?
- How are the program goals reflected in the setting?
- How do philosophy and environment affect each other?
- What is the self-help, anti-bias environment?
- What adult needs must be considered in setting an environment?
- What health and safety measures must be considered when planning the total environment?
- How are materials selected for a classroom?
- What are routines and how do they affect planning?
- How does the interpersonal tone affect learning?
- How can the environment guide children's behavior and highlight learning goals?

# WHAT IS THE ENVIRONMENT?

What does it mean to create an environment appropriate for young children? What makes up the environment? The environment is the stage on which children play out the themes of childhood: their interests, triumphs, problems, and concerns. An environment for children, therefore, includes all of the conditions that affect their surroundings and the people in it.

Each environment is unique. There is no such thing as a model or ideal setting for children. Each school has goals that reflect the values of its own program. When the goals and the setting mesh, the individual atmosphere of the school is created.

But just what does *environment* mean? What do teachers mean when they say they want to create:

- environments for learning?
- optimal growth environments?
- positive learning environments?
- child-centered environments?
- favorable classroom environments?

## Definition

The *environment* is the sum total of the physical and human qualities that combine to create a space in which children and adults work and play together. Environment is the *content* teachers arrange; it is an *atmosphere* they create; it is a *feeling* they communicate. Environment is the total picture—from the traffic flow to the daily schedule, from the numbers

**FIGURE 9.1** Each environment is unique, and children respond to whatever is offered. Does this equipment challenge the physical skills of young children? Is it safe for youngsters? Can it be properly supervised? For what age range would this playground be most appropriate?

*textable* ✱

**Physical Environment**

- room arrangement
- activity area
- storage space
- materials/equipment
- physical plant
- amount of space
- windows, doors
- lighting
- safety equipment
- health supplies
- bathroom facilities
- eating facilities
- living things
- personal space (lockers, etc.)
- tables, chairs
- rugs, pillows, flooring
- display areas
- colors
- evaluation of physical setting
- resting space

**Temporal Environment**

- daily schedule
- weather/climate
- blocks of time for:
    free play
    routines
    groups
    eating/toilet/dressing
- transitions
- evaluation of time schedule

**Interpersonal Environment**

- atmosphere, tone
- people: kinds of children, adults
- kinds of interactions between children and children, children and adults, adults and adults
- feeling of control of room
- flow of activity
- health and safety maintained
- how limits are made, followed through
- traffic patterns
- noise level and its regulation
- consistency between what room says and teacher behavior actually is

**FIGURE 9.2**    The environment is not only physical space and materials; it also includes aspects of time and interpersonal relationships.

of chairs at a table to the placement of the guinea pig cage. It is a means to an end. The choices teachers make concerning the *physical* setting (the equipment and materials, the room arrangement, the playground and the facilities available), the *temporal* setting (timing for transitions, routines, activities), and the *interpersonal* setting (number and nature of teachers, ages and numbers of children, types and style of interactions among them), combine to support the program goals. The environments teachers create should be safe, effective, challenging, and in concert with the theoretical framework of the early childhood program. Figure 9.2 illustrates this.

# CRITERIA FOR CREATING ENVIRONMENTS

Creating environments for children and adults is a practical matter, yet it can be exciting and challenging. Although there are endless variations in planning for children, certain common elements must be considered: (1) the physical plant, (2) available resources, and (3) program goals.

## Physical Plant

Before creating an environment for children, the early childhood teacher must analyze the physical plant. Many settings use space designed for other purposes, such as a church basement or an empty elementary school classroom. The size and shape of the designated space determine how to plan for safe and appropriate use. To rescale the space, teachers shift from an adult perspective to a child's scale. Getting on one's knees provides a glimpse of the environment from the child's point of view; child space is measured from the floor and playground up. A child's stature determines what is available to and noticed by that child. For crawling infants, space consists primarily of the floor, while school-aged children can use and learn from the space up to about five feet, roughly their own height (Rambusch, 1982). It is this perspective that teachers must remember as they plan the physical space for children (see Planning section in this chapter for details).

## Resources

In planning the environment, it is essential to know what kinds of resources are available. Rarely do teachers have unlimited dollars: "This year we can only afford..." determines many of the decisions made about the environment. Priority is usually given to teacher salaries and benefits, equipment and materials for the school, and other related services (maintenance, office help, bus service). Despite budget constraints, teachers must beware of operating on too low a materials budget. Lack of necessary materials can create increasingly passive, angry, and unhappy children out of sheer boredom. Only by knowing the extent of the fiscal boundaries and budget limits can a teacher plan a complete environment.

There are ways to stretch that budget, however. Good environmental principles are not dependent upon numerous or expensive equipment, materials, or buildings. A creative child-centered environment can happen in any setting, regardless of the lack of financial resources. Some equipment can be made, borrowed, or purchased second-hand. In church-based schools, annual rummage sales at the church provide a wealth of dress-up clothes, books, toys, and some appliances. Resource books are filled with

ideas for recycling materials into usable equipment for young children. Parents and others can provide computer paper, wood scraps, or office supplies for dramatic play kits. Community sources, such as the public-library storyteller or a senior citizens group, may be available for extended experiences for the children. Effective fund raising provides an added source of revenue in many schools and centers.

The human resources must also be identified. Adults do their best with children when their abilities, experience, and availability are matched with what is expected of them. Volunteers, for instance, will feel satisfied if their time is organized and spent in ways meaningful to them. A first-year teacher's resources are best expended in the classroom rather than on administrative projects. A master teacher is ready to be challenged in other ways, such as orienting parents or evaluating curriculum materials. Just as we try to match children's developing skills to the tasks at hand, so, too, should we consider individual people as part of an environment's resources.

## Program Goals

The program must be defined in relationship to the physical space, since the goals and objectives of the program are expressed directly in the arrangement of the environment. As Dr. Harms suggests in the Guest Editorial that introduces this section, teachers must ask themselves what sorts of goals we should have for children and then should plan the environment accordingly. The physical space and materials should tell the children exactly what is going to happen and how they are to go about their work. In every program, consideration of what children are to accomplish puts goals and environments together.

The goals of an early childhood program will vary widely because early childhood settings contain such a wide range of age and experience. Some programs are housed in large centers, others in homes; children may attend all day or for part of the day and for educational, recreational, or even custodial reasons. The important point is that good environments for children must reflect clear and reasonable program goals. Once we know what we wish to do, and why we want to do it, we can create space, timing, and an atmosphere in which to meet those goals.

## How Program Goals Are Reflected in the Environment

In creating an environment, teachers plan a program directed toward their goals:

1. They take care to arrange the daily schedule in ways that provide the time blocks needed to teach content when and how they want to teach it.

2. The room and yard are arranged to give maximum exposure to the materials and equipment they want children to use.

3. They see that a warm relationship exists among the teachers and in their interactions with children.

It is essential that teachers have a clear idea of their program goals before they begin to arrange the environment for children. When they invite children in to work, play, and learn, teachers must be sure that the way they have expressed goals through room arrangements, daily schedules, and personal styles, matches what they believe. Blending all the factors that create an environment for children uses the environment to its fullest and demonstrates a belief in how and what children need for learning to take place.

If a goal of the program is to have children practice cognitive and fine-motor skills, games using prereading and writing materials should be prominent. Puzzles and table toys should have a central place in the classroom. Enough tables and chairs should be provided to accommodate all the children. Larger amounts of time should be made available for children to work on these activities every day, and teachers should be available to reinforce and encourage children as they play.

When children walk into a classroom, the environment should communicate how they are to live and work in that setting. Children should receive clear messages about what they can and cannot do there as well as cues that tell them:

- Where they are free to move to and where they cannot go.
- How they will be treated.
- Who will be there with them.
- What material and equipment they can use.
- How long they have to play.
- That they are safe there.
- What is expected of them.

Teachers communicate these messages in many ways. Figure 9.3 describes how teachers use the environment to tell children what is important there. For instance, when it is time to go outside, the doors are opened. If children need to stay off a piece of equipment, it is marked by dividers or a flag, and a teacher stationed nearby explains the instruction. Children know that they matter when they are welcomed each day, and they know their time is valued when teachers tell them how long they have to complete a project or play sequence and when that time is nearly up.

The teacher is the key element in making a creative environment. It is not the facility itself that counts as much as the teacher's understanding of the use of all the environmental factors and how they relate to one another. A room is just a room and a yard is just a yard until a teacher makes them environments for learning. The teachers themselves are the most responsive part of the environment; it is they who converse, hug, appreciate, give information, and see the individuality of each child. They are the ones who create the space, the time, and the atmosphere that will engage children's curiosity and involvement. Figure 9.3 summarizes these environmental goals.

## The Self-Help Environment

There is one common goal in most early education programs which can be demonstrated through the careful use of environmental factors. Promoting *self-help* and independent behavior in children is a

| Children Need to | So the Environment Should |
|---|---|
| Have an opportunity to make choices and participate in independent learning. | Be arranged to encourage free exploration and a clear view of what is available. Offer a variety of activity centers so children can explore, manipulate, probe. Allow large blocks of time for free play so children can make more than one choice. Provide an adequate number of trained teachers to support self-discovery. |
| Be treated as individuals, with unique strengths and developmental goals. | Ensure that the teacher–child ratio supports one-to-one interactions. Provide private as well as public spaces so children can experience group and solitary play. Ensure that children have ready access to teachers and materials. Be staffed by teachers who will set goals for each child based on observation and assessment. Be equipped with materials that will match the developmental level of the group. |
| Learn to be part of a group. | Be set up for group play with four to six chairs around the tables, easels adjacent to one another, more than one telephone, carriage, wagon. Facilitate regular scheduling of small and large group times, which children are expected to attend and participate in. Include trained staff who select appropriate group activities for the age range. Allow children to use each other as resources. Provide activities that will stress cooperation and social interaction. |
| Become responsible for the setting and take care of the equipment and materials. | Schedule cleanup times as part of the daily routine. Include teachers and children working together to restore order. Allow time for children to be instructed in the proper use of materials and be made aware of their general care. |
| Be aware of the behavioral limits of the school setting. | Ensure that the teachers and the daily schedule reflect the important rules of behavior. Include teachers who deal with behavior problems in a fair and consistent way. Allow plenty of time during transitions so that children can move from one activity to another without stress. Be arranged to avoid runways and dead ends created by furniture. |
| Be with adults who will supervise and facilitate play, and encourage learning throughout the day. | Be set up before children arrive so teachers are free to greet them. Encourage teacher–child interactions through the use of small groups, and a time schedule that allows for in-depth interactions. |

**FIGURE 9.3** The environment mirrors the goals of the program.

widespread practice. In planning the environments, teachers attempt to create situations and settings where this is likely to happen.

A self-help environment has as one of its fundamental goals the development of children's own skills—fostering their mastery of basic abilities that will allow them to become responsible for their own personal care, their own learning, their own emotional controls, their own problem solving, and their own choices and decisions. A self-help environment gives children the feeling that they are capable, competent, and successful. It allows children to do for themselves, to meet the challenge of growing up. A self-help environment reflects the belief that autonomy and independence are the birthright of every child.

Nothing renders people more helpless than not being able to maintain their own needs or to take care of themselves in basic ways. Children are still in the process of learning about what they can and cannot do. They need many different kinds of experiences to help them learn the extent of their capabilities. Most of all, they need adults who understand their tremendous drive to become self-reliant, adults who will not only encourage their abilities and provide the time for them to practice skills, but adults who understand that it is the nature of the child to develop this way.

*Self-concepts* are based on what we know about ourselves, which includes the ability to take care of one's own needs. To care for oneself, to feel capable of learning, to solve problems, are all related to feelings of *self-esteem*. Self-esteem is the value we place upon ourselves; how much we like or dislike who we are. Helping children achieve positive self-concepts and self-esteem is the most important part of teaching. The development of a strong sense of self-esteem is a lifelong process; its origins are in the early years.

For all of these reasons, teachers establish settings that promote self-help. They want children to feel good about themselves and they want to foster that growing sense of self-esteem. This happens in classrooms which allow children to do what they are capable of doing. For the teacher, the reward comes from each child who says, "I can do it all by myself."

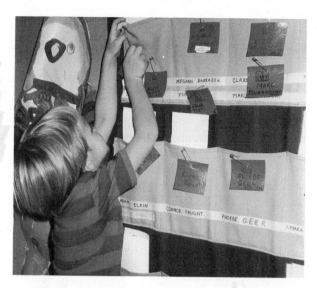

**FIGURE 9.4** Through self-help environments, children become independent.

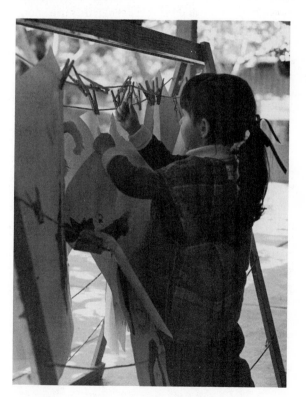

**FIGURE 9.5** "I can do this by myself."

Planning an environment designed to promote self-help skills is the teachers' responsibility. Every aspect of the environment, from the room arrangement to the attitudes of the teachers, supports children in doing all they can for themselves. Each activity is designed to foster self-reliance, thereby building self-esteem. The supermarket is a good example of an environment created for maximum self-reliance. Shelves are accessible and the products are clearly marked and attractively displayed. It takes that kind of thoughtful preparation to create space that says to children, "Do me. Master me. You are capable." Teachers want to communicate to children that they value self-help skills as much as they appreciate an art project or science experiment. The ultimate goal is for children to see self-reliance as valuable. If Claudia feels that learning to tie her shoes is worth doing just because of the pleasure it gives her to manipulate the strings, weave them through the holes, and bring them together in a knot, then that becomes her reward. She becomes capable of reinforcing herself and leaves the way open for adults to praise her for other important learnings.

## An Invitation for Success: The Anti-Bias Curriculum

Among the core values (see Professional Ethics in Chapter 5) in any good early childhood program is the recognition of each child as unique, as deserving of respect, and as a part of a family. Each child has the right to achieve full potential and to develop a positive self-esteem. Each family deserves support for the unique role it plays. Part of the commitment of the early childhood teacher is to help children learn to value one another's uniqueness, the differences as well as the similarities. Teachers do this, in part, by expressing such inclusive attitudes.

The *anti-bias curriculum,* developed at Pacific Oaks College, encourages children and adults

1. To explore the differences and similarities that make up our individual and group identities, and

2. To develop skills for identifying and countering

the hurtful impact of bias on themselves and their peers (Derman-Sparks, 1987).

The physical and interpersonal environment can be used to help children see that culture consists of the various ways people do similar activities. This approach is different from the tourist curriculum, which provides only superficial information that is often detached from the child's own life. It is also different from an approach that builds only on the interests of the class. There is an inherent feeling of fairness to self and others in the anti-bias approach, as children explore the many ways people do the basic human tasks of everyday life. Think of the diverse cultures expressed in how babies and things are carried from place to place in different parts of the world. How many ways do people eat? Cook? Shop for food?

A value common to all early childhood programs is expressed in this anti-bias curriculum: that every person is valuable and so diversity is valuable, and peaceful and just cooperation among all is possible. In this curriculum, the environment and the activities are derived from three sources: the children and their behavior, the teachers' awareness of the developmental needs and learning styles of the group, and societal events. Teachers, of course, make general selections of what children are to learn and arrange the environment for learning to begin. Then, the environment, which includes the children themselves, begins to change. If children are especially interested in making things, perhaps the theme "All people live in homes" emerges, with activities that focus on how people build things, what they use the buildings for, and how they work to get something built. As day-to-day problems and conflicts arise, teachers bring up problem-solving activities in a natural manner. Thus, the interpersonal tone of the class is one of trust and time for resolving conflicts.

The anti-bias approach to creating environments has its roots in the theories of Maslow and Erikson (see Chapter 4). Early childhood programs must develop a child's basic sense of trust and mastery so that children can learn to understand themselves and become tolerant and compassionate towards others. The anti-bias approach to a classroom goes hand in hand with self-help principles:

- *Positive self-concept.* Curiosity and creativity stem from being able to affect the environment and what is in it. When Jamal says his baby's hair is fuzzy like his, his smile tells how good he feels about it.
- *Awareness.* All people have interests and feelings, both about themselves and about others. Yoko notices that her classmate Julie runs and throws her arms around her dad, while she prefers a less demonstrative greeting.
- *Respect for diversity.* This stems from the ability to classify similarities and differences and then to appreciate both. For example, when the children create self-portraits for their class books, some choose different colors of paper for drawing faces, but all of them use the same markers to draw in their features.
- *Skills in communication and problem solving.* Learning how to express thoughts and feelings includes being able to hear others and finding peaceful ways to resolve conflicts. Jim and LaNell are quick to tell Eben he can't play, but they find out that telling him he is "too little" does not work. He does not accept that simply being three years old is enough reason to leave him out, and they must either try to include him or make a claim for privacy.

Both the self help approach and the anti-bias curriculum differ from traditional educational practices often seen in classrooms for older children in that the self-help, anti-bias environment is pluralistic and developmental. As Elizabeth Jones (1984) stated:

> The pluralistic view assumes that (1) people are different from each other and (2) differences are valuable; they add to the richness of everyone's experiences. The task of the worker with children, then, is to acknowledge and appreciate differences. The developmental view assumes that growth and learning are spontaneously

motivated. The task of the teacher is to provide a supportive environment that frees each individual to grow and learn—to empower children so that they will assert their needs and develop thoughtful strategies for meeting them.

## Principles of Successful Environments

- *Give children ways to identify their own space.* Label their cubbies with their names, a photo, or a familiar picture so that they can see where to put up their wraps, artwork, and other personal belongings.

**FIGURE 9.6** Children develop a sense of self when they have their own space, labeled with a photo or other visual clue so that they can easily identify it as their own. (Courtesy of Stephanie Barry Agnew.)

- *Give children an opportunity to make choices.* Both indoors and out, children should be given an abundance of materials and a range of activities from which to choose so that they will decide how they spend their time. Choosing to play with the hamster rather than in the block corner helps children practice self-direction. Children should also be able to decide with whom they would like to play and with which teachers they would like to establish close relationships.

- *See that children are responsible for caring for the equipment and materials.* Establish a cleanup time in the daily schedule and allow children time to help restore the room and yard. Label shelves and cupboards with pictures or symbols of what is stored there so that children can readily find where thing belong. Outlining block cabinets with the specific shape of the blocks that are stored on each shelf will encourage children's self-help skills. Outdoor areas, clearly marked for wheel toys, help children function independently. A drying rack with large clothespins that is accessible to children tells children that they are expected to care for their own artwork.

- *Involve children in the process of planning and setting up the environment.* Let the children help decide what they want to learn by developing areas and units around what they bring into class. For instance, if a child's pet has babies, encourage a visit and then send a newsletter asking for other pets, arranging a field trip to a pet store, and organizing a dramatic-play corner as a pet hospital or pet shop. When furniture or outdoor equipment needs moving, include the children in planning what the changes will be and then assist them in moving the pieces themselves. Make the yard more interesting by encouraging the children to rearrange climbing boards. Let them choose what game from the shed will be used that day. And the class feast is made more exciting when the children themselves move all the tables together.

- *Provide children with enough time.* One of the ways children learn is to repeat an activity over and over

again. They explore, manipulate, experiment, and come to master an 18-piece puzzle, a lump of clay, or how to brush their teeth. Large blocks of time in the daily schedule—especially for routines—let children proceed to learn at an unhurried pace.

- *Allow children to solve their own problems without adult interference whenever possible.* See how far a child can go in discovering how to manipulate a pin so that it will close, or work out with another child who will use the red paint first. In solving social or mechanical problems, young children can begin to find out for themselves what is or is not successful. One mark of a good teacher is a person who can let a child struggle sufficiently with a problem before stepping in to help.

- *Accept children's efforts.* To support children in their quest for independence, the adult must be satisfied with children's efforts, and be ready to accept the way Tom made his sandwich or Shelley's boots on the wrong feet.

- *Communicate expectations.* Let children know what they are expected to do. Tell them in both verbal and nonverbal ways. "You don't have to hurry; we

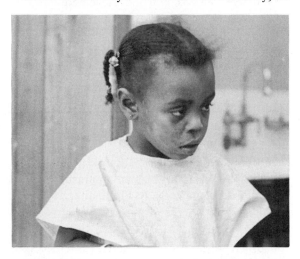

**FIGURE 9.7** The self-help environment says "You can do it!" Even paint smocks are designed so that children can take care of themselves. (Courtesy of Stride Rite Children's Centers, Cambridge, Mass.)

**FIGURE 9.8**    Children's drive for independence is expressed early; this infant is ready to help herself, and the environment can be designed to encourage such initiative.

have plenty of time for cleanup" lets children know they can do a job without pressure. Prompt children by giving them clues that indicate how to proceed: "If you pull up your underpants first, it will be easier to get your trousers up," can be said to Raymond who is waiting for an adult to dress him. Give him feedback on what is working. "Good. You've got the back up. Now reach around the front." Focus on how Raymond is succeeding and communicate your confidence in his ability to finish the task.

- *Be sure staff expectations are consistent.* The teaching team should set common goals for each child and reinforce them consistently. Janice will become confused if one teacher tells her to get her cot ready for nap and another teacher does it for her.

- *Consider the developmental level of the child.* Recognize that there are many things young children will not be able to do for themselves, but

**FIGURE 9.9**    Help yourself! (Courtesy of Stephanie Barry Agnew.)

allow them the chance to do all they can. Be developmentally aware—know what children in the class are capable of, where they are now in their development, and what the next step should be. Perhaps two-year-old Sophie can zip her jacket now. Soon she will be able to put the zipper in the housing by herself. Recognize her readiness for taking the next step.

- *Make it safe to make a mistake.* Children learn from their own actions and their own experiences. Let them know it is perfectly acceptable, indeed inevitable, that they will at times make mistakes. Children need to be accepted for who and what they are, and this includes when they are in error. Help them deal with the consequences of their mistakes. Adults in the preschool can provide models for children in coping with unexpected results and how to bring forth a positive resolution. When Chelo spills her juice, she is encouraged to find a sponge and clean up the table. The teacher reinforces Chelo's efforts and comments on her scrubbing ability or her swift action in preventing the juice from going on the floor.

- *Give credit where it is due.* Provide feedback so that children will know when they have been successful. Compliment Chaz on the length of time he took sorting through the nails to find the one he wanted. Tell Ellen she worked hard at opening her own thermos bottle. Let children take some credit for their own accomplishments.

- *Be sure children have access to enough toys and materials.* Help children imagine and live in alternative worlds, in communities and homes where things are different. Show children respect by giving them the option to take care of themselves. Make sure that supplies are stored in such a way that adults do not have to hand them to children each time they will be used. Equipment placed at a child's height on open, low shelving permits children to proceed at their own pace and select materials without depending upon adults to serve them.

- *Let children teach one another.* Encourage children to share the skills they have mastered with their peers. Actively seek out each child's way of doing things; support a diversity of approaches. Those who can tie shoes enjoy helping their friends with stubborn laces or slippery knots. Whether reading or telling stories to one another, or showing a friend a fast way to put on a jacket, children benefit from helping each other.

Adults who work with children should remember to interact with children in ways that will help them grow toward independence. To perceive children as helpless is to rob them of the satisfaction of achievement. A well-planned environment opens up infinite possibilites for children to achieve a feeling of self-satisfaction while they explore the boundaries of their own beings.

# PLANNING FOR THE ENVIRONMENT

## Who Is in the Environment?

Many people live and work in the early childhood environment. Cooks, bus drivers, office personnel, yard and building maintenance people are but a few. Each of these persons has special demands on the environment in order to do the job they are hired to do.

Teachers, parents, and children have the greatest influence on the early childhood environment; their needs are outlined below.

### Children

Children's needs are met through the environment. The physical, social, emotional, and intellectual requirements of children suggest the type of building, the size of the furniture, the choice of equipment, the size and age range of the group, the number of teachers who lead and supervise, and the budget allocations. Guided by child development principles, teachers match the setting to the children who will learn and play there. The individuality of a particular group of children, a school, and its

*Eating Teaches Health:*
Introduction to new and different foods, good nutritional habits

*Eating Teaches Social Skills:*
How to manage oneself in a group eating situation, focusing on eating *and* conversing; acceptable meal-time behavior and manners

*Eating Teaches Small Motor Skills:*
Pouring; handling spoons, forks; serving self; drinking, eating without spilling

*Eating Teaches Independence Skills:*
Finding and setting one's place, serving self, making choices, cleaning up at snack and lunch times

*Eating Teaches Individual Differences:*
Likes/dislikes; choices of food; fast/slow pace of eating

*Resting/Sleeping Teaches Health:*
Personal care skills; relaxation habits; internal balance and change of pace; alternating activity to allow body to rest

*Resting/Sleeping Teaches Independence Skills:*
Preparing own rest place; selecting book/toy; clearing bed things after rest

*Dressing Teaches Independence Skills:*
Self-awareness: size of clothes, comparisons between clothes for girls and boys, younger and older, larger and smaller children, and children in and out of diapers or training pants

Self-esteem: caring for one's own body; choosing one's own clothes.

*Dressing Teaches Fine-Motor Skills:*
How to manage snaps, buttons, zippers; handling all garments; maneuvering in and out of a snowsuit or jacket, matching hands and feet with mittens and boots or shoes.

*Toileting Teaches Emotional Skills:*
Self-awareness: body functions, comparisons between boys and girls, learning the names and physical sensations that go with body functions.

Self-identity: what girls/boys do

Self-esteem: caring for one's own body without guilt, fear, shame

Human sexuality: in a natural setting, promotes healthy attitudes toward the body and its functions; that adults can be accepting, open, and reassuring about the body and its care

**FIGURE 9.10**  Every routine can be used as a vehicle for learning within the environment.

philosophy is expressed by the arrangement of the environmental factors. First and foremost, though, is the question: Who are the children who will use this space? What are their needs? How can those needs be met in this particular setting?

**Routines.** What is meant by a *routine?* Routines are the framework of programs for young children. A routine is a constant; each day, certain events are repeated, providing continuity and a sense of order to the schedule. Routines are the pegs on which to hang the daily calendar. When should children eat? Sleep? Play? Be alone? Be together? These questions are answered by the placement of routines. The rest of the curriculum—art activities, field trips, woodworking—works around them. Routines in an early childhood environment setting include:

| Self-care: | Group times |
| --- | --- |
| Eating | Task completion |
| Naps, sleeping | Making choices |
| Dressing | Transitions between activities |
| Toileting | Beginning and ending the day |
| | Room cleanup and yard restoration |

Most routines are very personal and individual rituals in children's daily lives. Children bring to school a history firmly established around routines, one that is deeply embedded in their family and culture. Routines are reassuring to children, and they take pride in mastering them; they are also a highly emotional issue for some.

The self-care tasks—eating, sleeping, dressing, and toileting—can be difficult issues between adult and child, virtually from the moment of birth. Everyone can recall vivid memories associated with at least one routine. They seem to become battlegrounds on which children and adults often struggle. Many times this is where children choose to take their first stand on the road to independence.

The early childhood teacher must be able to deal with the issue of self-care routines in sensitive and understanding ways. Children adjust to routines

when they are regularly scheduled in the daily program and when there are clear expectations.

Routines are an integral part of creating a good environment for children. All three environmental factors are influenced by routines:

1. *Physical:* Child-sized bathroom and eating facilities; storage of cots, blankets, and sleeping accessories; equipment for food storage and preparation.

2. *Temporal:* Amount of time in daily schedule for eating, resting, toileting, cleanup.

3. *Interpersonal:* Attitudes toward body functions; willingness to plan for self-care tasks, interactions during activities and transitions, expectations of staff, parents, and children.

As teachers plan for children's basic needs, they are aware of the learning potential of ordinary, everyday routines. Figure 9.10 illustrates how self-

**FIGURE 9.11** Cleanup time. How can this routine be made interesting and appealing to children?

care routines teach the young child important skills and habits.

## Teachers

What about the needs of the teachers who work in the setting? Do they have an office? A teachers' room? A place to hold conferences? Where do they keep their personal belongings—or the materials they bring to use at school? Do they have a place to park? All teachers need a room in which to create curriculum materials, or evaluate their programs, to review other educational materials, to meet with their peers. How well teachers are provided for helps to determine the atmosphere they will establish in their classrooms for children.

## Parents

The needs of parents will differ, depending upon whom the program serves. Parents who bring their children to child care or school need adequate and safe parking facilities. In settings where parents are free to stay, a reading room, resource library, and a comfortable place to talk with other parents is desirable. Parents who participate in the class are welcomed by a teacher, shown a place to put their belongings, and given a name tag and task card.

There are many reasons parents may need to contact the school or center. Are there ways for parents to reach teachers and children in emergencies? How welcoming is the environment to parents as they enter the building? The office? The classroom? What does the environment say about parent involvement and interest?

To meet parents' needs, the school environment can be made accessible and welcoming in several ways. Posting telephone numbers at which school authorities and teachers can be reached when the school is closed assures parents that teachers are available whenever needed. A bulletin board for community notices and for parent use can be put up along with mail pockets. Written communication can go between parents and teachers and among families. The classroom that offers both the teacher and other resources helps parents feel that their children and families are important.

# Health and Safety in the Environment

Regardless of how many children are in the setting and for how long, the first priority is to provide for their health and safety. Government regulations vary, but all establish some kind of standards to ensure good health and safety practices.

## Keeping Children Healthy

**Sanitation.** When groups of people live in close quarters, proper sanitary conditions are imperative to prevent the spread of disease. For an early childhood center, the physical plant must have adequate washing and toileting facilities for both children and adults. The number and size of toilets and wash basins are usually prescribed by local health or other regulatory agencies. The classrooms require daily cleaning, and equipment that is used regularly should be sanitized on a periodic basis. Nontoxic paint must be used in all circumstances, including on outdoor equipment, cribs, and for art activities with children. Classroom dress-up clothing, pillows, nap blankets, and cuddle toys all need regular laundering, either at school or at home.

**Temperature, Ventilation, and Lighting.** Heating and ventilation should be comfortable for the activity level of the children and should change when weather conditions do. Adequate, nonglare lighting is a necessity. Rooms should have some means of controlling light (shades, blinds). Cross-ventilation is necessary in all rooms where children eat, sleep, or play. Proper heating and insulation are important.

**Communicable Disease.** This is an important issue when dealing with young children in group care. Some people question the advisability of early group care on the grounds that it exposes children to too much illness. Others claim that such exposure at an early age helps children build up resistance and that they are actually stronger and healthier by the time they enter primary grades.

Parents should be notified when normal childhood diseases (such as chicken pox) or common problems (such as head lice) occur in the classroom. A description of the symptoms and the dates of exposure and incubation period may be helpful to parents. They can then assist the school in controlling the spread of the disease in question.

In group care, children can contract a fair number of colds and viruses, especially when they are eating and sleeping in close proximity. The school and its staff have a responsibility to ensure that good health standards are instituted and maintained to keep illness to a minimum.

**Health Assessment and School Policies.** Every early childhood center should establish clear health policies and make them known to parents. A daily inspection of each child will help adults spot nasal discharge, inflamed eyes, and throat and skin conditions of a questionable nature. This daily check will screen out more serious cases of children too ill to remain at school, and may be done by a teacher, nurse or administrator. Educating parents about the warning signs of illness will encourage sick children to be cared for at home.

It is very important for the school to inform parents about what happens when children are refused admittance or become ill during the school day. Every school should provide a place for sick children where they can be isolated from others, kept under supervision, and be made comfortable until they are picked up. For their part, parents must arrange to have sick children cared for elsewhere if they are unable to take them home. School policies on these issues must be *explicit* and upheld consistently and compassionately, for the sake of all the children.

Teachers must be sensitive to parents' feelings and situations when sending a sick child home. This situation often produces guilt feelings in parents and work-related stress. Working parents may need school assistance in locating alternatives for care of a sick child.

Most schools require, under state or local laws, a doctor's examination and permission to participate in an early childhood education program before a child can enter the program. This includes a record of immunizations and the child's general health. Parents, too, should submit a history of the child, highlighting eating, sleeping, and elimination habits. It is critical to note any dietary restrictions or allergies and then post them in the classrooms for a reminder.

**Clothing.** The health and safety of children is affected by the clothing they wear. A simple way to be sure children stay healthy is to encourage them to dress properly for play and for varying weather conditions. Children need clothing in which they can be active—clothing that is not binding, and is easy to remove and easy to clean. Pants are a good choice for both boys and girls; long dresses can become a hazard when climbing, running, or going up and down stairs. The safest shoes for active play should have composition or rubber soles. Whenever possible, it helps to keep changes of clothes at school.

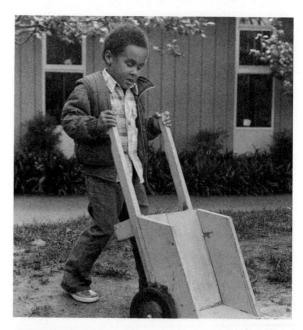

**FIGURE 9.12** Clothing should allow children freedom. Pull-on pants encourage self-mastery, and layers allow for movement and adjustment to changing weather.

**Health of the Staff.** A responsible early childhood center is one that supports and maintains a healthy staff. Teachers should be in good physical and mental health to be at their best with children. It is wise to check the health regulations and benefits of the individual school when employed there. Many states require annual chest X rays as a condition of employment. Sick leave policies should be clearly stated in print.

Early childhood education is an intense job involving close interpersonal contact. Most teachers work long hours, often with low wages and few health benefits, and with clients in various stages of health. Such working conditions produce fatigue and stress, which can lead to illness or other stress-related problems. For more on the issues of teacher burnout, see Chapter 15.

## Guarding Children's Safety

Everything is planned with the children's safety in mind. Creating a hazard-free environment for children takes careful observation and attention to detail. A quick walk around the room and yard will reveal potential problems:

- Are there any sharp corners at children's height?
- Are rug edges snagged or loose?
- Are absorbent surfaces used wherever there is water? Are mops and towels available for spillage?
- Is hot water out of the reach of children?
- Are children allowed to run inside?
- Are there rules governing the children's use of scissors, hammers, and knives?
- Are safety rules explained to children and upheld by adults?
- Are electrical outlets covered when not in use?
- Do open stairwells have gates?
- Do adults monitor the use of extension cords and appliances?
- Is broken equipment removed promptly?
- Are fences high enough to protect and safe to touch?
- Are there areas where wheel toys can move freely without fear of collision?
- Are swings placed away from traffic areas and set apart by bushes or fences?
- Can a child's foot or ankle be caught on equipment; under a chain-link fence?
- Does traffic flow easily?
- Are the toys safe for children's use?

**FIGURE 9.13** Teachers create safe environments.

**First Aid.** Every school should establish procedures for dealing with children who are injured on the property. First aid instructions should be required of all teachers and made available as part of their in-service training. Teachers should know how to treat bumps and bruises, minor cuts and abrasions, bleeding, splinters, bites and stings, seizures, sprains, broken bones, and minor burns. Each classroom should be equipped with two first aid kits. One is for use in the classroom and yard, the other should be suitable for taking on field trips. The kit should be readily available to adults, but out of children's reach, and supplies should be replenished regularly.

Emergency numbers to be posted near the telephone in each room include those of the ambulance squad, fire department, police, health department, nearest hospital, and a consulting physician (if any). All families enrolled at the school should be aware of school policy regarding injuries at school and provide the school with emergency information for each child: the name of their physician, how to locate the parents, and who else might be responsible for the injured child if the parents cannot be reached. The school in turn must make sure they notify parents of any injuries the child has incurred during the school day.

**Fire Safety.** Most local fire regulations require that fire extinguishers be in working order and placed in all classrooms and the kitchen area. Fire exits, fire alarms, and fire escapes should be well marked and functioning properly. Children and teachers should participate in fire drills regularly and, in some areas of the country, earthquake and tornado drills. These experiences can reinforce in parents the need for establishing similar procedures at home.

**Automobile Safety.** Automobile safety is a related concern when considering potential hazards for preschool children. The use of approved car seats and restraints for children riding in automobiles has received national attention in recent years. Some states have passed legislation requiring the use of specific devices to ensure safer travel for young children. Whether or not they walk to school, children should also be aware of basic rules for crossing streets. The school parking lot can be a source of danger unless the school articulates policies to parents regarding the safety needs of children. There are potential risks when cars and children occupy the same space. Children should not be left unattended in parking lots.

**FIGURE 9.14** A hazard-free environment can still be challenging. How can the children feed the animals without risking their safety?

**Nutrition.** What children eat is also important for proper health. Places where food is prepared and stored must be kept especially clean. The child who has regular, nutritious meals and snacks will likely be healthier and less susceptible to disease. Many children do not have the benefits of healthy meals

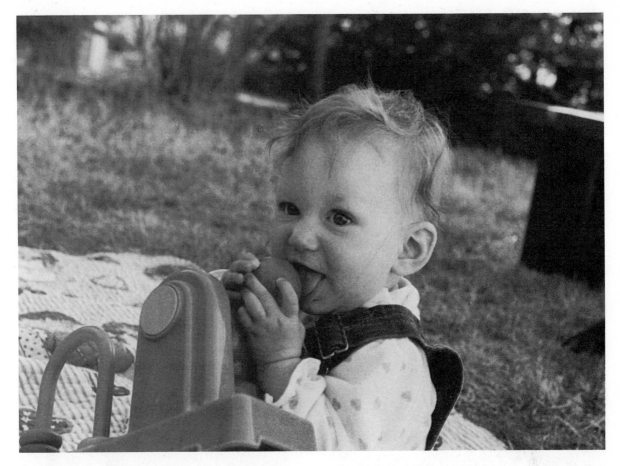

**FIGURE 9.15**  When planning for infants and toddlers, toys must be checked carefully, as children explore them with all their senses. (Courtesy of Adele Morse O'Connell.)

and snacks. Some do not receive adequate food at home; others are used to sugar-laden treats and "fast foods." Education about nutrition becomes the responsibility of a school that is concerned with children's health and physical development. The need for educating parents regarding child nutrition exists in virtually all early childhood programs, regardless of social or economic status. Some centers establish food regulations in an attempt to ensure that nutritionally sound meals are served to children. Most schools attempt to provide a relaxed atmosphere at meal and snack time. Children are asked to sit and

eat, sharing conversation as well as food. Since lifelong eating patterns are established early in life, teachers of young children have a responsibility to understand the critical role nutrition plays in the child's total development.

The health, safety, and nutritional needs of the children are of primary and fundamental importance. The National Academy of Early Childhood Programs has established explicit guidelines for health, safety, nutrition, and food service (NAEYC, 1984). When the basic needs of children are protected, the foundation for sound development has been laid.

# CREATING THE ENVIRONMENT

## The Physical Environment

Every school setting is organized fundamentally around physical space. This means teachers work with the size and limitations of the facility, both inside and out-of-doors. The building itself may be new and designed specifically for young children. More than likely, it is a converted house or store, a church basement, a parish hall, or an elementary classroom. Sometimes a program will share space with another group so that mobile furniture is moved daily or weekly. There may be a large yard or none at all. Some playgrounds are on the roof of the building, or a park across the street may serve as the only available playground. (See Playgrounds in Chapter 12.)

Restraints also come in the form of weather conditions. Outside play—and therefore large-muscle equipment—may be unavailable during the winter months. This may suggest that room for active, vigorous play is needed inside during that time. Hot summer months can make some types of play difficult if there is little or no shade outdoors. Weather conditions must be taken into consideration when planning programs for children.

Early childhood programs have specific needs that must be met by the buildings they occupy. Although the choice of building is generally determined by what is available, at a minimum the setting should provide facilities for:

| | |
|---|---|
| playing/working | food preparation |
| eating | storage |
| washing/toileting | office |
| sleeping/resting | clothing and wraps |

Courtesy of Jeanne Brannan, College of Notre Dame of Md.

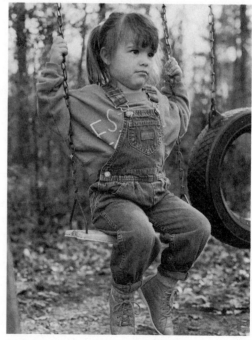

Courtesy of Lyolia Humphries, NLU Monroe.

**FIGURE 9.16** The swing, a staple of the early childhood playground, elicits many kinds of interactions, skills, and moods.

Courtesy of Mike Millikin.

Courtesy of Laurie Leach, Salt Lake Community College, Utah.

Courtesy of Mary Ann McFarlane, Sierra College, Calif.

Courtesy of Julia Kate Dow, Colby Sawyer College, N.H.

Ideally, the setting should have enough rooms to house these various activities separately. In practice, however, rooms are multipurpose and more than one event takes place in the same space. A play room doubles as an eating area, since both require the use of tables and chairs. When a school room serves many functions (playing, eating, sleeping), convenient and adequate storage space is a necessity. The amount of teacher time needed to prepare the room for each change of activity is worth consideration when planning the daily schedule.

## General Requirements

Ground floor classrooms are preferable for young children to ensure that they can enter and leave with relative ease and safety. For noise reduction, the walls and ceilings should be soundproofed. Carpeting, draperies, and other fireproof fabrics in the room will help absorb sound. Floors must be durable, sanitary, and easily cleaned. They should be

free from drafts. Rugs should be vacuumed each day. Room size should be sufficient to allow for freedom of movement and the opportunity to play without interference. Some licensing agencies may suggest minimum room and yard size standards.

Many local and state agencies have regulations regarding the use of space for children in group care settings. The fire marshall, health department, and similar agencies must be consulted and their regulations observed. It is wise to consider their requirements when arranging space.

The National Academy of Early Childhood Programs has developed guidelines for indoor and outdoor facilities that promote optimal growth. Besides floor and play space (minimum 35 square feet indoors and 75 square feet outdoors), the guidelines suggest how to arrange activity areas to accommodate children and what kinds of activities and materials are safe, clean, and attractive. Dr. Thelma Harms, whose guest editorial appears at the

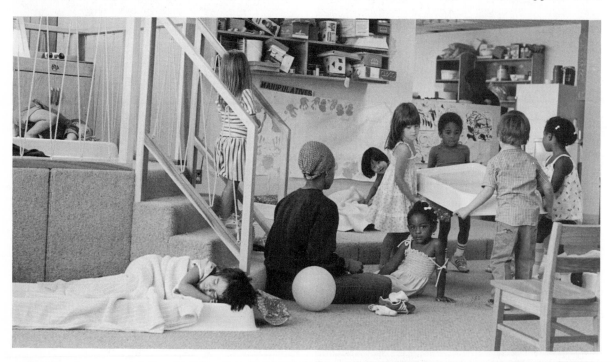

**FIGURE 9.17** The classroom serves many functions, such as sleeping or resting, storage, and playing or working. (Courtesy of Stride Rite Children's Centers, Cambridge, Mass.)

introduction of this section, has developed an environmental rating scale. The sections on Materials and Equipment and on Organizing Space in this chapter draw on these two exemplary works, which are cited in the chapter bibliography.

## *Bathrooms*

These should be adjacent to the play and sleeping areas and easily reached from outdoors. Child-sized toilets and wash basins are preferable, but if unavailable, a step or platform may be built. In most early childhood settings, the bathrooms are without doors, for ease of supervision. Toileting facilities for children should be light, airy, attractive, and large enough to serve several children at a time. An exhaust fan is desirable. Paper towel holders should be at child height and waste baskets placed nearby.

If diapering is part of the program, areas for this purpose should be clearly defined and close to hand-washing facilities. Handwashing regulations for the staff should be posted, and an area should be provided for recording children's toileting and elimination patterns. Closed cans and germicidal spray must be used, and diapering materials should be plentiful and handy.

## *Room to Rest*

Schools that provide nap and sleeping facilities require adequate storage space for cots and bedding. Movable screens set up throughout the classroom allow for privacy and help reduce the noise level.

Cots or cribs should be labeled with children's names and washed regularly. They should be placed consistently and in such a way that children feel

A poster on the wall encourages self-help skills in daily routines.

Courtesy of Stride Rite Children's Centers, Cambridge, Mass.

**FIGURE 9.18** Every routine—eating, resting, handwashing, dressing, toileting—has a place in the early childhood classroom.

familiar, cozy, and private—not in the center of the room or in rows. Teachers can develop a "nap map" that places children so they can all get the rest or sleep they need while still feeling part of the group.

### Out of Doors

A wide porch or covered patio is ideal for rainy days or days when the sun is too severe. Many activities can be extended to the outside area with this type of protection. The physical plant should include adequate playground space adjacent to the building. A variety of playground surfaces makes for more interesting play and provides suitable covering for outdoor activities. Tanbark can be used in the swing area, cement for wheel toys, and grass for under climbers. Sand is used for play, but can also cushion falls from climbing equipment. No matter what the surface, the yard should be constructed with a good drainage system. Trees, bushes, and other plantings will allow for both sunshine and shade. Fences are *mandatory*. They must be durable, an appropriate height, with no opportunity for a child to gain a foothold.

### Food Service

All schools for young children serve some sort of refreshment during the daily session. In an infant program, formula and milk storage is a necessity. Whether involved in a light snack or full meal program, the center must adhere to the most rigid standards of health protection and safety provisions. Every precaution must be taken to ensure maximum hygienic food service. Daily cleaning of equipment, counters, floors, and appliances is a necessity. Proper disinfecting of highchairs and tables requires half a cup of bleach to one gallon of water; bottles of this solution can be stored away from children's reach yet handy for teachers.

Local school districts, Coordinated Community Child Care (4Cs), or affiliates of the National Association for the Education of Young Children may be consulted for guidelines on serving nutritional foods and may even offer financial subsidies. For infant/toddler programs and in many full-day programs, space for recording feeding information

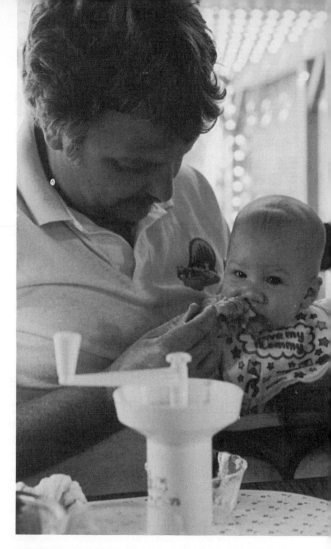

**FIGURE 9.19** No matter the age, snacks are a favorite part of the day. Feeding an infant involves the adult in a special, playful interaction.

must be designated, and enough highchairs or low tables must be provided to prevent an unreasonable wait for eating. Each age has its unique food service needs. Infants will need to be held or seated near an adult. Toddlers should not be fed popcorn, nuts, or raw carrots because of the hazard of choking. All children must be served food on disposable dishes or on dishes cleaned in a dishwasher with a sanitation cycle. Lunches brought from home by school-age and full-day children must be checked for spoilage. Information about eating patterns, proportions, and nutritional needs should be regularly shared with parents.

## Basic Materials in an Early Childhood Classroom

### Art Supplies
Easels, paints, watercolors
Plastic dough, clay
Pens, pencils, brushes
Scissors, holepunches
Glue, paste
Collage materials
Assorted paper

*Infants/toddlers:* Limit materials. Do not use open shelves.

*School age:* Have self-help table and teacher-guided projects.

### Discovery and Science
Nature materials
Textured materials
Water/sensory table and materials
Magnifying glasses, mirrors
Scales
Small pets

*Infants/toddlers:* Simplify, watch for safety. Aquarium.

*School age:* Display to read, computer.

### Dramatic Play
Furniture: child-sized, versatile
Clothing: variety, nonstereotyped
Dolls: variety, and accessories
Cooking utensils
Food items
Purses, suitcases, briefcases, backpacks

*Infants/toddlers:* Limit the choice, add hats or dolls that can get wet.

*School age:* Varied units such as prehistoric cave, moonscape

### Blocks and Manipulatives
Unit blocks
Block accessories: people, animals, vehicles
Puzzles
Construction toys: Lego®, Tinkertoys®
Stringing beads, dressing frames

*Infants/toddlers:* Push-pull toys, nesting toys, soft blocks

*School age:* Diversify accessories, increase complexity, add math materials.

### Language and Books
Books
Flannel board, accessories
Photos
Lotto games
Records, tapes
Writing center: typewriter, pads, and pencils

*Infants/toddlers:* Cardboard books; use others with adults only.

*School age:* Readers, listening post

### Outdoors
Large building blocks
Sand/water toys
Wheel toys
Dramatic-play props
Balls and game materials
Workbench materials
Dancing materials

*Infants/toddlers:* Omit workbench; simplify choices.

*School age:* Team-games equipment. Sequence projects, such as building bird feeders, piñatas.

**FIGURE 9.20** A sample materials and equipment list for an early childhood program. While not comprehensive, the list helps organize the environment for a variety of play. Note the adjustments that must be made to accommodate different ages.

## Materials and Equipment

Selection of materials and equipment is based on a number of criteria. Out of necessity, most school budgets limit the amount of dollars available for such purchases. To make every dollar count, teachers select materials that:

• Reflect the age-level characteristics of the group.

• Relate to the school's philosophy and curriculum.

• Reflect quality design and workmanship.

• Are durable.

• Offer flexibility and versatility in their uses.

• Have safety features (for instance, nontoxic paints, rounded corners).

• Are attractive and appealing to children.

• Are easy to maintain and repair.

• Reflect the cultural makeup of the group and the diversity of the culture overall.

• Are nonsexist, nonstereotypical, and anti-bias.

Materials should be appropriate for a wide range of skills since children within the same age group develop at individual rates. Many of the materials can be "*open-ended*," that is, they can be used in their most basic form or they can be developed in a variety of ways. Unit blocks, clay, and Lego® are examples of materials that children can use in a simple fashion; as skills develop these materials can be manipulated in a more complex manner.

Children are active learners, and their materials should provide them with ways to explore, manipulate, and become involved. Teachers encourage the use of fine and gross motor skills by providing equipment that involves their use. Children learn through all their senses, so the materials should be appealing to many of the senses.

## Organizing Space

There are many different ways to arrange and organize the living space in an early childhood setting; the final result expresses the diversity of the program. Most early childhood centers are arranged by *interest areas, learning centers,* or *activity areas.* These will most likely include:

| Indoors | Outdoors |
|---|---|
| Blocks | Sand |
| Manipulatives/table toys | Water play/sensory play |
| Art | Woodworking |
| Science | Wheel toys |
| Music | Climbers |
| Math | Swings |
| Dramatic play | Ball games |
| Books/language/listening center | Art |
| Water play/sensory play | Science/nature |
| Housekeeping | Dramatic play |

Figure 9.21 shows an environmental plan for optimizing learning and interaction for three- and four-year-olds; Figure 9.22 shows indoor alternatives for toddlers and school-age children.

The room arrangement and the choice of activity centers show what is being emphasized in the program. The amount of space devoted to any one activity says a great deal about its value to the staff. A housekeeping area with plenty of space encourages active use by a number of children. Social play is promoted when two or more items are available. Four telephones, three doll buggies, or two easels can be tools for social interaction.

Some activities are noisier than others, so the placement of the interest centers is important. Balance the number of noisy and quiet activities, both indoors and out. Quieter activities, such as puzzles, language games, story telling, take place in areas away from blocks, water play, or dramatic play, since the last three tend to kindle animated, active, and sometimes noisy behavior.

When arranging environments, there must be enough play spaces for the number of children in the group. Kritchevsky and Prescott (1969) analyzed the number of play opportunities in school settings, both

**FIGURE 9.21**  Layout for a preschool child care environment, ages three to five

For a group of children, teachers plan an indoor/outdoor environment that is challenging and uncrowded.

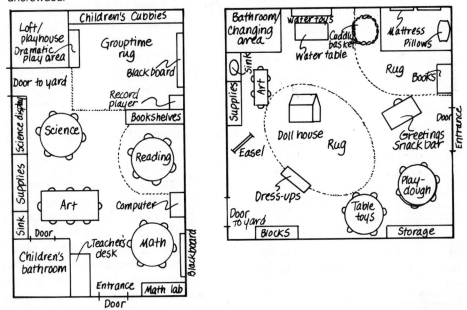

**FIGURE 9.22**  Room layouts for school-age and toddler groups differ according to the developmental needs of the group. These plans accommodate up to 20 K-1s and 12 two-year-olds

indoors and out. Areas and activities were assigned a value.

- A simple area (swings, climbers) counts as one play space.
- A complex area (housekeeping/dramatic play) counts as four play spaces.
- A super area (sand and water play combined) counts as eight play spaces.

The value assigned to the three areas generally coincides with the number of children who might be accommodated in that space. When the total is figured, it is matched against the actual number of children in the group to see if there is a place for everyone to play.

Adult needs also should be met through proper organization of classroom and yard. How can the teachers supervise all areas while ensuring cozy spots for children's privacy? Are the teachers deployed evenly throughout all the space? Is storage integrated so that equipment is located near the place where it will be used? Is the space arranged for cooperation and communication among the adults as well as the children? In other words, is this a workplace that is accepting, inviting, and challenging to all?

Clearly defined boundaries and obvious pathways make it easy for children to live and work in the space. There should be enough space for larger groups to gather together as well as small groups.

A good environment for children reflects the teachers' knowledge of how children play, what skills they possess, what they know, and what they need to learn. The settings are arranged to promote those aspects of child growth and development. In summary, the physical environment should be organized for children according to these criteria:

- *Availability:* open, low shelving with visual cues for placement of toys, equipment—aids in cleanup and room setup
- *Consistency in organization:* neat, systematic, in logical order
- *Compatibility:* noisy activities are grouped away

from quiet ones; art needs natural light when possible; water play near a bathroom or kitchen; messy projects on washable floors
- *Definition:* clearly defined boundaries indicating available space and what is to take place; obvious pathways outlined in class and yard; ways to get in and out of an area without disrupting activity in progress; no dead ends or runways
- *Spacing:* interest areas with enough space to hold the children who will play there; one-third to one-half of the surface should remain uncovered (Kritchevsky and Prescott, 1969); materials stored near space where they are used; storage and activity space has visual cues
- *Communicability:* tells children what to do instead of relying on adult to monitor activities; communicates to children what behavior is expected; arrangement suggests numbers of children, levels of activity.

# The Temporal Environment

## *Daily Schedule: Time to Learn*

The daily schedule defines the structure of each program. It creates the format for how children will experience the events of the day—in what order and for what length of time.

No two schedules are alike, since each reflects the program it represents. The amount of time devoted to specific activities communicates clearly what value the school places on them. The amount of time given to certain aspects of the curriculum, the variety of events, and the flexibility tell children and adults what is important in this particular setting.

In developing a schedule by which to function on a daily basis, teachers first decide what is important for children to learn, how that learning should take place, and how much time to allow in the daily program. If small-group work and individual attention are program goals, enough time will have to be set aside to ensure its success. More time is needed to allow children a number of curriculum choices than if they only had one or two activities from which to select. Three-year-olds need more time for toileting activities than do five-year-olds, who are considerably more self-sufficient.

The physical plant itself may dictate a portion of the daily schedule. If toilet facilities are not located adjacent to the classroom, then more time must be scheduled to travel to and from the bathrooms. If the building or space is shared with other groups, some portion of the program may be modified. Many schools housed in church buildings schedule field trips during the annual church rummage sale in order to free up the space for the church's use.

The daily schedule is important for everyone in the setting. When the time sequence is clear to all, then everyone can go about the business of learning and teaching. Children are more secure in a place that has a consistent schedule; they can begin to anticipate the regularity of what comes next and count on it. In that way they are then free to move, explore, and learn without hesitation. Children can freely involve themselves without fear of being interrupted. Adults, too, enjoy the predictability of a daily schedule. By knowing the sequence of events, they are then free to flex the timing when unforeseen circumstances arise.

## *Developmentally Appropriate Schedules*

Just as the arrangement of space should reflect the group of children within, so does the daily schedule allow for appropriate growth at the developmental level of the group. There are common factors to consider for all children in the early years, as well as some developmental distinctions at the various ages.

There are common elements in all schedules, whether they are designed for toddler groups or five-year-olds, all-day programs or half-day nurseries. Sound child development principles provide the framework on which the daily schedule is structured. The individual schools then adapt these requirements to their own philosophy as they work out their individual daily schedule. All schedules must:

- Include time for routines (to eat, rest, wash, toilet) as well as time for *transitions* (what happens when there is a change from one activity to another).
- Alternate quiet and active play and work to help children pace themselves.
- Provide opportunities for both inside and outside play.
- Allow children to participate in structured activities as well as those of their own choosing.
- Make it possible for children to work individually, in small groups, or in larger ones.
- Gear the time to the age and developmental levels of the group.
- Provide for flexibility so that children's interests can be maintained and emergencies met.
- Have a beginning and an end. Some provisions must be made for children to be met and greeted when they enter. The day is brought to closure with a review of the day's activities and a daily class anticipation of what will come tomorrow. Allow time for dismissal.
- Involve the adults in daily planning and review; include a regular meeting time for more substantial discussion of children, long-range planning, and evaulation.
- Include time for cleanup and room restoration.
- Incorporate the teachers' roles and assignments so that they will know their area of responsibility.
- Be posted in an obvious place in the classroom for all to see.

Schedules have a great deal in common, but certain age-related differences can be seen. Figure 9.23 outlines three typical daily schedules for: (1) a half-day toddler class, (2) a full day for preschoolers, and (3) a kindergarten. Notice, for instance, that more choices are available to children as they grow. Two-year-olds could be overstimulated by a selection of materials appropriate for school-aged children. Older children can move through some transitions as a group, which is difficult for younger ones to do. Therefore, the toddler door opens quietly, allowing children to wander out slowly, avoiding a rush with pushing and shoving. In the second example, the full

**Half-Day Toddler Program**

| | |
|---|---|
| 9:00-9:30 | Greet Children |
| | Inside Activities |
| | • playdough and art/easel |
| | • housekeeping |
| | • blocks and manipulatives |
| | • books |
| 9:30 | Door to outdoors opens |
| 9:45-10:20 | Outdoor Play |
| | • large motor |
| | • social play |
| 10:20 | Music/movement outdoors |
| 10:30 | Snack/"Here We Are Together" song |
| | • washing hands |
| | • eating/pouring/cleanup |
| 10:45-11:45 | Outside |
| 11:15 | "Time to Put Our Toys Away" song |
| | • all encouraged to participate in clean-up |
| 11:20 | Closure |
| | • parent-child together |
| | • story or flannelboard |

**Full-Day Program for Preschoolers**

| | |
|---|---|
| 7:00 | Arrival, breakfast |
| 8:00 | Inside free play |
| | • arts/easels |
| | • table toys/games/blocks |
| | • dramatic play center: house, grocery store, etc. |
| 9:00 | Cleanup |
| 9:15 | Group time: Songs/fingerplays and small-group choices |
| 9:30 | Choice Time/small groups |
| | • discovery/math lab/science activity |
| | • cooking for morning or afternoon snack |
| | • language art/prereading choice |
| 10:00 | Snack (at outside tables/cloths on warm days) |
| 10:15 | Outside free play |
| | • climbing, swinging; sand and water, wheel toys, group games |
| 12:00 | Handwash and lunch |

| | |
|---|---|
| 12:45 | Get ready: toileting, handwashing, toothbrushing, prepare beds |
| 1:15 | Bedtime story |
| 1:30 | Naptime for the whole group |
| 2:30 | Outdoors for those awake |
| 3:30 | Cleanup outdoors and singing time |
| 4:00 | Snacktime |
| 4:15 | Free play: some outdoor/indoor choices, fieldtrips, story teller |
| 5:30 | Cleanup and read books until going home |

**Half-Day Kindergarten Plan**

| | |
|---|---|
| 8:15-8:30 | Arrival: |
| | Getting ready to start |
| | • checking in library books, lunch money, etc. |
| 8:30 | Newstelling |
| | • "anything you want to tell for news" |
| | • newsletter written weekly |
| 9:00 | Work assignment |
| | • write a story about your news or |
| | • make a page in your book (topic assigned) or |
| | • work in math lab |
| 9:30-10:00 | Choice of indoors (paints, blocks, computer, table toys) or second grade tutors read books to children |
| | • when finished, play in loft or read books until recess |
| 10:00 | Recess |
| 10:30 | Snack |
| 10:45 | Language: chapter in novel read or other language activity |
| 11:15 | Dance or game or visitor and snack |
| 11:45 | Ending: Getting ready to leave |
| | • check out library books |
| | • gather art and other projects |
| 12:00-1:30 | for part of group each day: |
| | Lunch, then: |
| | • field trips |
| | • writing lesson |
| | • math or science lab |

**FIGURE 9.23** Daily schedules reflect the children's needs and ages while meeting the program's goals. The time and timing of the school day show the values in that program.

day for preschoolers reflects their age and their growing ability to handle longer free-play periods and proportionately fewer teacher-directed activities. The kindergarten schedule provides more structure both in individual work projects and teacher-focused time; such a schedule is developmentally appropriate for older children in a half-day time period. Thus does the temporal environment mirror the child's stage of life.

## The Interpersonal Environment

A child responds to everything in school: the color of the room, the way the furniture is arranged, how much time there is to play, and how people treat one another. To the child, everything is a stimulus. The *feeling* in a room is as real as the blocks or the books. Thus, the interpersonal or social aspects of an early childhood setting are powerful components of the environment.

Children are the most important people in the setting; they should feel safe and comfortable. A warm, interpersonal environment invites children to participate and to learn. When children feel secure with one another and with the setting, they will be able to engage more fully in the total program.

Parents are an important part of school, especially in the early years. The interpersonal connection between parent and teacher can bolster what happens to the child within the classroom and can offer the child a smooth transition between school and home. Learning is enhanced when parents and teachers come to communicate in supportive, nonthreatening ways.

Teachers are the most critical element in creating environments with positive interpersonal goals. What teachers do—and how they do it—determines the learning that takes place in the class. The attitudes and behaviors of teachers affect children's behaviors. Questions teachers can ask themselves as they evaluate the quality of the environment are:

- Is there a feeling of mutual respect between children and adults?
- How do children treat one another?
- Do teachers model cooperative behavior with other adults and children? Do they show by example how to work through a disagreement or problem?
- Does the physical setup allow the teacher to focus on the children?
- Do housekeeping details keep teachers disconnected from children?
- Do teachers encourage children to use one another as resources?
- Do teachers take time to show children how to accomplish a task by themselves?
- Do teachers use reasoning and follow-through?
- How and when do teachers interact with children?
- What is the teacher's posture and facial expression when involved in a problem situation?
- If I were a child, would I like to come to school here?

The answers to these questions provide teachers with a barometer of how well they are maintaining an atmosphere of positive social interaction. The most important thing to remember is that the way people feel about each other and how they express it has an impact on children. Teachers must focus as much attention on the interpersonal part of the environment as they do on buying equipment or arranging the room. Chapter 11, on play, and Chapter 14, on social and emotional skills, will emphasize the interpersonal aspects of the environment further.

## SUMMARY

A good environment for young children is a combination of many factors. Teachers must take into consideration the needs of the children, teachers, and parents as well as the program goals and objectives.

The physical environment includes the buildings and yard, the equipment and materials, and the way the space is organized and used. The setting is organized to support the program's goals and must meet necessary health and safety standards.

The daily schedule outlines the timetable of events. Time blocks are arranged around the daily routines of food, rest, and toileting. The temporal environment is balanced so that children alternate indoor and outdoor play, quiet and active play, and self-selected activities with teacher-directed learning. It is the interpersonal relationships that set the tone in each environment. The size of the group, the number of teachers per child, and the quality of relationships affect the interpersonal environment.

It is essential to have a clear idea of program goals before arranging the environment. The environment mirrors those goals in the way the room is arranged, teachers are deployed, and the time schedule is framed. In early childhood settings where children's independence and self-reliance is valued, the environment is created to enhance the child's budding sense of autonomy. Self-help environments reflect the goals through careful application of the environmental factors.

Creating good environments for young children does not require great sums of money or newly designed buildings. In most settings, teachers can adapt general principles of environments to create challenging, safe, and effective group settings for children.

## REVIEW QUESTIONS

1. Why is there no standard or ideal environment for early childhood schools? How would you describe a good environment for one-year-olds? For three-year-olds? For six-year-olds? Why?

2. What are the three aspects of environments to consider when planning programs for children? What do you think of first and why?

3. Why is self-help a common goal in most early childhood settings? How can teachers support self-help in infants? In toddlers? In nursery schoolers? In school-aged children?

4. Discuss three school health and safety policies that help keep illness and injury to a minimum. Include how you would explain these guidelines to parents, and how you would handle a problem.

5. What messages should the total environment communicate to children? How would these messages change with the age of the group? With the size of the group?

6. Look at the daily schedule of an early childhood program. What transitions occur in the daily schedule, and how are they handled?

# L E A R N I N G   A C T I V I T I E S

1. Hunch down on your knees and look at a classroom from the child's perspective. Describe what you see in terms of the principles of successful environments.

2. Examine a daily schedule from an early childhood center. What do you think are the program goals of the school? How can you tell? Compare this to a daily schedule of a family day care home. How are they alike? How are they different?

3. Below are listed some common problems that can be remedied by changing the environment. List at least one solution for each problem.
   a. Too many children crowding into one area
   b. Overcrowded shelves
   c. Grabbing or arguments over the same toy
   d. Hoarding of materials
   e. Lack of cooperation during cleanup
   f. Wheel toy collisions
   g. Children crying when others' parents leave

4. Visit a toddler program, a four-year program, and a kindergarten. How are the learning centers defined? Name the centers of interest and indicate which of them are for quiet play and which are for active play and work.

# B I B L I O G R A P H Y

Anselmo, Sandra, and Petersen, J.D. *A Manual for Caregivers of Infants and Toddlers.* San Francisco: R & E Research Associates, 1978.

Bredekamp, Sue (ed.), *Developmentally Appropriate Practice in Early Childhood Programs Serving Children From Birth Through Age 8,* expanded edition. Washington, D.C.: National Association for the Education of Young Children, 1987.

Cherry, Clare; Harkness, Barbara; and Kuzma, Kay. *Nursery School Management Guide.* Belmont, Calif.: Fearon Publishers, 1973.

Clark, Barbara. *Optimizing Learning: The Integrative Model in the Classroom.* Columbus, Oh.: Merrill Publishing Company, 1986.

Derman-Sparks, Louise. "'It Isn't Fair!' Anti-Bias Curriculum for Young Children." In Neugebauer, Bonnie (ed.), *Alike and Different: Exploring Our Humanity with Young Children.* Redmond, Wash.: Exchange Press, 1987.

*Found Spaces and Equipment for Children's Centers.* New York: Educational Facilities Laboratory, Inc., 1971.

Godwin, Annabelle, and Schrag, Lorraine. *Setting Up for Infant Care: Guidelines for Centers and Family Day Care Homes.* Washington, D.C.: National Association for the Education of Young Children, 1988.

Harms, Thelma, and Clifford, Richard M. *Early Childhood Environment Rating Scale.* New York: Teachers College Press, 1980.

Hendrick, Joanne. *Why Teach?* Washington, D.C.: National Association for the Education of Young Children, No. 20, 1987.

Jones, Elizabeth. Personal notes, 1984.

Kendall, Frances. *Diversity in the Classroom.* New York: Teachers College Press, 1983.

Kritchevsky, Sybil, and Prescott, Elizabeth. *Planning Environments for Young Children—Physical Space.* Washington, D.C.: National Association for the Education of Young Children, 1969.

National Association for the Education of Young Children. *Accreditation Criteria and Procedures of The National Academy of Early Childhood Programs.* Washington, D.C.: National Association for the Education of Young Children.

Phyfe-Perkins, Elizabeth. "Children's Behavior in Preschool Settings—A Review of Research Concerning the Influence of the Physical Environment." In Katz, Lillian (ed.), *Current Topics in Early Childhood Education.* Norwood, N.J.: Ablex Publishing Corporation, Volume II, 1980.

Rambusch, Nancy M. "The Organization of the Environment." In Donald Streets, *Administering Day Care and Preschool Programs.* Boston: Allyn & Bacon, 1982.

Spodek, Bernard; Lee, R.C.; and Saracho, O.N. "Mainstreaming Handicapped Children in the Preschool." In Kilmer, Sally (ed.), *Advances in Early Education and Day Care,* Vol. 3. Greenwich, Conn.: JAI Press, 1983.

Sprung, Barbara. *Non-Sexist Education for Young Children.* New York: Citation Press, 1975.

# CHAPTER 10

## Evaluating for Effectiveness

LOVE
ALEX

## QUESTIONS for THOUGHT

- What is evaluation?
- Why is evaluation important?
- What are the components of good evaluations?
- What are the areas of concern when using evaluations?
- Who is evaluated in the early childhood setting?
- How does evaluating children, teacher, and program increase effectiveness in the early childhood setting?

# INTRODUCTION

Evaluations are a part of everyday life. We look out the window and assess the weather situation, then decide if we want to carry an umbrella. Before making a purchase, we read the label on the box of crackers. We size up a person we have just met. We check the newspapers to find out where our favorite football team is ranked.

We are constantly evaluating, judging, and rating. In education, we evaluate:

- *Curriculum.* Will this language game help develop the listening skills of three-year-olds?

- *Materials and equipment.* If we order the terrarium, will there be enough money for the math lab?

- *The environment.* Should the children begin school with free play or a group time? Where can we store the nap cots? Do the cubbies create a hazard out in the hallway?

- *Children's behavior.* Evan and Francie interrupt each other too much. Should they be placed in separate work groups?

- *Teacher effectiveness.* Sandra has a knack for making parents comfortable in her classroom. Audrey finds leading large groups difficult. Karl supervises student teachers with great skill. How can each be challenged supportively? How can each learn from the other?

## What Is Evaluation?

### *Definition*

Evaluation is a process. It is at once a definition, an assessment, and a plan. Defining the kind of weather outside helps a person evaluate what to wear. Assessing a person's manner and style determines whether or not to talk with that person at a party. Planning a meal involves evaluating who will be eating and what their food preferences may be.

**FIGURE 10.1** Evaluations are part of everyday life in an early childhood setting. Can these children handle animals safely? How will having a pet chicken affect the program?

Evaluation involves making decisions, choices, and selections.

In educational circles, evaluations involve materials, people, and processes. Programs may be evaluated by taking an inventory of a school's curriculum and educational materials. Classroom organization may require mapping the environment, counting the number of play spaces in a room or yard, and evaluating the daily schedule. Observing and recording children's behavior could effectively evaluate behavior management techniques. Assessing teacher effectiveness requires gathering information about what teachers do and how they work. Feedback about performance is based on specific information concerning teacher behavior. Program evaluation might involve analyzing children, teachers, parents, and administration, and how they all work together to meet the goals of the program.

## Premises

All evaluation procedures are based on three important premises:

1. *Evaluation must be part of the goal-setting process.* Without evaluation, goals are meaningless. Evaluation helps shape a goal into a meaningful plan of action. For instance, a family who wants to go weekend camping will have to decide what they need in order to pack their suitcases. In the classroom, teachers decide what they want their children to learn before ordering equipment for the program.

2. *Goals are based on expectations.* Everyone has standards for themselves and others. Standards are used to anticipate performance and behavior. Should the office buy a block of tickets to the upcoming soccer match? Many people would consider the team ranking and likelihood of a victory before making the decision. Teachers think about how two-year-olds will use puppets or what use the four-year-olds will make of wheel toys before purchasing equipment.

In every early childhood setting, more than one set of expectations is at work. The director has job expectations of all the teachers. Teachers have

standards of performance for themselves, the children, and parents. Parents have some expectations about what their children will do in school and about the role of the teachers. Children develop expectations regarding themselves, their parents, teachers, and the school.

3. *Evaluations determine the degree to which expectations are met.* By evaluating, people check to see if their goals have been realized. This can be as simple as listening for the doorbell after hearing a car stop outside. It can be as complex as changing the curriculum to match the group as its needs and interests emerge during a school year, or as complex as analyzing questionnaires returned by parents. A good evaluation tool outlines clearly and specifically how expectations have been met. Evaluation is a system of mutual accountability. It is a way of stating expectations and defining how they are being met.

## Why Evaluate?

In early childhood education, evaluations are used for several reasons. Teachers are aware that *evaluation* and *education* must be linked when creating good programs for children. To evaluate is to test the quality of the educational endeavor. Teachers are becoming more sophisticated in informal and formal assessments, in combining their daily observations with high-quality instruments that give a rich and full picture of each child or of the class as a whole. Evaluation of children, teachers, and programs monitors growth, progress, and planning.

Evaluation is a way to look at where and how improvements can be made; to challenge methods, assumptions, and purposes. Teachers and children are rated for their level of development and areas of growth. Environments are assessed to see if they foster behavior and learning according to their stated goals. Total programs are evaluated to see if they accomplish their objectives. In fact, evaluations provide information by which to rate performance, define areas of difficulty, and look for possible solutions.

Setting goals is a third reason for evaluating. In order to be useful, an evaluation must include suggestions for improving the performance or behavior. The assessment tool that only describes a situation is an unfinished evaluation; goals for improvement must be established.

## Components of a Good Evaluation

Certain elements are common to all evaluations. The following criteria serve as a guideline to good evaluations:

1. **Select who or what will be evaluated.** Decide how often and under what circumstances the evaluation will take place.

2. **Have a clear purpose or motive.** Know the reasons you are making an evaluation and consider who or what will benefit from the process. State what you expect to gain from it.

3. **Decide how the data will be collected.** Have a good understanding of the process or format that will be used. For a report, discover what tools you might need and what is available to you. Outline who will collect the data and make the report. If more than one person is reporting, check for consistency among the evaluators. Sample tools for data collection may be found in Chapter 6 as well as later in this chapter.

4. **Know what use will be made of the evaluation.** Be aware of what decisions will be made from the results. Know who receives this information and how they will interpret it.

5. **State goals clearly.** Make sure goals and objectives are outlined in ways that can be measured and observed easily. State behavioral goals in terms of what the person will *do*.

6. **Make a plan.** Be prepared to act. Use the results to motivate people to put into action what they learned from the evaluation. Set new goals. Continue the process for another stated period of

**FIGURE 10.2** Know the reasons you are making an evaluation. Some assessments take into consideration children's activity preferences or their participation in small and large groups. (Courtesy of Denise Strus.)

time. Set up a timetable to check progress on a regular basis.

Evaluations are deliberate and systematic ways to judge effectiveness. Since they are based on goals and expectations, all evaluations need some kind of *feedback loop* to recycle what is perceived (Steps 1–4) into action for improvement (Steps 5 and 6). The important point to remember is that evaluation should be a continuous process, for without follow-through, long-lasting improvement is unlikely to occur.

## Cautions

A number of concerns have been voiced about assessment procedures. Anyone involved in evaluation should avoid:

1. *Unfair comparisons.* Evaluations should be used to identify and understand the person or program involved, not to compare one to another in a competitive manner.

2. *Typecasting.* Evaluations can label unfairly or prematurely the very people they are intended to

help. Insufficient data and overemphasis on the results are two areas that need close monitoring.

3. *Overemphasis on norms.* Most evaluation tools imply some level of normal behavior or performance, acceptable levels of interaction, or quantities of materials and space. People involved in an evaluation must remember to individualize the process, rather than try to fit a person or program into the mold created by the assessment tool.

4. *Interpretation.* There is sometimes a tendency to overinterpret or misinterpret results. Whether the evaluation assesses a child's skill, a teacher's performance, or an educational program, it must be clear *what* is being evaluated and *how* the information will be used. It is particularly important to be sensitive to the feelings of those being evaluated when communicating the results of the assessment. Parents and teachers need to interpret evaluations clearly and carefully if they are to understand the findings and feel comfortable with them.

5. *Too narrow a perspective.* An evaluation tool may focus too much on one area and not enough on others. Moreover, no single occasion or instrument will tell teachers all they need to know about a child's abilities, a teacher's performance, or a program's effectiveness. It is essential that information be gathered in many ways and on several occasions. Using a single yardstick to assess program effectiveness, for example, would ignore the comprehensive nature of the goals that most early childhood programs are designed to attain. These goals may encompass all areas of development while providing services for children and their parents that affect the health and well-being of the whole family. Sampling only children's skills as the single measure would lead to conclusions that were neither reliable nor valid. An imbalanced assessment gives an incomplete picture.

6. *Too wide a range.* An evaluation should be designed for a single level or age group and not cover too wide a range. It is appropriate to measure a child's ability to print at age six but not at age two. A teacher's aide should not be evaluated with the same method used to rate head or supervising teachers. The expectations of the person or task should be taken into account and the evaluation method modified accordingly.

7. *Too little or too much time.* The amount of time necessary to complete an evaluation must be weighed. The evaluation that is too lengthy loses its effectiveness in the time it takes. Time for interpretation and reflection must be included in the overall process.

For evaluations to be most productive, teachers must use caution in selecting an assessment method. Often, they will rework a common technique to meet their needs better. For instance, a testing tool could be used to describe children's skills, but the averages that accompany the test could be discarded. In this

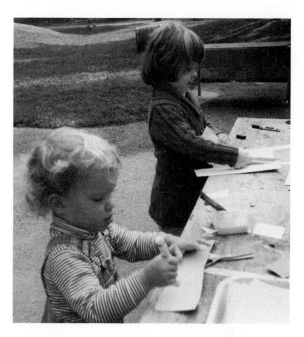

**FIGURE 10.3** Evaluations in programs with a wide age range may need to be individualized to adequately record children's skills.

way, teachers would avoid overemphasizing norms (Caution 3), making unfair comparisons (Caution 1) or typecasting the children according to the results (Caution 2).

Sometimes a staff or administrator will design an instrument, rather than using one already devised. Individualizing the evaluation process can thus balance an assessment, giving a perspective that is more in tune with the individual or program in a particular setting (Caution 5). Periodic evaluation checks give more than one set of results, so that early childhood personnel are less likely to misinterpret or overemphasize the data (Caution 4). A comprehensive evaluation done semiannually is more time efficient than a lengthy, detailed one done only once every year or so (Caution 7). In all evaluations, it is important to keep in mind that children and teachers are at various stages of development and skill; an assessment that is individualized or one in which a range of scores is acceptable allows for these variations (Caution 6).

## Evaluations in the Early Childhood Setting

In the educational setting, the process of evaluation is separate from the teaching or instructing process (Spodek, 1978). Judging an activity, a child's growth, or a teacher's performance is something "extra," apart from the everyday routine of the class. But evaluation is also related to teaching since it is a way of rating how effective are the teaching methods. Teaching and evaluating are closely integrated. As teachers examine how they work, they look at the effect this has on the children, the curriculum, the program, and themselves. Evaluating is a tool for improvement as well as a method of seeing what works well.

The teacher plays a critical role in the evaluation process. Through evaluation, teachers link specific goals to larger, more encompassing objectives, such as those illustrated in Figure 10.4.

These goals focus on the relationship between teaching in the classroom and the overriding educational objectives. The teacher sees the broad picture and keeps a perspective on education that includes the children, the program, and the teaching staff.

The three areas of evaluations we will discuss in this chapter are: (1) evaluating children; (2) evaluating teachers; and (3) evaluating programs. The purposes underlying each type of evaluation will be examined, followed by specific techniques for effective evaluations.

## EVALUATING CHILDREN

How do we evaluate children? What do we look for? How do we document growth and difficulties? How do we communicate our findings to parents? These questions focus our attention on children's issues and the evaluation process.

| Educational Aims | Behavioral Goals |
| --- | --- |
| To achieve independence and autonomy. | Children separate from their parents successfully; can manage their own clothing needs; initiate own activities. |
| To become a functional part of a larger society. | Children participate actively in small and large groups. |
| To learn to live effectively with others. | Children develop social skills with peers and adults, show tolerance of differences. |
| To learn basic tools for acquiring knowledge. | Children show signs of curiosity, memory, and symbol recognition. |

**FIGURE 10.4** Teachers relate what happens in the classroom (behavioral goals) to traditional educational goals.

# Why Evaluate?

Children are evaluated because teachers and parents want to know what the children are learning. Evaluations set the tone for a child's overall educational experience. Highlighting children's strengths builds a foundation from which to address their limitations or needs. The process of evaluating children attempts to answer several questions: Are children gaining appropriate skills and behaviors? In what activities does learning take place? What part of the program supports specific learning? Is the school philosophy being met? Are educational goals being met?

In evaluating children, teachers first decide what it is they want to know about each child, and why. With an understanding of children in general, teachers then concentrate on individual children and their unique development. Goals for children stem from program objectives. For instance, if the school philosophy is, "Our program is designed to help children grow toward increasing physical, social, and intellectual competencies," an evaluation will measure children's progress in those three areas. One that claims to teach specific language skills will want to assess how speaking and listening is being accomplished.

Evaluations provide teachers with an opportunity to distance themselves from the daily contact with children and look at them in a more detached, professional way. Teachers can use the results to share their opinions and concerns about children with each other and with parents. This concentrated effort expands everyone's vision of who and what the child can be, highlights patterns of the child's behavior, and helps in understanding the meaning of that behavior. It gives teachers the chance to chart growth and acknowledge progress and, in doing so, sets the child apart as an individual and unique human being. Evaluations are a reminder to all that they work with *individuals* and not just a group. Of course, evaluations contain varying degrees of subjectivity and opinion. Chapter 6 contains specific tools for establishing objective and descriptive data on which to base assessments.

In general, evaluations are made to:

1. Establish a baseline of information about each child by which to judge future progress.

2. Monitor the growth of individual children.

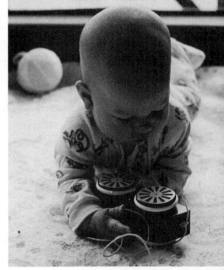

**FIGURE 10.5** A baseline is a picture of a child framed at a particular moment. Infants' use of materials, small muscle control, and task persistence can all be seen in these assessments.

3. Have a systematic plan for intervention and guidance.

4. Plan curriculum.

5. Provide parents with updated information on their child.

6. Provide information for making administrative decisions.

### To Establish a Baseline

One purpose of evaluating children is to establish a starting point of their skills and behavior. This is the beginning of a collection over a period of time of important information on each child. Through this cumulative record, teachers learn a great deal about the children: whom they play with, how they spend their time, how they handle problems, what fears and stress they show. In other words, they learn a lot about how children live their lives.

A *baseline* is a picture of the status of each child; an overview of individual development. It shows where the child is in relation to the school's objectives since the child is being measured according to program expectations. Baseline data give a realistic picture of a child at that moment in time, but there is a presumption that the picture will change.

**A Baseline Tool.** The beginning of the school term is an obvious time to start collecting information. Records of a child are established in the context of the child's history and family background. Parents frequently submit this information with an application to the school. Teachers can gather the data by visiting the child at home or holding a parent conference and speaking directly with the parents about the child's development.

An *entry-level assessment* made during the first few weeks of school can be informative, particularly when added to the child's family history. The

---

**ENTRY-LEVEL ASSESSMENT**

1. Child's name _____ Teacher _____
   Age _____ Sex _____ Class _____
   Major language_____ Fluency in English? _____
   Any previous school experiences? _____
   Siblings/others in household _____
   Family situation (one/two parents, other adults, etc.) _____

2. Separation from parent:
   Smooth_____ Some anxiety _____ Mild difficulty ___ Unable to
   separate _____
   Did parent have trouble separating? _____
   Comments: _____

3. How does child come to and leave from school?
   Parent _____ Carpool _____ Babysitter _____ Bus _____

4. Physical appearance:
   General heal'' . _____
   Expression _____
   Dress _____
   Body posture _____

**FIGURE 10.6** Entry level assessments collect baseline information. Once teachers and children have had some time together, these first impressions can be documented.

5. Self-care:
   Dressing: Alone _____ Needs assistance _____
   Toileting: By self _____ Needs help _____
   Eating: _____
   Toothbrushing: _____
   Sleeping/resting: _____
   Allergies/other health-related problems: _____

6. Child's Interests:
   *Indoors:*
   Clay ___ Books ___ Puzzles ___ Water play ___ Easels ___
   Language ___ Table/rug toys ___ Sensory choices ___
   Art ___ Science ___ Blocks ___

   *Outdoors:*
   Swings ___ Climbers ___ Sandbox ___ Water play ___
   Wheel toys ___ Animals ___ Group games ___ Woodworking ___
   Group times (level of participation): _____

7. Social-emotional development:
   a. Initiates activities ___ Plays alone ___ Seems happy ___
      Has to be invited ___ Brings security object ___
      Seems tense ___
   b. Plays mostly with children of: Same age ___ Younger ___
      Older ___
   c. Moves into environment: Easily ___ Hesitantly ___
      Not at all ___ Wanders ___
   d. Special friends: _____
   e. Does the child follow teachers? ___ Anyone in particular? _____

8. Cognitive development:
   *Use of language:* Follows directions ___ Clear pronunciation ___
   Memory ___ Curiosity ___ Holds conversations ___
   Words/Phrases _____

9. Physical development:
   Climbs safely ___ Uses scissors ___ Hand preference ___
   Runs smoothly ___ Uses pens, brushes ___ Foot preference ___
   Handles body well ___

10. Goals/Points to Remember: _____
    _____
    _____
    _____

**FIGURE 10.6 Cont.**

evaluation itself can be done informally. A few notes jotted during the first month of school can serve as a beginning collection of pertinent data about the child. Or the format can be more structured, such as in Figure 10.6.

**Application.** Teachers then use this information to understand children and their various levels of development. They can see children's strengths and weaknesses and where future growth is likely to occur. When the information is shared with parents, they feel more relaxed about their child and even laugh when they recall those first few days of school. One must remember, however, that the entry assessment is only a first impression. Care must be taken to avoid creating a self-fulfilling prophesy by labeling children so that they become shaped into those beginning patterns. Again, teachers must be mindful of the cautions associated with all assessments (pages 272-273) as they document children's early behaviors. Still, so much happens in that short period of time; the rich information we gain from documenting this growth is invaluable.

**Goals and Plans.** Teachers use baseline data to set realistic goals for individual children. They tailor the curriculum to the needs and interests they have observed. An entry-level assessment is a vehicle for watching children's growth throughout the year. For instance, after setting a baseline of Mariko's language ability in English, teachers plan activities to increase her understanding and use of language. Then, they make periodic checks on her increased vocabulary as the school year progresses.

### To Monitor Children's Progress

Teachers use evaluations to document children's growth. Data collected provide evidence of children's growth or lack of progress. A careful evaluation of each child furnishes the teaching staff with the necessary foundation from which they can plan the next steps.

Hita has mastered the brushes at the easel. Now we can encourage her to try the smaller brushes in table painting.

Enrico has been asking how to spell simple

**FIGURE 10.7** An evaluation can reflect teachers' perceptions of children's development in all skill areas, including self-concept. (Courtesy of Michelle Black.)

words. Let's see that he gets some time away from the blocks to work with him.

All the children seem able to separate from their parents and say goodbye comfortably. How can we celebrate this progress with the group?

**A Progress Tool.** Figure 10.8 is a sample *midyear evaluation.* Criteria for each area of development are included to build a profile of the whole child. Teachers note the intervention and guidance steps they plan, where appropriate. While a general form is outlined here, early education teachers individualize their assessments to specify the skills of their group; an infant/toddler group would have different age-appropriate skills than those of a preschool or primary-age class. Such a revised form should include what the child will do to show a suitable level of behavior in each developmental level.

**Application.** Information about a child will be used to assess growth and change. How often this happens can vary. Although many changes occur in rapid succession in these early years, it takes time for a child to integrate life experiences and for teachers to see them expressed as a permanent part of behavior.

## A TOOL FOR MONITORING CHILDREN'S PROGRESS

Check one of the evaluations below for each skill area; for those that need work, document with specific examples.

| Developmental Area | Age Appropriate | Highly Skilled | Needs Work |
|---|---|---|---|
| *Self-Management* Personal care Making choices Following routines | | | |
| *Physical/Motor* 1. Fine Motor     Art materials     Woodworking tools     Manipulatives 2. Gross Motor     Ball handling     Balancing     Jump/hop/skip | | | |
| *Communication and Language* Vocabulary Articulation Comprehension English as a second language Converses with children Converses with adults Listens Expresses self (needs,    ideas, feelings) | | | |
| *Cognitive Development* Sees cause and effect Processes and uses    information Solves problems with:    objects    peers    adults Premath (sequencing,    measuring, numbers) Prereading concepts (size,    colors, shapes, letters,    position) | | | |

**FIGURE 10.8**  A midyear evaluation is a more detailed description of the child. It highlights areas of concern and progress. (Developed by Bing Nursery School, Stanford University, 1975 to present.) (Chart continues on p. 280.)

**A TOOL FOR MONITORING CHILDREN'S PROGRESS**

| Developmental Area | Age Appropriate | Highly Skilled | Needs Work |
|---|---|---|---|
| *Social-Emotional* | | | |
| Independence/initiative | | | |
| Positive self-concept | | | |
| Recognizes/accepts own feelings | | | |
| Deals with frustration | | | |
| Flexibility | | | |
| Leadership | | | |
| Initiates social contacts | | | |
| Prosocial behaviors (friendly, sharing, inclusive, cooperative, empathetic) | | | |
| Child–child interactions | | | |
| Child–adult interactions | | | |

OVERALL STRENGTHS:                    GOALS:

**FIGURE 10.8 Cont.**

Evaluating too frequently does not reveal sufficient change to make it worthwhile and places an added burden on the teaching staff as well.

Once the initial baseline data has been gathered, a progress evaluation approximately every three months seems reasonable. In a normal school year, this would mean establishing a baseline in the fall and checking progress in the winter and the spring. For centers operating on a year-round basis, a brief summer report would be in order. These need not be time consuming. Many evaluations take the form of a checklist and can be accomplished while the class is in session.

**Goals and Plans.** Goals are established for children as a result of an assessment. These goals are changed as growth takes place. A good assesssment tool monitors progress in each developmental area so that plans can be made to challenge the child physically, socially, emotionally, creatively, and intellectually.

At the same time, theory reminds us that the child develops as a whole, with each area of growth influencing and being influenced by what changes take place in other areas. Evaluations that document growth include information so that all teachers see the interrelationships among areas of development. By assessing growth in individual areas, teachers relate that development to the child's collective abilities, as in this example:

Dylan's midyear report shows that he lacks dexterity in running and climbing, and that he is exceptionally strong in verbal and listening skills. This influences his development in the following areas:

*Emotionally.* He lacks self-confidence, and his self-esteem deteriorates the longer he feels inept at physical skills. He may even be afraid to master the art of climbing and running for fear he will fail.

*Socially.* Children tease Dylan because he cannot possibly keep up with them while playing outside. He often ends up playing alone or watching the other children in more active pursuits.

*Intellectually.* There is a lack of risk taking in Dylan's whole approach to play. Because of his slow physical development, he seems unlikely to challenge himself in other ways.

Dylan's progress report thus sets a primary goal in physical/motor skills, with the knowledge that such growth can positively affect learning in other areas. Teachers also plan the strategy of helping him talk about what he likes and dislikes about the outdoors and collecting some stories that depict characters persisting to master difficulties (such as *The Little Engine That Could*), using his strength as a springboard for growth.

## To Plan for Guidance and Intervention

A third purpose for evaluation is to help teachers determine guidance procedures. These are based on insights and perceptions brought into focus through the evaluation. This process serves as a primary tool on which guidance and planning are based.

**A Guidance Tool.** Evaluations help in behavior management. Once a need has been pinpointed, the teaching staff decides how to proceed. Individual problems are highlighted when teachers make a point of concentrating on the child's behavior. Figure 10.10 illustrates a form used to determine intervention. Used at a team meeting, this form demonstrates what steps are to be taken in addressing the concern directly. It also helps teachers clarify how to talk to parents in a concerned and supportive manner.

**Application.** The following case studies demonstrate how information from evaluations are used for guidance and intervention:

Elizabeth's recent evaluation revealed an increase in the number of toilet accidents she has had. The staff noted a higher incidence during midmorning snacks, but came to no conclusion

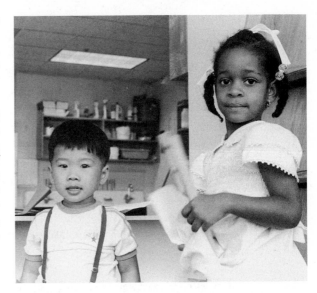

**FIGURE 10.9** What do these children need from the program? From teachers? Evaluation assesses each individual's needs for guidance and intervention. (Courtesy of Stride Rite Children's Centers, Cambridge, Mass.)

as to the cause. They agree to continue to treat her behavior in a relaxed manner, and have one teacher remind Elizabeth to use the toilet before she washes her hands for snack. At the same time, they make plans to contact the parents for further information and insights. They will confer again afterwards and agree upon an approach.

Trevor's parents report that he says he has no friends at school. At their staff meeting, the teachers make plans to suggest that Trevor's parents invite Ryan and Brooke to play with Trevor at home. Teachers have seen both children approach him, but he didn't seem to know how to respond. At school, the teachers will give Trevor verbal cues when children make attempts to play with him.

**Goals and Plans.** An evaluation tool, such as the *child guidance form* in Figure 10.10, helps teachers set goals for children. By narrowing the focus to include only those behaviors that concern the staff, the needs of many children can be reviewed quickly.

CHILD GUIDANCE FORM

*Presentation of Problems* (In behavioral terms)

What behaviors are causing the staff concern? Be specific. Limit to three problems or concerns.

1.
2.
3.

*Family History* (Information from family, medical info if needed)

*School History* (Child's relations to adults, children, materials, activities)

*Intervention* (What procedures have and have not worked? What strengths does the child bring to this issue?)

*Future Plans* (What is going to happen as a result?)

1. In classroom

2. With parents

3. Date for reviewing results

**FIGURE 10.10** One purpose of evaluating children is to plan for guidance and behavior management. A good evaluation form will include how to follow through on the plans made for intervention. (Adapted from K. McLaughlin and S. Sugarman.)

## *To Plan Curriculum*

Teachers plan curriculum based on children's evaluations. Translating the assessment to actual classroom practice is an important part of the teacher's role. A thorough evaluation helps teachers plan appropriate activities to meet children's needs.

**Planning Tools.** All three of the previous evaluation tools can be used to plan curriculum. The entry-level assessment and midyear report are often summarized in a group chart, such as in Figure 10.11. One such chart, made at the end of the first semester of a prekindergarten class, revealed this pattern:

At least one third of the class was having trouble listening at group time, as evidenced by the group chart that identified "Group Time" and "Language Listening Skills" as areas for growth for nearly half the children. The staff centered their attention on the group time content. It was concluded that a story made the group times too long; the children were restless throughout most of the reading. It was agreed to move storytime to just before nap and shorten the group time temporarily.

Summary of Development/Fall Progress Reports (see forms for details)
Developmental Area: + = fine; − = needs work; ? = don't know

| Child | Physical | Language | Cognitive | Social | Emotional | Creative |
|---|---|---|---|---|---|---|
| Greg | − | + | + | + | − | ? |
| Anwar | ? | − | + | − | − | + |
| San-Joo | + | ? | ? | − | + | + |
| Reva | + | + | + | + | + | + |
| Katy | − | + | ? | ? | ? | − |

Group Goals for Winter:
- Emphasize social and emotional areas of curriculum.
- Plan physical games (indoor games because of weather).

Individual Goals for Winter:
Greg: Encourage some creative arts, games. Observe creativity in intellectual activities.
Anwar: Needs to be helped to feel confident and express himself; don't push too hard on physical risks yet.
San-Joo: Need assessment of language and cognitive skills; observe use of table toys, receptive language at group time.
Reva: What is the next step? Is she ready for helping the others? Involve her with 100-piece puzzles and the computer.
Katy: Need to focus on her overall development; too many unknowns—is she getting enough individual attention?

**FIGURE 10.11**  A group chart. Teachers can use individual assessment tools to plan for the entire group and for each child in the class.

Evaluation also applies to daily events, such as individual projects and the day as a whole. One tool for curriculum evaluation reviews the results of a specific activity. Figure 10.12 is a sample of that kind of curriculum assessment. Chapter 11 discusses the planning of curriculum in further detail.

**Application.** Evaluation results assist teachers in seeing more clearly the strengths and abilities of each child in the class. Curriculum activities are then planned that will continue to enhance the growth of that child. Also, areas of difficulty will be identified:

Jolene has trouble mastering even the simplest puzzle. Provide her with common shapes found in attribute blocks (small plastic shapes of varying color, thickness, size) and do some matching exercises with her.

The younger children in the class are reluctant to try the climbing structures designed by the older ones. Build an obstacle course with the youngest children, beginning with very simple challenges and involving the children in the actual planning and building as well as rehearsing climbing techniques with them.

**Goals and Plans.** Each of the previous case studies demonstrates how evaluation tools can be used to plan curriculum. By analyzing both group and individual skills through periodic assessment, teachers maintain a secure and challenging environment.

## To Communicate with Parents

Plans for evaluating children should include the means by which parents are to be informed of the

Activity _____

How many children participated? _____ Did any avoid the activity? _____

How involved did children become? Very ___ Briefly ___ Watched only ___

What were children's reactions? Describe what they said and did. _____

_____

_____

_____

_____

What did you do to attract children? To maintain their interest? _____

_____

_____

_____

_____

How would you rate the success of this activity? Poor ___

Adequate ___ Good ___ Great ___ Why? _____

What skills/abilities were needed? Did the children exhibit the skills? ____

_____

_____

What parts of the activity were most successful? Why? _____

_____

_____

Describe any difficulty you encountered. Give reasons and tell how you
would handle it if it happened again. _____

_____

_____

_____

If you did this activity again, what would you change? _____

_____

In light of your evaluation, what would you plan for a follow-up activity?

_____

_____

How did this activity compare with your goals and expectations? _____

_____

_____

**FIGURE 10.12** Evaluating daily activities lets teachers use assessment as a planning tool. (Adapted from Vassar College Nursery School.)

results. Once the teachers have identified a child's needs and capabilities, parents are entitled to hear the conclusions. The teaching staff has an obligation to provide a realistic overview of the child's progress and alert the parents to any possible concerns. (See Chapter 8 for details about parents and teachers working together.)

Using the child guidance form (page 282), teachers define problem behavior for a child and work closely with the parents to reach a solution:

Yum-Tong refuses to let his mother leave. The teachers agree that there are two issues: (1) Y.-T.'s screaming and crying as his mother leaves, and (2) his inability to focus on an activity while she attempts to go (though she stays as soon as he starts screaming). The family has told them that their other two children had separation problems as preschoolers. The previous school asked the parents to stay until the children stopped protesting, although the parents report that this took nearly six months and so was a hardship for them in their work places.

The teachers choose to intervene by asking Yum-Tong's mother to plan ahead with Y.-T., deciding before school how they will spend five minutes together each morning. After playing and helping him to settle in, she will then say good-bye and leave Y.-T. with Pete, his favorite teacher. Pete will be prepared to be with him at the departure and stay with him until he calms down. They also plan to have a conference date after two weeks of this intervention plan to follow through and review how it is working for everyone.

**A Tool with Parents.** Teachers and parents need to talk together, especially when problems are revealed by the evaluation. As parents and teachers share knowledge and insights, a fuller picture of the child emerges for both. Each can then assume a role in the resolution of the problem. The role of the teacher will be defined in the context of the parents' role, and the parents will be guided by the teacher's attitudes and actions.

Evaluation tools can help parents target areas in which their child may need special help. A child guidance form (Fig. 10.10) is an effective tool for parent–teacher conferences and as a method for forming intervention plans. Chapter 8 discusses the parent–teacher relationship and offers guides for effective parent–teacher conferences. The tool that works best is one that summarizes the school's concerns and solicits high parent involvement.

**FIGURE 10.13** Assessing group skills is one reason to evaluate children. These children are ready for curriculum challenges in group time.

**Application.** Aside from identifying normal behavior problems, evaluations may raise questions concerning a child's physical development, hearing and visual acuity, or language problems. Potentially serious problems may emerge from the evaluation, and parents can be encouraged to seek further professional guidance.

**Goals and Plans.** Since evaluation is an ongoing process, reevaluation and goal-setting are done regularly. Communicating to parents both progress and new goals is critical for the *feedback loop* of an evaluation form to be effective.

### To Make Administrative Decisions

Evaluation results can help a school make administrative decisions. They can lead to changes in the overall program or in the school's philosophy. For example, a child care component might be added to the half-day program after learning that most children are enrolled in another child care situation after nursery school. Or an evaluation might conclude that there is too little emphasis on developing large motor skills and coordination. To invite more active play, the administration might decide to remodel the play yard and purchase new equipment.

In the early childhood setting, both *informal* and *formal methods* are used for evaluating children. *Informal* and *homemade methods* such as those in Chapter 6 and Figures 10.6, 10.8, 10.10, 10.11, and 10.12 include observation, note taking, self-assessments, parent interviews and surveys, samples of children's work, and teacher-designed forms. More *formal* kinds of *evaluations* are used also, although somewhat less frequently in the early years. These include standardized tests and various "screening" instruments. The yearly tests taken in school, using a Number 2 pencil, are an example of such procedures. Those and other standardized forms are examples of formal methods of evaluation. Commercially developed, these tests usually compare the individual child's performance to a predetermined norm. It is important to choose assessment tools and techniques that are appropriate for the group or the child under consideration. Informal observations

can be made more systematic (see Chapter 6) or comprehensive to gain more information about a specific problem. Formal, commercially developed instruments need to be used more carefully (see Standardized Testing).

**An Administrative Tool.** Many kindergartens and some nursery schools use various kinds of "screening" tests, before children begin school in the fall. The usual purpose of these evaluations is to determine readiness; that is, to verify that the child will be able to cope with and succeed in school. These tools are best devised with the individual child in mind. Their purpose is positive: to highlight the skills the child has and to identify the areas in which the child may need help in the next class. Figure 10.14 shows a homemade screening evaluation that was developed for individual four-to-five-year-old preschoolers who were leaving for kindergarten. The activity

**SKILLS INVENTORY**

Child _____ Age ____ Teacher _____ Date _____

| **Task** | **Teacher Comments** |
|---|---|

*Cognitive Skills*

1. Can you say the alphabet?
2. Can you tell me what these letters are?
3. Can you count for me?
4. Please point to the number.
5. Can you put these in order from smallest to biggest? Which is the largest? Smallest? First? Last?
6. What color is this? If child cannot, then ask to "Point to the red one," etc.
7. What shapes are these? If child cannot, then ask to "Point to the circle," etc.
8. Can you find your shoulders? Elbow? Thumb? Neck? Lips?

1. Sequence correct? Yes ___ No ___ Length:
2. Number of letters correct ___ Comment:
3. Note how far: Sequence correct how far? ___
4. 3-1-6-4-8-2-9-7-5 How many correct? ___
5. Three sizes of triangles. Comments:
6. Point to red, blue, yellow, black, green, orange, brown, purple, Comments:
7. Point to circle, square, triangle, rectangle. Comments?
8. Comments:

**FIGURE 10.14** By creating effective tools for assessment, we are able to evaluate children's developing skills and their readiness for the next educational step. (Developed by Bing Nursery School, Stanford University, 1975 to present.)

| Task | Teacher Comments |
|---|---|
| 9. Name all the animals you can think of. | 9. Comments: |
| 10. Please put these animals into two groups. One has the animals that live in water, and the other the ones that live on the land. | 10. Giraffe, deer, cat, frog, alligator, shark, goldfish |
| 11. Here is a bear and a cube. Put the cube on top of the bear. Under the bear. Behind the bear. Beside the bear. | 11. Check correct responses: |
| 12. Here are three pictures. Can you put them in order so that they tell a story? | 12. Tree with green leaves. Tree with orange/red leaves, falling. Bare tree. Comments: |

### Auditory-Perceptual Listening Skills

| Task | Teacher Comments |
|---|---|
| 1. Please repeat these numbers after I say them (Practice with 6–3–1–4):<br>    5–3–8–2<br>    2–7–9–3 | 1. Sequence correct? Numbers correct? |
| 2. Tell me the sentence in the same order as I say. (Practice with "The dog ran to the park.")<br>The mother pointed to the airplane in the sky. | 2. Sequence correct? Words correct? |
| 3. Listen to what I say, and then do what my words tell you. (Practice with "Put your hands on your head.")<br>Stand up, go to the door, and walk back to me. | 3. Comments: |

### Fine Motor Skills

| Task | Teacher Comments |
|---|---|
| 1. Print your name. | 1. Note grasp, hand preference. |
| 2. Draw a circle, square, triangle, rectangle. | 2. Comments: |
| 3. Write the letters:<br>    O  E  P  A  J | 3. Comments: |
| 4. Write the numbers:<br>    1  3  7  2  5 | 4. Comments: |
| 5. Cut out a circle. | 5. Note scissor grasp, hand preference. |
| 6. Draw the best person that you can. Have you left anything out? | 6. Comments: |

### Gross Motor Skills

| Task | Teacher Comments |
|---|---|
| 1. Jump on two feet from A to B. | 1. Note balance. |
| 2. Hop on one foot from B to A. | 2. Note balance. |
| 3. Skip from A to B. | 3. Comments: |
| 4. Walk backwards from B to A. | 4. Comments: |
| 5. Stand on one foot while I count to three. | 5. Note balance. |
| 6. Walk across this balance board. | 6. Note balance. |
| 7. Can you jump over these poles with your feet together? | 7. Comments: |
| 8. How high can you climb our climber? Go up our slide? | 8. Comments: |
| 9. Now run from the climber to the fence and back to me as fast as you can! | 9. Note gait and balance. |
| 10. Please throw the ball to me. Catch it. Kick it. | 10. Comments: |

**FIGURE 10.14  Cont.**

employs a one-to-one, game-like approach in which a child and a favorite teacher can explore both strengths and difficulties in a safe, supportive setting.

Some teachers conclude the year with a summary report. This evaluation serves as an overview of what a child has accomplished, what areas of strength are present, and what future growth might occur. These records are useful to parents as a summary of their child's learning experiences. Teachers may use them as references should they ever be consulted by another school about the child. Again, it is critical to administer these assessments in a sensitive and accepting manner, and to communicate the results in the same tone. If this is not done, the child's self-esteem may be damaged and the parents' trust may be lost. The disadvantages of these tools parallel those of standardized tests (see next section).

**Application.** Making administrative decisions based on evaluation results is a sound idea. Assessments give administrators specific and verifiable information on which to base decisions.

The issue of readiness or placement of children is difficult and complex. The section Standardized Testing, which follows, describes the potential problems and misapplications of tests in this regard. Whether or not a child is ready to succeed in a program affects parents and children personally. Having a good evaluation tool helps in making such decisions equitably and in communicating results in a clear and kind manner.

**Goals and Plans.** The evaluation tool that gives a specific profile of a child's skills will allow an administrator to share information with a family clearly and honestly. By carefully choosing a tool, administrators give the parents information they can use to plan for the child's development.

## Standardized Testing

The practice of testing and screening for readiness, which has increased in the last decade, raises some practical and philosophical issues. The use of

**FIGURE 10.15** Motor skills are one indicator of an ability to succeed in school, and should be assessed as regularly as cognitive or socio-emotional abilities. (Courtesy of Dori Salladay, Eva's Little School, Sacramento, Calif.)

tests for admittance to kindergarten or promotion to first grade has resulted in more and more children being denied entrance to a school system, being put in extra-year programs, or being placed in kindergarten twice. The 1988 *Position Statement on Standardized Testing of Young Children* of the National Association for the Education of Young Children states the problem clearly and succinctly:

Such practices (often based on inappropriate uses of readiness or screening tests) disregard the potential, documented long-term negative effects of retention on children's self-esteem and the fact that such practices disproportionately affect low-income and minority children; further, these practices have been implemented in the absence of research documenting that they positively affect children's later academic achievement.

(NAEYC, 1988)

Most tests focus on cognitive and language skills. This narrow focus ignores areas of development that most early childhood programs include and emphasize, such as self-help skills and motor, socioemotional, and creative development. Moreover, the practice of standardized testing has caused early childhood curriculum to be increasingly academic. Indeed:

> Many kindergartens are now structured, "watered-down" first grades, emphasizing workbooks and other paper-and-pencil activities that are inappropriate for 5-year-olds. The trend further trickles down to preschool and child care programs that feel that their mission is to get children "ready" for kindergarten. Too many school systems, expecting children to conform to an inappropriate curriculum and finding large numbers of "unready" children, react to the problem by raising the entrance age for kindergarten and/or labeling the children as failures.
>
> (NAEYC, 1988)

The implications of such testing further erode the curriculum when teachers, wanting their classes to do well on the test, alter activities to conform to what will be tested. They then begin teaching children to learn "right" answers rather than to engage in active, critical thinking. Rather than making teachers more accountable, "the overuse (and misuse) of standardized testing has led to the adoption of inappropriate teaching practices as well as admission and retention policies that are not in the best interests of individual children or the nation as a whole" (NAEYC, 1988).

Testing does have appropriate uses, as described in the section Evaluating Children. Moreover, nonstandardized assessments like those found throughout the chapter can and should be used to plan and implement programs for young children. In addition, NAEYC has adopted specific guidelines for the use of standardized testing to help early childhood professionals make decisions regarding the appropriate use of testing.

# EVALUATING TEACHERS

It is understood that teachers are the *single most important* factor in determining program quality. What makes "the effective teacher" has no one simple answer. However, there are ways to evaluate teachers that guide them toward more effective teaching, in their work with children, coworkers, parents, and administrators.

Think of teachers as conductors of a symphony orchestra. They do not compose the music. They do not design or build the instruments, nor do they decide which ones will be played in the orchestra pit. They may even have limited choice of the music that will be played. Yet, it is their job to lead a group of musicians through a medley of songs, bringing out the best in each. And all under the intense scrutiny of a critical audience. Teachers must do this with care and expertise under the watchful eyes of parents, boards, and funding agencies.

Many teachers do this well, often with little training except direct experience. As teachers' effectiveness is measured, they can learn better techniques for working with children, for planning environments and programs. The process for establishing and meeting these goals is evaluation. Teacher evaluation forms in this chapter can be adapted for use with student teachers and aides. Chapters 5 and 6 also address the work of the student teacher.

## Why Evaluate?

Teachers are evaluated for several reasons. The end result of an assessment may be setting guidelines for what kinds of teaching are expected. Or the intent of an evaluation might be to set clear goals for job improvement. The first part of any effective evaluation procedure is a statement of purpose.

### To Describe Job Responsibilities

It is essential for teachers to understand their job to do it well. A good job description outlines what is expected. One purpose of an evaluation is to see how those expectations are being met.

In an infant/toddler center, for example, teachers try to help children learn to separate comfortably from their parents. Evaluation in this setting could focus on the exact skills needed to implement this goal. How does a teacher help a parent separate from a young child? What environmental cues does the teacher prepare? How is the child in distress comforted? What teaching strategies are important?

Evaluation for specifying job responsibilities is a part of one's professional self-definition as well as a clarification of actual duties. Studying ourselves helps us know who we are and what we do. Assessing job responsibilities aids in this process.

### To Monitor Job Effectiveness

Once clear guidelines are set for teaching expectations, a method is needed to monitor actual teaching. Most evaluation systems attempt to check teacher effectiveness. It is important to establish a process for analyzing how teachers are doing their job.

This process may vary from school to school. In some schools, teaching effectiveness is measured, in part, by child achievement, such as how children score on tests. Other centers may solicit parent opinion. A teacher's coworkers may be part of an assessment team. For the most part, an evaluation for job effectiveness will include an observation of teaching time with children.

### To Clarify Strengths and Weaknesses

An evaluation procedure preferred by many teachers is one that identifies specific areas of strength and weakness. Feedback about actual teaching and other job responsibilities is helpful to all teachers, whether beginners or experienced personnel. As assessment that offers teachers information about how to perform their job better contributes to job competence and satisfaction. By recognizing strengths, teachers receive positive feedback for high-quality work. By identifying weaknesses, they can begin to set realistic goals for improvement.

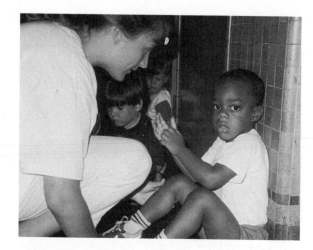

**FIGURE 10.16** Evaluating teachers includes assessing their work with children.

**FIGURE 10.17** Teacher evaluations monitor job effectiveness as teachers work with people in several dimensions. This teacher demonstrates skill with groups as well as with individual children and adults. (Courtesy of Dori Salladay, Eva's Little School, Sacramento, Calif.)

### To Set Professional Growth Goals

One function of teacher evaluation is to foster professional development. Teachers do not become "good" and then stay that way for life. Regardless of their stage of development, teachers need goals in order to continually improve.

Regular feedback to staff can help in setting goals for continual professional growth. Beginning teachers will need to work on skills that apply their educational training or background to the classroom and children. A professional with 15 years of experience might need to polish skills acquired a decade or more ago, or try another educational challenge, such as developing curriculum or planning a workshop.

### To Determine Employment

An evaluation can also be used to decide whether teachers should be "retained, promoted, or released" (Stoops et al. *in* Hatfield, 1981). Assessment procedures are an administrator's most valuable tools in performing these tasks. With a clear and effective evaluation tool, a teacher's performance can be monitored and specific areas targeted for improvement. The administrator then has a fair and equitable way to determine promotional status of each employee.

## Critical Issues in Teacher Evaluation

*How* to evaluate is an important issue in teacher assessment. A system for evaluating employees can be one of trust and mutual respect or of anxiety and tension. The method often determines how successful the entire evaluation will be.

### Preliminary Steps

To begin with, a school follows the same guidelines for developing a teacher evaluation as for child assessment. That is, the process includes determining a purpose, establishing who will collect the data and how, and clarifying how the evaluation will be used. When assessing teachers, the important components are: purpose (as described earlier in the chapter), evaluators, process, and follow-through.

### Evaluators

Several models have been developed around the issue of who will assess teacher performance.

**Self-Evaluation.** This can be an effective starting point. Self-assessment is used in the Child Development Associate's evaluation system, for these rea-

sons (Ward and CDA staff, 1976):

- The candidate is a valid source of information for use in assessment. Certain information is available only from the candidate's perspective.
- The candidate is able to clarify information or his or her performance, thereby adding to the assessment team's evidence for a valid decision.
- The candidate is better able to identify strengths and weaknesses and to receive recommendations for continued professional growth.

Figure 10.18 illustrates one type of systematic self-assessment. Another self-assessment technique, somewhat less formal, is to ask questions about yourself and your job, such as:

- What aspects of my work give me the greatest sense of satisfaction and achievement?
- What changes in my work assignment would increase my contribution to the school and my own personal satisfaction?
- What additional development activities would help me do a more effective job or prepare me for the next step on my career path?
- What would improve the effectiveness and quality of my relationship with my supervisor? (Young-Holt et al., 1983)

The answers to these few questions can provide a solid base for discussion between teacher and supervisor or assessment team.

One drawback of self-assessment is its subjectivity. We see ourselves too closely, too personally, to be able to be entirely objective about our teaching. Therefore, self-assessment must be accompanied by other evaluating feedback.

**Supervisory Evaluation.** Supervisors, or head teachers, are usually part of the evaluation process. Job performance is an administrator's responsibility; therefore, teachers can expect their supervisors to be involved in their evaluation. Supervisors often use a single form combining a teacher's self-assessment

---

## SAMPLE SELF-EVALUATION

Rate the following items on the scale below, based on your performance in the classroom. (Note: This form allows for a yes/no response if desired. Supervisors may use this same form to rate the student following the self-evaluation.)

| Superior Perf. | Acceptable Perf. | Unacceptable Perf. | Not Applicable |
|:---:|:---:|:---:|:---:|
| 3 | 2 | 1 | 0 |

*Relationship to Children*

_____ I am able to understand and accept a child as he/she is and recognize individual needs.
_____ I use knowledge and understanding of child development principles to understand children.
_____ I use information regarding home, family, and sociocultural background to understand children.
_____ I am able to forestall situations before negative behavior occurs.
_____ I use positive suggestions and choices to redirect behavior.
_____ I use prescribed limits and follow-through.
_____ I adapt methods of guidance to the individual and adjust guidance measures to fit the situation.
_____ I avoid the use of threats.
_____ I express positive reinforcement when appropriate.
_____ I can verbalize my own feelings in an honest, open, and humane manner when interacting with children.
_____ I avoid using baby talk.
_____ I relate to individual children.
_____ I relate to children in small groups.
_____ I relate to children in large groups.

*Developing the Program*

_____ I permit the children to explore materials in a variety of ways.
_____ I recognize and use spontaneous happenings to help children's learning.
_____ I make use of child development principles to plan curriculum for children.
_____ I offer a wide range of experiences so children can make choices according to their interests and needs.
_____ I allow for various levels of ability among children.
_____ I utilize a variety of media when developing instructional materials.
_____ I use a note-taking system to assist in planning and evaluating experiences for children.
_____ I maintain equipment and materials in good order and consider health and safety factors.

*Relating to Parents*

_____ I recognize parents by name.
_____ I converse with parents at appropriate times.
_____ I incorporate the cultural backgrounds of families into the program.
_____ I facilitate a free flow of information between staff and parents.
_____ I communicate concerns to parents in both written and verbal forms.
_____ I recognize and appreciate parental values and priorities for their children.
_____ I communicate children's school experiences with parents.

*Administration and Professional Development*

_____ I recognize and use policies and procedures of the program.
_____ I attend and participate in staff meetings.
_____ I inform the administrative staff correctly of illness, time off, vacation, etc.
_____ I am a member of at least one professional organization in the field of early childhood.
_____ I attend meetings conducted by professional groups.

---

**FIGURE 10.18** Self-evaluation can be an insightful and useful process. (Adapted from Young-Holt et. al. [1983], and Hatfield [1981])

_____ I make use of professional resources and contacts.
_____ I maintain professional confidentiality and discretion.

*Working with Other Staff Members*
_____ I show positive attitudes toward other staff members.
_____ I give directions carefully.
_____ I take directions from others.
_____ I participate as a team member.
_____ I coordinate my efforts with those of my coworkers.
_____ I share my time, interest, and resources with other staff members.
_____ I listen and hear staff feedback regarding my teaching.
_____ I act on suggestions.
_____ I communicate my perceptions of my teaching in an honest and clear manner.

**FIGURE 10.18  Cont.**

and the supervisor's evaluation. This kind of form simplifies the paperwork and assures both teacher and supervisor that both are using the same criteria for evaluation. They may, however, develop a different kind of form, such as the one in Figure 10.19.

**Coevaluation.** Evaluation by others associated with the teachers is a welcome addition to the evaluation process. Often a system includes more than a teacher's supervisor. Possible combinations are:

• Teacher (self-evaluation) and supervisor

• Teacher, supervisor, and parent

• Teacher, supervisor, and another team member (coteacher, aide, student teacher)

A team evaluation is a more collaborative approach. More information is collected on the teacher's performance. A team approach may be more valid and balanced, since a decision about teaching will be made by consensus and discussion rather than individual, perhaps arbitrary, methods. And the evaluation will have a wider perspective, evaluating a teacher's job performance from several viewpoints.

Coevaluation does have its disadvantages, however. It is a time-consuming process since more than one person is asked to evaluate a teacher. Feedback may be contradictory; what one evaluator sees as a strength, another may view as a shortcoming. The system can be complicated to implement. For instance, how do teachers work in a classroom and evaluate another team member at the same time?

Can funds be found to bring in substitutes? Do fellow teachers have the time to devote to evaluating each other? How and when does a parent evaluate a teacher? Clearly, a school must weigh these issues carefully as evaluation systems are devised.

## *The Process*

The evaluation tools used determine the information gathered. Informal techniques often use information that is gathered sporadically, and conclusions may be unreliable or based on opinions. A process that is formalized and systematic has a greater chance of success. Such evaluations will be based on observable, specific information on what the teacher actually does. This is known as *performance-based assessment*. When paired with specific goals and expectations, this system is known as competency-based assessment.

*Competency-based assessments* outline exactly what teachers must do to demonstrate their competency, or skill, in their job assignment. Criteria are set as a teacher begins working (or a student starts a class or teacher education program). Areas are targeted that pinpoint what knowledge, skills, and behaviors the teacher must acquire. Figure 10.20 is an example of an evaluation based on defined areas of competency.

## *Follow-Through*

What happens after the evaluation is critical to the overall success of an evaluation system. For instance, after gathering information for an

## Teacher Evaluation Form

**Instructions**: This form is designed to be used by the center director for evaluating teachers. To the left of each characteristic listed below write an **E** if the teacher's performance in this area is **excellent**, **S** if it is **satisfactory**, and **N** if it **needs improvement**. Make any explanatory notes to the right.

**Name of Teacher:** _____ **Classroom:** _____

____ 1. Friendly, with ability to relate positively to people.
____ 2. Enjoys the egocentricity of children.
____ 3. Speaks clearly, distinctly, and grammatically.
____ 4. Demonstrates tact, compassion, empathic concern for children and families.
____ 5. Tolerant and considerate of differences in children and adults.
____ 6. Understands humor, humorous incidents, and jokes of children.
____ 7. Displays a sense of humor with children and enjoys laughing with them.
____ 8. Smiles and shows enjoyment often.
____ 9. Is dependable and energetic.
____ 10. Makes real effort to become very involved in the program.
____ 11. Enthusiastic and excited about teaching.
____ 12. Indicates a desire to keep up in the field of ECE.
____ 13. Grows in ability to critically evaluate self.
____ 14. Can follow directions.
____ 15. Accepts and uses suggestions to improve teaching.
____ 16. Accepts share of responsibility for classroom preparation, gathering of materials, and other tasks assigned.
____ 17. Accepts individual differences.
____ 18. Uses a positive approach with all children.
____ 19. Alert to total group of children even when dealing with an individual child or small group.
____ 20. Remains controlled in *startling* or difficult situations.
____ 21. Assists children in gaining self-confidence and in becoming communicative.
____ 22. Makes an effort to joyously participate with children in small groups or 1:1 basis, indoors and outdoors.
____ 23. Displays a general positive attitude toward other adults in place of a negative, criticizing attitude.
____ 24. Responds well to adults.
____ 25. Respects the rights and teaching techniques of others in the group.
____ 26. Welcomes new ideas and demonstrates flexibility with willingness to consider new ideas.
____ 27. Realizes that situations cannot always be handled at home as they are at school.
____ 28. Evidences growth and potential for teaching young children.
____ 29. Demonstrates knowledge about growth and development of young children.
____ 30. Demonstrates knowledge about the meaning of specific activities for children.
____ 31. Is positive and supportive of parents as partners in ECE.

**Signed:**_____ **Date:**_____

**FIGURE 10.19** A teacher may be evaluated by the center director or supervisor using an evaluation tool such as this form, by the late Carol Murphy of La Crescenta, Calif. (Reprinted with permission of CCIE, Issue 51, Sept. 1986; a management magazine for center directors, P.O. Box 2890, Redmond, Wash., 98073.)

Competency Area:
1. Establishes and maintains a safe and healthy learning environment.
2. Advances physical and intellectual competence.
3. Builds positive self-concept and individual strength.
4. Promotes positive functioning of children and adults in a group.
5. Brings about optimal coordination of home and center child-rearing practices and expectations.
6. Carries out supplemental responsibilities related to children's programs.

**FIGURE 10.20** One type of competency-based assessment has been developed by the Child Development Associate Consortium. Competency areas are further elaborated with specific examples of teacher behavior. (Adapted from Ward and CDA staff, 1976.)

evaluation session, a supervisor and teacher might discuss and evaluate concrete examples and live performance. Together they can establish goals for changing what may be ineffective or problematic.

Follow-through is the final part of a continuous *feedback loop* in a good evaluation system. Data is collected on teacher behavior and given to the teacher in person. Goals are set to improve teaching. A follow-up check is done periodically, to see how—and if—goals are being met. Teaching improves as recommendations are put into practice. Follow-through makes the *feedback loop* complete as information about improvement is communicated. Figure 10.21 illustrates this cycle.

Evaluation takes hard work, time, and dedication to a higher quality of teaching. It is also a shared responsibility. The supervisor must be explicit about a teacher's performance and be able to identify for the teacher what is effective and what is problematic. The teacher is responsible for participating in the evaluation.

## Techniques for Productive Evaluation Sessions

Teachers must value the process itself. Evaluations emphasize how valuable the work of profes-sional teachers is, and the benefits of productive evaluation sessions are clear. They range from improved self-esteem, higher levels of job effectiveness, and less absenteeism and turnover, to assessment-related salary raises and other job benefits. Teachers need to analyze and take seriously the substance of the evaluation and understand its implications for their teaching. To further their professional growth, they must use this opportunity to improve the tools of their trade.

Certain techniques help make evaluation sessions productive for teachers:

**1.** Become involved from the beginning as the evaluation procedure is established. Know what is expected and how you will be evaluated.

**2.** Set a specific meeting time for your evaluation. Ask your supervisor for a time that works for you both.

**3.** Set some goals for yourself before meeting with your supervisor. If you know what you want to work on, you are more likely to get help achieving your goals.

**FIGURE 10.21** A "feedback loop" is a continuous cycle in which teacher behavior is observed for a performance evaluation. The evaluation is offered through growth goals, which are set to affect teacher behavior. Thus, the circle is continuous, with each part helping the next.

4. Develop a plan for action. Be prepared to set a timeline for when and how you will work on your goals.
5. Establish a feedback loop. Make a follow-up date and make copies of your goal sheet for both you and your supervisor.
6. Approach the meeting with a sense of trust, respect, and openness. Planning ahead promotes these attitudes.

What results from productive feedback sessions is better teaching and continued professional growth. Teacher evaluations help recognize strengths and build upon them. They identify areas where growth is needed. They individualize the process itself. No two teachers are identical; each evaluation must be interpreted in terms of the behavior and stage of development of the individual person. As teachers become more effective in their work with children, the quality of the entire program is improved.

# EVALUATING PROGRAMS

## Why Evaluate?

### To Gain an Overview

Evaluating a program gives an overview of how all the various components function together. Looking at children, teachers, and the total environment reveals the entire system as an integrated whole. Program evaluations add an awareness of how one area relates to another and how the parts mesh in a particular setting. To a great extent, evaluating a program amounts to asking, "What is a good program for children?"

To answer that question, a program evaluation looks at several issues:

- children's progress
- teacher performance
- curriculum development
- the financial structure
- the parents
- the community at large

- the governing organization of the school

In evaluating programs, each of these is assessed for how it functions alone and how each works in concert with the others.

### To Establish Accountability

Besides providing an overview, a program evaluation establishes *accountability*. This refers to a program's being answerable to a controlling group or agency, for instance the school board or the government office. These groups want to know how their funds are being spent and how their philosophy is being expressed through the overall program. Just as a teacher's evaluation is sometimes linked to salary increases, a program evaluation may be related to future funding. This can add stress to the evaluation process since teachers and administrators must justify their worth in dollars and cents.

### To Make Improvements

A third purpose of a program evaluation is to determine where and how improvements can be made. Program evaluations are an opportunity to take an objective look at how the goals of the school are being met. A good evaluation will support the strengths of the existing program and suggest where changes might improve overall effectiveness. An in-depth assessment increases the likelihood that program goals and visions will be realized. The evaluation helps determine the direction the program may take in the future.

### To Acquire Accreditation

Finally, evaluations are a necessary step for some schools who wish to be approved for certification or accreditation by various organizations. Such groups require that a school meet certain evaluation standards before the necessary permits are issued or membership is granted. The National Academy of Early Childhood Programs, a division of the National Association for the Education of Young Children, has established an accreditation system for improving the quality of life for young children and their families. The *Focus* discussion by Dr. Sue Bredekamp describes this system.

# FOCUS

## IMPROVING PROGRAM QUALITY THROUGH NATIONAL ACCREDITATION

*Dr. Sue Bredekamp*

Parents want the best for their children. Teachers want to work in programs that provide good quality care and education for children. Program administrators want to provide a high quality service to their clients. Program funders want to know that their investment is sound.

Parents, teachers, administrators, and funders involved in early childhood programs now have a system for helping ensure that their programs are of the highest quality. That system is the National Academy of Early Childhood Programs, a division of the National Association for the Education of Young Children (NAEYC). The academy administers a national, voluntary accreditation system for child care centers and preschools. This system, initiated in 1985, is designed for any full-day or part-day group program serving children from birth through age five and/or school-age children in before- and after-school care. Accredited programs represent the diversity of the field of early childhood education—church-housed and church-sponsored; private, for-profit; community-based, non-profit; employer-sponsored; university-sponsored; parent cooperatives; Head Start programs; and public school prekindergarten and kindergarten.

The goal of NAEYC's accreditation system is to *improve* the quality of care and education provided for young children in group programs. The accreditation system achieves its goal by establishing high standards of quality for programs and recognizing programs that achieve substantial compliance with the criteria. The criteria for accreditation were developed over a three-

year period with input from thousands of early childhood professionals.

How does the academy define a high quality early childhood program? A high quality program provides a safe and nurturing environment while promoting the physical, social, emotional, and intellectual development of young children. In accredited programs, you will see:

- Frequent, positive, warm interactions among adults and children
- Planned learning activities appropriate to children's age and development, such as block building, painting, stories, dress-up, and active, outdoor play
- Teachers who are specially trained in child development and early education
- Enough adults to respond to individual children, adequate ratios of staff to children, and reasonable group sizes
- Many, varied age-appropriate materials, accessible to children
- A healthy and safe environment for children
- Nutritious meals and/or snacks
- Regular communication with parents, who are welcome visitors at all times
- Effective administration designed to meet the needs of adults as well as children
- Systematic and ongoing program evaluation

Early childhood educators often stress process over product. The same is true of the accreditation system. The criteria form the basis for the system, but the accreditation process is what accomplishes the goal of program improvement. The three-step accreditation system is designed to bring about real and lasting improvements in the program. The first step is a thorough *self-study*. Using an observation form and questionnaires provided by the academy, the teachers, director, and parents evaluate how well the program is meeting the criteria and set goals for improvement. After improvements are made, the director reports the results of the self-study by completing a rating form, called the Program Description. During step two, the accuracy of the program description is verified during an on-site visit by trained early childhood professionals, called validators. The verified program description is then reviewed by a three-person commission that makes the accreditation decision on the basis of professional judgment. The accreditation decision considers all the criteria but weighs most heavily the criteria that directly affect children such as the quality of interactions with adults, the appropriateness of the curriculum, and the safety of the environment.

The accreditation system benefits the early childhood profession in many ways. It establishes professional consensus regarding program standards. It provides a goal that programs can use in working toward improvement. It provides tools for self-evaluation by administrators and teachers as well as overall program evaluation. It provides a mechanism for identifying programs that exceed the minimum requirements for operation and strive toward achieving professional standards. It provides additional assurance for parents as they make important decisions about the care and education of their children.

Although accreditation is a relatively new concept for the field of early childhood education, accreditation is a well-known and trusted concept in other professions. Most of us would not want to send our child to a nonaccredited college, nor would we want to be treated in a nonaccredited hospital. The implementation of a national accreditation system indicates that the early childhood profession, like other professions, is willing to establish standards for practice and to monitor the quality of services offered on behalf of the profession. Thus, accreditation is one of several recent trends that enhance the professional image and status of early childhood educators.

But the major benefactors of accreditation are the children. Directors and teachers whose programs participate in the accreditation process report that it works! It improves the quality of care they provide for children. And after all, all children deserve the best.

*Dr. Bredekamp is director of the National Academy of Early Childhood Programs at NAEYC.*

## Guidelines for Program Evaluation

### Defining the Objectives

A program evaluation begins with a definition of the program's objectives. Knowing why a program is to be evaluated indicates how to tailor the procedure to the needs and characteristics of an individual school. With the objectives defined, the choice of evaluation instrument becomes clear. If, for example, a program objective is to provide a healthy environment for children, the evaluation tool used must address the issues of health, safety, and nutrition.

### Choosing a Tool

Evaluation instruments vary with the purpose of the program evaluation. Moreover, a survey of various program evaluations shows that many are designed to be program-specific; that is, the evaluation itself is devised to examine one program only. Individualized assessments are difficult to generalize. However, it appears that most program evalua-

**FIGURE 10.22**  Program evaluations should represent the diversity of the field of early childhood education, from family day care for infants to after-school programs for primary school children.

tions assess several, if not all, of the following areas:

*The Physical Environment*

Are the facilities clean, comfortable, safe?

Are room arrangements orderly and attractive?

Are materials and equipment in good repair and maintained?

Is there a variety of materials, appropriate to age levels?

Are activity areas well-defined?

Is cleanup and room restoration a part of the daily schedule?

Are samples of children's work on display?

Is play space adequate, both inside and out?

Is personal space (e.g., cubby) provided for each child?

*The Staff*

Are there enough teachers for the number of children? How is this determined?

Are the teachers qualified? What criteria are used?

Is the staff evaluated periodically? By whom and how?

Does the school provide/encourage in-service training and continuing education?

Do the teachers encourage the children to be independent and self-sufficient?

Are the teachers genuinely interested in children?

Are teachers aware of individual abilities and limitations?

What guidance and disciplinary techniques are used?

Do teachers observe, record, and write reports on children's progress?

Are teachers skilled in working with individual children, small groups, and large groups?

**FIGURE 10.23** A program evaluation can determine if the curriculum materials are varied enough to provide opportunities for children to use a wide range of equipment that fits their developmental skills. (Courtesy of St. Thomas Episcopal School, New Haven, Conn.)

Does the teaching staff give the children a feeling of stability and belonging?

Do teachers provide curriculum that is age-appropriate and challenging?

How would you describe the teachers' relationships with other adults in the setting? Who does this include, and how?

Can the teaching staff articulate good early education principles and relate them to their teaching?

*Parent Relationships*

How does the classroom include parents?

Are parents welcome to observe, discuss policies, make suggestions, help in the class?

Are different needs of parents taken into account?

Where and how do parents have a voice in the school?

Are parent–teacher conferences scheduled?

Does the school attempt to use community resources and social service agencies in meeting parents' needs?

*The Organization and Administration*

Does the school maintain and keep records?

Are there scholarships or subsidies available?

What socioeconomic, cultural, religious groups does the school serve?

What is the funding agency, and what role does it play?

Is there a school board and how is it chosen?

Does the school serve children with special needs or handicaps?

Are the classroom groups homo- or heterogeneous?

What hours is the school open?

What age range is served?

Are there both full- and part-day options?

Is after-school care available?

Does the school conduct research or train teachers?

What is the teacher–child ratio?

*The Overall Program*

Does the school have a written, stated educational philosophy?

Are there developmental goals for the children's physical, social, intellectual, and emotional growth?

Are the children evaluated periodically?

Is the program capable of being individualized to fit the needs of all the children?

Does the program include time for a variety of free, spontaneous activities?

Is the curriculum varied to include music, art, science, nature, math, language, social studies, motor skills, etc.?

Are there ample opportunities to learn through a variety of media and types of equipment and materials?

Is there ample outdoor activity?

Is there a daily provision for routines: eating, sleeping, toileting, play?

Is the major emphasis in activities on concrete experiences?

Are the materials and equipment capable of stimulating and sustaining interest?

Are field trips offered?

Do children have a chance to be alone? In small groups? In large group?

Tools for program evaluation, then, include criteria about the teacher, the child, and the environment. They are woven together to give a more comprehensive look at the total program. The result is that the whole is greater than the sum of its parts. More is learned about the program than if teachers, children, and the environment were measured by themselves.

### Developmentally Appropriate Practices

To augment its accreditation program (see *Focus* discussion), NAEYC has developed an extensive list of publications that provide guidance in establishing and operating a program of quality. This series, *Developmentally Appropriate Practice*, provides informative, specific descriptions of early childhood programs serving children from birth through age eight. Teachers and administrators should become familiar with these documents and should use them as standards for program excellence. Material from these guidelines may be found in Chapters 11 through 14.

## HOW EVALUATIONS AFFECT AN EARLY CHILDHOOD SETTING

A useful assessment encourages positive change. It is easy to continue the same program, the same teaching techniques, even the same assessment techniques, year after year when a school is operating smoothly. Sometimes it is not clear what—or how—improvements could be made. A regular evaluation keeps a system alive and fresh.

Evaluations help give meaning and perspective to children, teachers, and programs. An assessment that helps clarify these processes brings renewed dedication and inspiration.

Assessments of children, teachers, and programs can blend together for positive results. Children and program evaluations often work in tandem, as program goals must be defined in terms of children and their growth. How well the children are doing is a measure of program success.

Teacher evaluations may relate to program assessment when they include an *upward evaluation,*

**FIGURE 10.24**  Evaluations give an overview of how children, teachers, and the environment interrelate.

or teacher evaluation of administrators. The program effectiveness is checked by the people who are responsible for its implementation.

A teacher's effectiveness is evaluated everyday by how the children respond to the environment, the schedule, teaching techniques and relationships, and each other. No more effective test exists than the dynamics of the children at work and play in a class.

As teachers, we learn to accept evaluation as a process, rather than a series of static endpoints. In doing so, we see that there can be continuity and consistency in how evaluations of the people and programs in early childhood education work together to enhance learning and growth at all levels.

## SUMMARY

Evaluation is a way of taking stock; it is an opportunity to look at how things are going. We can assess where we are now and where we want to be. A good evaluation instrument may even suggest ways to achieve our goals. A good evaluation process includes a clear purpose, knowing who and what will be evaluated, and what use will be made of the results.

Any program designed to meet the needs of children must be evaluated on a regular basis. Teachers, children, and the program must be assessed individually and then evaluated as a whole. Each supports and depends upon the other; an evaluation is a way to look at how those relationships are working. It can identify specific concerns and determine the areas of growth and potential development.

Setting goals is an important part of the evaluation process. Evaluating goals is a measure of success or lack of it. We judge whether or not we have met our goals effectively and whether or not the goals are reflective of the program.

Evaluations serve many purposes. Assessing individual children highlights their growth and potential more clearly. One method, standardized testing, is being used extensively in early childhood settings and can be misapplied and inappropriately used. Evaluation gives teachers information about their own performance and suggests ways to strengthen their teaching style. Examining the total program reveals a better picture of how all its aspects work in unison. The National Academy of Early Childhood Programs has established an accreditation system that encourages developmentally appropriate practices in settings for children from birth to eight years of age.

The process of evaluation can be positive and can encourage growth for all involved. The choice of evaluation instruments is important, as is the use made of the data collected. Programs will keep pace with their children and professional teachers if evaluation is considered an integral part of the program structure.

## REVIEW QUESTIONS

1. List three reasons for evaluation in the early childhood setting. Which do you think would be the hardest? Why?

2. What are the components of all good evaluations? What are the problems? Include some suggestions for solutions.

3. What are the reasons for assessing children's progress? How can you communicate both strengths and weaknesses to parents?

4. Describe some of the problems with standardized testing of young children. How can you address these problems if you are required to administer a standardized test to your class?

5. Who can be involved in evaluating teachers? Who would you prefer? Why?

6. How can teachers help to make their evaluation sessions productive?

7. Name three purposes of program evaluations.

8. What is the National Academy of Early Childhood Programs and how does it attempt to improve program quality?

## LEARNING ACTIVITIES

1. Does your own setting have an evaluation plan? Which of the evaluation criteria does it include?

2. Develop an informal assessment tool to evaluate children's skills in a toddler

class. Discuss how this would differ from one for a preschool, and from a school-age day care program.

3. Try to establish goals for your own growth as a professional in the following areas:

|  | Goal | Objectives/ Implementation | Timeline |
|---|---|---|---|
| Programmatic |  |  |  |
| Administrative |  |  |  |
| Staff Relations |  |  |  |
| Professional Growth |  |  |  |

Ask your supervisor or a colleague to help you make a realistic timeline for each goal.

## BIBLIOGRAPHY

Bredekamp, Sue. *Developmentally Appropriate Practice in Early Childhood Programs Serving Children From Birth Through Age 8,* expanded edition, Washington, D.C.: National Association for the Education of Young Children, 1987.

Harms, Thelma. "Evaluating Settings for Learning." In Baker, Katherine Read (ed.), *Ideas That Work Well with Young Children.* Washington, D.C.: National Association for the Education of Young Children, 1972.

Hatfield, L.M. "Inservice Evaluation in Early Childhood Education." *Young Children,* November 1981, pp. 59–65.

McLaughlin, Karen, and Sugarman, S. Personal communications, 1982.

Murphy, Carol. "Teacher Evaluation Forms." *Child Care Information Exchange,* No. 51, September 1986.

NAEYC. "Position Statement on Standardized Testing of Young Children 3 Through 8 Years of Age." *Young Children,* Vol. 43, No. 3, March 1988.

National Academy of Early Childhood Programs. *Accreditation Criteria and Procedures.* Washington, D.C.: National Association for the Education of Young Children, 1984.

Shapiro, Edna. In Boegehold, Betty D., et al., (eds.). *Education Before Five.* New York: Bank Street College of Education, 1977.

Spodek, Bernard. *Teaching in the Early Years,* 2nd Ed. Englewood Cliffs, N.J.: Prentice-Hall, 1978.

Ward, E.H., and CDA Staff. "The Child Development Associate Consortium's Assessment System." *Young Children,* May 1976, pp. 244–255.

Young-Holt, C.; Spitz, Gay; and Heffron, M.C. *A Model for Staff Evaluation, Validation, and Growth.* Palo Alto, Calif.: Center for the Study of Self-Esteem, 1983.

# SECTION 5

# THE 'MISEDUCATION' OF YOUNG CHILDREN

*David Elkind*

What is happening in the United States today is truly astonishing. In a society that prides itself on its preference for facts over hearsay, on its openness to research, and on its respect for "expert" opinion, parents, educators, administrators, and legislators are ignoring the facts, the research, and the expert opinion about how young children learn and how best to teach them.

All across the country, educational programs intended for school-aged children are being appropriated for the education of young children. In some states. . .educational administrators are advocating that children enter school at age 4. Many kindergarten programs have become full-day kindergartens, and nursery-school programs have become pre-kindergartens. Moreover, many of these kindergartens have introduced curricula, including work papers, once reserved for 1st-grade children. And in books addressed to parents a number of writers are encouraging parents to teach infants and young children reading, math, and science.

When we instruct children in academic subjects, or in swimming, gymnastics, or ballet, at too early an age, we miseducate them; we put them at risk for short-term stress and long-term personality damage for no useful purpose. There is no evidence that such early instruction has lasting benefits, and considerable evidence that it can do lasting harm.

Why, then, are we engaging in such unhealthy practices on so vast a scale? Like all social phenomena, the contemporary miseducation of large numbers of infants and young children derives from the coming together of multiple and complex social forces that both generate and justify these practices. One thing is sure: miseducation does not grow out of established knowledge about what is good pedagogy for infants and young children. Rather, the reasons must be sought in the changing values, size, structure, and style of American families, in the residue of the 1960s efforts to ensure equality of education for all groups, and in the new status, competitive, and computer pressures experienced by parents and educators in the 1980s.

# What Is Being Taught?

While miseducation has always been with us—we have always had pushy parents—today it has become a societal norm. If we do not wake up to the potential danger of these harmful practices, we may do serious damage to a large segment of the next generation....

...[T]he social revolutions of the 1960s effectively transformed our conception of out-of-home programs and of children's readiness to cope with and profit from such programs. The statistics tell the tale. In 1966, only 60 percent of 5-year-olds attended kindergarten, while in 1985, 82 percent of 5-year-olds were attending public, private, or church-sponsored kindergarten programs. Only 25 states provided aid for public kindergartens in 1965; by 1985, all 50 states were providing some form of public support for kindergarten and, increasingly, for pre-kindergarten programs as well.

The proliferation of educational programs for young children is not limited to 5-year-olds. The number of nursery schools has increased a thousandfold since 1965, and the number of licensed day-care centers has grown 234 percent between 1978 and 1985. In 1985, some 2.5 million children (39 percent) attended pre-kindergarten programs compared with only 700,000 (11 percent) in 1965. Never before in our history have so many of our infants and young children been enrolled for extended periods in regular out-of-home programs....

No authority in the field of child psychology, pediatrics, or child psychiatry advocates the formal instruction, in any domain, of infants and young children. In fact, the weight of solid professional opinion opposes it and advocates providing young children with a rich and stimulating environment that is, at the same time, warm, loving, and supportive of the child's own learning priorities and pacing. It is within this supportive, nonpressured environment that infants and young children acquire a solid sense of security, positive self-esteem, and a long-term enthusiasm for learning....

The boom in early-childhood education is, it very much appears, becoming a boom in miseducation. The extent of miseducation of young children has recently elicited a joint statement of concern by a group of national organizations involved in elementary and early-childhood education. These organizations include the Association for Childhood Education International, Association for Supervision and Curriculum Development, International Reading Association, National Association for the Education of Young Children, National Association of Elementary School Principals, and National Council of Teachers of English. [See Appendix C.] Some of the concerns mentioned in the joint statement were as follows:

- Many pre-1st-grade children are subjected to rigid formal pre-reading programs with inappropriate expectations and experiences for their level of development.

• Little attention is given to individual development and individual learning styles.

• The pressures of accelerated programs do not allow children to be risk takers as they experiment with language and internalize concepts about how language operates.

• Too much attention is focused upon isolated skill development or abstract parts of the reading process, rather than upon the integration of oral language, writing, and listening with reading.

• Too little attention is placed upon reading for pleasure; therefore children do not associate reading with enjoyment.

Each of these concerns is centered on one or another facet of miseducation, the many ways we can place children at risk for learning problems to no purpose. The potential dangers of the miseducation practices described above far outweigh any potential gains.

It is not only the schools that are introducing formal instruction to young children; parents are doing so as well. Parents have been barraged with commercial programs and books which promise them that if they follow certain procedures they can not only teach infants and young children reading and math, but also make their offspring brighter and raise their I.Q.—in a phrase, make them "superkids." . . .

Nothing new is offered in these books. . . . The authors are merely extending well-known learning principles downward to infants and young children or formalizing procedures parents use spontaneously when they interact with their offspring. There is absolutely no evidence that such teaching gives children any lasting advantage in reading or that it has any effect on a child's brightness. There is evidence, however, that too early formal instruction can do harm.

The miseducation of infants and young children is not limited to unwarranted efforts to teach them academics; it has extended to all facets of young children's development. The idea that young children can benefit from a program of formal instruction has spread to sports and to exercise, to music and gymnastics, to ballet, beauty contests, and karate. Done well, with a sensitivity to children's physical and intellectual limitations and to their psychological vulnerability, such programs need not necessarily be harmful. Nonetheless, because such programs put infants and young children in inappropriate learning situations, they also put them at risk of physical and/or psychological damage—and this despite the fact that such programs have no proven long-term benefit for youngsters. . . .

[The] study of gifted and talented people who were successful adults gives no support to the idea that early formal instruction creates intellectual giftedness or creative talent. Rather, what is consistent in these autobiographical statements [prepared by mathematicians under 40 who had won Sloan Foundation Fellowships] is that the parents of people who have attained eminence were careful not to impose their own priorities on their children but, instead, to follow each child's lead. In this regard, and in their concern with having their children be well-rounded persons, these parents are exponents of healthy, child-centered early-childhood education.

A recent study of the MacArthur Fellows reinforces [these] findings. . . .

These findings point up the fallacy of early instruction as a way of producing children who will attain eminence. Miseducation, in fact, reverses the natural order of development. With gifted and talented individuals, as with children in general, the most important thing is an excitement about and enthusiasm for learning. Skills are easily learned when the motivation is there. Miseducation, by focusing upon skills to the detriment of motivation, pays an enormous price for teaching infants and young children what amounts to a few tricks. An ounce of motivation is worth a pound of skills anytime.

Another popular argument for early instruction is that children now are intellectually more able at earlier ages because of the modern technology with which they are surrounded....

Actually, this argument has two parts, one having to do with the direct impact of technology itself and the other with the indirect effect of the information conveyed by that technology.

In response to the first half of the argument, there is no evidence that early exposure to a technology in any way accelerates mental development. The overall direct effect of technology on human nature is to extend and amplify but not alter our biological capacities....

Eyeglasses do not improve our visual system any more than a hearing aid enhances our auditory system. In the same way, a computer does not increase our ability to remember any more than using a lever makes us stronger....

Now for the second part of the argument. If technology does not directly improve our sensory or motor capacities, doesn't it do so indirectly through the information it provides? Doesn't this information improve our brains and make us more sophisticated and knowledgeable than if we did not have the technology?

To be sure, there is a point here. Children today do indeed have access to more information than did children of earlier generations. Yet many years ago John Dewey wrote that learning is the "representation of experience," by which he meant that experience, raw information, does not teach in and of itself. It is only when we talk about and reflect upon the experience or information we receive that we learn from it....

For children really to profit from the barrage of information to which they are exposed, they must also be given the time and opportunity to reflect upon that experience. Yet parents today are spending less time talking with their children than in the past....

It is all too easy for us as adults to forget just how inexperienced infants and young children really are and how much they have to learn about the world that we have already conceptualized and now take for granted....

Infants and young children are not just sitting twiddling their thumbs, waiting for their parents to teach them to read and do math. They are expending a vast amount of time and effort in exploring and understanding their immediate world. Healthy education supports and encourages this spontaneous learning. Early instruction miseducates, not because it attempts to teach, but because it attempts to teach the wrong things at the wrong time. When we ignore what the child has to learn and instead impose what we want to teach, we put infants and young children at risk for no purpose.

*DAVID ELKIND is currently Professor of Child Study and Senior Resident Scholar at the Lincoln Filene Center at Tufts University. He was formerly Professor of Psychology, Psychiatry and Education at the University of Rochester. After taking his doctorate at UCLA, Dr. Elkind spent a year as a postdoctoral fellow with David Rapaport at the Austen Riggs Center. In 1964-65 he spent a year at Piaget's Center D'Epistemologie Genetique in Geneva. He has attempted to build upon the research of Jean Piaget in the areas of cognitive and perceptual development.*

*Dr. Elkind has authored three hundred items, including research studies, review and theoretical articles, book chapters, books, and articles and children's stories for popular magazines. Among his most recent books are* Children and Adolescents: Interpretive Essays on Jean Piaget, 3rd Ed.; The Hurried Child: Growing Up Too Fast Too Soon; All Grown Up and No Place to Go; *and* Miseducation: Preschoolers at Risk. *Dr. Elkind is a consulting editor to many psychological journals, a member of ten professional organizations, and a consultant to government agencies, private foundations, state education departments, clinics, and mental health centers. He lectures extensively and has made many television appearances.*

# CHAPTER 11

## Play: The Curriculum of the Child

SOW

HMAAR
Hammner
HUMMER

## QUESTIONS for THOUGHT

- What is curriculum in the early childhood setting?
- What is developmentally appropriate curriculum?
- What is the process of developing curriculum for young children?
- What is the value of play?
- How are play and curriculum related?
- How do children learn through play?
- Why is dramatic play important to the young child?
- What is the role of the teacher?
- How do teachers support the play process?

# CURRICULUM

## What Is Curriculum?

Curriculum is considered to be one individual course of study or many courses. In elementary and secondary schools, social studies, geography, math, English, and art are part of curriculum. In an early childhood setting, curriculum consists of the art activity and language game; it is also the spontaneous gymnastics on the climbers and the song that accompanies digging in the sand. It can become, literally, everything that happens in the course of a school day.

Curriculum is the planned and the unplanned. Young children are like sponges; they absorb everything going on about them. Since they are young, the whole world is new and fresh. Therefore, children do not discriminate between what is prepared and structured for them to learn and whatever else happens to them at school. It is *all* learning.

Ira, a two-year-old, is more interested in the process of pouring milk (especially what happens after the cup is filled) than in eating and conversing at snack time.

Kindergarteners Bert and Leo become absorbed in watching a snail make its way across the sidewalk, ignoring for the moment the lesson on running relays.

Creating a good curriculum for young children is not simply a matter of practicing curriculum planning. It is a matter of understanding the process on which the practice is based. The basis of curriculum planning is an understanding of how children interact with people and materials to learn. Teachers apply what they know about children when they plan classroom activities; that is curriculum planning. It is the sum of a teacher's knowledge about children's needs, materials, and equipment, and what happens when they meet. Curriculum translates theories of education into practice.

### Two Approaches

There are two general approaches to curriculum that are common in early childhood settings. The

**FIGURE 11.1** Curriculum happens when child meets materials. (Courtesy of Dori Salladay, Eva's Little School, Sacramento, Calif.)

first is based on the premise that curriculum is everything that happens throughout the course of a day; it is all of the children's experiences as they interact with people and materials. The emphasis is on children's interests and involvement in their learning and in their ability to make constructive choices. Teachers set up the room and the yard, sometimes planning one or two activities that will invite children to participate. For the most part, teachers respond by watching and evaluating what children do and support what use children make of their experience. This is a process-oriented approach; curriculum content is apparent, but an end product or result is not the major focus. It is sometimes known as the emergent curriculum.

A second approach to curriculum development requires more formal, organized planning. Comprehensive lesson plans are developed and usually include *objectives,* the stated concepts that children will learn through this experience. These are commonly called *behavioral objectives.* The lesson plans include specific, stated, observable behaviors that children will be able to demonstrate to show that the teaching objective has been met. In other words, a behavioral objective states clearly what children will actually *do* (be able to hold scissors properly; grasp a pencil between thumb and first two fingers). If the behavioral objective is to improve fine motor skills, the lesson plan includes activities and events that foster children's use of their fine motor skills. Several objectives may apply to a given activity. It is then important to order the objectives so that the purpose of the lesson remains in focus. To plan successfully, the teacher needs to know developmental and behavioral theory (Chapter 4), to have good observational strategies (Chapter 6), and to possess tools to assess whether or not the objective was accomplished (Chapter 10).

## Developmentally Appropriate Curriculum

Appropriate early childhood curriculum is based on the theory, research, and experience of knowing how young children develop and learn. An infant

**FIGURE 11.2** Children enjoy and get involved with developmentally appropriate materials. Finger painting is fun and a popular sensory experience. (Courtesy of Pam Briggs, Beary Best Academy, Waco, Texas.)

curriculum meets the basic needs of young babies; a toddler curriculum takes into consideration the emerging independence and mobility of toddlers. Four-year-olds require different materials and teaching techniques, as do five- or eight-year-olds. Each age level deserves special consideration when curriculum is being planned.

Just what is meant by appropriate programs, curricula, or practices? The National Association for the Education of Young Children (NAEYC) defines appropriateness in terms of developmental principles as follows:

- *Appropriateness:* Programs and practices are based on knowledge of normal development within a given age span.
- *Individual appropriateness:* Programs and practices are based on respect for the individual child, the individual rate of growth, and the unique learning style.

Developmentally appropriate curriculum is integrated curriculum, that is, woven across many subject areas. For instance, mathematical principles are not taught to the young child by formal instruction but are an integral part of the child's curriculum:

- *In music:* Singing "Five Little Pumpkins"
- *In routines:* Waiting for a turn because "too many" are brushing teeth already
- *In reading:* Reading *Inch by Inch* by Lionni
- *In block play:* Observing the fractions and wholes that make up a set of unit blocks
- *In physical development:* Playing hopscotch
- *In cooking:* Measuring and counting items in the recipe
- *In dramatic play:* Noting there are only four hoses but there are five firefighters

This is how young children learn. The principles of an integrated curriculum are depicted in the following illustrations:

- Planning the curriculum: Figure 11.3
- Using the theme of the five senses: Figure 11.4
- Use of learning objectives: Figure 11.6
- Classification: Figure 11.7
- Using the theme of castles: Figure 11.8
- Water play: Figure 11.13
- Learning through play: Figure 11.14
- Using play to develop toddlers' sensory skills: Figure 11.15
- Creating curriculum through cooking: Figure 13.5
- Developing reasoning skills: Figure 13.6
- Using the theme of dinosaurs: Figure 13.9
- Using the theme of babies: Figure 13.15
- Reading: Figure 13.20
- Using the theme "Who am I?" Figure 14.10
- Fostering cooperation through the curriculum: Figure 14.21

The NAEYC's recent position statements and guidelines on appropriate program practices and curriculum for early childhood settings can be used as a basis for sound curriculum planning. These materials cover the age span of birth through age eight; developmental characteristics unique to each age group (infants, toddlers, preschoolers, and primary ages) form the basis for determining appropriate practices. A resource of this kind should be consulted before curriculum plans are developed.

# Planning Curriculum

## Written Plans

When using either approach to curriculum, written plans are helpful, especially for the beginning teacher. A written plan is an organized agenda, an outline to follow, a framework for the curriculum. It may include a list of activities, goals for children's learning experiences, the process or method of instruction, the teacher's responsibilities, the time of day, and other special notations. A curriculum may be developed for a day, a week, a month, or for a specific unit or theme. Figure 11.4 illustrates a weekly curriculum based on the theme of the five senses.

This and the next three chapters contain many different examples of written lesson plans:

- Figure 11.3 describes in-depth planning for a single activity.
- Figure 11.4 shows a weekly curriculum based on a theme of the five senses for children aged four and five. Figure 11.15 does the same for toddlers.
- Figure 11.6 stresses learning objectives in planning for young children.
- Figure 11.7 and Figure 14.21 both look at a specific skill and demonstrate how it is integrated throughout the curriculum.
- Figure 12.16 matches motor skills to specific activities in a theme of *Cinco de Mayo*.
- Figure 13.9 shows how to use the theme of dinosaurs to enhance cognitive development.

- Figure 14.10 illustrates the way a theme may be integrated throughout the curriculum and adapted to all activity centers.
- Figure 14.20 shows a week-long plan for developing social skills through specific small group experiences.
- Figure 14.28 develops a science theme for both indoors and out-of-doors.

Activity _____

 1. Brief description _____
 _____

 2. What will the teacher's role be? _____
 _____

 3. What will the children do? _____
 _____

Where in the room/yard will this be set up? _____
_____

How many children will participate at once? _____
_____

How will the activity be limited to the desired number of children? _____
_____

What equipment and materials are needed? _____
_____
_____

How much time will this activity require? Where in the daily schedule will it take place? _____
_____

Why was this activity selected? What are the learning objectives? _____
_____
_____

List comments and questions that will help involve children in the activity and enrich their experience. _____
_____

List any related projects that might expand this as a learning experience (activities, books, accessories, etc.) _____
_____
_____
_____

What are the clean-up provisions? Will children be involved? _____
_____
_____

**FIGURE 11.3**  Curriculum planning form. An example of a lesson plan outline for one activity. Good planning takes time and thought. See Chapter 10, page 284 for a follow-up form to evaluate the activity. (Adapted from Vassar College Nursery School.)

In each of these plans, the teacher started with an objective—a goal or desired result. The objective may be for the child to learn a specific skill or concept in an intentional way, to sequence a series of nature activities for a month, or simply to list what children will be doing in art for the next week.

Two important factors in developing curriculum objectives are (1) how much knowledge and understanding children have, and (2) what children are interested in. The most effective curriculum grows out of the child's interests and experiences. As they play, children reveal their levels of experience and information as well as their misconceptions and confusions, providing the clues from which teachers can develop curriculum that is meaningful.

> . . . Curriculum derives from several sources: the child, the content, and the society. The curriculum in early childhood programs is typically a balance of child-centered and content-centered curriculum . . . Good preschools present rich content in a curriculum that is almost entirely child-centered . . . [in] the primary grades the emphasis on content gradually expands as determined by the school, the local community, and the society. The challenge . . . is to ensure that the content of the curriculum is taught so as to take optimum advantages of the child's natural abilities, interests, and enthusiasm for learning.

(Bredekamp, 1988)

Setting lesson plans to paper has many advantages. Doing so:

- Helps teachers focus on the nature of the children they teach—their interests, their needs, their capabilities, their potential.

- Encourages thorough, in-depth planning of curriculum in a logical progression; provides a direction.

- Helps teachers clarify thoughts and articulate a rationale for what they do.

- Stimulates teamwork when teachers plan together, sharing their ideas and resources.

- Allows everyone to know what is happening; in case of absences, a substitute teacher can carry out the plans.

- Gives a foundation from which changes can be made; allows for flexibility, adaptation, and on-the-spot decisions.

- Allows for time to prepare materials, to see what is needed and what resources to gather or contact.

- Provides a concrete format from which evaluation and assessment can be made.

- Serves as a communication tool for the teaching staff, for parents, and for the governing agency. Teachers see how much they have offered children, and the program's worth is communicated to others.

Written plans may or may not include all of the other activities normally available in the interest centers all week. Blocks, manipulatives, and dramatic play, as well as science, math, and language materials remain available for children to choose, but some teachers include only planned learning experiences and teacher-directed activities in their written plans. Certain activities are part of the everyday routine. The more focused (and probably written) planned learning experiences are integrated with them to provide challenge and variety.

## Teacher Considerations

The aim of curriculum is to help children acquire the skills and behaviors that will promote their optimal growth physically, socially, emotionally, and intellectually. Teachers consider a number of factors in developing a curriculum to provide maximum learning opportunities.

Among these are the educational philosophy and goals of the program. A family day care provider plans activities for a few children in an intimate setting while the kindergarten teacher arranges small working groups so that the large group will not seem overwhelming. The activities should support the goals of the program and result in the goals being accomplished.

Probably the single most important determi-

Curriculum Planning for Week of _____ May 17-21 _____

Theme: _____ My Senses and Me _____

Objectives: To foster a greater understanding and awareness of the five senses through the use of various media, to have a series of positive science activities, and to experience "messy" activities in a legitimate way.

| Day | Indoors | Outdoors | Group Time | Other |
|---|---|---|---|---|
| Monday:<br><br>Sense of smell | Printing with fresh fruits and vegetables<br><br>Make scented play dough: peppermint | Identify mystery food by smells: onion, garlic, lemon, cinnamon, clove, peppers | Read: *Arthur's Nose;* discuss animal noses, which ones have strong sense of smell and why | Add scent to water table<br><br>Make popcorn<br><br>Take a Smell Walk: outside |
| Tuesday:<br><br>Sense of touch | Collage of various seeds and pods, legumes, assorted sizes and shapes | Texture walk with hands: bins of fabric, feathers, styrofoam, yarn, paper, popcorn | Read: *Going Barefoot;* touching game: touch parts of body that are soft, hairy, fat, thin, hard, soft, cool, warm | Texture puzzles<br><br>Fingerpainting<br><br>Make oobleck (cornstarch and water): outside |
| Wednesday:<br><br>Sense of sound | Make a sound mobile: a hanger with metal products | Explore variety of musical instruments: drums, bells of varying sizes and shapes | Read: *Too Much Noise;* sing *John Jacob Jingleheimer Schmidt*<br><br>Learn to sing a round *Row, Row, Row Your Boat* | Children play musical instruments<br><br>Parent volunteer plays instrument<br><br>Parade of sounds: outside |
| Thursday:<br><br>Sense of sight | Shrink art<br><br>Crayon melt<br><br>Ink blot butterflies | Use color paddles<br><br>Mix colors with water and food coloring<br><br>Use magnifying glasses with variety of objects | Read: *Little Blue and Little Yellow*<br><br>Discuss eyebrows, eyelashes, tears<br><br>Use braille sample, talk about being blind | Display of items that help us see in the dark<br><br>Mix two colors of dough<br><br>Shadow games: outside |
| Friday:<br><br>Sense of taste | Collage of food products: popcorn, dry macaroni, peas, legumes | Make ice cream<br><br>Make fruit salad<br><br>Make vegetable salad | Read: *The Very Hungry Caterpillar;* show pictures of pig, chicken, cow; identify where milk, eggs, meat come from | Identify tastes: salty, sweet, sour, bitter, no taste |

**FIGURE 11.4**  A unit approach to curriculum planning for four- and five-year-olds. Are the activities developmentally appropriate? Is the theme meaningful? Are the objectives realistic and achievable?

nant the teacher must consider is the children themselves. Their ages, developmental levels, individuality, and learning styles are barometers of what will be successful and stimulating curriculum. The number of children in the class will affect the teacher's planning, as will their ethnic and cultural backgrounds. Teachers like to plan curriculum experiences that draw on children's prior knowledge and experience, but which also extend their thinking.

Effective curriculum planning stems from a knowledge of young children. Teachers ask themselves what concepts children should learn and how they will teach those concepts. What does the child already know, and how can the teacher build on that? What is the most effective way to teach a particular concept to this group of children—through sensory exploration or large-muscle practice? In many ways, teachers start at the end: they look at what they want the child to accomplish or to learn as a result of this experience and then plan the curriculum to lead toward those results.

Planning for a broad range of developmental skills and interests is a key factor in creating a classroom curriculum. Because the abilities of children even of the same age vary, activities must be open-ended and flexible enough to be used by a number of children with varieties of skills. Remember, too, that some children may not be interested in formal or organized art projects or science experiences. These children may learn more easily through self-selected play: by wearing a space helmet and fantasizing a trip to the moon, by building with blocks for long periods, or by running and climbing out of doors. The developmental Word Pictures of children from birth through age eight found in Chapter 3 can be useful in determining what kinds of activities appeal to young children.

All activities—expecially those that are planned and formal—should be conducted in an atmosphere of play that offers the children options in choosing what they need to learn.

A *prerequisite* for planning is the availability of people and material resources and ways to use them. What are the strengths of the teaching staff? Are there enough supplies and equipment available? Are there enough adults to supervise the activities?

The amount of time available in the daily schedule and the amount of space in the room or yard affect a teacher's planning. Fingerpainting requires time for children to get involved, a proximity to water for cleanup, and an area in which to store wet paintings. All of these elements must be considered when teachers plan to include fingerpainting in the curriculum.

## Guidelines for Planning Curriculum

The process of developing curriculum is the process of teaching children who and what they are. It begins with understanding what goals are set for learning and then choosing the most pressing ones for attention. Using available resources, teachers plan effective curriculum for young children. The five steps below are guidelines to sound curriculum planning.

1. *Set goals.* Decide what it is you want children to learn. What do you want them to know about themselves? Others? The world? State goals clearly, preferably in behavioral terms so results can be measured.

2. *Establish priorities.* Make a list of three to five goals or objectives you consider most important. State the reasons for your choices; your own values and educational priorities will emerge more clearly.

3. *Know the resources.* A rich, successful, and creative curriculum relies on a vast number of resources. To create a health clinic in the dramatic play area, for instance, you might need the following resources:

   - *Materials:* Props, such as stethoscopes, X rays, tongue depressors, band aids, medical gowns, and masks.

   - *People:* Parents and/or community people in the health care professionsl to visit the class.

   - *Community:* Field trips to nearby clinics, hospitals, dentist's office.

4. *Plan ahead.* Set aside a regular time to meet for

curriculum planning. This may be on a weekly, monthly, or seasonal basis. Discuss the curriculum activities as well as the daily routines in order to integrate the two.

**5.** *Evaluate.* Reflect on the outcome of your planning. Consider what worked and what did not, why it was successful or not. Look at the part of the experience that did not work as well as you would have liked. How can it be improved? What can you change about it? An evaluation should be immediate, precise, and supportive. Teachers need feedback about their planning and implementing skills. By refining and improving the curriculum, the needs of children are better served.

# Curriculum Focus

Curriculum, as defined here, is all-encompassing. How then do teachers select from all the possibilities that afford the potential for learning? How do teachers begin to focus on projects and activities in a balanced, integrated way? Three common approaches are to look at (1) the activity or learning centers in the classroom; (2) the skills of the children; and (3) themes.

## Classroom Activity Centers

The activity centers in most early childhood programs consist of:

| Indoors | Outdoors |
|---|---|
| Creative arts | Climbing equipment |
| Blocks | Swings |
| Table toys/manipulatives | Sand/mud/water |
| Science/discovery | Wheel toys |
| Dramatic play | Woodworking |
| Language arts/books | Hollow blocks |
| Math | Music |
| Music | Nature/science |

All of these centers offer activities and materials for children to choose from during free play time—the

**FIGURE 11.5** Teachers of toddlers encourage touching and feeling, simple problem solving, and choosing play materials. They remain patient as children explore the environment. (Courtesy of Trinity Preschool, New York, N.Y.)

greatest portion of their school day. Paints are in the easel trays, puzzles on the tables, dress-up clothes and props in the housekeeping/dramatic play center, blocks and accessories in the block corner, and books and tapes in the language area. Teachers plan the resources and materials and place them so that children readily see the alternatives available to them. Some of these activities might be teacher-directed on occasion: cooking snacks in the housekeeping area, fingerpainting in art, creating castles with blocks. For the most part, however, these activities will be self-initiating and child-directed. At all times, the emphasis will be on providing a child-centered curriculum.

Whatever the area, it needs attention and planning. Wherever children are present, learning and playing will take place. Since each play space will make a contribution to children's experiences, teachers should develop appropriate curriculum for that learning area. Figure 11.6 demonstrates curriculum potential, both indoors and out.

## Children's Skills

Just as curriculum can be developed by focusing on the activity or learning centers, so, too, can an early childhood program be planned around the skill levels of the children in the class.

The first decision teachers must make concerns what particular skill they wish to help children develop. The skill can be in the area of physical, cognitive, language, creative, social, or emotional development. The nature of the individual class and the program philosophy will help teachers establish priorities for these skills. Teachers then select the activities and materials that will enhance the development of any one or more of those particular skills. Figure 11.7 shows how the cognitive skill of classification can be implemented in the classroom, making it the focus of the entire curriculum.

## Themes

A common method of developing curriculum is to focus on themes also known as units. While used interchangeably, themes are generally a smaller part of a unit allowing for a more specific focus. For example, a unit on the body may have "What I can do with my hands" as one theme. This mode of planning is used in many early childhood and elementary settings; it is often a way to emphasize holidays. Focusing on themes, however, can and should be much more than that.

Themes that are of great interest to young children are those that directly concern themselves. The body as a theme suggests many avenues for development; body parts may be emphasized; exploration using the senses may be stressed; measuring and weighing children may be used to demonstrate growth of the body. Another subject to which children readily respond is that of home and family. Animals, especially pets, are appealing to young children and can lead into further curriculum areas of wild animals, prehistoric animals, and so on.

The more in touch with children the teachers are, the more their classroom themes should reflect the children's interests and abilities. Children who live in Silicon Valley in California, in Houston, Texas, or in central Florida will have a local interest in space shuttles and computers. The urban child of New York, Detroit, or Washington, D.C., will relate more readily to themes about subways, taxis, and tall buildings. Children's interests often focus on, but are not necessarily limited to, what they have experienced. By choosing themes that coincide with children's daily lives, teachers promote connected and relevant learning.

Television, travel, and older brothers and sisters enlarge a child's vision so that the themes a teacher chooses do not have to reflect only the world in which the child lives. With appropriate visual aids and manipulative materials, a child in the sunbelt can experience snow and ice *vicariously* or enjoy learning a song and dance from Spain.

Some themes in an early childhood setting can address children's own issues. All young children share similar fears and curiosity about the world they do not know but imagine so vividly. The cues children give, particularly about their concerns, suggest to the observant teacher some important themes of childhood. During Halloween, for example, it can be helpful and reassuring to children if the theme of masks is developed. Select some masks that have a function, such as hospital masks, ski masks, safety glasses, sun glasses, snorkel masks, or wrestling and football helmets. Children can try them on and become comfortable with the way their appearance changes. They can laugh with friends as they look in the mirror to see how a mask changes the appearance but does not change the person.

Prehistoric animals are another theme that calls attention to the natural world and deals with issues of monsters, both real and imaginary. Learning about sea animals and the ocean can give young children an opportunity to talk about the wild and noisy waves, sharks, and just getting their faces wet in salty water.

Through holiday themes, teachers can reinforce the multicultural nature of the curriculum. Ethnic, national, and religious holidays from all over the world help children celebrate the differences and similarities in people and their heritage. Themes

| Learning Objectives | Area | Activity |
|---|---|---|
| | OUTDOORS | |
| Observing/finding materials; experimenting (Why does the leaf stick and not the pine cone?) | Art | Use nature material for collage |
| Counting nails, hammers, C-clamps; classifying (Which nail will go into the redwood, the pine, the plywood?) | Small toys/ manipulatives | Woodworking |
| Locomotion; force/physics; change in matter (What happens when the sand is wet? Can I carry, pull, slide, push it the same as when it is dry?) | Science | Wet or dry sand |
| Communication/observation; reasoning and problem solving (What is the nest made of? Where do birds find the materials for it? How do young birds learn how to fly?) | Language arts | Discovering birds' nests |
| Social conflict resolution; acting out people, places; symbolic representation (using a map) | Dramatic play | "Camping out" dramatic play accessories |
| | INDOORS | |
| Tactile stimulation; awareness of textural design, small-motor coordination; use of imagination | Art | Painting with corn cobs |
| Creating an awareness of body parts and their use; small-muscle coordination, awareness of body and clothing; identification of body parts, self, clothing | Small toys/ manipulatives | Flannel board cutouts in adult and children's shapes with clothes to dress them |
| Learning about cause/effect relationship; small-muscle development; language development; awareness of milk by-products | Science | Making butter |
| To stimulate discussion about weather and seasons; differences between hot and cold climates; to compare and contrast seasons; vocabulary words related to temperature | Language arts | Read *Katy and the Big Snow, The Snowy Day* |
| To experiment with other roles; to reinforce letter concepts; to encourage social interaction; to learn about the mail process | Dramatic play | Post office and office dramatic play accessories |

**FIGURE 11.6**  Learning objectives may be the focus of curriculum planning. They define the goal and describe the desired behavior or outcome.

relating to children's cultural and ethnic backgrounds and their neighborhood environments also provide rich curriculum potential.

The following description of a unit based on castles, written by a teacher of four- and five-year olds, traces the evolution of the idea over a two-month period. The unit originated with a school event based on children's ethnic and cultural heritage. Its scope was then enlarged to encompass additional interests of the children and the teacher's sensi-

tive integration of real-life experiences. Figure 11.8 uses a chart to outline the various learning areas contained in this same unit employing a castle theme.

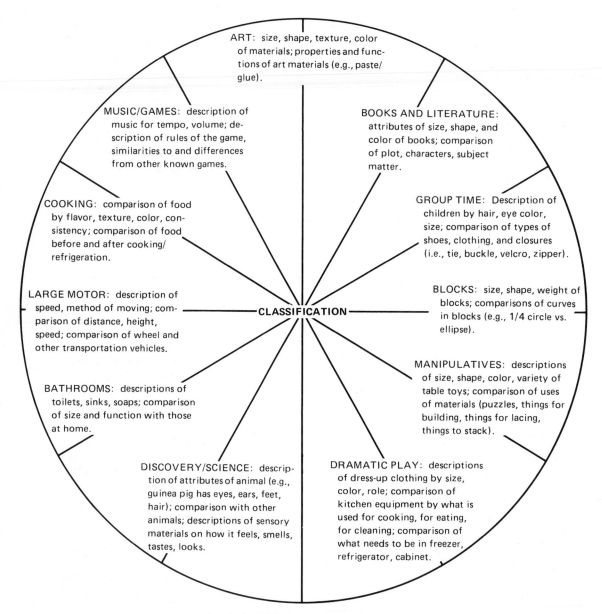

**FIGURE 11.7** Curriculum can be developed with a focus on a particular skill. Classification skills can be enhanced throughout the curriculum and in activity centers.

**FIGURE 11.8** A rich curriculum can be developed from ideas based on children's family history and cultural background. In this unit, children will gain a greater understanding and awareness of the world and a sense of pride in their own history. What else would you add to develop the activities areas further?

## The Castle Unit

This unit took place over a two-month period. It originated with our International Fete Celebration, a party held at the school to celebrate the children's individual ethnic backgrounds. The parents brought ethnic foods and set up displays depicting their countries of origin. The entire school participated. Tickets were sold and the proceeds went to our twin school in Nicaragua.

We wanted to integrate the theme of castles with concepts such as houses, maps, and countries. We started with maps of the country of origin. Germany, England, and France were dominant. One of the children had recently visited England and France, where she had seen a number of castles. She returned to school busily making crowns and teaching the other children to make them. We naturally moved into the castle theme. We read books about castles, the geography of a good castle location, how to build them, the customs of castle living, the

ecology of castles. We learned that castle waste was thrown into the moat; the idea was "dirty your castle and move on to a clean one." A staff was left behind to clean up the castle. We brought this up to date by comparing the castle to our planet, seeing that once you dirty this planet you can't move on to a new one."

We read "Farmer Giles of Ham," a Tolkien story about castles, dragons, kings, knights, and giants. We paraphrased it, broke it into chapters, and read it piece by piece.

We visited a castle in Central Park. The children designed a lot of castles in block building. We then moved on to our individual homes—where we live now—and to "my home as my castle."

We also read the African Masai tale "Who's in Rabbit's House" as retold by the Aardemas. We later made masks and performed this story as it would have been told by the storyteller and villagers in Africa. (Contributed by Judith Caden, Trinity Preschool, New York City, 1988.)

# CURRICULUM EXPRESSED THROUGH PLAY

## What Is Play?

Play! What a wonderful word! It calls up images from the past, those childhood years when playing was the focus of our waking hours. "Will you play with me?" is one of the most expressive, expectant questions known. It carries with it hope and anticipation about a world of fun and make-believe, a world of adventure and exploration, a world of the young child.

Elizabeth Jones expresses a pertinent and timeless view of play in the following *Focus*.

**FIGURE 11.9** Planning for physical skills is part of good curriculum development. (Courtesy of Craig Kessler.)

---

### F O C U S

# WHAT'S THE POINT OF PLAY?

*Elizabeth Jones*

*Bianca:* "This is our new house." She looks around. "Oh, my baby's coughing up blood. (Laughing) She's coughing up green...red blood."

*Marquita:* "Here's the doctor."

*Bianca:* "I have to lie down. I'm sick too."

• • •

*Michael:* "Get out!"

*Bianca:* "Speak nice to me. Like my funny hat?"

• • •

*Bianca* (alone, playing with Legos®: "This airplane has guns. BRRR! BRRR!"

• • •

*Bianca:* "I don't want you to play. My bear!"

*Michael:* "I got the bear."

*Bianca:* "I'm going to find the other bear."

*Michael* (on phone): "911...Hello, I need...yes, of course her sick. Hello."
(to Bianca): "They are going to come in 15 minutes."

*Bianca:* "O.K."

*Michael* (on phone again): "I need paramedics."

*Marquita to Michael:* "Can you tie this?"

*Michael:* "I *can* tie."

*Bianca:* "I can't, I'm dead."

• • •

*Bianca to Glory Beth:* "You can't play. You can't play. I'm the boss of the house. I can say who can play and who can't. Get out! Don't do that! And I mean it!"

*Bianca to Marquita:* "You are in the game. I'm the sweetheart, I'm the baby." (Observed by Barbara Creaser)

What's the point of play? It's how children reconstruct their world in order to understand and master it. To be a child is to be little and powerless; someone big is always in charge, telling you what to do. In play the child is in charge. Bianca can build an airplane all by herself and, if she chooses, shoot its guns. Michael can call the paramedics and they'll come in 15 minutes. Bianca can be the boss of the house and say who can play and who can't.

In play, children are autonomous; they're independent. They make the decisions, solve the problems, deal with the consequences. As Piaget has said, autonomy should be the aim of education, and to understand is to invent. In play, children are autonomous inventors.

What's play? Choosing for oneself. As an adult, you probably engage in some kinds of play that other adults would never do unless they were forced to (in which case it wouldn't be play for them). Maybe jog, dance or shop. Maybe you do jigsaw puzzles, surf, sing, or knit. It's play because *you* decide to do it, and when, and for how long, and with whom. If someone started telling you how to do it, or to do it because it's good for you, it wouldn't be play any more.

But if children are just playing, how will they ever learn? Each child learns by asking his or her own next questions and trying out the answers. Often both the questions and the answers take the form of actions rather than words; children learn by doing. If I stand this long block on end, will I have a skyscraper or a crash? If I pick up your bear, will you be the daddy or will you hit me? If I set the table with this many plates, how many cups do I need to go with them so all my dolls can have coffee?

Reading, writing, and arithmetic all begin with play. The child who pretends a doll is a baby is making something stand for something else: that is, the doll is a symbol. The child who is drawing is also inventing a symbol system: marks on paper to represent a house. The word *house* is a symbol, too: a more abstract way of representing a house. Understanding proceeds slowly from concrete to abstract, at each child's own rate of growth. If young children play with the real things that symbol systems represent, and if they have access to symbol-making tools like pencils and paper, they will grow in their understanding of words and numerals without being interrupted, and often confused, by formal teaching.

To learn through play, children need choice: materials, space, permission, and time—lots of time, to start when they're ready and stop when they're finished. There's no need to hurry children in preschool. If we slow down and listen, we can share the children's discovery of their world.

*Elizabeth Jones teaches human development at Pacific Oaks College.*

City streets, parks and fields, tenements, huts, empty rooms, and backyards are all settings for play. Play is a way of life for children; it is their natural response. It is what children *do* and it is serious business to them. Any activity children choose to engage in is play; it is neverending.

Play is the essence of creativity in children throughout the world. Play is universal and knows "no national or cultural boundaries" (Frost, 1985).

What is play? Educators and psychologists have called play the work of childhood, a reflection of the child's growth, the essence of the child's life, a window into the child's world. It is a self-satisfying activity through which children gain control and come to understand life. Play teaches children about themselves; they learn how tall—or short—they are, what words to use to get a turn on the swing, and where to put their hands when climbing a ladder. Through play, children learn about the world: what the color purple is, how to make matzoh balls, and how to be a friend. Play helps children define who they are.

**FIGURE 11.10** Play: The essence of childhood. (Courtesy of Trinity Preschool, New York, N.Y.)

Play takes many forms. Children play when they sing, dig in the mud, build a block tower, or dress up. Play can be purely physical (running, climbing, ball throwing) or highly intellectual (solving an intricate puzzle, remembering the words to a song). Play is creative when crayons, clay, and fingerpaint are used. Its emotional form is expressed when children pretend to be mommies, daddies, or babies. Skipping rope with a friend, playing jacks, and sharing a book are examples of the social side of play.

## Types of Play

There is a general sequence to the development of social play. Babies and toddlers have a clearly defined social self. Infant play begins with patterns established at birth: babies gaze, smile, and make sociable sounds in response to the quality and frequency of attention from a parent or caregiver. Socialization of infants occurs through interaction. By the end of their first year, infants smile at and touch one another and vocalize in a sociable effort (Charlesworth, 1987). Toddlers play well on their

own (*solitary play*) or with adults. They begin solitary pretend play around one year of age. During the toddler years, as children become more aware of one another, they begin to play side by side, without interacting (*parallel play*). They are aware of and pleased about the other person, but are not directly involved with them. It is during this second year that toddlers begin some form of *coordinated play,* doing something with another child. This is similar to the preschooler's *associative play.* The preschool years bring many changes for children in relation to social development. The number and quality of relationships outside the home increases as does the ability to play with other children. At first, this is accomplished just by a child's presence in a group: playing at the water table with four other children or joining a circle for fingerplays (*associated play*). When children join forces with one another in an active way, when they verbalize, plan, and carry out play, *cooperative play* is established. This is the most common type of peer interaction during these preschool years. Figure 11.11 shows a timeline of social play development.

Most play is unstructured and happens naturally when the curriculum is designed for play. *Spontaneous play* is the unplanned, self-selected activity in which children freely participate. Children's natural inclinations are toward play materials and experiences that are developmentally appropriate. Therefore, when they are allowed to make choices in a free play situation, children will choose activities that express their individual interests, needs, and readiness levels.

*Dramatic play*—or imaginative play—is a common form of spontaneous play. Three- and four-year-olds are at the peak of their interest in this type of activity. In dramatic play, children assume the roles of different characters, both animate and inanimate. Children identify themselves with another person or thing, playing out situations that interest or frighten them. Dramatic play reveals children's attitudes and concepts toward people and things in their environment. Much of the play is wishful thinking, pretending great strength and deeds. This is the way children cope with their

Infant play is solitary. (Courtesy of Lynda Spahr, Asbury College, Fla.)

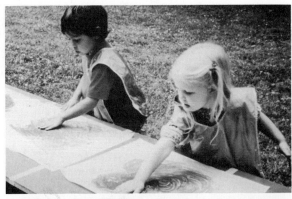

Associative play: nearby but alone.

Parallel play: side by side. (Courtesy of Trinity Preschool, New York, N.Y.)

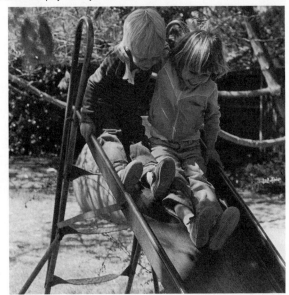

Joining forces in cooperative play.

**FIGURE 11.11**    A timeline of social play.

smallness or lack of strength. Superhero play is appealing, since it so readily addresses a child's sense of helplessness and inferiority. Pretending to be Wonder Woman makes it easier to understand and accept the limitations of the real world. Dramatic play provides the means for children to work out their difficulties by themselves. By doing so, they become free to pursue other tasks and more formal learning. For all these reasons, play is invaluable for young children.

## Values of Play

In their classic book, *Understanding Children's Play* (1952), Hartley, Frank, and Goldenson define

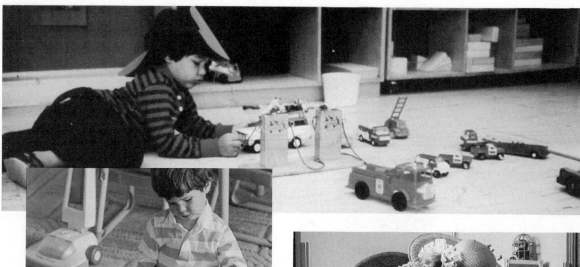

Courtesy of Susan Thibodeau, College of Notre Dame of Md.

**FIGURE 11.12** Dramatic play reaches its peak in the preschool years.

eight functions of play:

- to imitate adults
- to play out real-life roles in intensive ways
- to reflect home relationships and real-life experiences
- to express pressing needs
- to release unacceptable impulses
- to reverse roles usually taken
- to mirror growth
- to work out problems and experiment with solutions

The main theme of these functions is the emotional release they provide children. Play becomes a suitable outlet for expressing negative feelings, hostility, and aggression. Clay can be pounded, balls can be kicked and thrown, dolls can be spanked. Young children

Courtesy of John Zacher, St. Jude's Children's Research Hospital.

give free expression to a wide range of emotions, playing them out and releasing tension.

But play is more than an avenue for emotional release. Rubin, Fein, and Vandenberg (1983) cite three common factors that emerge from the many definitions of play: (1) children's feelings and motivations, (2) how children behave when they play, and (3) the environment that supports play and where play occurs. The early childhood curriculum is developed with all three aspects of play in mind.

Why do children play? Why is play so universal

to childhood experiences? One answer may be that play is intrinsically motivated, that is, it is naturally satisfying to children. Rubin and associates suggest other reasons as well:

- Play is relatively free of rules except for what children will impose themselves.
- Play is controlled and dominated by the children.
- Play is carried out *as if* the activity were real life.
- Play focuses on the activity—the doing—rather than on the end result or product.
- Play requires the interaction and involvement of the children.

Play promotes learning for the whole child as well. A wide range of learning opportunities are inherent in any single play activity. Water play is a popular activity in most early childhood settings. What specific learnings take place as children explore the properties of water? How are their developmental needs challenged? Figure 11.13 highlights

| Water play promotes: | By teaching children: |
|---|---|
| Emotional growth | The soothing effect of water; the pleasure of playing with a messy, sometimes forbidden medium; sensory pleasure in splashing, trickling, swirling water through fingers, hands, and feet. |
| Language development | Play with words of alliteration (swish, swirl, splish, splash); new words: funnel, eyedropper, siphon, float. |
| Creativity | New ways to store, move, and pour water. |
| Social growth | To share space at a water table as well as to share some of the equipment; to be next to or across from a friend; to have fun with others; to wait for a turn. |
| Cognitive development | Problem solving with tubes, sieves, pipes; experimenting with measurement, float and sink properties, volume, quantity, fractions, weight, comparisons, numbers, temperature. |
| Physical coordination | Eye-hand coordination; small-motor control in learning to pour, squeeze, balance. |

**FIGURE 11.13**   Water play is fun—and promotes learning.

Courtesy of Traci Marla Probst, Glenville State College.

some of the learning that is likely to occur. In water play, block play, sand or art activity, children play because they enjoy the activity. In their play they feel competent as they learn to control the environment, match the new with the known, elaborate and complicate the play, experience success, and do so with their minds, their bodies, and their hearts (Rogers and Sawyers, 1988).

All play activity holds this potential for growth and learning. Blocks, easel painting, woodworking, and clay could also be analyzed for how they contribute to the development of the child as a whole. Figure 11.14 demonstrates further the learning possibilities in all play activity.

## Play as a Cornerstone of Learning

Play is the cornerstone of learning, the foundation from which children venture forth to investigate, to test out. Curriculum takes on expression through play; teachers plan curriculum that uses play as the medium for learning. As they mature, children integrate and assimilate their play experiences. What started out as play—the sheer fun of it—is transformed into learning experiences. Curiosity about magnets at age five nourishes a scientific attitude for the later years, as well as a foundation for studying gravity, planetary movements, and the like. Feeling free to sing out at group time at age three can prepare a child to be an active participant in the kindergarten classroom at age six.

Teachers want children to learn about *themselves,* to learn about the *world around them,* and to learn how to *solve problems.* A childhood filled with play opportunities should culminate in these three types of learning.

1. *Learning about themselves* includes developing a positive self-image and a sense of competence. Children should know and feel good about themselves as learners. They should develop a sense of independence, a measure of self-discipline, and knowledge based on full use of their sensory skills.

2. *To learn about others and the world around them* means developing an awareness of other people. Teachers want children to perfect their communication and social skills so that they will be more sensitive participants in the world in which they live. This means that children learn and appreciate some of the values of their parents, the community, and society at large. When children become aware of the demands of living in today's society, it can help them become more responsible citizens. The emphasis on social interaction and group relationships in the early childhood setting underscores this goal.

3. *To learn to solve problems,* children need to be accomplished in observation and investigation. When exploring a puzzle, for example, children need to know how to manipulate it, take it apart, and put it back together, to see how other people solve puzzles, and to know how to get help when the pieces just do not seem to fit together. They should know how to predict and experiment. What will happen, wonders a kindergartener, when a glass is placed over a glowing candle? How will that change if the glass is large or small? What is the effect if the glass is left over the candle for a long time or for a second? Young children also need to learn how to negotiate, discuss, compromise, and stand their ground, particularly when they encounter and solve problems socially. "I want the red cart and someone already has it," thinks the preschooler. "Now what? How can I get it? What if the other person says no? Will the plan that works with my best friend work with someone else? When do I ask for help? Will crying make a difference?" In order to be effective problem-solvers, children must know and experience themselves and others.

## Teacher Considerations

Play is a window to the child's world and the adult who knows the value of play is committed to learning about children while they play. The vast knowledge of human development and behavior comes from researchers who spent countless hours observing and recording children playing.

COGNITIVE/LANGUAGE

Distinguishes between reality and fantasy
Encourages creative thought and curiosity
Allows for problem solving
Encourages thinking, planning
Develops memory, perceptual skills, and concept
  formation
Learns to try on other roles
Takes initiative
Acquires knowledge and integrates learning
Learns communication skills
Develops listening and oral language skills

PHYSICAL

Releases energy
Builds fine and gross motor skills
Gains control over body
Provides challenges
Requires active use of body
Allows for repetition and practice
Refines eye–hand coordination
Develops self-awareness
Encourages health and fitness

SOCIAL

Tries on other personalities, roles
Learns cooperation and taking turns
Learns to lead, follow
Builds a repertoire of social language
Learns to verbalize needs
Reflects own culture, heritage, values
Learns society's rules and group responsibility
Shows respect for other's property, rights
Teaches an awareness of others
Learns how to join a group
Builds awareness of self as member of a group
Gives sense of identification
Promotes self-image, self-esteem
Experiences joy, fun

EMOTIONAL

Develops self-confidence and self-esteem
Learns to take a different viewpoint
Resolves inner fears, conflicts
Builds trust in self and others
Reveals child's personality
Encourages autonomy
Learns to take risks
Acts out anger, hostility, frustration, joy
Gains self-control
Becomes competent in several areas
Takes initiative

**FIGURE 11.14**    Play is the cornerstone of learning.

Classroom teachers continue to learn about children by listening to and observing spontaneous play activity and planning curriculum that encourages play. They discover each child's individual personality, learning style, and preferred mode of play.

Genuine interest is one way teachers show their approval of the play process. Creating a safe environment where children feel physically and emotionally secure is another. To establish play as an important part of the curriculum, teachers must:

• *Understand*, appreciate, and value play experiences for young children.

• *Focus* on the process of learning rather than on the process of teaching.

• *Reflect* on their observations in order to know what activities, concepts, or learning should be encouraged or extended.

The two major roles of teachers in promoting spontaneous play environments are (1) as facilitators or supervisors of play, and (2) by setting the stage and creating an atmosphere for play.

### *The Teacher as Facilitator*

One of the most difficult tasks teachers face is knowing when to join children at play and when to remain outside the activity. They must ask themselves whether their presence will support what is happening or whether it will *inhibit* the play. Sometimes teachers are tempted to correct children's misconceptions during play. Abby and Salina, deeply involved in their grocery store drama, are making change incorrectly. A teacher must judge whether or not to explain the difference between nickels and quarters at that time or create an opportunity at a later date. Teachers must be aware of what happens if they interrupt the flow of play and how they influence the direction it takes. If Abby and Salina begin to talk about their coins, showing an interest in learning how to compute their change, the teacher can move into the discussion without seeming to interfere.

When do teachers interact and intervene? Many adults enjoy playing with the children in their class.

Others feel more comfortable as active observers. Every teaching situation will demand the teacher's involvement at some level. The hesitant child may need help entering a play situation; children may become too embroiled in an argument to settle it alone; play may become inappropriate, exploitative, or dominated by a particular child.

The following guidlelines are ways teachers facilitate play. A good teacher:

• Guides the play, but does not direct or dominate the situation or overwhelm children by participation.

• Capitalizes on the children's thoughts and ideas; does not enforce a point of view on them.

• Models play when necessary. Shows children how a specific character might act, how to ask for a turn, how to hold a hammer when hammering. Models ways to solve problems that involve children interacting on their own behalf.

• Asks questions; clarifies with children what is happening.

• Helps children start, end, and begin again. Gives them verbal cues to enable them to follow through on an idea.

• Focuses the children's attention on one another. Encourages them to interact with each other.

• Interprets children's behavior aloud, when necessary; helps them verbalize their feelings as they work through conflicts.

• Expands the play potential by making statements and asking questions that lead to discovery and exploration.

### *Creating the Environment for Play*

To structure the environment for play, teachers include uninterrupted time blocks in the daily schedule (at least forty-five minutes to an hour) for free-play time. This allows children to explore many avenues of the curriculum free from time restraints. It is frustrating to young children to have their play cut off just as they are getting deeply involved.

A variety of activity areas and learning centers

**Curriculum Through Play for the 1½-Year-Old**

Sensory Stimulation

Objective: To help toddlers begin to explore and understand the five senses

|  | **Activity** | **Small-Group Focus** | **Other** |
|---|---|---|---|
| Monday | Soap painting | Guessing game: textures. Distinguish soft/hard from familiar objects | Play hide-and-seek with two or three. |
| Tuesday | Water table play | Guessing game: smells. Identify familiar scents in jars. | Blow bubbles. |
| Wednesday | Fingerpainting | Guessing game: weights. Distinguish heavy/not heavy using familiar objects such as book or doll. | Talk walk to collect collage materials of different textures. |
| Thursday | Making collages of textures collected day before | Guessing game: shapes. Use puzzles of shapes and shape-sorting boxes. | Have a parade of sounds from many musical instruments. |
| Friday | Playdough | Food fest of finger foods: Try different textures, sizes, shapes, and flavors. | Make foot or hand prints on large mural paper. |

**FIGURE 11.15**    Examples of teacher-directed activities to help toddlers explore their sensory skills.

set up with specific play and learning materials provides children with choices for play. There should be enough to do so that each child has a choice between at least two play options. Established routines in the schedule add to the framework of a day planned for play. The raw materials of play—toys, games, equipment—are changed periodically so that new ones may be introduced for further challenge.

In choosing materials, teachers select dress-up clothes and accessories that appeal to all children's needs, interests, and emotions. Props are required for a variety of roles: men, women, babies, doctors, nurses, grocers, mail carriers, teachers, and fire fighters. Hats for many occupations help a child establish the role of an airline pilot, tractor driver, construction worker, police officer, or baseball player. Large purses are used for carrying mail and babies' diapers; they also double as a briefcase or luggage. Simple jackets or capes transform a child for many roles. Things that represent aspects of the

**FIGURE 11.16**    A good teacher guides the play but does not dominate the action. (Courtesy of Stephanie Barry Agnew)

child's daily life are important; children need many opportunities to act out their life stories.

For younger children, teachers make sure there are duplicates of popular materials. Group play is more likely to occur with three telephones, four carriages, eight hats, and five wagons. Social interaction is enhanced when three space shuttle drivers can be at the controls.

Play is further enlarged by materials that are *open-ended*. These are materials that will expand the children's learning opportunities because they can be used in more than one way. Blocks, a staple of the early childhood curriculum, are a case in point. Children explore and manipulate blocks in many ways. The youngest children carry and stack blocks and also enjoy wheeling them around in wagons or trucks. They also enjoy the repetitious action of making small columns of blocks. As children learn to make enclosures, they add animals, people, and transportation toys to their block play. Older preschoolers build multistoried structures as part of their dramatic play—offices, firehouses, garages, and the like.

Play is the way curriculum is expressed in the early childhood setting. The function of play in the life of a young child is more than sheer enjoyment. Play provides an avenue for growth in social, emotional, intellectual, and physical development. Teachers, aware of play as a foundation for learning, provide an atmosphere that supports the play process. They provide a setting in which play is recognized as the curriculum of the child, the primary process through which children learn. Curriculum comes alive as children discover and take pleasure in learning.

## OTHER CURRICULUM PERSPECTIVES

A sound curriculum is the *linchpin* of a quality program for children. Curriculum planning and development is a creative act, one that is rewarding for teachers. In the next three chapters, curriculum implementations will be explored from another perspective, that of the major areas of development in the child's growth. In Chapter 12, the focus will be on how curriculum affects the growing body. Chapter 13 will emphasize the curricular role in developing the mind, and Chapter 14 will explore the curricular issues surrounding social and emotional growth.

## SUMMARY

Curriculum encompasses the planned and unplanned events children experience in group settings. Curriculum can include whatever happens to a child while in school or day care, or it can be a syllabus with detailed lesson plans.

Developing curriculum includes setting goals, establishing priorities, knowing what resources are available, planning ahead, and then evaluating the process. As teachers develop their curriculum plans, they may focus on the classroom activity or learning centers, the skills of the children, or a particular theme. All three lend themselves to a basis for curriculum planning, and all are important vehicles for creative and effective curriculum for young children.

## R E V I E W   Q U E S T I O N S

1. Define developmentally appropriate curriculum for early childhood programs. What two principles determine whether or not curriculum is "appropriate"? Describe the difference between infant/toddler and preschool curriculum.

2. Name five steps to effective curriculum planning.

3. How are written curriculum plans useful to the beginning teacher?

4. How is play beneficial to the child's development?

5. Define four stages of play.

6. How are reading concepts learned when children play (a) in the sand area; (b) easel painting; (c) on the climbers; (d) during housekeeping dramatic play?

## L E A R N I N G   A C T I V I T I E S

1. Consult Figure 11.4. Add two columns on Music and Math. Develop curriculum for the week, with five senses as a theme, in these two areas.

2. Develop a curriculum for a week-long celebration: (a) for three-year-olds in a half-day nursery school; (b) for six-year-olds in an after-school extended day program; (c) for a family day care home. Use a non-holiday theme.

3. What do you think of superhero play in the preschool years? Research recent articles on the subject and prepare to present an argument for or against this type of play. Ask a classmate to prepare an opposing viewpoint.

4. Observe teachers as children play. What is the difference in the play when (1) a teacher interacts with children in their play and (2) a teacher intervenes? What happens to the play immediately after teacher contact is made? How long does the play last? What is your conclusion?

5. Develop a dramatic play kit for your school. Select a theme and collect appropriate props and accessories. Describe why you chose this theme and what you expect children to gain from this experience.

6. Describe a series of activities, to be used over several months, to enhance (a) infant social development and (b) motor development.

## B I B L I O G R A P H Y

Bredekamp, Sue (ed.). *Developmentally Appropriate Practice in Early Childhood Programs Serving Children From Birth Through Age 8,* expanded edition. Washington, D.C., National Association for the Education of Young Children, 1987.

Cataldo, Christine Z. *Infant and Toddler Programs.* Reading, Mass.: Addison-Wesley, 1983.

Charlesworth, Rosalind. *Understanding Child Development.* Albany, N.Y.: Delmar, 1987.

Fein, Greta, and Rivkin, Mary (eds.). *The Young Child at Play—Reviews of Research,* Vol. 4. Washington, D.C.: National Association for the Education of Young Children, 1986.

Frost, J.L., and Sunderlin, S. (eds.). *When Children Play.* Wheaton, Md.: Association for Childhood Education International, 1985.

Hartley, Ruth E.; Frank, Lawrence K.; and Goldenson, Robert M. *Understanding Children's Play.* New York: Columbia University Press, 1952.

McKee, Judy Spitler (ed.). *Play: Working Partner of Growth.* Wheaton, Md.: Association for Childhood Education International, 1986.

Rogers, Cosby S., and Sawyers, Janet K. *Play in the Lives of Children.* Washington, D.C.: National Association for the Education of Young Children, 1988.

Rubin, K.H.; Fein, G.G.; and Vandenberg, B. "Play." In E.M. Heatherington (ed.), *Handbook of Child Psychology,* vol. 4. Socialization, Personality and Social Development. New York: Wiley, 1983.

Schwartz, Sydney L., and Robison, Helen F. *Designing Curriculum for Early Childhood.* Boston: Allyn and Bacon, 1982.

# CHAPTER 12

## Planning for the Body: Physical/ Motor Development

# INTRODUCTION

Teachers often characterize children through their movements. Movements are one of the most notable features of young children's behavior. Pregnant mothers are aware of fetal motions and often assign personality traits to their children by these movements. What is striking about newborns is the extent of their full-bodied, random movements when they cry, roll over, follow, and reach for a crib mobile. Learning to walk is a major milestone in a child's development. Holding a pencil, cutting with scissors, tying a shoe are further illustrations of how motor development signifies growth. Motor skills are a good indication of how the child is progressing.

Basic motor skills develop in the early childhood years. As in other areas of development, by six or seven years of age, most motor skill development has been accomplished. These years form the foundation for movement and motor proficiency. Though skills will improve throughout a lifetime, it is generally believed that after the early years, no new basic skills will be added to children's movement repertoire (Malina, 1982).

## Learning Through Movement

Motor abilities affect other areas of development. Recent research reinforces this notion. Malina (1982) claims that motor development greatly affects "the child's cognitive development, the child's own self-discovery, and the child's ability to communicate." There is evidence of such interrelationships in children.

Tim is reluctant to climb outside. He is easily frightened when he—or anyone else—is up in a tree or on any climber. Because he cannot risk using his body in space, he stops himself from playing with anyone who invites him to try these activities. Thus, Tim's lack of gross-motor development is affecting his social skills.

Samantha loves to draw and cut. She chooses the art area every day she attends the two-year-old class. Not only are her fine motor skills well

developed for her age, she takes great pride in her creations. Her motor skills enhance her self-confidence in school. In turn, she receives praise and attention from others as she communicates with both adults and children through her work.

The greatest portion of the young child's day is spent in physical activity. Quality early childhood programs recognize this, providing for a full range of physical and motor experiences. Indoors, children use puzzles, scissors, and dressing frames as they practice fine motor skills. They dance with scarves and streamers to music. *Perceptual-motor development,* as with body awareness, occurs when children learn songs and games ("Head and Shoulders, Knees and Toes" or "Mother May I Take Two Giant Steps?") or while fingerpainting. Outdoors, gross motor skills are refined by the use of climbers, swings, hopscotch, and ring-toss.

Throughout the program, physical/motor development is emphasized as an important part of children's learning. Children will need time as well as equipment and and activities to practice their skills. The value teachers place on physical/motor development is directly related to the time allotted in the daily schedule for children to pursue them.

For years, early childhood programs have made an outdoor environment available to children, assuming a great need for physical activity and that children will find ways to fill that need themselves. However, many school outdoor areas contain few challenges, perhaps only a blacktop for bouncing balls and a small, metal climber for hanging and climbing. Moreover, American children are exposed to a value system in which physical/motor fitness is not always a high priority. Children live with adults whose primary sport is as spectator only, and they are often encouraged toward *sedentary* activities themselves at an early age, such as watching TV and using computers.

Physical/motor development is the central focus of the needs and interests of young children; it should play a central role in planning the curriculum. Teachers must recognize that children have different needs from adults; they are growing, developing, emerging beings with a set of physical needs and interests that are quite different. Too often, adults try to develop miniathletes without first developing the child's fundamental movement activities.

# PHYSICAL GROWTH/ MOTOR DEVELOPMENT

## Physical Growth

According to Bee (1985), an understanding of physical development is important to teachers and parents for a number of reasons. For example:

- New behavior is made possible through physical change: a toddler can be toilet-trained once anal sphincter muscles develop.
- Growth determines the child's experiences: observe the new vistas that open up to the brand new walker.
- Growth changes the way people respond to the child: the mobility of crawlers and toddlers leads to more restrictions from parents.
- Self-concepts are profoundly related to physical development: an obese kindergartener avoids the running and chasing games during recess.

**FIGURE 12.1** Children are the picture of movement, spending the greatest portion of their day in physical activity.

**FIGURE 12.2** Growth follows a predictable pattern: large muscles develop before smaller ones.

Early childhood is the time of most rapid growth, though development does not take place at an even pace, but in starts and spurts. A child will tend to grow rapidly in infancy and as a toddler, with the growth rate beginning to taper off during preschool and middle childhood years. While there are individual differences in the rate of maturation among children, growth follows a sequential pattern.

Development seems to follow a directional pattern as well. Large muscles develop before smaller ones—one reason why most preschoolers are more proficient at running than at cutting with scissors. Growth also starts at the center of the body and moves outward. Watch a toddler walk using whole-leg action and compare that with a five-year-old whose knees and ankles are involved in a more developed response. Children also tend to develop in a head-to-toe pattern. Infants move their eyes, head, and hands long before they learn to creep or crawl.

Tremendous growth takes place just within the first two years of life and continues through the

| Age | Weight | Height | Proportion | Teeth |
|-----|--------|--------|------------|-------|
| Newborn | 7 pounds | 20 inches | Head = ¼ of length | None |
| Infancy (up to 18 mos.) | Gains 15 pounds (now 20–25 lbs.) | Adds 8 inches (now 28–29″) | About the same | 6 |
| Toddler (18 mos. to 2½ yrs.) | Gains 5 pounds (now 28–30 lbs.) | Adds another inch or two (now 29–33″) | Legs = 34% of body | 20 |
| Preschool (2½ to 5 yrs.) | About 5 pounds/yr. (now 30–40 lbs.) | Adds 14–15 inches from birth; at age 3 = ½ of adult height (now 35–40″) | Head growth slows; legs at age 5 = 44% of body | 20 |
| Early–middle childhood (5–8 yrs.) | Doubles before adolescence; (age 6 = 45–50 lbs.) | Adds 9–10 inches (age 6 = 44–48″) | Continues to move slowly towards adult proportions | Begins to lose baby teeth; replaced by permanent teeth (age 6 = 20–24) |

**FIGURE 12.3** An overview of growth shows how rapid is physical growth in childhood.

preschool years. Figure 12.3 shows an overview of these dramatic changes.

Growth is influenced by a variety of factors. Genetic makeup, disease, and injury all play a part in how children grow. Environmental influences, such as nutrition and experience, have their greatest effect during the early years.

There are gender differences as well. Boys have a larger proportion of muscle tissue than girls, and, from the beginning, girls have more fat tissue than boys. Each of these differences becomes more obvious at adolescence. In regard to physical development, girls mature earlier than boys and their growth is more regular and predictable. In motor skills, preschool girls exhibit greater skill than boys in jumping, hopping, and balancing. Elementary-school boys excell in running, jumping, and throwing (Bee, 1985).

Always, while looking at general growth patterns of children, parents and teachers must keep in mind the wide individual differences in the rates at which children grow and in the timing of each change. As a general rule, the pattern within individuals is consistent; that is, a child who is early, average or late in one aspect of physical development will be so in all aspects (Bee, 1985). Bee also found that as a group, poor children grow more slowly and are shorter than middle-class children, a finding attributed to diet. Even though the *rate* of physical development may differ, however, the *sequence* of development remains the same. This holds true even for children who are physically or mentally handicapped.

## Motor Development

Motor development consists of ''complex changes in the child's body activities and movements'' (Bee, 1985). It is a process of continuous modification based upon the interaction of (1) *maturation* (i.e., the genetically controlled rate of growth); (2) *prior experiences;* and (3) *new motor activities.* Like physical growth, motor development is a sequence of stages that is universal but still allows for individual differences. Each stage is different from, yet grows out of, the preceding level. Figure 12.4 charts motor development through the early years.

# PHYSICAL/MOTOR SKILLS IN EARLY CHILDHOOD

## Types of Movement

Physical/motor skills involve three types of movement: gross motor, fine motor, and perceptual-motor.

### Gross Motor Activity

*Gross motor* activity involves movements of the entire body, or large parts of the body. Using various muscle groups, children try to creep, crawl, roll, bounce, throw, or hop. Activities that include balance, agility, coordination, flexibility, strength, speed, and endurance foster gross motor development.

### Fine Motor Activity

*Fine motor* activity uses the small muscles of the body and its extremities (the hands and feet). Such movement requires dexterity, precision, and manipulative skill. Grasping, reaching, holding, banging, pushing, spinning, and turning are all activities that refine these skills.

### Perceptual-Motor Activity

*Perceptual-motor activity* involves both how children move (motor) and what they perceive (perceptual). As Gallahue (1976) puts it:

> The dash that appears in the term ''perceptual-motor'' signifies the interdependence of one on the other. This becomes apparent when we recognize that efficient and effective movement is dependent upon accurate perceptions of ourselves and our world and that development of one's perceptual abilities is dependent, in part, on movement.

In a sense, every movement is perceptual-motor activity, since the body and mind must work together to complete all motor tasks. The perceptual task is to process information; the motor response activates what is received in a physical way. The complex

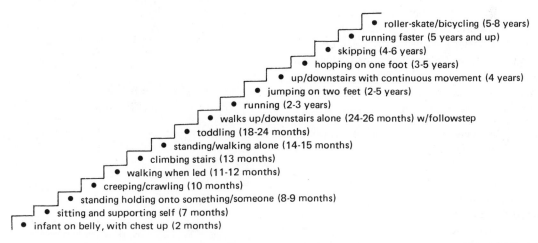

**FIGURE 12.4** Motor development follows a developmental sequence. (Adapted from Shirley [1931] in Roberton and from Shirley [1933] in Teeple [both in Ridenour, 1978].)

nature of perceptual-motor development can be seen when examining its three elements, those of spatial, temporal, and sensory awareness.

**Spatial Awareness.** For children, spatial awareness means a sense of their own bodies and the body's relationship to space, as well as a knowledge of what the body parts can do. For the toddler, concepts of spatial relationships are developed through motor activity: dropping objects from a high chair or forcing a large stuffed animal into a small box. Their definition of space is related to the action and movement involved in specific activities. A sense of relationship to less immediate things and places (knowing a specific route, making simple maps) develops in the preschool years. Not until ages six to eight do children develop the more abstract spatial ability of distinguishing left from right on their own bodies and on others'. Specifically, spatial awareness refers to left and right, up and down, front and behind. To illustrate, let us look at 2½-year-old Tamara. She demonstrates her awareness of spatial relationships as she moves herself up to a table (without bumping into it), reaches to her left to pick up a ball of clay, and turns around behind her to choose a rolling pin.

**Temporal Awareness.** Temporal awareness is the child's inner clock, a time structure that lets the child coordinate body parts. Dancing to a rhythmic beat develops this kind of skill. For instance, seven-year-old Luis and Aref ask if it is time to clean up as they finish their game of soccer. The after-school center has sports time for about an hour before cleaning up for snack; the children have an inner sense of time that parallels their knowledge of the daily schedule.

**Sensory Awareness.** Sensory awareness refers to use of the senses. It is another way the body gives the mind information. Vision is the dominant sense for young children. Auditory (hearing) skills help children process information about language. Babies seem to put everything in their mouths to learn. When four-year-old Stephanie picks up each object at the display table, she is using her sense of touch to discover size, shape, and volume.

**FIGURE 12.5** Gross motor activity uses the various large-muscle groups so that children can move their entire bodies.

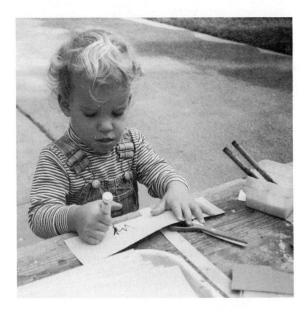

**FIGURE 12.6** Fine motor activity requires using the small muscles of the body with dexterity and precision.

**FIGURE 12.7** To learn a motor skill, children must combine memory with experience, taking advantage of opportunities to try something new and to practice what has already been learned.

# Learning Motor Skills

Children must use their bodies in order to learn motor skills. They acquire these skills by making comparisons between their past experience and new actions. Such comparisons use memory and experience.

## *Memory and Experience*

Memory plays an important part in learning motor movements, since children need to recall what they just did in order to make corrections or refinements. In the short term, the ball that does not reach the basket is tossed further on the next shot. To get the puzzle piece to fit, a child remembers other ways to manipulate the pieces. A long-term memory of movement is one that may go unrehearsed for longer periods of time. The experience of swimming, for example, may be recalled only in the summer. Whether using short-term or long-term memory, children learn motor skills by remembering what they have already learned and by practice.

The experiences children have and the ability to recall those experiences are necessary to the process of gaining motor skill. Rehearsal is as important to the young child as it is to the actors in a play. "Overt practice, repeating a specific movement over and over again, provides a motor rehearsal young children display everyday" (Clark *in* Ridenour, 1978).

## *Practicing Basic Skills*

A child's typical day, at home or at school, provides numerous opportunities to practice motor skills. Through *play,* the child can practice fine motor skills such as:

- holding a paintbrush, scissors, or rattle
- tiptoeing to music
- grasping a bottle, a hand, a toy
- threading a bead, a wide needle, a sewing board

and such gross motor skills as:

- pumping on a swing
- climbing a tree
- digging a garden
- balancing on a board, on one foot

Through *self-help activities* the child can practice fine motor skills such as:

- buttoning a coat or dolls' clothes
- brushing teeth, hair
- turning a faucet handle or doorknob
- feeding self with utensils

gross motor practice includes:

- moving a nap cot or table
- kicking covers off
- walking, holding onto furniture
- climbing into crib, bed

Children learning motor skills need experience in basic skills; they must learn simple skills before combining them into complex activities. To gain mastery over a skill, there must be an opportunity for practice. Children must have time to try, refine, and try again.

### *Feedback*

Children modify and improve their motor skills as they receive information about their movements, both *intrinsic* (the paintbrush makes marks when it is pushed across the paper) and *extrinsic* ("I notice that your legs are very far apart as you try the somersault; how about holding them together as you roll next time?").

### *A Range of Developmental Levels*

Any group of young children will have various levels of motor growth and physical development. An individual child may have different abilities and skills in gross, fine, and perceptual-motor areas; activities should, therefore, be offered on several developmental levels. Climbing boards put on several levels and puzzles ranging from six to sixty pieces are two examples of how teachers can meet the need for success and challenge.

## ROLE OF THE TEACHER

## Considerations

As teachers plan programs for physical/motor development, they reflect on several important issues.

### *Sex-Role Stereotyping*

Is motor behavior different for boys and girls? If so, why? Research indicates that there are differences between girls and boys in these areas. For example, behavioral differences in motor development are apparent in early life: one-year-old girls already spend more time in fine motor tasks, while baby boys are more engaged in gross motor activity. Preschool boys, on the average, are better in activities requiring speed or strength, while girls excel in jumping, hopping, and balancing. Yet by five or six, boys have begun to do better in most gross motor tasks (Malina, 1982).

**FIGURE 12.8** Teachers provide many opportunities to practice motor skills through finger plays, games, and songs.

Why does this happen? Probably some sex differences are the result of genetics. At the same time, sex role expectations profoundly affect the motor and physical development of young children. This is the crucial issue for teachers, for their attitudes can either encourage or discourage children from developing to their fullest potential. Teachers must acknowledge the differences that exist, and then ask themselves:

- What messages do I give children about physical activity? Do I value it for myself? For children? Do I value physical expression for girls as well as boys?

- Do I emphasize sports as a way to have fun? A way to be healthy? Do I only praise the "winner"?

- Can I provide male and female role models for physical activities using parents, grandparents, older siblings, staff, visitors, and guests?

- Do I encourage children to wear clothing that allows them the freedom to run, climb, tumble? What do I do when girls arrive in long dresses and party shoes? What should I wear?

- Are all physical/motor activities made equally available and attractive to boys and girls? What happens if some children dominate these activities, while others never choose them?

- How do I actively engage all children in every form of physical activity? Do I let them know I think it is important?

One often overlooked area is that of gross motor development as an everyday occurrence. Teachers sometimes take for granted children's progress as they walk up and down stairs, climb on and off platforms and benches, and dance with abandon. Favorite rainy-day activities such as moving around like *Tyrannosaurus rex* or spinning like a top are exercises in physical/motor development using gross motor skills. Remember that the normal classroom setting can promote physical development every day through established routines and curriculum.

## A Safe and Challenging Environment

First and foremost, teachers ensure the safety of the children. To maintain a safe physical environment, they see to it that materials and equipment are in usable condition, and that overall traffic patterns are hazard-free. For example, to make a gymnastic activity safe, teachers would provide mats and make sure that only one child is tumbling at a time.

Psychological safety requires an even finer sensitivity on the part of the teaching staff. Fear is a learned response and teachers must be careful not to discourage children from using their full range of abilities, creating overly anxious and fearful children. The new teacher is often concerned about children's safety, particularly when they are climbing. It helps to remember that children generally climb to heights that are comfortable for them; in other words, they set their own limits.

The practice of picking children up and placing them on equipment, often at their own request, is questionable. If teachers comply with children's wishes to be lifted and set somewhere high, they are placing those children in situations outside of their natural limits. The children may see this as saying, "You are incapable of climbing up there yourself," or "It is too dangerous for you to try that alone." Also, this does not allow children to gain experience

in basic skills first, but puts them in a situation that calls for skills more complex than they have at the time. This denies the child the opportunity to practice those skills. Children learn their capabilities by being held responsible for what they do. When they must seek solutions to getting up, out, in, or down, they learn to handle realistically their current level of physical and motor development. Teachers lend encouragement and confidence to children by saying, "I can't put you up there, but I will help you try."

## Playground Enrichment

The playground is the natural arena for optimal physical development and the ideal environment to promote physical fitness. On the playground, all motor skills are called into play.

> Carmen *grabs* a scarf and begins to dance, *twirling* and *whirling, hopping* and *bending* in time to the music. Following the teacher's lead, Carmen *balances* on his toes and *waves* his scarf high over his head.

> Tina *walks* to the climber, *grasps* the highest rung she can *reach, pulls* herself up by *lifting* one leg and then the other until she *stretches* vertically full-length along the climber bars. Satisfied, she *pushes* off with her feet and *jumps* backward to the ground. She *bends* her knees as she lands, *balances* herself to an upright position, and *runs* off.

> Ramon *toddles* over to *pick* up the large red ball. Momentarily overwhelmed by its size, he *falls* backward to *sit* on the grass. As a teacher approaches him, he *rolls* the ball toward her. She *throws* it back to him and Ramon imitates her movements. Soon they are involved in *kicking* and *tossing* the ball to each other.

Using both small and large muscles, children gain control over their bodies as they run and play. The playground provides open space where full-bodied action takes place, providing many opportunities to develop balance and coordination.

Physical skills, however, are not the only benefit

---

### MAKING PLAYGROUNDS SAFE

---

*Safety in the yard means:*

- Enough room for the number and age of children who will use it
- Adequate empty space
- Availability of both hard and soft surfaces
- Absorbent surfaces under any equipment from which a child might fall
- Shady areas alternating with sunny spots
- No standing water—good drainage
- No poisonous or thorny plants
- Areas of play clearly defined and differentiated from one another
- Sand area protected at night from animals
- Fences high enough and in good repair
- Gates secure with latches out of children's reach

*Equipment is:*

- Well maintained—no exposed nails, screws, sharp edges, chipped paint
- Chosen with children's ages in mind in regard to height and complexity
- Stable and securely anchored
- Repaired immediately or removed if damaged
- Varied to allow for wide range of skills
- Not crowded
- Smooth where children's hands are likely to be placed
- Checked frequently
- Placed appropriately: slides facing north, swings away from other structures and busy areas
- Scaled to age level: steps and other openings are four inches or less apart *or* eight to ten inches apart
- Modified for age levels: swings have soft seats

*Teachers:*

- Reinforce safe practices
- Wear appropriate outdoor clothing
- Check frequently *where* children are playing
- Involve children in safety checks of yard, equipment, and grounds
- Provide continual, adequate supervision
- Avoid congregating to talk
- Get involved with children
- Provide enough activities and challenges
- Watch for sun exposure, especially with toddlers
- Assist children when they want to rearrange movable equipment

---

**FIGURE 12.9** Before children are allowed to use a playground, teachers should use a checklist such as this to ensure that safety standards are met.

of outdoor play. Social and cognitive skills are enhanced as well. On the playground, children must negotiate turns with the wagons, ask for a push on the swing, and wait in line going up the slide. Some of the most intricate and involved dramatic play takes place outdoors. Problems get solved when two trikes collide. Science experiences are all around—finding a bird's nest or planting a garden. According to Frost, "good playgrounds increase the intensity of play and the range of play behavior" (McKee, 1986).

On the playground no one says "Be quiet!" or "Quit wriggling!" It is a place of motion and space, filled with the special sensations found only out-doors.

When creating and maintaining a challenging environment, teachers consider both variety and level of challenge. A choice of surfaces encourages a variety of movements. Cement may be appropriate for transportation toys, but climbing/hanging/dropping are more likely to occur with tanbark or rubber mats. Varying the equipment also stimulates motor activity. Equipment that is mobile allows for greater range of uses, and allows children to manipulate their own environment. By creating their own physical challenges with wooden crates, children make platforms, caves, and houses to crawl in, over, and through. Another way to provide variety is to focus on the less-developed skills, such as catching and throwing, rolling, latching, snapping, or zipping. When children are encouraged to discover their own physical capabilities, they learn to solve problems of movement defined by the limits of their own abilities rather than by performance. This kind of learning encourages self-confidence as children find success through their own challenges.

## A Child's Self-Concept

The image of physical self is an important part of self-concept. How people feel about themselves is rooted in the way they feel about their bodies and what they can or cannot do with them. Attitudes about the body and its abilities directly affect the types of activities children will try. Studies show that skill in games appears tied to peer-group acceptance (Gallahue, 1976). Psychologists and teachers often notice a link between learning problems and clumsiness. Children with problems seem to have motor difficulties more often than those who do well in the classroom (Cratty, 1971).

Physical activity, then, contributes to a child's self-concept. With practice comes a sense of competence. Children can learn to relax as they gain experience in physical activities, and thus reduce the stress of anticipating failure. Competence breeds self-confidence, and a willingness to try greater challenges. As children try new activities, they learn more about themselves. And physical activity increases awareness of what fun it is to move—to run through a field or pump a swing just for the sheer joy of it!

Teachers support positive self-concept through physical and motor development in several ways. They let children discover their own physical limits, rather than warning or stopping them from trying out an activity for themselves. "I'm stuck!" a child shouts across the yard. Rather than rushing to lift down the child, the teacher might reply, "Where can you put your foot next? How can you find a way to get across?" To the child afraid to climb, the teacher might stand close by, responding to the fear by saying, "I'll stand close to the climbing ropes so you will feel safe." Using positive reinforcement encourages children in physical and motor endeavors. Teachers notice children who try something new: "Greg, it's good to see you cutting out the pumpkin yourself." They congratulate efforts for the achievements they really are: "Your hands reached the top this time, Shannon! I'll bet you are feeling proud of yourself." Children who stand on the sidelines observing others may need some encouragement from the teacher to take the first step in mastering the climbing frame or slide. "Here's a good place for you to put your foot, Arturo. I'll hold onto your hand until you tell me to let go."

It is often not so much what teachers say to children that influences their feelings about themselves as it is the way in which children are treated. Children value themselves to the degree they are valued by others. The way teachers show how they feel about children actually builds their self-confidence and sense of self-worth. Children create a picture of themselves from the words, attitudes, body language, and judgment of those around them.

### Encouraging Physical Play

The vital role of physical activity is best fulfilled when teachers:

- Create time in the daily schedule for periods of physical activity, preferably outdoors.

- Actively participate while supervising and encouraging *all* children to become involved in strenuous activity.

- Set goals for children's motor development and physical fitness.

- Use a variety of activities including science, art, and music to stimulate physical development.

- Select age-appropriate equipment and materials, providing a variety of props to enhance their use.

- Give children opportunities to repeat, practice, and refine the skills they learn.

When children develop their physical and motor skills under this kind of encouragement, their confidence and sense of competence grow.

Observing children while they play outdoors allows teachers an opportunity to assess potential problems in motor development. The checklist in Figure 12.11 indicates some areas to observe.

**FIGURE 12.10** From early infancy, parents and teachers encourage physical play.

---

**Check whether child:**

- ☐ 1. Has trouble holding or maintaining balance
- ☐ 2. Appears to have difficulty balancing and moves awkwardly
- ☐ 3. Cannot carry self well in motion
- ☐ 4. Appears generally awkward in activities requiring coordination
- ☐ 5. Has difficulty making changes in movement
- ☐ 6. Has difficulty performing combinations of simple movements
- ☐ 7. Has difficulty in gauging space with respect to own body; bumps and collides with objects and other children
- ☐ 8. Tends to fall often
- ☐ 9. Has poor eye-hand coordination
- ☐ 10. Has difficulty handling the simple tools of physical activity (beanbags, balls, other objects that require visual-motor coordination)

---

**FIGURE 12.11** A checklist of possible problems in physical/motor development serves as a guideline when devising a developmentally specific profile for spotting problems.

## Curriculum Planning for Physical/Motor Development

Teachers plan activities that promote physical/motor skills in the areas of gross motor, fine motor, and perceptual-motor development. They look at the environment, both indoors and out, to see that all three areas of physical growth are encouraged.

### In the Classroom Setting

When thinking of physical/motor development in the classroom and yard, teachers tend to focus on the fine motor (or small-muscle) tasks for the classroom, and gross motor (or large-muscle) tasks for the outdoor play space. The indoor area lends itself more readily to activities with less movement, and the outdoor area encourages whole-body play. Yet children can have a wider variety of activities if teachers remember that both gross and fine motor projects can happen everywhere in the environment.

FIGURE 12.12  Many times, creativity combines with a physical skill and gives the young child great satisfaction. (Courtesy of Rachell Feldman, Nassau County Community College, N.Y.)

**Indoor Areas.** Indoors, the art area is stocked with pens, crayons, scissors and hole punches that develop the fine motor skills. Add large brushes or rollers to the easel, or plan fingerpainting, and the art area now includes gross motor development. When children use templates to trace both inside and outside spaces, they develop perceptual-motor skill. In the science area, getting "just a pinch" of fish food is a fine motor activity; cleaning out the turtle house requires larger muscles to move rocks and sant. Perceptual-motor development occurs as children use pitchers to fill the fish tank or turtle tub and learn about water levels. When a child puts pegs into a pegboard, fine motor skills are used in the manipulative area. Removing puzzles from a shelf and carrying them to a table brings in gross motor skills. Add nuts and

bolts and the child's perceptual-motor skills are called into play. The block area has endless possibilities, from lifting and carrying (gross motor), to balancing and stacking (fine motor), to building a space so that an animal or car will fit through (perceptual-motor). The language and library areas are places for turning pages or looking at words and pictures (fine motor). They also involve taking books off shelves and replacing them, and trying out the movements and activities read about in books. For instance, Tana Hoban's *Is It Hard? Is It Easy?* encourages children to act out the scenes pictured in the story, all gross motor tasks. With a listening post nearby, children listen for the "beep," and coordinate what they hear (perceptual) with turning the pages (motor).

**Outdoor Areas.** Outdoors, children develop motor skills of all kinds. In the sand, children dig, a gross motor activity. As they judge how big a hole is, or how much water will fill it, they are practicing and improving their perceptual-motor skills. Turning on

FIGURE 12.13  The outdoor sand area has great potential for developing *gross motor skills* (bending, digging), *fine motor skills* (grasping, scooping), and *perceptual motor skills* (sensory motor, eye-hand coordination).

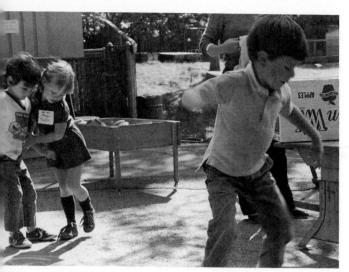

**FIGURE 12.14** At an early age, children take pride in their physical accomplishments. "I feel strong," or "I feel capable," enhance self-confidence.

a faucet, planting seeds, and making mudpies are for fine motor development.

Wheel toys offer children opportunities in all motor areas. Pushing someone in a wagon develops arm and leg strength—gross motor development. Guiding tricycles and carts on a path and around obstacles requires perceptual-motor skill. Trying to "repair" or "paint" a wheel toy with tools or with large brushes, tying wagons together, or weaving streamers through the spokes of a bicycle all use fine motor skills. By looking at the classroom and yard with one eye to physical and motor development, teachers can plan activities that support growth in all skill areas.

**Transitions and Group Times.** Every part of the daily schedule can be planned to use all physical/motor skills. For instance, getting in and out of coats and snowsuits is a large-muscle activity. Children learn perceptual-motor skills as they try to get their arms in the correct sleeves. Buttoning, zipping, and tying are fine motor activities. As children get ready for group time, often a difficult transition, they might practice drawing faces in the air, or making their bodies into the shape of letters, both perceptual-motor tasks.

Group times also include activities for motor development. When there are balloons, scarves, or a parachute at music time, children practice gross motor skills. Fingerplays at group time are a fine motor task. Activities for developing the senses of hearing and sight are two areas of sensory growth that can be utilized as content for group times.

## Focus on Skills

The physical/motor skills include those that use large muscles, the smaller muscles, and the coordination of perception and motor response. Teachers planning activities for children can focus on any one of these as a basis for curriculum planning. For example, the skills of eye-hand coordination (perceptual-motor) and of walking on a balance beam (gross motor) are elaborated below. They show how teachers can focus on a single skill and develop a rich curriculum for children.

**Eye-Hand Coordination.** Developing stitchery skills uses the perceptual-motor skill of eye-hand coordination. A series of activities can be planned to help children learn these skills. This learning begins in infancy, when the baby first begins to manipulate and examine an object, learns to grasp with thumb and forefinger (*pincer grasp*), and shows a hand preference. Stringing large wooden beads is a first step and leads to using pieces of straw and punched paper, with somewhat smaller holes. Macaroni can be strung on shoe laces or stiff string, then onto yarn, which is softer and more challenging. Sewing cards made by punching holes in styrofoam trays can be introduced as the next activity. Large, plastic needles can be used with the lacing cards or with styrofoam trays; large embroidery needles with big eyes can be used for stitching yarn onto burlap. Children may be ready to use embroidery hoops, with which they can make a design on burlap first and then stitch over the outlines. Buttons can be sewn on burlap or other fabric. Popcorn can be strung using a needle. A final project might be to make a group wall hanging, with squares of children's stitchery sewn together. Simple backpacks and coin purses might be made, with the children sewing most of it themselves.

**Walking on a Balance Beam.** Teachers might want to focus on the skill of walking on a balance beam, a gross motor activity. Using any kind of beam requires more balance and slower movements than regular walking. Teachers place tape on the floor and ask children to walk forward and backward. Use a rope on the floor and everyone can pretend to be a tightrope walker. Place a wide board flat on the floor, then substitute a narrow one (still on the floor itself). Next, place the wide board at a minimal height (perhaps 2 inches off the ground). Once children have mastered walking on this board, they are ready to try a narrower board at the same height. Set some boards at a slant, from the ground level up, providing a challenge that allows children to move their bodies off the ground as gradually as they wish. By planning activities for walking on wide and narrow boards of various heights, teachers help children of all levels acquire the gross motor skills necessary to master these tasks. Malina (1982) suggests three categories

| Type of Motor Skills | Infants 0-1½ years | Toddlers 1½-3 years | Preschoolers 3-5 years | Early School Years 6-8 years |
|---|---|---|---|---|
| **Locomotor:** Walking Running Jumping Hopping Skipping | Safe areas to explore body movements Balls to roll Hanging jumpseats Walkers on wheels Simple obstacle course | Walker wagons Pull/push toys Dancing Wide balance board Toddler gym—stairs and slide Ring Around the Rosey | Hippity-hop balls Sled Beginning skis Trampoline Rollerskates Jumprope Balance beam Climber Dancing | Jumprope Rollerskates Ice skates Climbing rope Tumbling mats Hopscotch |
| **Nonlocomotor:** Pushing Pulling Bending | Large, safe areas for exploration Parent/caregiver play: holding, pushing arms, legs, sturdy push toys Soft obstacle course of pillows | Pounding board Simple, low rocking horse Ride-on toys Toddler-type swing Large Legos® Sturdy doll buggy Wagon Fabric tunnels Blocks Cars, trucks to push | Shopping cart/doll carriage Wheelbarrow Pedal toys, trike Rakes, shovels Slide Swing Punching bag | Scooter Two-wheel bike Sled, toboggan Exercise mat Acrobatics Diving mask for swimming Doorway gym bar |
| **Manipulative:** Grasping Throwing Catching Kicking Receiving/ moving objects | Mobile attached to crib—kicking feet moves it Rattles, teething rings Crib activity board Soft foam blocks Snap beads Floating bath toys | Variety of balls Stacking, nesting toys Activity box—on floor Shape sorters Large, fat crayons Large pegs and board Water/sand table | Crayons, markers Clay, dough Bowling games Puzzles Woodworking tools Balls Lacing board Water/sand table | Baseball glove/bat Ring toss game Full-size balls Oversize bat Frisbee "Miss Mary Mack" |

**FIGURE 12.15** Toys and games to help develop specific motor skills in young children.

for motor skills: (1) locomotor; (2) nonlocomotor, and (3) manipulative. Figure 12.15 shows age-appropriate equipment that fosters the development of those three types of skills.

## Use of Themes

When beginning teachers plan activities, they often have a theme or unit as their focus. Themes can be used to encourage physical and motor involve-

### CINCO DE MAYO

| Activity | Skill |
|---|---|
| 1. Make a piñata | |
|   a. make strips of newspapers for paper maché; cut and paste colored tissue paper | Fine motor |
|   b. feel the flour paste; choose the colors that go together | Perceptual–motor (sensory) |
|   c. organize the children by height | Perceptual–motor (spatial) |
|   d. try to break it with a bat; clap and jump each time someone swings at the piñata | Gross motor and perceptual–motor |
| 2. Cook corn tortillas | |
|   a. mix the masa with water | Perceptual–motor (measuring) Fine motor (mixing) |
|   b. roll the masa into balls; put into tortilla press | Fine motor and gross motor |
|   c. put onto griddle, flip, eat! | Perceptual–motor (sensory) Fine motor |
| 3. Using music | |
|   a. dancing "La Raspa": | |
|     hearing the rhythm | Perceptual–motor (sensory) |
|     learning the steps | Perceptual–motor (temporal) and gross motor |
|     using costumes | Gross motor (getting in and out) Fine motor (doing fastenings) |
|     dancing the steps | All three |
|   b. making and playing maracas | |
|     using shakers/hearing sounds, | Fine motor/perceptual–motor |
|     making shakers | Fine motor |
| 4. Learning Spanish words and stories | |
|     hearing and trying new words | Perceptual–motor (sensory, both hearing and speaking) |

**FIGURE 12.16** When teachers use a theme to develop physical/motor activities, they are matching children's interests and cultural awareness with activities to practice the skills they need to learn.

ment. A unit of "Outerspace" involves gross motor skills (jumping around on the moon, taking a space walk, getting in and out of the rocketship, building a spaceship with large blocks). Fine motor skills are needed to manipulate knobs on the instrument panel, to draw maps of the stars or write out a countdown on a chalkboard. Perceptual-motor skills are needed to work out how to get ready for a trip to Mars, what happens on the trip, and when and how to get back to Earth. Use the sample forms in Figures 11.3, 11.4, and 11.15 to develop an outer-space unit as well as other appropriate themes to encourage motor skills.

Once teachers realize which physical/motor skills the children possess and what the group is ready to learn, they can plan activities around a classroom unit. Figure 12.15 outlines a theme familiar to Mexican-American children that will encourage physical/motor skills as well as an appreciation for cultural diversity.

Curriculum planning for motor and movement skills requires teachers to know principles of physical growth and motor development. They then can use this knowledge to plan activities that encourage children to master their own movements and to learn other skills through movement. In the early childhood setting, curriculum can be planned by concentrating on activity areas, focusing on a specific motor skill, or using a classroom theme.

# SUMMARY

Children are in motion virtually from conception and develop their abilities to move their bodies as they grow. Young children spend most of the day in physical activity; therefore, the development of physical and motor skills must take a high priority in early childhood programs. Physical growth, that which pertains to the body, is for teachers an issue of fitness and health. They need to have an overview of growth in order to help children develop functional and flexible bodies. Motor development means learning to move with control and efficiency. Development involves maturation and experience. Teachers must know the sequence of development and what part they play in providing physical and motor experiences for the young child.

Muscular movements can be categorized as gross motor, fine motor, and perceptual-motor. Gross motor movements use the entire body or large parts of it, such as the legs for running or the arms and torso for throwing. Fine motor movements, such as manipulating objects, are those that use smaller muscles and that require precision and dexterity. Perceptual-motor movements are those that combine what is perceived with a body movement. Spatial, temporal, and sensory awareness all play an important part in the development of perceptual-motor skills.

In the early childhood years, children need exposure to many motor activities. They need a chance to practice, to get feedback, and to have a broad range of experiences of variety and challenge. Since children acquire motor skills through short- and long-term memory, rehearsal plays an important role as well.

When planning curriculum, teachers must have an awareness of sex-role stereotyping and must consider safety as well as challenge. A child's self-concept is linked with the concept of physical self and skill, so teachers keep in mind which behaviors should be encouraged, and which behaviors may indicate potential problems. As they plan activities for children, teachers use classroom and yard areas, focus on a specific skill, or use a theme to develop curriculum for physical/motor skills.

## R E V I E W   Q U E S T I O N S

1. How does physical growth differ from motor development in young children?

2. What factors influence motor development in young children?

3. What physical/motor skills are appropriate for young children to develop?

4. How can the teacher of young children support motor development in classroom areas?

5. How can the teacher support acquisition of specific motor skills in young children?

6. Follow (a) a toddler, (b) a 3½-year-old, and (c) a six-year-old during a typical play period at school or home. Observe the child for as long as possible but at least for one hour. Describe the specific motor skills you observe that child using/practicing during your observation.

## L E A R N I N G   A C T I V I T I E S

1. Map the classroom in which you are currently working. List at least one activity in each area that develops physical motor skills. Add one more activity of your own that widens such development.

2. In what ways does a school program you know reinforce sex-role stereotyping in motor activities? What could be done to change this?

3. Try to develop the theme of "at the beach" or "camping" in your setting in such a way that physicial/motor skills are used. Be sure to include gross motor, fine motor, and perceptual-motor activities. List at least six other themes around which you could build a similar curriculum.

# B I B L I O G R A P H Y

Ames, Louise Bates, et al. *The Gessell Institute's Child from One to Six.* New York: Harper and Row, 1979.

Bee, Helen. *The Developing Child.* Cambridge, Mass.: Harper & Row, 1985.

Cataldo, Christine Z. *Infant and Toddler Programs.* Reading, Mass.: Addison-Wesley, 1983.

Frost, J.L., and Sunderlin, S. (eds.). *When Children Play.* Wheaton, Md.: Association for Childhood Education International, 1985.

Gallahue, David L. *Motor Development and Movement Experiences for Young Children.* New York: John Wiley & Sons, 1976.

Javernick, Ellen. "Johnny's Not Jumping—Can We Help Obese Children?" *Young Children,* January 1988, pp. 18-23.

Lovell, Penny, and Harms, Thelma. "How Can Playgrounds Be Improved?" *Young Children,* March 1985, pp. 3-8.

McKee, Judy Spitler. *Play: Working Partner of Growth.* Wheaton, Md.: Association for Childhood Education International, 1986.

Malina, Robert M. "Motor Development in the Early Years." In Moore, Shirley G., and Cooper, Catherine R. (eds.), *The Young Child: Reviews of Research,* vol. 3. Washington, D.C.: National Association for the Education of Young Children, 1982.

Oppenheim, Joanne. *Buy Me! Buy Me!* New York: Pantheon Books, 1985.

Ridenour, Marcella V., ed. (Contributing Authors: Clark, Herkowitz, Roberton, Teeple) *Motor Development: Issues and Applications.* Princeton, N.J.: Princeton Book Company, 1978.

Riggs, Maida L. *Jump to Joy: Helping Children Grow Through Active Play.* Englewood Cliffs, N.J.: Prentice-Hall, 1980.

Sprung, Barbara. *Non-Sexist Education for Young Children.* New York: Citation Press, 1975.

Stone, L. Joseph, and Church, Joseph. *Childhood and Adolescence.* New York: Random House, 1979.

# CHAPTER 13

## Planning for the Mind: Cognitive and Language Development

Dinosaurs ate
dinosaurs or
meat or plants or trees.

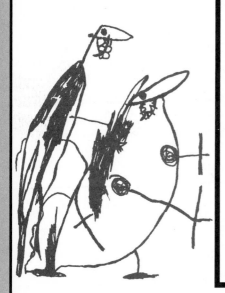

## QUESTIONS for THOUGHT

- What is the relationship between cognitive and language development?
- What is meant by cognitive development?
- How can the teacher support cognitive development?
- What language skills are developed in an early childhood setting?
- What is the teacher's role in supporting and extending language development in young children?
- How does the teacher introduce and develop reading and writing in the early childhood setting?
- What can children's literature offer young children?
- How might computers be used with young children?

Portions of this chapter were developed with the assistance of Gay Spitz, Salinas Adult School, Salinas, Calif.

# PREFACE

The relationship between language and thought cannot be overemphasized. Thoughts are produced when people internalize what they experience. Language is the powerful tool that turns actions and events into thought. Language also shapes the way thoughts are produced and stored; language brings a semblance of order to the thought processes. It is, according to Bruner, a "logical and analytical tool in thinking" (Vygotsky, 1962).

Psychologists and educators today acknowledge the interdependent nature of cognition and language. People are molded by the tools they use; language and thought are the instruments people use to interact with the world.

For these reasons, this chapter contains curriculum planning units for both cognition and language rather than treating them in separate chapters. Inclusion in the same chapter emphasizes their close relationships.

Graphic language—reading and writing—is a major avenue for creating curriculum that stimulates and encourages language and cognitive skills. A third unit addresses these special topics as vehicles for language and intellectual development in the young child.

# INTRODUCTION

Ah, to be a child again! The world is a place of wonder and promise. There are worlds and people to discover, explore, and understand. Childhood is a time:

- Of self . . . a baby plays with his hands and feet for hours, and rolls over just for the sake of doing it.
- Of things everywhere . . . a toddler invades the kitchen cabinets to see what treasures can be found.
- Of people . . . a preschooler learns the teachers' names and then makes a first "friend."
- Of faraway places . . . a kindergartener packs for the first "sleepover."

The amount of learning that takes place in early childhood is staggering. How do children manage to absorb the sheer quantity of information and experience they accumulate in their first few years of life?

Every child accomplishes this mighty feat by *thinking*. Theories about cognition have been based on the idea that intelligence is a general capacity or potential that can be measured by standardized tests (such as I.Q. tests) and, therefore, that cognition can be developed by a specific, rather narrow, set of teaching techniques. Recent research expands this notion of intelligence significantly. Articulated by Harvard University psychologist Howard Gardner (1985), current theory suggests that there are at least seven types of intelligence, or "frames of mind":

1. Linguistic intelligence (language ability)

2. Musical intelligence (the earliest talent to emerge)

3. Logical mathematical intelligence (the ability to manipulate, order, and assess both quantity and quality)

4. Spatial intelligence (the capacity to perceive the visual world, to change one's perceptions, and to be able to re-create aspects of what one sees without its being in view)

5. Bodily/kinesthetic intelligence (the ability to control body motions and to handle objects)

6. Intrapersonal intelligence (access to one's own feelings and a range of emotions)

7. Interpersonal intelligence ("the ability to notice and make distinctions among other individuals, and in particular among their moods, temperaments, motivations and intentions").

To think, then, is to be able to acquire and apply knowledge. By using conscious thought and memory, children think about themselves, the world, and others. Educating the thinking child is a critical function of every teacher and parent. Curriculum in the early years of school must address the skill of *cognition*, the mental process or faculty children use to acquire knowledge.

**FIGURE 13.1** As children investigate the world of people and places, they ask themselves and others what they want to know.

*Language* is the primary form of expression through which people communicate their knowledge and thoughts. A baby does not start life with language, but always communicates. In fact, oral language begins early, as infants learn to express themselves with sounds if not words. The growing child communicates needs, thoughts, and feelings through meaningful language. Thus, language and thought are intertwined.

Yet, the two are also separate. Cognition can occur without the language to express it. For example, when the infant laughs during a game of peek-a-boo, it indicates the child's knowledge that the hidden face will reappear. Conversely, the use of language can occur without *cognition* (i.e., without knowing the meaning). A child counting from one to twenty (". . . 11,13,17,19,20!") is a case in point.

Cognition and language generally become more interdependent as development progresses. Children expand their knowledge base through language. They listen, question, tell. The child with good language skills can thus apply them to widen the horizons of knowledge.

Cognition and language relate not only to the developing mind, but also to all areas of the child's growth. Young thinkers are at work no matter what they are doing. For example, physical/motor development is also a cognitive process. Learning to roller-skate involves skinned knees and learning to balance (motor tasks), along with analyzing, predicting, generalizing, evaluating, and practicing the art of locomotion on wheels (cognitive skills). When trying to enter into group play (a social task), children will think of strategies for how to get started (cognitive skill).

Children use language in developing emotionally. They listen, label, describe, elaborate, and question (language skills) as they learn to tell themselves and others how they feel (emotional tasks). And anyone who has heard a child mumbling instructions on how to get down from a tree knows that language can be of great help in using physical skills.

This chapter will explore in depth the framework for planning curriculum for the mind. For the purposes of clarity, cognition and language will be separated into units. However, teachers must remember that these work together constantly in the minds and lives of young children. Planned programs for early childhood will be more successful if that link is recognized.

# UNIT 13–1   COGNITION

## THE DEVELOPMENT OF COGNITION: A PERSPECTIVE

### An Eclectic Point of View

In trying to enhance cognitive development, early childhood educators draw upon developmental and learning theories and their direct experiences with children. By combing theoretical and practical viewpoints, teachers take a blended, or *eclectic*, perspective on the development of the thinking process. They work with children to encourage their ability to formulate ideas and to think rationally and logically.

Most important, the early childhood professional works toward helping children acquire skills that will lead to the development of:

*Concepts:* labeling or naming an idea, moving from the specific to the abstract
"What is a grape?"

*Relationships:* What is the association between two or more things? How are they similar or different? What are their functions, characteristics, attributes?
"How many colors of grapes are there? Do all of them have seeds? Are they different sizes? Do they taste alike?"

*Generalizations:* Drawing conclusions from relationships and concepts/ideas. This means grouping into classes and finding common elements.
"Are grapes a fruit or meat? How do grapes grow?"

### A Piagetian Perspective

Developmental psychology, particularly through the works of Jean Piaget, has provided a deeper understanding of cognitive development. Piaget's view of cognition is twofold: First, learning is a process of discovery, of finding out what one needs to know to solve a particular problem. Second, knowledge results from active thought, from making mental connections among objects, from constructing a meaningful reality for understanding.

Piaget divided knowledge into three types:

- *Meaningful knowledge* is what children learn gradually, adding new concepts and ideas to what they already know. For example, being able to explore magnetism with horseshoe and bar magnets gives the child the opportunity to connect objects to thoughts.

- *Rote knowledge* is just what it implies: information with no particular meaning to the learner. In this case, an explanation of magnetism might be given to a class without a chance to handle or explore magnets.

- *Social knowledge* comes from our culture, the rules of the game, the right vocabulary, the moral codes. Value-laden and often arbitrary, this knowledge can rarely be constructed logically. Still, social knowledge is learnable and a crucial part of children's cognitive development. A new set of magnets is brought to school. Who gets to play with them? When is it someone else's turn?

In developing cognitive curriculum, teachers plan experiences that enhance those types of knowledge they feel are most important for children.

## COGNITIVE SKILLS IN EARLY CHILDHOOD

The actual skills children acquire as they learn to think are considerable. A basic skill is defined by two fundamental qualities:

- A skill is basic if it is transcurricular: that is, if the child can use it in a variety of situations and activities throughout the school day. For example, children who can express feelings and opinions clearly—who can let adults know when they are having difficulties with a particular task or social situation—have acquired a skill that is useful anywhere.

- A skill is also basic if it has dynamic consequences: that is, if it leads to other worthwhile responses. For instance, children who are articulate tend to elicit more verbal responses from adults. Consequently, they are exposed to more verbal stimulation, which in turn strengthens their verbal abilities, and so on. Thus, having this skill leads to major dynamic consequences in a favorable direction, while *not* having the skill leads to dynamic consequences in an unfavorable direction (Katz, 1985).

Most skills fall into the nine categories below. The list, while long, is a comprehensive one; what children learn in the thinking realm of their development will fall into one of these categories. The teacher plans activities for all cognitive skills to ensure challenging children's thinking.

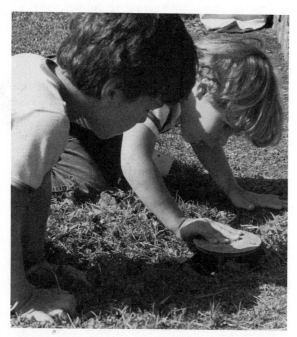

**FIGURE 13.2** Being able to explore actual materials and objects encourages children to use and assimilate new knowledge.

## Skills of Inquiry

Young children are curious, watching the world carefully. Through exploration and examination, they increase their attention span. Inquisitive children begin to organize what they see, analyzing and identifying confusions or obstacles for themselves. The next step is communication; the child asks questions, listens, gets ideas, and makes suggestions. This includes interpreting what others communicate. Then children are ready to use resources, seeking assistance from other people and materials.

Reasoning and problem solving are also inquiry skills. As children examine alternatives, they choose a course of action, revising their plans as needed. Young children thrill in making educated guesses, then checking their *hypotheses* by experimenting and taking risks. In doing so, they learn to evaluate, to use the judgments and opinions, and to distinguish between fact and opinion, reality and fantasy. These basic skills of inquiry are the foundation for thinking; as such, they are far more important to develop than simple prereading or number skills.

## Knowledge of the Physical World

How do children learn about the physical world? First, they use objects, spending plenty of time exploring, manipulating, choosing, using toys and natural materials. Babies search for something to suck; they begin to grasp objects and let them go. Toddlers will pick up and throw things or drop objects from a highchair to see what happens. Children observe reactions, discover relationships, and try to predict what will happen. Six-year-olds with balloons and water explore how to fill, roll, throw, and burst the balloons. As they learn the properties of objects, children gain a better understanding of the concept of cause and effect.

## Knowledge of the Social World

Learning about others is hard work, since the social world is not concrete and is often illogical. The child needs an awareness of self before developing an awareness of others and how to interact socially. Infants begin by distinguishing friends from strangers. Toddlers learn to use "mine" and then to use others' names as well. The next step is to expand their knowledge of roles to include those of family, school, and the community. Four- and five-year-olds are provided with daily opportunities to cooperate, to help, and to negotiate with others about their needs and wishes.

Children are encouraged to notice both similarities and differences in people and then are led to develop tolerance for both. School-aged children seek small-group teamwork and moments of private time with a close friend. Children in the primary grades experience the development of conscience and learn rules for social living. In these ways children learn what is appropriate conduct in various situations—indoors or out, happy or sad, at the grocery store or at the dinner table.

## Classification

Knowledge of the physical world teaches children to have different responses to different objects. *Classifying* this knowledge is a lengthy process. To clarify this process, consider how two-year-old Tisa learns to classify:

> What can Tisa do to the stuffed bear *and* the pet dog? What can she do with one and *not* the other? Which are her toys? Rover's? Which ones have fur? What is different about them?

Tisa learns the *attributes* of the objects by exploring, learning the class names of "toy" and "pet." She makes collections, sorting by similarity those that are Rover's toys and those that are her own. She uses class relationships to understand that both animals have fur, but she can tug on only one animal's ears without encountering a problem.

## Seriation

How do children learn to seriate, or to arrange items according to a graduated scale? Like classification, *seriation* can appear confusing at first glance. To illustrate its development, look at some of the materials designed by Dr. Maria Montessori. These toys were developed to make clear to children exactly what seriation is and how it can be learned. Many of these toys distinguish grades of intensity by size, color, weight, number. Children build pyramid towers, fit nesting blocks together, and use the counting rods. By noting differences, often through trial and error, children learn seriation systematically. For instance, the pyramid tower is ordered from largest piece to smallest as it is built. Boxes are nested, one inside the other, by their graduated size or volume. The counting rods can be put into a staircase array, the units building on each other from one to ten. Children can arrange several things in order and fit one ordered set of objects to another.

## Numbers

Understanding the concept of *number* means learning about quantity; that is, understanding amount, degree, and position. Once infants develop an understanding of *object permanence* (that an object exists whether or not it can be seen), they are ready to learn about quantity as they compare objects—for example, by stacking rings on a stick. Toddlers and twos can sort by groups (large versus small, hard versus soft) and start noticing what is "more." To learn about the names of numbers, one begins with their sound. Settings for children under five have plenty of songs, chants, and fingerplays that include numbers ("One Potato, Two" or "Five Speckled Frogs"). Once children comprehend numbers, they are ready to use mathematical terms and forms of expression. For instance, after singing about the frog that jumped into the pool in the song "Five Speckled Frogs," Chantel can begin to understand that four is one less than five.

But a knowledge of number is neither complete nor meaningful unless children have direct experience with materials and objects. Learning about quantity also means comparing amounts (as when children work with table toys, blocks, sensory materials, and the like) and arranging two sets of objects in one-to-one correspondence ("Each person needs one and only one napkin for snack, Tyler"). Children can also count objects and begin computation

("Parvin, you have three shovels. Here is one more; now how many do you have?"). With countless experiences such as these, children in kindergarten through third grade will be ready and excited to learn more mathematical skills.

## Symbols

A symbol stands for something else; it is not what it appears to be! Young children have to think hard and long in order to symbolize. It is a task of some skill to imitate or use one object to represent something else.

Children begin by using their bodies. Infants and toddlers love to play peek-a-boo, reacting to "Boo!" with full-bodied excitement each time it is said. Preschoolers revel in playing favorite characters. Primary school children make up plays and puppet shows. Make-believe helps in the process of symbolizing, as does making sound to represent objects ("Choo-choo" is a train, for example). Using and making two- and three-dimensional models are other ways children symbolize, when they transfer what they see to the easel or to the clay table. Children are also symbolizing when they dress up in costumes and uniforms. Teachers add to the symbolizing process when they use descriptive words. Description games encourage children to do the same. For example, "It is round and red and you eat it. What is it?" (An apple!) After all these skills have been mastered, children are ready for written symbols, when they can use the written word to label, take dictation, or write notes.

## Spatial Relationships

Spatial relationships develop early. Infants visually track what they see, trying to reach and grasp. As they experience one object's position in relation to another, they begin to have a mental picture of spatial relationships. Toddlers find this out as they learn to steer themselves around tables and seat themselves on the potty. The concept of "close" (the chair) and "far away" (the quesadilla cooling on the counter) give clues to length and distance ("How far

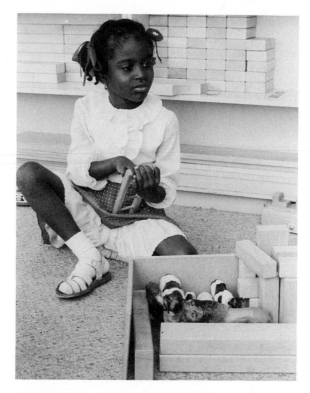

**FIGURE 13.3** Small animals and blocks symbolize a farm: cognitive skills at work. (Courtesy of Stride Rite Children's Centers, Cambridge, Mass.)

do I have to reach to get one?"). As spatial skills develop, children learn to fit things together and take them apart. They rearrange and shape objects. They observe and describe things from different spatial viewpoints. This perspective is learned only through experience. The child under five needs to describe and then try out the notion that what one sees from the side of the hill is *not* what can be seen from the top.

Adults help children learn such skills by letting them locate things at home, in the classroom, in the department store. They encourage children to represent such spatial relationships in their drawings, with pictures, and in photographs.

# Time

Understanding time is a complicated affair, since time is composed of at least three dimensions: time as the present, time as a *continuum,* and time as a sequence of events. Children must learn each of these to fully understand the concept of time. In some settings children learn to stop and start an activity on a signal (when the teacher strikes a chord on the piano for cleanup time). They try to move their bodies at different speeds, indoors and out. Older children begin to observe that clocks and calendars are used to mark the passage of time. Specifically, children come to know the sequencing of events in time: which comes first, next, last? Having an order of events through a consistent daily schedule helps children learn this aspect of time. They also benefit from anticipating future events and making the appropriate preparations. Planning a course of action and completing that plan gives meaning to the idea of time (Furth, 1970; Ginsburg & Opper, 1969; and Piaget, 1969).

What children learn intellectually in the early years is massive in quantity and quality. Yet young children are ready—eager, in fact—to engage themselves with the world around them in order to acquire these cognitive skills. By remaining aware of how much is to be learned, educators keep a realistic—and humble—appreciation for the "work" of children.

# THE TEACHER'S ROLE

# Considerations

When considering children's intellectual development, teachers should keep in mind:

- *Education is exploration.* The process of education is more than its products. Teachers enhance learning by allowing children to interact with the environment. The teacher is a source of information and support rather than one who gives answers or commands. The goal is to have children ask their own questions and create their own challenges.

- *Children do not think like adults.* Children think and perceive in their own ways. They think in concrete terms and come to conclusions based on what they see and touch.

- *Children's thinking is legitimate and should be valued.* Their thought processes and perceptions are as valid as adults'. Teachers support those processes by asking questions to stimulate further thought and by providing materials for exploration.

- *The language of the teacher should support cognitive development.* Throughout their interactions with children, teachers help children use words, terms, and concepts correctly:

  Mariko (at water table): I need that suckup.
  Teacher: The baster really does suck up water, doesn't it?

Teachers' questions are open-ended; they are not to be answered with a simple yes or no. For example, Tony asks his kindergarteners what will happen if they do not count the cups of flour while making bread. What he is really asking them to do is to predict what will happen and consider the results. The goal is to use language to help children to *think.*

Sometimes teachers use their own language skills to define a problem, help children figure out what they are doing, and decide what they need to do next. They leave the child with something to ponder.

  Teacher: I wonder why the turtle's head went back in its shell when you put your finger close by.
  Teacher: If you want to play with José, how can you let him know?
  Teacher: What *do* we need from the woodworking shelf to make a spaceship?

Figure 13.4 shows further how teachers' use of language helps children think and develop cognitive skills as part of their early childhood experience.

| Skill | Teachers Can |
|---|---|
| Inquiry | • Ask questions so children make statements about their conversations.<br>  *Example:* "What do you notice about the guinea pig?"<br>• Try to be more specific if such questions seem overwhelming or if they elicit little response.<br>  *Example:* "What sounds do you hear? What can you find out by touching her?"<br>• Ask how children arrived at their answers.<br>  *Example:* "How did you know that the marble wouldn't roll *up* the ramp?"<br>• Ask questions that expand the process.<br>  *Example:* "Can you tell me anything else about your doll?" |
| Social Knowledge | • Try not to respond to unstated needs.<br>  *Example:* "Do you want something? Can I help you?"<br>• Help children define what they want or need, so that they learn how to ask for it.<br>  *Example:*   Marie: I wonder who is going to tie my shoes?<br>        Teacher: So do I. When you want someone to tie your shoe, you can say, "Would you tie my shoe?"<br>        Marie: Would you tie my shoe?<br>        Teacher: I'd be glad to. |
| Classification | • Ask questions that will help children focus on objects and see differences and details.<br>  *Examples:* While cooking, ask<br>    Which things on the table do we put in the bowl? Which are made of plastic? Which go in the oven?<br>    What on the table is used for measuring? How do you know?<br>    Now look carefully—what do you see on the measuring cup?<br>    What do those little red lines mean? |
| Spatial Relationships | • Ask for the precise location of an object the child asks for or is interested in.<br>  *Examples:* "Where did you say you saw the bird's nest?"<br>           "You can find another stapler in the cabinet underneath the fish tank." |
| Concept of Time | • Use accurate time sequences with children.<br>  *Example:* Teacher: Just a minute.<br>        Milo: Is this a real minute, or a "wait a minute"?<br>        Teacher: You're right. I'm with Phoebe now. I'll help you next. |

**FIGURE 13.4**  Teachers' use of language affects how children develop cognitive skills. The more children are allowed and encouraged to think for themselves, the more their cognitive skills will develop.

# Curriculum Planning for Cognitive Development

## *In the Environment*

Teachers can plan cognitive curriculum for their children by considering the class setting, both indoors and out, throughout the daily schedule. Each activity center can be used to encourage intellectual development with a variety of curriculum materials and methods. Remember that children think differently from adults (see Chapter 4). Children learn through direct and sensory exploration with concrete objects.

**Indoor Areas.** The indoor areas might have some of the following materials and activities:

*Art:* Include a shelf for self-chosen projects. A variety of paper, drawing implements, and tools encourages children to re-create their own reality, using representational art forms that show how children see the physical and social worlds.

*Blocks:* Have paper models of each block shape to help children with classification by shape and size. Accessories, such as animals and homemade trees and lakes, help children symbolize.

*Discovery/Science:* Rotate a display of "touch me" materials. This gives children first-hand experience with plants, seeds, animals, magnets, seashells, foods, etc.

*Dramatic play:* Stock this area with materials for role playing, puppet making, and acting out of adult activities. Have boy and girl dolls, anatomically complete and as physically like the children as possible. Include clothing for all types of work, equipment for carrying things and babies, that reflect the homes of all the children in the group but also extend the play to include new ways of dressing, eating, and playing. Children learn to understand the world of people as they pretend to be adults with adult occupations and responsibilities.

*Language/Library:* Choose books that focus on both the physical and social worlds. Children's interests in numbers, symbols, and time can also be extended by selecting literature that reflects their level of understanding. Look for the message in children's books and choose good stories that reflect diversity, such as *Helping Out* (Ancona), and *George the Babysitter* (Hughes). Be sure to listen to the group's interests, and make a point to place books that respond to those interests in the library.

*Manipulatives (table toys):* The manipulatives area is an ideal place for materials that encourage cognitive development; highlight this area with both favorites (Lego® or Crystal Climbers®) and new items (Construx® or sewing cards). Counting cubes aid in classification and seriation, while puzzles or nesting blocks focus on spatial relationships. Homemade lotto games or puzzles with the children's photos encourage self-esteem and group identity as well as cognitive and motor development.

Figure 13.5 shows how an indoor activity contributes to the development of children's thought processes across the curriculum areas.

**Outdoor Areas.** The outdoor area provides opportunities for children to plan and organize their own thoughts. Toddlers can classify what they find as they look for balls, sand buckets, and toy trucks hidden around the yard. Kindergartners playing tag need inquiry skills. Preschoolers in the sand pit predict how water will affect the sand. using their growing knowledge of the physical world. Children learn to classify water table and wheel toys; they learn seriation when they select sand buckets by size. Counting shovels to see that there are enough to go around, building with large, hollow blocks and watching the seasons change are all cognitive skills children gain as they play outside.

**Transitions.** Groups, transitions, and routines all play a part in developing children's knowledge base of the social world. As children learn to conduct themselves in school, they learn:

- To enter a class and start to play (transition).
- To take care of their own belongings and those of their school (routines).
- To concentrate on an activity with others around (group times).
- To interact with others while at the same time pay attention to a leader or task (group times).
- To end an activity, an interaction, a school day (transition).

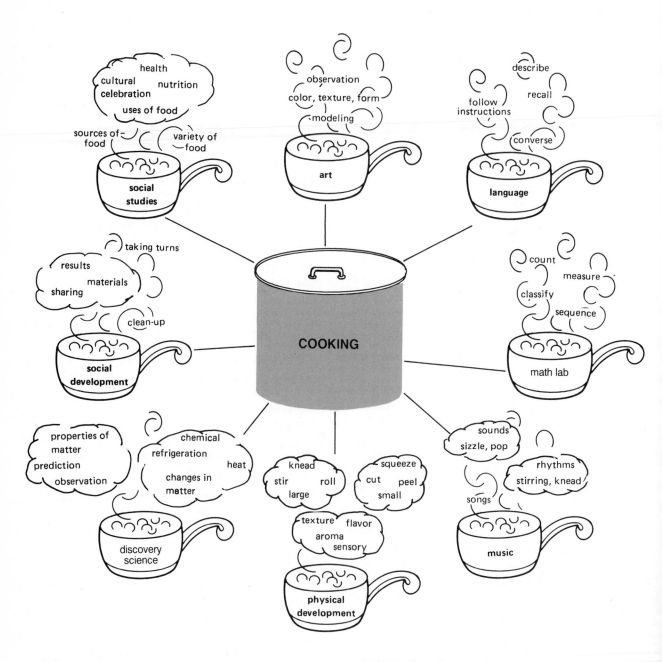

**FIGURE 13.5** Each activity in the environment, such as cooking, can enhance cognitive development throughout the curriculum.

Teachers plan environments, activities, and grouping of children to give the class experience in all these cognitive challenges.

## *Focus on Skills*

After choosing a specific skill, teachers identify the process, the concepts, and the vocabulary involved. Any skill can be the focus of curriculum development. The skill of inquiry is one that teachers can develop throughout the classroom and yard.

They ask children to observe what others are doing, to see how children play and work. They ask questions to model such a technique, showing their own curiosity about process:

Teacher: I wonder which piece of wood you'll

---

*The Concepts:* Selecting a course of action
Making educated guesses
Making and revising a plan
Risking and evaluating the results

*The Vocabulary:* Guess
Plan
Problem
Solution/solve
What? why? how?

*The Process:*

| Activity area | Process question |
|---|---|
| Art | How many ways can you use the brush (pen, squirt bottle) to make a mark on the paper? Why is it dripping? How can you stop it when you're ready? |
| Bathrooms/cubbies | You found Paul's sweater . . . How can you find where it goes? Where did the water come from? How can you clean it up? |
| Blocks | What makes the tower of blocks fall over? How can a block be used to connect two others? |
| Cooking | How do we mix these ingredients together? What will happen when it is put in the oven? |
| Discovery/science | Why did the magnet pick up the nail and not the pen? What is the difference between the rabbit and the guinea pig? How are they alike? |
| Dramatic play | Who will be the dad? What happens when these other children want to play? How can you get to wear the costume you want? |
| Language/library | What happens next in the story? Why do you think so? Why did the child feel unhappy at first? Then what happened? |
| Large group | Why can't you see/hear the leader? What can you do about feeling too crowded? What can you do when your friend keeps whispering to you during storytime? |
| Large motor | How do you jump rope? What do you use to pump yourself on a swing? How will you find a ball? |
| Manipulatives | How do you figure out what puzzle piece fits? Do you see a pattern on the peg board? What is it? |
| Sensory | How do you get the water from the large pitcher to the small cup? How will you get the wet sand through the funnel? |

---

**FIGURE 13.6** To help children with the skills of reasoning and problem solving, be sure to ask real questions so that children believe they are worth exploring and answering fully.

**FIGURE 13.7** A small-group time allows teachers to plan a curriculum that meets cognitive needs of a select group of children.

choose to glue on your board next?

Teacher: What part do you want to play in our grocery store?

Teacher: How can we find out how long your road of blocks is?

When children see that it is all right to ask "Why?", they feel encouraged to ask questions themselves. *Brainstorming* is a technique that helps children get ideas and use resources to find out how many ways there are to make a kite or build a castle.

Outdoors, inquisitive children explore their environment. Children ask questions: "Can we turn on the water? What if we bury all the toy bears in the gravel?! Could we use the ladder to see over the fence? Let's all hide from the teacher?!" The way teachers handle inquiries from children about what they want to do sends a message that supports—or discourages—this cognitive skill. When there is no harm in *asking* (though the answer may be "No"), children are encouraged to develop further the skill of inquiry. Figure 13.6 illustrates exactly how the cognitive skills of reasoning and problem solving could serve as the basis for curriculum development around the entire classroom.

## Use of Themes

A specific theme can be chosen for cognitive development. Units based on things in the physical world (season changes, pets, the garden), on un-expected or current events (a new load of sand, a community fair, road work nearby), or the special interests of the children (sharing the African mask or spacesuits, using the puppet stage, studying reptiles) are all appealing. Figure 13.9 illustrates a dinosaur theme.

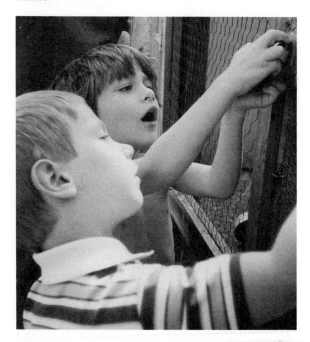

**FIGURE 13.8** The skill of inquiry: "How does this lock work?"

**THEME: DINOSAURS**

| Area | Cognitive Skill(s) | Activity |
|------|-------------------|----------|
| *Indoors* | | |
| Art | Organization | Papier mâché model of a dinosaur; make a "dinosaur world" mural. |
| Blocks | Seriation | Use blocks to compare relative sizes of dinosaurs. |
| Cooking | Relationships | Prepare vegetarian snack (herbivores), then meatballs for the carnivores. |
| Discovery | Observation | Get fossils, other skeletons. |
| | | Collect books on how scientists learn about dinosaurs. |
| | | Compare relationships (size, stature, etc.) of prehistoric to common animals. |
| | | Hide bones in the sand table to dig up and role-play paleontologist. |
| Dramatic play | Symbols | Dinosaur puppets. |
| | | Masks of dinosaurs. |
| Library | Label/recall; use of resources | Provide books about dinosaurs. |
| | | Make dinosaur books with stamps and children's words. |
| Manipulatives | Reasoning; problem solving | Individual and floor dinosaur puzzles. |
| | | Templates to trace and cut. |
| *Outdoors* | | |
| Sensory | Symbols | Rubber dinosaurs in pebbles; dinosaur cookie cutters in clay/play dough. |
| Large motor | Symbols | Measure children's bodies with a rope the length of various dinosaurs. |
| Sand | Symbols | Act out digging up dinosaur bones. |
| Games | Social world | "Tyrannosaurus, May I?" game, naming and taking steps of various dinosaurs. |
| *Groups* | | |
| Large | Label/recall; educated guessing | "Who Am I?", verbally describing dinosaur. |
| | | Mystery Pictures, showing parts of dinosaurs and having children guess. |
| Music | Symbols | Acting out dinosaurs to the record, or to music of various tones. |
| Small | Label/communicate | Draw your favorite dinosaur; dictate what you like about it and what you know. |
| | | Dinosaur sheet, folded in quarters, with a sentence to fill in and space to draw: The dinosaurs laid. . . / |
| | | Some dinosaurs lived. . . / |
| | | Dinosaurs ate. . . / |
| | | Dinosaurs died because. . . / |

**FIGURE 13.9** Using a theme of special interest, such as "Dinosaurs," teachers can develop children's cognitive skills in many classroom areas.

Current events must be chosen carefully, as young children may have only passing knowledge or interest in most of them. Meaningful events might be a space shuttle mission or a solar eclipse. More likely, the event will be a local one, such as a children's fair or someone's new baby. Units based on these happenings might be named "Space and Travel" or "Our Beginnings As Babies."

Themes can change with the seasons. Fall is the time for a unit on "Harvest Time," "Corn," or "Masks and Hats." Winter may mean a unit on how water changes with the seasons, since snow, sleet, hail, and rain are a regular part of most winter months. Spring is a time for green and growing things, and a unit could focus on the physical world of growing plants from seeds, hatching chicks, visiting a farm. Summer weather on the coasts sends everyone to "The Seashore," or at least the local lake or river.

The theme of friendship during Valentine's Day expands children's knowledge of the social world, as they increase their awareness of others through the giving and receiving of letters and cards. Cooperation and group conflict resolution expand the friendship theme. A unit can also focus on symbolizing through use of names, letters on a "post box," or the numbers and location of people's houses and apartments.

One special interest of young children is dinosaurs such as in Figure 13.9. Another way to plan curriculum is to focus on the group of children and their particular developmental level. Infants and toddlers have less need for theme curriculum; curriculum ideas for them concentrate on cognitive stimulation at their particular level of development, such as in Figure 13.10.

## Unit 13–1 Checkpoint

Cognition is the ability to learn, remember, and think abstractly. Children's cognitive development relates to learning in all other skill areas. Early childhood educators see cognitive development from

---

### Curriculum Planning for Cognitive Development with Infants and Toddlers

**The Environment**
- Contains soft items (such as pillows) and hard elements (such as mirrors) to see, taste, and touch.
- Has contrasts of color and design.
- Changes periodically, from the floor to strollers to swing.
- Is decorated with pictures of people's faces, animals, families.

**The Skills**
- Include self-help activities of eating, toileting/changing, and dressing.
- Highlight language and thinking as the adults label objects, describe events, and reflect feelings in a simplified, conversational manner.
- Encourage listening to a person, a story, a flannelboard song, a fingerplay.
- Use appropriate art media to explore and manipulate, not to produce a finished product.

**The Themes**
- Are loosely defined and flexible, as is the schedule.
- Are of family and belonging, of self and bodies, of babies.
- Are dictated more by children's needs than by adults'.

---

**FIGURE 13.10** Planning for infants and toddlers involves understanding specific development and intimate knowledge of the individual child. Consistent caregiving and flexibility are as important to effective planning for children under two as are the actual activities offered.

an eclectic point of view and draw heavily from the works of Jean Piaget.

Cognitive skills in the early years can be put into several categories. The teacher's role is to understand how cognition develops in children and to put that knowledge to work in the classroom. While creating curriculum, teachers keep certain attitudes and ideas in mind. Then, they set about planning for their programs.

The methods of developing children's cognitive skills are as varied and creative as the teachers—and children—can be. By focusing on the class setting, a specific skill, or a theme, teachers help children acquire and use the skills of thinking to understand themselves and the world around them.

*Ask yourself:*

- What perspective do early childhood teachers have on the development of cognition?
- What are nine cognitive skills of the early years?
- What should teachers consider when defining their role in cognitive development?
- How can cognitive curriculum be developed in the class setting?
- What skills could be the focus for curriculum planning?
- What are three themes that encourage the development of cognitive skills?

# UNIT 13-2  LANGUAGE

| | |
|---|---|
| Alexis: | Laleña, will you help me full this pitcher up? |
| Laleña: | No, becuse my ponytail is keeping me in bothers. |
| Veronique: | Hey, come here! I accidentally dropped a piece of bread and the birds yummed it right up! |
| Abhi: | I know, that's what the tooth fairy did to my tooth. |
| Marty: | I'm going to keep *all* my baby teeth in a jar and the next time a baby comes along, I'll give him my baby teeth. |

Language is the aspect of human behavior that involves the use of sounds in meaningful patterns. This includes the corresponding symbols that are used to form, express, and communicate thoughts and feelings. Any system of signs used for communication is language. For the developing child, language is the ability to express oneself. Language is both *receptive*—listening, understanding, and responding—and *expressive*—pronunciation, vocabulary, and grammar. In other words, as illustrated above, language has meaning.

# THE DEVELOPMENT OF LANGUAGE

Language seems to be an innate characteristic of humankind. Wherever people live together, language of some form has developed. Languages worldwide vary remarkably in their sounds, words, and grammatical structure. Nonetheless, young children around the world acquire language.

## What Research Tells Us

Research into language development and expression reveals several interesting characteristics. First, the language of children is different from adult language (deVilliers and Jill, 1981). Children's language deals with the present and is egocentric, taking into account only the child's own knowledge. There appears to be a lack of awareness on the child's part of language form and structure. In other words, children use language to communicate but seem to have no understanding of language as an entity itself.

Language is not learned simply by imitating adult speech (Beck, 1979). Child language is not garbled adult language, but rather unique to the child's age and linguistic level. Children are not just trying to imitate others and making mistakes, but are trying to come to terms with language themselves. A child will try out theories about language in attempts to understand its patterns. In language, as in so many areas of cognition, children are involved as active participants in their own learning. The use of speech is not merely imitative but productive and creative.

Moreover, language development is a process of maturation. Just as in the development of cognitive skills, there are stages of language growth that follow a specific sequence. There are also variations in timing that are important to remember.

# Stages of Language Development

Children follow a six-step sequence in language development, one that seems *invariable* regardless of what language is being learned.

1. *Infant's Response to Language.* Babies begin by attending to speech, changes in sound, rhythm, and intonation. These are the *precursors* of speech, and young infants are especially sensitive to some sound differences. Infants need to hear speech, and plenty of it, to develop the foundations of sound.

2. *Vocalization.* By three to four months of age, infants begin cooing and babbling. Babbling increases with age and seems to peak around nine to 12 months. This is a matter of physical maturation, not just experience; deaf children do it at the same time as those whose hearing is normal. Furthermore, there are similar patterns across different languages.

3. *Word Development.* According to de Villiers and Jill (1981), the child must first separate the noises heard into speech and nonspeech. The speech noises must be further separated into words and the sounds that form them. The growing infant starts to shift from practice to playing with sounds. The end result is planned, controlled speech.

   Children begin playing with sounds around 10 to 15 months of age. From this point, the development of speech is determined as much by control of motor movements as by the ability to match sounds with objects.

   Most children can understand and respond to a number of words before they can produce any. Their first words include names of objects and events in their world (people, food, toys, animals). Then the child begins to overextend words, perhaps using "doggy" to refer to all animals. Finally, single words can be used as sentences: "Bye-bye" can refer to someone leaving, a meal the child thinks is finished, the child going away, a door closing.

4. *Sentences.* Children's sentences usually begin with two words, describing an action ("Me go"), a possession ("My ball"), or a location ("Baby outside"). These sentences get expanded by adding adjectives ("My big ball"), changing the verb tense ("Me jumped down"), or using negatives ("No go outside"). Children learn grammar not by being taught the rules, but as they listen to others' speech and put together the regularities they hear.

   Child language, while not identical to that of adults, does draw upon language heard to build a language base. Children incorporate and imitate what they hear to refine their own language structures.

5. *Elaboration.* Vocabulary begins to increase at an amazing rate. Sentences get longer, and communication begins to work into social interaction. In the hospital corner of a nursery school, this conversation takes place:

   | | |
   |---|---|
   | Chip: | I'm a nurse. |
   | Brooke: | I'm going to try to get some patients for you. |
   | Megan: | Do I need an operation? |
   | Chip: | Yeah, if you don't want to be sick anymore. |

6. *Graphic Representation.* By five or six years of age, reading and writing emerge as children become aware of language as an entity itself and of the written word as a way of documenting what is spoken. Awareness of print and emerging literacy are the outgrowth of this last stage of development. These areas are developed in the elementary school years, yet teachers can begin this process with preschool children in an interesting and child-oriented fashion. The *Special Topic Units* on Reading and Writing and Children's Literature

**FIGURE 13.11** Children's language skills reach their peak when they begin to represent language graphically.

as well as Dr. Calfee's *Focus* discussion address the issue of language and literacy. Additionally, six professional associations who serve as advocates for literacy standards have issued a joint statement of concerns about practices in pre-first grade reading instruction. See Appendix C, Literacy Development and Pre-First Grade. Figure 13.11 is a sample of a child's beginning writing skills.

# LANGUAGE SKILLS IN EARLY CHILDHOOD

Teachers translate language development theory into practice as they work with children. Language skills in the early childhood setting include articulation, receptive language, expressive language, and enjoyment.

## Articulation

*Articulation* is how children actually say the sounds and words. Children's ability to produce sound is a critical link in their connecting the sounds to form speech. As children talk, teachers listen for their ability to hear and reproduce sounds in daily conversation. Can they hear and produce sounds that differ widely, such as "sit" and "blocks"? Can they produce sounds that differ in small ways, such as in "man" and "mat"?

## Receptive Language

*Receptive language* is what children acquire when they learn to listen and understand. It is what they hear. With this skill children are able to understand directions, to answer a question, and to follow a sequence of events. They can understand

relationships and begin to predict the outcome of their behavior and that of others. They develop some mental pictures as they listen.

Children begin early and can become experts in reacting to words, voice, emphasis, and inflection. How many times does the child understand by the *way* the words are spoken?

"You finally *finished* your lunch." (Hooray for you)

"You *finally* finished your lunch." (You slowpoke)

Children learn to listen for enjoyment, for the way the wind sounds in the trees, the rhythm of a storytelling, or the sound of the car as it brings Mom or Dad home.

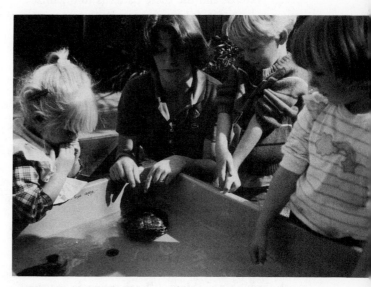

**FIGURE 13.12** Children learn language when they hear important people share with them interesting facts and stories.

# Expressive Language

*Expressive language* in the early years includes words, grammar, and elaboration.

## Words

Expressive language is the spoken word. Children's first words are of what is most important to them (Mama, Da-Da). Adults help children extend their knowledge and vocabulary by using the names of objects and words of action (walk, run, jump) and feelings (happy, sad, mad). By describing objects in greater and greater detail, teachers give children new words that increase their skills. Children are then ready to learn that some words have more than one meaning (the word "orange," for example, is both a color and a fruit) and that different words can have the same meaning (such as "ship" and "boat" as similar objects, or *muñeca* and "doll" as the same word in different languages).

## Grammar

Basic grammatical structure is learned as children generalize what they hear. They listen to adult speech patterns and use these patterns to organize their own language. It helps to hear simple sentences at a young age, with the words in the correct order. Next, children can grasp past tense as well as present, plural nouns along with the singular. Finally, the use of more complex structures is understood (prepositions, comparatives, various conjugations of verbs).

## Elaboration of Language

*Elaboration* of language takes many, many forms. It is the act of expanding the language. Through description, narration, explanation, and communication, adults elaborate their own speech to encourage children to do the same. For instance, communication for children includes talking to oneself and others. When a teacher verbalizes a process aloud, children see how language helps them work through a problem. ("I am trying to get the plant out of its pot, but when I turn it upside-down, it doesn't fall out by itself. Now I'll use this shovel to loosen the dirt from the sides of the pot, and hope that helps.") Communicating with others involves giving and following directions. ("It's time to make a choice for cleanup time. You find something to do and I'll watch you.") It means asking and answering questions. ("How do you feel when she says she won't play with you? What can you say? What can you do?") Sticking to the subject keeps communication flowing: "I know you want to play kickball, but first let's solve this problem between you and Conor about the wagon." Children are encouraged to communicate verbally with others as they see teachers using speech to get involved in play themselves. ("What a great house you have built. How do you get inside? Do you need any dishes?")

# Enjoyment

To encourage language is to promote enjoyment in using it. Teachers converse with children, parents, and other adults, modeling for children how useful and fun language can be. Children learn to enjoy language by participating in group discussions and being encouraged to ask questions. Reading and listening to stories and poems everyday is an essential part of any program. The program should also include children's literature and stories children dictate or write themselves.

Word play and rhyming are fun as well as educational. Group language games are useful, such as asking the question, "Did you ever see a bat with a hat? a bun having fun? a bee with . . .?"and letting the children add the rest. Begin a song, for instance, "Do You Know the Muffin Man?", and add the children's names. Whatever contributes to the enjoyment of language supports its growth, from varying voice and tone to fit the situation (in storytelling, dramatic play, and ordinary activity periods) to spontaneous rhyming songs.

# THE TEACHER'S ROLE

## Considerations

When considering how to work with young children in language development, teachers should keep several things in mind.

**FIGURE 13.13**  Teachers and children can share intimate moments when they enjoy using language together.

**Children Must Use Language to Learn It.** Adults who are unaware of this sometimes spend a lot of their time with children talking to, at, and about them. Children need time, place, and support for practicing language. Practice must include time with peers and adults, and in both structured (group time) and nonstructured (free play) situations.

**The Most Verbal Children Tend to Monopolize Language Interactions.** Research shows that teachers interact verbally with the children who are most skilled verbally (Cazden, 1979). Seek out and support language development in those with fewer skills, generally by drawing them out individually through (1) reading the unspoken (body) language that communicates their ideas, needs, and feelings, and (2) helping them express verbally those ideas, needs, and feelings.

**Adults Should Know the Individual Child.** Consistency in adult–child relationships may be as important for language as for affective development during the early years (Cazden, 1979). If so, teachers must have a meaningful relationship with each child. This includes knowing the parent(s) and how they communicate with their child.

**Bilingualism.** In early childhood terms, *bilingualism* is the acquisition of two languages during the first years of life. The bilingual child must learn to comprehend and produce aspects of each language and then develop two systems of communication. Bilingualism in early childhood also occurs under these general conditions:

**1.** Children can comprehend and produce some aspects of both languages.

2. Through natural exposure, such as in a classroom, children get experience in both languages.

3. Development occurs simultaneously in both languages (Garcia, 1983).

The preschool setting is an excellent laboratory for studying exactly how children meet these conditions. Unfortunately, little systematic research has been done of children who acquire two languages at the same time. The challenge to a young child is enormous, particularly since acquiring a second language is more than linguistics. The issue of bilingualism must include cognitive and social considerations as well as linguistic ones.

What can be concluded at this time, however tentatively, is that:

• Children can and do learn two languages at an early age.

• Two languages can be learned at the same time in a parallel manner. The depth of knowledge of one language may be different from the other, or the two may develop equally.

• The acquisition of languages may mean a "mixing" of the two, as heard in children's speech when they use words or a sentence structure of both languages.

• Learning two languages does not hurt the acquisition of either language (Garcia, 1983).

Teachers must understand the increased workload bilingualism creates, and they must keep in mind that learning another language affects cognitive and social development.

**Speech and Language Disorders.** Early childhood professionals should have knowledge of speech and language disorders. Disorders of both receptive and expressive language can be detected early. The perceptive teacher does a great service to children and parents by discovering potential problems. Special needs are normal and common, and Chapter 3 elaborates how these are dealt with in early childhood settings.

**The Language of the Teacher.** What teachers say—and how they say it—is important. Moreover, it is often what they do *not* say that communicates the most to children in their struggle to gain mastery of the language. For instance, when a child is stumbling over a word or phrase, teachers must give the child the time to work through the difficulty, rather than correcting or "helping" by finishing the sentence themselves. Teachers provide a rich environment and a high quality of interaction with the child that encourages articulation, receptive language, expressive language, and graphic language (the written word).

To *articulate* means to speak distinctly and with moderate speed. Teachers reinforce clear speech by giving frequent opportunities for children to practice speech.

*Receptive language* can be developed by using several strategies.

1. Give clear directions: "Please go and sit on the rug next to the chairs," instead of "Go sit over there."

2. Let children ask questions, and give them acceptable answers. For example, repeat a phrase from the child's last sentence that asks the child to try again: "You want *what?*" or "You ate *what?*". Or cast the question back to a child by changing the phrase "Where did you put it?" into "You put it *where?*".

3. Give instructions in a sequence: "Put your lunch on your desk, then wash your hands. Then you are ready to go to lunch." It often helps to ask the children what they think they are to do: "How do you get ready for lunch? What comes first? Next?"

4. Try to understand what the child means, regardless of the actual language. Look for the purpose and intent beyond what the child may have said. This is particularly important with toddlers, non–English speakers, and newcomers.

5. Ask children to state their thoughts out loud. "Tell me what you think is going to happen to the

eggs in the incubator. Why do you think some might hatch and some might not?"

6. Use literature, poetry, and your own descriptions to give children an idea of how words can be used to paint verbal and mental pictures. Ask questions about children's own images and dreams. To older children read aloud from books without pictures.

*Expressive language* is encouraged when teachers focus on the spoken word. They use short, concise sentences to frame or highlight a word. If a child says, "Look at that!", teachers reply, "That's a butterfly," or "I see; do you think it's a butterfly or a bee?"

One way children gain a greater awareness of themselves is by describing their own actions in words. To make sure that all children experience the art of conversation, be sure to provide plenty of opportunities for them to converse with adults as well as peers to help them learn the reciprocal nature of communication. Ask them to say what they are doing. Make a statement describing the child's behavior or actions. This is particularly helpful when dealing with feelings, such as the statement "It looks like you are feeling angry" (when confronted with a frown and clenched fists).

**Curriculum Planning for Language Development: The Teacher Talks**

*Description*
- Use nouns for people, places, events: "We are going to visit Grandma now. That means we need to get dressed and walk to her apartment."
- Use modifiers: "That is your uncle's truck outside" or "Can you find your sister's teddy bear?"
- Use relational terms: "You are taller than the chair; the wagon is wider than the bed."
- Try more differentiated words to express differences: Instead of just "big/ little," try "fat/thin" and "tall/short."

*Narration*
- Describe simple relationships of time: "Yesterday you stayed at home. Today is a school day. Tomorrow is Saturday, a stay-home day."
- Clarify a sequence of events: "When you come to school, first you put your things in your cubby, then you make an inside choice."
- Use words to describe repetition, continuation, and completion: "We are going to the store again, to buy food for dinner" or "I see that you and Juana are still playing together today" or "You finished building the box last time; now you are ready to paint it."

*Explanation*
- Point out similarities and differences: "Both Cathi and I have brown hair, but what is different about us? Yes, she has on shorts and I am wearing overalls."
- Try classifying what you see as well as asking children to do so: "I notice that all these shells have ridges on the outside; what do you see that is different about them?"

**FIGURE 13.14** Several aspects of language development affect how teachers speak to children in the early years.

Teachers help children by directing their attention to objects, events, and relationships.

Michelle: I have something to show you.
Teacher: Can you give us some clues?
Michelle: It's not a record and it's not a book, and you can't play with it.
Teacher: Can you hold it in your hand?
Michelle: No, silly; it's a kiss!

Give children opportunities to describe what they are going to do and what they have done. Through this, teachers discover what is meaningul to children and what they remember, and it gives them the chance to plan and review. When the class celebrates a birthday, children will want to discuss when their birthday is, what they will do, or how they feel. The answers may range from "July thirty-last" to "We're going to the moon" to "On my birthday my heart is filling me with lightening."

"Why do you think that happened?" is a thought-provoking question for children. Questions that encourage children to expand on their thoughts include those that ask for classifications ("Who has short-sleeved shirts on today?"), seriation ("If the blue ball is smallest, which one comes next?"), and other concepts of cognition.

An interesting and revealing aspect of working with children is listening to how they communicate and to the kinds of confusions that arise. "I can see you are really thinking about..." supports children's self-talk and concentration.

Developing communication skills with others is particularly important for children in the early years. Encouraging active listening and repeating one child's words to another ("Bahrain, did you hear what Joanna said about the sandtruck?") give children support. Expressing thoughts and feelings in words offers a model. By telling a child what works for you ("I like it when you listen to my words"), a teacher provides a good example of how to communicate. Helping children stick to the subject shows that there is a topic at hand: "Stevie, now we're talking about our field trip to the track. You can tell us about your new dog next." Figure 13.14 elaborates three ways to enhance language development.

## Curriculum Planning for Language Development

Teachers who plan curriculum for language skills, just as for cognitive development, focus on the class setting, specific skills, and themes. They organize the environment and activities to help children acquire linguistic skills of their own.

### In the Environment

**Indoors.** Teachers arrange space so that children will practice speaking and listening and, in programs for older children, reading and writing. For example, a restaurant in the dramatic play area encourages the use of language. There are many signs: the name of the restaurant, OPEN and CLOSED, and COME AND GET IT! The children help create what is written on the menu. They can suggest "daily specials," and how to advertise them. Stories are written as a group-time project. A follow-up activity to encourage graphic language might be a newsletter about the restaurant corner, signed by the children themselves.

There is new vocabulary to learn in the restaurant unit: names of objects (menu, waiter, customer), action (serving, eating, paying), and feelings (waiting, impatient, hungry, finished). Children describe to one another where things are located, how much food to serve, how to pay for the meal.

The following dialogue shows expressive and receptive language as overheard in the restaurant:

Jean: I'm the cooker! Torrey, you make the money.
Frankie: What's going on around here?
Jean: We're the rest'rant. Whadda you want to eat?
Frankie: I'm thirsty. Where's my coffee?
Teacher, who is watching nearby: What happens when someone comes into a restaurant?
Torrey: We need a waitress, man. Emily, come here!
Emily: Tell me what you want to eat.
Frankie: Don't give me rabies; I'm allergic to them but my mom makes me eat them all the time.

Teacher:  What's rabies?
Frankie:  Oh, that's meatloaf and other yucky stuff.
Emily:  All we have is scrambled eggs.
Jean:  Here's your eggs.
Frankie:  Hey, my eggs are gooder than these. Yuck.
Torrey:  Come back here! You haveta pay me! He's a robber!

Other indoor areas can also be arranged to enhance language development:

*Art*
- Design menu cover.
- Offer templates for tracing letters.
- Have signs and pictures that show where things are kept.
- Ask children to describe the materials they use.

*Blocks*
- Ask children to give each other directions for where blocks go and what they are used for.
- Label block shelves with shapes and words.
- Sketch children's structures and then write their word descriptions.

*Cooking*
- Label utensils.
- Describe actions (pour, measure, stir).
- Use recipe cards with both pictures and words.

*Discovery/Science*
- Label all materials.
- Ask questions about what is displayed.
- Encourage children's displays, with their dictated words nearby.
- Graph growth and changes of plants, animals, children, and experiments.

*Language*
- Label the bookshelf, record player, other equipment.

- Help children make their own books that involve description (My family is...), narration (It is winter when...), and recall (Yesterday I...).
- Have children "write" notes, lists, or letters, to one another, the teachers, and their families.
- Develop a writing center with a typewriter, office supplies, and so on.

*Manipulatives*
- Recognize this area as a place for self-communication, as children talk and sing to themselves while they work.
- Explain similarities and differences of materials and structures.

Another way to develop language along with cognitive and socioemotional skills is to build a "Talkalot Kit" (Jones, 1987). These collections of materials with something in common stimulate conversation as well as classification and dramatic play. Kits could be made of buttons, gloves, shoes, brushes, face coverings, containers: use your imagination!

**Outdoors.** Outdoors, motor skills can be described and pointed out by teachers and children, as both use words of action and of feeling. For example, what actions does it take to get a wagon up the hill? How does a child's face feel when swinging up high? How do people sit? move? carry things?

**Transitions.** Transitions and routines are more manageable if the children understand what is happening and exactly what they are to do. Teacher language helps talk children through the process so that they can internalize what they are asked to do. A teacher can write a note to "Please save" for the child who does not have time to finish a project, or they can write children's dictated notes to parents.

Group times, with fingerplays, songs, and stories, are language-intensive activities. Children's articulation skills are strengthened, as is receptive language through listening to others. Group times are also opportunities for children to express themselves. When children discuss daily news and important events, brainstorm ideas about a subject, or report on what they did earlier in the day, they gain experience in listening and speaking. Children can also dramatize familiar stories and fingerplays.

Using visual aids or name cards gives children experience in *graphic language*. These might include having felt letters for the song "B-I-N-G-O," numbers for the fingerplay "One, Two, Buckle My Shoe," or name cards for the activity "I'm Thinking of Someone . . . " And children enjoy the cadence and rhythm of language spoken or chanted.

## Focus on Skills

Language development involves five different skills. Teachers can plan a curriculum focusing on a single skill, be it articulation, receptive, expressive, or graphic language, or the enjoyment of language. After choosing one of the skills, they look at the environment to see how that skill can be developed.

To focus on expressive language, teachers remember that children learn to express themselves by practicing words and grammatical structure, and by elaborating on their own expressions. A teacher asks three-year-old Ceva to describe what she is doing with the art materials. "I'm dripping my paint," she replies. Outdoors, two-year-old Hadar describes her actions: "Teacher, look at me! I'm taller than you!" The teacher responds, "You climbed up the ladder to the top of the tunnel. Now, when you stand up, your head is above mine." At group time, the whole class makes a group story about "The Mystery of Space." Then they separate into small groups with second-grade helpers to write their own books in story form, complete with illustrations.

## Use of Themes

How could using themes for curriculum planning be used to develop language skills? One unit with universal appeal is "Babies," charted in Figure 13.15. Other units that elicit an extensive use of language are:

- *Thanksgiving.* Activity area: Make a display of food from a harvest feast in the past—for instance,

**THEME: BABIES**

*Art:* Limit the art materials to just what toddlers and infants can use.
*Cooking:* Make baby food.
*Discovery/science:* Display baby materials, then bring in baby animals.
*Dramatic play area:* "The Baby Corner" with dolls, cribs, diapers.
*Manipulatives:* Bring in several infant and toddler toys.
*Large motor/games:* Make a "crawling route," an obstacle course that requires crawling *only*.
*Field trip/guest:* A parent brings a baby to school to dress, bathe, or feed.
*Large-group time:* Sing lullabies ("Rock-a-Bye-Baby").
*Small/large group:* Children discuss "What can babies do?"
 Joshua: Babies sleep in cribs. They wear diapers. Babies can't talk.
 Becky: They sometimes suck their thumbs. Babies cry when they are hungry.
 Dennis: Babies go pee in their diapers.
 Stevie: Babies sit in highchairs. Babies eat baby food that looks like squished bananas.
 Corey: Babies sleep in a basinette. Then they crawl and bite your finger.

**FIGURE 13.15** Teachers plan a unit to promote the skills they are focusing on in the class. To encourage language, a "babies" theme brings out the "expert" in all children.

of Native Americans as well as the colonists—and then of foods today.

Group time: Begin a group story using the sentence "I am thankful for . . . "

Special project: Plan a feast, with the children creating the menu and preparing both the food and the table for their families at the school.

- *Summertime.* Activity area: Children bring a piece of summer clothing for a display and "try-on" corner.

  Group time: Children respond to the phrase, "One summer morning . . . " with stories and pictures.

  Special project: A trip to the beach, or a treasure hunt for buried shells in the sand area outside.

- *Celebrations.* Activity area: Decorate each corner of the room with materials from different countries or ethnic groups, including party clothes and gift wrap.

  Group time: "People celebrate when . . . "

  Special project: Children make a gift for someone they love.

- *Favorite Foods.* Activity area: Make a salad from everyone's favorite vegetable, or follow the storyline of *Stone Soup.*

  Group time: Discussion topic: "My favorite fruit is . . . " (Example: "An apple because it is crunchy and is big enough to share.")

  Special project: Make recipe cards to send home. (Example: Chicken—"First you get seven pounds of skin. Then you get flat pieces of roast chicken. Then you put some bones in. Then you get one pound of pickle seeds and put them on the chicken. Then cook it in the oven for about five hours!")

Any theme can be developed, so long as it brings out oral and graphic language experiences.

While preschool and school-age children are challenged by specific themes, curriculum development for infants and toddlers does not always need this kind of focus. Rather, these classes look to the developmental level of the group to encourage language growth for the very young. Figure 13.16 describes curriculum ideas for language development in an infant/toddler class.

---

**Curriculum for Language Development of Infants and Toddlers**

**The Environment**
- Is gentle and supportive, with adults who listen and respond to sounds made and who let the children initiate language.
- Is explained simply, such as what the caregiver is doing during clothing or diaper changing.
- Is responsive, as adults respond quickly to crying and redirect what the children can do and express.

**The Skills**
- Adults expand on the children's own words. Toddler: "The shoe." Adult: "Oh, that's your shoe you are holding."
- Adults model for children the words to say. Adult: "Elenoa, I want the puppet now."
- Children listen in small groups of two or three, on laps or next to adults, and are allowed wide variation in their participation.

**The Themes**
- Revolve around the children's individual interests.
- Include favorite stories presented in several ways: reading *The Three Bears,* doing a flannelboard story, singing a fingerplay, having bear puppets and stuffed animals.

---

**FIGURE 13.16** Language experiences for infants and toddlers take into consideration the developmental milestones and the individual child's level of self-expression.

## Unit 13–2   Checkpoint

Children develop language in their own ways, following patterns consistent over different cultures and countries. In the early years, language consists of several skills. The teacher's role is one of knowing how language develops and what skills to encourage in a class setting.

Then, teachers plan curriculum for language development. They organize the environment and schedule by focusing on the various areas and activities, a specific skill, or a unit.

*Ask yourself:*

- What does research tell us about child language and its development?

- What are the six stages of language development?

- What are the five language skills in early childhood education?

- What are six teacher considerations in planning for language development?

- How can teachers plan a curriculum that uses language skills?

- What themes promote language skill in the classroom?

# UNIT 13–3   SPECIAL TOPICS IN COGNITION AND LANGUAGE

## READING AND WRITING

*Graphic language* is the written word. For the young child, what once looked like dots and lines becomes letters and words. How does the early childhood teacher help children in this process?

The ability to read and write does not just happen when children reach a certain age. Their readiness for graphic language must be nurtured. A child's language proficiency will determine readiness for reading. Teachers identify this readiness by knowing how well a child understands the structure and vocabulary of the language. Therefore, a program to encourage beginning reading will offer experiences in oral language. Research shows that successful readers see a relationship between spoken language and the written word. They are aware that sounds are how language is put together (Nurss, 1980). So teachers plan activities that make connections between what is said and what is written.

# F O C U S

## LANGUAGE AND LITERACY: FROM HOME TO SCHOOL TO LIFE

*Robert Calfee*

More than once a youngster has nudged my arm at the end of a lesson to say, "That was fun. I thought it was supposed to be a reading lesson..."

Reading *is* fun. It's also work, and it can be power. The trek today from kindergarten through third grade is often unhappy. At best the barrage of rote questions and repetitive worksheets leaves children bored and disinterested; at worst the child fails—and is labeled *learning disabled*.

It's wonderful when a five-year-old tells you that you've done well as a teacher! But how can reading have such a poor reputation so early in life? From my earliest memories, books opened doors to new worlds, to the minds of others. Equally marvelous is the power of writing—to influence others through the printed page.

These experiences are not felt by children in today's classrooms. What's wrong? One answer is *nothing*. The present system needs technical refinement, but standardized tests of vocabulary and comprehension have stayed steady over recent decades. Not to worry.

A second answer, "You learn to read by reading," confuses the public. This answer posits that simply engaging youngsters in the richness of literature will do the trick. Reading should be an experience that is purposeful and whole, not a collection of objectives.

Neither answer fits our time. In past years, schools served for daycare and for selection. Like today, we needed to offer children a haven. But schools also identified youngsters who (for whatever reason) entered with academic promise. The latter rode the high track to high school, college, and professional status. Competence in reading and writing was their touchstone. The future has changed. We must now educate virtually every youngster entering the school door, even though demographics tell us that many in the next generation will not fit expectations.

How to resolve this problem—the critical challenge for education in the next decade? I've thought a lot about this matter and I've spent considerable classroom time testing my hypotheses. Some references to these studies are included in the bibliography for this chapter in order to provide additional detail for this brief note.

First, we need to change our definition of reading from a *technical skill* (translating print to spoken language) to the conception of a *different mode of language usage*. For some purposes, in

some times and societies, decoding is enough. But for our future, youngsters need the capacity to employ language as a tool for thinking and for communicating.

Second, we need to gather the scattered objectives of present-day curricula into a coherent image of literacy as the core of the elementary grades. You may hear about the *integrated language curriculum*: reading, writing, speaking, and listening joined rather than separated. On the other hand, teaching literacy as a lump rather than a mess is not much of an advance. Literacy has *separable components*, each with a distinctive technical language: vocabulary and concept development, narrative and expository forms, decoding and spelling. The literate person commands all these forms.

Third, the informed teaching professional is the key to guiding youngsters along the path from home through school to success in society (more than work, to be sure). The teacher without a road map must "follow the directions." The teacher who knows the territory can, in contast, help students stand away from language and appreciate the deeper meaning of literary works—the comparison of characters, the understanding of feelings, the grasp of theme, the reach that moves a child to authorship. The process holds magic but also entails solid grounding in the technology of language, rhetoric, and learning. It requires both head and heart.

*Robert Calfee is a professor of education at Stanford University.*

---

There is an important role, then, for teachers of young children in the early stages of reading and writing. Teachers can influence positive attitudes toward reading and writing. Supporting children's interest in learning to read and write is a part of this role. The *Focus* discussion in this chapter, by Dr. Robert Calfee, explores the place of language and literacy at home, in school, and for life. Teachers encourage children to talk and converse with others about what they see and do; this gives them increasing experience in using and attaching experiences to words. When adults take the time to write down what children say and then read it back, it gives a sense of importance to children's language and their ability to express themselves. In these ways, teachers can help children get involved with print in natural and unpressured ways.

When is your birthday?
- Where is your name?
- How many children have birthdays in April? February? December?
- How many children have birthdays on the 10th? the 2nd? At the end of the month?

| JAN. | FEB. | MAR. | APRIL | MAY | JUNE | JULY | AUG. | SEPT. | OCT. | NOV. | DEC. |
|---|---|---|---|---|---|---|---|---|---|---|---|
| 13 Ann | 1 José | 3 Leon | 2 Mrs. K. | 16 Brian | 11 Katie | 5 Mr. W. | 2 Carrie | 8 Jim | 21 Chris | 7 Nick | 13 Keesha |
| 19 Bill | 3 Mary | 7 Kirk | 10 Peter | 27 Adele | | 9 Panya | | 29 Danny | 30 Jay | | 25 Carol |
| 26 Judy | 6 Sue | 15 Roberto | 11 Jon | | | 12 Kevin | | | | | 30 Mrs. M. |
| 24 Tom | 11 Andy | | 18 Jill | | | | | | | | |
| | 19 Sean | | 23 Libby | | | | | | | | |
| | | | 30 Mia | | | | | | | | |

**FIGURE 13.17** A language experience chart involves children through the subject matter and through the way the information is displayed.

# Children and Reading

The role of the adult is one of engaging children with print in ways that make sense to them. By creating an environment that provides rich opportunities to use the printed word, teachers help motivate children toward reading. Research tells us that children who are successful readers in elementary school are typically those who have a history of successful reading in their early years (Schickedanz, 1983).

At the preschool level, we often find a stereotypical concept of reading. Both children and adults associate the ability to read with the literal translation of signs and symbols on a printed page (called *decoding*). But for the young child, learning to read is not merely decoding the symbols. It is attaching experiences and knowledge to those words and understanding the use of the written word in their daily lives. Many parents and teachers believe that reading instruction begins in elementary school, so little is done to expand a child's simplified concept of reading before first or second grade.

In the early childhood setting, there is an opportunity to teach a broader concept of reading that goes beyond decoding and permeates children's lives. To do this, reading should not be taught as "basal reading," but instead should be treated as part of a child's immediate and ongoing life. This can help create positive attitudes about reading before the decoding process begins.

It is up to adults to provide children with opportunities that will enlarge their concepts of the power of the written word. Teachers and parents can wield a great deal of influence in communicating positive feelings about reading. One way to do this is by providing real and valid prereading experiences.

Children can learn to recognize, read, and write their names when given interesting ways to do it. A popular technique in many early childhood centers is to use a waiting list for highly desirable activities. By learning to read or print their names, children receive a tangible benefit: they can sign up for the activities they want and check the list to see where their names are. Some computer programs now allow children to manipulate letters for making their names, then print them (see computer section in this chapter). Through these experiential activities in reading and writing, children learn that words are useful and can be fun.

In her book *Teacher*, Sylvia Ashton-Warner describes another technique for introducing printed language to young children. A kindergarten teacher who believed strongly in children's innate creativity and curiosity, Ashton-Warner developed a system of "organic reading" in which the students themselves build a key vocabulary of words they wish to learn to read and write. This method was effective for her classes of native Maori children in New Zealand, for whom the British basal readers held little meaning. Ashton-Warner's personal, culturally relevant teaching works well, since it flows naturally from the child's own life and interests.

The child's readiness to read is related to the development of certain skills (see Figure 13.18).

| Reading Readiness Is | Teachers |
| --- | --- |
| 1. Oral vocabulary | 1. Encourage talking, learning new words and phrases, singing, fingerplays, remembering and reflecting verbally. |
| 2. Curiosity about/for reading | 2. Provide a separate area for books (and are available to read to children), language games (lotto), dictation from children ("If I could fly I would . . ."), notes about children that the children deliver themselves to other adults. |
| 3. Auditory discrimination (the ability to detect sound differences) | 3. Create sound discrimination boxes in the science area, a "listen-to-the-sound" walk, guessing games with musical instruments, activities that teach letter sounds by using the children's names. |
| 4. Visual discrimination | 4. Support directionality: left and right (in the "Hokey-Pokey" dance and labeled on shoes and mittens), up and down, top and bottom, likeness and differences. |
| 5. Awareness of print | 5. Help the children name and label the classroom (door, tables, book corner), with bilingual signs as appropriate. Bring children's native languages into print by asking parents for the names of common objects, numbers, and so on for use around the classroom and in song and fingerplay charts. Encourage children to help print their own names on creative works. Write group newsletters to send home. Make flannelboard letters for free play and for use in songs, such as "Bingo." |

**FIGURE 13.18** Children gain reading readiness skills through activities for oral vocabulary, curiosity about reading, and auditory and visual discrimination.

Readiness skills can be acquired through planned experiences in the school program that:

- Promote meaningful interaction with words.
  *Example:* Writing children's names on their drawings; labeling cubbies with children's names and pictures.
- Are age-level appropriate.
  *Example:* For 2½-year-olds, play lotto games using pictures of familiar objects; for four-year-olds, use animal pictures; for six-year-olds, use alphabet letters.
- Are fun and enjoyable for children.
  *Example:* Creating a class newspaper to take home.
- Take a gradual approach through the use of non-reading materials.
  *Example:* Label toy storage boxes with pictures. Later in the year, add the words alongside the pictures.
- Acknowledge the child's ability to read the environment, to read events, to read other people.
  *Example:* Clark, looking out the window at the darkening sky, says, "Looks like it's gonna rain." Margo "reads" her painting as she describes the vivid monster to the teacher.
- Involve the use of children's senses.
  *Example:* Display baskets of vegetables and foods along with the book *Stone Soup.*

The school will have many activities in the area of "reading readiness." Recent research implies that an early childhood program promotes and awareness of the graphic aspects of language by:

1. Developing children's speaking and listening proficiencies through the use of conversation, descriptive language, oral feedback, and meaningful listening comprehension activities.

2. Helping children hear phonemes (language sounds) through oral language activities such as rhyming, initial consonant substitution, and the use of alliterations in jingles and language play.

3. Providing many opportunities for children to make the connection between spoken and written language.

4. Emphasizing children's own language in beginning reading activities.

5. Filling the environment with printed words and phrases, so children become familiar with meaningful print.

6. Highlighting the language used in beginning reading instructions; for example, use the terms, "letter," "sound," "word," and "sentence."

## Children and Writing

Children learn about words in print much the same as they learn about reading and other aspects of language; that is, by seeing it used and having plenty of opportunities to use it themselves. Writing can be as natural for children as walking and talking. Children begin to write when they first take a pencil in hand and start to scribble. Later, they can write a story by drawing pictures or by dictating the words and having someone else write them down.

The early childhood classroom heightens an interest in writing through a writing center. It can be part of a language area or a self-help art center. Wherever it is located, this center will include a variety of things to write with and write on, and "writing helpers." Children write with pencils (fat and thin, with and without erasers), colored pencils, narrow and wide marking pens, and crayons. They enjoy having many kinds of paper products, including computer paper, old calendars, data-punch cards, and colored paper. Children also enjoy simple books, a few blank pages stapled together. Carbon paper, dittos, and lined paper will add variety. "Writing helpers" might be a picture dictionary, a set of alphabet letters, a print set, an alphabet chart, chalkboard, or magnetic letter board. All of these serve to help children practice writing skills.

Writing materials can be available throughout the room and yard. Paper and pencils come in handy in the dramatic play area. Menus, shopping lists, prescriptions, and money are but a few uses children will find for writing equipment. The block corner may need traffic signs; the computer, a waiting list. Outdoors, pictures can label the location of the vegetables in the garden; markers indicate where children have hidden "treasures," or where the dead bird is buried.

The "language experience" approach involves taking dictation, writing down and reading back to children their own spoken language. It is important to use the child's exact words so they can make the connection between their speech and the letters on the page. This is true for group stories, for children's self-made books, or for descriptions of their own paintings. A useful technique in taking dictation is to say the words while writing them, allowing the child to watch the letters and words being formed. When the content is read back, the child has a sense of completion. Figure 13.19 is an example of this kind of language experience in a classroom of five- and six-year-olds.

---

*If I were a musical instrument:*

Dennis: I would be a violin. Someone would play me with a bow and I would make a beautiful sound.

Janette: I would be a drum. I would be hit and I wouldn't be happy because they would make me hurt.

Corey: I would be a flute and someone would play my keys and it would craze me out. I would feel funny and I would play with my keys so hard that my wits would jump out and then my feet would jump out.

Michelle: I would be a piano with strings and lots of sparklies on top. And, you could play me even if you were blind.

Stevie: I would be a guitar because my friend is a guitar player.

Sara: I would be a flute. I would go whistle, whistle, whistle. And if I was a triangle I would go dong, dong, ding, ding. If I was a triangle they would use me for dinner so everybody would come.

Matthew: I would be a flute. I would make noise. I would make music.

Joshua: I would play the trombone 'cuz I would play songs. It has buttons. I would put it away up high where my sister couldn't reach it.

Matt: I would be a rattle and I would sound like a rattlesnake when somebody shakes me. I would be happy.

Rohan: I would be a drum and somebody would hit me with a stick. I would go pum, pum, pum.

Jocelyn: I would be a triangle so I could hit myself. It would make a ding-dong, a ding, ding. If I was, I knew that if I hit myself it would hurt; if I hit myself, it would hurt real badly.

Gregory: I would be a trumpet. I would play and everyone would be happy.

Becky: I would be a flute. I would make all different kinds of sounds.

---

**FIGURE 13.19** Dictation, as a language experience approach, gives children a meaningful way to learn about the printed word.

The early childhood setting encourages an awareness of and interest in writing by having the printed word displayed regularly. Storage units are labeled with pictures and words of what belongs where (scissors, turtle food, blocks). Areas of the room are named, and stories, poems, or familiar fingerplays are hung on charts. Written signs remind children of the rules, such as "Inside Voices Here" in the book corner or "Wear an Apron" near the easels. Primary classes may add calendars and helper charts, visual cues for children to read and prepare for the next event. In these ways, teachers help raise awareness of the use and enjoyment of the printed word.

# CHILDREN'S LITERATURE

From the beginnings of education on this continent, literature has had a place in the curriculum. To be sure, from era to era, the emphases in the literary experiences of children . . . have changed; but the basic commitment to literature as a valuable . . . enterprise has been maintained. And today the potential of literature for children is greater than ever before. For we have more . . . beautiful books . . . more children who are capable of reading on their own . . . more good aids to teachers for selecting and utilizing literature in the education of youngsters. There is, indeed, little reason why any child . . . in these times should not be amply provided with . . . contact with literature throughout his entire . . . life.

(Jacobs *in* Rasmussen, 1961)

Literature does indeed have an important place in the curriculum today. It is especially valuable as a vehicle for cognitive and language development. Books help to acquaint children with new words, ideas, facts, and adventures. Planned and spontaneous reading experiences are a vital part of the young child's day.

Reading books to children introduces them to the reading concept, to a different form of communication from spoken language. It is a symbol system with which they will become familiar as they learn that words and pictures have meaning.

# Literature and Cognitive Development

Literature can perform several functions in aiding cognitive development. Through the use of good books, teachers can help children broaden their interests and concepts. Books that are primarily used for transmitting information expand the child's knowledge base. Thoughtful books that draw on children's everyday experiences widen their understanding of themselves and others. Through books, children can learn to see things in an endless variety of ways. Five different books will describe and illustrate behavior of cats in five different ways. Exposure to *Millions of Cats* (Gag), *Angus and the Cats* (Flack), and *The Cat in the Hat* (Dr. Seuss), as well as to the cats portrayed in *Peter Rabbit* (Potter) or *Frog Went A-Courtin'* (Langstaff), will enlarge the child's concepts of cats. Different cultures are also represented in any number of children's books, teaching a greater awareness of all of humankind.

Teachers have an opportunity to encourage divergent thinking through the use of children's literature. Children gain more than facts from books; they learn all matter of things, providing they can interpret the story rather than just hear the individual words. Quizzing children about whether the dinosaur was a meat- or plant-eater will bring about responses that are predictable and pat, but comprehension does not have to be joyless. Zingy questions will provide not only thought but also interest. "Would a brontosaurus fit in your living room?" will get children to think about *Danny and the Dinosaur* (Hoff) in a new way. "Is the troll bigger or smaller than your brother?" might be a point of discussion after reading *The Three Billy Goats Gruff*. The point is not to have children feed back straight factual information, but to get them involved in the story.

Selection of books obviously plays a part in using literature to stimulate thought and conversation about what was read. The wise teacher will choose books that invite participation. Everyone can "roar a terrible roar, gnash their terrible teeth, and show their terrible claws" during a rendition of *Where the Wild Things Are* (Sendak). Meaning for children lies more in action than in words. Children will be more apt to talk about stories that have in some way touched them and stimulated their involvement.

Questions for thought and children's participation must be related to children's experiences and knowledge, yet lead them toward discovery. Books provide a pleasurable avenue for this type of intellectual growth.

## Literature and Language Development

A great many language skills are learned when children are exposed to good literature in the classroom. The value lies in the use of language by the author and the use the teacher makes of the language potential.

If language development is the goal, auditory appeal is one of the best reasons for choosing a book. The actual sounds of the words catch children's attention and imagination. Familiar sounds of animals or objects reinforce and provide new ways to express thoughts. "Buzz" and "humm" are playful words that have a great appeal to children. Sensory words, such as cold, soft, and slippery, capture children's attention.

Building and extending vocabulary is another function of literature in the language arts curriculum. Old familiar words take on new meaning as they reflect the content of each different story. Children love new words, especially big ones, and they do not necessarily need them defined. If used correctly in the context of the storyline, the words will be self-explanatory. Many children memorize phrases from favorite books, sometimes unaware of their meaning, but fitting the rhythm and pattern into their play.

When Andrea was struggling to find the words to describe a large amount, Mitra began to recite: "Hundreds of cats, thousands of cats, millions and billions and trillions of cats!" (*Millions of Cats,* Gag)

Riding home in the car after school one day, Parker chanted: "Tik-ki tik-ki tem-bo no sa rembo, chari bari ru-chi, pip peri pembo." (*Tikki Tikki Tembo,* Mosel)

Derek and Shigeo were playing grocery store. In order to attract customers they called out: "Caps for sale! Fifty cents a cap." (*Caps for Sale,* Slobodkina)

Language—and vocabulary—come alive with such repetition, as children integrate the words into their play. This demonstrates another benefit of books and literature in language development: that of learning the skill of listening. Teachers could ask for no better activity to promote good listening habits than a wealth of good children's books.

## Creating a Rich Literary Environment

The comics of yesterday are far outdistanced by the television and video games of today. How can teachers give children experiences in literature in the face of such competition?

The field of children's literature is rich in its variety, including both great classic stories and those of present-day situations and concerns. Fiction and informational books, children's magazines, and poetry add balance to the literary curriculum. Every classroom should contain representative works from each of these areas.

Provide plenty of time for using books and other materials. Children need time to browse, to flip through a book at their own pace, to let their thoughts wander as they reflect on the storyline. They also enjoy retelling the tale to others. Be sure to plan enough time for children to be read to every day.

Make a space that is quiet and comfortable. In addition to soft pillows or seats, locate the reading area where there is privacy. Crashing blocks and messy fingerpainting will intrude on the bookreader. A place to sprawl or cuddle up with a friend is preferable.

Have plenty of books and supporting materials. The language arts center might contain a listening post, with headsets for a record or tape player. Perhaps there is even a place where books can be created, a place supplied with paper and crayons. There may even be a typewriter, puppet stage, or flannel board nearby so that stories can be created in new ways.

Display children's literary creations. The efforts of children's stories and bookmaking should be honored by establishing a place in the room where they can be seen and read. Children then see how adults value the process of literary creation and the final product.

Teachers must model how to care for a book and keep classroom books in good repair. Children can come to realize that a book is like a good friend and should be given the same kind of care and consideration.

Fostering children's reading at home is one of the important contributions a teacher can make to the reading process. Attitudes about reading are communicated to children from the important people in their lives. Because teachers do not have a direct influence on the home environment, their route to the home is through the children. A child who is enthusiastic about books and carries them home is likely to involve parents in the quest for good books and stories. Teachers encourage this in a number of ways. Posting the local library hours, establishing a lending library, and providing parents with lists of favorites will reinforce the child's interest in literature.

Use books around the room. Don't confine them to just the book corner or the book shelf. Demonstrate their adaptability to all curriculum areas by displaying a variety of books in the activity centers. Ask children to help you retell or emphasize parts of a story (see Storytelling section), and ask them questions informally afterwards: "How many bowls of porridge were on the kitchen table? Which one did Goldilocks like best? How did you know?" Figure 13.20 shows how books can enhance play and learning throughout the school room.

# Extending Literary Experiences

Good literature comes in many forms and can be presented in a variety of ways. A creative teacher uses books and literature to develop other curriculum materials. Translating words from a book into an activity helps a child remember them. Books and stories can be adapted to the flannel board, storytelling, dramatizations, puppets, book games, and audiovisual resources.

## Storytelling

Storytelling is as old as humanity. The first time a human being returned to the cave with an adventure to tell, the story was born. Storytelling is the means by which cultural heritage is passed down from one generation to another.

Children's involvement with a story being told is almost instantaneous. The storyteller is the medium through which a story comes to life, adding a unique flavor through voice, choice of words, body language, and pacing.

The beginning teacher will want to start with a familiar story, perhaps a classic like *The Three Little Pigs*. Props can be added to draw attention to the story. Flannel board adaptations of stories are helpful; they give the storyteller a sense of security and a method for remembering the story. Children can be involved in the action by placing the characters on the felt board at the appropriate time. Puppets or an assortment of hats can be used as props. Good storytellers enjoy telling the story and communicate their enthusiasm to children.

## Dramatizing Stories

Acting out characters from a favorite story has universal appeal. Young preschoolers are intoduced to this activity as they act out the motions to fingerplays and songs. "They Eensy-Weensy Spider" and its accompanying motions is the precursor for dramatization.

Stories such as *Caps for Sale* (Slobodkina) and *Swimmy* (Lionni), as well as fairy tales, are popular choices for reenactment by four- and five-year-olds. They need plenty of time to rehearse, and simple props help them focus on their role. A red scarf helps Jeannada become *Little Red Riding Hood;* an old pair of sunglasses transforms Joaquin into a character from *Goggles* (Keats).

## Puppet Shows

Puppet shows can involve a large number of children as participants and audience. Children of all

### DISCOVERY SCIENCE: SEA LIFE

*Swimmy* (Lionni)
*One Morning in Maine* (McCloskey)
*Houses from the Sea* (Gaudy)
*I Saw the Sea Come In* (Tressault)
*What Does the Tide Do?* (Kinney)
*Ranger Rick* magazine (National Wildlife
   Federation)
*My Big Backyard* magazine (National Geographic)
*Little Tim and the Brave Sea* (Ardizzone)
*The Sand The Sea and Me* (Craig)

### MUSIC

*Hush Little Baby* (Aliki)
*I Know an Old Lady* (Bonne)
*Ben's Trumpet* (Isadora)
*Frog Went A-Courtin'* (Langstaff)
*One Wide River to Cross* (Emberley)
*Over in the Meadow* (Wadsworth)
*Fox Went Out on a Chilly Night* (Spier)

### LIVING TOGETHER: REFLECTING DIVERSITY

*Mei Li* (Handforth)
*The Quilt* (Jones)
*Helping Out* (Ancona)
*Stories for Free Children* (Pogrebin)
*Tikki Tikki Tembo* (Mosel)
*Umbrella* (Yashima)
*The Fish from Japan* (Cooper)
*The Trip* (Keats)
*First Pink Light* (Greenfield)
*On Mother's Lap* (Scott)
*Why Mosquitoes Buzz in People's Ears* (Aardena)
*Stevie* (Steptoe)
*Arrow to the Sun* (McDermott)
*Gilberto and the Wind* (Ets)

### TO READ ALONE: WORDLESS BOOKS

*Gobble Growl and Grunt* (Spier)
*A Boy, a Dog, and a Frog* (Mayer)
*Rosie's Walk* (Hutchins)
*Out! Out! Out!* (Alexander)
*Look What I Can Do* (Aruego)
*Apples* (Hogrogian)
*The Grey Lady and The Strawberry Snatcher* (Bang)

### BLOCKS

*Changes Changes* (Hutchins)
*The Big Builders* (Dreany)
*Boxes* (Craig)
*Shapes* (Schlein)
*Who Built the Bridge?* (Bate)
*The Giant Nursery Book of Things That Work*
   (Zaffo)

### MATH LAB: PASSAGE OF TIME

*The Very Hungry Caterpillar* (Carle)
*When Sheep Cannot Sleep* (Kitamura)
*Lifetimes* (Mellonic and Ingpen)
*Goodnight, Moon* (Brown)
*Carrot Seed* (Krauss)
*Inch by Inch* (Lionni)
*The Growing Story* (Krauss)
*Annie and the Old One* (Miles)
*Fast Is Not a Ladybug* (Schlein)

### ART

*Start with a Dot* (Roberts)
*I Like Red* (Bright)
*Little Blue and Little Yellow* (Lionni)
*The Color Kittens* (Brown)
*Red Light, Green Light* (MacDonald)
*Hailstones and Halibut Bones* (O'Neill)
*A Color of His Own* (Lionni)
*My Very First Book of Colors* (Carle)
*The Great Blueness and Other Predicaments*
   (Lobel)
*Black Is Brown Is Tan* (Adoff)

### DRAMATIC PLAY: LIVING AND DRESSING

*Martins' Hats* (Blos)
*Curious George Goes to the Hospital* (Rey)
*Madeline* (Bemelmans)
*George the Babysitter* (Hughes)
*There's a Monkey in My Closet* (Mayer)
*When You Were a Baby* (Jonas)
*All Kinds of Families* (Simon)

**FIGURE 13.20** Reading around the curriculum. When good literature is a natural part of the environment, children learn to appreciate and use it.

ages enjoy watching and putting on a puppet show. Teachers can support their efforts by helping them to take turns, suggesting questions and dialogue to them, and involving the audience. The project of puppet making can be quite elaborate and very engaging for older children.

### Book Games

Book games are a good way to extend the literary experience. Buy two copies of an inexpensive book with readable pictures, such as *The Carrot Seed* (Krauss). Tear out the pages and cover with clear plastic. Children must then read the pictures in order to put the book into proper sequence. A book of rhymes, *Did You Ever See?* (Einsel), lends itself to rhyming games. Children can act out the rhymes from the storyline or match rhyming phrasing from cards the teacher has made.

### Audiovisual Resources

Records, cassettes, and filmstrips enlarge the child's experience with books. The auditory and the visual media reinforce one another. The pictures can show children new aspects of the words; sometimes the music or the voices bring the book to life. Often both happen. Hundreds of children's stories— classics and modern day—have been translated to these media.

### Computers in the Classroom

A computer can be as nonthreatening as a watercolor brush. In the hands of a child it can be a tool for experiencing the world. Early childhood classrooms are arranged so that children learn about the world directly, by piling blocks, molding sand and clay, bouncing a ball. Through these experiences, children gradually form concepts about how the world works and how they can affect it. As children touch the keys of a computer, they are challenged to explore and discover in ways never before possible.

Discovery-oriented experiences with computers enhance children's learning, especially in stimulating their cognitive thought processes. Children

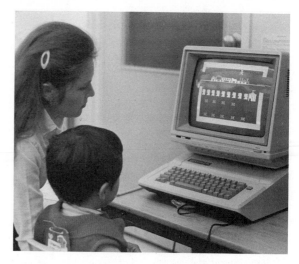

**FIGURE 13.21** Using the computer in a classroom can help individualize a child's educational experience.

form new knowledge as they interact with computer-based programs to form what is described as "microworlds" (Papert, 1980). Children design and control places of their own choosing, such as building a house, the seashore, or a face. Then they create events that challenge them to think through consequences of their actions. Moreover, computer programs can be "process highlighters" for children (Haugland & Shade, 1988). That is, the program can speed up or detail hidden processes and cause:effect relationships that are more difficult to observe, such as a plant growing, a face changing expression upon command, or a dance put together with a special sequence of steps.

**Developmentally Appropriate Software.** Just a few years ago, computers were seen as a wave of the future. Now computers have become firmly established in early childhood classrooms, particularly in kindergarten and primary grades but also in many preschools. This is because the *hardware,* or actual machinery, has become less expensive while being sturdy and workable for busy teachers and young children alike. The most dramatic change, however, has been in the proliferation of *software,* the computer programs themselves.

**FIGURE 13.22** When child meets computer, the results can be challenging and exciting. (Courtesy of St. Thomas Episcopal School, New Haven, Ct.)

It is in the areas of software that teachers of young children have a multitude of choices. These choices must be carefully made. Not every program intended for children is developmentally appropriate, and teachers must pay thoughtful attention to the program and to what they know about their own group of children. Teachers must know what to look for and how to choose programs that will be useful and appropriate for the specific age of the group. Haugland and Shade (1988) have developed ten criteria for evaluating computer programs. Not all software will meet all the criteria, but it is important to view the criteria as a continuum for considering computer programs for young children. Computer software should:

1. Be age appropriate.

2. Allow children to control it (children setting the pace and being active participants).

3. Include clear instructions.

4. Have expanding complexity.

5. Support independent exploration.

6. Be "process oriented" (having the software program so engaging that the product of using it is secondary).

7. Include real-world representation.

8. Have high quality technical features (colorful, uncluttered, and realistic).

9. Provide trial-and-error opportunities.

10. Have visible transformations (being able to affect the software, for example, by transposing objects).

Appendix D offers other points to consider when choosing computer software.

**When Child Meets Computer.** Specific methods have been devised for teaching young children to work successfully with computers (Davidson, 1989). For instance, a child must be able to maneuver a joystick, find the keys on the keyboard, and insert a floppy disk into the computer correctly. Since very young children cannot read, they will need help getting started. Teachers must be able to help children learn by setting up their classrooms with a computer positioned in a safe yet accessible place, structuring activities and the daily schedule to give children plenty of time to manipulate the machinery and programs, and choosing specific hardware and software that works with the class.

**Integrating the Computer into Learning.** One of the most exciting aspects of computers in the classroom is their ability to support other learning. Teachers who use the computer effectively as an educational tool integrate their program goals to use the computer with individual children. What happens at the keyboard matches each child's individual needs. Jane Davidson (1989) suggests using computers to support a classroom unit on three levels:

1. Specific software can provide unit-related information. For instance, the program "Dinosaurs" can be in place while developing a theme such as in Figure 13.9.

2. Tool software—such as graphics or writing programs—can be used for creating unit-related products. For example, a program such as "Explore-a-Story" can help primary-age children write stories about their own interests and responses to whatever unit is being studied. With a younger group, the teacher could help the class make a group story to send home.

3. Computer-related activities can be designed to support the unit theme. One idea is using the program "Name-Jumping," which asks children to jump around a floor-sized keyboard. Both computer concepts and the words of a unit or theme are reinforced using children's full-body involvement.

## Unit 13–3  Checkpoint

The special topics on cognition and language includes reading, writing, and computers. Each offers a unique extension to children's learning in the classroom. Clearly, language and thought are learned both at home and in school and can be connected in meaningful ways.

Children and books belong together. Good literature gives insight into human behavior. Books teach children less important though exciting things such as how to play peek-a-boo or escape a hungry lion. But they also teach matters of substance and character such as how to go to sleep, make a friend, be brave. The early years should lay a foundation in literature upon which children can build throughout their lives.

> Books are no substitute for living, but they can add immeasurably to its richness. When life is absorbing, books can enhance our sense of its significance. When life is difficult, they can give a momentary relief from trouble, afford a new insight into our problems or those of others, or provide the rest and refreshment we need. Books have always been a source of information, comfort, and pleasure for people who know how to use them. This is as true for children as for adults.
>
> (Arbuthnot and Sutherland, 1972)

The computer is a twentieth century creation, yet it can stimulate the timeless, innate characteristics of curiosity, creativity, and discovery. A major challenge for teachers is to provide curriculum that will develop these "dispositions," or habits of the mind (Katz, 1985), so that children will be willing as well as able to develop skills. As a teacher, ask yourself:

• How do teachers help children become ready to read?

• What should a writing center in an early education classroom look like?

- How does literature support cognitive development? Language development?
- What literacy software could be used that would entice the reluctant school-aged child?
- What language activities would be appropriate with toddlers?
- What are the guidelines for creating a rich literary environment?
- What are five ways to extend literary experiences?

# SUMMARY

People entering early childhood education as a profession are challenged to develop children's minds and language. This chapter begins with the premise that intellectual development and language are interrelated. As teachers help children learn how to think, they learn about children's thinking processes by listening to what they say, and observing how they respond to others' words, thoughts, and actions.

Much of cognitive development theory has its roots in the work of Jean Piaget. Cognitive development includes the areas of inquiry, knowledge of the physical and social worlds, classification, seriation, numbers, symbols, spatial relationships, and time. Language development, on the other hand, takes into consideration how children learn articulation, receptive and expressive language, graphic representation, and enjoyment of language.

Teachers plan curriculum to develop these skills in several ways. Many class settings offer children an opportunity to refine cognitive and language skills. At times, teachers focus on a specific skill, such as reasoning or conversation, and adapt the curriculum to emphasize those areas.

The teacher's role also requires an understanding of bilingualism and a working knowledge of speech and language disorders. Early childhood teachers use their own language abilities to stress and support the language development of their students.

Reading and writing are part of the language and thought processes. Adults in early childhood seek ways to involve children with the printed word in ways that have meaning to the here-and-now in children's lives. Books, literature, and computers further the development of reading and writing skills and provide enjoyable tools for the enhancement of cognition and language.

## REVIEW QUESTIONS

1. How are cognition and language related?

2. Match the cognitive skill with the appropriate activity:

| | |
|---|---|
| inquiry | being aware of others |
| physical world | learning to locate things |
| social knowledge | pretending to be a puppet |
| classification | asking questions |
| seriation | sequencing events |
| numbers | using nesting blocks |
| symbols | expressing amounts |
| spatial relationships | sorting objects |
| time | manipulating materials |

3. What kinds of questions does the teacher ask to help children to think?

4. How does the teacher help children develop speech and language skills in planning curriculum?

5. The way teachers use language is critical in encouraging children's own language. Name the four areas of language and what a teacher can say to encourage growth in those areas.

6. What are some of the criteria for evaluating computer software for early childhood? What traps are to be avoided?

7. Describe some curriculum activities for cognition and language development. Simplify them for infants/toddlers/twos and elaborate for the primary-aged youngsters.

## L E A R N I N G   A C T I V I T I E S

1. Look at the program in which you now teach, or recall your own first classrooms. Find at least one example of rote knowledge, social knowledge, and meaningful knowledge.

2. Take one cognitive skill and trace how it could be developed in each curriculum area of the program.

3. Observe block play at your school. Make a chart, as in Figure 13.5, that describes the learning processes involved.

4. How does teacher language affect how children develop cognitive skills? Give several examples of what discourages such growth; counter that with how what a teacher says encourages skills.

5. Make a list of the classroom areas. Beside each, name one activity that would foster cognitive development and one that calls for language skills.

6. One theme often used in early childhood programs is that of the changing season in the fall. How can that theme develop language and thinking skills in preschoolers?

7. Teaching reading readiness involves trying to develop oral language and listening skills. What could a teacher of toddlers plan for each? A kindergarten teacher?

8. Describe three ways children's books and literature help to develop intellectual skills and language proficiency. Through what techniques can literary experiences be extended in the curriculum?

9. Consider the use of a computer in the following classrooms:
   toddler day care program
   preschool half-day program

kindergarten

after-school primary program

Is a computer appropriate in each of them? Why and how? What guidelines, if any, would be needed in each setting? What would be the adult's role in each?

## BIBLIOGRAPHY

### GENERAL

Bredekamp, Sue, (ed.) *Developmentally Appropriate Practice In Early Child-hood Programs Serving Children From Birth Through Age 8* (Expanded Edition). Washington, D.C.: National Association for the Education of Young Children, 1987.

Brown, Janet F., (ed.) *Curriculum Planning for Young Children.* Washington, D.C.: National Association for the Education of Young Children, 1982.

Katz, Lillian G. "Dispositions in Early Childhood Education." *ERIC/EECE Bulletin,* Vol. 18, No. 2, 1985.

Piaget, Jean. *The Language and Thought of the Child.* Cleveland: World Publishing Co., 1969.

Schickendanz, Judith A.; York, M.E.; Stewart, I.D.; and White, D.A. *Strategies for Teaching Young Children,* 2nd ed. Englewood Cliffs, N.J.: Prentice-Hall, 1983.

Vygotsky, L.S. *Thought and Language.* New York: M.I.T. Press and John Wiley and Sons, 1962.

### COGNITION

Clark, Barbara. *Optimizing Learning: The Integrative Model in the Classroom.* Columbus, Oh.: Merrill, 1986.

Furth, H.G. *Piaget for Teachers.* Englewood Cliffs, N.J.: Prentice-Hall, 1970.

Ginsburg, H., and Opper, S. *Piaget's Theory of Intellectual Development.* Englewood Cliffs, N.J.: Prentice-Hall, 1969.

Hohlmann, Mary; Banet, B.; and Weikart, D.P. *Young Children in Action.* Ypsilanti, Mich.: The High/Scope Press, 1979.

Hunt, J. McVicker. *Human Intelligence.* New Brunswick, N.J.: Transaction Books, 1972.

Katz, Lillian. "Fostering Communicative Competence in Young Children." *ERIC/EECE Newsletter,* Vol. 18, No. 2, 1985.

Whitchurch, Janet. "Block Play at Bing Nursery School." *Bing Bulletin,* Vol. VIII, Spring 1987.

### LANGUAGE

Barton, J., and Calfee, R. "Theory Becomes Practice: One Program." In Lapp, D.; J. Flood and N. Farnan, (eds.) *Content Area Reading and Learning: Instructional Strategies.* Englewood Cliffs, N.J.: Prentice Hall, 1989.

Beck, M. Susan. *Baby Talk: How Your Child Learns to Speak.* New York: New American Library, 1979.

Bolles, Edmund B. *So Much to Say.* New York: St. Martin's Press, 1982.

Calfee, R. "Those Who Can Explain, Teach. . ." In *Educational Policy,* 1, 1987.

Calfee, R.C., M.K. Henry, and J.A. Funderburg, "A Model for School Change." In Samuels, S.J., and P.D. Pearson (eds.), *Changing School Readiness Programs.* Newark, Del.: International Reading Association, 1988.

Cazden, Courtney B., ed. *Language in Early Childhood Education.* Cambridge, Mass.: Harvard University Press, 1979.

deVilliers, Peter A., and Jill, G. *Early Language.* Washington, D.C.: National Association for the Education of Young Children, 1981.

Garcia, Eugene. "Bilingualism in Early Childhood." In Brown, Janet S. (ed.), *Curriculum Planning for Young Children.* Washington, D.C.: National Association for the Education of Young Children, 1983.

Jones, Elizabeth. Staff Development Guide, personal communication, January 1987.

MacIntosh, Helen K., ed. *Children and Oral Language.* Washington, D.C.: Association for Childhood Education International, 1964.

## LITERATURE

Arbuthnot, May Hill, and Sutherland, Zena. *Children and Books,* 4th ed. London: Scott, Foresman and Co., 1972.

Ashton-Warner, Sylvia. *Teacher.* New York: Bantam Books, 1963.

Neugebauer, Bonnie (ed.), *Alike and Different: Exploring our Humanity with Young Children.* Redmond, Wash.: Exchange Press, 1987.

Trelease, Jim. *The Read-Aloud Handbook.* New York: Penguin Books, 1982.

## COMPUTERS

Davidson, Jane I. *Children and Computers Together in the Early Childhood Classroom.* Albany, N.Y.: Delmar, 1989.

Haugland, Susan W., and Shade, Daniel D. "Developmentally Appropriate Software for Young Children." *Young Children,* Vol. 43, No. 4, May 1988.

Margot, Charlene, and Armstrong, N. "Learning Basics with the Computer: Preschool." Reston, Va., Reston Publishing Company, 1984.

Papert, Seymour. *Mindstorms: Children, Computers, and Powerful Ideas.* New York: Basis Books, 1980.

Piestrup, Ann. "Silicon Chips and Playdough." In Gordon, Ann M., and Browne, Kathryn W. *Beginnings and Beyond,* 1st Ed: Albany, N.Y.: Delmar, 1985.

Scharf, P., and Chattin-McNichols, J. *Understanding the Computer Age.* Hasbrouck Heights, N.J.: Hayden, 1986.

# CHAPTER 14

## Planning for the Heart and Soul: Emotional, Social, and Creative Growth

STEVEN

THANK YOU

FOR

THE NICE

YEAR AT BING

Portions of this chapter were developed with the assistance of Gay Spitz, Salinas Adult School, Salinas, Calif.

# PREFACE

The heart and soul of any good program for young children is a commitment to help children as they struggle with (1) the reality of emotions; (2) the awareness of the need for social skills; and (3) the creative urge. The foundation must be laid in these early years for children to understand themselves and others.

Emotional, social, and creative development are related to the child's self-concept and self-esteem; the child must have an understanding of self before seeing that self in relation to others. It is primarily through emotional, social, and creative growth that children learn who they are, and they must have self-confidence to experience and learn the necessary skills.

This chapter contains three separate units. Each area—emotional, social, and creative growth—is explored individually to give a greater understanding of its importance to the developing child. An overview of development is followed by a discussion of the skills children learn in the pre-school years. The crucial role of the teacher is emphasized next, followed by curriculum planning to reinforce each developmental area. At the end of each unit, a checkpoint and review serve as a short summary.

# INTRODUCTION

The first thing one notices upon entering an early childhood classroom is the children at play. A quick survey of the area shows who is playing together, whether or not there is crying and fighting, and how happy or sad the children look. This overview gives an immediate sense of the emotional, social, and creative climate in that early childhood setting.

- *Emotional:* Toddler Abier giggles as she runs her hands across the water table, then cries after she splashes soap suds in her eyes and needs to be comforted.
- *Social:* Preschooler Danny wants his favorite red wagon so Pat, the student teacher, helps him negotiate a turn with Christa.
- *Creative:* Kindergartners Fabio, Erika, and Benjy work steadily to build a tall, intricate block structure. When it is finished, the three children stand back and marvel at their creation.

Together these three factors—emotional mood, social dynamics, and creative tone—define the overall atmosphere in which children play and work.

Emotional, social, and creative well-being are woven together in the developing child. Children who are sensitive to their own feelings and moods are able to begin understanding other people and thus become more socially effective and successful. Children with experience in many creative endeavors have the self-confidence that comes from having an outlet for self-expression.

These three areas are also linked to other aspects of the child's growth:

- *Creative/Physical:* Physical skills can define and limit children's creative abilities. Two-year-old Andrea, whose physical skills do not yet include balancing objects, plays with blocks by piling them on top of one another, filling her wagon with blocks, and dumping them or lugging them from place to place.
- *Social/Cognitive:* It is hard for five-year-old Karena to share her best friend Luther with other children. Her intellectual abilities do not yet allow her to consider more than one idea at a time, so she cannot understand that Luther can be her friend and Dana's at the same time.
- *Emotional/Language:* Tyler is upset at his mother's refusal to let him play outside. "I hate you!" he screams, "I want a new mommy!" Children learn to label and express their emotions through words.

It is difficult to observe and measure the child's growth in creative, social, and emotional areas; it is easier to determine a child's progress in physical, cognitive, and language development. After all, a child counts or doesn't count, is either 40 inches tall or not, and speaks in full sentences or short phrases.

**FIGURE 14.1** The emotional, social, and creative growth of children is the heart and soul of any early childhood program. (Courtesy of Stephanie Barry Agnew.)

Emotional, social, and creative expressions are more subtle and subjective. A child usually gets immediate and concrete feedback when playing lotto, calling for a teacher, or riding a tricycle. That does not always happen when children express their feelings, encounter others, and create something important. Talbot may feel rejected and sad if no one greets him as he enters the playhouse. He may mistake the children's busyness as an act of exclusion. In reality, the children did not even know he was there. Teachers can play a critical role helping children interpret their emotional, social, and creative interactions.

Traditionally, early childhood educators have concerned themselves with children's well-being, knowing that in the early years the foundations must be laid for children to understand themselves and others. Social growth, creative expression, and experience with a wide range of emotional behaviors

also help children develop a strong self-concept and positive self-esteem.

*Self-esteem* is an individual's sense of personal worth and an acceptance of who one is. Children's self-esteem (the way they feel about themselves) is expressed through children's behavior. They make judgments about themselves as they confront the world. To the extent that children feel worthy and capable, they are ready to succeed. If children disapprove of themselves, they may feel like failures and expect to do poorly.

Self-esteem develops as a reflection of experiences: the way people respond to you gives you some indication of your importance or value. Newborn infants have no concept of self and no past experience to judge their own worth. A young child who has positive experiences with others will more likely have a high sense of self-esteem than one who has felt unloved or unnoticed.

Planning for children's success builds self-esteem. It includes the following four components, which we call the "Four I's":

• *I:* When children enter the classroom, the message they receive is "I am important and this is my place." The physical environment, the daily schedule, and the curriculum are designed to give all children permission to express themselves.

• *Initiative:* Children are encouraged to initiate their own learning, to make contact with others, to take action.

• *Independence:* Self-management tasks of dressing, eating, toileting are given an important place in the curriculum. Children are assisted in taking care of their own belongings and in developing independent judgment about events and activities.

• *Interaction:* Social interaction has a high priority in the program. The room and yard are busy places with children moving about and talking among themselves and with adults. Conflicts are accepted as a natural consequence of social life. In the spirit of John Dewey (see Figure 1.4, Chapter 1), democratic group living will encourage children to interact and foster a consciousness of interdependence.

Eventually, the child becomes independent of others' opinions, but early in life self-esteem is tied to family, friends, and other important people. There appear to be four components of self-esteem (Clemes and Bean, 1980; Brophy and Willis, 1981):

1. A sense of one's own identity.

2. A sense of belonging.

3. A sense of one's uniqueness is recognized and respected.

4. A sense of self through the use of the power of self-definition.

Children with these characteristics are ready to meet the emotional, social, and creative challenges of the early years. They will have the self-confidence to deal with the reality of their emotions, the adaptability of their social learnings, and the risk of creativity.

## UNIT 14–1 EMOTIONAL GROWTH

## THE DEVELOPMENT OF EMOTIONS

Emotions are the feelings a person has—joy and sorrow, love and hate, confidence and fear, loneliness and belonging, anger and contentment, frustration and satisfaction. They are responses to events, people, and circumstances. Feelings are an outgrowth of what a person perceives is happening. Emotionally healthy people learn to give expression to their feelings in appropriate ways. They do not allow their feelings to overshadow the rest of their behavior. The optimal time to learn these skills is in the early years.

Early childhood teachers encourage children to identify and express their emotional nature so that they can learn to live with these powerful forces.

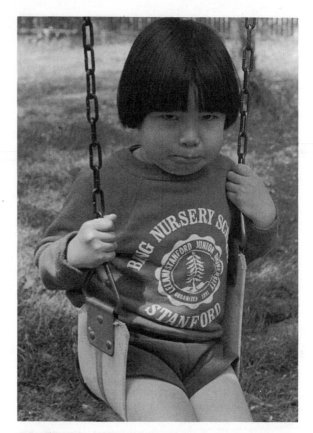

**FIGURE 14.2** Young children feel their emotions strongly.

When a child begins to understand and communicate feelings, the emotions are no longer in control of the child; the child is becoming the master of the emotions.

Infants respond in agitated emotion whether wet, hungry, hurt, or bored. Gradually, the expression of the emotion becomes more refined and varies with the situation. A toddler's cry of distress is different from the cry of discomfort or hunger. As children get older, their emotional expressions change as they gain control over some of their feelings and learn new ways to express them.

Strong external forces are also at work. Parents, family members, teachers, and friends are social influences, helping the young child learn socially acceptable behavior. Much of what children learn is by example; therefore, children learn more from adult models than from simply being told how to behave (Clemes and Bean, 1980; Jensen and Wells, 1979).

# EMOTIONAL SKILLS IN EARLY CHILDHOOD

The emotional skills children learn in their early years are substantial. Research shows that humans seem to possess a relatively small set of emotions (Izard, 1971). In fact, Alan Fogel (1980) reports that our "basic" emotions include enjoyment, interest, excitement, surprise, fear, sadness, disgust, shame and anger. He cites the evidence of Charlesworth and Kreutzer (1973) indicating that the facial expressions which correspond to each of these emotions are present in newborns or very young infants. These expressions have been observed in a wide range of cultural and ethnic groups (Eibl-Eibesfeldt, 1971).

In early childhood, children learn to respond to new situations and to react and connect with a teacher, both very emotional experiences. Good teachers stimulate an emotional response to themselves and the curriculum that is a balance between interest and overwhelming fear. "Creating the 'right' emotional conditions is the path toward gaining access to the child's capacity for learning" (Fogel, 1980). Young children are not yet limited by *social mores* and standards of conduct that prevent them from sincere and truthful self-expression. Teachers observe children and learn how youngsters feel about facing their own feelings, the feelings of others, and the range of skills categorized as emotional growth.

## Ability to Deal with Feelings

Dealing with feelings involves four steps. Each builds upon the other so that they follow a developmental sequence; the learning that takes place at one level affects the development of what follows. Figure 14.3 describes how the early childhood classroom and teacher help children deal effectively with their feelings.

### To Notice and Label Feelings

This is the first step. The sobbing one- or two-year-old may have many reasons for feeling in distress. As parents recognize the cries of hunger, hurt, and fear, they name these feelings. The child will learn to notice what the feeling is and recognize it. Preschoolers are quite verbal and curious about language and ready to learn words that describe a wider range of feelings. They can learn "lonely," "scared," "silly," and "sad," and "happy." Labeling what one feels inside is a critical skill to learn. It is a healthy first-grader who can say, "I have tried to cut this string three times and the scissors aren't working. I am frustrated. I need some help!"

### To Accept Feelings

Teachers recognize that children are capable of strong feelings. Children can feel overwhelmed by the very strength and intensity of a feeling, be it one of anger or of love. As children come to accept feelings, they learn how to handle the depth of the feeling and not let it overpower them. The changing nature of feelings is also part of accepting the feeling. It can be a source of comfort and relief for young children to discover that the strong emotion they experience now will pass. Adults who work with young children help them work through those feelings safely. Carlos feels sad as his mother prepares to leave. His teacher walks them to the door, then bends down and puts an arm around him as his mother waves goodbye. Acknowledging that he is sad, the teacher stays with Carlos, reminding him that his mother will return and that the teacher will take care of him while he is at school. Since the child is allowed to feel the sadness that is natural in leave-taking, the tense feelings are over in a few minutes. The teacher smiles and encourages Carlos to find something fun to do. Once he has recovered his composure, the teacher can point this out, and Carlos can feel proud for having lived through and grown from saying goodbye. Acknowledgment of the feeling and his ability to accept it help give Carlos the confidence to move on.

---

**Developing Emotional Skills in the Early Childhood Classroom**

---

1. IN-CLASS SETTINGS
   *Art*
   a. "You look like you're enjoying yourself." "Your face tells me that it feels funny to you." Such statements reflect children's expressions and help them become aware of how they are feeling.
   b. Write the words children use at work and at play. This can be at the bottom of their individual artwork, or on a sheet of paper you post alongside several examples as a display.

   *Blocks:*
   As children play in this area, be aware of what they do, and ask them how it feels when:

   - you make a structure all by yourself
   - it falls down
   - someone knocks it over (accidentally and on purpose)
   - someone laughs

   *Discovery/Science:*
   Use the words "curious" and "proud" to describe what children do as they explore and experiment with materials. Ask them to describe both their feelings and the objects.

   *Dramatic Play:*
   a. Have a full-length mirror so children can try on expressions with their roles.
   b. Provide a variety of role-play materials.
   c. Include in the wall display pictures of a variety of expressions, with mirrors nearby to aid imitation.

   *Language/Library:*
   a. Have books that reflect a variety of feelings and ways to deal with them, such as:
      Fear: *There's a Nightmare in My Closet* (Mayer)
      Self-Esteem: *The Growing Story* (Krauss)
      Loss: *The Maggie B* (Keats); *Amos and Boris* (Steig)
      Change: *Changes, Changes* (Hutchins)
      Friendship: *Two Is a Team* (Bemelman); *That's What Friends Are For* (Kidd)
      Security: *One Step, Two* (Zolotow); *The Bundle Book* (Zolotow); *Big Sister, Little Sister* (Zolotow)
   b. Include books on themes, particularly when a child or group is dealing with an emotional issue:
      Death: *Death and Dying* (Open Family Series, by Sara Bonnet Stein); *The Dead Bird* (Brown); *Nana Upstairs, Nana Downstairs* (de Paoli)
      Divorce: *Two Places to Sleep* Schuchman
      Doctor/Dentist: *Curious George Goes to the Hospital* (H.A. Rey); *Your Turn, Doctor* (Robison and Perez); *My Doctor* (Harlow)
      Moving: *Mitchell Is Moving* (Sharmat); *Jamie* (Zolotow)
      New Baby: *Baby Sister for Frances* (Hoban); *I Want to Tell You About My Baby* (Banish); *Peter's Chair* (Keats)
      Nightmares: *Where the Wild Things Are* (Sendak); *In the Night Kitchen* (Sendak); *There's a Nightmare in My Closet* (Mayer)
      Spending the Night: *Ira Sleeps Over* (Waber)
   c. When reading stories, stop and ask how a particular character is feeling.
   d. Tie in children's lives to books. For example, have children bring a special object or toy to share. A warm cuddly can be tied into the stories of *Goodnight Moon* (Brown) or *Teddy Bear's Picnic* (Kennedy).

   *Movement:*
   a. "How would you walk if you were glad?" (sad, mad, worried, giggly?)
   b. "A Tiger Hunt" (this game is known by many names). Go on a "hunt" with children, using their bodies to describe

---

**FIGURE 14.3** Whether two years old or in second grade, children learn about their feelings when teachers plan programs that encourage self-expression.

such movements as opening/shutting a gate, swishing through tall grass, climbing a tree, swimming in water, going through mud, looking in a cave, running home so that the "tiger" doesn't catch us.

*Music:*
   a. Choose several cuts of music that differ in tone and type. Ask children how each makes them feel, then have them show you with their bodies.
   b. Write songs/chants about feelings.

2. AT GROUP TIMES
   a. Use children's faces as a focus: Practice facial expressions with mirrors; have them draw facial expressions; have them tell you how they are feeling and show you on their faces; show photographs of children's faces and expressions and ask the group how the child in the picture is feeling, and why.
   b Try idea completions:
      "I feel glad when . . ." (also mad, sad, bad, safe, excited, scared, silly)
      "I like school when . . ." (also don't like; also my friend, mom, it)
   c. Use situations to elicit feelings:
      1. "Here's a picture of a family. What are they doing? How does the child feel? The grown-ups? What happened?"
      2. "I'm going to cover part of the picture of the face to see if you can guess what expression it's going to be."
      3. "These are cards of situations that the teachers have seen happen in our class. Let's read them and then ask ourselves, 'How do I feel? What can I say? What can I do?'"
   d. Using circles already drawn with various facial expressions and labels, the teacher can ask each child to assess the state of feelings at that time, and even try to give some reason.
   e. Use songs and fingerplays that reflect expressions.

3. DURING ROUTINES AND TRANSITIONS
   a. Respect children's feelings of anticipation. Have a chart of the daily schedule; discuss upcoming field trips or visitors ahead of time when possible.
   b. When unexpected changes occur, discuss them with individuals and the group. "Andy isn't here today. He has a sore throat, so he is staying home. Esther will be the teacher in his group today."
   c. When possible, let children set the stage for themselves by encouraging them to take responsibility for known sequences. Let them use the toilet without you there, set their own snack table, get flowers for the table, help clean a place for the next children.
   d. Self-help: Provide time for children to do things for themselves, such as dressing, putting on a name tag, washing hands and drying them without too much hurrying. Reflect their pride in being able to do it "all by myself."

**FIGURE 14.3   Cont.**

## To Express Feelings in an Appropriate Way

This is a two-part process. First, children must feel free to express their feelings; second, they must learn ways of expression that are suitable to their age and to the situation. Many beginning teachers are uncomfortable because children express themselves so strongly (and often aggressively). Yet the child who is passive and unable to express feelings freely should be of equal concern and should be encouraged in self-expression.

As children grow, they acquire the modes of expression that are developmentally appropriate for their age. Babies and toddlers without language cry to express their feelings; thus this type of crying calls for the same kind of immediate response given to other forms of communication in later years. Two-year-olds express their displeasure by pushes and shoves, while four-year-olds use their verbal power and argue. By six or seven, children learn to tell others—clearly and with reasons—what they are feeling. The ability to express feelings is intact, but the methods of expression change as children grow.

**FIGURE 14.4** Children learn to appreciate and understand one another as they see each others' feelings. How can these boys learn to express hurt and comfort? (Courtesy of Kathye Garner, Mississippi State University.)

### *To Deal with the Feelings of Others*

This is the culminating step in the development of emotional skills. Feelings are the spark of life in people: the flash of anger, the "ah-hah" of discovery, the thrill of accomplishment, the hug of excitement. Helping children to tolerate and appreciate how different people express their emotions leads to understanding and cooperation.

## Ability to Deal with Change

Change is inevitable. Many people fear or reject change. Chidren can learn that change is a constant part of their lives and to cope with the challenges changes present. Fear, insecurity, and uncertainty are some of the emotions felt when people experience changes in their lives or routines. Many times, these feelings arise from not knowing what to expect or how to behave or from not understanding different sets of values.

Inevitably, changes will happen in children's lives, bringing with them a measure of stress. The very

act of being born is a change, marking the beginning of a life in which stress is part of the act of developmental achievement. Witness the toddler's numerous falls towards walking, the separation of parent and child at the nursery-school doorway, the concentration and frustrations of the six-year-old on roller skates.

Stress and coping are part of the ability to deal with change. Much has been researched and written of stress in children's lives (Selye, 1982; Honig, 1986), and stages of dealing with stress have now been identified:

- *Stage 1:* Alarm—arousal and fear of the new situation.

- *Stage 2:* Appraisal—attempts to understand the problem.

- *Stage 3:* Search for a coping strategy, selection from what is at hand.

- *Stage 4:* Implementing a coping strategy—trying to take care of the stress.

Teachers can thus help children to deal with change by supporting them in working through these stages, as they cope with changes in their lives at school, at home, and in the world at large.

For instance, teachers can help children accept change in several ways. Anticipating changes that are likely to occur and identifying the process for children is very important. "Junko, your mother will be leaving soon. We'll go looking for that favorite puzzle after you say good-bye to her." If the daily routine is altered, children should be notified. "We won't be having snacks inside today; let's use the patio table instead." When children are informed that change is anticipated, accepted, and not necessarily disrupting, they become more relaxed about handling the unpredictable. Teachers become resources for helping children cope in ways that are appropriate to the child and the situation at hand, be this by crying in sadness or fear, ignoring an unpleasant situation, finding a compromise, or accepting comfort.

## Ability to Exercise Judgment

The ability to exercise judgment is an important skill, for it helps children make decisions and figure out what to do in new situations. On entering school, a child faces many decisions: Where shall I play? Who shall I play with? What if my friend wants to do something I know is wrong? Who will I turn to for help when I need it? Judgment is selecting what to do, when to do it, with whom to do it, and when to stop.

There is no easy way to teach children how to make decisions since each situation must be dealt with on an individual basis. The judgment a child exercises in choosing a friend to play with today may have other factors to consider tomorrow. Instead, teachers help children base their decisions on the best judgment they are capable of in each instance. As they mature, children are able to sort out what judgments might be made here, what factors need to be considered there.

## Enjoying One's Self and One's Power

Teachers want children to feel powerful—to know that they can master their lives and feel confident in their own abilities. This feeling of power is particularly important in the early years when so much in a child's eyes is out of reach, both literally and figuratively.

Responsibility and limits, however, go hand in hand with power. The child who is strong enough to hit someone has to learn not to use that strength unnecessarily. The child who shouts with glee also finds out that noise is unacceptable indoors. By holding children responsible for their own actions, teachers can help chidren enjoy their power and accept its limitations.

One kind of fantasy play most teachers encounter is that of superheroes. Common to young children as young as two, *superhero* play is exciting and rowdy, usually active and loud, playacting of heroic roles that give children powers they lack in everyday life. It is the embodiment of control and strength, even wisdom, and the parts to be played are clear for everyone involved.

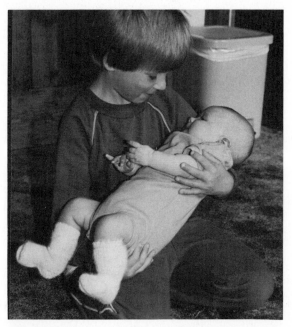

**FIGURE 14.5** An awareness of their own power can bring enjoyable rewards to children. This boy discovers the rewards in holding and responding to a baby.

Children's natural struggles for mastery and the attraction of rough-and-tumble play collide with teachers' concerns about fighting, aggression, and letting the play get out of hand. Kostelnik and others (1986) have described this special type of dramatic play in detail, offering suggestions for managing it:

- Help children recognize humane characteristics of superheroes.
- Discuss real heroes and heroines.
- Talk about the pretend world of acting.
- Limit the place and time for superhero play.
- Explore related concepts.
- Help children de-escalate rough-and-tumble play.
- Help children deescalate rough-and-tumble play.
- Make it clear that aggression is unacceptable.
- Give children control over their lives.
- Praise children's attempts at mastery.

Teachers can help children learn to appreciate and enjoy themselves. Each time a child is acknowledged, a teacher fosters that sense of uniqueness. "Carrie, you have a great sense of humor!" "Freddie, I love the way you sing so clearly." Saying it aloud reinforces in children the feeling that they are enjoyable to themselves and to others.

# THE TEACHER'S ROLE

## Considerations

The first step in helping children develop healthy emotional patterns is for adults to acquire and use a "feeling" vocabulary. Words of an emotional nature can be used to label and identify feelings as teachers talk with young children.

There are many ways to develop a list of words related to emotions. Figure 14.6 illustrates one way. Identify some of the feelings children express; then describe how the children look and act when experiencing those emotions. This helps to build a vocabulary and an understanding of children's emotional expressions.

Teachers can also become more attuned to the emotional climate in the classroom by knowing when and how feelings are expressed. To gain insights, teachers might ask themselves:

- What causes children in the class to become excited? Frightened? Calm? Loud? How does this knowledge guide curriculum planning? How can it help a teacher handle an unplanned event or change in the schedule?

| Feeling | Behavioral Definition |
|---------|----------------------|
| 1. Fear | Pale face, alert eyes, tense mouth, rigid body. |
| 2. Surprise | Wide eyes, eyebrows uplifted, involuntary cry or scream, quick inhale of breath. |
| 3. Anger | Red face, eyes staring, face taut, fists and jaw clenched, voice harsh or yelling, large gestures. |
| 4. Joy | Smiling face, shining eyes, free and easy body movements, laughing. |
| 5. Pride | Head held high, smiling face, jaunty walk or strut, tendency to announce or point out. |
| 6. Embarrassment | Red face, glazed and downcast eyes, tight mouth, tense body, small and jerky movements, soft voice. |
| 7. Sadness | Unsmiling face, downturned mouth, glazed and teary eyes, crying or rubbing eyes, limp body, movements are slow or small, voice is soft, trembly. |
| 8. Anxiety | Puckered brow, pale face, tight mouth, whiny voice, jerky movements, lack of or difficulty in concentration. |
| 9. Curiosity | Raised brow, shining eyes, perhaps tense body in absorption of the object of curiosity, often hand movements to touch and pick up object, sometimes mouth agape. |

**FIGURE 14.6** As we observe children's behavior, we understand how their feelings are expressed. Expressions of fear, anger, sadness, disgust, and happiness are universal, and the face can be read and understood long before children understand language.

- How do I anticipate children's emotional behavior? How do I follow through?
- What can teachers do to handle children's emotional outbursts and crises?
- What happens to the rest of the class when one teacher is occupied in an emotional incident with one or more children?
- What do I do when a child shows emotion? How do I feel when a child displays emotion?
- What types of emotions are most common with the young child?

In the early childhood setting, teachers help children come to grips with their strong feelings by discussing these feelings openly. They take the time to help children find names for feelings, to speak of their own feelings, and begin to be aware of the feelings of others.

When teachers perceive that children are ready to talk about their feelings, small group discussions or individual conversations can be helpful. Good books that touch upon sensitive issues (being excluded, being blamed, caring for others) offer possibilities for teachers and children to talk about feelings. Games, joking, and teasing can help children to feel relaxed and to explore feelings in an accepting way. Classroom problems (not sharing materials, pushing on the climbers) offer topics for discussion. The ability to express emotions verbally gives children the power to deal with them without resorting to inappropriate behavior.

When adults show an understanding of feelings, children come to believe that adults are able to help them with their emotions, and the children become more at ease with their own feelings. When something painful happens to a child, adults can express what the child is feeling. "It really hurts to bend your knees now that you have scraped them." "You look so sad now that Gabi is playing with someone else." Children then become familiar with ways to express how they feel in a variety of emotional situations.

Adults can also help children become aware of the emotional states of others. "Look! Paul is crying. Let's go over and see if we can comfort him."

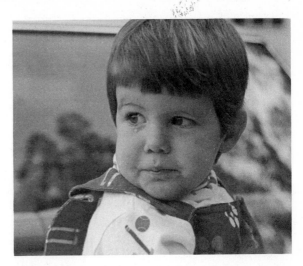

**FIGURE 14.7**  What causes children to become frightened? Sad? What can teachers do to handle children's emotional outbursts and crises? (Courtesy of Susan Thibodeau, College of Notre Dame of Md.)

Teachers can encourage children to help care for each other's hurts and needs. A child can ease the pain of a friend by sitting nearby as a wound is cleansed or by giving a hug when an achievement is made. Teachers must be sure to allow children to express their concern and to help them learn ways to respond to the emotional needs of others.

# Curriculum Planning for Emotional Growth

## *In the Environment*

Teachers set up their classrooms and yards to promote emotional growth. Materials and activities enhance self-esteem and self-expression. How activities are presented and carried out is also a factor. In looking at the class setting, it is important to remember that the "how" is as critical as the "what" in curriculum planning for emotional development. Refer to Figure 14.3 to see how curriculum can be developed to encourage emotional growth.

Select materials that enhance self-expression. Indoors, children's inner thoughts and feelings are best expressed through:

- *The Arts.* Clay or dough lets children ventilate feelings, since it can be pounded, pinched, poked, slapped, and manipulated. Fingerpainting and painting on broad surfaces with large brushes encourage a freedom of movement that permits children to express themselves more fully.

- *Blocks/Manipulatives.* Vary the materials regularly to help children adjust to change and to allow them to exercise judgment about playing with different materials. A variety of props—motor vehicles, animals, people, furniture—gives children the opportunity to reenact what they see of the world.

- *Discovery/Science.* Often science projects are geared toward cognitive and language development. This need not always be so; some activities can focus on feelings. Caring for pets, for instance, brings out feelings of nurturing and protectiveness. Making "feeling clocks" can emphasize emotions. Blank clock faces are used as a base upon which children draw or paste pictures of people showing various emotional states. Display these at children's eye level so they can be changed frequently.

- *Dramatic Play.* Home-life materials give children the props they need to express how they see their own world of family, parents, siblings. Mirrors, telephones, and dress-up clothes encourage children to try out their emotional interests on themselves as well as each other.

- *Language/Library.* Stories and books in which characters and situations reflect a wide range of emotions are readily available (see Figure 13.20 and Figure 14.3 for some suggested titles). Children enjoy looking at photographs of people and guessing what the person in the photo is feeling. This encourages children to find words that label feelings; their responses can be recorded and posted nearby. Once children seem at ease in using feeling words, the discussion can continue when the teacher poses the question, "Why do you think this person is sad/happy/angry?"

- *Music/Movement.* Music of all kinds encourages self-expression and permits an endless variety of movement and feelings to be shown openly and freely. Children can be introduced to classical, ethnic, jazz, or rock music while dancing with scarves or streamers or marching with rhythm sticks, as well as singing and dancing to children's recordings. Since musical knowledge is the earliest of human intellectual competencies (see Chapter 13), music can be part of the curriculum for children as young as toddlers. Pounding on drums and dancing both relieve tension in a socially acceptable manner. More structured activities, such as showing children how to use musical instruments, must be balanced by plenty of freedom for individual musical expression.

- *Outdoors.* The environment itself encourages self-expression. Whether in the sand or on a swing, children seem to open up emotionally as they relax in the physical freedom the out-of-doors fosters. Outdoor games are usually highly emotionally charged. Running, chasing, and the dramatic play of superheroes provide emotional release for children.

The outdoor area is an ideal place for large, noisy, and messy activities. It is ideal for tracing body outlines, for instance. These life-size portraits of each child reinforce self-concepts and encourage a feeling of pride in one's self. Woodworking is an outdoor activity that allows children to vent anger and tension. Nails won't be hurt no matter how hard they are pounded; there is satisfaction in sawing a piece of wood into two pieces. Music offers numerous opportunities for self-expression. Children can dance with scarves or streamers, march through the yard with drums pounding, imitate Wild Things, make a maypole around the tree, and create a Chinese dragon for a parade. A rich musical repertoire of band instruments, phonograph records, tapes, and voices can stimulate children to pretend to be elephants, tigers, and dinosaurs, as well as circus performers and ballet artists. Even a simple project such as water painting becomes an avenue for self-expression as children use paint brushes and buckets of water on trees, cement, and buildings, giving them all a fresh coat of "paint."

Figure 14.8 outlines how specific materials and activies can be developed for emotional growth. Using the senses and sensory activities, teachers can promote an atmosphere in which emotions can be explored.

| Emotion/Skill Developed | Sensory Activity (Senses Used) |
|---|---|
| *Self-Esteem* | |
| 1. Identity: "Look at what I can do, the noise I can make, the weight I can pick up and move!" | Use rocks of various sizes with balances, so that children can touch and hear when they move things around. |
| 2. Connectedness: "I can make the same snakes as you, we can all make cakes." | A malleable material such as playdough can be used first alone, then with tools. |
| 3. Uniqueness: "I'm pouring mine; you're dripping yours, and she is squeezing her stuff out her fingers!" | Make "oobleck," a mixture of cornstarch and water, in separate tubs for each child. Children can manipulate it in their own ways. |
| 4. Power: "I can make this water go anywhere I want; look out for the tidal waves!" | Water play offers the child choices: pour into any of several containers, fill or empty the jug, use a funnel or a baster to squirt the water, make waves or splash hands. |
| *Feelings* | |
| 1. Identification: "Does it feel very smooth, slippery, slidy? Is it soft and soothing?" | When fingerpainting, the teacher can describe what it appears the child is feeling. Children can identify their feelings as the teacher describes them while they use the materials. |
| 2. Acceptance/Mastery: "She took your baker's dough and that made you angry. You can tell her you don't like it when she grabs what you are using." | Whether the sensory material is clay, cornmeal, soapy water, or fine sand, the issues of ownership and use of materials arise. Then, teachers reflect children's feelings and help them take responsibility for their own feelings. |
| 3. Appropriate Expression:<br>Child: "Tami has all the big pitchers."<br>Teacher: "How can you let her know you want one?"<br>Child: "And she splashed me two times!"<br>Teacher: "If you feel too crowded, you need to tell her so." | As children begin to use the sensory materials, they need to communicate to others. Usually the issues are about wanting more material and personal space. |
| 4. Appreciation of Feelings: "Whee! Yuk! Mmm! Ha!" | When children share in a sensory activity, such as a feeling walk through tubs of cornmeal, lentils, flour, and soapsuds, they have the delightful experience of enjoying their own feelings with another. |

**FIGURE 14.8** Sensory materials offer a sensorimotor opportunity to deal with materials in a nonstructured way. Because children relax with open-ended activities, they will often share their feelings as they use sensory materials in a comfortable atmosphere.

## Focus on Skills

Emotional development is a lifelong process, requiring experience with one's own feelings. Each child has a unique emotional foundation, which the knowledgeable teacher assesses. Only then can teachers plan curriculum with realistic goals in mind for the children in that class. The goals teachers set for children will determine which emotional skills will be the focus as they individualize the curriculum. Maggie has difficulty with changes in the routine, Caroline never cries, no matter how she hurts, and Clyde screams when he is frustrated. To help children like these learn to express and control their emotions, teachers plan programs like the one illustrated in Figure 14.3 and Figure 14.8.

**FIGURE 14.9** Teachers and children explore emotions together.

### Use of Themes

One particular theme, that of "Who Am I?", is useful when developing curriculum for emotional growth. Figure 14.10 outlines how this theme can be incorporated in many ways, both indoors and out. A number of other units can be developed to extend the theme of "Who Am I?" Some of these are: "My Body," "The Senses," "The Community Where I Live," and so on.

## Unit 14–1  Checkpoint

Emotional growth is a crucial part of children's development in the early years. Emotions develop as children respond to life experiences with a full range of feelings. An undifferentiated state of emotions during infancy evolves into a more refined array of feelings in childhood. Children gain control of their emotions through maturation and experience.

Emotional skills learned in the early years are: the ability to deal with feelings and with change, to be able to exercise judgment, to know and enjoy one's power. Teachers help children develop these skills by building a vocabulary of feeling words, by an awareness of the emotional climate in the classroom, by talking with children about their feelings, and by helping children sense the emotional framework of others. Self-esteem and self-concepts are enhanced by positive emotional growth.

Curriculum planning for emotional development involves an emphasis on many avenues for self-expression in the class setting, sometimes focusing on one particular emotional skill or theme that emphasizes emotional expression.

**THEME: WHO AM I?**

1. *Art:* Body outlines
      Facial expressions pictures—variations: (a) look in a mirror, (b) have a blank face and you draw in the features, (c) have a face partly done and you complete, (d) magazine cut-outs
   Face painting
   Fingerprinting (hand and foot)
2. *Blocks:* People, furniture, structures people live in
      Pictures of same
3. *Cooking:* Share ethnic dishes (tortillas, pasta, things you like to cook at home)
4. *Discovery/science:* Height–weight charts
      Drawing around hands and feet and comparing sizes
      Doing body outlines of a large group of children, each with a different color, and comparing sizes
      Mapping—where people live, charts of phone numbers
      Put out a globe
      Weather–homes connections
5. *Dramatic play:* Lots of mirrors
      A variety of dress-up play for taking on a variety of roles and seeing how they feel
6. *Language/library:* Have children write books about themselves—variations: (a) use *Is This You?* (Krauss) as model, (b) loose-leaf binder of their own books they can add to themselves, (c) "My house is me" as title, (d) families
      Books on families of various sorts; books about other children and what they are like (Corduroy lives in an apt.)
      Where animals live
      Feelings about where children live
7. *Manipulatives:* Puzzles with body parts, with people and clothing
      Self-help skills with dressing frames
      Encourage children to build a structure that things could live in; i.e., lincoln logs.
8. *Sand and water play:* Bubble-blowing
      Using your bodies to build—digging with hands and feet, encouraging sensory exploration
      Use body parts to help you, like using your foot on the shovel.
9. *Swinging/climbing:* All these activities use body parts; teachers emphasize this when watching children at play.
10. *Games:* Rolling the barrel, rolling yourself      Hide and Seek and Tag
      Mother May I?                                      Dramatic play games with family members
11. *Large block-building:* Making house-like structures
      Using vehicles that need your body's force to move
12. *Woodworking:* Using body parts
      Make a map board of school, neighborhood, a city.
13. *Routines:* Self-help: Awareness of what you can do by yourself; by definition all "Who Am I?" tasks; teachers use verbal and musical reinforcement.
14. *Transitions:* Use physical characteristics of children for transitions—"Everyone who has brown eyes . . . freckles . . . blue jeans can go outside . . . "
15. *Group times:* "Head and shoulders"
      Description games—describe someone and guess who it is as a game "I'm thinking of someone" or with song "Mary Has a Red Dress"
      "Little Tommy (Tina) Tiddlemouse," voice recognition
      "Good morning little Teddy Bear," with bear going around circle and saying names
16. *Snacktime/bedtime:* Mark places with names and pictures, such as beds or placemats
      Try to coordinate the nametag, bed, or placemat with symbol on cubby.

**FIGURE 14.10**   A child's school experience is strongly related to how emotional events are handled.

*Ask yourself:*

- What are the principles of emotional development?
- What emotional skills are learned in early childhood?
- What is the role of the teacher in emotional development?
- What are three ways to plan curriculum that will enhance emotional growth?

## UNIT 14–2  SOCIAL GROWTH

# THE DEVELOPMENT OF SOCIALIZATION

Social development is the process through which children learn what behavior is acceptable and expected. A set of standards is imposed on the child at birth that reflects the values of the family and the society in which the child lives.

Social development begins in the crib. Within the first few months of life, the infant smiles, coos, and plays in response to a human voice, face, or physical contact. Young children are influenced from birth by a conscious attempt on the part of adults to guide them in ways that society expects. Parents attempt to transmit behavior patterns that are characteristic of their culture, religion, gender, educational, and ethnic backgrounds. Children imitate what they see; they adapt social expectations to their own personality.

This process—called *socialization*—includes learning appropriate behavior in a number of different settings. Children learn very early to discriminate between the expectations of each environment. At school, free exploration of play materials is encouraged, but in a church pew it is not. Grocery stores, circuses, libraries, and Grandma's home call for a repertoire of fitting behaviors.

In general, the socialization process in a school setting revolves around a child's relationships with other people. During this time of their lives, children work out a separate set of relationships with adults other than their parents. They also establish different relationships with adults than they do with other children.

Through socialization, the customary roles that boys and girls play are also transmitted. Children come to understand how teachers, mommies, daddies, grandparents, males, and females are expected to act.

Children also learn social attitudes at an early age. They learn to enjoy being with people and participating in social activities. Favorable attitudes toward people and a strong desire to be part of the social world, to be with others, are established in the early years.

The child's social development is an integral part of the total growth process. Cognitive and social growth are related. In order to consider the consequences of one's actions, for instance, there must be a certain level of intellectual understanding. Accord-

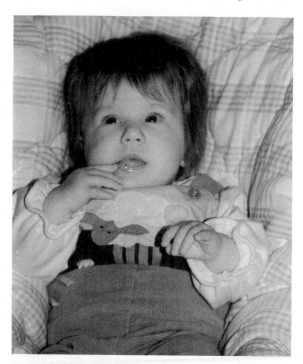

**FIGURE 14.11**  Infancy: the beginning of socialization. (Courtesy of Michael Neilan.)

ing to Smith (1982), the manner in which children define their appearance influences their attitudes toward themselves and their relationships with others. Emotional development is affected also. When children conform to the behavior expected of them, they have a greater self-acceptance and like themselves better. Language, of course, is what allows the socially developing child to communicate with others as part of the social process.

In the early years, children mature socially in discernible developmental stages. From birth to age three, children's interest in others begins with a mutual gazing and social smile in the early months (birth through eight months), continues with an exploration of others as well as some anxious behavior around strangers in the crawler and walker stages (8 to 18 months), and develops into an enjoyment of peers and adults along with an awareness of others' rights and feelings as a toddler and two-year-old (18 months to 3 years) (Lally, 1987).

For preschool children, there are four basic social expectations: (1) that they will show affection and interest in family members; (2) that they will learn right from wrong and act accordingly; (3) that they will learn to get along with other children; and (4) that they will learn to play an appropriate sex role (Hurlock, 1972). Children of the primary years (five to eight years) show an increased interest in peers and social competence, and group rules become important. The development of a social conscience and of fairness rounds out the primary-grade developmental milestones (Bredekamp, 1987).

It is through play (as discussed in Chapter 11) that children learn much of their social repertoire. Dramatizations, role playing, and dramatic play provide opportunities to act out many roles and help children deal with some of the demands placed upon them. In play, the child experiments with options: finding out what it feels like to be the boss, to be the baby, to behave in ways that might otherwise be unacceptable. Carla was the oldest of three children and had many "big girl" expectations placed on her within the family setting. At school, Carla enjoyed being the baby, acting out a helpless infant role whenever she could. Under the guise of play,

**FIGURE 14.12**   Through play, children learn to get along with one another as they experiment with how it feels to be silly, sad, or even adorned with a broad-brimmed hat! (Courtesy of Stride Rite Children's Centers, Cambridge, Mass.)

children, like Carla, rehearse for life without suffering the real-life consequences.

## Peer Relationships

For the young child, social development means moving away from adults toward people of one's own age. During the early years, the child learns to socialize outside the family; social contacts outside the home reinforce the enjoyment of social attitudes and prepare the child for future group activity.

*Peer interactions*, that is, associating with friends of the same age group, become important to the child once infancy and early toddlerhood are past. Through peer interactions, children can identify with models who are like themselves and can learn from each other's behavior. Friends provide models for imitation, for comparison, for confirmation of themselves, and are a source of support.

Playing with other children begins with solitary parallel play at around two years of age, where two or more children are in the same area with each other

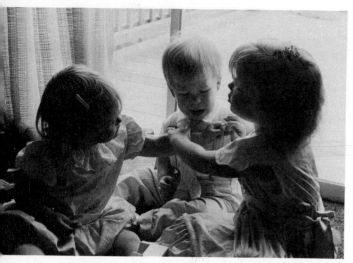

**FIGURE 14.13** Socialization involves learning how to solve problems and interact with others, particularly in conflict resolution. (Courtesy of Jeanne Brannan, College of Notre Dame of Md.)

**FIGURE 14.14** Peer relationships are a source of pleasure and support. As social understanding develops, children shift from a preoccupation with themselves to an awareness of the thoughts and feelings of their friends.

but do not initiate social interaction. By the ages of three and four, more interaction takes place: there is conversation as well as cooperation in playing together.

A peer group is important for a number of reasons. Social development is enhanced because a child learns to conform to established social standards outside of his home setting. The expectations of the larger society are reinforced. In order to become autonomous, the child must also learn to achieve independence from the family, especially parents. Young children must also come to understand themselves as part of society. Their self-concepts are enlarged by a group of peers as they see how others respond to them and treat them.

Smith (1982) states that three trends emerge in the way children relate to each other. First, children become more sensitive to their play partners; then they begin to use language more effectively in their interactions. Finally, cooperative play increases as parallel play decreases. Rubin (1980) defines three stages of social understanding through which children pass: (1) they shift from a preoccupation with self to an awareness of the thoughts and feelings of another; (2) they shift from the observable, physical qualities of the play partner to an awareness of their friend's less obvious characteristics; and (3) they begin to perceive the friendship as long lasting (Smith, 1982).

## SOCIAL SKILLS IN EARLY CHILDHOOD EDUCATION

*Social skills* are strategies children learn that enable them to behave appropriately in many environments. They help children learn to initiate or manage social interaction in a variety of settings and with a number of people.

*Social cognition* plays a part in the development of social skills. It is the application of thinking to personal and social behavior; it is giving meaning to social experience (Smith, 1982). Nadia used her cognitive skills in memory when she wanted to play with Paul, a very popular four-year-old. She remembered Paul's interest in the rope swing and challenged him to swing higher than she did. Bruno, on the other hand, is well known throughout the group for his inability to share materials. When Sandy wanted to play with the small fire trucks (Bruno's favorite toys), she used cognitive skills to negotiate the use of one truck. Social cognition requires children to interpret events and make decisions, to consider the impact of their behavior on others, and to consider the cause as well as the consequence of an action. Cognitive skills are necessary when we ask children to seek alternative solutions to social problems: "How else could you ask him for a turn, Pete?" These are all social cognition skills, and they serve as the basis for the acquisition of other skills.

In an early childhood setting, children learn a great deal about social behavior and expectations. They develop many skills as they learn to interact with adults other than their parents and children other than their siblings. Social skills emerge as children learn to function as members of a group and as they come to understand themselves as social beings. The social skills of early childhood, then, are complex and change with the age and experience of the individual child. Broadly, the following are some of the specific skills and values young children learn.

## Skills Learned with Adults

In their relationship with adults, children learn:

- They can stay at school without parents.
- They can enjoy adults other than parents and respond to new adults.
- Adults will help in times of trouble or need.
- Adults will assist in learning social protocol.
- Adults will keep children from being hurt and from hurting others.
- Adults will not always take a side or solve the problem.
- Adults will work with them to solve problems.
- Adults believe that every child has a right to a satisfying social experience at school.

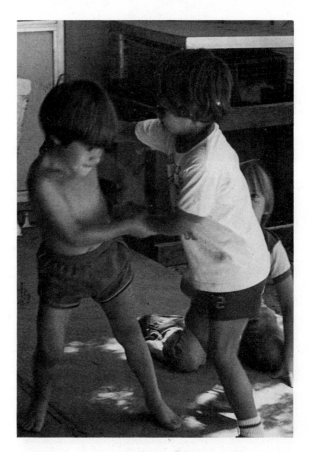

**FIGURE 14.15** Quarreling is a common form of social behavior in young children. In the early years, children need to learn to resolve conflicts without retreat or force. (Courtesy of Stephanie Barry Agnew.)

## Skills Learned with Peers

In their relationship with other children, children learn:

- There are different approaches to others; some work, some don't.
- Interactive skills, and how to sustain the relationship.
- How to solve conflicts in ways other than retreat or force.
- How to share materials, equipment, other children, friends, teachers, and ideas.

**FIGURE 14.16** Cooperation: "You push me—then I'll push you!"

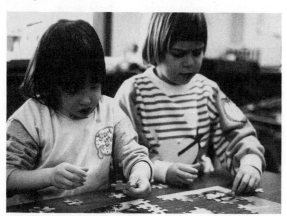

**FIGURE 14.17** Friendship: "We can work on the puzzle together." (Courtesy of Denise Strus.)

- How to achieve mutually satisfying play.
- Self-defense, and how to assert their rights in socially acceptable ways.
- How to take turns and how to communicate desires.
- Negotiating skills.
- How to be helpful to peers with shoelaces, information, and by modeling behavior.
- To anticipate/avoid problems.
- Realistic expectations of how other children behave and respond toward self.

## Skills Learned in a Group

In groups, children learn:

- How to take part as a member and not as an individual.
- That there are activities that promote group association (stories, music).
- A group identity (center room class, Mrs. T's group, four-year-old group).
- To follow a daily schedule and pattern.
- To adapt to school routines.
- School rules and expectations.
- Interaction and participatory skills: how to enter and exit from play.
- To respect the rights, feelings, and property of others.
- How to work together as a group, during clean-up time, in preparation for an event, etc.
- How to deal with delay of gratification: how to wait.

## Skills Learned As an Individual

As individuals, children learn:

- To take responsibility for self-help, self-care.
- To initiate their own activities and to make choices.
- To work alone in close proximity to other children.
- To negotiate.
- To cope with rejection, hurt feelings, disappointment.

- To communicate in verbal and nonverbal ways, and when to use communication skills.
- To test limits other people set.
- Their own personal style of peer interaction: degree, intensity, frequency, quality.
- To express strong feelings in socially acceptable ways.
- To manage social freedom.

Specific skills within these four areas include the social/moral aspects of nurturance, kindness, and sharing (Melson & Fogel, 1988; Krough, 1985; Smith, 1986). As children get older, these skills become more specific, including truth telling, taking turns or reciprocity, promise keeping, property rights, and rules (DeVries & Kohlberg, 1987).

# THE TEACHER'S ROLE
## Considerations

A major role for the early childhood teacher is to see that children have enjoyable social contacts and to help motivate children toward a desire to be with others. The early childhood setting affords children numerous learning opportunities for social development.

The teacher has an important role to play as children learn the give-and-take of social interaction. In the role of social organizer, the teacher creates a physical and interpersonal environment that promotes the development of children's social skills. A first consideration is to *plan and arrange a social environment* to enhance appropriate social behaviors. To stimulate child-initiated activities, self-care, and group responsibility, the use of low, open shelves and furniture scaled to size is a necessary ingredient. Group activities, toys, materials, and placement of furniture should be structured in ways that allow children to play alone or with someone. Many areas lend themselves to group play, such as dramatic play corners or blocks. Books, puzzles, and easels, on the other hand, can be a singular experience or can generate associative play. Cooperative play is suggested in the environment when there is more than one piece of equipment. The placement of two telephones, three wagons, and eight fire fighter hats fosters child–child interactions. The teacher must also allow enough time in the daily schedule for children to get thoroughly involved in playing with one another.

The teacher's role in social development is also one of *facilitating children's interactions and interpreting their behavior.* In order to help young children understand each other and to pave the way for continued cooperation, the teacher reports and reflects on what is happening. In the classroom setting, during an active, free-play period, the teacher might:

| *Reflect the Action:* | *Say:* |
| --- | --- |
| Call attention to the effect one child's behavior is having on another. | "Randy, when you scream like that, other children become frightened and afraid to play with you." |
| Show approval and reinforce positive social behavior. | "I like the way you carefully stepped over their block building, Dannetta." |
| Support a child in asserting her rights. | "Chrystal is hanging on to the doll because she isn't finished playing yet, Wilbur." |
| Support a child's desire to be independent. | "I know you want to help, Keyetta, but Sammy is trying to put his coat on by himself." |
| Acknowledge and help children establish contact with others. | "Omar would like to play, too. That's why he brought you another bucket of water. Is there a place where he can help?" |
| Reflect back to a child the depth of his feelings and what form those feelings might take. | "I know George made you very angry when he took your sponge, but I can't let you throw water at him. What can you tell him? What words can you use to say you didn't like what he did?" |

**FIGURE 14.18** Helping: "Let's take turns feeding the baby." (Courtesy of Beverly Thornton.)

Adult responses to children's play are particularly critical in supporting positive social development. The teacher has a powerful, emotional role in children's lives at school. How does a teacher engage children in acting on their social environment so that they learn from one another and accept the realities and benefits of living together? In carefully observing and participating with children, the teacher must decide when and how to intervene and tap into children's own developing social skills and social/moral judgment—without taking over. This is perhaps the most dynamic and challenging part of teachers' jobs, the heart of the profession. Conflicts and their resolution illustrate the interaction between teacher and children, and the critical part teachers play in children's lives. Illustrated in Figure 14.19, the social problems in early childhood range from possession of toys, to hitting others, to keeping promises. *How* a teacher helps children identify and resolve their own conflicts is often more important than the specific problem or solution may be.

# Curriculum Planning for Social Growth

## *In the Environment*

Teaching social behavior in most classrooms usually occurs in response to spontaneous situations.

The teacher's direct involvement in children's social interactions is the most frequent method used. Occasionally, teachers will approach the acquisition of social skills in a more formalized way through planned curriculum activities. The way the environment is arranged has a profound effect on social interaction among children. Most indoor activities are planned and set up to encourage participation by more than one child at a time. Specific areas that enhance social relationships indoors are:

- *The Arts.* At the art table, four or more children will share collage materials, paste, and sponges that have been placed in the center of the table. When easels are placed side by side, conversation occurs spontaneously among children. A small table, placed between the easels, on which a tray of paint cups is placed, also encourages children's interactions. If there is only one of each color, the children will have to negotiate with one another for the color they want to use.

- *Blocks/Manipulatives.* A large space for block cabinets gives children a visual cue that there is plenty of room for more than one child. Puzzle tables set with three or four puzzles also tell children that social interaction is expected. Many times children will talk, play, and plan with one another as they share a large bin full of Lego® or plastic building towers. A floor puzzle always requires a group: some to put the picture together, others to watch and make suggestions. As children build with blocks next to one another, they soon share comments about their work; many times this leads to a mutual effort on a single building.

- *Discovery/Science.* Many science projects can be arranged to involve more than one child. A display of magnets with a tray of assorted objects can become the focus of several children as they decide which ones will be attracted to the magnets. Cooking together, weighing and measuring one another, and caring for classroom pets can be times when teachers reinforce social skills.

- *Dramatic Play.* This area more than any other seems to draw children into contact with one another. Provide an assortment of family life acces-

---

### The Five-Step Approach to Problem Solving

**SCENARIO:** Two children run outdoors to get the available wagon. They reach it simultaneously and start pulling on the handle, yelling "Mine!" One child starts shoving the other child out of the way.

**Step 1: Approach:**
—Get close enough to intervene if necessary.
—You signal your awareness and availability.

**Step 2: Make statement:**
—*Describe the scene.*
—Reflect what the children have said.
—*Offer no judgments, values, solutions*
   "It looks like you both want the wagon."
   "I see you are yelling at each other."

**Step 3: Ask questions:**
—Don't direct questions toward pinpointing blame.
—Draw out details; define problems.
—Help kids communicate versus slugging it out.
   "How did this happen?"
   "What do you want to tell her?"
   "How could you solve this problem?"
   "How could you use it without fighting?"

**Step 4: Pose alternatives:**
—Give children job of thinking and figuring out.
—What are *they* going to do to solve *their* problem?
   "You could take turns,
   You could both use it together,
   You could both do something else, or
   No one could use it."

**Step 5: Follow through physically:**
—Model appropriate behavior.
—*Bottom line goal* is to get social conflict resolved.
—If they can't solve it, you do.
   "It's too hard for you to figure it out. Here's what we'll do."

---

**FIGURE 14.19** Teachers should remember always to start with as little as the children need. Do not use step 5 when step 1 or step 2 will do. The goal is to maximize children's *self*-resolution.

sories, dress-up clothes, kitchen equipment and utensils, and children have little trouble getting involved. A shoe needs to be tied, or a dress zipped up. Someone must come eat the delicious meal just cooked or put the baby to bed. A medical theme in this classroom area also enhances children's social skills. They learn to take each other's temperature, listen to heartbeats, and plan oper-

ations, all of which require one or more people.

• *Language/Library.* Children enjoy reading books and stories to one another, whether or not they know the words. Favorite books are often shared by two children who enjoy turning the pages and talking over the story together. Lotto games encourage children to become aware of one another, to look at each person's card in order to identify who has the picture to match. Name songs and games, especially early in the year, help children learn to call each other by name.

- *Music Movement.* Build in regular times for music and movement activities. The entire group can participate in familiar songs, which builds a sense of community by everyone's participation. Activities during free choice times usually involve smaller numbers, where group members can challenge one another to new ways to dance with scarves or use the tumbling mat. Finally, one-to-one experiences encourage new friendships as the intimacy of a shared musical experience brings two children or a teacher and child together.

Outdoors, the environment can be structured in ways to support group play. Painting or pasting on murals or drawing chalk designs on the cement are art activities that promote social interaction. Planning and planting a garden is a long-range activity that involves many children. Decisions must be made by the group about what to plant, where to locate the garden, how to prepare the soil, and about the shared responsibilities of caring for the garden.

Most gross motor activities stimulate group interactions. Seesaws, jump ropes, and hide-and-seek require at least two people to participate. A-frames, boards, and boxes, as well as other moveable equipment, need the cooperative effort of several children in order to be rearranged. Sand play, when accompanied by water, shovels and, other accessories, draws a number of children together to create rivers, dams, and floods. Ball games and relay races also encourage social relationships.

As a directed learning experience, small-group times afford an opportunity to focus on social skills in a more structured way. Small groups provide a setting for children and teachers to participate in more relaxed, uninterrupted dialogue. The intimacy of the small group sets the stage for many social interactions.

Group-time discussions can focus on problems

that children can solve, for instance. Too many children crowding the water table, a child's fear of fire drills, or the noise level on a rainy day are subjects children will talk about in small groups. The most relevant situations are ones that occur naturally in the course of a program. Another curriculum idea is to make "Situation Cards" of these and other common incidents. For instance, teacher can create illustrated cards that pose situations such as:

- You tell your friends to "stop it" when they take part of the toy you are using, but they do it again.
- You open your lunch and your mom or dad has packed your favorite foods.
- You come down the slide and your teacher calls "Hooray for you!"
- You promise your friend you'll play with him at recess, but then someone else you like asks you to play with her.

The teacher then guides a discussion around the questions "How do you feel? What can you say? What can you do?" This activity can be simplified or elaborated depending on the individuals and group involved.

Solutions may emerge when the teacher supports active and involved participation. Teachers pose the problem and ask children to respond in several ways: "How does it make you and others feel when that happens? What can you and others do about it? What are some alternatives?" The problems must be real, and they must be about something that is important to children. Figure 14.20 is an example of a sequentially planned curriculum that fosters the development of social skills in small group settings.

### Focus on Skills

Social development for the preschool child includes gaining an awareness of the larger community in which the child lives. The early childhood curriculum contains elements of what is often in the later grades called social studies. Visits from police

## THEME: LEARNING SOCIAL SKILLS

| Day | Skill | Activities |
|---|---|---|
| Monday | Developing a positive self-image | Do thumb print art.<br>Make foot and hand prints.<br>Compare children's baby pictures to current photos.<br>Play with mirrors: make faces, emotional expressions.<br>Dress felt dolls in clothing.<br>Sing name songs: "Mary Wore Her Red Dress."<br>Make a list: "What I like to do best is . . ." Post in classroom.<br>Do a self-portrait in any art medium.<br>Make a silhouette picture of each child. |
| Tuesday | Becoming a member of a group | Take attendance together: Who is missing?<br>Play picture lotto with photographs of children.<br>Play "Farmer in the Dell."<br>Share a favorite toy from home with other children.<br>Tape record children's voices; guess who they are.<br>Have a "friendly feast": each child brings favorite food from home to share. |
| Wednesday | Forming a friendship within the group | Provide one puzzle (toy, game, book) for every two children.<br>Take a "Buddy Walk"; return and tell a story together of what you saw.<br>Play "Telephone Talk": pretent to invite your friend over to play.<br>Play "copy cat": imitate your friend's laugh, walk, cry, words.<br>Practice throwing and catching balls with one another.<br>Form letter together with two children's bodies: A, T, C. K. etc.<br>Play tug-of-war with your friend.<br>Build a house out of blocks together.<br>Make "mirror image" movements with your friend. |
| Thursday | Working together as a group | Play with a parachute; keep the ball bouncing.<br>Make snacks for the rest of the class.<br>Plan and plant a garden.<br>Make a mural together to decorate the hallways.<br>Play "Follow the Leader."<br>Celebrate a holiday with a pinata.<br>Sing a round: "Row, Row, Row Your Boat." |
| Friday | Learning a group identity | Make a map of the town and have children place their house on it.<br>Take a field trip together.<br>Print a newspaper with articles by/about each child.<br>Select and perform a favorite story for the rest of the class.<br>Take a group snapshot.<br>Make a "family tree" of photos of children in group.<br>Learn a group folk dance.<br>Make a mural of handprints joined in a circle. |

**FIGURE 14.20** Building social skills through small-group experiences, beginning with an understanding of self and moving toward an appreciation of group membership.

officers, mail carriers, fire fighters, and other community helpers are common in many programs. Learning about children from other cultures, exploring the neighborhood around the center, and making maps are other ways children learn social studies skills.

Learning how to cooperate with others is one primary social skill in which young children need plenty of practice. Toddlers and two-year-olds can begin to see the benefits of cooperation as they become more aware of others' feelings and wishes, and as teachers help all children get what they want through taking turns, dividing materials, looking for another item when it is in demand. Three- to five-year-olds become more cooperative as they learn more self-help skills (motor development) and can express themselves (language development) as well as remember guidelines and understand reasons for

LANGUAGE

Plan and perform a favorite story.
Choose a story at the listening post together.
Learn "I love you" in sign language.
Copy someone's motions, dance, block patterns.
Put on a puppet show.
Develop a "What Can I Share?" chart.
Discuss how new toys, equipment will be shared
   so everyone gets a turn.

SCIENCE

Care for classroom pets.
Have group cooking projects.
Plan and plant a garden.

MUSIC

Sing together each day.
Have a rhythm band.
Dance in groups of two or three.
Dance with a parachute.

ENVIRONMENT

Schedule cleanup daily.
Have two children share cubbies.
Bring snacks from home to share.
Set tables for two or more children.
Use large bins to store some materials; children
   will need to share contents.

SOCIAL STUDIES

Make a group gift for hospital, rest home.
Create an art display for the local library.
Make cookies to sell at the school fair.
Run errands for teachers, each other.
Develop dramatic play themes of: shoe stores,
   hospital, doctors, ecology.
Collect and sort recycling materials.
Take a field trip to the town dump for recycling.

OUTDOORS

Push someone on a swing.
Pull a friend in a wagon.
Make bird feeders.
Set up bowling alley, with bowlers and pin setters.
Make an obstacle course.
Use seesaws.
Play group jump rope.
Play "Follow the Leader".

COOPERATION

ART

Trace each other's bodies on paper.
Share paste and collage materials.
Share paints.
Make a mural.
Make litter bags.
Create a wall hanging: fabric, crayons
   and sheets; each child draws part.
Create a class quilt: each child sews a square;
   teacher puts it together.

GAMES

Play Simon Says
Play board games:
   Winnie-The-Pooh
   and Candy Land
Play Lotto
Play Bingo

**FIGURE 14.21** The social skill of cooperation can be fostered throughout the curriculum.

prosocial behavior (cognitive development). School-age children develop an emotional sense of competence (see discussion of Erik Erikson's work in Chapter 4). They do this by acquiring knowledge and skills recognized by our culture as important (e.g., the cognitive tasks of reading and writing) and then using them with peers. The opportunity for children to learn and rehearse this skill takes place in many areas of the classroom. Figure 14.21 illustrates this.

## Use of Themes

A popular theme that lends itself to social growth is that of friendship. This has particular appeal during the month of February when the meaning of friendship is enhanced by the celebration of Valentine's Day. At other times, relay races and noncompetitive games (those in which everyone is a winner) promote working with friends to achieve a goal. Teachers who encourage children to help each other read, tie shoes, pour milk, fasten a smock, or sponge a table reinforce what friendship can be in the early years. Many books and songs can be found that emphasize friendship. Group discussions can help children define what is a friend. Figure 14.22 illustrates how a friendship unit can be developed for an early childhood setting.

**THEME: FRIENDSHIP**

| Concepts Children Will Learn | Activity |
| --- | --- |
| Everyone has a name and likes to have it used. | Friendship songs, using children's names |
| Each person is something special and unique. | Make a "Friend Puppet" with paper plates, tongue depressor handles. Child decorates it with felt pieces and yarn to look like a friend. |
| Friends are different; they do not all look the same. | Children respond to: "Tell me about your friend Alice. She . . ." (Child describes a friend as teacher writes the words.) |
| Having friends is fun. | Make a friendship ring: each child traces own hands on mural, making a circle. |
| Friends enjoy doing things together. | Go on a scavenger hunt with a friend. |
| Adults can be your friends. | Teacher helps child solve conflict or gives comfort when child is hurt. |
| Animals and pets can be your friends. | Children have an opportunity to bring small house pets to school to share with rest of class. |
| To have a friend is to be a friend. | Children respond to: "A Friend Is Someone Who . . ." (They describe their impressions while teacher writes down their words.) |
| Friends enjoy doing things for one another. | Children respond to: "Being A Friend With Someone Means . . ." (Teacher writes down children's dictation.) |
| Everyone can have a friend. | Teacher reads stories about friendships: *Will I Have A Friend?* (Cohen), *Corduroy* (Freeman), *Play With Me* (Ets), *Little Bear's Friend* (Minarik), *A Letter To Amy* (Keats), *Hold My Hand* (Zolotow). |
| You can show someone you want to be friends. | Write a letter to a friend; invite a friend over to play. |
| Friends will help you. | Form a relay team and have a race. |

**FIGURE 14.22** A friendship unit can encourage children to express positive emotions while they use their cognitive, language, and motor skills to enhance their social development.

Dusty, a four-year-old, is clear about what quality he has that makes him a good friend:

Dusty (to Nathan): Be my friend?
Nathan: No!
Dusty (thoughtfully): You really should, you know, because I'm FUNNY!
Nathan (appreciatively): Okay.

## Unit 14–2 Checkpoint

Early in life children become aware of their social nature. The socialization process begins under the guidance of parents and family members. When children enter group settings, they are further exposed to behavior, social roles, and attitudes that foster social development. Much of a child's social repertoire is learned by playing with other children.

Children learn a great many social skills in these early years. They learn to enjoy and trust adults other than their parents. In their relationships with others, children learn ways to cooperate, disagree, share, communicate, and assert themselves effectively.

Children also learn how to be a member of a group—to take part in group activities, adapt to school expectations, and to respect the rights and feelings of others. The young child also learns to express feelings in appropriate ways and to begin self-care tasks.

Teachers plan and arrange the early childhood environment in ways that will promote social growth and interaction. The adults help children understand each other's actions and motivations by interpreting the behavior to children as they play.

Curriculum to develop social skills in young children can be spontaneous as well as planned. Much of the focus in an early childhood setting is on social interactions throughout the day. At other times, social growth is enhanced by group-time discussions, awareness of the community and society at large, and an emphasis on specific social skills.

*Ask yourself:*

- What are social expectations of infants and toddlers? the pre-schooler? school-aged children?
- Why is peer group experience important?
- What social skills do children develop with adults? With other children? In a group? As individuals?
- How do teachers help children develop social skills?
- How are social skills fostered in the curriculum?

**FIGURE 14.23** Creativity is the ability to be original and imaginative; to soar above the commonplace. (Courtesy of Thomas J. Ranney, Milwaukee Area Technical College, Wis.)

# UNIT 14–3 CREATIVE GROWTH

## THE DEVELOPMENT OF CREATIVITY

Creativity is the ability to have new ideas, to be original and imaginative, and to make new adaptations on old ideas. Inventors, composers, and designers are creative people, as are those who paint and dance, write speeches, or create curriculum for children. When people think in a different way than they usually do, when they change in how they learn or see something, that is creativity (Adams, 1987). The more teachers realize they are a part of a creative act, the more sensitive they become in helping young children develop creatively.

Creativity is a process; as such, it is hard to define. As one becomes involved in creative activity, the process and the product merge.

> . . . It is probably best to think of creativity as a continual process for which the best preparation is creativity itself. . . there is real joy in discovery—which not only is its own reward, but provides the urge for continuing exploration and discovery.

(Lowenfeld and Brittain, 1975)

The young child is open to experience, exploring materials with curiosity and eagerness. For young children, developing the senses is part of acquiring creative skills. Children are also quick to question, wonder, and see things that do not quite match up. These are traits of creative children.

# CREATIVE SKILLS IN EARLY CHILDHOOD

There are characteristics common to creative people. For the teacher interested in fostering creative growth in children, these are the skills they should help children learn.

## Flexibility

Flexibility, or fluency, is the ability to produce many ideas and the capacity to shift from one idea to another. Children who are flexible in their thinking have original ideas and usually demonstrate a unique perspective on issues. This is a natural trait and can be encouraged by teachers who are aware of its relationship to creative growth. Children are challenged, for instance, if they must think of another way to share the wagons when taking turns doesn't work.

## Sensitivity

Being creative involves a high degree of sensitivity to one's self and one's mental images. Creative people, from an early age, seem to be aware of the world around them: how things smell, feel, and taste. They are sensitive to mood, texture, and how they feel about someone or something. Seeing detail, noticing how a pine cone is attached to the branch, is a detail the creative person does not overlook.

Creative children take delight and satisfaction in making these images come to life. Their creative response is in the way they paint a picture, dance with streamers, or find a solution to a problem. Figure 14.24 shows how a 5½-year-old's sensitivity to perspective and detail comes out through a drawing.

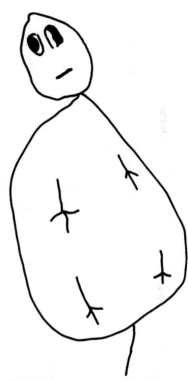

**FIGURE 14.24** Sensitivity to one's own mental images, such as perceiving direction and movement, are part of creativity in the young child. A 5½-year-old sketched how a rat looked from below after picking it up often and watching it run on its exercise wheel.

## Use of Imagination

Imagination is a natural part of the creative process. Children use their imagination to develop their creativity in several ways.

**Role Playing.** In taking on another role, children combine their knowledge of the real world with their internal images. The child becomes a new character, and that role comes to life.

**Image-Making.** When children create a rainbow with a hose or with paints, they are adding something of their own to their understanding of that visual image. In dance, children use their imagination as they pretend to be objects or feelings, images brought to life.

**Constructing.** In building and constructing activities, children seem to be re-creating an image they have about tall buildings, garages, or farms. In the process of construction, however, children do not intend that the end product resemble the building itself. Their imagination allows them to experiment with size, shape, and relationships.

## A Willingness to Take Risks

People who are willing to break the ordinary mental set and push the boundaries in defining and using ordinary objects, materials, and ideas are creative people. They take risks. Being open to thinking differently or seeing things differently is essential to creativity.

Self-esteem is a factor in risk-taking since people who are tied to what others think of them are more likely to conform rather than follow their own intuitive and creative impulses. People usually do not like to make mistakes or be ridiculed; therefore, they avoid taking risks.

A teacher concerned about creative growth in children realizes that it will surface if allowed and encouraged. When a child is relaxed and not anxious about being judged by others, creativity will more likely be expressed. With support, children can be encouraged to risk themselves.

## Using Self as a Resource

Creative people who are aware of themselves and confident in their abilities draw upon their own perceptions, questions, and feelings. They know they are their own richest source of inspiration.

MacKinnon found that those who excelled in creative productivity had a great deal of respect for self, that they used the self as a resource (Shallcross and Sisk, 1982).

## Experience

Children need experience in order to gain skills in using materials creatively. They must learn how to hold a paint brush before they can paint a picture; once they know how to paint, they can be creative in what they paint. When the skill of the medium is mastered, the child is ready to create.

# THE TEACHER'S ROLE

## Considerations

The early childhood curriculum offers many rich avenues for self-expression and creativity. Beyond art and music, there is the ability to think and question, to find more than one answer to a problem. Blocks, climbing equipment, and social relationships offer risk-taking opportunities. Children use themselves as resources as they play outdoor games, experiment with science projects, and participate in dramatic play. Taruna exhibits many creative traits as she attempts to enter into play with two other children. She first asks if she can play, and when met with rejection, she demands to be one of the mommies. Taruna finally offers her doll as a prop and is accepted into the group. Her persistence is exceeded only by her creative problem solving.

Regular creative opportunities give children the necessary experience and skill to be creative. Children need frequent occasions to be creative in order to function in a highly creative manner (Eisner, 1964). When children have a chance to create, their skills in perceiving the world are enhanced.

One of the teacher's most crucial considerations for supporting creative growth is that of *divergent thinking*. To diverge means to take a different line of thought or action, deviating from the normal. Finding ideas that branch out rather than converge and center on one answer is divergent thinking. Recent

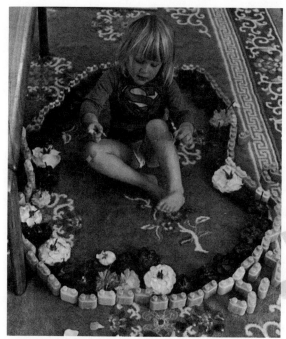

**FIGURE 14.25**  When children have a chance to create, with permission to use an abundance of materials, the results are creative.

works suggest that creativity and problem-solving may stem from similar sources (Hitz, 1987). Real life problem-solving calls for creative thinking as well as logic and concept development (Feldheusen and Treffinger, 1984). The creative arts are important if only because they tend to stress this kind of thinking. Where there are no "right" or "wrong" answers, there will undoubtedly be many solutions for problems.

Children and teachers can discuss issues and seek solutions to problems when divergent thinking is encouraged. In a child care center, for instance, children were fighting over the use of the two swings. The children's responses indicate their willingness to take a different line of thought:

Teacher: How do you think we could share the swings?
David: The kids who give me a turn can come to my birthday party.
Sabrina: No. We will have to make a waiting list.

Xenia: Only girls can use the swings; the boys can have all the carts.
Frederico: Buy a new swing set.

Talking with young children about what they create—be it their artwork, table toy creations, dramatic play sequences—is an important consideration. Robert Schirrmacher (1986) offers some suggestions about talking with children about art; these hints could apply to all creative endeavors. Rather than approach children's work with compliments, judgments, or even questions:

- allow children to go about their artistic discoveries without you comparing, correcting, or projecting yourself into their art...

- shift from searching for representation in children's art to a focus on the abstract, design qualities...

- use reflective dialogue...

- smile, pause, and say nothing at first...

(Schirrmacher, 1986)

In other words, teachers allow children to take the lead in their own creative works from start to finish. Adults do not need to take over at any point, particularly at the end with questions ("What is it?") or praise ("I like it!"). If a child seems to want more response, comment on the color or texture ("What a lot of blue you used" or "I see wiggly lines all down one side"). Then reflect their own ideas back to the children:

Child: The monster's gonna get you and eat you up!
Teacher: You made a monster with the wood scraps.
Child: Yes and it's for my daddy.
Teacher: Let's put it on the counter so it will be dry when he picks you up.

Teacher timing and attitudes are also important in stimulating creative development in young children. The early childhood years are probably the most crucial time to encourage creative thinking. "It is here that initial attitudes are established...and school can be a fun place where the individual's contribution is welcome and where changes can be sought and made." (Lowenfeld and Brittain, 1975)

Children need plenty of time and a relaxed atmosphere to be creative. They need encouragement and respect for the process and products of their creative nature. The teacher's attitude tells the children that what they do is important, and how they do it makes a difference. Rather than expecting a predetermined right answer, the teacher encourages creativity by valuing the answers the children give even when they appear unusual or illogical.

## Curriculum Planning for Creative Growth

### In The Environment

Teachers set up an environment that promotes creative expression; they choose activities and materials that can be used in many ways. These *open-ended materials* provide a continuing challenge as children use them repeatedly in new and different ways. Clay, playdough, paints, crayons and pens, blocks, water, sand and other sensory materials, and moveable outdoor equipment are good examples of open-ended materials that stimulate creativity. Particularly in the area of creative art, it is important to *avoid* projects that masquerade as crative activities, such as:

- duplicated, photocopied, or mimeographed sheets
- cut-and-paste activities
- tracing patterns
- coloring-book pages
- dot-to-dot books (Schirrmacher, 1988)
- any art "project" that is based on a model for children to copy or imitate.

Children are motivated to try new ways to use materials when they are flexible and challenging.

Every classroom has a potential for creative activity. Children use their imagination when blocks

**FIGURE 14.26** Creative people use themselves as a resource; children will draw on their own ideas for creating their own activities and play spaces.

become castles, tunnels, corrals, and swamps. Using all their senses to explore a medium helps children discover many approaches to creativity. Teachers enhance imaginative thought when they introduce questions to ponder that are out of the ordinary. "What would you wear if you were twins? What would you eat? Where would you live?" are ways to help children reflect on subject matter in a different light. Songs that use children's ideas become creative as well as socially inclusive. For example, the song that begins "Did you ever see a whale...?" asks for creative language and thought with answers that may rhyme ("flipping its tail") or not ("spouting chicken soup!").

Creativity happens out-of-doors also. Large, hollow blocks can become a stairway, and wagons and carts become fire engines, buses, doll carriages, moving vans, or trucks. Dancing with ribbons, making a Chinese dragon for a parade, rearranging equipment to make a tumbling or obstacle course all combine children's motor skills with music for creative growth. the use of these activities is limited only by the creativity of the children. Sand, water, and mud provide a place for children to dig, haul, manipulate, and control in any number of ways.

Teachers can apply their own creativity to many routine situations. When looking for a lost mitten, a "hunt" is organized; pretending to be vacuum cleaners, dump trucks, or robots gets the blocks picked up faster.

The dramatic arts offer opportunities for children to express themselves. In order to perform "Goldilocks and The Three Bears," for instance, children will have to create costumes. At music time, children use their creative skills to play drums: tapping, brushing, pounding the drums. Figure 14.26 is a photograph of safe and durable equipment that children can use creatively.

## Focus on Skills

The wide range of skills necessary for creative development can be supported throughout the early childhood program. The creative thinker is one who finds many ways to solve a problem, approach a situation, use materials, and interact with others. The teacher's role is one of supporting imaginative use of equipment.

To encourage creative thinking, teachers also look at the ways they ask children questions. How can they prompt children to view the unusual and think of the exceptional? How can they encourage divergent thinking? What will encourage children to use their cognitive and language skills in creative ways? Figure 14.27 illustrates some of the ways teachers can focus on creative skills through the use of questions.

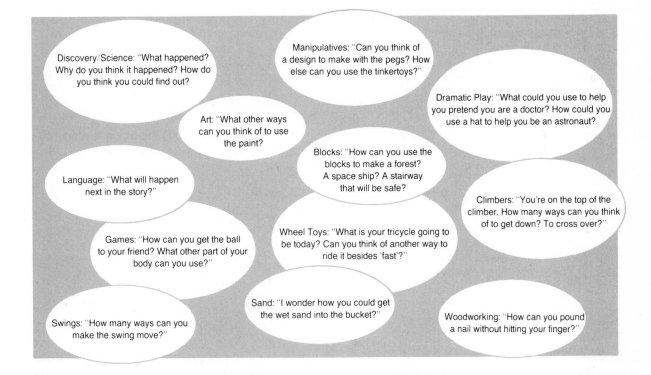

**FIGURE 14.27** As teachers focus on the skills of creativity, they ask children questions to stimulate creative thinking.

## OUTDOORS

1. Plant a garden in a corner of the yard, in an old barrel, or in a box flat on a table. Children learn through experimentation why some things grow and others don't. Make space for a compost heap.
2. Add wheelbarrows to the transportation toys.
3. Take a field trip to a farm, at planting time if possible.
4. Add gardening tools to the sand area. With proper supervision, children can see how trowels, hand claws, rakes, and shovels can be used to create new patterns in the sand and mud.
5. Plan group games that emphasize green and growing things. Older children could run wheelbarrow races, using one child as the wheelbarrow and other as the driver.

## INDOORS

1. Leaf rubbings, printing with apples, onions, carrots, potatoes, lemons, oranges, and celery, and painting with pine boughs are ways children can create art with green and growing things.
2. Block accessories might include blue felt forms for lakes, hay for corrals and barns.
3. In the manipulative area, match a photo of familiar plants with a sample of the plant. Add sorting trays with various kinds of seeds to count, feel, mix, and match. Match pictures of eggs, bacon, milk, and cheese with the animals from which they come.
4. In the science area, grow alfalfa sprouts and mung beans. Let children mix them in salads and feed to classroom pets. As the sprouts grow, children can chart the growth. This can lead to charting their own development, comparing it to when they were infants.
5. The dramatic play center can be transformed into a grocery store to emphasize the food we buy to eat, how it helps us, and why good nutrition is important. Other dramatic play units are a florist shop or nursery, stocked with garden gloves, seed packets, peat pots, and sun hats.
6. The language area can be stocked with books about how plants, baby animals, and children grow. In small groups, children can respond to "When I plant a seed . . ." or "When I was a baby I . . . Now I . . ." to stimulate creative expression.
7. Songs and fingerplays can help focus on green and growing things, children's growth, and animals. "The Green Grass Grows All Around" can be sketched by a teacher so that children will have visual cues to each successive verse. A favorite fingerplay, "Way Up in the Apple Tree," can be adapted to a number of fruits and vegetables. When it comes to lemons, children can be encouraged to think of what rhymes with "sour." Children use just their hands to accompany the verse, or they can use their whole bodies.

> Way up in the apple tree
> Two little apples smiled down at me.
> I shook that tree as hard as I could!
> Down came the apples!
> Mmmmmmm, they were good!

**FIGURE 14.28** "Green and Growing Things," a spring science theme, lends itself to creative development.

## *Use of Themes*

As teachers plan curriculum around a theme, they keep in mind what creative skills can be developed. Figure 14.28 charts the theme of "Green and Growing Things," and can bring out the child's creative nature.

## Unit 14–3 Checkpoint

Young children are open to the creative process and to creative experiences. The early years are a good time to acquire the skills of flexibility, sensitivity, imagination, risk-taking, resourcefulness, and experience.

The role of the teacher is to plan curriculum that will help develop children's creativity. An atmosphere conducive to creative work is one that supports children's divergent thinking, encourages them to take risks, and provides ways they can use themselves as resources.

*Ask yourself:*

- What are the creative skills learned in early childhood?
- What is the teacher's role in the development of creativity?
- What classroom area, skill, or unit promotes creative thinking?
- How can I ask children to use language to promote creative thinking?

# SUMMARY

Emotional, social, and creative growth development are at the center of the early childhood

**FIGURE 14.29** Creativity and problem solving may stem from the same source. Real-life experiences, such as how to plan and build a garden, call for both logic and creative thinking.

curriculum. Planning for these areas involves an understanding of how each develops in the young child and how they are interrelated. Children learn many skills in these three areas as they interact with each other, with adults, and in the environment.

Planning curriculum for emotional, social, and creative growth calls upon teachers to play a supportive role, facilitating children's involvement with the materials and each other. Only then can children discover themselves, explore their relationships, and develop the ability to use their imagination and resources.

## REVIEW QUESTIONS

1. How do emotional, social, and creative growth relate to each other?

2. How can these three areas affect growth in other developmental areas?

3. What are the advantages of and problems with superhero play?

4. List some of the developmental milestones and expectations for socialization of young children.

5. How can teachers support conflict resolution and problem solving?

6. What kinds of activities masquerade as creative art?

## LEARNING ACTIVITIES

1. Name five people you consider creative. Match their skills with those we have identified in early childhood. Where are they similar? Different?

2. How does your center promote positive self-concept? What else could be done?

3. Observe a group of four-year-olds at play. How do they decide what roles each one takes? Are they clear in their expectations of what sex roles are appropriate for boys and girls? Is there sex-role stereotyping?

4. Taking turns and sharing equipment and materials is difficult for young children. Cite three examples you have seen where children used their social skills to negotiate a turn. Was teacher intervention necessary?

5. Make behavioral definitions of emotions you think you will see in the children you teach. Observe the children, then check the accuracy of your definitions.

6. Give three examples of children in your center trying to "break mental set." In what area of the classroom did it occur? What were the adults' responses?

7. How do teachers in your setting plan for creativity? What place does such expression take in the priority of the school philosophy?

## BIBLIOGRAPHY

### GENERAL

Baruch, Dana, and Brown, Roger. "Building Self-Esteem in Children: A Valuable Goal for Parents and Teachers." *The Bing Bulletin,* Vol. VI, Spring 1986.

Brophy, Jere E., and Willis, S.L. *Human Development and Behavior.* New York: St. Martin's Press, 1981.

Clemes, Harris, and Bean, Reynold. *How to Raise Children's Self-Esteem.* San Jose, Calif.: Enrich, 1980.

Shallcross, Doris J., and Sisk, D.A. *The Growing Person.* Englewood Cliffs, N.J.: Prentice-Hall, 1982.

Weber, Evelyn. *Ideas Influencing Early Childhood Education.* New York: Teachers College Press, 1984.

### EMOTIONAL GROWTH

Charlesworth, W., and Kreutzer, M. "Facial Expressions of Infants and Children." In P. Eckman (ed.) *Darwin and Facial Expression.* New York: Academic Press, 1973.

Eibl-Eibesfeldt, I. *Love and Hate: The Natural History of Behavior Patterns.* New York: Holt, Rinehart & Winston, 1971.

Fogel, Alan. "The Role of Emotion in Early Childhood Education." In Katz, L.B. (ed.) *Current Topics in Early Childhood Education,* Vol. III. Norwood, N.J.: Ablex Publishing Corporations, 1980.

Honig, Alice S. "Stress and Coping in Children." *Young Children,* Vol. 41, Nos. 4 and 5, May and July 1986.

Izard, C. *The Face of Emotion.* New York: Appleton-Century-Crofts, 1971.

Kostelnik, Marjorie; Whiren, A.P.; and Stein, L.G. "Living with He-Man: Managing Superhero Fantasy Play." *Young Children,* Vol. 41, No. 4, May 1986.

McDermott, Jeanne. "Making Faces Just Comes Naturally." In *Smithsonian,* Vol. 16, No. 12, March 1986.

Selye, Hans. "History and Present Status of the Stress Concept." In L. Goldberger and S. Breznitz (eds.), *Handbook of Stress.* New York: The Free Press, 1982.

## SOCIAL GROWTH

Bredekamp, Sue (ed.), *NAEYC Position Statement on Developmentally Appropriate Practice in the Primary Grades, Serving 5- Through 8-Year-Olds.* Washington, D.C.: NAEYC, 1987.

DeVries, Rheta, and Kohlberg, Lawrence. *Programs of Early Education.* New York: Longman, 1987.

Krogh, Suzanne L., and Lamme, L.L. "But What About Sharing?" *Young Children,* Vol. 40, No. 4, May 1985.

Lally, J. Ronald; Provence, S.; Szanton, E.; and Weissbourd, B. "Developmentally Appropriate Care for Children from Birth to Age 3." In Bredekamp, Sue (ed.), *Developmentally Appropriate Practice in Early Childhood Programs Serving Children from Birth Through Age 8,* Washington, D.C.: NAEYC, 1987.

Melson, Gail, and Fogel, Alan. "Research in Review: The Development of Nurturance in Young Children." *Young Children,* Vol. 43, No. 3, March 1988.

Rubin, Zick. *Children's Friendships.* Cambridge, Mass.: Harvard University Press, 1980.

Smith, Charels A. *Promoting the Social Development of Young Children.* Palo Alto, Calif.: Mayfield Publishing Co., 1982.

Smith, Charles A. "Nurturing Kindness Through Storytelling." *Young Children,* Vol. 41, No. 6, September 1986.

## CREATIVE GROWTH

Adams, James. *The Care and Feeding of Ideas.* Reading, Mass.: Addison-Wesley, 1987.

Eisner, Elliot. *Think with Me About Creativity.* Dansville, N.Y.: F.A. Owen Publishing Co., 1964.

Feldheusen, J., and Treffinger, D.J. *Teaching Creative Thinking and Problem Solving.* Dubuque, Iowa: Kendall/Hunt, 1984.

Hitz, Randy, "Creative Problem Solving Through Music Activities." *Young Children,* Vol. 42, No. 2, January 1987.

Lowenfeld, Victor, and Brittain, W.L. *Creative and Mental Growth.* New York: Macmillan, 1975.

McVickar, Polly. *Imagination: Key to Human Potential.* Washington, D.C.: National Association for the Education of Young Children, 1972.

Schirrmacher, Robert. "Talking with Young Children About Their Art." *Young Children,* Vol. 41, No. 5, July 1986.

Schirrmacher, Robert. *Art and Creative Development for Young Children.* Albany, N.Y.: Delmar Publishers, 1988.

van Oech, Roger. *Whack on the Side of the Head.* New York: Warner Books, 1983.

# SECTION 6

# ISSUES FOR THE FUTURE

*Bettye M. Caldwell*

Can you remember your excitement the first time you looked under a microscope at a droplet of your drinking water? Surely it was not possible that all that life, all that movement, all those amoebae and paramecia could be there, moving around in a gracefully patterned cellular ballet! Were we able to put the field of early childhood under a microscope at this point in the eighties, we would react with similar astonishment at the extent to which synchronous activities are taking place in our little droplet of history. From the mid-sixties to the present, the field of early childhood development has impacted modern society and reciprocally has been impacted by modern society, so that neither will ever again be quite the same. It has been a period of intense activity, and all of us who have been part of it can legitimately feel that our efforts will affect children in all areas of the world for decades to come.

And activities of the next two decades will be every bit as exciting as those of the past two. At this point in history, I feel confident in identifying the following four trends as representing major conceptual and programmatic developments in the field of early childhood education.

1. *Extra-home services will become the norm, rather than the exception, for young children.* At this point in history, the first half of the eighties, we have crossed the magic fifty percent mark in terms of enrollment of young children in early childhood programs. Throughout this century, there has been a steady climb in the percentage of children younger than age six—our former traditional age for putting children in formal school programs—who are enrolled in some type of early childhood program. As utilization of such services varies with economic need and educational level of parents, it is difficult to cite any one figure that accurately represents the entire population. However, across all census categories, more than half the children under six participate in some type of early childhood program. About two fifths of the children younger than three are enrolled, which represents a truly dramatic rise over the past 20 years. These increases represent changes in family styles in America—the rising divorce rate, the

# How Do We Teach for Tomorrow?

greater social acceptability of parenthood out of wedlock, the increase in the number of women who choose to or who must, for economic reasons, work outside the home.

As these increases began to register with demographers, there were many who decried the changes and predicted disaster for the future of our children. These predictions were based partly on the fear that participation in group programs would weaken the ties that children have to their parents and partly on a concern that most of the available programs were of poor quality. Fortunately, we now have information to reassure us that out-of-home care part of the time need not weaken a child's basic tie to her or his parents or stunt cognitive development. Also, we have now developed professional consciousness to the point where program directors and child care givers are acutely aware of their responsibility to offer quality programs that will enhance, not distort, the development of the children in their care. With this reassurance, which comes from both research-based knowledge and practical experience, has come greater social acceptance and increased public awareness of the importance of quality early childhood programs. Within the next ten years, it will become a rarity to hear people speak of age six as the age of beginning school. Far more likely, will they speak of age three, two, or even one.

2. *We will recognize that early childhood services lie along a continuum.* Let me clarify this point. At present, some people make a big point of trying to differentiate among various kinds of early childhood programs. And certainly we have enough names for describing our programs to make it easy to play this game! For example, we speak about early childhood education, preschool education, nursery schools, play schools, day nurseries, cooperative nurseries, day care, child care—and on and on. The public is legitimately confused by our proliferation of terminology. Furthermore, we have subtle ways of implying that some of these services are good for children, whereas others should be avoided. The "outcast" of the field has been day care (or child care, to use the most common synonym). Many professionals, policy makers, and parents often seem to imply that anything called "early childhood education" is good for children and anything called "day care" is potentially harmful. Such attitudes are based on the false impression that services provided under these two labels are drastically different—as, indeed, they might be. However, it is not inevitable that they be different except in the number of hours per day that each service is offered.

Particularly damaging in these implicit attitudes has been the assumption that children enrolled in day care programs are somehow not being reared by their families.

No matter how many hours per day or per week a child might be enrolled in an early childhood program (whether labeled education or day care), that child is being primarily reared by its own family, with supplementation from the professionals who staff the early childhood program. The task for policy makers and service providers is to make available in all communities a broad array of services—a continuum of early childhood services—that will match the need for supplementary care found in all types of family settings. It is my confident prediction that, in the future, we will do a better job both of realizing that such a continuum exists and of providing a full array of needed services.

3. *New and better ways of integrating intra- and extra-family services will be devised.* As early childhood programs have moved more toward the long day, and as more parents are themselves fully occupied with work during the school day, it has become increasingly difficult to obtain as much involvement of parents in the children's programs as most educators and care givers would like to have. The old patterns of after-school and evening programs are less successful than used to be the case because more and more parents are tired in the evenings and need that time for additional work in the home or for private time with their children or one another. This has led to a certain degree of pessimism on the part of professionals in early childhood education about the likelihood of achieving a high level of parental commitment to program quality. It can also be frustrating when teachers need to consult with parents about difficult behavior, about parental goals for the children, and about needed support for the early childhood service. But just as societal changes have brought about the increased need for early childhood services, so will the ingenuity and creativity of professionals lead to the development of new types of services adapted to new family realities. If professional early childhood programs are indeed but a supplement to family care, then new ways of creating a collaborative relationship between the family and the early childhood program will be necessary.

4. *Programs for young children will be considered as a routine part of public policy.* At present, young children tend to be considered by our public policy makers as something of an after-thought. We *have* to have public schools for children between the ages of six and 21, so funds are appropriated and programs launched. Fortunately, the need for adequate health care for young children (and their mothers) has sufficiently intruded into the consciousness of most of our citizens that more and more health programs are becoming available for families at all income levels. But we still seem to labor under the false idea that just *anybody* can take care of young children and that, therefore, only minimal standards of quality need be guaranteed for child care programs for very young children. Some people will maintain that no particular level of training is necessary for those who will be care givers and teachers of the very young. After all, they assert, people have been taking care of young children for centuries without any specific training! Now, of course, during those same centuries, we have had countless children victimized by abuse and neglect and by having to grow up in environments in which childhood was not valued. Fortunately such attitudes are changing. More and more new parents are utilizing books and nonprint media to learn more about how children grow and develop, and they are eager to improve their skills in this most important of human tasks. And more of them are becoming advocates for children and are working to ensure that our

government does not slight appropriations that affect the availability of quality early childhood programs.

The parents of the children we serve are our most influential advocates and helpers. As we improve in our ability to serve families, to meet the needs of both the children and their parents, we will find the support we need in the public arena to ensure that children of the future will not be overlooked or forgotten. Developing advocacy skills and strengths within the profession of early child development will go a long way toward ensuring that a reasonable portion of our public assets will be reserved for the development and maintenance of quality programs for children and families.

*BETTYE CALDWELL directed the Children's Center at Syracuse University, one of the first infant child care programs in America and one that served as a model for similar programs in many other states. She has been active in child development research since the early sixties and has published over 100 articles and edited three books in the field. She also edited the prestigious journal* Child Development.

*Dr. Caldwell has served on many governmental task forces and review boards, including the 1970 White House Conference on Children and the 1980 White House Conference on Families. She has received a number of public honors for her work with children and families, most notably Woman of the Year in Humanitarian and Community Service in 1976 by the* Ladies' Home Journal. *She is a past president of the National Association for the Education of Young Children and has served on the faculties of Northwestern University and the Washington University School of Medicine. She developed and directed the Kramer Project in Little Rock, Arkansas, a comprehensive early childhood and elementary school that was open year round and provided extended day care for all participating children. Dr. Caldwell is currently the Donaghey Distinguished Professor of Education at the University of Arkansas at Little Rock.*

# CHAPTER 15

## Issues and Trends in Early Childhood Education

## QUESTIONS for THOUGHT

- What are the major issues facing early childhood educators today?
- What programs and services should be available for young children and their families?
- What are the crises children and their families face, and what can we do to help them?
- How are the role and structure of the family changing and how does this affect the children we teach?
- What is the impact of the school reform movement on early childhood?
- What challenges will we face when dealing with diversity in schools, neighborhoods, and families?
- How do we become advocates for children who will have to cope with the demands of the twenty-first century?

# INTRODUCTION

Early childhood education has undergone remarkable changes in the past thirty years. It has evolved from being an option for middle-class preschool children to a necessity for millions of families with children from infancy through the primary years. These changes have signaled a new level of professionalism and training for teachers. Such transformations are a reflection of the economic, social, and political climate of the times. Changes in education historically have been linked to societal reform and upheaval. Issues of today and trends for tomorrow grow out of the problems and solutions in the past.

In the 1960s, social action and a war on poverty captured the American interest and spirit. Head Start programs opened around the country and were the symbols of social action of that era. The 1970s brought changes related to economic crisis. Social services were scrutinized to determine their worth and value. The family unit was affected by the job market, the end of the Vietnam War, an energy crisis, inflation, rising divorce rates, and the feminist movement. All of these factors led more women toward work in the marketplace rather than in the home. One of the expansions in public funding at this time was in the services to the handicapped and bilingual populations.

The 1980s have meant further budget cuts, reduced services for children and families, and an altered state of childhood. Computers are being installed at all grade levels. Children are often in group care for most of their waking hours. They are growing up with change, rather than stability, as a constant in their lives. Child abuse has become a national cause for alarm. Obviously, the need for early child care and educational services is here today and will be here for the next several decades. To ignore this need is to deny the reality of family life today.

The renaissance in general education that began in the early 1980s has brought about reforms in early childhood education. As people became aware of the shortcomings of education at higher levels, they could view the early years as a starting point for

**FIGURE 15.1** How do we prepare our children to live successfully in the future? (Courtesy of Trinity Preschool, New York, N.Y.)

improvements. Interest in young children flourishes along with reforms at other grade levels. How will young children be affected by these two forces—the need for child care and the growing call for excellence in education?

Looking ahead to the twenty-first century, we see a wide range of issues affecting children and society and, hence, all early childhood educators. In this chapter, we look at some current points of discussion and controversy on raising and educating children in America today. Six major questions deserve serious considerations:

1. What programs and services should be available for young children and families?

2. What are the crises children face, and what can we do to help them?

3. How are the role and structure of the family changing, and how do these changes affect the children we teach?

4. What is the impact of the school reform movement on early childhood?

5. What challenges will we face when dealing with diversity in schools, neighborhoods, and families?

6. How do we become advocates for children who will have to cope with the demands of the twenty-first century?

# CHILD CARE IN THE UNITED STATES

## Extending School Services

As child care has become a real and pressing concern for the majority of U.S. families, schools are under pressure to provide a longer school day and expanded services for more children. Parents and educators are asking for public programs to provide a wide range of educational and recreational activities for children up to their early teens. Beyond the home and the regular school day, these programs would offer local support for families so that children could learn and live in caring environments.

The public school is seen as the obvious solution to many child care issues. Indeed, it is the largest single program for child care in our country today. The buildings and staff are already in place and community use of schools after hours is a well-established precedent. Using existing school buildings at a time they are not otherwise in use is considered to be a good *stewardship* of community resources. Four particular programs under consideration are: (1) programs for three-and four-year-olds; (2) all-day kindergartens; (3) after-school care for children; and (4) year-round school.

### *The Controversy*

Controversy surrounds all four issues. Should three- and four-year-olds be exposed to formal education? Will children be rushed in their development if they have a longer school day or school year? Will schools be burdened by after-school responsibilities? How will programs be financed? Underlying these questions are concerns that the academic quality of the regular school curriculum might suffer if these extra programs are put into operation and become an added responsibility of the school.

The need for providing care beyond the regular school day is well-documented. Millions of children are without adult care after school while their parents work. Many of these are cared for by older siblings who arrive home with a house key around their necks. These *"latchkey children"* are responsible for the safety and well-being of themselves and often of younger brothers and sisters. The social, emotional, even physical effects on these unsupervised children have not been researched extensively at this time, but the need to develop after-school alternatives seems clear nonetheless. Stress, fear, isolation, boredom, even resentment at having to care for others younger than themselves have been cited as some of the negative consequences for children who are left without adults after regular school hours.

### *Future Directions and the Role of Educators*

The answers to the debate over extended school services will depend on how these programs are perceived and put into effect. The major concern of parents and educators is the question of how extra time in school will be spent. If public schools are kept open until early evening for preschool, elementary, and middle-school students, what will be the shape of the program?

Consensus among educators is that a longer school day, school term, or school year does not necessarily mean more "schooling." They envision programs that will provide continuity in children's lives. Taking place at the same setting as their formal education, these programs would provide a balanced day. Most likely the curriculum of after-school care would focus on the physical, social, emotional, and creative aspects of children's development, as the academic content of the regular school day concentrates on cognitive and language skills. Program quality will be the key, and supervision by qualified adults is imperative. The critical issue of child care for older children could be resolved if the doors were open before and after school. The time is right for schools to consider ways to merge care and learning.

See the discussion by Dr. Bettye Caldwell in the *Guest Editorial* on pages 434–437, especially the fourth point on public policy and children's programs.

# Providing Child Care

The continuing need for quality child care programs cannot be ignored. By 1995 more than three-quarters of U.S. school-age children and two-thirds of preschool children will have mothers in the labor force (Children's Defense Fund, 1988). The needs of parents who work must be recognized and addressed. Part of the solution can be found in the extension of school services; however, programs for the child under three years of age are still difficult to find and increasingly difficult to afford. Child care that meets parents' work schedules is increasingly hard to find. Thus, the issue of providing child care is a serious one. In fact, child care today is no longer being talked about in terms of "when" it will happen. The debate today focuses on the "who" and "how" of the needed services to families.

At present, child care in the United States is a loosely organized, underfunded system for those who need it:

- Two-parent families in which both adults work and rely on child care services
- Single-parent families for whom employment, job training, or completing an education is dependent on affordable, readily available child care
- Teenaged parents, 60 percent of whom have not completed high school, who need child care in order to finish their education.

## *Need for Standards and Accessibility*

Child care services lack consistent and appropriate regulations and are scattered throughout the country in a variety of separate agencies. Churches, through programs affiliated with religious groups of all kinds, are probably the largest single child care providers in the country today, with 25,000 churches serving more than two million children (Lindner et al., 1984). Franchised and industry-sponsored child care, family day care homes, family members, and an increasing number of unlicensed facilities provide the bulk of child care services. According to the United States Census Bureau, 37 percent of all preschoolers are in family day care settings, and 60 to 90 percent of those homes are unlicensed (Levin, 1988). This hodgepodge of care urgently needs a set of national standards and policies to ensure safe and caring environments for the youngest of children.

At this writing, Congress is debating comprehensive legislation designed to improve the quality, affordability, and accessibility of child care services. Standards and guidelines for implementing quality programs are included in this legislation. One such bill, the Act for Better Child Care Services, inspired a national campaign for child care launched by a coalition of leaders from the fields of social welfare, education, religion, labor, public policy, and child advocacy. Over 130 national organizations are cooperating to increase awareness of and support for child care as a national issue.

In the 1988 election year, child care became a major campaign topic nationwide. The momentum created by the interest and activity of Congress and political candidates suggests to many that the passage of comprehensive child care legislation will soon be a reality.

Calling on his state to "make the next 10 years the Decade of the Child," Governor Mario Cuomo of New York exemplified current political attitudes. He said, in part, that "the problems of our children demand a bold and broad commitment of government at all levels, in partnership with the whole community" (Snider, 1988).

Availability of child care services is much too dependent upon the ability to pay. Single-parent families (generally headed by women) and poverty-level families (usually ethnic minorities) often do not have access to child care because of its cost. Federal cutbacks on social service programs have affected these groups more than any other (Children's Defense Fund, 1988). Middle-income parents also suffer the lack of child care options as costs increase. Child care should be made available (by government, industry, and private agencies) as a voluntary program for those who want and need it.

For a further discussion of critical issues in child care, see Chapter 2.

## *Future Directions and the Role of Educators*

The two issues of extended school services and child care raise questions concerning the institutionalization of children. Is it in the best interests of children to be raised primarily in group care away from their homes? How can we ensure that we are supporting, not undermining, family life and responsibility by providing these services? And, finally, who should be responsible for child care . . . the government? parents? schools? the local community?

Regardless of the politics of funding, we must respond to the wave of demand in the child care area. In our view, the welfare of children should be the concern of everyone. It is our responsibility as citizens, as it is their right and privilege, to care for children, to broaden their educational opportunities, and to use community resources to the fullest extent.

In the following Focus discussion, Ellen Galinsky stresses the need for addressing the child care crisis now. She also raises critical questions regarding some of the solutions proposed. (For more information, see the section on the child care controversy in Chapter 2.)

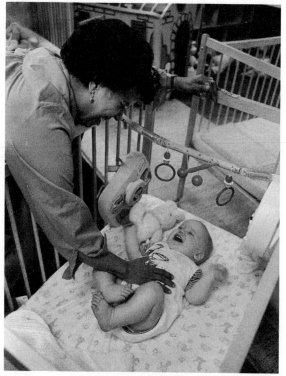

**FIGURE 15.2**   The need for quality child care cannot be ignored. (Courtesy of Trinity Preschool, New York, N.Y.)

## F O C U S

# THE CHILD CARE CRISIS

*Ellen Galinsky*

In the past year, I have participated in child care conferences in 29 states, and in every one of them, professionals from the field have defined the situation as not just problematic, but as a virtual crisis.

Throughout the United States, women have entered the labor force in unprecedented numbers: 52 percent of the mothers of infants, 57 percent of the mothers of preschoolers, and 72 percent of the mothers of school-aged children are working. Not only do more mothers work outside the home, but for the first time in several decades, the U.S. population of young children has risen—up from 19.6 million preschoolers in 1980 to 21.7 million in 1986. These demographic changes have strained the child care system to the point of crisis.

The conferences have crystallized the difficulty parents face in finding child care. In Minnesota, a parent told of going to program after program only to find them filled. At a New Jersey conference, a mother told of putting her name on a waiting list right after learning she was pregnant. Eight months after her son's birth, she still faced a year's wait.

A recent Bank Street College study of employees at three New Jersey companies found that 54 percent of the parents had experienced extreme difficulty in finding their current child care arrangement. Sixty-five percent of parents of infants reported extreme difficulty. All of our studies linked scarcity of child care to higher rates of job absenteeism.

Our research has also shown that parents put together patchwork arrangements for each of their children. Many of these arrangements are tenuous and fall apart easily. The below-poverty-level wages paid to child care workers (under $10,000 per year) encourages an annual turnover rate of 40 percent for center teachers and 60 percent for in-home providers. This instability in turn forces parents to deal with frequent breakdowns in their child care arrangements, at a high cost to themselves and their workplace. Parents miss work more often, are less able to concentrate while on the job, and experience stress and its related health problems.

Despite the fact that child care providers are vastly underpaid, the average expense of $2,000 per year for preschoolers and as much as $6,000 or more for infants is prohibitive for many parents, who have to settle for lower quality care or even for leaving their children home alone.

The uneven quality of child care is the final aspect of this crisis. We know from numerous studies that group size in a center is integral to a child's learning and safety. Yet according to the Children's Defense Fund, 32 states do not specify group size for preschoolers, and 25 states do not regulate group size for infants. Further, 22 states do not require any prior training for teachers in child care centers. When children are in poor quality child care, the societal cost is enormous—

we are wasting the potential of our next generation.

As the news of this crisis spreads and is discussed in states and in the federal government, a number of issues deeply disturb me:

- One of the first solutions proposed by states is to provide schooling for four-year-olds; yet many states plan to provide only part-day (three-hour) or full-day (six-hour) programs. For employed parents, this will mean even more patchwork arrangements.

- The communities that have discussed full-working-day options are considering a "school" program with child care before and after. But children cannot be divided up; they are learning and needing care at all times. Why not develop programs that minister to the needs of children—learning and care—rather than shuttle them from one program to another? Thus, parents could select from part-day and full-day programs.

- Some states and federal legislators propose that the schools become the principal child care system for preschoolers. This strategy neglects the fact that we already have a child care system within every community. We need both systems to work side by side, recognizing that we must strive to bring the salaries of child care staff in line with those of public school professionals.

- In focusing on four-year-olds we neglect the reality that the greatest need is for high quality infant and toddler care. Our policy initiatives must focus on these problems.

- When we debate a federal role in mitigating the child care crisis, some assume that parents are abdicating their rights and turning child care over to the government. In my view, the federal government needs to become involved but not take over. We need coalitions of parents; local and state governments; child care providers and schools; the federal government; philanthropic, social service, and religious organizations; business; and labor. The goal of such coalitions should be to help parents in their primary role of child-rearing.

The child care crisis has been brewing for a long time. Its resolution will not be a quick fix, but we do have the American know-how to fashion solutions. Our children and employed parents deserve no less.

*Ellen Galinsky is Project Director of The Work and Family Life Studies at Bank Street College, and is President of the National Association for the Education of Young Children.*

---

## F O C U S

# CANADA: LEADING THE WAY IN CHILD CARE

*Heather J. Burke-Clarke*

In July 1988, Canada's Health and Welfare Minister unveiled the appropriation of $6.4 billion for early childhood education in Canada as part of the government's efforts to support child care initiatives. Of this total, $2.3 billion will provide enhanced tax assistance to families with young children.

Canada's Child Care Act (Bill C-144) was designed to double day care spaces to 200,000 over a seven-year period, to offer tax breaks to parents who pay for child care services, and to improve working conditions in child care settings.

Under this national strategy, the federal government will pay 50 percent of the operating costs for commercial and non-profit day care centers, and 75 percent of the start-up costs for new non-profit centers. This financial mechanism will allow the provinces to address their child care needs on a regional basis.

Although Canada's 25 million citizens have eagerly awaited the child care act, many child care advocates and women's groups have expressed the following concerns:

## Additional Child Care Spaces

The promise to help provinces set up an additional 200,000 day care spaces will only satisfy one quarter of Canada's space requirements. The province of Ontario alone, comprising one third of Canada's total population, needs 170,000 more spaces by 1995. Ontario's plans might be cut by almost 12,000 spaces because the federal funding is inadequate.

Smaller provinces such as New Brunswick, however, will benefit greatly by doubling their 5,200 child care spaces over the next seven years.

However, the Act does not address the current problems of quality, affordability, low wages for child care workers, and poor working conditions in centers. In fact, if we add spaces without attacking these problems, we may magnify some of our current problems. We must commit to adding quality to our programs as we add spaces.

## Tax Breaks to Parents

Critics of the child care act have suggested that the act is really being used as a voting strategy by offering Canadian parents $2.3 billion in tax benefits, when the revenues could have been used to add new day care spaces. However, day care is not the only option for working parents. If all of this money were allocated to day care spaces, parents who might use other child care arrangements would find their choices narrowed. The tax break to parents actually expands child care choices.

## Government Funds for Non-profit and For-profit Centers

A long-standing argument in the child care field is whether profit-making centers should turn over their profits to benefit the children. Ontario favors non-profit centers, while other provinces make no distinction between the two.

Some critics argue that profit-making centers have fewer trained staff, high turnover rates, lower wages, and are less likely to meet the provincial standards and regulations.

However, low wages, high turnover, and poorly qualified day care personnel have always been problems for both profit and non-profit centers.

To maintain standards for commercial day care centers, these facilities should be licensed with the province and follow the same rules as non-profit centers. The government could require any commercial day care centers established with the new funds to follow these licensing requirements. Further, the government should require those who run centers to meet minimum requirements in early childhood education. This measure will ensure that teachers and administrators understand the demands of the profession.

Proponents of this parallel funding hope that commercial day care centers will become more financially self-sufficient during the seven-year period. This development would free government funding to address the deeper problems of quality, affordability, and wage issues. Financially self-sufficient centers will also free the government from funding the same programs year after year, which fosters little progress and perpetuates the same internal day care problems.

## Provincial Autonomy

Some fear that once the $4.1 billion is gone, the provincial governments will not be able to maintain their own programs. A federal mandate can only tackle general day care issues, while the provinces know what their own problems are and how best to solve them. Accordingly, the federal government has structured its program to encourage the provinces to become self-reliant. Funding is available and awaits spending proposals from each province. It is now up to the provinces to make their own child care choices—we hope the best child care choices based on their regional needs—since they will have to live with these choices after the seven-year period.

Canada's commitment to its future is made concrete in the child care act. Research affecting the direction of our early childhood education industry remains a priority. Our progress cannot come fast enough, but we must still recognize that for the first time in Canada's history, we are witnessing efforts to raise society's consciousness of the importance of early childhood education.

Canada has offered valid and unprecedented incentives to establish and maintain the best possible early childhood education programs. Still, many unresolved issues regarding the use of national funding will continue to challenge us as we make good child care accessible and affordable to families across this nation.

*Heather Clarke is an instructor in the Child Care Assistant, Day Care Training, and Human Service Counselor Programs at New Brunswick Community College, St. John, Canada.*

# CRISES IN CHILDREN'S LIVES

## Endangered Childhood

Children and childhood have changed. Gone are the days when the majority of children arrived home from school to be greeted by Mom in the kitchen, serving milk and homemade cookies. To-day's child spends the bulk of time in child care centers or with a neighbor while the parent is at work. Too many arrive at empty homes and spend the next few hours alone or caring for younger siblings. As often as not, the child of today lives with just one parent at best.

### *Emphasis on Survival*

A decade or two ago children seemed to be more protected than they are today; they seemed more innocent. Adults of yesteryear perceived their roles as protectors of children, keeping them at arm's length from life's stresses. Today's parents, on the other hand, are concerned that their children learn to survive, to cope with problems at an early age. They believe the best way to teach children survival skills is to expose them to adult experiences and "reality" early.

The impact of social changes in the last twenty years has been hardest felt by the children of the nation. The breakdown of the nuclear family unit, the sexual and feminist revolutions, television, drugs, and worldwide violence have thrust children into adult situations with adult troubles. Dual-parent careers and single working parents, together with the lack of extended families, have meant that children's behavior is not as closely monitored as it once was.

### *The Television Set*

In many homes and other settings, the television set has replaced the adult supervision of the past. Ninety-eight percent of the homes in the United States have televisions, and the average set is on for more than six hours each day (Trelease, 1984). When we know that the average kindergarten grad-uate has already seen more hours of television than

the time it takes to get a bachelor's degree from college (Waters *in* Trelease, 1984), several areas of concern arise regarding the use of television as a child care method.

Television watching is a passive way for chil-dren to spend their time. It is a method that encour-ages children to watch life rather than actively pur-sue it in vigorous activity. Growing children need to exercise their bodies and perfect their physical skills. Too much television detracts from more lively pursuits.

While the content of most television programs is questionable, there is no doubt that children are not discriminating viewers. They will watch most anything they are allowed to watch. Children at home alone have the opportunity to select inappro-priate programs. Too many programs portray life issues in unrealistic ways. Solutions by violent means, a disrespect for human life, and disregard for

**FIGURE 15.3** Every child has the right to a full and wondrous childhood.

family values are shown as amusing and acceptable ways to cope. Violence is shown as the way to get what you want and is used by the "good guys" as well as the "bad guys." The consequences of violence are rarely shown. The portrayal of life situations in unreal or humorous forms presents children with life views that ignore the real issues of childhood and distort the ways humans deal with reality.

Research appears to show a strong link between television violence and aggressive behavior; it seems that children do learn specific aggressive acts from television watching and that those who watch violent television are more aggressive with other children (Bee, 1985). Educators have cause for concern for other reasons as well. A survey of teachers cited television watching as having negative effects on learning and attributes the following behaviors to excessive television watching: limited attention span, lack of enthusiasm for reading and writing, impaired listening skills, and reduced motivation (Winn, 1985).

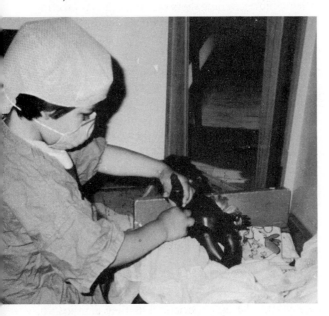

**FIGURE 15.4**  A positive use of television watching encourages children's fantasy and imaginative play. They can then live out many exciting roles when they have an opportunity for dramatic play.

Deregulation of the television industry by the Federal Communications Commission in the early 1980s has produced yet another phenomenon that creates further problems for parents and teachers: the program-length animated commercial. This involves the marketing of licensed popular characters and has created a multibillion-dollar industry. Good programs for children, such as *Captain Kangaroo,* were phased out of commercial network television after the deregulation took effect. From 1979 to 1983 the average time commercial stations allotted for children's programming dropped from 11.3 hours per week to only 4.4 hours. During that period, not one commercial network regularly scheduled programs for children during the after-school hours (Engelhardt, 1986).

Without guidelines for children's programming and restrictions on the amount of commercials in a given time period, new shows for children were created primarily to sell a special toy or series of products. Aside from the purely commercial implication of these shows, educators criticize the content of the program-length commercial. The plots confuse fantasy with reality, and most characters encourage racist and sexist stereotypes.

The decline of good television programming for children is best demonstrated by Engelhardt's (1985) description of the four major categories of commercial children's programs:

- *The action-figure superhero in the afternoon:* Emphasis is on team action to encourage purchase of multiple figures and accessories; terrorism is a major theme.
- *Specials aimed at little girls:* While less violent than superhero programs, these specials also encourage the purchase of complete sets of figures or dolls and promote role stereotyping of little girls as being passive.
- *Saturday morning programming:* Licensed characters abound, but some remnants of shows with human actors and old favorite cartoons may be found. The potpourri of programs communicates mixed messages to children. Prosocial talks from

popular television actors, interspersed throughout the morning, contradict the aggression and violent problem-solving models of the actual shows.

- *Advertisements:* Presweetened cereals, toys, and candy are the major products advertised. Many of the ads are clustered for effect; as a group they promote some questionable values of consumerism.

Public television does offer some age-specific programs for young viewers, but the number is limited. The power of television is well documented. High quality television for children must become a national priority as an integral part of reforming child care and education.

The role of the teacher is to help parents become more effective in the use of television. To do this, they both give information and teach strategies:

*Giving information* includes:
- Providing lists of good programs, channels, and times.
- Holding parent meetings to discuss available programming, including research on program selection and its effect on children's behavior.
- Positive use of television through science, nature, and music programs as well as shows depicting other cultures in nonstereotyped ways and those in which helping others is a central theme.
- Discussing alternatives to television watching and providing lists of good books for families to read aloud. Also include lists of good home video movies for child and family viewing.

*Teaching strategies* include:
- Encouraging parents to watch television with their children.
- Suggesting ways to rate television shows for violence and aggression, prosocial behavior, fantasy and reality, and advertising messages.
- Observing children as they watch TV to see the effects, listening to their comments, and answering their questions.
- Ways to respond to children's viewing with clarification, interpretation, and elaboration of what children see.

- Learning what teachers can do to encourage children's fantasy and imagination and its effect on dramatic play. This helps parents see the relationship between many of the make-believe shows and children's lives. (Also see Chapter 14 on superhero play.)
- Assisting parents in establishing limits regarding the amount of time children watch television and their choice of programs.

## Stress and Changing Parent–Child Relations

Childhood has been misplaced. The boundaries between adults and children are hazy. Adults exert pressure on children to hurry and grow up, to achieve and succeed, to perform and to please. Children respond by doing their best, all the while sensing the pressure to mature (Gordon, 1986).

People are dealing with their children differently than did their parents. They are opening up to their children, telling them of (rather than protecting them from) their own fears and anxieties. Children have been enlisted as coparents in their own upbringing, collaborating with their parents on child-rearing practices, dress codes, and behavior expectations. While this is obviously more democratic and less authoritarian, the results have been that the boundaries between children and adults have become increasingly hazy. It would appear that we are asking young children of today to assume a mantle of maturity before they are capable. We are requiring them to respond to life as adults, not as children. We no longer assure children that the adult is in charge and that their needs will be met. Instead, we ask children to share that burden with us.

Another type of parent has emerged in the 1980s, the creator of the "superbaby" (Langway et al., 1983). These children begin life enrolled in a series of classes by parents who hope to give them as many stimulating experiences as they can absorb. Infant gymnastic workouts, alphabet flash-cards in the nursery, and violin or acting lessons to supplement preschool signal parental expectations for these children. These wonderkids, children of the post–World War II "baby-boom" children (who now are affluent, knowledgeable, and generally over 30), must fulfill every conceivable potential as early as possible. They are being pushed toward success by parents who themselves are more successful than their parents were. "The more, the better" sometimes seems the motto of the day.

The focus for these parents is often on infant academics and superior physical achievement. This raises concerns about the welfare of the child. When the emphasis is on performance and not on unconditional acceptance or feelings, the development of the child may be focused on only one or a few areas of the child's growth. It raises questions as to whether all the basics are being met—social and emotional needs as well as creative, intellectual, and physical ones.

Today's children are also expected to cope with changing family structures. Only a small percentage of U.S. households are traditional, nuclear families. Instead, children face divorce, single parenthood, sexuality issues, dual-career parents, poverty, homelessness, and other late twentieth century phenomena that produce stress. Adult coping skills are expected of two-, four-, and seven-year-olds, rather than allowing children to respond to life as children (Gordon, 1986).

For many children, the result has been a hurried childhood (Elkind, 1982). Parents push their children through the early years, urging them to grow up fast, succeed, achieve. Designer clothes are just the outward trappings these parents use to encourage adult attitudes and behaviors. The loss of childhood seems to have brought with it new problems for children. Clinicians are seeing more children with stress-related problems: headaches, abdominal pains, and even ulcers are occurring in children three and four years old.

Many common experiences that produce stress in young children are family related. (Further on in this chapter is a discussion of the relationship between poverty and stress.) Most adults would identify divorce, a move to a new home, prolonged visits from a relative, and a new sibling as classic stress situations for children. Yet there are homlier and less dramatic sources of stress, the simple everyday occurrences that children face: being told not to do something, not having a friend, being ignored by a parent, experiencing changes in the routine, not being able to read or zip a zipper or put a puzzle together (Gordon, 1986). Stress may also occur in families where both parents pursue high-powered careers and children feel the need to live up to exceptional standards in academic achievement or sports proficiency. Apathetic parents, parents who ignore their children or have no time for them, and parents who push children into frantic schedules of activity also cause stress in their children. Stress can result from happy occasions as well—holidays, vacations, or a new puppy may be overanticipated, overstructured, and overstimulating to a child.

Children respond to stress in many ways. In adults, and sometimes in older children, depression, substance abuse, underachievement, and obsession with financial success are common responses to stress. In children, signs of stress include sleeping problems (such as nightmares or sleepwalking), depression, regression to the behavior of an earlier stage, aches and pains, acting out, eating problems, and overreactions, as well as medical problems (such as headaches, upset stomach, and bleeding ulcers) (Reed, 1986).

Stress is a natural part of life and is a factor in every child's development. From the efforts of crawling to playing the piano to learning a physics equation, children's developmental milestones contain the normal stress that it takes to make an effort. Societal changes in the last two decades, however, are combining with normal stresses to produce unusual pressure on children and their families.

Several factors affect how a child responds to stress. Personal variables, such as temperament, sex, age, and intellectual capacity are factors in how a child will react. Other external, ecological circumstances can also stress children. Poverty, joblessness, and homelessness put children at risk as they then have inadequate housing, a troubled neighborhood, and infrequent health care along with emotional unrest. Individual catastrophes, such as separation and divorce, hospitalization, war or terrorism, the death of a parent or other family member, even a disaster such as an earthquake or the space shuttle explosion, can shake a child's sense of security and well-being.

When many stressors occur at once, or are chronically present, children cannot cope. Since no one can predict exactly what stresses will be difficult for an individual child, adults must be sensitive to the *meaning* of an event or situation. All children must have parents and teachers who work together in meaningful ways, to be available and reassuring when the child needs it. Some successful coping responses include:

- flexible and inventive creation of response options
- open consideration of options and choices
- orientation to reality and to future implications of situations
- rational, conscious consideration and purposeful thinking (Haan in Honig, 1986)

Both parents and children will need support in working through the natural stages of stress response (see chapter 14).

### Future Directions and the Role of Educators

Children are not the same as adults and are unable to assume the responsibility for their own care. Children need to be nurtured and protected, to have the time of childhood in which to discover themselves and to be guided and directed toward maturity. Children need adults, teachers, and parents who understand this, who respect childhood and children, and who will help them achieve their potential in supportive ways.

Parents and teachers can work together to reduce unnecessary stress in children's lives by teaching children coping skills that help them react to their circumstances in productive ways. Observe children, locate their points of stress, and listen to what they say. Let them know that what they say matters. Let them know you recognize their attempts to cope and respect their efforts to do the best they can. Allow children to fail; make it safe to make a mistake and also give them opportunities to make

decisions and succeed at tasks appropriate to their skills (Gordon, 1986). Most important, adults must make themselves available to children—to be there to provide the emotional response whenever possible.

Family stress is a normal part of growing up. As children move through developmental stages, sensitive adults can help them discover their own potential and their own inner resources to overcome stressful demands. The bonus will be strong self-worth and a feeling of being competent and worthwhile.

## Child Abuse and Neglect
### The Crisis

In 1986, 1.9 million children were reported abused and neglected; 40 percent of them were preschoolers. This is an increase of more than 50 percent since 1981 (Children's Defense Fund, 1988). Cases of substantial sexual abuse of children increased approximately twenty times between 1976 (6,000 cases) and 1986 (113,000 cases) (Galtney, 1988). Respect for children and childhood is seriously eroded when adults violate the trust of and responsibility for children through neglect and abuse. Social change over the last few decades has put many of our children at risk. The changes in the family unit, unemployment, loss of funding for programs and subsidies for families, and rising divorce rates have put parents under stress and are having a negative effect on children's well-being. When children are cared for improperly, the results are often child neglect and abuse.

A neglected child may be one whose waking hours are mostly unsupervised by adults, in front of the television or simply unconnected with—and unnoticed by—parents or an important caregiver. *Neglect* takes other, more hazardous, forms, however. When the basic needs of adequate food, clothing, shelter, and health are unmet, parents are being neglectful. Failure to exercise the care that children need shows an inattention to and lack of concern for children.

*Child abuse* is the most severe form of disrespect for children. Violence in the form of physical maltreatment and sexual abuse is an improper treatment of children, regardless of their behavior. Abusive language and harsh physical aggression are other forms of child abuse that occur in families and, unfortunately, some settings for child care.

Publicized investigations into sexual abuse of children in child care centers, preschools, and family situations have brought national attention to this hideous violence. A recent study, however, reported a higher incidence of child abuse at home rather than in child care centers (Jennings, 1988). Whether or not its increased incidence is due to a change in reporting practices, it is clear that the abuse of children knows no social, racial, or economic barriers. It is happening to children at all levels of the social spectrum.

## *Standards of Care*

For child care workers, the heart of the issue lies in the regulation and licensing of early childhood programs. In light of recent disclosures concerning incidents in centers, we need to take a long, hard look at who is caring for children. In what physical, emotional, and interpersonal environments are our children living? Licensing regulations for schools and teacher certification vary greatly throughout the country. Primarily they ensure only minimum health and safety standards of the physical environment. The great number of unlicensed child care facilities and the quality of children's programs are urgent issues. Governing and regulatory agencies in most states are inadequately staffed and insufficiently budgeted to handle the monitoring of child care settings.

A national call to action to increase public awareness and understanding of child abuse is underway. Standardized licensing procedures, upgrading of the certification of child care workers, and national *accreditation* of all preschools are some of the most frequently mentioned solutions to the problem. Helping parents identify what qualities to look for when placing their children in someone else's care is another way to prevent child abuse in centers.

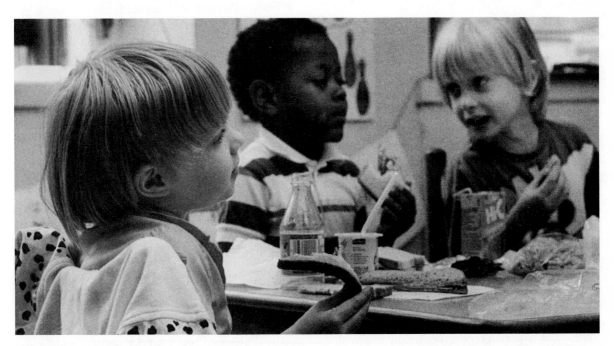

**FIGURE 15.5**   When basic needs such as food and shelter are met, children are free to develop interests in other people, other things. (Courtesy of Trinity Preschool, New York, N.Y.)

Child abuse should be suspected if a child:
- Is constantly late, stays away from school for long periods of time, or arrives early and stays late, avoiding going home.
- Is withdrawn, passive, and uncommunicative or aggressive, destructive, and nervous.
- Has unexplained injuries, too many "explained" ones, or has an injury that is inadequately explained.
- Complains of numerous beatings, of someone "doing things," whether or not the parents are home.
- Goes to the bathroom with difficulty; has burns, limps, or bruises, patches of hair missing, bad teeth.
- Wears clothing that is too small, soiled, or inappropriate for the weather, or uses clothing to cover injuries.
- Is dirty, smells, is too thin or constantly tired; exhibits dehydration or malnutrition.
- Is usually fearful of other children or adults.
- Has been fed inappropriate food, drink, or drugs.

**FIGURE 15.6** A child who exhibits several of these signs should be investigated as a possible victim of child abuse. (Adapted from Fraser, 1977.)

## Future Directions and the Role of Educators

Teachers have a role to play. Reporting suspected child abuse is mandated by law in *all* states (Fraser, 1977). Educators must assume the responsibility to inform the proper authorities if they suspect that a child in their care is being abused by adults (see Appendix C for excerpts from the California Penal Code). Figure 15.6 lists the signs a teacher should look for if child abuse is suspected.

The mandate to report suspected child abuse applies to teachers, principals, counselors, school nurses, and staff members of child care centers and summer camps. Certain knowledge that abuse took place is not required; reports are legally required if there is reasonable cause to suspect a child has been mistreated. To protect anyone reporting abuse or neglect, the person filing the report is held immune from civil or criminal liability if the report was made in good faith.

### What to Do If You Suspect Child Abuse

- Make notes of child's appearance—any bruises, marks, or behaviors that cause you concern.
- Inform the director of the program and/or your immediate supervisor; plan together who will inform the proper authorities and how to contact the parent(s).
- Discuss ways to support the staff members who make the report, the parent(s), and the child.
- Call the locally designated agency for child abuse. A written report may be required within 24 to 48 hours.
- Support the parent(s) throughout the investigation. Be available to the parent(s) and the child as they deal with the other agencies who are trained and equipped to handle this problem.
- Follow through with assistance or support if requested to do so by the child-protective service agency. Help the family by working with others who are counseling them and performing parent support services.

### What to Do If a Child Tells You He or She Has Been Abused

- Believe the child; children rarely lie about sexual abuse.
- Commend the child for telling you what happened.
- Convey your support for the child. Children's greatest fear is that they are at fault and responsible for the incident. It is important to help children avoid blaming themselves.
- Temper your own reactions, recognizing that your perspective and acceptance are critical signals to the child. Do not convey your own feelings about the abuse.
- Report the suspected abuse to the child's parent(s), the designated social service agency, and/or the police.

• Find specialized agencies that evaluate sexual abuse victims and a physician with the experience and training to detect and recognize sexual abuse.

**Source of information:** *Child Sexual Abuse Prevention,* Washington, D.C.: U.S. Department of Health and Human Services, 1984.

In some early childhood programs, teachers and other specialists have started programs for young children that will help them recognize and avoid abuse. Perhaps most important, teachers must stay in close touch with the parents of all their children. By knowing parents personally and being in contact with them regularly, an early childhood professional may be able to detect early signs of impending problems of both abuse and neglect. The perceptive teacher can then support parents through their difficulties, offering them help by informing them of a parental stress hotline, suggesting strategies to avoid stress and violence, and recommending professional help.

## Missing Children

The phenomenon of missing children is another national problem. Each year approximately 1.2 million children disappear from their homes and neighborhoods (Bridgeman, 1984). Some are runaway children; others are kidnap victims, most of whom are snatched from one divorced parent by the other. To help locate missing children, national efforts have focused on a massive fingerprinting campaign to identify those missing. Dramatic presentations on television with case histories and photographs of missing children have contributed to an increased level of public concern. The U.S. Congress established a National Center for Missing and Exploited Children in late 1984. Teachers can help by supporting these steps. And they can ensure that children are not taken from their care unless written permission is given by the parent with whom the child lives.

## The Problem of AIDS

*Acquired Immune Deficiency Syndrome* (AIDS) is a communicable disease that breaks down the body's immune system, leaving it unable to fend off harmful bacteria, viruses, and the like. Illnesses that are not usually life-threatening to a healthy person can result in death for someone who has AIDS. At this writing, the mortality rate for those with AIDS is 100 percent (Skeen and Hodson, 1987). Forty-five percent of all AIDS patients will die within a year after diagnosis; 85 percent die within three years. When reading this section, the student is reminded that statistics and information on AIDS is constantly changing; the reader is strongly urged to consult the most recent research data.

AIDS is caused by a virus (HIV) that is primarily sexually transmitted, although it can pass from one person to another by contact with blood, blood products, or through bodily secretions that mix with a person's blood. The AIDS virus may be present in the blood even though the full AIDS syndrome does not develop. The infection, however, can be transmitted to someone else even if the person carrying it has no symptoms.

AIDS is thought to have first occurred in the 1970s, although documentation of AIDS patients did not begin until 1979. In the United States the disease is prevalent among males (90 percent of the AIDS victims are men) and occurs primarily in homosexuals, in intravenous drug users, and in hemophiliacs and other persons who receive contaminated blood transfusions.

Children, too, are AIDS victims. Those at greatest risk are:

• Infants born to mothers who have AIDS

• Infants who are breast-fed by mothers with AIDS

• Infants and children who receive blood transfusions (blood screening programs may have reduced this risk)

• Sexually abused children

The greatest fears—and misconceptions—about AIDS are how contagious is the disease and how is it transmitted. "People seem to find it hard to believe that a virus which can cause such a cruel and fatal disease is not easily caught from people who are infected" (Aronson, 1987). Sexual contacts and mingling of blood are the two known routes of infection, and not one case is known to have been transmitted any other way, even to close family members of AIDS patients (Aronson, 1987). No children have caught AIDS from ordinary contact with other children. None of the cases of AIDS in the United States has been transmitted in a school or child care setting nor through hugging, sharing a glass or a plate, sharing bathrooms, or in kissing that is not mouth to mouth kissing (Aronson, 1987).

### *Future Directions and Role of the Educator*

The numbers of AIDS victims multiply rapidly. The Centers for Disease Control predict a continued increase in the heterosexual population and in babies. One source estimates that by 1991, almost 4,000 babies will have contracted the disease from their mothers during pregnancy (Aronson, 1987). Early childhood professionals clearly have a role to play regarding this misunderstood disease:

- Be an informed resource to parents and other teachers. Keep abreast of current data and educate others about the *facts* of AIDS.

- Know how to answer the questions a preschooler will ask. Begin to educate children.

- Examine your own attitudes about homosexuality and drug usage.

- Keep up to date on research about AIDS; information changes rapidly and is released frequently.

- Take appropriate precautions—careful handwashing and use of plastic gloves when contact with blood may occur.

- Be prepared to counsel children and their families through long illness and death in the same way as with other fatal diseases.

- Develop school policies that reflect the current knowledge and recommendations of medical experts.

## At Risk: Children in Need

Of major concern to educators for the twenty-first century is a "growing underclass of Americans" (Olson, 1987) who are destined for limited participation in the social, political, and economic mainstream of national life. Millions of children are poverty-bound and are at risk to repeat the cycles that keep them poor and disadvantaged. These children and youth are undereducated, marginally literate, and lacking the necessary skills for employment. They are high risks for dropping out of school and becoming teenaged parents who will perpetuate the cycle again. One-quarter of U.S. children live in poverty, one in five is likely to become a teen-age parent, and one in seven will drop out of school (Children's Defense Fund, 1988).

There is a striking correlation between poverty and school failure. Children who start out at a disadvantage fall farther behind in academic achievement throughout their school years. Unless quality education for *all* children is a national priority, we risk the creation of an "education third world," according to Ernest L. Boyer, President of the Carnegie Foundation for the Advancement of Teaching (Nienhuis, 1986).

The changing school population suggests that these problems will only increase as the proportion of minority groups expands, as a larger and larger percentage of children fall below the poverty line, and as traditional patterns of child-rearing and marriage change so that fewer children will have the emotional and educational advantages of a two-parent family (*Education Week*, 1988).

### *Future Directions and the Role of Educators*

To date, schools seem ill equipped to deal with the complex and comprehensive needs of disadvantaged children. The reform movement of the 1980s has not yet addressed this population. It is estimated that approximately one-third of the school population is at risk (Olson, 1987). Reform strategies must include the critical early years when early and sustained intervention is known to bring success.

Quality child care for teen-aged parents and quality preschool programs for disadvantaged three- and four-year-olds, parent education, and developmental screening are a few of the proposals made by 225 corporate executives and college presidents in their report, *Children in Need: Investment Strategies for the Economically Disadvantaged* (Olson, 1987). School reforms would include smaller schools and smaller classes, programs for pregnant teenagers, local autonomy in school management, and the support of business with job training and work experience programs. A dramatic and intensive reform effort is needed for at-risk children for, as the report states:

> This nation cannot continue to compete and prosper in the global arena when more than one-fifth of our children live in poverty and a third grow up in ignorance. And if the nation cannot compete, it cannot lead. If we continue to squander the talents of millions of our children, America will become a nation of limited human potential. It would be tragic if we allow this to happen. America must become a land of opportunity—for every child.
>
> (Children's Defense Fund, 1988)

# FAMILIES

How has the American family structure changed in the last two decades? With the social changes of the 1960s came changes in the ways people looked at themselves and their opportunities. Children raised on Dr. Spock's philosophy of freedom of movement became adults who wanted to express themselves more freely. "Without consciously setting out to do so, American adults have spent the last decade and more trying to adjust the way society works—giving themselves a bit more freedom (to move, to play, to work, to divorce) while devising alternative arrangements for bringing up the kids." (Murphy, 1982) Thus, the family is undergoing serious transformations in the last quarter of this century. Who the family is, how much time children spend with their parents and with other children, and family relationships and attitudes are important issues.

## Divorce and Change

Today more than 12 million children younger than 18 live in homes marked by divorce (Talan, 1986). That means more than one fourth of the nation's children are confronted with the trauma that the breakup of a family can bring. Divorce affects the family structure in far-reaching ways.

### Financial Impact

After a divorce, the family usually must survive on one income. The median annual income for families with children under six is $6,114, and for families with children 6 to 17 it is $12,152 (Galinsky, 1986). When the estimates for quality child care are $3,000 to $4,000 per year, it is no wonder that more than 60 percent of female-headed households with young children are poor (Halpern, 1987). The face of poverty is becoming younger, complicating the emotional problems of divorce with serious financial woes.

### Effects on Parents

Having only one parent to handle the daily struggles of family life alters family patterns. If the single father is busy with food preparation, there is no other parent available to help children with homework, listen to how their school day went, or watch them play. The single mother who is with the toddler in the tub cannot help the first-grader with reading.

To be sure, two-parent families experience similar incidents. However, in a single-parent household, children may find themselves needing to wait more often, perhaps for longer periods of time. And the parent may not get the adult support, or respite from a relentless child, that is so helpful when raising young children.

After divorce, parents are confronted with many pressing issues all at once. Generally speaking, single parents have fewer financial and socially supportive resources to rely on (Galinsky, 1986). Their own emotional needs are often left unmet. Their main contact is no longer at home. Privacy is difficult when young children's needs are so immediate. And these parents get very tired. We know from family therapists that many problems are either created or made worse by fatigue.

Parents must address their own needs for privacy and for socializing in order to be able to share themselves with their children in meaningful and untroubled ways. Single parents must take care to avoid making their children their confidantes. Further, parents need to establish an adult support network of their own. As the family structure changes from a two-parent, nuclear family to that of a single-parent family (with little or no contact with the other parent), the challenges for parents and children alike are tremendous. Growing up without two parents often puts a household in continual difficulty.

## Impact on Children

Most children exhibit classic reactions to divorce: shock, depression, denial, anger, low self-esteem and, among younger children, a sense of blame. Some studies show that divorce may have a more negative effect on boys, that the timetable for adjustment for them is twice that for girls, and they may express their concerns more aggressively (Francke, 1983). Some researchers have found that these descendents of divorce have lower academic scores, problems with friendships, and emotional difficulties (Talan, 1986). These results, however, are complicated by the poverty often associated with divorce, and many of the negative effects may well be the result of severe financial difficulties.

The economic status of the parents does affect children seriously. In the United States, average child support is less than $1,800 per year, and one out of every three mothers entitled to payments does not receive them (Galinsky, 1986). Since children of poverty will be at risk for poorer health care, inadequate intellectual stimulation, and little social support (Halpern, 1987), the personal costs of divorce are high for the children.

In early childhood, children show emotional changes and behavioral reactions to divorce. These responses tend to differ for each age group. Two-year-olds may regress in their speech and toilet training. They may show increased irritability and crying, outbursts of separation anxiety, and may even ask questions about things they already know (*cognitive confusion*). Preschoolers will likely show

more sadness and confusion and develop strong fears (*phobias*) of death, loss of both parents, of injury. Early school-age children may become anxious and aggressive or extremely moody and depressed. Often these children act as if they do not need or want *anyone* and, at the same time, are quite possessive of a parent's attention or possessions (Family Service Association of Santa Clara County, 1982).

It is clear that at all ages, children in divorce situations experience some insecurity and possibly even regressive behavior until the family structure becomes more stable. Children sometimes become pawns of angry parents, receptacles of resentment each parent feels for the other.

## Future Directions and the Role of Educators

Adults in the school setting can help these children by minimizing the stress for children at school and providing them with a safe, supportive, and constant environment until their lives have adjusted to a new routine at home. Teachers can be good resources for both children and parents in this critical, sensitive time.

Children need help from adults to deal with the loss of a parent and the resulting changes. Teachers can help children of all ages cope with divorce by:

- Being available for some one-to-one time together.
- Answering any and all questions children may ask.
- Sharing openly feelings of sadness, loss, anger, and confusion in an appropriate way so that children feel less alone and feel safe in expressing their own feelings.
- Explain that the child is not to blame whenever the divorce issue arises.
- Provide books that both explain family changes and show different kinds of families.
- Maintain as much of a stable, caregiving role as possible.

For parents, teachers can be sources of information and support, whether by providing books (for adults and children), suggesting participation in parental support groups, or giving specific referrals of family or individual counselors. Teachers are most helpful when they can be available to listen to and confer with parents about their child's behavior, their feelings, and their adjustment to the new situation. Support of the family—whether it involves one parent or both—should be the goal of every early childhood center, especially when divorce is involved.

# Family and Work

The nuclear family—two parents with mother at home full time—is fast becoming the exception rather than the rule, more a myth than reality. More than 51 percent of mothers with children under three are in the labor force (Galinsky, 1986) and fewer than one-fifth of American families fit the traditional mold (Wallis, 1987). All signs indicate that the family of the 1990s will be of various structures, and that few children will have mothers who do not work outside the home.

How is the change toward more working mothers affecting the family structure? Caretaking arrangements are becoming a major issue and a part of daily life in every socioeconomic group. Working parents find themselves in a triple bind: finding child care that is of high quality, affordable, and flexible seems nearly impossible. This affects both the workplace for adults and the school place for children.

## *Impact on Adults*

As adults become more aware of their children's caretaking needs, they begin to look to their employers, the government, and the school system to provide some kind of support. Child care costs, after all, are becoming a large part of a family's budget. In fact, after housing, food, and taxes, they are the average American family's biggest expense (Kolben *in* Sommers, 1983). Quality child care is expensive— more than $4,000 per year per child. Yet child care workers are among the lowest-paid wage earners in this country. Consequently, turnover is high, and the quality of child care is compromised (Bank Street, 1986). Alternatives in child care must be

sought, with solutions that work for both parents and teachers as well as children. Employers must recognize the importance of the child care issue. Dialogue about employer-supported child care, tax credits, flexible working hours, paternity and maternity leaves, job sharing, cash subsidies, and extended school hours encourages society to get involved in child care at a meaningful level.

## *Impact on Children*

How will the increase in the number of working parents change children's lives? Today's child is likely to be cared for outside the home in an alternative child care arrangement. Census Bureau statistics for the years 1984 and 1985 show that 39 percent of children under five are cared for in their own home by a relative or hired help, 37 percent are cared for in someone else's home (usually by a nonrelative), and 23 percent are in organized child care facilities. Less than 1 percent are in kindergarten. Significantly, nearly half of the children cared for in their own home are cared for by their fathers (Lewin, 1988).

Alternatives other than kin networks and nonrelatives in the home include children brought to the parents' worksite, care by older siblings, a larger child care center, or small neighborhood groups such as family day care. Families with young children are turning to agencies and people beyond kin and friends for support in child-rearing. What this means for children is that their social and emotional nurturance, in addition to their intellectual and language stimulation, will be in different and more adult hands. Parents and children will need to develop relationships with caregivers that are mutually supportive, both financially and psychologically. This will take time and perseverance on the part of the adults but will be critical to ensure children's well-being.

## *Future Directions and the Role of Educators*

For children, these arrangements mean that, from early morning until evening, they will be socializing with each other. And, while adults will be available, they may not be interacting with an individual child very often. Therefore, adults must structure adequate private time to ensure that children get to be alone with an adult and to reenergize themselves. They must balance the day so that it is not too peer oriented. Children who are with each other all day may find themselves unwilling or unable to relate significantly to adults, who bring to children their knowledge, affection, and values. Losing such connection is risky, particularly if we value children learning about societal values, rules, and codes of conduct.

# Sex-Role Changes

Married, unmarried, or divorced, women with children have entered the work force of America in great numbers. Whether from necessity or choice, women have become part of the labor force and are unlikely to leave it. One result of working has been a change in women's self-images and in their ideas about the roles that men and women play in today's and tomorrow's world.

## *Parents as Adults*

How people look at themselves and their roles in life is undergoing considerable transformation. Women who are heads of households are likely to deal with their children differently than did those in the old-style, traditional families. They will question how parents and children treat each other, what they do and talk about together, and who is responsible for the children's upbringing. Blended families (families following remarriages that include parents, step parents, children, step children, half-siblings, etc.) will be headed by women and men who have experienced another kind of "parenting," different from the intact nuclear family of the past.

Any adult who becomes a parent and can talk with his or her own parents about raising children should take advantage of that opportunity. The insight and support adults get from their own parents will temper the fact that contemporary families *look* different. Yet the appearance of the family, such as its structure or actual members, may not change the deeper values and attitudes that

**FIGURE 15.7** Adults bring knowledge, affection, values—and sometimes a helping hand.

parents wish to instill in their own children. Connecting the generations may help today's parents raise tomorrow's children, who, as adults, will enter society and become parents themselves with the stamp of their own family experiences upon them.

## *Children Becoming Parents*

One side effect of the changing sex roles and attitudes of the last quarter-century has been the increase in sexual activity among teenagers. Each year one U.S. teenager in ten becomes pregnant (Children's Defense Fund, 1988). This ratio is among the highest in developed, industrialized nations. Among the consequences of teenage births and families are birth defects and low birth weight. Teenage women may not be able to finish school or get a job and may become dependent on welfare. Only half of the teenagers who bear babies before they are 18 finish high school (Children's Defense Fund, 1988). When children are raising children, all are at risk. Moreover, the cycle of teenage pregnancies, like those of child abuse and poverty, is too often self-perpetuating. Over 80 percent of teenagers with a first child before their fifteenth birthday had mothers who were also parents in their teen years (Murphy, 1982).

## Impact on Children

Children will be exposed to and live with models of women, mothers, and adults that are different from those of 30 or more years ago. What the effects will be on children is difficult to predict. Some say that a less stable, more *androgynous* outlook and upbringing may blur children's identity and views of sexuality, causing confusion and *aberrant* behavior. Others claim that children will now have a more realistic outlook. With a wider range of choices in personal life-style and habit, they will ultimately be freer to express themselves fully and authentically. Regardless of personal opinion, the changes in sex roles will influence children's behavior and attitudes about themselves and each other.

## Parents' Roles

As the family structure changes, so, too, will the role of each parent. As the mother takes a job outside the home, the family feels her absence and must create new ways to handle family matters. Combining career and family puts new stresses on women as well as men. For example, husbands have traditionally assumed that careers are combined with family by taking little responsibility for child care or home management. As women have jobs and careers to maintain, the needs of children must be shared.

Fathers need a nurturing role in families. In finding new ways to cope with the demands of both profession and family, the father takes on more of the caretaking, just as the mother becomes more responsible for material support. This applies to an absent father as well. When adults divorce, both parents change their parts in the family. Yet the father can still take an important and caring part in the family.

Power and custom can make way for the needs of children.

## Future Directions and the Role of Educators

Early childhood educators have long recognized how important it is for children to understand their world, particularly of family, interpersonal dynamics, and the roles people play in life. Adults have a critical part in helping children develop a realistic and clear view of themselves and the world around them. How a young child perceives the world of people and their roles influences self-concept, future attitudes, and behavior in significant ways.

The role of the teacher is to accept children and families for who they are, to clarify sex roles for children, and to interpret others' behavior to children so that they learn to understand and are able to act for themselves. In our view, teachers fulfill these responsibilities best when they offer choices in class that invite a freedom of response, rather than ones that dictate behavior with restrictions according to sex, dress, age, etc.

The teacher organizes space and develops materials that encourage broad participation. Varying art, dramatic play, and outdoor games with an eye toward including girls and boys will stimulate skill development and interest in all areas. Books chosen to depict men and women in a variety of roles encourage children to do the same, widening their possibilities rather than narrowing their world view.

Throughout the day and with all children, a teacher must be sure that all children know their biological sex. Matter-of-fact references to a number of children regarding their body parts and uses helps define this. Helping children learn appropriate gender role behavior is the next step in learning. However, present trends appear to point to a future with changed views of such behavior. Already, dress and activity level for young boys and girls have undergone attitude changes: it is acceptable for girls to be athletic and active physically, just as it is appropriate for boys to cook in the kitchen and be nurturing parents. The teacher must balance professional training and experience with the personal

**FIGURE 15.8** Changing sex roles will influence future generations.

viewpoints of both self and parents. In this way, educators can take an authoritative yet even-handed approach to sex-role changes and the changing family structure.

### The Family and Its Values

The major changes in family structure—from divorce to work and sex role changes—call for new ways of thinking in order to preserve the family and its values. To deal with the changes taking place in our society, we must consider different possibilities, from economic issues to gender-role differentiation. New ideas about the way people are reared, how they see their place in life, and their attachment to their children will be needed to preserve old values of freedom, democracy, and equality. How we help the family is the issue most important to the future of our society (Friedan, 1987; Fuchs, 1984).

When a substantial number of children spend their lives in a family with no man at its head, the image and even the definition of the family must change. Adults must question and clarify their values about children, caretaking, and child-rearing,

and the role of society—both individuals and institutions—in caring for the common good. The social and demographic trends of the 1980s lead us to these conclusions:

- Families with young children are increasingly dependent on agencies outside their informal social networks for the emotional, informational, and material support underlying nurturant child-rearing.

- Our sense of collective responsibility for other people's children, never strong to begin with, is deteriorating further.

- The stress on parents of trying to provide both adequate economic support and adequate care and nurturance is likely to intensify.

- We as a society face the urgent task of renewing and redefining our social contract with each other, and with young families in particular; the early childhood care and education community has a central responsibility with respect to this task. (Halpern, 1987)

How we deal with these trends will have important implications for both children and families in the next century. With commitment and will, the values of this society for democratic freedom and a quality life for families can coincide.

### Ecology of the Family

Bronfenbrenner (1979) uses the phrase "ecology of development" to describe the system or network of family and cultural relationships that significantly influence how children develop—and which children themselves significantly influence. This relatively new principle suggests looking beyond the ages and stages of child development to a larger context in which the child grows.

It makes good sense to look at ways parents and children affect one another's growth. Galinsky (see Chapter 8) sets out some of these changes and how they occur through the life cycle of both parents and children. Parents are also growing, changing human beings, and they are influenced by their children's personalities, demands, and needs. In turn, they influence their children by the way they discipline, the way they show affection or withhold it, the toys they provide, and the attention they give.

Society and the culture in which children are raised also affect their development. Children who have enough nutritious food, a home, and a supportive, loving family develop in ways unknown to a child in a ghetto or a war zone.

As Bee (1985) points out, this is a new, integrated way of looking at child development and bears consideration as an important finding that requires further research and study.

The current generation of Americans is materially the richest in our history. Yet no other generation has experienced so much divorce, so much shifting family structure. No other children have been exposed to such different sex-role models, nor have adult American women and men had so much to question so freely. While we may not know the effects of such changes for some time to come, we are assured that children and their parents will need our help in significant ways.

# EDUCATION REFORM

## Issues for Educators

In the spring of 1983, the National Commission on Excellence in Education issued a report on American schools that precipitated the current reform movement. *A Nation at Risk,* as the report was called, was soon followed by a number of other significant publications which defined the educational crisis at hand and offered a variety of solutions. Early childhood education; vocational education; elementary and secondary schooling; urban schools; teacher education, preparation and recruitment; character development; literacy; dropouts; and disadvantaged children all came under scrutiny by blue-ribbon panels.

By 1988, education emerged as a dominant issue in the presidential campaign. American public schools faced a crisis of quality; a national educational problem was identified and a sense of urgency instilled in the public mind. In the first wave of

reform, virtually every state enacted reform measures of some kind. The focus was on higher standards of student performance through the upgrading of curricula, increased requirements for homework, and firmer disciplinary methods.

A recent shift in the focus of the reform movement is notable. The "unfinished agenda" (Boyer in Nienhuis, 1986) of the reformation must center on the disadvantaged students and schools who are at greatest risk. These are primarily minority students in urban schools and in small rural districts where poverty factors and school failure are closely related.

Some of the most important issues to come out of the school reform movement are:

- *Professionalization of teaching:* To place teaching on a par with other professions, such as law and medicine; looking at the ways in which teachers are educated and trained in four-year institutions.

- *School governance:* The need for more on-site autonomy, involving teachers as well as administrators.

- *Giving parents a choice:* Allowing parents to select their children's school from a range of options throughout the school district, public as well as private.

- *Teacher recruitment:* Providing professionally competitive salaries to attract good teachers; using merit pay schedules and master teacher roles to keep qualified teachers in the classroom.

- *Experimental programs:* The use of smaller school settings, smaller classes, and magnet schools.

- *Involvement of the larger community:* To support schools in new ways; to provide more child care functions wherever necessary.

- *Equal access:* To ensure that disadvantaged students, minority students, handicapped students, and others at risk, have their needs addressed and specific, more comprehensive programs to prepare them as adequately as middle-class students.

### *Future Directions and the Role of Educators*

Although the current reform movement was

initiated by critical appraisals of public high schools, it bears heavily on those of us in early childhood education. A number of the concerns relate directly to our own profession, but equally as important is the obligation of all education professionals to understand the role of education in contemporary society. We can then reflect on the role of early childhood education in the larger context of societal and educational reform.

Common factors in the reform agenda that early childhood educators share with other education professionals are those related to the professionalization of teaching, parental choice, program quality, and serving all children equally. There are specific issues, however, which apply primarily to the early years.

## Care and Education

The early childhood profession includes both the caregiving and educating aspects of teaching. Child care has historically been identified with custodial care in child care centers. Educational programs traditionally focus on the enrichment of the child's social and cognitive growth. In recent years, the distinction between the two has blurred within the profession and the two have been intentionally linked. There is a greater acknowledgment that caretaking and educational factors are involved in all programs that serve very young children. However, the general public, as well as government agencies, tend to be unaware of the critical relationship between these two factors and to perpetuate the division. This dichotomy between care and education must be eliminated (Kagan, 1988). Read again Bettye Caldwell's *Guest Editorial* on page 434, especially point two.

## Wages

According to the Bureau of Labor Statistics, two out of every three child care workers earn below-poverty wages. They are paid less per hour than animal caretakers or bartenders. Staff turnover in child care centers averages 42 percent per year (Children's Defense Fund, 1987). Each year thousands of teachers and child care workers leave the early childhood field because of the low pay and low status accorded them.

To improve teaching and provide a high quality of education and care for children, the field of child care and early childhood education must attract superior talent. Business, medicine, law, and also the military attract intelligent young people with good pay and benefits. Considering how many early childhood teachers support themselves and a family, the financial aspects of the field are dismal. Poor wages, difficult working situations, and overall low job status contribute to job dissatisfaction.

In the past, teaching was one of the few professional opportunities open to women and minorities; thus, the lower pay was accepted. Now, however, more options are open. Unless education can improve teacher pay, the field itself will neither attract nor keep people of high caliber.

## Economics

Economic issues boil down to these questions: How much will teacher and school improvements cost, and what are the possible funding sources? The answer to the first depends on what kinds of improvements are made. If teacher salaries are improved at the entry level, rather than across the board, the overall increase in cost would be gradual. If the school day or term—either preschool or kindergarten/elementary—is lengthened, the costs would be considerable. For the thousands of child care centers already operating fulltime, the issue is more complicated. Raising tuition fees may not be a solution if the result is shutting out families in need. Merit pay and master teacher plans may be workable, depending on the type and extent of each. Caregivers, parents, and communities joining together in efforts to improve teacher salaries may become essential for maintaining any quality at all in the teaching field.

The answer to the second question—where the money comes from—depends, again, on the type and scope of school improvements. Some advocate a return to the post-Sputnik 1960s with massive federal support. Others, remembering that those funds did not solve all our educational problems, advocate more local control through state and community resources. We are inclined to believe that the task of teacher and school improvement is so large that more than one financial source will be needed.

Finally, we think it critical that each beginning teacher enter the field of early childhood education with the understanding of the financial issues facing educators today. No serious improvement in fiscal status will occur without our own support and advocacy. If we feel strongly that our society needs good teachers, we must make our voices heard to have teachers compensated fairly for their work.

## Curriculum

The critical issue of how and what to teach young children is discussed in chapters 11 through 15 and in David Elkind's *Guest Editorial* on "miseducation" (pages 304-308). Dialogue about appropriate curriculum practices will continue to dominate the field of early childhood; the profession will need to be vigilant in protecting young children from being subjected to early academics and highly structured programs before they are developmentally ready.

## Solutions

Changes in education are historically linked to social reform. Nowhere is this more clearly demonstrated than in the current reform movement. The link between poverty and school failure has been recognized and clearly demonstrated. The reform itself was spurred in part by one of the most powerful social and economic changes in this century: the employed mother.

The problems that have been raised cannot be solved by any single agency or institution. They will be solved by a coalition of state and federal governments, joined by business and industry, with the assistance of research and education. Together these groups, supported by parent involvement and commitment, can coordinate cohesive and comprehensive programs and services for all young children.

# Back to Basics

The rise of the *back-to-basics* movement that began in the mid-1970s is understandable in light of the history of educational reforms. As with so many movements in the past, "back to basics" seems as much grounded in the desire for social, political, and economic reform as in educational philosophy. A review of Chapter 1 will show that these same forces historically have created the necessary climate for change—from the Renaissance to the Reformation to the War on Poverty.

By the end of the 1970s, we experienced a wave of political and economic conservatism, extensive inflation, and high unemployment. A ten-year decline in national test scores of high school students was observed. There was a general but rampant feeling that "Johnny and Jane" could neither read nor write very well, barely able to decipher a menu or fill out a job application. All these became evidence of a failing public school system. Parents became discontent about the nature of education in their schools. Thus, the back-to-basics movement emerged.

Much of the pressure for this movement came from parents who experienced school policies they did not understand. Parents were reacting to some of the educational innovations of the 1960s and early 1970s. These included shortened school days and curricula that confused parents, such as the "new math" and courses in "psychology" or "human sexuality and family life." Letter grades were dropped in favor of teachers' written comments about a student's progress. Children were promoted to the next grade regardless of whether or not they had passed all their coursework. Parents were puzzled; they felt their standards and values were being rejected. In their eyes, the self-directed and open education of the 1960s and 1970s was just another name for inadequate teaching. When their children graduated from high school without basic reading and writing skills necessary to find and keep a decent job, parents demanded reform.

## Issues and Implications

But the back-to-basics movement is more complicated than it appears. There are fringe issues—many with religious and moral overtones—that are relevant to the general question. The return to strict, if not harsh, disciplinary procedures, the restoration of school prayer and dress and behavior codes for students are a few of the concerns that have attached themselves to the cause. In the emotional climate created, the main point is sometimes lost.

The major issue of the back-to-basics movement is the desire for schools to return to teaching the *basic skills*. The main emphasis in such a schoolroom is continual rehearsal of those fundamental skills, usually defined as the classic "3Rs" of reading, 'riting, and 'rithmetic. Learning by rote is common. That often means that art, music, drama, and other subjects of the humanities are curtailed or modified. In some cases, these "extras" are eliminated from the curriculum, so that teaching time is spent practicing the "basic" skills. Supporters of back to basics would institute these methods at every level of education, preschool through high school.

In the early childhood realm, this approach is implemented in classes for children in several ways. Formal reading programs, often with basal readers and regular formalized tests, may be an early and regular part of kindergarten. Memorizing letters and practicing printing may be required in preschool and day care centers. Drills in beginning sounds and flashcards may take precedence over songs and fingerplays in groups.

Clearly, a back-to-basics approach has an impact on the teaching and learning process:

*Teaching is affected when:*
- The teacher becomes the dominant figure; it is a teacher-centered, teacher-controlled approach.
- The teacher's role is to instruct, to tell how, or to give a lesson.
- The teacher has a prescribed standard to measure and test all student response against.

*Children are affected when:*
- Intellectual skills are stressed, and there is a lack of emphasis on the whole child.

- Child-centered learning through exploration, choice, and discovery are valued less than teacher-directed instruction.

*The learning process is affected when:*
- There is a deemphasis on the arts and humanities.
- Testing and measuring for gains made by children is frequent.
- There is less creativity in the teaching and learning/response methods and in the content of the curriculum itself.

**FIGURE 15.9** Early childhood educators support each other and the issues they care about. (Courtesy of Noah's Ark Preschool, Richmond, Calif.)

## Future Directions and Role of Educators

Many parents and educators on both sides of the argument would agree that there is a need for curriculum reform. The importance of having children learn basic skills is not really in question. The debate begins by first defining exactly what are "basic skills," particularly in the early years, and then deciding how they should be taught. For the teacher who is concerned with total growth and the individual child, a back-to-basics approach could be difficult to implement. In our view, the early childhood educator recognizes that the more child-centered style of teaching has greater meaning to the child than one determined entirely by grown-ups. And the early childhood teacher knows that the full range of children's skills and developmental needs must be addressed for well-rounded and complete growth to occur.

We face some serious issues as educators in the 1980s and beyond.

> For generations, the American Dream has been to live in freedom and to have the opportunity to pursue a satisfying life, reap the benefits of economic prosperity, and partake of the privileges and responsibilities of citizenship in the world's foremost democracy. But as we stand on the threshold of the 21st century, that dream is in jeopardy.
>
> *Children in Need*, Committee for Economic Development, 1987

# DIVERSITY

## Multicultural Education

### Issues

America as a "melting pot," where all cultures and ethnic groups blend together smoothly and completely, is a myth. Unfortunately, much of American society historically can be characterized as racist and *ethnocentric* in nature. The gap between our ideals—equal opportunity and freedom to pursue life, liberty, happiness, and self-expression—and daily reality can be narrowed only if we recognize its existence and then set concrete goals and plans to change it.

What is needed is to form a new concept of society and, as educators, of programs for children. It is imperative that we bring an awareness and sensitivity to children concerning the diversity of mankind. Diversity means difference—how we each express our unique cultural, religious, and ethnic heritage. There is strength and positive power in cultural and ethnic diversity. Our goal in early childhood education is to have children appreciate and respect those differences as they are socialized into the larger community beyond their homes.

Education has always been a process of socialization; early childhood education is the transition from the child's first socializing experience to that of mainstream society, as expressed in schools. By knowing a child's family and background, teachers work to make this enormous and important transition smoother and less stressful. And when the goal of the program is to accept children for who they are (rather than to change their identities), cultural pluralism is respected and celebrated.

We must equip children to live in the United States of the twenty-first century, an era when the white population will become a minority group. Children will need to learn about a variety of cultures and their expressions in people; *cultural pluralism*

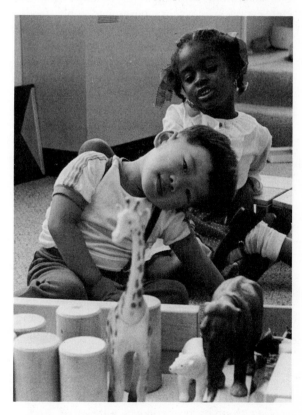

**FIGURE 15.10** Early childhood classrooms reflect the diversity that is the cornerstone of modern society. (Courtesy of Stride Rite Children's Centers, Cambridge, Mass.)

will mark that century as it has never before. As children maintain identification with their own culture within the broader framework of schools and society, they can better come to tolerate and appreciate a genuine variety of ethnic groups. Society will run smoother and survive with less violence if the cultures of all its citizens are respected.

### *Future Directions and the Role of Educators*

Curriculum can become rich when based on a commitment to help children learn to know and understand people. Our classrooms are a good place to begin teaching a crosscultural perspective. With the young child, we begin closest to home with concrete experiences (celebrations, songs, books, foods) about people close by: class members, neighbors, all the people children see in their everyday settings. Local celebrations and holidays may be used to bring the black, native American, Hispanic, and Asian cultures into the classroom. Parents can help their children share their diverse heritages with one another.

The model of family and school as partners is of particular importance when working toward multicultural education. No one knows better what is meaningful to a child's personal cultural experience than the family. Of course, teachers expand their own information base with educational classes, books, and materials. However, this is a supplement to a regular dialogue between themselves and parents.

Moreover, teachers must not assume, when faced with a monochromatic group of children, that there is no cultural diversity. Scratch the surface and there are family histories from all parts of the globe. These profiles and the children themselves tell personal family stories that can be the basis of curriculum units or an entire class approach. No one needs to lose ethnic identity in order to be part of another group or society in which they live.

We cannot, however, just pad the curriculum with interesting ethnic celebrations and consider that we have fulfilled the responsibilities of multicultural education. By teaching about our differ-

**FIGURE 15.11** A crosscultural, anti-bias curriculum helps children understand similarities and differences. (Courtesy of Stephanie Barry Agnew.)

ences we are, in fact, teaching about our similarities as people. The accent does not have to be on food, clothing, song and dance, and language as setting people apart from one another. Rather, the focus can be on how very similar are the components of many cultural and religious celebrations. Eggs, for instance, are a common theme in spring holidays around the world. Gift giving and creating presents for the family can be another theme to cross cultural and religious barriers. Emphasizing commonalities brings depth and interest to the curriculum, not simply a look at something different and therefore less valued.

We want to teach the values of a pluralistic society, but we also want to teach the values our diverse cultures hold in common. No one culture or religion should feel less valuable than any other. As teachers, we must be certain that we respect the values of others and that our own standards are in no way demeaning to the heritage of any child we teach.

## Bilingual Education

The late 1980s have left unresolved the basic questions concerning bilingual education. The goals and purposes of bilingual education remain little understood by the American population. Disagreements persist over how to define bilingualism, how to determine who needs it, and who is primarily responsible for providing the service. The long-term impact of current bilingual programs remains in dispute.

## Issues and Implications

Bilingual education has been part of the American experience since before the Revolutionary War, when school was taught in any one of the more than 18 languages that were spoken by the colonists. As early as 1870, U.S. Commissioner of Education William T. Harris argued that "national memories and aspirations, family traditions, customs and habits, moral and religious observances cannot be suddenly removed or changed without disastrously weakening the personality" of the immigrants who bear them (Castellanos, 1987).

Nonetheless, cultures have been suppressed with regularity in the United States. Both Native American and immigrant groups have categorically faced discrimination. Speaking English is only part of bilingual education: at issue are the civil and educational rights of people who speak limited English, the respect or assimilation of their culture, and their participation and acceptance in society.

Changing populations and the influx of immigrants from Asia as well as from the Hispanic nations have brought with them today new challenges of bilingual education. Bilingual programs serve primarily Spanish-speaking students. The U.S. Hispanic population grew by 30 percent between 1980 and 1987. Some states will probably reach "minority majority" status by the turn of the century. It is estimated that the number of school-age Spanish-speaking children in the country will increase by 50 percent by the year 2000 (White, 1984). How will this affect the early childhood teacher?

**The School-Age Child.** The questions about bilingualism for the school-age child are different from those for the young child. In elementary school, teachers and children are forced to deal with issues beyond those of receptive and expressive language. Learning graphic language (reading and writing),

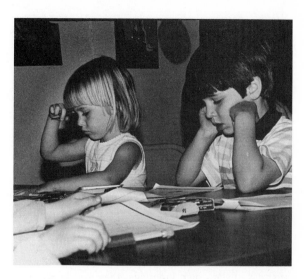

**FIGURE 15.12**   What price do children pay for academic achievement? How can we help them succeed without adding to their stress? (Courtesy of Dori Salladay, Eva's Little School, Sacramento, Calif.)

acquiring concepts in other subject areas through listening, and dealing with the more complex social patterns and interpersonal issues are just a few of these issues. Moreover, the age at which children should be taught a second language is highly controversial. Research shows that children *can* acquire nativelike mastery of a second language if they learn to speak the language before the age of five. Others will argue that a child should learn all the fine points of the first language before being exposed to a second one and that this exposure should not occur prior to the age of six.

Much research is centered on how children achieve second-language competence and performance. We do know that by age five, children know most of the sounds and grammatical structure of their native tongue and appear to learn a second language in a similar way. With a bilingual child, the level of competence in both languages may be low while gaining mastery in the second language.

The two pieces of legislation that have most influenced the bilingual issue in our time are the 1968 Bilingual Education Act and the 1974 *Lau* v.

*Nichols* Supreme Court decision. In 1974, the Supreme Court determined that a lack of instruction in one's first language is a violation of children's civil rights.

Since 1968, Title VII programs (the Elementary and Secondary Education Act, also known as the Bilingual Education Act) addressed the needs of students with limited proficiency in English. State bilingual education laws followed, requiring special instruction for children who lack competence in English.

The result is that children are taught, in public kindergarten and elementary schools, by using both the primary language and English. For instance, children may be taught to read in their primary language first; once they have learned the reading process in their own language, they are then taught to decode in English. Yet bilingual programs are so varied that it is difficult to assess them. Some work to mainstream children into regular classrooms as quickly as possible, while others try to maintain the child's native language. A more recent program, the *dual* or *bilingual immersion method,* attempts a blending of language instruction by putting both English speakers and those with limited English into classes together, and teaching "two-way" bilingual education. By bringing together both groups for language instruction, this method also indicates respect for both languages as assets. It shows promise as a truly multicultural tool for desegregation.

Still, the controversy continues. Another political backlash is occurring in the late 1980s against non-English speakers. The U.S. Office of Education has claimed bilingual education programs have not helped children learn English. California voters declared English as the official state language, and its governor vetoed state bilingual funding in 1988. Without consensus on the effectiveness and goals of bilingual education, educators must press for continuing research and clarity.

**The Young Child.** In preschools and child care centers, children are still taught in a regular class setting, often with little extra instruction. This means they are learning English through the "immer-

sion method," hearing mostly English at school. Teachers report success with this method, since much of the curriculum is developed for learning by *doing,* not just by listening. Moreover, children hear English throughout the day but may not be required to produce it until they are ready. Finally, children's play for those under five years of age is often carried out without the need for much spoken language. Yet we do not know definitively if this method of language acquisition really serves the non-English speaker well. Early childhood programs—both public and private—need more research to be able to take a clear direction in the area of bilingual education.

**The Immigrant.** Another serious challenge for schools is posed by the educational needs of immigrant children. Nationwide, there are more than 2.5 million school-age immigrants, countless children under five years of age, and thousands of other undocumented entrants. Immigrant enrollment in school can, in some places, reach more than 95 percent (Jennings, 1988).

The language barrier is the most immediate problem, followed by that of acceptance of the immigrants' native culture. Further, many newcomers arrive from countries racked with war, violence, and poverty. These children and families are under tremendous pressures and need help coping with the overwhelming stress (see Chapters 14 and 15). The way schools place and monitor these immigrant children—both their educational progress and their general well-being—challenges educators and all American citizens to clarify the responsibilities our society has toward its newcomers.

## Future Directions and the Role of Educators

We need appropriate measures to determine which children need bilingual services and what those services should be. Assessment of the methods for teaching bilingual children should be examined: Is a bilingual program still immersion in English or is it a true two-language experience? Do the same needs apply to all children in the early childhood years?

For the teacher working with young bilingual children, "caretaker language," noted by Krashen (Gingras, 1983), can be useful. This is the language that researchers found was used by adults who deal with young children. Specific features are that the caretaker:

- Does not teach language acquisition as such, but helps children understand the meaning of what is being communicated.
- Deals with the here and now.
- Uses short, simple sentences that increase in complexity as the child matures.
- Uses slightly more complex sentences than children are using.
- Repeats syntactic patterns frequently and slows down by pausing longer when speaking.

(Gingras, 1983)

Social and political forces affecting bilingualism must be addressed as we look at methodology and curriculum. The real world and education cannot be isolated from one another. The impact of poverty and discrimination as a barrier to language acquisition and academic achievement are crucial factors in bilingual education.

## Equal Play and Gender Segregation

There is ample research to confirm the widespread occurrence of gender segregation in childhood (Lockheed and Klein, 1985; Maccoby and Jacklin, 1985). While adults may not directly contribute to biased development, teachers and parents are indirectly responsible for the inequity between the sexes in their children. For instance, in unstructured play situations, the free-play backbone of early education programs and most at-home play, children will choose playmates and play situations that are comfortable to them. They will not, typically, choose those activities with which they have had little or no experience, nor will they ordinarily choose cross-sex playmates (particularly as peer pressure increases with age). Further, boys still get more attention than

girls do at most grade levels and subject areas (Sadler, 1985). Sexist treatment in the classroom encourages the formation of patterns of power and dominance that occur very early (Maccoby and Jacklin, 1985), though it is inappropriate to our current culture.

Teachers and parents must take an assertive role in recognizing this sexist bias and replacing it with more equitable experiences for all children. Girls need more experiences with spatial exploration and gross motor coordination as well as quality attention from—without dependence on—adults. Boys in particular need experiences in flexibility, nurturance, and learning from modeling. Strategies for all children include:

- Providing activities that all children may use, that are sex fair and sex affirmative in content.
- Developing verbal and physical interactive patterns that make all children equal participants.
- Using strategies such as teacher proximity and structured playtime to involve children in activities they may otherwise avoid (Greenberg, 1984).

## Society of the Sandbox: Class Differences

The early childhood field is at the center of the family and the school. It is here that children are taught the social order: values, attitudes, and behavior are transmitted from one generation to the next in these two institutions. As parents and teachers we re-create society through our children. To do this responsibly means to deal with our *real* values.

Schools are places were children learn what it means to be a person, and how to survive in their society. If the world values each individual, schools enhance who each child is and what that child needs to accomplish. Education that values cultural and personal diversity will try to strengthen each child's own family and cultural values.

This requires hard work. First, being clear about our beliefs is important. So is understanding the reality behind these beliefs. For instance, diversity brings great strength to a classroom, and also conflict. Differing points of view do not threaten the class but will define its tone and even its curriculum. Encouraging diverse views in early childhood means inviting families' styles and values to enter the classroom. The teacher will not be bored but will certainly need to be alert!

If diversity is a program priority, the staff and the classroom will reflect it (Carter, 1988). Activities and daily schedules will show which life experiences are valued (Olson, 1988). A teacher may try to promote sameness and homogeneity, or a teacher can try to foster uniqueness and individuality. The teacher who wishes to take the latter path must learn to deal with each child as the unique, distinctly different person he or she is (Wasserman, 1985).

# Special Education

## *Issues*

In 1976, Congress passed the Education for All Handicapped Children Act, which stated that by 1978 all children three to 18 years of age were to have access to public educational facilities. Since then, handicapped and normal youngsters have spent more time together in school because this federal legislation requires that handicapped children be placed in the least restrictive environment possible. That attitude has led to greater acceptance of the handicapped in many other areas of daily life.

Many handicapped children now participate in the full range of programs offered to normal children, from gymnastics to summer camps. The law that required their inclusion also mandated individual education plans (IEP) for each handicapped child. Thus, all handicapped children can have an education that is designed to meet their needs. The results of removing these barriers have been to encourage the handicapped to travel, work, shop, and play in the mainstream of American life. Public Law 99-457, as described in Chapter 3 (see Children with Special Needs), promises to have an even greater impact on early childhood education with even greater integration of handicapped children in regular school settings at an earlier age.

Public institutions have been forced by the law to include handicapped children in their programs. Three important issues must be addressed.

## *Implications*

First, an important question concerns the private sector. Are private schools taking the initiative in enrolling and educating the special child? Early childhood educators in these settings have a responsibility to help others see this issue as critical to the nature of teaching.

Second, teachers must be trained and supported in methods that will integrate the handicapped in school so that quality education is maintained for all children. The teacher cannot be expected to provide for children's special needs alone, without help. At the same time, most activities offered in early childhood programs, especially for children under five years of age, can be made appropriate for children with a variety of handicaps. The key issue here is teacher training and ongoing support.

A final issue is the value of mainstreaming for all children. One of the goals of mainstreaming is to give both nonhandicapped and handicapped children an opportunity to interact with each other and develop more tolerance and acceptance of people with handicapping conditions. Is this happening? If so, what works well? What does not work? Research in this area would enlighten both families and educators as they plan programs in special education.

# TEACHING FOR THE TWENTY-FIRST CENTURY

Every day, teachers open their classroom doors to young children by the thousands. As they do so, they are influencing the course of our nation in the next century. If this statement seems overwhelming, consider this: the child who is born in 1990 will be school-age in the twenty-first century. We are teaching the children of the future. What is the kind of world our children will face, and what skills will they need to deal with that world?

**FIGURE 15.13** What kind of world will our children face? How do we support parents in their roles as the 21st century draws near?

## Issues

Early childhood education is a broad field that encompasses children, parents, communities, and a staggering variety of programs. The issues of the day have changed over the last thirty years. A review of these gives teachers a perspective on what has been and may become important in our profession:

- *The 1960s:* How important are the early years for the field of formal education? Can education in those years compensate for inadequate childhood experiences? What kind(s) of schooling makes a difference?

- *The 1970s:* What kind of early childhood program is best? Which one(s) are financially efficient?

- *The 1980s:* What are the effects of child care on children's development? What is the best match between programs and their participants? How do the family and children interact?

We cannot envision the exact issues of the 1990s. The evolution of the problems that have faced teachers give clues to what may arise. We predict that child care, crises in children's lives, the changing family, school reform, and diversity will be among the most important. They combine to form the three trends of (1) supporting parents, (2) teaching values, and (3) advocating for children.

## Implications

Changing family concepts and structures call for renewed support for parents. Whether for reasons of economics or personal fulfillment, mothers' need to work intersects with children's need for healthy development. These needs do not have to conflict if adequate child care is available. Fathers must be supported in developing a nurturing role in the family and in maintaining contact (both financial and emotional) in the case of divorce. Teachers will have to develop strategies for helping both parents function effectively and with care in whatever role each plays in the life of a young child.

# Peace Education: Living with Diversity

In the broadest sense of the term, educating for diversity means preparing children to choose a life of peace. The world needs children who can both tolerate and embrace diversity in its many forms:

**FIGURE 15.14** What values do we teach children? How do teachers transmit values? (Courtesy of Trinity Preschool, New York, N.Y.)

language, skin and hair color, dress, customs, beliefs, opinions, and ways of behaving. People need the skills to care about and for others.

All life is vulnerable and fragile, but with today's capacity to annihilate and to use and pollute the entire planet, humankind will need to develop new and careful ways to live with one another. Children and adults must become capable of controlling themselves and their anger, of making decisions and solving conflicts peacefully, and of relating to each other without the use of power or force as solutions (see Chapters 7, 9, and 14 for specifics).

In learning to live with diversity, children can be taught new lessons for "Einsteinian reality" (Lally, 1984), to bring our ways of living together in line with our advanced science concepts. These lessons include creating experiences for children to learn about:

- The power of varied perspectives
- The many definitions that can be given to the same matter or the same event
- The importance of relationship to harmonious functioning
- The dependence of life on connection (Lally, 1984)

## Teaching Values

Education has never been free of values. Whenever someone chooses to teach something to another person, a choice of what and how to teach it implies what that person values. In early childhood education in particular, teachers and parents know that a neutral education is not possible. Our values reflect what we believe is important, what is acceptable, and what we will not tolerate. Teaching our children our belief system is part of their education. (See Multicultural Education, Chapters 9 and 14).

What is critical for us to realize is that we *are* teaching values. Children learn about themselves, their place in the school setting, and how to get along with others in the same classroom where they discover how to mix colors, memorize a fingerplay, and ride a tricycle.

Teaching values starts with knowing your own belief system and its place in your career. Ask yourself:

- Why am I teaching? Why young children? Why children at all?
- What made me choose early childhood education as my career?
- What do I stand for? Why?
- How did I come to have my beliefs?
- Do I allow others their beliefs?
- How do I state my values to children? To parents?
- How do I keep my values and integrity while allowing myself to grow and change?

The answers to these questions may strike a raw nerve here and there. If so, congratulations for being courageous enough to look at personal values honestly. The teacher who believes in such a process is one who has a gift for every student in class: that of a conviction to values, purpose, and sharing.

Each generation of Americans has the responsibility to prepare future generations for the world that will confront them. Our forefathers prepared us to cope with the complicated world we live in, and we, as the current adult generations, must fulfill our responsibility for preparing our children for the . . . world of the future. We must heed H.G. Wells' warning that "human history becomes more and more a race between education and catastrophe." Action is required now to ensure that America's people are prepared for the twenty-first century. (National Science Foundation Commission, 1983)

How do we prepare our children to live successfully in the future? We begin by looking ahead to predict what intellectual, social and emotional tools our children will need. We embrace the willingness to change while at the same time holding to our beliefs of personal choice, integrity, equality, and opportunity.

## Child Advocacy

Teachers are, by definition, advocates for children as they are dedicated to providing a better future for America's children.

With the issues of money and educational reform of such immediate concern, teachers need to understand the forces that affect how these issues are resolved. Teachers will have to educate themselves about the political process. They will need to know the rules and regulations regarding public funding sources. It is important to know how monies are allocated and who to work with in order to affect the decisions regarding education. By being acquainted with legislation, teachers can rally support for bills that will help children, families, and schools.

Teachers have long kept out of the political process, not unlike many minorities. But they have not been immune from its effects. As teachers, we must become informed in order to increase our power in the political and financial arenas of daily life. Just as we encourage children to help themselves, we must support each other in taking the initiative for our own profession's well-being.

One particularly promising piece of legislation in 1988 was the Act for Better Child Care, which spelled out a comprehensive partnership between the federal government and state governments, local agencies, private charities, employers, and families to make child care services more affordable and available. A coalition of agencies, coordinated by the lobbying group of the Children's Defense Fund, worked together under the banner "Alliance for Better Childcare." Cooperation such as this will increase the chances of political success on behalf of children.

Every teacher can become a child advocate. By working for children and children's services, teachers advocate for themselves as well. Effective legislative involvement proceeds through these steps:

1. Make a personal commitment.

2. Keep informed.

3. Know the process.

4. Express your views.

5. Let others know.

6. Be visible.

7. Show appreciation.

8. Watch the implementation.

9. Build rapport and trust.

10. Educate your legislators (Pearce, 1983).

The teacher who works to ensure high-quality programs and services for children and their families also increases the likelihood of achieving the improved working conditions, professional opportunities, and public recognition that the field of early childhood education so richly deserves.

## SUMMARY

Early childhood educators are facing issues today that challenge the very definition of childhood. How society handles these issues will help determine where we are headed—as teachers, children, families, a nation.

Some of the issues presented here may seem somewhat personal and even political. This is deliberate: as caretakers of the future—our children—we have serious and far-reaching questions that we must ask ourselves *now*. This book is dedicated to the quest for knowledge and action concerning a most important endeavor of the twentieth and twenty-first centuries: teaching young children. We can hardly do anything less than address those topics that are critical to the success of this task and of our profession.

## TOPICS FOR DISCUSSION

1. Why do you think child care workers have low salaries? How can you work to change these conditions?

2. Is it possible for child care centers to provide quality programs at the same time they pay fair wages and work benefits? How?

3. What can you say to parents who ask what you teach their child? How can you respond to their insistence on teaching children to read and print before kindergarten?

4. What would you do if you suspect a child in your center is being seriously neglected or abused?

5. What can you say to help children handle separation and divorce? How will you deal with *both* parents?

6. How can you articulate your own aspirations for yourself as a professional?

7. How can you provide for and deal with diversity in the classroom? What can you do to support both cultural pluralism and a sense of togetherness and mutual respect?

8. How will children develop acceptance, not intolerance, of multicultural and handicapped children? What can you do to deal with teasing and exclusion of children different from themselves?

9. How will you prepare yourself and your profession for the twenty-first century?

10. Research changes in AIDS statistics since this text was published.

## BIBLIOGRAPHY

## CHILD CARE IN THE UNITED STATES

Children's Defense Fund. *A Children's Defense Fund Budget.* Washington, D.C.: Children's Defense Fund, 1988.

Lindner, Eileen; Mattis, Mary C.; and Rogers, June R. *When Churches Mind Children.* Ypsilanti, Mich.: High/Scope Press, 1984.

Modigliani, Kathy. "Twelve Reasons for the Low Wages in Child Care." *Young Children,* March 1988, pp. 14–15.

Snider, William. "Cuomo Sets 'Decade of the Child' as Goal." *Education Week,* January 13, 1988, p. 12.

# CRISES IN CHILDREN'S LIVES

"A Demographic Portrait of America's Future Students." *Education Week,* April 27, 1988, p. 17.

Aronson, M.D., Susan S. "AIDS and Child Care Programs." *Child Care Information Exchange,* November 1987, pp. 35–39.

Bridgeman, Anne. "Schools Joining National Fight Against Child Abuse." *Education Week,* January 18, 1984, pp. 1, 16.

Bee, Helen. *The Developing Child.* Cambridge, Mass.: Harper and Row, 1985.

Children's Defense Fund. *A Children's Defense Fund Budget.* Washington, D.C.: Children's Defense Fund, 1988.

Elkind, David. *The Hurried Child: Growing Up Too Fast Too Soon.* Reading, Mass.: Addison Wesley, 1982.

Engelhardt, Tom. "Saturday Morning Fever—The Hard Sell Takeover of Kids' TV." *Mother Jones,* September 1986, pp. 39–54.

"Excerpts from the C.E.D.'s New Report, 'Children in Need.'" *Education Week,* September 9, 1987, p. 42.

Fraser, Brian G. *The Educator and Child Abuse.* Chicago: National Committee for Prevention of Child Abuse, 1977.

Galtney, Liz. "Mothers on the Run." *U.S. News and World Report,* June 13, 1988, pp. 22–33.

Golden, Nancy. "Children and AIDS." *Newsletter* of the Peninsula Chapter of the Association for the Education of Young Children, June 1987, pp. 1–2.

Gordon, Ann Miles. "Ministries to Childhood." *National Association of Episcopal Schools Journal,* Winter 1986, pp. 22–26.

Jennings, Lisa. "More Abuse Found at Home than in Day Care." *Education Week,* March 30, 1988, p. 7.

Langway, Lynn, et al. "Bringing Up Superbaby." *Newsweek,* March 28, 1983, pp. 62–63.

Murphy, Cullen. "Kids Today." *Wilson Quarterly,* Autumn 1982, pp. 61–82.

Nienhuis, Marleen. "Boyer Urges Schools to Focus on Plight of 'At-Risk' Youth." *Education Week,* September 10, 1986, p. 1.

Olson, Lynn. "Reforms 'Doomed,' Says Panel, Without Early Family Aid." *Education Week,* September 9, 1987, p. 1.

Reed, Mary S. "Stress at an Early Age." *San Francisco Chronicle and Examiner,* Sunday supplement *This World,* March 2, 1986, p. 13.

Skeen, Patsy, and Hodson, Diane. "AIDS: What Adults Should Know About AIDS (And Shouldn't Discuss With Very Young Children)." *Young Children,* May 1987, pp. 65–71.

Trelease, Jim. *The Read-Aloud Handbook.* New York: Penguin Books, 1984.

United States Department of Health and Human Services. *Child Sexual Abuse Prevention—Tips to Parents.* Washington, D.C.: 1984.

Van de Kamp, John. *Child Abuse Prevention Handbook.* Sacramento, Calif: Child Prevention Center, 1983.

Waters, H.F. "What TV Does for Kids." *Newsweek,* February 21, 1977, pp. 62–70.

Winn, Marie. *Children Without Childhood.* New York: Penguin Books, 1984.

Winn, Marie. *The Plug-In Drug: TV, Children, and the Family.* New York: Viking-Penguin, 1985.

## FAMILIES

Bank Street School of Education Faculty. "Who Will Pay the Piper?" Seminar at NAEYC National Convention, November 1986.

Bee, Helen. *The Developing Child.* Cambridge, Mass.: Harper & Row, 1985.

Braun, Linda. "The Changing American Family, Implications for Home–School Relationships." Seminar at NAEYC National Convention, November, 1987.

Bronfenbrenner, U. *The Ecology of Human Development.* Cambridge, Mass.: Harvard University Press, 1979.

Buscaglia, Leo F. "Nurturing Dads Are Real Men." San Francisco Chronicle, June 16, 1985.

Children's Defense Fund. *Child Care: The Time Is Now.* Washington, D.C.: Children's Defense Fund, 1987.

Family Service Association of Santa Clara County. "Anticipating Children's Reactions to Separation and Divorce." Santa Clara, Calif.: Family Service Association of Santa Clara County, 1982.

Francke, Linda Bird. *Growing Up Divorced.* New York: Ballantine Books, 1983.

Friedan, Betty. "Families in Transition." Stanford University Conference, "You Can Make a Difference." February, 1987.

Fuchs, Victor. "Preservation of Family Most Crucial Issue." *Stanford Campus Report,* October 31, 1984.

Galinsky, Ellen. *Investing in Quality Child Care.* Report prepared for AT&T, November 1986.

Haan, N. "The Assessment of Coping, Defense, and Stress." In Honig, A.S. (ed.) "Research in Review: Stress and Coping in Children." *Young Children,* May 1986.

Halpern, Robert. "Major Social and Demographic Trends Affecting Young Families: Implications for Early Childhood Care and Education." *Young Children,* September 1987.

Kolben, as quoted in Sommers, Carl. "What's News in Corporate Day Care: Consciousness Raising for Executives." *The New York Times,* July 24, 1983.

Lewin, Tamar. "Day Care Becomes a Growing Burden." *New York Times,* June 5, 1988, p. 22

Murphy, Cullen. "Kids Today." *The Wilson Quarterly,* Autumn, 1982.

Talan, Jamie. "What Divorce Does to Kids." *San Francisco Chronicle and Examiner,* October 1, 1986.

Wallis, Claudia. "The Child Care Dilemma." *Time,* June 22, 1987.

"When Children Bear Children." Editorial. *The New York Times,* August 1, 1983.

## EDUCATION REFORM

Elkind, David. *Miseducation—Preschoolers at Risk.* New York: Alfred A. Knopf, 1987.

Kagan, Sharon Lynn. "Current Reforms in Early Childhood Education: Are We Addressing the Issues?" *Young Children,* January 1988, pp. 27–32.

Nienhuis, Marleen. "Boyer Urges Schools to Focus on Plight of 'At-Risk' Youth." *Education Week,* September 10, 1986, p. 1.

Reeves, M. Sandra. *Education Week,* April 27, 1988, pp. 14–21.

# DIVERSITY

## Multicultural Education

Lubeck, Sally. *Sandbox Society.* London: The Falmer Press, 1985.

Morgan, Dorothy, and York, Mary E. "Ideas for Mainstreaming Young Children." *Young Children,* January 1981.

Neugebauer, Bonnie. "Evaluating Resources for Attitudes about Diversity." *Child Care Information Exchange,* March 1987.

Rosenmann, Alba A. "The Value of Multicultural Curricula." *Education Week,* November 11, 1987.

## Bilingual Education

"Bilingual Education: Language, Learning, and Politics: A Special Report." *Education Week,* April 1, 1987.

Gold, Deborah L. "Two Languages, One Aim: 'Two-Way' Learning." *Education Week,* January 20, 1988.

Gingras, Rosario C. "Early Childhood Bilingualism: Some Considerations from Second-Language Acquisition Research." In Spodek, B. and Saracho, O. (eds.), *Understanding the Multicultural Experience in Early Childhood Education.* Washington, D.C.: National Association for the Education of Young Children, 1983.

Jennings, Lisa. "Panel: Schools Must Aid Immigrants in 'Struggle to Succeed.'" *Education Week,* April 27, 1988.

Rashid, Hakim M. "Promoting Biculturalism in Young African-American Children." *Young Children,* January 1984.

White, Eileen. "Bilingual Education in the 1980s: Basic Questions Remain Unresolved." *Education Week,* February 8, 1984, p. 13.

## Equal Play and Gender Segregation

Carter, Marie. "Honoring Diversity: Problems and Possibilities for Staff and Organization." *Child Care Information Exchange,* January 1988.

Greenberg, Selma. "Recommendations for Creating the Five Es: Educational Equity in Early Educational Environments." In Klein, S. (ed.). *Achieving Sex Equity Through Education.* Johns Hopkins Press, 1985.

Lockheed, M., and Klein, S. "Sex Equity in Classroom Organization and Climate." In Klein, S. (ed.). *Handbook for Achieving Sex Equity Through Education.* Johns Hopkins Press, 1985.

Maccoby, Eleanor, and Jacklin, Carol N. "Gender Segregation in Nursery School: Predictors and Outcomes." Paper presented to the National Convention of the Society for Research in Child Development, Toronto, April 1985.

Olson, Lynn. "Bigotry: A Teacher's Voyage into the Eye of the Storm." In *Education Week,* April 6, 1988.

Sadler, Myra, and Sadler, David. "Sexism in School." *San Francisco Chronicle and Examiner,* Sunday supplement *This World,* June 16, 1985.

Wasserman, Selma. "Even Teachers Get the Blues." *Childhood Education,* Sept./Oct. 1985.

# TEACHING FOR THE TWENTY-FIRST CENTURY

Castillo, Cathy. "Computers in California Schools." *San Francisco Chronicle and Examiner,* April 29, 1984.

Clarke-Stewart, K.A. "Evolving Issues in Early Childhood Education." *Viewpoints,* University of California at Irvine, 1986 (ERIC document 278 481).

"Educating Americans for the Twenty-First Century: Excerpts from the National Science Foundation Commission's Report." *Education Week,* September 14, 1983, pp. 14–18.

Engle, Patricia. "The Intersecting Needs of Working Mothers and Their Young Children: 1980–85." *Viewpoints,* January 1986 (ERIC document 275 393).

Lally, J. Ronald. "Preparing Children to Choose a Life of Peace: Lessons for Einsteinian Realities." Keynote address to the California Association for the Education of Young Children, Santa Barbara, Calif., March 1984.

Pearce, Marilyn. "Child Advocacy in 10 Easy Steps." *On The Capitol Doorstep* (handbook), Sacramento, California, 1983.

"Public TV Still Big in the Classroom." *San Francisco Chronicle and Examiner,* June 13, 1984.

Williams, Linda. "Creating the Caring, Capable Kid." Personal communication, 1985.

# APPENDIX A

## KATZ' TEACHERS' DEVELOPMENTAL STAGES

A beginning teacher moves from one stage to the next on the way to maturity. At each stage, there are unique issues, concerns, and needs.

| Stage | Name | Time Span | Teacher Concerns | Teacher Needs |
|---|---|---|---|---|
| I | Survival | First year or two of teaching | Questions ability to do this daily; feels inadequate, ill-prepared | Support, guidance, comfort from someone on-site; skill instruction |
| II | Consolidation | End of first year into third | Begins to focus on individual children and specific problem behaviors | Continued on-site support and consultation; open to other professional resources in related fields |
| III | Renewal | Third or fourth year | Tired of doing same old thing; ready to explore new developments in the field | Likes to meet other teachers; goes to conferences; joins professional organizations |
| IV | Maturity | Third to fifth year on | Has come to terms with self as teacher; searches for insight, perspective | Might work on advanced degree; reads widely; participates in teacher conferences |

Adapted from Katz, Lillian G., *Talks with Teachers*, Washington, D.C.: National Association for the Education of Young Children, 1977, pp. 7–13.

# APPENDIX B

## COMPUTER SOFTWARE: WHAT TO LOOK FOR

Too many programs available for young children offer only a thin veneer of learning over a slow video game. Of the thousands of programs available, very few were designed by people who understand child development. In evaluating a program to use in your classroom, consider these points:

- Does the program present basic concepts and encourage children to learn basic skills, or does it merely recite a few facts and ask children to repeat them?

- Is the child continually active, or is the computer having all the fun? Some programs display animated graphics that are appealing, but the child is passive, watching the show. Better programs are more interactive.

- Is there a sequence to the program, and enough depth to hold a child's interest? Are difficult topics presented from several perspectives to assure understanding?

- Is the program open-ended, encouraging exploration and invention, or are there only "right" and "wrong" answers? Does the program use a rigid, narrow path that traps the child, or can he or she move freely from one activity to another?

- Is the program internally consistent, easy to use, and intuitive, so that it is fun to use? Many public domain programs are not designed for easy use. Unfortunately, that is also true of many commercial programs.

How can you know whether a program is worthwhile before you buy it? Try to preview the program, if possible, in a store or resource center. Look for endorsement of the program by the National Educational Association or other groups of educators. Read reviews in magazines like *Family Computing, Popular Computing* and *Electronic Learning*. Ask other teachers and librarians whose judgment you trust.

---

*Courtesy of Ann Piestrup, The Learning Center, Menlo Park, California.*

# APPENDIX C
# LITERACY DEVELOPMENT AND PRE-FIRST GRADE

*A Joint Statement of Concerns about Present Practices in Pre-First Grade Reading Instruction and Recommendations for Improvement*

- Association for Childhood Education International
- Association for Supervision and Curriculum Development
- International Reading Association
- National Association for the Education of Young Children
- National Association of Elementary School Principals
- National Council of Teachers of English

## Objectives For A Pre-First Grade Reading Program

Literacy learning begins in infancy. Reading and writing experiences at school should permit children to build upon their already existing knowledge of oral and written language. Learning should take place in a supportive environment where children can build a positive attitude toward themselves and toward language and literacy. For optimal learning, teachers should involve children actively in many meaningful, functional language experiences, including *speaking, listening, writing* and *reading*. Teachers of young children should be prepared in ways that acknowledge differences in language and cultural backgrounds and emphasize reading as an integral part of the language arts as well as of the total curriculum.

## What Young Children Know About Oral and Written Language Before They Come To School

1. Children have had many experiences from which they are building their ideas about the functions and uses of oral language and written language.

2. Children have a command of language, have internalized many of its rules, and have conceptualized processes for learning and using language.

3. Many children can differentiate between drawing and writing.

4. Many children are reading environmental print, such as road signs, grocery labels, and fast food signs.

5. Many children associate books with reading.

6. Children's knowledge about language and communication systems is influenced by their social and cultural backgrounds.

7. Many children expect that reading and writing will be sense-making activities.

## Concerns

1. Many pre-first grade children are subjected to rigid, formal pre-reading programs with inappropriate expectations and experiences for their levels of development.

2. Little attention is given to individual development or individual learning styles.

3. The pressures of accelerated programs do not allow children to be risk-takers as they experiment with language and internalize concepts about how language operates.

4. Too much attention is focused upon isolated skill development or abstract parts of the reading process, rather than upon the integration of oral language, writing and listening with reading.

5. Too little attention is placed upon reading for pleasure; therefore, children often do not associate reading with enjoyment.

6. Decisions related to reading programs are often based on political and economic considerations rather than on knowledge of how young children learn.

7. The pressure to achieve high scores on standardized tests that frequently are not appropriate for the kindergarten child has resulted in changes in the content of programs. Program content often does not attend to the child's social, emotional and intellectual development. Consequently, inappropriate activities that deny curiosity, critical thinking and creative expression occur all too frequently. Such activities foster negative attitudes toward communication skill activities.

8. As a result of declining enrollments and reduction in staff, individuals who have little or no knowledge of early childhood education are sometimes assigned to teach young children. Such teachers often select inappropriate methodologies.

9. Teachers of pre-first graders who are conducting individualized programs without depending upon commercial readers and workbooks need to articulate for parents and other members of the public what they are doing and why.

## Recommendations

1. Build instruction on what the child already knows about oral language, reading and writing. Focus on meaningful experiences and meaningful language rather than merely on isolated skill development.

2. Respect the language the child brings to school, and use it as a base for language and literacy activities.

3. Ensure feelings of success for all children, helping them see themselves as people who can enjoy exploring oral and written language.

4. Provide reading experiences as an integrated part of the broader communication process, which includes speaking, listening and writing, as well as other communication systems such as art, math and music.

5. Encourage children's first attempts at writing without concern for the proper formation of letters or correct conventional spelling.

6. Encourage risk-taking in first attempts at reading and writing and accept what appear to be errors as part of children's natural patterns of growth and development.

7. Use materials for instruction that are familiar, such as well-known stories, because they provide the child with a sense of control and confidence.

8. Present a model for students to emulate. In the classroom, teachers should use language appropriately, listen and respond to children's talk, and engage in their own reading and writing.

9. Take time regularly to read to children from a wide variety of poetry, fiction and non-fiction.

10. Provide time regularly for children's independent reading and writing.

11. Foster children's affective and cognitive development by providing opportunities to communicate what they know, think and feel.

12. Use evaluative procedures that are developmentally and culturally appropriate for the children being assessed. The selection of evaluative measures should be based on the objectives of the instructional program and should consider each child's total development and its effect on reading performance.

13. Make parents aware of the reasons for a total language program at school and provide them with ideas for activities to carry out at home.

14. Alert parents to the limitations of formal assessments and standardized tests of pre-first graders' reading and writing skills.

15. Encourage children to be active participants in the learning process rather than passive recipients of knowledge, by using activities that allow for experimentation with talking, listening, writing and reading.

*Prepared by the Early Childhood and Literacy Development Committee of the International Reading Association, December 1985. Reprinted with permission of the Association.*

# APPENDIX D

# CHILD ABUSE CODE

Following are excerpts from the California Penal Code regarding the responsibilities of child care personnel in reporting suspected child abuse.

## REPORTING CHILD ABUSE

While *everyone* should report suspected child abuse and neglect, Article 2.5 of the Penal Code provides that it is a crime for certain professionals and laypersons who have a special working relationship or contact with children *not* to report suspected abuse to the proper authorities. Following are excerpts and summaries of sections from this article regarding child abuse reporting:

> . . . any child care custodian, medical practitioner, nonmedical practitioner, or employee of a child protective agency who has knowledge of or observes a child in his or her professional capacity or within the scope of his or her employment whom he or she knows or reasonably suspects has been the victim of child abuse shall report the known or suspected instance of child abuse to a child protective agency immediately or as soon as practically possible by telephone and shall prepare and send a written report thereof within 36 hours of receiving the information concerning the incident. For the purposes of this article, 'reasonable suspicion' means that it is objectively reasonable for a person to entertain such a suspicion, based upon facts that could cause a reasonable person in a like position, drawing when appropriate on his or her training and experience, to suspect child abuse. (Penal Code Section 11166.)

Failure to report by telephone and in writing within 36 hours is a misdemeanor punishable by six months in jail or a $500 fine, or both. (For those required to report who do not do so, there may also be civil liabilities.) Basically, this penalty ensures that those required to do so will report all suspected incidents of child abuse immediately to a child protective agency (the local police authority, sheriff's department, juvenile probation department or the county welfare department).

Those required to report should be aware that mere reporting does not always mean that a civil or criminal proceeding will be initiated. However, all reports are investigated.

Those agencies to whom reports are made are obligated to follow procedures in the reporting law which ensure that all reports of suspected abuse or severe neglect reach the Department of Justice statewide central index.

It is important to note that reporting under the law is an *individual* statutory responsibility, and that no one should in any way interfere with an individual's legal obligation to report. Additionally, no individual required to report is relieved of his or her obligation by depending on another person or a supervisor to report the suspected incident.

Those professionals required to report by Penal Code Sections 11165 and 11166 are:

> *"Child care custodian"* means a teacher, administrative officer, supervisor of child welfare and attendance, or certificated pupil personnel employee of any public or private school; an administrator of a public or private day camp; a licensed day care worker; an administrator of a community care facility licensed to care for children; headstart teacher; a licensing worker or licensing evaluator; public assistance worker; employee of a child care institution including, but not limited to, foster parents, group home

personnel and personnel of residential care facilities; a social worker or a probation officer, as well as others.

Employees of community service programs or organizations for abused or neglected children under contract or agreement with a county to provide shelter, care or counseling are also considered "child care custodians." (Welfare and Institutions Code Section 307.5.)

*Persons required to report are not liable either in civil damages or for criminal prosecution as a result of making a report. Other persons are not liable either civilly or criminally, unless it can be proven that a false report was made and that the person knew that the report was false.* (Penal Code Section 11172.)

When making the telephone report, the following information is to be provided:

name of the child;
whereabouts of the child;
character and extent of injuries and/or molestation, and any other information which led person to suspect child abuse;
age of child; and
address of the child and parents.

# WHAT HAPPENS TO THE REPORTS?

Reports are investigated by either the local law enforcement agency or by the county children's protective services agency assigned to handle dependency cases (the welfare department or juvenile probation department). If the investigation reveals evidence of criminal child abuse, the local law enforcement agency has the authority to: take the child into protective custody, file criminal charges against the parent(s) or responsible parties and/or to refer the case to probation, welfare or another service agency (counseling, church, etc.). Ideally, this decision is made after consultation with representatives from other disciplines.

# GLOSSARY

**Abberant.** Deviating from the usual or natural type; abnormal, atypical.

**Accommodation.** A concept in Piaget's cognitive theory as one of two processes people use to learn and incorporate new information; the person adjusts what is already known to "accommodate" new learning. Children usually will change their way of thinking into a "schema," once they see that their usual ways do not take new information into account; they then will add new thought patterns to handle the new knowledge.

**Accountability.** The quality or state of being answerable to someone or of being responsible for explaining exact conditions; schools often must give specific account of their actions to a funding agency to assure the group that the funds and operation of the school are being handled properly.

**Accreditation.** A system of voluntary evaluation for early childhood centers. The goal is to improve the quality of care and education provided for young children. Accreditation is administered by the National Academy, a branch of the National Association for the Education of Young Children.

**Active Listening.** A child guidance technique of reflecting back to the speaker what the listener thinks has been said.

**Activity Areas.** Similar to learning centers and interest areas; areas in a classroom or yard that are designed and arranged for various activities to take place. An early childhood setting will offer several centers, or stations, for children that are based on both children's interests and what the staff hopes for them to learn in class.

**Advocate.** One who maintains, defends, or pleads the cause of another; in early childhood terms, an advocate is someone who furthers the principles and issues of the field by speaking to others about such issues.

**After-School Care.** Programs designed to care for children after the regular academic school day.

**Age-Level Characteristics.** Those features of children's development and behavior that are most common among a given age group.

**Androgynous.** Having to do with either sex; associated with both the male and female identity, behavior, etc.

**Anti-bias.** A phrase describing the development of curriculum that emphasizes an inclusive look at people and problems, extending the tenets of multicultural education and pluralism.

**Articulation.** The manner in which sounds and words are actually spoken.

**Assess.** To make an evaluation or determine the importance, disposition, or state of something or someone, such as in evaluating a child's skills, a classroom environment, or a teacher's effectiveness.

**Assimilation.** A concept in Piaget's cognitive theory as one of two processes people use to learn and incorporate new information; the person takes new information and puts it together with what is already known in order to "assimilate" the new information intellectually, such as when a toddler shakes a toy magnet first, as with all other toys, in order to get to know this new object. Children usually first try to put new experiences into the "schema," or categories, they already know and use.

**Autonomy.** The state of being able to exist and operate independently, of being self-sufficient rather than dependent upon others.

**Baby Biographies.** One of the first methods of child study, these narratives were written accounts by parents of what their babies did and said, usually in the form of a diary or log.

**Back to Basics.** A movement of the 1970s and 1980s prompted by a desire for schools to return to teaching the "basic" skills usually associated with academic learning, such as reading, writing, and arithmetic.

**Baseline.** A picture of the status of a child, teacher, or environment that serves as the basis for evaluation and later comparison.

**Basic Needs.** Conditions, described by Abraham Maslow and other humanists, that are necessary for growth; these needs, such as physiological conditions and safety and security, are critical for a person's survival.

**Behavior Swings.** Shifts from one behavior to another, usually by a sharp change in what one is doing; e.g., from highly active to motionless, or from gregarious to shy.

**Behavior Theory.** A psychological theory developed in the United States in the twentieth century, which states that all important aspects of behavior and people are learned and can be modified or changed by varying external conditions.

**Bilingualism.** The acquisition of two languages during the first years of life; using or being able to use two languages.

**Brainstorming.** The process of thinking that involves bringing up as many ideas as possible about a subject, person, event, etc.

**Cephalocaudal.** In the direction of head (cephalic) to toe (caudal, of the tail or hind part of the body), as in how children develop physically.

**Cerebral Palsy.** A disorder that is the result of damage to a certain part of the brain (motor cortex); "CP," as it is commonly called, is a nonprogressive disorder (does not get worse as the child grows older); usually movement dysfunction is paired with some intellectual and perceptual impairment.

**Child Abuse.** Violence in the form of physical maltreatment, abusive language, and sexual harassment or misuse of children.

**Child Care Center.** A place for care of children for a large portion of their waking day; includes basic care-taking activities of eating, dressing, resting, toileting, as well as playing/learning time.

**Child-Centered Approach.** The manner of establishing educational experiences that takes into consideration children's ways of perceiving and learning; manner of organizing a classroom, schedule, and teaching methods with an eye toward the child's viewpoint.

**Child Neglect.** The act or situation of parents'/adults' inattention to a child's basic health needs of adequate food, clothing, shelter, and health care; child neglect may also include not noticing a child or paying enough attention in general.

**Church-Related Schools.** Educational programs affiliated with a church or religious organization; they may have a direct relationship with the church by including religious education, by employing church members as teachers, or by being housed in a church building and using the facilities for a fee.

**Classical Conditioning.** The most common and basic category of learning in behavior theory, involving an association between a stimulus and response so that a reflex response (eye-blinking, salivating, etc.) occurs *whenever* a neutral and new stimulus is activated ( a bell for a light, food, etc.); conditioned-response experiments conforming to the pattern of Pavlov's experiment, sometimes known as "stimulus substitution."

**Clinical Method.** An information-gathering technique, derived from therapy and counseling fields, in which the adult observes and then interacts with the client (in this case, children) by asking questions and posing ideas to the person or group being observed.

**Cognition.** The act or process of knowing, thinking, and perceiving. Cognition involves perceptual, intellectual, and emotional skills that begin as a child makes connections among objects and people and later extends to formulating mental representations (see Flavell Focus in chapter 4).

**Cognitive Confusion.** State of being unsure or forgetful about what is already known, such as becoming perplexed about things or facts already learned.

**Cognitive Theory.** The psychological theory developed by Jean Piaget and others; the theory focuses on thought processes and how they change with age and experience; this point of view contrasts with the stimulus-response aspects of behavior theory.

**Compensatory Education.** Education designed to supply what is thought to be lacking or missing in children's experiences or ordinary environments.

**Competency-Based Assessment.** Evaluation in which a teacher is judged or rated in comparison with a predetermined set of skills, or competencies, related to the job.

**Comprehensive.** Inclusive, covering completely, such as a program for children that concerns itself with the physical, intellectual, social, emotional, creative, and health needs of the children.

**Concrete.** Concerning the immediate experience of actual things or events; specific and particular rather than general or symbolic.

**Continuing Education.** The commitment of teachers to learning new approaches and ideas and to continuing to challenge themselves to higher levels of learning and competence.

**Continuum.** Something that is continuous; an uninterrupted, ordered sequence.

**Core Values.** The basic purposes or issues a professional group acknowledges as common concerns to all its members.

**Cultural Pluralism.** A state or society in which members of diverse ethnic, racial, or cultural groups maintain participation in and development of their traditional culture within the common society.

**Custodial.** Those tasks relating to guardianship of a child's basic needs for food, clothing, and shelter; they include providing for eating, dressing, toileting, resting, and appropriate protection from physical hardships such as weather, danger, etc.

**Decoding.** Converting from code into ordinary language; in terms of language development, decoding is the process of making sense out of printed letters or words.

**Developmental Schedules.** Arrangement of a daily plan for children that is based on both individual and group levels of development.

**Developmental Tasks.** Those functions or work to be done by children at a particular point in their development.

**Discipline.** Ability to follow an example or to follow rules; the development of self-control or control in general, such as by imposing order on a group. In early childhood terms, discipline means everything adults do and say to influence children's behavior.

**Disequilibrium.** Loss of balance, or a period of change.

**Divergent Thinking.** The processes of thought and perception that involve taking a line of thought or action different from what is the norm or common; finding ideas that branch out rather than converge and center on one answer.

**Down's Syndrome.** A genetic abnormality that results in mongolism, one of the most common and easily identified forms of mental retardation.

**Dramatic Play.** Also known as imaginative play, this is a common form of spontaneous play in which children use their imagination and fantasy as part of the setting and activity.

**Early Childhood Education.** Education in the early years of life; the field of study that deals mainly with the learning and experiences of children from infancy through the primary years (up to approximately eight years of age).

**Eclectic.** Choosing what appears to be best in various doctrines, methods, styles; comprised of elements drawn from various sources.

**Educaring.** A concept of teaching as both educating and care giving; coined by Magda Gerber in referring to people working with infants and toddlers.

**Elaboration.** The act of expanding language; developing language by building complex structures from simple ones and adding details.

**Emerging Literacy.** The process of building upon prereading skills in a child-centered fashion, so that the ability to read evolves from children's direct experiences.

**Emotional Framework.** The basic "feeling" structure of a classroom that determines the tone and underlying sensibilities that affect how people feel and behave while in class.

**Employer-Sponsored Child Care.** Child care supported in some way by the parents' employers. Support may be financial (as an employee benefit or subsidy) or physical (offering on-site care).

**Environment.** All those conditions that affect children's surroundings and the people in them; the physical, interpersonal, and temporal aspects of an early childhood setting.

**Environmental.** Forces that are not innate or hereditary aspects of development; in early childhood terms, environmental aspects of growth are all those influences of physical conditions, interpersonal relationships, and world experiences that interact with a person to change the way he or she behaves, feels, and lives.

**Ethics.** A theory or system of moral principles and standards; what is "right and wrong"; one's values; the principles of conduct governing both an individual teacher and the teaching profession.

**Ethnocentric.** Having one's race as a central interest, or regarding one's race or cultural group as superior to others.

**Experimental Procedure.** An observation technique that gathers information by establishing a hypothesis, controlling the variables that might influence behavior, and testing the hypothesis.

**Expressive Language.** Those aspects of language development and skill that deal with expression: pronunciation, vocabulary, and grammar, as well as speaking and articulation.

**Extrinsic.** Originating from or on the outside; external, not derived from one's essential nature.

**Family Day Care.** Care for children in a small, home-like setting; usually six or fewer children in a family residence.

**Feedback Loop.** In terms of evaluation, *feedback loop* is used to describe the process whereby an evaluator gives information to a teacher, who in turn uses this information to improve teaching skills.

**Fine Motor.** Having to do with the smaller muscles of the body and the extremities, such as those in the fingers, toes, and face.

**Formal Tests.** Evaluation instruments that are administered in a conventional, "testlike" atmosphere for use with groups of children, and may or may not be developed commercially.

**Four "I"s.** The four components (I, Initiative, Independence, and Interaction) of early childhood curriculum for building self-esteem.

**Genes.** The biological elements that transmit hereditary characteristics.

**Gifted Children.** Children who have unusually high intelligence, as characterized by: learning to read spontaneously; being able to solve problems and communicate at a level far advanced from their chronological age; excellent memory; extensive vocabulary; and unusual approaches to ideas, tasks, people.

**Gross Motor.** Having to do with the entire body or the large muscles of the body, such as the legs, arms, and trunk.

**Growth Needs.** Conditions, as described by Abraham Maslow and other humanists, that are important to a person's well being; these needs, such as love and belonging, self-esteem and respect for others, playfulness, truth, beauty, etc., while not critical to a person's survival, are necessary for growth.

**Holistic.** A viewpoint that takes into account several conceptions of a child or situation to form a wider, more rounded description; in early childhood terms, this view includes a child's history, present status, relationships with others, and the interrelationships of development to arrive at a picture of the child; in medicine, this view includes dealing with a person's mental and emotional state, relationships, etc., as well as body signs.

**Humanist Theory.** The psychological theory of Abraham Maslow and others; it involves principles of motivation and wellness, centering on people's needs, goals, and successes.

**Hypothesis.** A tentative theory or assumption made

in order to draw inferences or test conclusions; an interpretation of a practical situation that is then taken as the ground for action.

**Inadequacy.** The state of being or feeling insufficient, of not being or having "enough"; if feeling discouraged, children will display their feelings of inadequacy by misbehaving.

**Individualized Curriculum.** A course of study developed and tailored to meet the needs and interests of an individual, rather than those of a group without regard for the individual child.

**Inference.** A conclusion reached by reasoning from evidence or after gathering information, whether direct or indirect.

**Informal Assessment.** Evaluation based on methods and instruments that are not administered formally, as in paper-and-pencil tests, but rather are done while the subjects are at work or play in their natural environments.

**Initiative.** An introductory step; in early childhood terms, the energy, capacity, and will to begin taking action.

**Integrated Curriculum.** A set of courses designed to form a whole; coordination of the various areas of study, making for continuous and harmonious learning.

**Integrated Day.** A school schedule with no prescribed time periods for subject matter, but rather an environment organized around various interest centers among which children choose in organizing their own learning experiences.

**Integrated Development.** Growth that occurs in a continuous, interrelated manner; a child's progress as a whole, rather than in separate areas.

**Intelligence.** The cluster of capabilities that involves thinking (see chapter 13 for details).

**Interdependence.** Dependence on one another, as in the relationship between teachers' experience in the areas of discipline and their competence at knowing and using appropriate language for discipline.

**Interdisciplinary Approach.** A method of teaching/learning that draws from sources in more than one field of study; e.g., a course in education

that uses background from the fields of medicine, psychology, and social work as well as education itself.

**Interest Areas.** Similar to learning centers and activity areas; one way to design physical space in a classroom or yard, dividing the space into separate centers among which children move about, rather than assigning them desks.

**Interpersonal.** Relating to, or involving relationships with, other people; those parts of the environment that have to do with the people in a school setting.

**Intervene.** To enter into a situation between two or more persons or between a person and an object; to interpose oneself into another's affairs, such as when teachers enter into children's interactions when their behavior calls for some action on the part of an adult.

**Intrinsic.** Belonging to the essential nature of or originating from within a person or body, such as intrinsic motivation, whereby one needs no external reward in order to do something.

**Job Burnout.** Exhaustion and stress from one's job, characterized by a wearing down of body and attitude.

**Kindergarten.** A school or class for children four to six years old; in the United States, kindergarten is either the first year of formal, public school or the year of schooling before first grade.

**Kindergarteners.** (1) A modern term to describe the children who are attending kindergarten programs; (2) A term used in 19th century America to describe early childhood practitioners who worked in kindergartens patterned after Froebelian models (see Spodek Focus in chapter 1).

**Laboratory Schools.** Educational settings whose purposes include experimental study; schools for testing and analysis of educational and/or psychological theory and pactice, with an opportunity for experimentation, observation, and practice.

**Latchkey Children.** Children who are left home after school unattended or supervised by an adult; children who are responsible after school for themselves and perhaps younger siblings while their parents/guardians are not at home, usually working; such children have a "latchkey" (housekey) to let themselves into an empty home.

**Laterality.** Of or relating to the side, as in children having an awareness of what is situated on, directed toward, or coming from either side of themselves.

**Learning Centers.** Similar to interest areas and activity areas; hubs or areas in a classroom designed to promote learning; the classroom is arranged in discrete areas for activity, and children move from one area to another rather than stay at an assigned desk or seat.

**Limits.** The boundaries of acceptable behavior beyond which actions are considered misbehavior and unacceptable conduct; the absolute controls an adult puts on children's behavior.

**Linchpin.** Something that serves to hold together the elements of a situation.

**Mainstreaming.** The process of integrating handicapped children into classrooms with the non-handicapped.

**Maturation.** The process of growth whereby a body matures regardless of, and relatively independent of, intervention such as exercise, experience, or environment.

**Maturation Theory.** A set of ideas based on the notion that the sequence of behavior and the emergence of personal characteristics develop more through predetermined growth processes than through learning and interaction with the environment; the theory of growth and development proposed and supported by Dr. Arnold Gesell and associates.

**Merit Pay.** A system for teachers that gives pay bonuses for excellent teaching.

**Misbehavior.** Improper behavior or conduct.

**Miseducation.** David Elkind's term describing the end result of contemporary parents rushing their children into formal instruction too early.

**Modeling.** A part of behavior theory, modeling is a way of learning social behavior that involves observing a model (either real, filmed, or animated) and mimicking its behavior, thus acquiring new behavior.

**Negative Reinforcement.** Response to a behavior that decreases the likelihood of the behavior recurring; for instance, a teacher's glare might stop a child from whispering at group time, and from then on, the anticipation of such an angry look could reinforce not whispering in the future.

**Networking.** Making connections with others who can further career and professional opportunities.

**Nonpunitive.** Methods that do not involve or aim at punishment; for instance, letting a child be hungry later when he refuses to eat at snack time is a nonpunitive method of enforcing the need to snack with the group; hunger is a natural and logical consequence of the child's behavior, rather than a punishment meted out by the teacher (such as scolding or threatening).

**Norm.** An average or general standard of development or achievement, usually derived from the average or median of a large group; a pattern or trait taken to be typical of the behavior, skills, or interests of a group.

**Objectivity.** The quality or state of being able to see what is real and realistic, as distinguished from subjective and personal opinion or bias.

**Open-ended.** Activities or statements that allow a variety of responses, as opposed to those that allow only one response; anything organized to allow for variation.

**Open School.** A style of education, developed in progressive American schools and in the British infant schools, that is organized to encourage freedom of choice and that does not use predetermined roles and structure as the basis of education; an educational setting whose ultimate goal and base for curriculum is the development of the individual child, rather than of programmed academic experiences.

**Operant Conditioning.** A category of learning in behavior theory that involves a relation between a stimulus and response. The response is learned, rather than reflexive, and is gradually and carefully developed through reinforcement of the desired behavior as it occurs in response to the stimulus; behavior leading to a reward.

**Organic Reading.** A system of learning to read, popularized by Sylvia Ashton-Warner, that lets children build their own vocabulary with the words they choose.

**Parent Cooperative.** An educational setting organized by parents for their young children, often with parental control and/or support in the operation of the program itself.

**Pediatrician.** A medical specialist in pediatrics, the branch of medicine dealing with children, their development, care and diseases.

**Peer Interactions.** Associations with people of the same age group or with those one considers equals.

**Perceptual-Motor Development.** The growth of a person's ability to move (motor) and perceive (perceptual) together; perceptual-motor activity involves the body and the mind together, to coordinate movement.

**Performance-Based Assessment.** Evaluation based on observable, specific information on what a teacher actually does (performance while on the job).

**Philosophy.** Concepts expressing one's fundamental beliefs; in early childhood educational terms, the beliefs, ideas, and attitudes of our profession.

**Phobia.** A strong, exaggerated, and illogical fear of an object or class of things, people, etc.; one of several reactions children often have to divorce.

**Phonemes.** Language sounds; the smallest units of meaningful speech; two examples of phonemes are /a/ (as in hat) and /p/ (and in sip).

**Pluralism.** (1) A theory that holds to the notion that there is more than one kind of reality or correct way of perceiving and acting upon the world; (2) A state in which members of diverse ethnic, racial, religious, or social groups participate in their traditional cultures while still belonging to the common society.

**Positive Reinforcement.** A response to a behavior that increases the likelihood of the behavior being repeated or increased; for instance, if a child gets attention and praise for crawling, it is likely that the crawling will increase—thus, the attention and praise were positive reinforcement for crawling.

**Practice Teaching.** The period of "internship" that students experience when working in a classroom with supervision, as opposed to having a role as a regular working staff member.

**Precedent.** Something done or said that serves as an example or rule to authorize or justify other acts of the same or similar kind; an earlier occurrence of something similar.

**Precursor.** What precedes and indicates the approach of another; predecessor or forerunner.

**Prejudices.** Ideas and attitudes that are already formed about other people, situations, ideas, etc., before hearing or experiencing full or sufficient information; in teaching terms, those attitudes or biases that may be based less on mature thought and reasoning than on incomplete or nonexistent personal experiences.

**Prepared Environment.** The physical and interpersonal surroundings of an educational setting that are planned and arranged in advance with the group of children in mind.

**Prerequisite.** Something necessary or essential to carrying out an objective or performing an activity; when early childhood teachers determine what skills children will need in order to successfully engage in an activity, they are clarifying the prerequisites for that activity.

**Professional.** One engaged and participating in a profession and accepting the technical and ethical standards of that profession; in early childhood terms, one who has accumulated methods, course work, and teaching experience with young children along with attitudes of competency, flexibility, and continual learning.

**Professional Organizations.** Those associations developed for the purpose of extending knowledge and teaching/learning opportunities in the field of education.

**Proximal to Distal.** In the direction from the center of the body (proximal) toward the outer part (distal, far from the center), as in the way children's bodies develop.

**Psychodynamic Theory.** The psychological theory of Dr. Sigmund Freud and others; it asserts that the individual develops a basic personality core in childhood and that responses stem from personality organization and emotional problems as a result of environmental experiences.

**Psychosocial.** Those psychological issues that deal with how people relate to others, and the problems that arise on a social level; a modification by Erikson of the psychodynamic theories of Freud with attention to social and environmental problems of life.

**Receptive Language.** Those aspects of language development and skill that deal with the ability to receive messages: listening, understanding, and responding.

**Reinforcers.** Rewards in response to a specific behavior, thus increasing the likelihood of that behavior recurring; reinforcers may be either social (praise) or nonsocial (food) in nature, and may or may not be deliberately controlled.

**Routines.** Regular procedures; habitual, repeated or regular parts of the school day; in early childhood programs, routines are those parts of the program schedule that remain constant, such as indoor time followed by cleanup and snack, regardless of what activities are being offered within those time slots.

**Running Record.** The narrative form of recording behavior; this kind of descriptive record of one's observations involves writing down all behavior as it occurs.

**Screening.** Evaluations to determine a child's readiness for a particular class, grade, or experience.

**Self-Actualization.** The set of principles set forth by Abraham Maslow for a person's wellness or ability to be the most that a person can be; the state of being that results from having met all the basic and growth needs.

**Self-Awareness.** An awareness of one's own personality or individuality; in teaching terms, an ability to understand one's self and assess personal strengths and weaknesses.

**Self-Concept.** A person's view and opinion of self; in young children, the concept of self develops as they interact with the environment (objects, people, etc.); self-concept can be inferred in how children carry themselves, approach situations, use expressive materials such as art, etc.

**Self-Correcting.** Materials or experiences that are built or arranged so that the person using them can act automatically to correct errors, without needing another person to check or point out mistakes.

**Self-Esteem.** The value we place upon ourselves; how much we like or dislike who we are; self-respect.

**Self-Help.** The act of helping or providing for oneself without dependence upon others; in early childhood terms, activities that a child can do alone, without adult assistance.

**Sensorimotor.** Relating to or functioning in both sensory and motor aspects of body activity.

**Sensory.** Having to do with the senses or sensation, as in an awareness of the world as it looks, sounds, feels, smells, tastes.

**Separation Process.** The act and procedure that occurs when parents leave a child at school.

**Sequential Learning.** Learning based on a method of consecutive steps; an arrangement of concepts or ideas in a succession of related steps so that what is learned results in continuous development.

**Seriation.** The process of sequencing from beginning to end or in a particular series or succession.

**Sex-Role Stereotyping.** A standardized mental picture or set of attitudes that represents an oversimplified opinion of people's abilities or behavior according to their sex; overgeneralizing a person's skills or behavior based upon an inequitable standard of sex differences.

**Social Cognition.** The application of thinking to

personal and social behavior; giving meaning to social experience.

**Socialization.** The process of learning the skills, appropriate behaviors, and expectations of being part of a group, particularly society at large.

**Social Mores.** Standards of conduct and behavior that are determined by society, as opposed to those established by family or personal preference.

**Social Skills.** Strategies children learn to enable them to respond appropriately in many environments.

**Spatial.** Having to do with the nature of space, as in the awareness of the space around a person's body.

**Special-Needs Children.** Children whose development and/or behavior require help or intervention beyond the scope of the ordinary classroom or adult interactions.

**Specific Development.** Area of a person's growth and maturation that can be defined distinctly, such as physical, social, emotional, intellectual, and creative growth.

**Spontaneous Play.** The unplanned, self-selected activity in which a child freely participates.

**Standardized Testing.** Formal assessment techniques whose results have been tabulated for many children and thus have predetermined standards, or norms, for evaluating the child being tested.

**Stewardship.** Responsibility for judicious management of resources; the obligation assumed by an individual or agency to act responsibly in the use of both personal and natural resources.

**Stimulus-Response.** The kind of psychological learning, first characterized in behavior theory, that makes a connection between a response and a stimulus; that is, the kind of learning that takes place when pairing something that rouses or incites an activity with the activity itself in such a way that the stimulus (such as a bell) will trigger a response (such as salivating).

**Stress.** The physical and emotional reactions and behaviors that come from having to cope with difficult situations beyond one's capabilities.

**Support System.** A network of people who support each other in their work and advancement.

**Surrogate.** Substitute, such as a teacher acting in the place of the parent, a school toy taking the place of a blanket from home, a thumb taking the place of a pacifier.

**Tactile.** Perceptible or able to be learned through the sense of touch.

**Teaching Objectives.** A set of goals teachers set for themselves as they plan activities for children; these goals remind teachers what they will do in order to help children learn.

**Temporal.** Having to do with time and time sequence; in the early childhood setting, refers to scheduling and how time is sequenced and spent, both at home and in school.

**Traditional Nursery School.** The core of early childhood educational theory and practice; program designed for children aged two-and-one-half to five years of age, which may be part- or all-day programs.

**Transcurricular.** Able to be used or applied in a variety of situations or activities.

**Transitions.** Changes from one state or activity to another; in early childhood terms, transitions are those times of change in the daily schedule (whether planned or not), such as from being with a parent to being alone in school, from playing with one toy to choosing another, from being outside to inside, etc.

**Upward Evaluation.** Assessment procedure in which employees evaluate their superiors.

**Vicariously.** Experienced or realized through the imagination or the participation of another, rather than from doing it oneself, as in learning vicariously about something by listening to a story.

**Volatile.** Easily aroused; tending to erupt into violent action or explosive speech or behavior.

**Word Pictures.** Descriptions of children that depict, in words, norms of development; in this text, these are age-level charts that describe common behaviors and characteristics, particularly those that have implications for teaching children (in groups, for curriculum planning, with discipline and guidance).

# INDEX